Essentials of Educational Psychology

Essentials of Educational Psychology

S.K. MANGAL
Formerly
Professor and Head, Department of Postgraduate Studies, and Principal
C.R. College of Education, Rohtak

PHI Learning Private Limited
Delhi-110092
2026

*In fond memory of **Shri Asoke K. Ghosh** (October 1942 – February 2024), Founder Chairman and Managing Director of PHI Learning, whose vision endlessly inspires.*

The Legacy Continues....

Published by Pushpita Ghosh, PHI Learning Private Limited, Rimjhim House, 111, Patparganj Industrial Estate, Delhi-110092 and Printed by Mudrak, C-55, Sector 65, Noida, U.P.-201301.

₹895.00

ESSENTIALS OF EDUCATIONAL PSYCHOLOGY
S.K. Mangal

ISBN-978-81-203-3055-9 (Print Book)
ISBN-978-93-5443-083-1 (e-Book)

To

my grandchildren

Lavanya, Anvit, Isha and Arnav

for giving a new meaning to my life

Contents

Preface

Educational Psychology is best defined as a science of education or in its most practical sense, it presents the application of the theory and practice of psychology in the field of education. In our school education set-up, it is mainly concerned with equipping the aspiring as well as practising teachers with the necessary knowledge and skills, interests and attitudes helpful in playing their roles as effective teachers. However, such a task is not as simple as otherwise visualized. For playing its role effectively, a course and text in educational psychology must be capable of providing the teachers and other personnel concerned with the development, progress and welfare of the children all the essentials that are helpful to them in understanding their wards in terms of their varying individual differences, particularly related to their abilities and potentialities, growth and development, habits, interests, attitudes and aptitudes, needs and motives and other likewise personality characteristics. Teachers can thus help their students through needed guidance and counseling in the tasks of their proper learning and behaviour modification for achieving maximum balanced development of their personality helpful in enjoying desired physical and mental health and overall adjustment to their self and the environment. As a result, the coverage of the topics related to a particular course in educational psychology is bound to be extensive, wide and enormous to meet the challenge of providing better teacher education.

The present text is designed to meet this challenge. To adjust to the varied requirements of the teacher preparation courses, the subject matter of the text has been organized in forty-five chapters. The flow of the topics follows the traditional organization for most courses of the B.Ed. and B.A. (Education) of the Indian universities. However, in doing so, the important principles of content organization like principle of logical sequence, proceeding from simple to complex, etc. have been well taken care of.

Starting with an introduction to the meaning, nature, scope and methods of psychology and its applied branch, educational psychology, the book throws light on the various aspects of human growth and development, particularly related to the stages of childhood and adolescence. In its subsequent chapters, it focuses on the nature and theories of learning in perfect coordination with a discussion on the learning conditions like factors affecting learning, maturation and training, psychology of individual differences, motivation and attention, interests and aptitudes, concept formation, habits and attitudes, memory and forgetting, transfer of learning, group dynamics and group behaviour, etc. Thereafter, it discusses the nature, types, theories, determinants and assessment of personality. It has also accorded due importance to the cognitive aspect of human behaviour by introducing topics related to intelligence, creativity, thinking, reasoning and problem solving. The mental health and overall adjustment of the learner have also been taken care of in the text with the inclusion of topics like mental health and hygiene, sex education, adjustment, frustration and conflicts, behavioural problems, along with their needed prevention and treatment. A full chapter has been devoted to the various categories of exceptional children with an objective of providing needed insight into the identification, etiology, treatment and educational provisions for them.

In the next four chapters, the text provides an essential knowledge and skill for the use of statistics in organizing educational data and computing statistics like Mean, Median, Mode and Correlation for its analysis. The text concludes with an important aspect of equipping the readers with the skill of performing various psychological tests for collecting essential information regarding the potential and progress of the children.

The text is adequately illustrated with examples, diagrams and tables for helping the readers in their understanding of the topics discussed. Every chapter of this text begins with its structural composition to provide a glimpse of what the chapter consists of. At the end of each chapter, besides giving a summary for the readily recollection of the subject matter discussed, appropriate references and suggested readings have been provided for the readers' further reference.

I express my gratitude to the various authors, research workers and educational psychologists, the views and opinions of whom I have freely incorporated in the work. Many of the students also have been a great source of inspiration for me during more than three decades of my association with them. I am also obliged to my wife Dr. (Mrs.) Uma Mangal, who besides being a constant source of inspiration, has helped much in the preparation of the manuscript. Besides, I would like to thank Shri Naresh Kaushik for typing the manuscript. Finally, I wish to thank the Publishers for the efforts taken in bringing this work in such a presentable and useful form.

It is hoped that the book will be read by a host of readers for whom it has been specifically designed and they will be duly benefited by it. Nothing is ever perfect and so any comments or suggestions for improving this work would be greatly appreciated and thankfully acknowledged.

With all good wishes to the readers,

S.K. MANGAL

1

Psychology—Meaning, Nature and Scope

CHAPTER COMPOSITION

- Introduction
- Defining Psychology
- Nature of Psychology
- Scope of Psychology
- Summary
- References and Suggested Readings

INTRODUCTION

The subject psychology is nowadays becoming more and more popular. In comparison to other subjects a larger number of students are opting for it at the senior secondary and degree levels. Even in the most prestigious competitive examinations like the IAS and the allied examinations or the Provincial Civil Service examinations, the number of students opting for psychology, for the preliminary and mains is increasing every year. The reason for its popularity lies with its body of knowledge, which is quite interesting, and its wide use and applications in almost all the walks and spheres of life.

However, there was a time when there was no such subject as psychology. The 'study of mind' was covered under a separate branch of philosophy called *Mental Philosophy*. Hence psychology is a legitimate child of philosophy. The break away of psychology from philosophy is said to be due to the fact that it gave up sheer speculation in favour of scientific procedure. This drift of psychology from philosophy to science took a long course swaying one way or the other. Such a movement has been responsible for the change in the meaning and definitions of psychology from time to time as can be observed from the following discussion.

DEFINING PSYCHOLOGY

Etymological derivation of the word 'Psychology' indicates that it has its origin from two Greek words—psyche and logos. The word 'logos' stands for rational discourse of a study. However, the meaning and interpretation of the word "psyche" has been in a state of change from time to time leading to subsequent changes in the ways of defining the term 'psychology' as may be evident from the following four stages of its evolution.

- **First Stage.** By taking the meaning of the word 'psyche' as soul, psychology was first defined as the "study of soul". Actually during these days, the subject philosophy almost dominated and influenced the views of the scholars including psychologists. Consequently, a philosophical meaning and interpretation was given to the word 'psyche'. However, soon such interpretation faced criticism like what is soul? How can it be studied? and so on. The inability to answer such questions led to the search for a new meaning of the word 'psyche'.
- **Second Stage.** At this stage, the philosopher cum psychologists tried to define psychology as the "study of the mind" by giving a new meaning and interpretation to the word 'psyche' in the form of 'mind'. Although the word 'mind' was less vague and mysterious than soul, it faced the same criticism with questions like what is mind? How can it be studied? and so on.
- **Third Stage.** The criticism and unacceptability of the meaning of the word psyche as soul or mind led the psychologists to a new search of its proper meaning. The initiative was taken by famous psychologists like William James (1890), Wilhelm Wundt and Edward Bradford Titchener (1894) who, while interpreting psyche as consciousness, defined psychology as a study of consciousness. According to these psychologists the description and explanation of the states of consciousness is the task of psychology which is usually done by introspection (the process of looking within). In the state of consciousness, we remain aware of the situation, conscious or alive to the task we are doing and the process of thinking and feeling which is growing in our mind.

  This definition too was rejected on the ground that it had a very narrow vision as it did not include the sub-conscious and the unconscious activities of the mind and also due to the most subjective nature of the method of introspection which it had taken into account.
- **Fourth Stage.** This stage in the evolution of the definition of the subject of psychology reflects the advent of the modern era of science and technology. Consequently, in the definition of psychology the word 'study' was replaced by 'science'. The first psychologist who, besides using the word science in place of study, replaced consciousness with total behaviour (conscious as well as unconscious) was the famous William Mcdougall. In the book *Physiological Psychology* published in 1905, he wrote: "*Psychology may be best and most comprehensively defined as the positive Science of the conduct of living creatures.*" Later in 1908, in his book *Introduction to Social Psychology*, he added the word 'behaviour' to his definition and finally in *An Outline of Psychology,* gave the following meaningful definition:

"*Psychology is a Science which aims to give us better understanding and control of the behaviour of the organism as a whole.*" (1949, p. 38)

In the same period, an American Professor Walter Bowers Pillsbury in his book *Essentials of Psychology* published in 1911 gave the same behavioural definition of the term psychology in these words "*Psychology may be most satisfactorily defined as the Science of human behaviour.*"

However, later in 1913, J.B. Watson, the father of behaviourism, proposed to elaborate the concept of the term behaviour by including in it both human and animal behaviours and consequently he defined psychology as "*The science of behaviour*" (taking into account the human as well as animal behaviour).

In the subsequent years of 20th century, the scholars and psychologists tried to similarly define psychology as a science of behaviour.

Let us cite a few important definitions for the purpose of illustration. First definition of this nature may be cited from the famous authors and psychologists, Woodworth and Marquis, who wrote:

"*Psychology is the scientific study of the activities of the individual in relation to his environment.*" (1948, p. 20)

Going further on similar lines, the famous writer on psychology N.L. Munn summarised it in one of his books as under:

"*Psychology today concerns itself with the scientific investigation of behaviour.*" (1967, p. 4)

Analysis of Definitions

A close analysis of the definitions of the subject psychology given above clearly reveals that starting from their vague and mysterious concepts having philosophical base, the definitions of psychology have now concentrated on the scientific investigation of behaviour. Commenting upon the history of evolution of these definitions, Woodworth (1948) writes, "*First psychology lost its soul, then its mind, then it lost its consciousness, it still has behaviour of sort.*"

Hence, as per the latest definition, psychology is a science of behaviour, or a scientific study of the behavioural activities and experiences. Here the main emphasis is on the term 'behaviour' whose scientific study or investigation is clearly aimed through the theoretical and practical activities to be organised under psychology.

However, the issues which remain unanswered, even at this stage may be put as under:

1. What should be clearly inferred from the term 'behaviour' whose study we aim at in psychology?
2. We aim to organise a scientific investigation of behaviour through psychology. It implies that psychology is a science quite capable of organising a proper scientific investigation or study of the behaviour. Is it true, therefore, that psychology is a science? If yes, then what kind of science is it?

Let us try to discuss and look for some answers to these issues.

BEHAVIOUR: MEANING AND NATURE

The latest concept of the term behaviour has a very wide and comprehensive meaning revealed as under:

(a) "Any manifestation of life is activity," says Woodworth (1948) and behaviour is a collective name for all these activities. Therefore, the term 'behaviour' includes not only motor (conative) activities like walking, swimming, dancing and so on but also activities like thinking, reasoning, imagining (cognitive activities) and feeling happy, sad, angry (affective activities) etc.

(b) It concerns all the segments of human mind — conscious, sub-conscious and unconscious, and, therefore, covers not only the overt behaviour but also inner experiences and mental processes *i.e.*, covert behaviour.

(c) In psychology, we study the behaviour of all living organisms. Therefore, it includes the behaviour of human beings as well as that of birds, insects, plants and animals, of normals as well as of abnormals and of children as well as of adults, etc.

In this way, the term behaviour is too comprehensive to cover all the life activities and experiences of all the living organisms.

NATURE OF PSYCHOLOGY

Whether to Consider Psychology a Science or Not?

After a long discussion among the scholars and psychologists on the acceptance of psychology as a science and its nature as scientific, the verdict has been in favour giving it the status of science. The observation and concluding remarks of the famous authority N.L. Munn may be cited as a solid evidence for this purpose. He writes—"*Psychology is a science and a properly trained psychologist is a scientist, or at least a practitioner who uses scientific methods and information resulting from scientific investigation.*" (1967, p. 4)

Besides such assertions and observations of the various authorities, we can put the following arguments to justify its status as a science

- Like sciences, it has an organised and systematic body of knowledge, facts, principles and theories which are subject to change on the discovery of new facts and emergence of new principles and theories.
- Like sciences, it believes in the cause and effect relationship. It declares that every behaviour has its roots, the factor of its causes and development.
- Like sciences, it emphasizes the search for truth. It studies facts of behaviour and describes the laws governing them.
- It adopts the method of systematic inquiry and scientific approach as used by sciences.
- Like other sciences, psychology too has its pure and applied aspects.

With all such evidences, it can be safely concluded that it is an accepted reality that psychology is a science.

Psychology as a Science

Science can be divided into two broad categories—Normative and Positive. The question arises as to which category should psychology be included in. Psychology studies facts and describes 'what is'. It does not concern with 'ought to be' as emphasized by Normative Sciences like Ethics, Logic and Philosophy etc. Therefore, it is quite proper to describe it as a positive science.

WHAT KIND OF POSITIVE SCIENCE IS PSYCHOLOGY?

(i) It is not as perfect a science as physics, chemistry or mathematics. It is a behavioural science which deals with the behaviour of an organism.

(ii) This behaviour is quite dynamic and unpredictable. We are not consistent in our behaviour. On the other hand, physical reactions which are studied by the natural sciences are always predictable. This makes the study in natural sciences more exact, accurate and objective. Psychology has not yet attained the status of these sciences although it is trying hard to be more objective, exact and accurate. Therefore, it is better to name it as a developing positive science.

In the end, we can conclude that psychology although termed as positive science, is not yet much developed as the natural sciences and therefore can be defined as:

Psychology is a developing positive science which enables us to study the behaviour of a living organism in relation to his environment.

SCOPE OF PSYCHOLOGY

What do we mean by the scope of a subject? The scope of a subject can usually be discussed under the following two heads :

1. The limits of its operations and applications.
2. The branches, topics and the subject matter with which it deals.

The field of operations and applications of the subject of psychology is too vast. It studies, describes and explains the behaviour of the living organisms. Here the terms 'behaviour' and 'living organism' carry quite comprehensive and wide meanings. Behaviour includes all types of life activities and experiences of a living organism—whether conative, cognitive or affective; implicit or explicit; conscious, unconscious or subconscious. Moreover, the term living organism is to be applied to all the living creatures created by the Almighty irrespective of their species, caste, colour, age, sex, mental or physical state. Thus normals, abnormals, children, adolescents, youth, adults, old, criminals, patients, workers, officials, students, teachers, parents, consumers and producers belonging to different stock, spheres and walks of human life are all studied under psychology. Moreover, as a subject psychology does not limit itself to the study of human behaviour only but also tries to study the behaviour of animals, insects, birds and even plant life.

In this way, where there is some life and there are living organisms, psychology may be needed for the study of the activities and experiences of these organisms. We know that the living organisms as well as their life activities are countless and consequently, no limit can be imposed on the fields of the operation and applications of the subject psychology either. Hence, it is quite appropriate to conclude that the scope of psychology can neither be adjudged as narrow nor be confined within boundaries. It has width and depth of an ocean. However, for the sake of convenience, as well as for proper specialized study and application, it can be divided into a number of branches and fields as discussed below:

Fields or Branches of Psychology

General psychology

It is relatively a large area or field of psychology which deals with the fundamental rules, principles and theories of the subject in relation to the study of the behaviour of normal adult human beings.

Abnormal psychology

It is that branch or field of psychology which describes and explains the behaviour of abnormal people in relation to their own environment. The causes, symptoms and syndromes, description and treatment of the abnormalities of behaviour form the subject matter of this branch.

Clinical psychology

Clinical psychology comes at the forefront after the work and operations of the knowledge and activities connected with abnormal psychology have been done. The knowledge about abnormality of behaviour and the underlying causes, symptoms etc. provide necessary framework to the subject matter and skills required for the study of clinical psychology. The abnormality and maladaptation of the behaviour leads to mental illness and diseases. A proper diagnosis of such illness and diseases is then the work of clinical psychology. It analyses the causes of such maladaptation and mental illness and then suggests ways and means for the proper treatment and rehabilitation of the patient. The experts, who provide such treatment to the patients attending the clinic or hospital, are known as clinical psychologists.

PHYSIOLOGICAL PSYCHOLOGY

This branch of psychology describes and explains the biological and psychological basis of behaviour. The study of the internal environment and psychological structure of the body, particularly brain, nervous system and functioning of the glands in relation to the conative, cognitive and affective behaviour of the human being form part of the subject matter of this branch.

SOCIAL PSYCHOLOGY

This branch of psychology studies the human behaviour in relation to his social environment. One's behaviour as a member of the group, the process of communication and inter-personal relationship, group dynamics and social relationship etc., are studied under this branch.

INDUSTRIAL PSYCHOLOGY

It is that branch of psychology which studies the human behaviour in relation to the situations and environment prevalent in the industrial world. It aims at bringing improvement in the working output of the human resources for the purpose of raising quality production. Consumer psychology, selection, training and placement of human capital, establishing harmonious relationship between the employee and the employer, strengthening morale of the workers and other employees etc., form the subject matter of this branch.

CRIME PSYCHOLOGY

This branch of psychology studies the behaviour of the criminals in relation to their situations and causes through behaviour analysis techniques and adopts behaviour modification devices for their proper reforms and rehabilitation.

EXPERIMENTAL PSYCHOLOGY

This branch of psychology describes and explains the ways and means of carrying out psychological experiments following scientific methods in controlled or laboratory situations for the study of mental processes and behaviour. It picks up animals, birds and human beings as subjects for these experiments.

CHILD PSYCHOLOGY

This branch of psychology deals with the study of the behaviour and the process of growth and development of children from birth to the beginning of the period of adolescence.

ADOLESCENT PSYCHOLOGY

In this branch of psychology, we study the process of growth and development during adolescence, and the personality characteristics, behavioural and adjustment problems faced by adolescents. It helps the elders to understand the adolescents in their proper perspectives and in helping them in their proper adjustment as well personal and social welfare.

ADULT PSYCHOLOGY

This branch of psychology deals with the study of the behaviour of adults. The characteristics of growth and development in various dimensions of their personality, their interests, aptitudes and attitudes, the typical behavioural and adjustment problems specially related to the period etc. are studied under this branch. The knowledge of adult psychology proves helpful to the teachers of adult education, workers and counsellors in teaching and guiding their subjects properly for their individual and social progress.

EDUCATIONAL PSYCHOLOGY

In this branch of psychology, we try to study the behaviour of the learner, with respect to educational environment. As a science of education, the subject matter of this branch helps in improving all the processes and products of education. The teachers can teach well and students can learn well with the help of the knowledge and skills gained through the study of this subject. It also helps the teachers in acquiring proper insight for bringing desirable modification in the behaviour and an all-round harmonious personality development of the students.

PARA PSYCHOLOGY

It is a relatively new branch of psychology. There are instances where people have sensed that somebody is in trouble despite being at a far away place, have foretold the coming events or have given an account of their previous births. Para psychology tries to go into the depth of such behaviour related to telepathy, extra-sensory perceptions and rebirth etc.

DEVELOPMENT PSYCHOLOGY

This branch of psychology deals with the processes and products of the growth and development of human beings at all stages of life—from conception till death—and in all the aspects of their personality. The study of this branch equips us well with the knowledge of expected behaviour patterns and personality characteristics at various stages of growth and development.

ANIMAL PSYCHOLOGY

This branch of psychology deals with the study of animal behaviour in controlled situations. The study of the behaviour patterns of the animals through various types of experiments and observations constitute the subject matter of this branch. Citable in this connection are the studies related with the behaviour of cats by Thorndike, dogs by Pavlov, rats and pigeons by Skinner and of the chimpanzees by Kohlar and Koffaka. Such studies help in understanding the behaviour of these animals in some or the other type of controlled situations. The other major benefit that can be derived from these studies is of comparative and inferential nature. We can derive comparative analysis of the behaviour of different types of animals in a particular situation or environmental set up. The results of these studies can then be generalized in dealing with of behavioural adjustment and development problems of the human beings.

COGNITIVE PSYCHOLOGY

This branch of psychology deals mainly with the study of the processes and products of growth and development of cognitive abilities and capabilities of the human beings. It studies the behaviour of the individuals in relation to the development of his cognitive strengths and their use in challenging circumstances. It emphasizes the role of one's cognitive abilities like reasoning and thinking; analysis and synthesis, inferring and generalizing, intelligence and insight etc. in the process of learning, problem solving, creative output and adjustment etc. The experts dealing with the study of the branch referred to as cognitive psychologists.

MILITARY PSYCHOLOGY

This branch of psychology studies the use of psychological principles and techniques in the world of military science. How to keep the morale of the soldiers and citizens high during war, how to fight a war of propaganda and intelligence services, how to secure better recruitment of the armed forces personnel and how to improve the fighting skills and organisational climate and leadership etc., are the various topics that are dealt with in this branch of psychology.

LEGAL PSYCHOLOGY

It is that branch of applied psychology which tries to study the behaviour of the persons like clients, criminals, witnesses and so on in their respective surroundings with the help of the application of psychological principles and techniques. The subject matter of this branch deals with improving the ways and means of detecting crimes, false witnesses and other complex phenomena. The root causes of a crime, offence, dispute or any legal case can be properly understood with the help of this branch of psychology, and proper reformatory and rehabilitation measures may be employed.

POLITICAL PSYCHOLOGY

This branch of psychology relates itself with the use of psychological principles and techniques in studying politics and deriving political gains. The knowledge of the dynamics of group behaviour, judgement of the public opinion, leadership qualities, psychology of a propaganda and suggestions, the art of diplomacy, etc., are some of the key concepts that find place in the subject matter of political psychology.

EXPERIMENTAL PSYCHOLOGY

This branch of psychology describes and explains the ways and means of carrying out psychological experiments following scientific methods in controlled or laboratory situations for the study of mental processes and behaviour. It picks up animals, birds and human beings as subjects for these experiments.

GEO-PSYCHOLOGY

This branch of psychology describes and analyses the relationship between physical enviroment, particularly weather, climate, soil and landscape, with behaviour.

HEALTH PSYCHOLOGY

In this branch, the facts, principles and theories of psychology are used in the task of preservation of the physical and mental health of individuals. Since many of our physical ailments are said to be due to of our anxieties, worries, stress, conflicts and frustrations, psychological handling of the affected individuals may help in the prevention and treatment of various physical and mental disorders, ailments and diseases.

SPORTS PSYCHOLOGY

This branch of psychology deals with the study of the behaviour of the players and sports personnel vis-a-vis the activities, experiences, situations and environment prevalent in the world of sports. Today, this branch of psychology is playing quite an effective role in bringing desirable improvement in the processes and persons connected with the sports world. This includes bringing improvement in the mental and physical health of the players, inculcating in them true sportsman's feelings through suitable behaviour modification and group dynamics techniques, providing sufficient motivation and raising their morale at the time of competition, devising training and coaching techniques so that the players excel in individual as well as group activities.

Environmental psychology

Environment plays a key role in affecting and influencing the process of growth and development, evolution of behaviour patterns, learning of specific personality characteristics, disorders and behaviour problems etc. The description and analysis of the process and the ways and the steps we can take for modifying and structuring environment for the social well-being—all these constitute the subject matter of environmental psychology. An environmental psychologist thus gives more emphasis and weightage to the environmental setting and facilities for moulding the behaviour of the individuals in the desired direction, solving their personal and social problems and working towards their individual and social progress.

Community psychology

A particular community, society or group is known to possess its own psychology of thinking, feeling and doing. Those belonging to this community have a unique style of living and behaving, coping with one's self and the environment, and maintaining intra-personal and interpersonal relations. The study of such behviour patterns and styles may thus help in knowing the individual and group behaviour of the members of this community, the merits and limitations of the community resources as facilitator or barrier in their progress and so on. Such knowledge and understanding of community psychology may then help the students, researchers and social workers for devising means and ways for the welfare and progress of the community.

Correctional psychology

This branch of psychology is concerned with the corrective measures and activities designed for modifying the undesirable, abnormal and maladaptive behaviour of the affected individuals. It discusses, explains and suggests the ways and means of the diagnosis, prevention as well as treatment of the deviant behaviour, so that it is brought back to the right channel.

Aerospace psychology

It is relatively a new development of psychology and studies the behaviour of aeronauts and astronauts, who venture to travel in space. They have to face the challenges of a new environment quite different from that on the earth. As soon as they go higher and higher in the space, there is tremendous change in their physiological functioning. Their mental functioning, emotional set up etc. are also affected accordingly. The new challenges faced on account of weightlessness, changed equations of gravitational powers and other special situations and difficulties created by the space related environment demand from them quite a lot in terms of adapting behaviour and sound mental health. Aerospace psychology tries to focus on these issues in order to find the ways and means of providing adequate behavioural training to all those who plan to become astronauts or inhabitants of the space colonies in the coming future.

Consumer psychology

This branch of psychology is concerned with the study of the behaviour of the consumers in relation to their present economic and social status and consumption related environment. The study is quite valuable for the manufacturers, advertisers, shopkeepers and salesman who wish to reach the mind and heart of the consumers for the sale of their products. What do the consumers need? What are their expectations from the products they wish to buy? What kind of behaviour do they expect from the shopkeepers and sales persons? How can they be approached, influenced or motivated to purchase a particular brand? and so on. A number of such questions can be successfully answered through the study of consumer psychology.

INDIVIDUAL PSYCHOLOGY

There are differences among individuals with respect to each and every aspect of human behaviour and personality traits. The nature and causes of such differences are studied under individual psychology.

PSYCOMETRICS

This branch of psychology is concerned with the construction and use of different tests and techniques meant for the measurement or assessment of the various types of human abilities and capacities, the processes and products of human behaviour and nature of the relationships and adjustment etc. Thus, the task of construction and standardisation of various intelligence tests, interest and aptitude tests, attitude scales, inventories and other techniques meant for the assessment of personality traits, behavioural characteristics and adjustment etc. are carried out through the study of this branch. Since statistical methods and techniques are very much needed in the construction, standardisation and application of these measures, these are also included in the subject matter of this branch of psychology.

ORGANISATIONAL OR MANAGERIAL PSYCHOLOGY

The popularity of this branch of psychology is on a continuous rise on account of its utility in bringing desired efficiency in the organisational climate and managerial capacities. With the help of the knowledge and skills acquired through the study of this branch, we can properly study the behaviour of the human resources related to the organisational climate of an establishment or institution. In the light of this study, we can devise suitable means and measures for maintaining proper co-ordination and inter-relationship among the personnel holding different positions in an establishment. We can help them in maintaining their zeal and enthusiasm for exercising their duties properly and co-operatively by seeking proper job satisfaction and adjustment in their work environment.

In this way, as done above we can try to provide an account of the scope of the subject psychology by dividing it into various branches on the basis of their fields of operation, nature of the subject matter included and experiences gained and advantages derived from their use. However, by this division, it should not be assumed that all these branches of psychology are highly independent, autonomous and unrelated to each other. On the contrary, all being the offshoot of the subject psychology are quite interdependent and related to each other. We have divided them into different branches only for the sake of our convenience with regard to their specialised study and application.

Applications of Psychology

Psychology is the science of behaviour and behaviour is the collective name of the various activities performed by us in various walks of life. In this sense, the fields of operation and application of psychology are quite extensive and wide. You may have gained some idea about this from the divisions of the subject psychology into various branches as described earlier in the chapter.

Actually, there is no corner or activity of our life which has remained untouched by the valuable use and application of the subject psychology. We live our lives through our behaviour which lies in the efficient hands of psychology. This is why the use and application of psychology is increasing day by day in all the spheres and walks of life. Let us have a look at its varied applications.

1. **In Education.** The main aim of education is to bring an all-round development in the personality and desired modifications in the behaviour of the students. To achieve this aim, it is important that those who are entrusted with the responsibility of helping the students are acquainted and equipped with the knowledge and skills needed for this purpose. This knowledge and skill can only be properly supplied through the study of a branch of psychology known as Educational Psychology. It teaches us what is behaviour and what is personality? What kind of behavioural changes are desirable at a particular stage of growth and development? What steps can be taken for the proper personality development of child? Through its body of facts, principles and theory, educational psychology equips the teachers, parents and all those, who are in one way or the other, connected with education, for exercising their responsibilities in the most economical and effective way. Truly speaking, the use of psychology in the field of education has resulted in the discovery of ways and means to provide better teaching, guidance, direction and help to the students at all levels of education for their better learning and development. Individualization of education, self-learning, child-centred approach, caring for the exceptionals, bringing the problem children and other types of deviant back into the mainstream, providing better guidance and counselling for the personal, educational and vocational adjustment of the children—all such tasks have been made possible with the use of relevant psychological knowledge and practice. Hence, all the aspects and dimensions of education related with the welfare of the students have been largely influenced and affected by the active involvement of theory and practical application of the subject psychology.

2. **In Guidance and Counselling.** The second major field of operation and application of the subject psychology is related with the task of rendering guidance and counselling services to all those who need such services. Each one of us at one stage or the other requires one or the other type of guidance or counselling for solving our personal, educational and occupational problems. Such type of help or assistance may be properly provided with the application and use of the psychological knowledge and practices. Guidance personnel and counsellors have to take up certain practical and theoretical courses and undergo relevant professional training for equipping themselves in a proper way for exercising their duties. These theoretical courses and practical training, as may be seen anywhere, are highly loaded, determined and controlled by the application of the psychological facts, principles and theories in the field of guidance and counselling. Equipped with such knowledge and skills, they can now know the behaviour of their client, his abilities and capacities, weaknesses and strengths, and so on, and help him accordingly in solving his problem.

3. **In Medicine.** Psychology has proved its worth in the field of medicine and cure. A doctor, nurse or any person who attends to a patient needs to know the science of behaviour to achieve good results. Behaviour has a bigger role than the medicines and this behaviour can only be learnt through psychology. The belief that sickness, whether physical or mental, may be caused by psychological factors has necessiated the use of psychology in this field. It has helped in weeding a lot of superstitions in the diagnosis as well as cure

of mental and physical sickness. Psychology has contributed valuable therapeutic measures like behaviour therapy, play therapy, group therapy, shock therapy, and psychoanalysis, for the diagnosis and cure of patients suffering from psychosomatic as well as mental diseases.

4. **In Business and Industry.** The use of psychology is increasing day by day in the field of business and industry. Those who have tried to utilize the theory and practices of psychology in their working and functioning, have been rewarded accordingly through name and fame in their world of work. In brief, the application of psychology in the field of business and industry may be described through the illustrations of its following types of uses.

   - Psychology through one of its branches, consumer psychology, may help the business establishments to know the psychology of the consumers. Accordingly, it may be known as to what type of behaviour and quality of the product is expected from them by the different sets of consumers. They may then plan and act accordingly for their desired success.
   - In the business and industrial world, style and quality of the propaganda and advertisement of the product play quite an effective role. Once again the service of psychology is needed here to search for an effective as well as economical means to create the required propaganda and advertisement for the sale of the manufactured items. The various types of psychological researches, field survey and samplings, methods and techniques then come in handy for those connected with the propaganda and advertisement tasks undertaken for popularising the products.
   - The organisation and management provide proper legs and wings for the success of any business concern or establishment. Psychology is contributing a lot of learning and is devising better ways and means for proper organisation, and management of all that is done and expected from the human capital. This is why we may find the inclusion of courses like industrial psychology, organisational and managerial psychology etc. in every management, administration and professional training classes like MBA, MSW, etc.
   - The sale or production may be increased if there is a proper work environment in any establishment and this depends upon how well the inter-relationships is maintained among the persons working in that concern. Psychology is then used by the employers directly or through special department established for this purpose to maintain a proper cordial and turstworthy relationships among the workers and other personnel. The provision of work incentives, bonus and other work and living facilities are then devised by observing the psychological principles for motivating, inspiring and adjusting the human capital according to the demands and progress of the establishment.
   - The efficiency of the staff working in an establishment depends upon the degree of job satisfaction. Such satisfaction is made possible through the use of psychological methods and techniques. Similarly, the selection and appointment of the right persons for a particular type of work, the division of work according to the workers' abilities and timely promotion and due incentives etc. also very much count towards the success of an establishment. Use of psychology again helps in all such tasks through its objective methods of testing and evaluation.

5. **In Law and Criminology.** Detection of crimes and dealing with criminals have been greatly influenced by psychology. The old adage, tooth for a tooth and eye for an eye, holds no ground today in dealing with offenders and criminals. No one is criminal by nature but circumstances lead to this maladaptive and criminal behaviour. He can be reformed, rehabilitated and made an useful organ of society if handled properly by making use of psychological knowledge and researches. The use of psychology has also resulted in a change of attitude of the general public as well as civil and judicial authorities in dealing with the so-called bad elements and criminals. In brief, the contribution and application of psychology in the field of law and criminology may be summarized as below:
   - To help in the detection and search of the crime and criminal by testing the validity of an evidence put up in court with the help of the psychology of evidence.
   - To suggest preventive measures for the prevention of offences and crimes in the light of proper analysis of the probable causes.
   - To suggest the ways and means for the proper behaviour modification and rehabilitation of the delinquents and criminals.
6. **In Politics.** Psychology has successfully demonstrated its usefulness in the field of politics. It has been almost customary for every student of Political Science and the politicians to get benefitted in their tasks by making use of the theory and practice of psychology. What is public opinion, how can it be moulded in one's favour or on the other side, what is needed for an effective leadership, what is the significance of the propaganda tactics, suggestions, timely decisions and responses etc. are many things the knowledge and understanding of which is quite essential for the students of politics and politicians. It can be acquired through the use of application of the psychological principles and practices. The game of politics needs to be played according to the changed situations and circumstances. A politician, who can mould himself according to the circumstances or can reverse the flow of the public opinions and attitudes according to his wishes, always proves winner in this game. It is no secret that such abilities, skills and will power can only be acquired through the learning and application of the knowledge of psychology.
7. **In Military Science.** The study of Military Science in theory and practice also makes use of principles and techniques of psychology. This is why in any academic course of military science or its professional training, psychology is given a due place. The reason lies in the multi dimensional use of this subject in all the aspects and dimensions of the world of work of the military personnel. In brief we can summarize the use and applications of psychology here as under.
   - To help in the selection, training, promotion and classification of military personnel.
   - To get acquainted with the adaptation or adjustment level and status of mental health of the soldiers and officers through a careful study of their behaviour and personality traits.
   - To bring desirable modifications and corrections in the environmental situations and work conditions of the defence personnel after analysing the needs to do so.
   - To make use of psychological propaganda, rumours and conversations etc. in maintaining the cold war diplomacy.

- In the time of war, to keep the morale of the defence personnel and that of the citizens quite high.
- To make the defence personnel capable of handling stress in the most difficult situations and odd circumstances.

In this way, the knowledge and application of psychology proves quite helpful in providing a desired channel to the behaviour and work environmental of defence personnel. With the use of its body of knowledge, principles and techniques like sympathy, suggestions, imitation, motivation, group dynamics, behaviour modification, propaganda techniques, quality of leadership and managerial or organisational techniques, psychology is proving its worth in the matters related to education, training, upkeep and progress of the defence personnel in all their dimensions and forms.

8. **In Adjustment and Mental Health.** It is quite essential to have adjustment with one's self and the environment to lead a healthy, happy and successful life. The key to one's adjustment, as explained by the studies and researches in the field of psychology, lies in the gratification of one's basic needs — psychological or socio psychological. The extent to which the needs are gratified or remain in the process of gratification one may feel adjusted. In the contrary situation, it may lead to maladaptation of his behaviour, dissatisfaction with his self and the environment. It paves the way for the deterioration of his mental health and abnormality of his behaviour. All such types of knowledge regarding the status of one's adjustment and nature of one's mental health, the causes leading to such status etc. can only be acquired with the help of the knowledge and skills provided by the subject psychology. Further when we need corrective and remedial measures for the treatment of maladaptive behaviour, abnormality, poor mental health and mental illness or diseases etc., we again have to seek the expert advice and technical help of the psychologists and therapists. Therefore, when we talk about securing one's proper adjustment to oneself and the environment, including security against the mental illness or disease, we have to call for the services and applications of the theory and practices of the subject psychology.

9. **In Human Relationship and World Peace.** One of the special and significant uses and applications of the subject psychology in our lives lies in its capacity to develop mutual understanding, peace and brotherhood among the human beings. Let us for a while search for the root causes of conflicts, fights, failed relationships, and even wars and conflict between individuals, groups or nations. The eruption of mutual distrust, doubts, fears, rivalries, cut throat competitions, the feeling to subjugate or exploit others, exhibitionism and enflated ego etc., may be cited as some of the reasons? Can't we understand that all such causes have come into existence only on account of lack of knowledge and mutual understanding of the behaviour of other persons, groups and nations. The task of psychology is to help us in knowing and understanding the behaviour with respect to others, and if tried honestly, there remains hardly any scope for mutual distrust or misunderstanding which can otherwise lead to unhappy and quarrelsome situations. That is why there is a vast scope of the use and application of the knowledge, skills and techniques of psychology for establishing trustworthy inter-relationship among the human beings crossing the barriers of caste, colour, religion, language and boundaries leading to universal brotherhood and world peace.

10. **In Development of the Self.** Psychology may provide valuable help and assistance for understanding one's self, plan about one's progrerss and actualize one's potential to the maximum in the interest of the self and the society. Psychology in true sense is the science of life. It provides us valuable directions for understanding our own abilities and capacities, develop them properly and then strive for an adequate adjustment with the self and the ever changing needs of the environment. There is an ever growing craving for self actualization and proper development of the abilities and capacities of the individuals since their conception. The knowledge of the various aspects of growth and development, modification of behaviour, the ways and means of seeking a proper harmonious development of the personality of the child helps the parents, teachers and elders to plan and implement all such schemes for self and their wards or children. One can use the knowledge of the many special branches like infant psychology, child psychology, adolescent psychology, adult psychology, psychology of teaching and learning, health psychology, psychology of adjustment, guidance and counselling, etc. for seeking such a proper development and self actualization. Psychology has also provided the ways and means of self development, self actualization, self instruction and self evaluation etc. for the help of all the individuals who wish to strive for the development of their self in tune with the development of the society.

In this way, it can be concluded that psychology has a wide field of application and utility. There is no profession in the world where we do not have an opportunity of utilising the principles and techniques of psychology. Children or adults, normals or abnormals, males or females, rich or poor, educated or uneducated belonging to all castes, colours or creeds, knowingly or unknowingly do make use of psychology and may derive more benefits by gaining proper training in this subject. There is no corner of one's life which cannot be illuminated or glorified with the help or knowledge of psychology. It helps the individual to grow and develop in totality with complete resonance to their environment to achieve happiness and contribute towards social progress and development. In a nutshell, where there exists any living organism, environment and behavioural response, the need for study of behaviour and a subject competent to perform this study will always be felt and where there is any craving or desire for self improvement, adjustment, happiness and social progress, we will have to call for the available or otherwise discovered services of the subject psychology.

SUMMARY

Historically, studied in the name of 'Mental Philosophy' as a separate branch of philosophy, psychology has gradually emerged into a separate discipline claiming the status of science. In doing so, its meaning has changed from time to time as the study of soul, study of mind, study of consciousness and finally as the study of behaviour. Today it is well defined as the science of behaviour by equating the term 'behaviour' with all the life activities and experiences of all the living organisms.

On account of its scientific nature and characteristics like its belief in cause and effect relationship, use of scientific methods in investigation and study of behaviour, it has been given the status of a science. However, it has not been yet developed on account of its limitation to study the behaviour as exactly as possible in other natural and applied sciences. Thereby it is designated as a developing science and not as a developed science.

The scope of psychology is quite extensive and wide. It covers the study of all types of behaviour of all the living organisms. As living organisms and their life activities are so diverse, no limit can be imposed upon the scope of this subject. It has many branches and fields for the study of all types of their behaviour in its theoretical and applied aspects like general psychology, abnormal psychology, industrial psychology, crime psychology, para psychology, legal psychology, experimental psychology, animal psychology, military psychology, educational psychology and sports psychology. Equipped with the knowledge, understanding and skills of its so many branches and fields of study, psychology has gained quite a wide and diversified applications in all the spheres and walks of life like education, guidance and counselling, medicine, military, adjustment and mental health, sports and games, industry and management, politics and law, development of the self and maintenance of human relationships and world peace.

References and Suggested Readings

Guilford, J.B. (Ed.), *Fields of Psychology*, Van Nostrand, New York, 1966.

James, W., *Principles of Psychology*, (2 Vols), Henry Holt, New York, 1890.

———, *Psychology* (Briefer course), Collier, New York, 1962.

Keller, F.S., *The Definitions of Psychology*, Appleton Century, New York, 1937.

McDougall, W., *Psychology—the Study of Behaviour*, Henry Holt, New York, 1912.

———, *An Outline of Psychology*, 13th ed., Methuen, London, 1949.

Munn, N.L., *Introduction to Psychology*, (Indian ed.), Oxford & IBH, Delhi, 1967.

Pilsbury, W.B., *Essentials of Psychology*, Macmillan, New York, 1911.

Watson, J.B., *Psychology as a Behaviourist Views It*, Psycho. rev. Vol. 20, 1913.

———, *Psychology from the Standpoint of a Behaviourist*, J.B. Lippincott, Philadelphia, 1919.

———, *Behaviourism*, Kegan Paul, London, 1930.

Woodworth, R.S., *Psychology*, Methuen, London, 1945.

———, R.S., *Contemporary Schools of Psychology*, Methuen, London, 1948.

Woodworth, R.S. and Marquis, D.G., *Psychology*, 5th ed., Henry Holt, New York, 1948.

2

Educational Psychology—Meaning, Nature and Scope

CHAPTER COMPOSITION

EDUCATIONAL PSYCHOLOGY—MEANING AND DEFINITION

The subject psychology like other natural sciences has two aspects—Pure and Applied. As pure psychology, it formulates broad principles, brings out theories and suggests techniques for the study of human behaviour which finds the practical shape in its applied aspect *i.e.* branches of applied psychology like occupational psychology, clinical psychology, crime psychology, industrial psychology, educational psychology, and so on.

In its pictorial form, these pure and applied aspects of the subject psychology, alongwith their branches, can be represented as shown in Figure 2.1.

Therefore, educational psychology is nothing but one of the branches of applied psychology. It is an attempt to apply the knowledge of psychology to the field of education. It consists of the application of psychological principles and techniques to human behaviour in educational situations. In other words, educational psychology is a study of the experiences and behaviour of the learner in relation to educational environment.

From time to time, psychologists have tried to define educational psychology in their own ways. Some of these definitions are given below:

1. Skinner defines it as: *"Educational Psychology is that branch of Psychology which deals with teaching and learning."* (1958, p. 1).

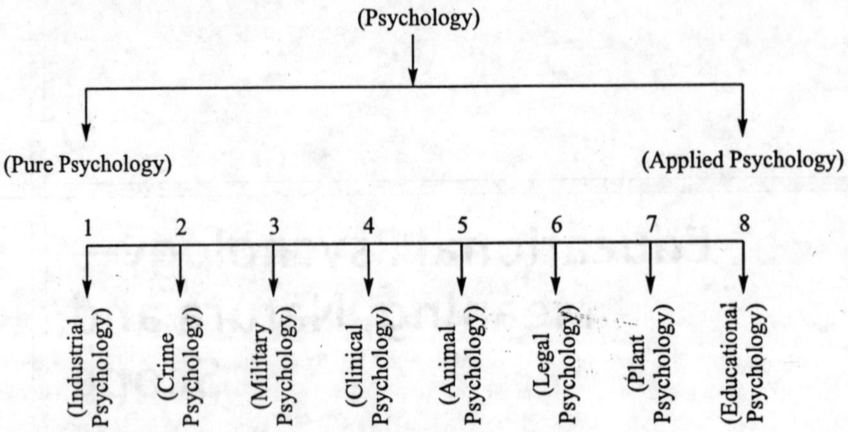

Fig. 2.1 Psychology and its branches.

2. Crow and Crow put it as: *"Educational Psychology describes and explains the learning experiences of an individual from birth through old age."* (1973, p. 7).

   Both these definitions emphasize that educational psychology is a psychology of teaching and learning. Teaching and learning are the main processes of education and pupil (learner) is the key figure in this process. Therefore, it is proper to define educational psychology as the study of the behaviour and experiences of the learner in response to educational environment.

3. There is one more definition of the term educational psychology given by Peel which, in my opinion, is the shortest and the best of all the definitions suggested so far. It states: *"Educational Psychology is the science of Education."* (1956, p. 8).

Let us analyse this branch of psychology in relation with education and see if terming educational psychology as 'science of education' is justified.

EDUCATION AND EDUCATIONAL PSYCHOLOGY

Education, by all means, is an attempt to mould and shape the behaviour of the students. It aims to produce desirable changes in them for the all-round development of their personalities.

The essential knowledge and skill to do this job satisfactorily is supplied by educational psychology as Peel puts it in the following words:

"Educational Psychology helps the teacher to understand the development of his pupils, the range and limits of their capacities, the processes by which they learn and their social relationships." (1956, p. 8).

In this way, the job of an educational psychologist resembles that of an engineer, who is a technical expert and supplies all the knowledge and skill essential for the satisfactory accomplishment of a job like construction of a bridge. In the same way, educational psychologist, who is a technical expert in the field of education, supplies all the information, principles and techniques essential for—

- Understanding the behaviour of the pupil in response to educational environment; and
- Desired modification in his behaviour to bring an all-round development in the student's personality.

In this way, it is quite reasonable to call educational psychology as a science and technology of education.

NATURE OF EDUCATIONAL PSYCHOLOGY

One question that is often put forward is—What is the nature of educational psychology?

The answer to this becomes quite clear when we try to examine the meaning and definitions discussed earlier. Its nature is scientific since it has been accepted that it is a science of education. The relationship between education and education psychology also throws light on its nature. We can summarise the nature of educational psychology in the following ways.

1. Educational psychology is an applied branch of the subject psychology. By applying the principles and techniques of psychology, it tries to study the behaviour and experiences of the pupils.
2. While psychology deals with the behaviour of all the individuals in all walks of life, educational psychology limits its study to the behaviour of the pupil (learner) in relation to educational environment.
3. It is not concerned with the 'what' and 'why' of education, it gives the necessary knowledge and skill (technical guidance) for giving education to the pupils in a satisfactory way.
4. It is not a normative science as it is not concerned with the values of education and does not concern itself with "what ought to be". It is an applied positive science.
5. Educational psychology is not a perfect science. It has its own drawbacks. The human (as well as animal) behaviour is unpredictable. It is more variable and less reliable. Therefore, educational psychology, the applied behavioural science, cannot claim objectivity, exactness and validity as claimed by natural sciences or even applied sciences like medicine and engineering.
6. It employs scientific methods and adopts scientific approach to study the behaviour of an individual in educational environment. Moreover, the controlling of the factors and prediction of the behaviour on generalized results gives educational psychology a complete scientific base. Therefore, it is proper to call its nature as scientific.

SCOPE OF EDUCATIONAL PSYCHOLOGY

When we are asked to point out the scope of a subject, following are the questions we need to answer:

1. What are the limits of its field of operation?
2. What is to be included in its study or what subject matter does it contain?

As pointed out earlier, educational psychology deals with the behaviour of the learner in educational situations (only). Therefore, it becomes imperative that educational psychology limits itself within the four walls of the teaching-learning process and educational environment. It must try to solve the problems evolving in actual teaching-learning situations and help the individuals involved in this process.

The key factors involved in an educational process may be listed as below:

1. Learner or Pupil.
2. Learning experiences.

3. Learning process.
4. Learning situations or environment.
5. Teacher.

The subject matter of education psychology, if it is at all necessary to draw its boundaries, revolves round these five pivots mentioned above.

- **Learner.** The total subject matter of educational psychology primarily revolves around this factor—learner. This section of the subject acquaints us with the need of knowing the learner and deals with the techniques of knowing him well. The topics like below may be included in this section:

  The innate abilities and capacities of the individuals, individual differences and their measurements, the overt, covert, conscious as well as unconscious behaviour of the learner and characteristics of his growth and development at each stage from his childhood to adulthood.
- **Learning experiences.** This is the second area of educational psychology and though the subject does not directly connect itself with the problem of what to teach or what learning experiences to provide the learner, it has the responsibility of suggesting the techniques on acquiring learning experience. Once the task of educational philosophy to decide the aims and objectives of a piece of instruction at a particular stage is finished, the need of educational psychology is felt. At this juncture, Educational psychology helps in deciding the kinds of learning experiences desirable at different stages of growth and development of the learner so that these experiences can be acquired with a greater ease and satisfaction. In this area, educational psychology has the subject matter which facilitates the selection of the desirable experiences for the learner.
- **Learning processes.** After knowing the learner and deciding on the types of learning experiences that are to be provided, the next problem arises when helping learner properly acquires these experiences with ease and convenience. Therefore, around this pivot, educational psychology deals with the nature of learning and how it takes place and comprises topics such as laws, principles and theories of learning, remembering and forgetting, perceiving, concept formation, thinking and reasoning process, problem solving, transfer of training, ways and means of effective learning and so on.
- **Learning situation or environment.** Under this topic, educational psychology focusses on the environmental factors and learning situations which come between the learner and the teacher. Topics like classroom climate and group dynamics, techniques and aids which facilitate learning, evaluation techniques and practice and guidance and counselling which help in the smooth functioning of the teaching-learning process, come under the purview of this pivot.
- **Teacher.** Last but not the least is the teacher. He is a potent force in any scheme of teaching and learning and educational psychology can not forget this key player either. It emphasizes the need of knowing the self for a teacher to play his role properly in the process of education. It discusses his conflicts, motivation, anxiety, adjustment, level of aspiration, etc. Moreover, it throws light on the essential personality traits, interests, aptitudes, characteristics of effective teaching, etc. so as to inspire him to become a successful teacher.

Educational Psychology beyond Boundaries

The five pivots mentioned above, however, do not show the complete picture of the boundaries and limits of educational psychology. In fact, sketching the full picture is quite a difficult task because of the fact that educational psychology is a developing and fast growing science. Like any other developing branch of science, it multiplies itself every year. New ideas keep pouring in because of the result of new researches and experiments. Change is the law of the nature and education, being a dynamic subject, is changing very fast. New problems are coming in the process of education at a faster rate forcing educational psychology to try harder for solution. As new concepts, principles, and techniques are taking birth in the sphere of educational psychology therefore, it is unwise to place a hedge or boundary around the fertile ground of educational psychology by defining its scope. It will not only hamper the progress of this developing subject but also prove an obstacle in the progress of education.

Therefore, educational psychology must be left free for future expansion so as to facilitate the inclusion of all that is created to solve the problems of education and help in the smoothening of teaching-learning process.

FUNCTIONS OF EDUCATIONAL PSYCHOLOGY

Educational psychology, as defined earlier, is definitely that branch of psychology which helps the cause of teaching and learning. As a science of education, it supplies all the information, principles and techniques which may help a teacher in better teaching and a learner in his better learning. Let us now see how the knowledge of this branch helps a teacher and a learner. In other words, let us analyze and elaborate the functions served by educational psychology in the field of teaching and learning.

In Teaching

Educational psychology, with its broad coverage of the content material principles, theories, techniques and applied experiences, first analyses the tasks of the teacher's teaching and then, in its light, tries to supply the knowledge and skills needed by the teacher. Factors required by the teacher in respect to his classroom teaching and other activities for the desirable behaviour modification and all-round growth and development of the students may be outlined as below:

TO KNOW THE LEARNER

Unless the teacher has some knowledge of the potentialities of his student, he cannot go ahead with his task. Educational psychology equips the teacher with the understanding of the child in the following ways:

(i) His interests, attitudes, aptitudes and the other acquired or innate capacities and abilities etc.

(ii) The stage of development linked with his social; emotional, intellectual, physical and aesthetic needs.

(iii) His level of aspiration.

(iv) His conscious and unconscious behaviour.

(v) His motivational behaviour.

(vi) The aspect of his group behaviour.

(vii) The conflicts, desires and other aspects of his mental health.

To select and organise the subject-matter or learning experiences

Once the teacher gets to know the child, the stage is ready for educating the child and following questions come in the way:

- What types of learning experiences or learning materials are to be provided?
- How should we organise or grade the materials or learning experiences?

To answer such questions, which are part of curriculum construction, one needs the knowledge of the characteristics of the learner at each stage of his development, the nature and laws of learning etc. and these questions can be answered through educational psychology.

To suggest art and techniques of learning as well as teaching

After deciding about the learner and the learning material, the next problem of 'how to teach or learn' is also solved with the help of educational psychology. Educational psychology explains the process of learning and suggests the means for effective and enduring learning. It reveals how to maintain interest in the learning process. In this way, it acquaints the teacher with the ways of making pupils learn and thus gives birth to the suitable methdology of teaching. It also suggests that no single method or technique is suitable for all kinds of learners in different circumstances. A teacher should select a proper device or method according to the learning situations he faces.

To arrange learning situations or environment

Midway between the learner and the teacher in an educational process are the learning situations or the environment. Much depends upon the appropriateness of this midway element. The knowledge of educational psychology equips the teacher to take care of the desirable learning situations and environment. Where should individual learning or self-study be implemented and when is group learning or project work suitable, it is suggested by educational psychology. The knowledge of group dynamics and group behaviour gives the necessary art for teaching or learning in a group. In other words, the study of the impact of the learning environment (including equipment facilities and aid material etc.) on the teaching-learning process equips the teacher to take care of the appropriate learning situations or environment.

To acquaint oneself with the mechanism of heredity and environment

The knowledge of the role played by heredity and environment in the process of growth and development of child is very essential for the teacher. Based on this he can weigh their relative importance and take a balanced decision for his work.

Helping in maintaining discipline

Knowledge of educational psychology helps the teacher to have a creative type of discipline as it acquaints him with the nature of the child, his strengths and weaknesses, his interests and aptitudes, etc. on one hand and the art and techniques of teaching and learning on the other. Moreover, his knowledge of the needs drives, fatigue and motivational aspects of the learner and above all, the knowledge of the behaviour pattern and personaiity characteristics of the children-all help him in the process of maintaining proper discipline.

Rendering guidance services

Educational psychology helps the teacher in rendering guidance services to his pupils. He is the person who can know the children better, even more than their parents. With the knowledge of educational psychology at his command, he is well aware of the methods of behavioural assessment and appraisal. He can better diagnose the abilities, interests and aptitudes of his pupils and consequently have an idea of the direction and speed of their development. In this way, with the help of educational psychology, a teacher can show the right direction to his pupils for their total development.

Helping in evaluation and assessment

While furthering in the teaching-learning process, one feels the need for evaluation. After imparting learning experiences to the child, the behavioural changes occurred in him need to be examined and also in the beginning the potentialities are to be known. In educational psychology, as applied behavioural science, evaluation, measurement and appraisal find its place, which make the teacher well-equipped in the task of evaluation with proper professional skill.

Solving classroom problems

There are innumerable problems like backwardness, truancy, bullying, cheating in the classroom situations which are to be faced by a teacher. Educational psychology helps the teacher on this front also. The study of the characteristics of problem children, the dynamics of the group, behavioural characteristics and adjustment etc. equip the teacher to solve the actual classroom problems.

Knowing About Oneself

Knowledge of educational psychology helps the teacher know about himself. His own behaviour pattern, personality characteristics, likes and dislikes, motivation, anxiety, conflicts, adjustment, etc. are all revealed to him. He also learns the psychology of being a teacher and acquaints himself with the traits of a successful teacher and characteristics of effective teaching. All this knowledge helps him in growing as a succeessful teacher.

However, we cannot say that the above mentioned areas are all for which a teacher needs the knowledge of educational psychology. A teacher's needs and problems are too many and have so many aspects. Educational psychology being a science and technology of education, helps the teacher in all the phases of teaching and learning—whether informal or formal, curricular or co-curricular. It does not only equip him for the classroom instruction but also for the other duties assigned to him like—construction of time-table, organization of co-curricular activities, to seek parental co-operation and so on.

Educational Psychology vis-á-vis Learning

Learning is to a large extent helped and facilitated by the knowledge, principle, theories and techniques of educational psychology. In other words, educational psychology may prove quite beneficial to the learners in the realization of the learning objectives in the manner summarized below:

1. Educational psychology may help the learner in the task of knowing one's self. They may thus be acquainted with their abilities and capacities, interests and aptitudes, likings and dislikings, attitudes and dispositions etc. related to the various aspects of their curricular courses and co-curricular means. Such knowledge of their strengths and weaknesses may go a long way and adjust their level of aspiration and mode of working in getting desired success in their learning attempts.
2. The theories, principles and techniques related to motivation, ways of learning and remembering may help them well in their tasks of learning.

3. The knowledge of the processes and factors helpful in paying attention and staying away from the forces of distraction may help them in attending to their studies and learning processes as effectively as possible.
4. To what extent is it essential to remain adjusted to one's self and the environment? The knowledge and techniques helpful in seeking such harmony and better mental health can be better acquired through the applied aspect of educational psychology. It is no denying the fact that those who remain adjusted and enjoy better mental health can be better learners and successful individuals in their lives.
5. The knowledge of the facts and principle related to group dynamics and group behaviour may help them to adjust and merge their behaviour according to the needs of the group learning situations—classroom and other cooperative ways of learning.
6. Through the study of mechanism of heredity and environmental, they may get acquainted with true roles of the hereditary and environmental forces in shaping and moulding their ways of learning and behaving, growth and development, and so on. They must thus protect their self from being damaged with the rumours and incorrect information spread in the society in the name of the perpetuation of caste, creed, colour and blood theories. As a result, a child born in the deprived section of the society may also acquire enough confidence to learn whatever he decides in the course of his life.
7. A student after learning the role of favourable and unfavourable factors, conditions, situations and resources may be able to utilize or make optimum use of the better learning environment on one hand and avoiding the situation or factors that may prove detrimental to his learning success on the other.
8. The theory and mechanism related to remembering and forgetting may help the learner to learn, retain, reproduce and thus fully utilize the fruits of learning as effectively as possible.
9. The knowledge of the mechanism of transfer of learning or training may provide them desired skill for getting proper help from their past and related learning in their present learning assignment as well as utilize their present learning stock in almost all the possible ways in the learning or problem solving behaviour of the future.
10. The knowledge of educational psychology may also equip them with the facts and principles of behaviour modification and other therapeutic techniques. How to acquire desirable habits and proper ways of learning and how to break the bad habits and unlearn the improper ways and means of learning can thus be better acquired through the study and practices of educational psychology.
11. The knowledge of educational psychology makes the learner aware of the developmental stages of human life and the needs and characteristics of the learners at these specific stages of life. Accordingly, the learner may direct and structure his path of learning and learning objectives according to the needs and characteristics of his developmental stage. It may in the long run help him to make his learning attempts and situations well in tune with his developmental characteristics and thus be able to seek harmony in terms of his adjustment with self and the environment.
12. Educational psychology makes the learner realize the importance and facts related to the all-round growth and development of the personality in order to become successful in the realization of the success in the processes and products of learning. It inspires him to strive for the harmonious and progressive growth and development of his abilities and capacities instead of one-sided or lopsided development of his personality.

Thus, it can be easily concluded that while knowledge and practices of educational psychology help the teacher in their tasks related to teaching and fulfilling their obligation as a teacher in all possible ways, the help rendered by it to the learners in their tasks of learning and shaping their lives in the desired ways is also praiseworthy. There is no aspect of the teaching-learning process that can remain untouched or unaffected by the positive results, impacts and influence of the knowledge and skill acquired by the teachers and students from educational psychology. It definitely makes a learner a better learner and a teacher a better teacher and here lies the worth and contribution of the subject in the field of education.

SUMMARY

Educational psychology as one of the branches of applied psychology deals with the study of the behaviour of the learner vis-a-vis his educational environment. Since the behaviour of the learner in relation to educational environment is almost centred around the teaching-learning process, it is designated as that branch of psychology which deals with teaching and learning or a subject of study that helps in better teaching and effective learning to the maximum extent possible. On account of its role as providing best output (in the results of teaching and learning) with the minimum input and efforts as the part of teacher and learner, it has been best described and defined as the science of teaching and learning or in brief, science of education (serving the cause of education as effectively as possible).

The nature of educational psychology like its mother i.e. psychology, is well assumed as quite scientific on account of its employment of scientific methods in the study of learner's behaviour, and the availability of its body of knowledge for further verification and modification through a continuous process of research and experimentation. However, like psychology, it can also not be regarded as perfect science as the natural and applied sciences and thereby we can only designate it as developing science of the learner's behaviour.

Scope of educational psychology is both limited and extensive. It is limited in the sense that being the science of teaching and learning, it should try to confine itself within the boundry walls of the teaching-learning process, comprising learner, learning experiences, the learning processes, learning situations or environment and the teacher. It should, therefore, cater to the better management and functioning of these five pillars of the teaching-learning process. However, as it is also designated and defined in a broader way as a 'Science of education', it has to serve the cause of education as a whole. Since the cause of education is so extensive and wide, its problems and demands so unending and by nature its process is so ever-evolving, it is neither possible nor desirable to put a hedge or boundary on the scope of educational psychology.

In its most applied form, the functions of educational psychology may be well studied in terms of its use and applications in the field of teaching as well as learning. On one hand, it may help the teacher in knowing the learner, selecting and organising the learning experiences and methods of teaching, analysing learning situations or environment, and in assisting him in exercising his duties concerned with maintenance of discipline, rendering guidance services, solving classroom and other behavioural problems of the children, evaluation and assessment and to adjust himself in the existing teaching, learning set up etc. On the other hand, educational psychology may also help the learner in almost all possible ways to attain utmost perfection on the path of learning to reach the desired teaching-learning objectives. Starting from helping him to know his self, it suggets ways and means for his self motivation, attention and goal-directed learning, overall adjustment to his self and environment leading to the overall development of his personality by bringing desirable modification in his learning behaviour and personality variables.

References and Suggested Readings

Bigge, M.L. and Hunt, M.P., *Psychological Foundations of Education*, Harper & Row, New York, 1968.

Crow, L.D. and Alice Crow, *Educational Psychology*, Eurasia Publishing House, New York, 1973.

George, J. Mouley, *Psychology of Effective Teaching*, Holt, Rinehart & Winston, New York, 1968.

Peel, E.A., *The Psychological basis of Education*, Oliver & Boyd, London, 1956.

Skinner, C.E. (Ed.), *Essentials of Educational Psychology,* Englewood Cliffs, Prentice Hall, New Jersey, 1958.

Smith, M. Daniel, *Educational Psychology*, Allyn & Bacon, New York, 1978.

Sorenson, H., *Psychology in Education*, McGraw-Hill, New York, 1964.

Stephens, J.M., *Educational Psychology*, Holt, Rinehart & Winston, New York, 1956.

3

Methods of Studying Behaviour

CHAPTER COMPOSITION

INTRODUCTION

Psychology, as you have read in chapter one, is concerned with the study of the behaviour of all living organisms. The various methods it adopts for such study can be named as below:

1. Introduction Method
2. Observation Method
3. Psycho-analytic Method
4. Experimental Method
5. Differential Method
6. Survey Method
7. Clinical Method
8. Questionnaire Method
9. Interview Method
10. Rating Method
11. Case Study Method

12. Sociometric Method
13. Projective Method

All these methods have their own merits and limitations with regard to their use in the study of behaviour. Therefore, decision of using a particular method or methods in a particular situation for studying the behaviour of particular subject depends upon many factors like whose behaviour is to be studied, what is the purpose of this study, what facilities, resources and equipment are available for the study, and so on. Keeping all these things in view, the task of behaviour investigation requires proper knowledge, understanding and skill of the various methods mentioned above. However, for the purpose of this text we are hereby focussing on those few important methods like Observation, Experimental, Interview, Survey and Case Study, that are frequently used in the field of educational psychology for studying the behaviour of learners.

OBSERVATION METHOD

Observation method may be regarded as one of the most convenient and appropriate methods for the study of human behaviour. We can get valuable information about the behaviour and personality traits of an individual by the systematic and careful observation of his behavioural activities related to his day-to-day life.

In some cases, we may create the situations or conditions for the occurence of a particular type of behaviour so that necessary inferences may be drawn by its observation. For example to draw inferences about the trait of honesty, we can leave or drop some cash or valuable to observe how an individual reacts to such an artificially created situation. In this way the situations, whether natural or artificially created, may be utilised for the observation of one's behaviour and the data collected from such observations, may be employed for drawing inference about one's behaviour or personality characteristics.

What is Observation Method?

Observation, as we know it in sciences, means knowing the environment through sense organs. In the field of psychology, it is concerned with the perception of an individual's behaviour by the other individuals and the interpretation and analysis of the perceived behaviour by them. By this method we can infer the mental processes of other persons through the observation of their external behaviour. In fact it is an indirect approach to the study of the mental processes. If someone frowns, howls, grinds his teeth, closes his fists, we can conclude by these external signs that he is angry. Similarly, as a result of observation—purposive perception—of human conduct we can know a lot about his mental processes and personality. Thus observation stands as one of the important methods of studying the human behaviour.

Styles and Ways of Observation

Observations may be carried out in many ways, forms and styles. Here we are describing a few of such forms and styles.

FORMAL OBSERVATION

Such an observation is carried out in quite a formal way by observing the necessary formalities like (i) providing the information to the individual or individuals about the nature and purpose of the observation; (ii) the date, timing and place of observation; (iii) the names and introduction of the observers; (iv) the necessary pre-preparation needed on the part of the subjects for such an observation just as showing of any maintained record or preparing them or their environment for such inspection and so on. However, such type of observation cannot prove very fruitful in terms of drawing some reliable and valid conclusions about one's behaviour or personality. For example, if we announce to the inmates of a hostel that there would be an inspection of their rooms regarding their habit of cleanliness on a particular date and time, such a formally announced observation will surely fail in its objective of knowing about the cleanliness habit of the boarders. The prior information will automatically make them quite alert. Thus the cleanliness behaviour shown at the time of such formal observation will not be a true representation of their real behaviour. It will have an artificial mask with the aim of turning the results of the observation in their favour. A similar thing may happen at the time of a school's formal inspection or inspection of the house of a bride or groom for the matrimonial purpose simply because on account of prior information, everything or behaviour under observation is hidden behind an artificial mask. Hence no real picture or conclusion about one's behaviour can ever be drawn through the method of formal observation.

Informal observation

Contrary to the formal observation, informal observation is carried out in quite a spontaneous and natural way. Here no prior information about the nature, purpose, timings and place of the observation is given to the individual or individuals. They are thus caught unaware, engaging in their behavioural activities in a quite usual and natural way. In such naturalistic observational situations, we may have a realistic and true picture of the things, events, traits and characteristics of one's behaviour.

Participant observation

In this type of observation, the observer tries to observe the behaviour of an individual or individuals by joining them as an associate or participant in any of their individual or group activities. For example, he may join them in their play activities or accompany them on tour and excursion activities to closely observe them. This may provide good opportunity for the observation of the behaviour of the individuals. However, it suffers from a serious limitation as the presence of an observer may obstruct the natural and spontaneous flow of the behavioural activities of those individuals.

Non-participant observation

This type of observation tries to do away with the above cited defect or limitation of the participant observation. Here the observer observes the behaviour of the individuals in such a way that they may not have any idea that their behaviour in any way is being observed. For this purpose, as an observer he may take his position in such a place and in such a way that while the individuals under observation may not see him, he can clearly watch and hear, if possible, all about their behaviour in action. There may be a screen or a curtain of such a nature as can help for real observation while hiding his presence.

The use of some modern equipment like secret cameras, video recording, audio recording etc. may also serve such purpose. While sitting at quite a far distance, the observer may also take the help of a telescope for a clear but secret observation. Whatever means and methods may be employed by the observer, his motive in such an observation is always to come in contact with the natural and spontaneous behaviour of the subject without making him aware of his presence.

How to Make Use of the Observation Method?

The use of the observation method for the investigation of behaviour generally requires the following four systematic steps.

Planning and Preparation for Observation

The success of an observation depends much on its proper planning and pre-preparation. This initial task requires proper attention on the following aspects.

— What type of behavioural activities or personality traits are to be assessed through observation?

— How the observation work is to be carried out, what type of methods or resources will be used for such observation?

— What type of situation or environment is to be maintained for carrying out the observation work?

— What type of difficulties or adverse situations may occur during the observation work and how can these be overcome for carrying out effective observation?

— How can the observation results be made more reliable, informative, objective and valid?

Observation of the Behaviour

The second step is related with the actual observation work done by the observer as per planning and preparation made in the first step. As far as possible the best methods and techniques should be used here for the observation of the behaviour depending upon the purpose of observation and availability of the resources and environmental situations at the time of observation. Hence, for obtaining better results, the following things should always be kept in mind.

— The subject should not have any idea that his behaviour is under observation. As far as possible, his behaviour is to be observed in a quite naturalistic condition for deriving the sample of his most natural and spontaneous behaviour.

— The observation work must be carried out properly in a quite effective way. The eyes have to play a key role in such an observation. If possible, one should also try to hear about the behavioural activities in action.

— It is always better to make use of a telescope for viewing the activities of individuals specially while sitting at a far off place.

— There must be an adequate arrangement for using the modern observation equipment like cameras, video and audio recording. The use of these appliances not only helps in proper observation of the behavioural activities but prove an automatic recording device for the proper analysis and interpretation of the behaviour.

— It is not proper to rely over the results of a single observation of the subject's behaviour for taking decision about his one or the other behavioural or personality trait. For a desirable objectivity, reliability and validity, such observation work must be repeated by the same observer for a desirable number of times or it should be carried out by a number of different observers at one or a number of times.

— The recording about the nature of the behavioural or personality traits should always be done side by side by the observer while making observation of his behaviour. The failure to do so proves quite costly as the observer may forget or miss some or the other important things or links regarding the observed behaviour. It is always better to prepare a check list for tallying or making the things to be observed in one's behaviour during the observation.

Analysis and Interpretation of the Observed Facts

In this third step, what is observed and recorded in terms of the behavioural or personality traits during the observation of one's behaviour is subjected to a close analysis for deriving the necessary interpretation about his behaviour and personality.

Generalization of the Results

The interpretation made and results arrived at are then used for establishing generalized opinion, facts of principles about the occurence of behaviour and existence of similar personality characteristics among similar individuals in similar situations. It can help us to predict behaviour in similar circumstances, search for the roots of a particular type of behaviour and study the effects of some remedial or treatment measure in the correction of a maladaptive behaviour.

Merits of Observation Method

For the investigation of behaviour the observation method is said to possess the following points to its credit:

1. Observation method makes it possible to study the behaviour in its quite natural and original form, the way it occurs or is performed spontaneously by the subject concerned.
2. Observation and experimentation are said to be the only reliable and valid measures and methods for carrying out any systematic and scientific study. However, it is neither practicable nor feasible to have valid experimentation (observations in the laboratory like controlled situations) for the study of human behaviour. We may have such experiments for the study of animals like cats, rats, pigeons, chimpanzee but in the case of the human behaviour, observation is the only reliable and valid measure that can be properly adopted for the investigation.
3. The observation method needs to study the behaviour of an individual in its present form or state. The method makes it possible to draw inferences about one's behaviour on the basis of the observation of his present behaviour. One does not need to care about his past behaviour or previous history for the investigation of his behaviour as happens with the methods like psychoanalysis and case study. In this way the difficulties faced in digging out the past is almost saved through the use of observation method.
4. There is greater scope for the proper verification of the derived results and conclusion reached through observation method. We can have repeated observations of the behaviour before taking decision regarding a particular behavioural characteristic and this can either be done by a single observer at different times or a team of observers at a single or number of times.
5. It is quite an economical method in terms of time, money and labour. We can collect huge information about the behaviour of a single subject or a number of subjects within the limited time and resources. We need neither any special type of laboratory facilities or controlled environment nor the services of any professionally trained or special psychologists or researcher for the investigation of behaviour by the observation method.
6. It is possible to study the behaviour of any living organisms like plants, animals, insects, birds, besides human beings, through the application of observation method. Thus

observation method has provided a wide scope and application to the study of psychology in our day-to-day lives.

7. Observation method proves helpful in carrying out the investigation of various behavioural characteristics of many individuals at a particular time and occasion.
8. It can be quite helpful in collecting not only the qualitative data but also the quantitative data. The quantification of the observed behavioural traits may thus help in the maintenance of the required objectivity, reliability and validity in the assessment and measurement of one's behaviour and personality.

Demerits of Observation Method

Observation method is said to pose following difficulties and limitations in its application:

1. **Lack of trained observers.** Observation method rests on the quality of a good observation. Such good observation requires the services of some relatively competent and skilled persons as observers. In the absence of such competent observers, observation work is bound to suffer, which may ultimately lead to the failure of the observation method in its objective.
2. **Subjectivity.** Subjectivity factors on the part of the investigator as well as in the process of observation also affect the results of observation. There may arise distortions of observable facts depending on the degree of care in observation. His interest, values, bias and prejudices may also distort the contents and results of observation. One may lay over-emphasis on some particular part of one's behaviour and may altogether neglect some other very important aspect. The interpretations of the recorded events may also be sufficiently coloured. One may read one's own thoughts, feelings and tendencies in the minds of others.
3. **Partial and revengeful attitude of the observer.** Besides subjectivity, a partial and revengeful attitude maintained by the observer towards the subject of observation may also colour and distort the results of the observation. As a result, the favourable and dear ones are always assessed and estimated on quite a higher footing whereas the unfavourable, disliked and thorny ones are looked down upon on one point or the other.
4. **Lack of reliability and validity.** The observation method suffers from lack of reliability and validity on account of its complete dependence on the observation of the external observable behaviour of the subject. Here it is impossible for the observer to know what is going on in the minds of the subjects. He is supposed to observe it through external signs of behaviour. It is quite a difficult task. There is every chance that the subject under observation may play hide and seek and use all his expertise to hide his feelings, emotions and inner personality. A crooked person thus may be able to disguise his evil nature in the garb of artificial sobriety. Similarly, we may mistakenly consider a person otherwise after observing his discipline bound rough attitude, cool temperament and unmixable indifferent behaviour. In this way, overdependence on the external signs of behaviour may make this method a failure when investigating the true nature of the individual concerned.
5. **Difficulty in the occurence and reoccurence of events.** Another serious limitation of the observation method lies in the fact that the behaviour observed is dependent on a particular time and place and on a particular individual or groups of individuals involved. It lacks repeatability as each natural situation can occur only once.

6. **Cause and effect relationship not established.** Another important limitation of the observation method lies in its inability to establish a proper cause and effect relationship. In case we observe that two phenomena, say poverty and delinquency behaviour, invariably occur together, we cannot infer from this that poverty is the sufficient and necessary cause of delinquent behaviour or vice versa.
7. **Total behaviour remains unexplored.** Observation method takes into account only the observation of the external or observable behaviour of the subject. External behaviour is quite an incomplete portrait of one's personality. The internal aspects of one's behaviour or inner mechanism of one's personality remain totally unexplored through the use of observation method. We can't reach the unconscious or even sub-conscious layers of one's mind through the observation of his observable behaviour. Thus, observation method fails in the objective of the investigation of one's total behaviour and aspects of personality.
8. **Difficulty in recording the observation data.** The other limitation of observation method lies with the proper timely recording of the observed events or data regarding the occurence of behaviour. As an observer, one has to observe one or the many things occuring at the same time in the behaviour of the subject. All his attention, concentration and energy is then directed to gather information about the ongoing behavioural activities. The task of simultaneous recording at this time becomes an extra burden. Both the tasks are serious and at best can be done properly by taking them one by one. Now if one does not record the observed phenomena side by side, one is to miss a few things or important links afterwards. In case he records them side by side, it may affect the process of proper observation. The subject may become overconscious that his behaviour is being noted down. Even in the case when the observer takes the help of recording devices like camera, video and audio recording etc., the behaviour of the subject cannot remain spontaneous or natural. As a subject one is quite intelligent to guess the arrangment of such a nature and then one may also like to cover up one's true nature and behaviour under artificial showism and sobriety.

Conclusion

In this way, we can observe that the observation method suffers from a few serious limitations and drawbacks, casting serious doubts about its objectivity, reliability and validity. However, these deficiencies in the application of the observation method cannot be termed as unrepairable. Much depends upon the sincerity, seriousness, abilities and skills of the observer. If he is determined he can find ways and means for the proper investigation of the behaviour of a subject within the limited resources at his disposal.

EXPERIMENTAL METHOD

What is Experimental Method?

In experimental method, due emphasis is laid on the experiments and their subsequent observed results. The word experiment comes from a Latin word meaning "to try" or "put to the test". Therefore, in experimentation we try or put to the test the material or phenomenon, the characteristics or consequences of which we wish to ascertain. In sciences, while doing such experiments in an indoor or outdoor laboratory in natural environment, we may be interested to learn the effect of friction on motion, the effect of sunlight on the growth of the plants, etc. In psychology also, we perform such experiments in our psychological laboratory or outside laboratory in the physical or social settings to study the cause and effect relationship regarding the nature of human behaviour, i.e. the effect of anxiety, drugs or stresses on human behaviour, effect of intelligence or the participation in co-curricular activities on the academic performance of the students. In performing all such experiments, we try to establish certain cause and effect relationship through the objective observations of the actions performed and the subsequent changes produced under pre-arranged or rigidly controlled conditions. From these observations, certain conclusions are drawn and theories or principles formulated.

Features and Characteristics of Experimental Method

Main features and characteristics of the experimental methods may be summarized as below :

- Psychological experiments performed in this method essentially require two persons, the experimenter and the subject or the person whose behaviour is to be observed.
- Psychological experiments are always conducted on living organisms in contrast to experiments in physical sciences which are generally conducted on inorganic or dead subjects.
- The key factor in this method is the controlling of the conditions or variables. By this control we can eliminate irrelevent conditions or variables and isolate relevant ones. Thus, we are able to observe the casual relationship between the two phenomena keeping all other conditions almost constant.

Let us illustrate this feature of experimental method with the help of an example.

Suppose under an experimental study of behaviour, we want to study the effect of intelligence on academic achievement. For such a study we will definitely need to discover the causative relation between the two phenomena (variables)—intelligence and academic achievement. One of these variables, the effect of which we want to study, will be called independent variable and the other as dependent variable. Thus independent variable stands for the cause and dependent variable is characterised as the effect of that cause. The other conditions like study habits, sex, socio-economic conditions, parental education, home environment, health, past learning, memory etc., which exercise desirable impact upon one's achievement besides his intelligence, are termed as intervening variables. In experimentation all such intervening variables are to be controlled, i.e. made constant or equalized and the effect of only one independent variable, is studied on the dependent variable. Here in the present case intelligence is the independent variable whose effect on academic achievement, the dependent variable we want to study. For experimental study we will now try to change and vary the independent variable (intelligence) for observing the concomitant changes in the dependent variable (academic achievement).

The further task concerns with the objective observation and measurement of these changes and then drawing the relevant conclusions about the relationship of intelligence with academic achievement.

Experimental Designs or Techniques

For exercising control over the intervening variables and studying the exclusive effect of the independent variable on dependent variable, the following experimental designs or techniques can be adopted by an investigator.

THE CONTROL TEST METHOD

In this method or technique we try to differentiate by observing the performance under different conditions. First we observe under normal conditions and then again with one condition changed. In this experimental design, there is no need of two different groups of subjects for the experiment. Only the measures can be taken several times under different conditions.

Example. Suppose we want to know whether students can do better on an intelligence test under the influence of a specific drug (like benedrine sulphate, caffeine or Brahmi).

For its finding, we will take only one group of some students preferably of the same age, sex, health conditions, etc. The process of experimentation will then run in the following steps :

(i) These students can be given sugar capsules. After giving the capsules they can be tested on some intelligence test. This will make the initial testing under normal conditions.

(ii) Sometimes later, they can be given drug capsules and tested on the same intelligence test. This will make a test under changed conditions.

(iii) The I.Q. scores under these two situations are noted down and the difference is calculated. If any significant difference is found, it is attributed to the influence of the drug.

CONTROL-GROUP METHOD

Control test method possesses a serious drawback known as positive practice effect. In control-group method we can minimise the practice effect. In this method, two separate groups, known as experimental group and control group, are taken. They are equated or matched on various traits like age, sex, intelligence and other personality characteristics. There is one to one correspondence in the two equated groups. Now the one group—control group—is given sugar capsules and tested on some intelligence test. At the same time, the experimental group is given drug capsules and tested on the same intelligence test. Then the differences in the intelligence scores of the groups are calculated. In case we find some significant differences, they are attributed to the effect of the drug.

ROTATION METHOD

This method consists of presenting two or more simulating situations to the experimental subjects in as many sequences as necessary to control the serial effects of fatigue or practice.

For example if we want to determine the relative influence of two specified conditions A and B (say praise and blame) on a group of subjects, we will not measure all the subjects under conditions A and then under condition B. Condition A might so fatigue or train the subjects that the measures under conditions B would not be independent of the fatigue or training effects. Here two alternatives can be adopted :

(i) We may obtain half the measures for condition A, all the measures for condition B and then the other half of measures for condition A. This technique is sometimes called the ABBA order.

(ii) Another alternative is to separate the subjects into two equated groups, one of which receives treatment A and then B, whereas the other group receives treatment B and then A. Both sets of A results and both sets of B results may then be combined and the difference between these calculated.

Limitations of Experimental Method

1. Experimental method advocates the study of behaviour under completely controlled rigid conditions. These conditions demand the creation of artificial situation or environment and the behaviour studied under these conditions may be or is usually different from spontaneous or natural behaviour. Therefore, experimental method fails to study the behaviour in naturalistic conditions as may be otherwise studied through naturalistic observation.
2. The second limitation or difficulty lies in exercising actual control or handling of the independent variable and the intervening variables. It is quite difficult to know and control all the intervening variables. Similarly we cannot always control the independent variable. Therefore, it is not always possible to create conditions in the laboratory as we would like to and consequently in the absence of the desired controlled conditions, the success of this method becomes quite unpredictable.
3. In the experimental method, we often make use of animals or birds as subjects for the experimentation. It is also debatable whether experimental results obtained from such sources are applicable to human beings or not.
4. The experimental method has a limited scope. All problems of psychology cannot be studied by this method as we cannot perform experiments for all the problems that may be raised in the heterogeneous subject matter of psychology.
5. The dynamic nature of human behaviour does not always allow the independent variable leading to the change in the dependent variable. Human behaviour is not like that of a machine. The anger or fear-producing stimuli or variables may or may not yield the required responses as desired under experiment and hence it is not possible to get the uniform responses or changes in the dependent variables on account of the concomitant changes in the independent variable.
6. The experimental method is both costly and time-consuming. Moreover, handling of this method demands specialized knowledge and skill. In the absence of such an exercise, this method is not functionable.

SURVEY METHOD

Survey method is also often utilised in social studies, including psychology, mainly to collect information about *what exists* by studying and analysing important aspects of a pattern of a particular behaviour, quality or characteristic related to an existing group. We can study the interests, aptitudes, attitudes, habits and many other temperamental and personality characteristics of a group with the help of the survey method. For example, a researcher can very well study the attitude of the young marriagable Indian boys and girls towards dowry system. For this study he has to interact with a group of youths (included in the appropriately chosen representative sample) for knowing their opinions, views, stereotypes and feelings etc. regarding the dowry system. Such contact with a wide variety of people in a group to arrive at a proper conclusion concerned with the objectives of psychological study can only be possible through survey method. As a result we can consider and define survey method *as a method of extensive study involving all the members of a population or its representative sample to derive the desired specific information for the realization of the objectives of the study.*

As a matter of collecting information from the required population or its representative sample in the survey method, there are two main modes that may be employed by the researchers. These are:

1. Use of Questionnaire technique.
2. Use of Interview technique.

Let us discuss these modes one by one.

Use of Questionnaires in Survey

Questionnaire, in general is referred to a device or instrument consisting of some systematically planned questions in the shape of a form which the respondents fill in to provide answers to the questions asked. In this way questionnaires are usually paper and pencil instruments (forms) that are filled up by the respondents of a given population or its representative sample for providing desired information.

TYPES OF SURVEYS USING QUESTIONNAIRES

Mail Survey. When most people think of questionnaires, they think of the mail survey. All of us have, at one time or another, received a questionnaire in the mail. There are many advantages of mail surveys. They are relatively inexpensive to administer. You can send the exactly similar instrument to a wide number of people. They allow the respondents to fill it at their own convenience. But there are some disadvantages as well. Response rates from mail surveys are often very low and mail questionnaires are not the best vehicles to ask for detailed written responses.

Group Administered Survey. A second type is the group administered survey. Here a sample of respondents is brought together and asked to respond to a structural sequence of questions. Traditionally, questionnaires were administered in group settings for convenience. The researcher could give the questionnaire to those who were present and be fairly sure that there would be a high response rate. If the respondents were unclear about the meaning of a question they could ask for clarification. Hence, there were often organizational settings where it was relatively easy to assemble the group (in a school or club or temple etc).

Door to Door Survey. A less familiar type of survey made with the help of questionnaires is the Door to Door survey. In this approach, a researcher goes to the respondent's house or work place and hands over the instrument to the respondent. In some cases, the respondent is asked to mail it back or the researcher returns to pick it up. This approach attempts to blend the advantages of the mail survey and the group or ask follow-up questions by taking the respondent in confidence.

Use of Interview Technique

Technique of Interview may prove an effective device for collecting information from the concerned persons very effectively through face to face contacts.

The use of interview as a technique may involve the features like below.

Formats of the Interview

Interview in view of its structural organisation may be shaped in the following two forms.

(*i*) Structured and standardized.

(*ii*) Unstructured and non-standardized.

Structured and Standardized Interview

In such a format the interview is structured as well as standardized well in advance before it is put to use for getting information from individuals as per the need of the survey study. This is done by taking care of the following:

- — Selection of appropriate questions to be put to the individuals.
- — Deciding about the order and sequence of the asked questions.
- — To decide on the type of answer or responses for an asked question that will be able to provide the required information in the light of the objectives of the study.

Hence, by taking proper definite decisions about the mode, procedure and outcomes of the interview, the desired control can be effectively exercised over the total operation of the inverview.

Such control and effective organization of the interview then automatically makes it more objective, reliable and valid. The path of the interviewer becomes totally clear as he has all the material with him (pre-planned, structured and standardized) for the achievement of the interview objectives.

Unstructured and Non-standardized Interview

In this type of an interview, the interviewer neither possesses the pre-prepared set numbers of questions with him for getting the individual's response nor does he have a set of prior decision about the evaluation of their responses in terms of the objectives of the study. The interviewer is totally free to ask any type of questions to the subject to get the desired information. He may go to any depth to seek such information. This unstructured, unplanned and non-standardized format of the interview may result in losing control over the systematic schedule of the interview. The interviewer may put up unnecessary questions after questions for going deep into a single direction, digging out a single aspect of one's knowledge or personality attribute. The subject may also go on elaborating his response and focussing on an irrelevant theme. Thus, this type of interview is regarded as less objective, reliable and valid in comparison to the structured interview. However, it scores a merit point over the structured interview in its characteristic of providing complete freedom to the interviewer and the subject for setting the direction of the interview as per their own perceptions and the needs of the situations. The subject gets enough opportunity for self expression through the spontaneously formed questions of the interviewer and hence there lies greater opportunity for the expression and assessment of the spontaneous behaviour in such kind of unstructured interview.

Interview as an Instrument in Survey

Application of the interview as an instrument of survey research is usually carried out through the following systematic steps namely (i) Preparation for the interview; (ii) Taking interview; and (iii) Closure of the interview.

Let us try to discuss the various activities carried out in these above mentioned steps.

Preparation for the Interview

The following pre-preparation on the part of interviewer may prove quite helpful in the proper application of the interview instrument in carrying out a survey.

- — Be definite about the objectives of the survey study and then plan accordingly what is to be asked and observed.

- Locate the population or sample of the individuals to be interviewed and try to enlist their cooperation in conducting the interview.
- Motivate respondents by convincing them about the importance of the study well in advance.
- Acquire enough knowledge and training about using interview technique for conducting the survey.
- Ensure that the physical and psychological conditions in which the interview is to be held is properly checked so that the respondent and interviewer do not feel uncomfortable.
- Ensure that the respondent feels as natural and spontaneous as possible for providing desired information.
- Have proper arrangement for recording the responses of the respondents.

Taking an Interview

The following essential points should be kept in mind while taking an interview:

- Introduce yourself with necessary legitimate identification as an interviewer to the respondent.
- Explain the purpose of your study by being as definite and short as possible.
- Give proper time to the respondent to get ready to be interviewed for your survey questions.
- Ask the questions very carefully but in a spontaneous and informal way, surely in the manner and order as planned in your study.
- Don't dominate or monopolise the conversation during the interview. Don't put words unnecessarily into the mouth of the respondent. Be a patient listener and never feel disappointed, irritated or surprised by what the respondent says.
- Use the silent probe technique for getting adequate responses. Just pause and wait. It really works by suggesting to the respondent that you are waiting for his response.
- Encourage the respondent by providing direct encouragement. However, this does not imply that the interviewer approve or disapprove his responses. It may be as simple as saying OK or nodding your head.
- Try to get more desired information by asking for elaboration, *e.g.* Is there anything else you would like to say?
- Ask for the desired clarification, if needed, by putting questions in some other ways or repeating your question.
- Demonstrate warmth and respect towards the respondent. Try to have a rapport by winning his confidence and assuring him of the secrecy of his thoughts and feelings.
- Try to accept the responses and reactions of the respondent in their original form and have its record as adequately as possible.

Closure of the Interview

The following things may be kept in mind at this final stage:

- Ensure optimum realisation of the objectives of the survey, as decided before holding the interview.
- The information collected should be as complete as possible.
- Thank the respondent for allowing you to take his interview.

— Assure the respondent to send the result of your study.

— Make the respondent feel natural and satisfied with the conversation held at the time of the interview. Allow a few minutes for winding up the interview and never make him feel as though you just rushed after realising your motives.

— Try to draw necessary conclusion from the recorded information and responses of the interview for realising the objective of your study.

Merits and Demerits of Interview

MERITS AND ADVANTAGES

The interview as instrument for carrying out survey studies is said to enjoy following advantages and merits:

(i) It provides face-to-face contact or relationship between the interviewer and the interviewee in comparison to the questionnaire.

(ii) Cent per cent answers of the questions put to the individual are obtained through an interview.

(iii) By establishing proper rapport, there is very little danger of not getting answers to the questions and, moreover, one can get most confidential information from the individual, which otherwise he may have hesitated to reveal.

(iv) Interview is relatively a more flexible tool. It pertains explanation, adjustment and variations according to the situation and thus proves one of the essential and important tools for the investigation of behaviour.

LIMITATION AND DRAWBACKS

Interview suffers from the following limitations and drawbacks:

(i) An interview is often held in artificial situation. Therefore, the behaviour as investigated may not be typical or representative of his usual behaviour.

(ii) It suffers from the subjective bias of the interviewer.

(iii) There is no safeguard to stop the individual to hide his feelings or to respond in terms of selective answers.

(iv) It needs a well trained competent interviewer.

(v) It is costly in terms of labour, time and money.

THE CLINICAL METHOD

It is used primarily for diagnosing and treating a problem case and is used extensively in Abnormal Psychology and Educational Psychology. The concept of this method is contained in the concept of the Clinical Psychology itself which can be put as: *Clinical Psychology is the art and technology of dealing with the adjustment problems of the individual.*

Consequently, Clinical method needs to possess the following characteristics:

(i) Clinical method is applicable to individual cases.

(ii) The individual has some problem.

(iii) Both methods of diagnosis and treatment are employed in dealing with these problems.

(iv) Clinical approach is an art as well as a science which means that everybody cannot treat every patient and it gives pleasure in making mankind healthier and better.

The basic factors in this method are the diagnosis and treatment of the individual. Merely detecting the causes of maladjustment is not enough. It should be supplemented by giving the individual fruitful suggestions and treatment.

Method of Diagnosis

Following are the important techniques for the diagnosis of maladjustment or problem behaviour:

Physical Examination

It is important that to modify the behaviour of any individual, the psychologist knows whether the behaviour exhibited is of a functional or of an organic basis. Hence, there should be a careful physical examination of the individual concerned.

Case History

Here, the psychologist tries to go deep into the past history of the subject in order to find out some of the important events or forces which are responsible for making him what he is.

Clinical Interview

Here, the psychologist tries to interview the individual concerned to secure and impart information. With the help of carefully planned questioning and understanding the responses of the patient, he tries to understand him.

Appraisal of Abilities and Aptitudes

Here the strengths and weaknesses of the subject are diagnosed by means of objective tests.

Method of Treatment

By giving the treatment, we try to bring a change in the attitude of the patient so that he may adjust well to his environment. Thus treatment involves a change in behaviour. The task of the psychologist is to arrange events and situations so as to bring about this change.

This can be done by either modifying the environmental forces or by modifying the client's attitude.

Ways of modifying environmental forces:

(i) Client may be physically removed from one situation and placed in another.
(ii) The attitude of parents, teachers and others towards the client may be changed.
(iii) More adequate recreational facilities and play activities may be provided or some suitable measures for sublimation and catharsis of repressed desires and wishes may be taken.

CASE STUDY METHOD

The term 'case' is used in a number of ways conveying different meanings in our day-to-day life. A lawyer helps his client by arguing his *case* in a court of law. A doctor attending a *case* diagnoses the disease of his patient and prescribes appropriate medicines. A Judge decrees after hearing and studying the *case* file of an offender. An officer disposes of a number of *cases* put up by his subordinate clerks.

In all such situations, the term 'case' is used for a person or matter put to examination, observation or investigation for the purpose of helping the concerned individual in deciding or solving the problem related to him. In the subject psychology, the term case is also used almost in the similar sense. Here the individual who is confronted with an educational, vocational, socio psychological or personal problem is termed as a 'case' and is subjected to proper study. Investigation, diagnosis and remedial or treatment measures on the similar lines as happens with the cases of the doctors or lawyers. Such investigation and study of one's behaviour related with the task of finding a solution of his problem is termed as 'Case Study' in the subject of psychology. This investigation or study is quite comprehensive as it covers one's past history related to the problem, the present status of the problem and the future possibilities of dealing with the problem.

Thinking on these lines, a workable definition of the term 'Case Study Method' for the investigation of human behaviour can be adopted as under.

The case study method is that method of behaviour investigation in which we try to study the behaviour of an individual in all the essential aspects by analysing the past record, present position and future possibilities regarding his felt problem or otherwise guidance functions.

Objectives of the Case Study

Case study is carried out mainly to serve the following two purposes:

- **Diagnosis and treatment of behavioural problems.** Some individuals may suffer from one or the other behavioural problems on account of their lack of adjustment to their self or the environment. For example, children may have emotional or social maladjustment or may be lagging behind in their studies or normal mental functioning. Such type of problem children, backward, slow learners, delinquents or antisocial personalities, need quite a careful attention and it is done here by studying them as individual and unique cases. The case study method thus aims at going into the depth of the nature of the problem, search for the probable cause of the eruption of this behaviour and then suggests the possible remedial or treatment measures for helping the sufferer get rid of the problem.
- **To provide better guidance and counselling.** The case study methods and techniques are quite helpful to guidance personnel and counsellors in exercising their responsibilities in an effective way. Whether it is the field of educational guidance or vocational and personal guidance, the assistance to the guidance seeker is given by treating him as a case, studying him in relation to his environment and his problem and then providing appropriate guidance. In this way whatever guidance or counselling is given to a guidance seeker or counsellee depends to a great extent on the results of his case study, much in the same way as a doctor has to carry out the proper diagnosis of his patient's problem before subscribing any medicines for the treatment.

Subjects of the Case Study

It must be clear by now that whosoever feels any kind of difficulty and problem in his adjustment, development or progress, or due to one reason or the other, if we as investigators are interested in the investigation or study of one's behaviour, then such individual may be treated as a case for carrying out the study in a quite professional and technical way. Thus all individuals, whether normal or abnormal, average, above average or below average in the possession of the abilities or capacities related to their growth and development, personality traits or adjustment, may be taken as a subject for the case study. However, in general, the case study is more particularly applied for those in search of any assistance or help for solving their felt problems or for those whose behaviour we want to study in bringing desirable modification for their necessary adjustment, development and progress. This is why case studies of the following types of children or individuals are more commonly carried out in the field of education and psychology—(i) Creative person; (ii) Gifted or Genius; (iii) Backward or Slow learners; (iv) Delinquents or Criminals; (v) Persons suffering from emotional, social psychological and educational problems or maladjustment; (vi) Addicted individuals; (vii) Antisocial personality, etc.

How to Make Use of the Case Study Method?

In the case study method, any individual who is under study, is treated as a unique or individual case in himself. Thus the study of his behaviour begins by giving due recognition and respect to his individuality. The next task is concerned with the establishment of a good rapport with him. He must be taken in confidence by winning over his trust and faith in the investigation. Henceforth all attempts are made to know him in relation to his personal identity, past history particularly regarding his felt problem of development and adjustment, all relevant information about the present status, circumstances and situations concerning his behaviour, development and adjustment, and so on. Truly speaking, case study aims to study the past and present of the subject thoroughly in all its aspects of behavioural or personality dimensions vis-a-vis his environment. In this way, it deeply studies the investigation of all the essential things related to the subject's case in a very comprehensive way. Technically it is quite proper to use a pre-prepared format for such a study. It may provide more objectivity, reliability and validity to the case study work. The use of such a format may be illustrated through the case study of a problem adolescent.

Case Study of a Problem Adolescent

1. Identifying Data

(i) Name	*Narender Chawla*
(ii) Sex	*Male*
(iii) Father's Name	*Sh. R.K. Chawla*
(iv) Address	*House No. 150, Model Town, Delhi*
(v) Date of Birth	*10.1.1989*
(vi) Name of the School	*Govt. Sr. Sec. School, Delhi*
(vii) Class	*X*
(viii) **Problems**	
— Emotional:	*Extremely Aggressive*
— Social:	*Excessive sex interests, teasing girls*
— Education:	*Little interest in studies.*

Source of identification: The parents and teachers have identified these problems and told about these in their own way to the investigator.

2. Birth Information

(i) Place of birth:	*Delhi*
(ii) The health of the mother at the time of his birth:	*Normal*
(iii) The health of the subject at the time of birth:	*Normal*

(iv) Any mishappening at the time of the birth:	*No mishap*	

3. Health Record

(i) General Health	Good/Average/Poor	*Good*
(ii) Height		*5'4"*
(iii) Weight		*50 kg*
(iv) Eyesight	Normal/Defective	*Normal*
(v) Power of Hearing	Normal/Defective	*Normal*
(vi) Power of Conversation	Normal/Defective	*Normal*
(vii) Condition of Teeth	Normal/Defective	*Normal*
(viii) Condition of Throat	Normal/Defective	*Normal*
(ix) Does the subject perform daily exercise for health.	Yes/No	*No*

4. Family Data

(i) Tell, if		
(a) Father is alive or dead		*Alive*
(b) Mother is alive or dead		*Alive*
(ii) If both alive, do they live together/ live separately/are divorced		*Live together*
(iii) Education of the Father		*M.B.B.S., M.D.*
(iv) Occupation of the Father		*Doctor*
(v) Education of the Mother		*M.B.B.S., M.S.*
(vi) Number of real brothers with their age		*No Brother*
(vii) Number of real sisters with their age		*Two (18 & 13 years)*
(viii) Total Members in the Family		*Five*
(ix) Joint Family	Yes/No	*No*
(x) The birth order of the Subject First/Second/Third/Fourth etc.		*Second*
(xi) Has the subject been brought up in the family	Yes/No	*No*
(xii) Does the subject get proper love and affection from his parents?	Yes/No	*No, lack of love and affection*
(xiii) Does the subject get proper recreational facilities at home?	Yes/No	*No*
(xiv) Does the subject get proper education?	Yes/No	*No*
(xv) Do the parents meet all the basic needs of the subject?	Yes/No	*His psychological needs are not satisfied*
(xvi) Do the parents provide due encouragement to the subject?	Yes/No	*No*
(xvii) Is the relationships between father and mother quite satisfactory?	Yes/No	*No*
(xviii) Is the relationship between the subject and parents quite satisfactory?	Yes/No	*No*

(xix) How does the subject spend his leisure time?

(a) Mostly with members of the family — Yes/No — *No*

(b) Mostly with friends — Yes/No — *No*

(c) Anywhere outside family — Yes/No — *Yes*

(xx) His attitude towards siblings — Positive/Negative *Negative*

(xxi) The attitude of siblings towards the subject — Positive/Negative *Negative*

(xxii) The discipline in the home — Strict/Loose *Loose*

5. Socio-Economic Status

(i) The total monthly income of the family — *More than Rs. 20000*

(ii) The source of the income — *Salary and some private practice*

(iii) Does the family own a house? — Yes/No *No*

(iv) The source of entertainment within the family environment—Radio/ Television/Magazines/Indoor games etc. — *Radio/Television Magazines*

(v) The surroundings where family is residing Lonely/Crowdy — *Not so crowdy*

(vi) The type of society in which the family resides : High/Middle/Low — *High, Middle class*

(vii) The status of the family in the society High/Middle/Low — *Middle*

6. (i) **Level of Intelligence**

(a) The opinion of the teachers — *Above average intelligence*

(b) The opinion of the parents — *Average Intelligence*

(ii) **Level of creativity**

(a) The opinion of the teachers — *Demonstrates creativity in his work and adjustment*

(b) The opinion of the parents — *Nothing creative can be expected from him.*

7. Educational Record

(i) Academic Achievements (Last three years)

Subjects	*Class VII Year 1998*	*Class VIII Year 1999*	*Class IX Year 2000*
Hindi	55/100	40/100	34/100
English	60/100	50/100	35/100
Mathematics	80/100	40/100	30/100
General Science	70/100	35/100	33/100
Social Sciences	65/100	35/100	33/100
Art	75/100	38/100	34/100
Total	405/600	238/600	199/600
The position in the class	II positon	30th out of 50	Passed with Grace marks 46th out of 50

(ii)	The subjects he likes most	*English and Art*
(iii)	The subjects he does not like	*Maths and Science*
(iv)	The relationship with the teachers Good/Satisfactory/Not satisfactory	*Not satisfactory*
(v)	The relationship with the colleagues Good/Satisfactory/Not satisfactory	*Not satisfactory*
(vi)	The opinion of the teachers about the subject	*Careless*
(vii)	The status of his attendance in the school Satisfactory/Unsatisfactory	*Unsatisfactory*
(viii)	Has he ever failed in the school examination?	*He has passed IX class with the grace marks*
(ix)	If yes, the name of the subject in which failed	*Mathematics*

8. Areas of Interests

(i) Co-Curricular Activities

The name of the activity	*Participated or not participated*	*The distinction if achieved*
(a) Drama/Play	Participated	—
(b) Music	Not participated	—
(c) On the spot painting	Participated	—
(d) N.C.C.	Not participated	—
(e) Social Sciences	Not participated	—
(f) Declamation/Debate	Not participated	—
(g) Games and Sports	Participated	Won some prizes
(h) Literary	Not participated	—
(i) Any other	Participated in excursion	—

(ii) What type of books does he want to read? — *Film magazines, love stories and detective novels*

(iii) His specific interests:

(a) *Reading novels and film magazines*

(b) Watching films

(c) Having friendship with girls and *teasing them.*

9. Adjustment

(i) *Home Adjustment*

(a)	Does the subject feel that his parents are disappointed with him?	Yes/No	*Yes*
(b)	Does the subject enjoy the family environment?	Yes/No	*No*

(ii) *Emotional Adjustment*

(a) Does the subject feel difficulty in talking to strangers? Yes/No *No*

(b) Does the subject usually remain anxious? Yes/No *No*

(iii) *Social Adjustment*

(a) Does the subject make friendship easily with others? Yes/No *Yes*

(b) Does he take interest in social work? Yes/No *Yes*

10. Behaviour in the Classroom

(i) Does the subject behave properly with his teachers? Yes/No *No*

(ii) Does the subject take interest in classroom activities? Yes/No *No*

11. Behaviour in the Classroom

(i) Does the subject demonstrate a socially responsive behaviour on the playground? Yes/No *No*

(ii) Does the subject remain aggressive and assertive on the playground? Yes/No *Yes*

12. Personality Traits

Traits	*High level*	*Middle level*	*Low level*
Self confidence	H	Ⓜ	L
Emotional stability	H	M	Ⓛ
Stability	H	Ⓜ	L
Leadership	H	Ⓜ	L
Persistence	H	M	Ⓛ

Note: The encircled M and L here are indicating the middle and low levels respectively of the possession of the related personality traits. The subject has not reached a high level in respect of the demonstration of any of the mentioned traits in his behaviour.

13. Educational and Vocational Plan or Ambitions

(i) What subjects would the subject prefer for his further studies after class X?

First choice *Dramatics*
Second choice *Fine Arts*
Third choice *Tourism*

(ii) What profession or occupation would the subject prefer to enter after his studies?

First choice *Hotel Management*
Second choice *Tourism*
Third choice *Commerce*

14. Follow up Work

After collecting relevant information in the above form by using a pre-structured pro forma through various sources, attempts were again made to seek interview with his parents, colleagues, family members and friends for bringing more objectivity, reliability and validity to the collected data. The observation of their behaviour was also subjected to repetition for arriving at more appropriate conclusions. All these above mentioned efforts related to the case study of our subject Narendra Chawla has finally led us to conclude about him as under:

Subject and His Problem. Narendra is enjoying a good physical health. He is above average in intelligence. He is ill tempered, emotional and aggressive in his behaviour. He faired well in his studies till class VII. His downfall began from class VIII. It was at this time when his mother joined a service and both his parents were quite occupied in their respective professions. The higher social status made them quite busy at the cost of looking after their home and children. Now there is free-for-all in the home environment. The impact of western culture is clearly reflected in the life style of all the family members. The elder sister has developed unhealthy heterosexual relationships. Following her steps, Narendra has developed an unusual excessive interest in girls to the extent of teasing and molesting them. He is maladjusted in the class and school and it has led to his truant behaviour. He has no attraction for the school life except taking part in dramatic or excursion activities for the sake of fun and enjoyment.

Probable Causes of His Present Behaviour. The more probable causes leading him to such present status may be listed as below :

(a) He is not receiving the desired emotional support from his parents.

(b) His sexually deviant behaviour may be the result of the impact of the sex behaviour of his parents and elder sister. There is no co-education in his own school and this has led him not to pay proper respect to the opposite sex. His interest in heterosexual behaviour has directed him to tease and harass girls.

(c) There is no proper provision and opportunities for the co-curricular and social activities in the school curriculum. Teachers are also indifferent to the children's need and there is no proper arrangement for the guidance and counselling services in the school.

Remedial Work and Suggestions

1. The parents should come to the reality. They must try to bring desirable changes in their attitude especially in dealing with their children. They must not neglect their children for their own enjoyment, professionalism and social life. Narendra should get the essential moral, emotional and educational support from his parents.
2. There is need of proper change in the attitudes, behaviour and inter-personal relationships on the part of every member of the family. The parents should produce better examples before the youngsters. The over indulgence in sex behaviour, especially in the presence or awareness of the children should be altogether avoided by the parents.
3. The school environment also needs to be restructured in terms of suitable modifications in the methods of teaching, individual attention and care, proper organisation of appropriate cocurricular activities and social work, group activities, tours and excursions, and the maintenance of proper discipline in classrooms and school etc. Narendra, for his behaviour modification, needs some extra care and attention from the teachers and school authorities. He should be properly attended to and given due recognition and appreciation for the goodness shown in any ongoing curricular or extra-curricular activities.

Merits and Demerits of Case Study Method

Merits: Case study method may be credited with some of the following merit points:

1. It provides quite a deep, intensive and overall investigation of the behaviour of the individual with respect to his past and the present. Here he is studied as a complete case in relation to his environmental surroundings, developmental characteristics and adjustment difficulties. Such thorough study and investigation of his behaviour is only possible through this method. As a result, the method has unique advantage of the subject under study.
2. The method can play an effective role in the proper identification, diagnosis and subsequent remedial work, adjustment and rehabilitation of the problem children, maladjusted or maladaptive personalities, emotionally or socially disturbed individuals, delinquents, criminals or antisocial persons by studying them thoroughly as individual cases.
3. In this method of behaviour study, the scope and range of study is quite wide and comprehensive. The information and data are collected from various persons and information sources. The behavioural data is subjected to repeated observation. All such efforts make the results of the investigation or study more objective, reliable and valid.
4. This method provides opportunity for collecting data on personal basis, by seeking personal interview, going close to the original source of information, etc. The rapport established and the closeness received may help the investigator to reach and search for the most secret and unconscious seated behaviour of the subject. In this way, the information received through the case study may prove more effective in the solution of the felt problems or rendering proper educational, vocational and personal guidance.

Demerits: The case study method suffers from some of the following limitations and defects:

1. The case study work is quite a technical and professional work. It can't be entrusted to the classroom subject teachers. There is a need for specially trained teachers or professionals for carrying out the studies.
2. There is a need of collecting so much of the information regarding a case from a number of persons or sources. The work is quite extensive and comprehensive. There are a lot of difficulties and utilization of individual resources in terms of time, labour and money causing a serious handicap to the collection of the required information for such a study.
3. There is no guarantee of objectivity, reliability and validity of the information or data collected from the variety of sources for the analysis and investigation of the behaviour of the subject.
4. The field of application of this method is quite narrow and limited. It can only be used properly for the investigation of the behaviour of the problem children or antisocial or deviant personalities.
5. There is no provision of studying the behaviour in a properly controlled laboratory like situation. Therefore we can not expect the required objectivity, reliability and validity in the results of the study carried out through the case study method like in the experimental or other scientific observations.
6. The task of proper analysis and interpretation of the collected information, drawing conclusions and then having its proper generalization is quite difficult and technical. There are plenty of chances of drawing erroneous conclusion about the causes and possible remedial work related to the problems and needed assistance to the subject.

Conclusion

Hence, the case study method may be seen to be affected with a few drawbacks and limitations. However, keeping in view the advantages of this method we must give it a due place in the task of investigating human behaviour. Afterall, it is the only method that strives hard for the thorough investigation of one's hebaviour in all its sorts, forms and dimensions by using one's past and present record for the future possibilities of one's better adjustment, development and progress in the interest of self and the society.

SUMMARY

For studying the behaviour of the learners in educational situations and learner's related environment, educational psychology more frequently makes use of the methods like observation, experimental, survey, clinical and case study.

In observation method the situations, whether natural or artificially created may be utilized for the observation of one's behaviour and the data collected from the observation may then be utilized for drawing interferences about one's behaviour or personality characteristics. The observation for the required purposes may be carried out in many ways and styles like formal observation (*e.g.* pre-informed formal inspection), informal observation (carried out in most informal, spontaneous and natural way without informing the subjects), participant observation (participation of observer in the events of observation), and non-participant observation (observing without letting the subjects know) etc. The success of the observation method lies in the proper planning and preparation of the observation task and then carefully observing and recording the events of the observed behaviour. However, as a matter of studying behaviour objective method suffer from a number of limitations and drawbacks casting serious doubts about its objectivity, reliability and validity.

Experimental method is considered to be the most scientific and objective method for studying behaviour. It allows to study the cause and effect relationship concerned with a particular type of behaviour by performing experiments in the psychology laboratory or outside laboratory in the physical or social settings, *i.e.* effect of intelligence or the participation in cocurricular activities on the academic performance of the students. The key factor in the method is the controlling conditions or variables for studying the cause and effect relationships. Independent variable stands for the cause and dependent on the effect of that cause. The other conditions or factors influencing the cause-effect relationship are called intervening variables. These variables need to be controlled by making use of various experimental designs like control test or single group design, control group design, matching group design and design involving relation depending upon the resources in hand and demands of the study.

Survey method is employed mainly to collect information about what exists by studying and analysing important aspects of a pattern of a particular behaviour, quality or characteristic related to a existing group, *i.e.* attitude towards dowry/population/education/birth control. Here the desired information is collected from the total population or its representative sample by adopting mainly two modes—questionnaire and interview techniques. Generally surveys like mail survey, group administered survey and door-to-door survey are carried out with the use of questionnaires. In interviews, we can have more personal touch and face-to-face contacts for collecting useful information. In general we may have three types of interviews for the required surveying task namely personal interview, group interview and telephone or electronic interview.

Clinical method is primarily used for diagnosing and treating a problem behaviour. The basic factors and steps involved in this method then lies in outlining the diagnosis and treatment procedure. Diagnosis is carried out by having physical examination, preparing case history, organising the clinical interview and getting appraisal of abilities and aptitudes etc. After collecting useful information through diagnosis, treatment measures are applied in the shape of (*i*) modifying the environmental forces and (*ii*) modifying the individuals' attitude for enabling him adjusting to his self and the environment to get rid of problem.

Case study method allows to study the behaviour of an individual in its totality by analysing the past record, present position and future possibilities regarding his felt problem or otherwise guidance functions. It can be utilised for the diagnosis and treatment of behavioural problems as well as for the purpose of planning better guidance and counselling to the normal and exceptional ones.

In this method, the individual under study is treated as a unique or individual case in himself and then attempts are made to know him in relation to his personal identity, past history particularly regarding his felt problem/exceptionality, all relevant information about the present status, circumstances and situations concerning his behaviour, development and adjustment etc. After collecting relevant information (preferably using a pre-structured pro forma) through various sources, attempts are then made to derive useful conclusions about the probable causes, needs and requirements, possible remedial tasks, etc. for the betterment of the individual.

References and Suggested Readings

Andrews, T.G. (Ed.), *Methods of Psychology*, John Wiley, New York, 1958.

Boring, E.G., *A History of Experimental Psychology*, 2nd ed., Appletion Century, Crofts, New York, 1950.

Horney, K., *New ways in Psycho analysis*, W.W. Norton, New York, 1939.

Wilson, E.B. Jr., *An Introduction to Scientific Research*, McGraw-Hill, New York, 1952.

Woodworth, R.S., *Experimental Psychology*, Rev. ed., Holt, New York, 1954.

4

Heredity and Environment

CHAPTER COMPOSITION

WHAT IS HEREDITY?

A cat gives birth to a kitten, a cow to a calf and a human being to a child. The members of one species resemble each other and possess characteristics that are common to their respective species. Now the question arises: what is responsible for a particular type of body, shape and other likewise characteristics in the members of one species. Furthermore we find that there are individual differences even in the members of the same species. A child resembles his sisters, brothers, parents, grandparents, and other members of the family more than the people unrelated to him at all. What is it that causes such similarities and dissimilarities? The answer to this is heredity which means that an offspring inherits most of the personality traits of his parents and forefathers that make him resemble them. It is in this sense that Douglas and Holland have defined heredity as follows:

"One's heredity consists of all the structures, physical characteristics, functions or capacities derived from parents, other ancestry or species." (1947, p. 51)

When does a child inherit such personality characteristics from his parents or forefathers and how is this process of inheritance performed? What helps in such inheritance? There are some of the basic questions that need some clarification at this stage. For the answers, let us try to understand how life begins.

How life begins: Life in human being actually begins with the conception, approximately nine months before birth. The mechanism of conception is explained below:

The male and female reproductive organs produce germ cells. In the males, their testes produce the male germ cells, the spermatozoa, while the females' ovaries produce the female germ cells, the ova. Life is the result of the union of these male and female cells.

As a result of coitus at the time of mating, numerous male germ cells try to come in contact with the female germ cells. The male germ cells are deposited at the mouth of the uterus and they try to make contact with the single ovum. (Normally only one ovum is produced in each menstural cycle). Out of the many spermatozoa, only one sperm comes in contact with the ovum and makes it fertilized. This fertilized ovum is the beginning of the life which starts the process of the child's development in the mother's womb.

The fertilized ovum consists of a semi-fluid mass called cytoplasm and within the cytoplasm lies the nucleus which contains the chromosomes. The chromosomes exist in pairs. In the fertilized ovum (zygote), there are 23 pairs of chromosomes, 23 of which are contributed by the father and 23 by the mother. (See Fig. 4.1).

Each chromosome consists of a number of minute particles called genes. The genes are the physical substances passed on from parents to offspring and thus, are the real carriers and determiners of the heredity traits. What we get out of the heredity is the net result of the traits and characteristics of the parents and forefathers transmitted to the zygote through the respective genes.

Therefore, the inherited characteristics are always transmitted through respective genes at the time of the fertilization of the ovum by the sperm and consequently *heredity refers to a biological mechanism as a result of which a child gets something from his ancestral stock through his parents. It points out the native capital and endowment of an individual, the sum total of the traits potentially present in the fertilized ovum at the time of conception.*

Heredity and Variations

With the discussion so far, we now know the cause of similarities between child and his immediate parents. However, it is still not clear as to why we sometimes find children possessing altogether different characteristics and traits from their parents. For example:

(i) Both the parents are of black complexion while the baby is white.
(ii) The parents are extra ordinarily genious while the child is not.
(iii) The child does not inherit the blindness, lameness or mental disorder of his parents.
(iv) The child does not resemble any of his sisters and brothers.

Let us try to seek clarification for these doubts. In fact, variations as observed above are the result of chance factors that work as under:

- It is purely by chance that a particular sperm fuses with a particular ovum to form a zygote. Moreover, in zygote there are 23 pairs of chromosomes, 23 of which are contributed by the sperm of the father and 23 by the ovum of the mother. Which chromosomes from ovum

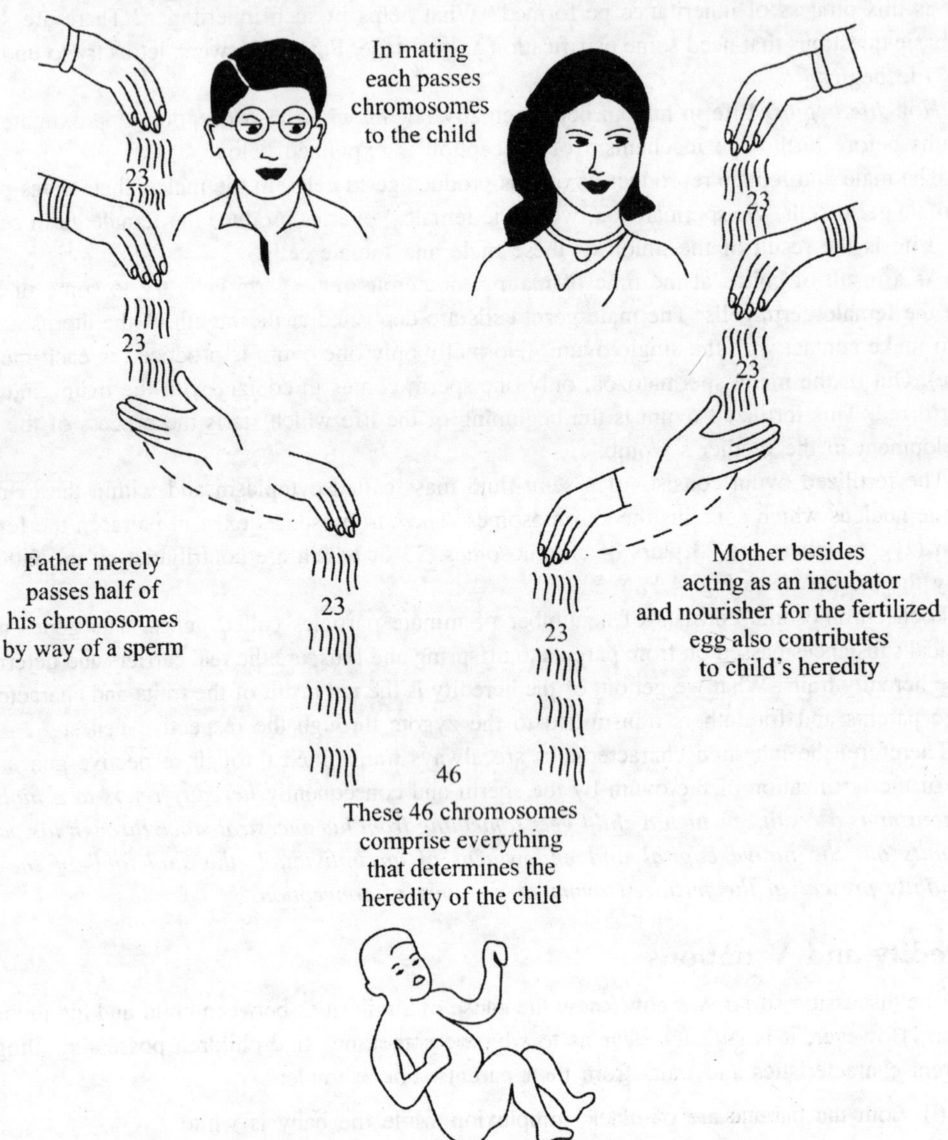

Fig. 4.1 Transmission of chromosomes at the time of conception.

will pair with which chromosomes from sperm depends upon chance. A million of permutation and combination is possible for the union of chromosomes which contain genes. This explains why no two individuals are perfectly identical.

- What does an individual get from heredity is determined by the genes which he received through his parents. The traits of the forefathers, besides those of immediate parents, are also transmitted to the offspring through these genes. Therefore, it is possible that a child may possess certain traits that are traceable to one or more of the ancestors, even though they may not be visible in either of the parents.

Twins and Heredity

Normally at the time of fertilization, a single ovum is fertilized by a sperm of the male. It results in the birth of a single offspring at one time. But sometimes this normal function is disturbed and there are cases of multiple births—the birth of two or more offsprings at a time. The birth of twins is one of such cases where two individuals are born at the same time. There are two types of twins namely Identical twins and Fraternal twins.

Identical twins. Usually the fertilization of one ovum by one sperm produces the offspring. Sometimes, however, it so happens that when the ovum splits, as a result of fertilization the two parts fail to unite together. The result is that each part develops into a complete individual. The twins formed thus are called Identical because they carry exactly same genes. They possess almost the same characteristics and are definitely of the same sex.

Fraternal twins. Normally in the ovary of the human female during each menstrual period, only one ovum is matured but it may happen that two or more ova mature simultaneously and be fertilized at the same time by two different sperms. The result is that two different zygotes are produced. The individuals thus produced are known as the Fraternal twins or Non-identical twins. They have different combination of chromosomes and genes as both ova are fertilized by different sperms. Fraternal twins, therefore, are sure to differ in many traits. Unlike the identical twins, they may not necessarily belong to the same sex.

Theories of the Mechanism of Heredity

Biologists and hereditarians, as a result of their studies and experiments, have come up with certain theories propagating their view points for explaining the mechanism and outcomes of the heredity endowments. Let us talk about some of them.

THEORY OF CONTINUITY OF GERMPLASM

Credit for the propagation of this theory goes to Weisman. According to him, there are two types of cells in the human body, namely—somatic cells and germ cells. While somatic cells are responsible for the maintenance and development of the somatic structure, germ cells contribute towards the hereditary endowments. These germ cells are formed through germ plasm which is subject to transmission from one generation to the other in a continuation process. As parents, the present generation is the trustee of the age-old hereditary germ plasm of their ancestors which is passed by them to their offsprings.

Thus, according to Weisman, child is as old as his remotest ancestors. All the traits of his first ancestors are to be found in the child. He does not inherit the modification of the intermediary generation in those traits. This continuity of germ plasm is the reason why man gives birth to a man and not a dog.

Weisman supported his viewpoints with his experiments on rats. He cut off their tails for several successive generations but each new generation got a tail at birth, concluding that modification in the bodily structure was not herited by the successive generation. The newborns continued to resemble their remotest ancestors.

In our day-to-day lives, we also observe that a son born to a physically handicapped person is normal and without any handicap. Similarly, the scars on either parents' face and body due to small pox are not inherited by their children. Thus, the theory of continuity of germ plasm clearly states that there is no transmission of acquired traits. It is only the inherited traits, the abilities and traits received from the parents (in the form of ancestral stock of germ plasm), that are transmitted from one generation to another. The fact thus remains that in any way there is no transmission of the acquired traits as Crow and Crow observe, *"A mother who may have acquired curly hair by ways of attending a beauty shop cannot transmit the acquired curl in her hair to her daughter. The son of a skilful carpenter may himself become a skilled worker in his father's vocation only if he inherits whatever potentialities are needed for the development of the skill and is simulated towards engaging in the kind of training which ensure for him competence equal to or superior to that of his father."* (1973, p. 36)

In conclusion, potentialities of development (the contribution of the hereditary transmission of germ plasm), and not acquired skills, knowledge and attitudes are transmitted from one generation to another.

GALTON'S BIOMETRY THEORY

On the basis of the statistical methods to study heredity, Galton concluded that not only the immediate parents but all their ancestors do contribute their shares of hereditary endowments to the child in a diminished order as stated by Galton himself in the following words:

"The two parents between them contribute, on the average one half of each inherited faculty, each of them contribute one quarter of it. The four grandparents one eighth, or each of them one sixteenth and so on. The sum of the series 1/2 + 1/4 + 1/8 + 1/16 + = ... 1 or the total inheritance of the organism."

In this way, the contribution towards the heredity fund of the child goes on diminishing in hierachical order as depicted below :

Contribution of the immediate parents—1/2 of the total
Contribution of the grandparent—1/4 of the total
Contribution of the great grandparents—1/8 of the total
Contribution of great great grandparents—1/16 of the total
And so on.........................

MENDEL'S THEORY OF HEREDITY

Gregor Mendal was a monk in Australia. He was fond of experimenting with garden peas. In one of his experiments, he used two varieties of peas, one tall and the other short. After cross-fertilizing them in the succcessive generations, he noticed the following developments:

(i) In the first generation, the hybrid peas were all tall.

(ii) In the second generation, there were three tall pea plants as compared to one short plant. In other words, the ratio was 3 : 1.

(iii) In the third generation, all the short type of peas plants produced peas of their own variety. In the case of tall types the result was as under:

1/3rd of the tall type produced their own type.

Remaining 2/3rd of the tall types produced both tall and short types in the ratio of 3 : 1.

The result of his above experiment can be diagrammatically represented as under:

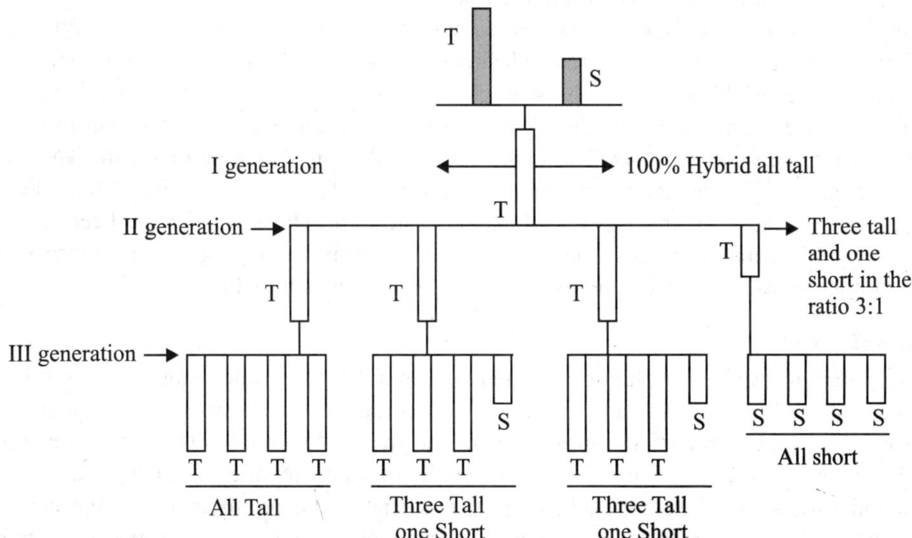

Fig. 4.2 The results of crossing the tall and short varieties of peas in three successive generations.

These experiments brought into light two main ideas or principles governing the mechanism of inheritance:

Principle of dominance: According to this principle, when two traits or characteristics are paired, one of them becomes dominant. (In the above experiment on peas, the tallness was a dominant trait and the shortness was recessive). This dominant trait has more chances to get stamped on the offsprings.

Principle of segregation: Basic traits like tallness and shortness in peas always try to retain their individuality. They give the proof of their existence in some way or the other. In the third generation the hybrid element was segregated as short peas produced all short plants and in the tall variety, majority produced tall plants. From this we can conclude that after some generations of hybrids produced, there happens always revision of the main type (short or tall) *i.e.* disappearance of hybrids. It may also be concluded that the recessive traits lie dormant in the offsprings and there are chances of their coming into picture even if in a limited ratio as and when they get an opportunity to do so.

All of the theories stated so far believe in non-transmission of the modification of intermediary generation or the acquired traits to the coming generation. In case such rigidity had been imposed in strict sense, then it would not have been possible to see the consequences of the process of evolution. Variations are bound to happen as we proceed from generation to generation and these variations are definitely brought out by the process of evolution. The two other theories given by Darwin and Lamark may throw light on the mechanism and consequences of the process of evolution in relation to its role in the transmission of modified and acquired traits to the progeny.

Let us discuss them one by one.

DARWIN'S THEORY

According to Darwin, life is full of struggles. One has to keep struggling for existence and survival. However, in this struggle only those species or individuals can survive who are the fittest and wise enough to adapt themselves to the changed circumstances of life. This has been happening since the starting of life on this earth. In the struggle for existence, only those species have been able to survive who were fortunate enough to get favourable variations through the transmission of the acquired traits of their predecessors. This process has resulted in the evolution of life. There has been a lot of changes, slight and major variations, in the characteristics and traits of the species from generation to generation in the process of natural selection. Those, who have been selected and favoured in this adaptation process, have been able to survive and progress and those who could not have either vanished or led quite a miserable or unsatisfactory life.

LAMARK'S THEORY

While according to Darwin, evolution was the result of a process of the struggle and survival of the fittest through natural selection and choice of inheriting favoured variation and acquired traits, Lamark emphasized the role of an inward urge of the species to adjust to the changed environment. According to him, there is an inner urge, a hereditary characteristic, in each organism to bring changes and variations in itself for adjusting it to the need and requirements of the environment. As a result of this, one introduces certain specific changes or acquire certain needed traits in one's behaviour and personality. These changes, variations or acquired, over the generations are then transmitted through the mechanism of heredity. Lamark has clarified his viewpoints by citing the example of giraffe.

According to Lamark, the giraffe, as the history of evolution would tell, did not originally possess a long neck but over the years it has enlongated due to the enhanced need and efforts of the species for generations, to stretch its neck in order to reach the leaves of tall trees. The slight changes and modifications in the length of the neck brought by the efforts of a particular generation might have been transferred to succcessive generations who made a further advance in the same direction resulting in the long neck, a permanent acquired feature transmissible to the coming generation.

LAWS OF HEREDITY

The above cited theories of heredity have further given birth to certain specific principles and laws for explaining the process and outcomes of the mechanism of heredity. These laws are briefly discussed below.

Law of Similarity (Like Begets Like)

According to this law of inheritance, children tend to be similar to their parents. Thus following the notion of like begets like, the children of fair coloured parents are likely to be fair, while those of the dark coloured are likely to be dark in complexion. Likewise, in inheritance of intellectual potentialities, bright parents are likely to have bright children, average parents—average children and dull parents—dull children. While the child of a German or Afghan national has all the possibilities of inheriting tall height and broad structure from his parents, a Japanese or Nepalese child is likely to inherit short structure and appearance resembling its parents.

This law of similarity and resemblance may thus work well in explaining the transfer of so many traits and characteristics from parents to their offsprings. However, it does not appear to be universal. There are many exceptions. Fair coloured parents may have dark complexioned children and dark-eyed parents may have blue-eyed children. Similarly bright parents may have dull children or dull parents may produce bright kids. The disparity or variation in the mechanism of inheritance thus needs some other laws or principles for its explanation.

Law of Variation

According to this law of inheritance, children may vary or differ from their parents with respect to one or the other traits or characteristics. As Sorenson (1948) puts it: *"The reason for such variations lies in the characteristics of the germ cells of the parents. Germ cells contain many determiners (in the name of chromosomes and genes) which are in fact responsible for the transmission of hereditary characteristics to the offsprings."* (p. 256).

The type of combination of genes and chromosomes (The determiners of traits and characteristics) a child gets from his immediate parents solely depends on mere chance. This explains the differences and variations among the children of the same parents, even the children of same sex and twins. Moreover, as pointed out by the already referred inheritance theory of continuity of germplasm, the parents are said to be the trustee of the age-old hereditary characteristics that they transfer in the form of germ plasm to their offsprings. In such a transfer, it may be possible that the child inherits many of the characteristics or traits of his ancestors that lie dormant in his immediate parents. It explains why parents with darker complexion may also have fair children. Children of the same parents may also differ widely in terms of the inheritance of one or the other traits.

The reason for such variations may also be explained on the basis of the findings of some other theories of inheritance (already discussed in the text) propagated by the well-known personalities like Mendel, Darwin and Lamark. While Mendel has explained the possibilities of variations in the succcessive generations through his findings in the characteristics of hybrids of peas and rats etc, Darwin and Lamark have supported the principle of variation through their own explanations of the process of evolution needed to bring bodily and behavioural changes in the species on account of the demands of their environment for survival and progress.

Law of Regression

This law of inheritance is governed by the phenomenon of regression which means that there is an inherent tendency in the human beings to move towards the mean or average for the transmission of traits and characteristics from one generation to another.

As a result *"Children of tall parents tend to be taller than the average but not so tall as their parents. The offspring of especially talented parent can be expected to be less gifted from their parents and similarly the children of less able parents probably will exceed parental ability."* (Crow and Crow, p. 38).

Thus, for any trait under transmission through hereditary mechanism, there is a tendency to move towards the average rather than farther below or above it. This is why son of a great artist or scientist seldom becomes as great as his father or the son of dull parents always show better performance than his parents.

EDUCATIONAL IMPLICATIONS

The above mentioned three principles or laws of inheritance have wide educational implications in terms of better understanding of the general characteristics and individual differences found in children. The findings of these three laws are not at all contradictory as they may appear at first instance. In fact, they provide solid support to each other for better understanding of the mechanism and outcomes of inheritance. Therefore, we should try to understand the outcome of inheritance by taking a synthesized view of all the three principles or laws in the manner summarized below:

(1) As a human being, a child will definitely inherit all those traits and characteristics which are generally attributed to human beings. Furthermore, he is likely to inherit (with some slight variations) all those traits and characteristics which are common and peculiar to the family lines (paternal and maternal) of which he is a product.

The understanding of such resemblance (like begets like) may prove thus, of wide educational implications to the teachers and educational thinkers and planners. They may very well estimate the potentialities of the children as members of the human race and also as a member of a particular family.

(2) Although a child has a tendency to resemble his parents, ancestors or members of the race in many of the traits or characteristics, yet he is not definitely a replica. According to the law of variation, he is bound to differ in one or the other ways from them. Therefore, we should not be surprised to observe significant differences or variations among the parents and their children or among the siblings. The hard realities related to such variations found in the children may help the teacher and parents be cautious in dealing with them. Accordingly, they should not expect or search for similar traits or potentialities in the children as found in the parents, certain members of the family or siblings who had earlier earned for themselves a good or bad reputation due to such traits or characteristics.

(3) The law of regression clearly states that for any trait there is a tendency for the children to regress towards the average. Here, there is a good news and ray of hope for the offsprings of the less capable, dull, idiot or below averages. Following the law of regression, their children will certainly be higher in those traits in which the parents are low. Here also lies a message for the teachers who tend to neglect the children of the less capable parents simply on the argument that like begets like.

They must take a synthesized view while taking into consideration the other laws and principles of inheritance. According to the law of regression, these children are likely to be better than their incapable parents. Moreover, a child's heredity does not solely rest on the traits and characteristics of the immediate parents. It is an age-old phenomenon that may be influenced or dominated by all or any of the ancestors (from paternal or maternal side). Therefore, the combination a child inherits at the time of conception in the form of chromosomes and genes is the matter of pure chance and thus, as a teacher or parent, we should never underestimate the potentialities of the child for his future progress and development.

(4) The theories and principles of inheritance especially related to the phenomenon of continuity of germ plasm, may reveal to the teacher, and parents that the germ cells (not the somatic or body cells) are the true basis for the transmission of hereditary characteristics. Therefore, deficiencies regarding the somatic or bodily structure of the parents are not transferred to the children. A son or daughter of a physically handicapped person is, therefore, not necessarily a born handicapped.

Similarly, only the potentialities of development, and not the acquired skills, knowledge and attitudes of the parents, are inherited by the children.
Therefore, it is not necessary that son of a musician will be a born musician or daughter of a dancer a born dancer. However, he or she may inherit such potentialities on its own, which may be further developed through well-planned efforts and training.

WHAT IS ENVIRONMENT?

From the above discussion, it is clear that a child inherits the traits and characteristics of his parents and forefathers through genes at the time of conception. Therefore, what he possesses at the time of conception is all due to heredity. It is the native capital given to him for starting his life. After conception, how he develops is the outcome of the interaction between his hereditary characteristics and environment. The forces of environment begin to play their part and influence the growth and development of an individual right from the time of the fertilization of the ovum by sperm. Therefore, from the environmental point of view, not only what happens after birth is important, but also what goes on inside the womb of the mother after conception has equal significance.

The above point of view has given birth to many meanings and definitions of environment and have been mentioned as follows:

Boring, Langfield and Weld
"The environment is everything that affects the individual except his genes." (1961, p. 422)

Wordworth and Marquis
"Environment covers all the outside factors that have acted on the individual since he began life." (1948, p. 156)

The views expressed by the above writers lead to the conclusion that environment consists of external forces, which influence the growth and development of an individual right from his conception. Before birth, the mother's womb is the place where these forces play their part. Nutrition is received by the embryo through the blood stream of the mother. The physiological and psychological states of the mother during pregnancy, her habits and interests, etc all influence the development of the baby. After birth, the child is exposed to numerous environmental forces that are purely external in nature. These can be divided into two parts, physical forces and social or cultural forces. The food, water, climate, physical atmosphere at home, school, village or city, all physical facilities available are all included in the physical forces while parents, members of the family, friends and classmates, neighbours, teachers, members of the community and the society, the means of mass communication and recreation, religious places, clubs, libraries, etc. constitute the social forces.

These different environmental forces have a desirable impact upon the physical, social, emotional, intellectual, moral and aesthetic development of an individual. Their influence is a continuous one, which begins with the emergence of life and continues till death.

HEREDITY Vs ENVIRONMENT

Arguments in favour of heredity and environment, showing the relative importance of one or the other, have given birth to an untangible controversy. On one end are the hereditarians who claim that heredity is all in all and decides and sets everything about the personality of an individual. No amount of education or training can change the individual from what he is or has been in his ancestral beings. Education to them is futile. The function of education or environment in the making of the personality, according to them, can be compared to the polishing or painting of a wooden furniture.

No polish or paint can change the basic qualities of the wood used in the furniture. It only improves its appearance and might increase its life a little.

The environmentalists, on the other hand, are of the opinion that heredity does not, in any way, affect the growth and development of an individual. Man is the product of his environment. He is what his environment has made him. There is nothing like definite heredity characteristics or inherited qualities. What a man has done another man can also do if he gets favourable opportunities. Watson, one of the prominent environmentalists, went much ahead. He declared—*"Give me any child, I will make him what you desire."* Thus, according to the environmentalists, environment is all in all. The growth and development of an individual is the net result of his environment.

Both hereditarians and environmentalists have engaged themselves in psychological experimentations since time immemorial and have put forward their experiments in support of their viewpoints. Some of the mentionable experiments are given below.

Experiments Performed by Hereditarians

F.N. Freeman's Study

This study is based on an experiment analysed through the calculation of coefficients of correlation and their comparison. The summary is given below:

Coefficient of correlation of the intelligence test score of

Identical twins	=	.90
Fraternal twins	=	.60
Siblings (brothers or sisters)	=	.50
Cousins	=	.25

The study shows the increased similarity in intelligence test scores with the increase in the amount of blood relationship. Mathematically, it concludes that blood relationship is directly proportional to the similarity in intelligence. According to herediatarians, this experiment gives sufficient evidence in favour of the theory of royal blood.

Studies of Family Histories

Two of the famous studies based on family histories are given below:

Kallikak Family Study

H.H. Goddard studied Kallikak family. Kallikak was a soldier who married two women. First was a feeble-minded girl and the other was a normal one. The family line established by the feeble-minded woman contained 480 direct descendents among whom only 46 normal individuals were found, the others were criminals, drunkards, feeble-minded, patients, sexually perverted, illegitimate, etc. However, among 496 direct descendents of the line established by the normal woman, all were normal with an exception of five.

Juke Family Study

This study was conducted by Dugdal. Juke was a corrupt fisherman. His wife was also corrupt. About

1,200 descendents of the family line established by them were studied. It was found that most of these descendents were paupers and prostitutes. Only a few of them were found normal.

Galton Francis's Study

In 1869, he prepared a list of 977 genius and well-to-do persons and investigated about their relatives. They were found to have 536 eminent relatives. For comparison he prepared another list of 977 average men and similarly investigated about their relatives. These 977 average men had but four relatives who were eminent. By this data, he concluded that intelligence and all other likewise personality characteristics are transmitted through blood.

Studies on Identical Twins

Various such studies have also been conducted. G.C. Schwesinger made one such study in the manner given below.

He took 10 pairs of identical twins for his study. The individuals in each pair were brought up separately in different environments. After attaining maturity, both the counterparts in a pair were compared. In six pairs, no difference in their intelligence quotient was noted and the remainder differed by 15 or 17 points. He, hence, concluded that heredity is an important factor in determining the intelligence and other likewise characteristics of personality.

Experiments Performed by Environmentalists

Newman, Freeman and Holzinger

In 1937, they reported a case study of 19 pairs of identical twins. They found that while the I.Q. difference of the identical twins reared together was 5.9 point, it was 8.2 for the twins reared apart. In this study, they tried to compare the impact of different environments on the pattern of development by making constant the heredity factor with the help of identical twins. It was found that environment plays a decisive role in bringing individual differences.

Kodak's Analysis

It is based on his experiment and it also emphasizes the importance of environment. He studied foster children. The true mothers of these children were tested on certain mental test. The average I.Q. of this group of 80 mothers was 87.7. The majority of the mothers fell "below average", 53.8 per cent had IQs below 90, 16.3 per cent were borderline and 13.8 were feeble-minded. Yet the average IQs of their children was 116. If heredity determines the future course, then these foster children could not have gained much in terms of I.Q. This study clearly shows the influence of environment on the growth and development of personality characteristics.

Case History of Ramu, the Wolf Boy

The case history of some children reared in the forest by wolves also throws light on the role of environment in the personality development.

One such child was Ramu, known as the wolf boy. When he was quite young, he was picked up by a wolf. He remained among the wolves for a pretty long time and became wolf-like in his food habits, speech and other traits. He could only crawl instead of walking and uttered sounds like a wolf.

Similar was the case with two sisters, Amla and Kamla, aged 2 and 9 years. They were found in the forest of Bengal in 1920 from the den of a wolf. They used to talk, walk and act like wolves. Amla died in an hospital after some time, but Kamla was subject to further study. By providing suitable environment and training, she was made to walk on foot and speak like a human child.

There are so many other studies which support the role of environment in the personality development. Notable among them are studies done by IOWA School of American Educational Psychologists and the Chicago Sociologists. These studies have concluded that environment plays a decisive role in moulding the patterns of one's life. Experiments with twins, siblings and foster children all seem to indicate that children getting privileged environment have all the chances to go ahead in life in comparison to the children getting less privileged environment.

Now, we can see that both hereditarians and environmentalists have conducted different experiments to support their viewpoints. Dr. Prem Pasricha has given beautiful concluding remarks about these experiments. She writes, *"It is quite customary for the Psychologists wedded to either side, viz. heredity and environment, to perform experiments and quote findings in favour of either of the factors. It has also been found that the findings of these experiments can be interpreted either way and can be easily made to support the opposite view. When analyzed in an objective manner, it indicates clearly that the two are so closely interwoven that it is difficult to separate the effect of one from that of the other."* (1963, p.18).

Let us see why it is difficult to conduct actual experiments for the study of the impact of pure heredity or environment on the growth and development of an individual.

To study the impact of environment, we have to take individuals with same heredity. After keeping them in different environments, the comparison can be made. Similarly, for studying the impact of heredity, environmental factor should be made constant. The individuals belonging to different hereditary stock and brought up in exactly similar environments can be compared for this purpose.

There are so many difficulties one faces while conducting these studies. These are listed below:

(i) In the first place, it is impossible to get individuals with the same heredity. Even identical twins are not supposed to have exactly the same genes and therefore, the same hereditary characteristics.

(ii) If we, for the time being, assume that identical twins at the time of conception, belong to approximately similar hereditary stock, then the question arises—is it possible to experiment upon them right from the time of conception? Right from the time of fertilization and division of ovum, can these twins be subject to different types of environments for studying the impact of environmental differences? The answer is 'No'. It is only after their birth—approximately 9 months after their conception—that the pair is available for experimentation. We cannot rule out the environmental effects inside the womb of the mother. Nor can these effects be ruled out as common influence upon the pair. It may happen that one of the twins gets a major share of nourishment and is favoured with the inner environment in one way or the other while the other is neglected to some extent. Therefore, it is difficult to get even the identical twins with the exactly similar heredity.

(iii) The environmental influence also cannot be controlled. It is very difficult to provide exactly similar environment to different individuals. Even a mother cannot show equal amount of love and affection to her own children. There are individual differences and as a result one individual is likely to be favoured in comparison to others. In the same foster home or orphanage, the various individuals may be subjected to different starta of environmental conditions depending upon their own nature as well as the attitude of the keepers and officials. Therefore, the uniformity with regard to the provision of same environment is hard to be maintained.

The main reason for the failure in controlling either the heredity or environmental factor lies in the plain truth that the influence of these factors on the growth and development of an individual is inseparable. Right from the time of conception, the two factors are so intermingled and interwoven that it is hard to say whether a particular characteristic is due to the genetic or the environmental influence.

Conclusions Regarding the Relative Importance of Heredity and Environment

1. The supposition, that a particular trait in an individual is exclusively the product of his heredity or environment, does not hold any ground. The individual's personality is the product of both heredity and environmental factors. In this connection, Mclver and Page have said very correctly that *"Every phenomenon of life is the product of both. Each is as necessary to the result as the other. Neither can ever by eliminated and neither can ever be isolated."* (1949, p.95).
   Whatever character or trait we may consider, it requires both heredity and environment for its development.
2. The controversial arguments regarding the relative importance of heredity and environment are quite useless. The question whether heredity is more important than environment or vice versa is same like asking whether seed or soil is more important for the proper development of a plant. The seed and the soil do not work independently, but are mutually dependent. The seed has the power to grow into a certain kind of plant but how well it will grow depends on what soil it gets. The plant cannot grow without either the seed or the soil. It needs both. We cannot do away with either of them. It is also useless to say that one of them contributes more in the proper development of the plant.
   In the similar way, it is hard to make any statement in favour of either heredity or environment in the process of development of an organism. Both are equally important and indispensable. Also, it is wrong to assume that they are opposed to each other. They are complementary and support each other. The remark made by Garrett is worth quoting. *"Nothing is more certain than that heredity and environment are coacting influences and that both are essential to achievement."* (1968, p. 34).
3. In judging the relationship between heredity and environment, it can now be said that it is absurd to make such statements as heredity or environment. The 'either' and 'or' relationship between these two terms does not exist. It is always heredity and environment. But now the question arises as to whether the relationship between them is simply of an additive nature or not. The personality of an individual is not just the sum total of his heredity and environment. In this connection, Woodworth and Marquis write: *"The relation of heredity and environment is not like addition, but more like multiplication. The individual does not equal heredity + environment, but does equal heredity × environment."* (1948, p. 158).

   They further declare that an individual is the joint product of his heredity and environment just like the area of a rectangle is the joint product of its length and breadth.

In this way, like the base of a rectangle, heredity provides us the structure on which, with the help of favourable environment, desired construction can be made. The native powers and energies of an individual, like the seed, lie in the heredity but it is up to the environment to extract these energies and make them able to reach their maximum limits.

4. Let us also study the relationship between heredity and environment from a diffferent angle. As a gift from heredity, we get our working capital but it is the environment which gives us the opportunity to invest it. The capital as well as the opportunities for its proper development are essential for the proper success in the business. There are instances where individuals starting with a very meagre amount have been able to earn in millions. Therefore, the extreme view of hereditarians like Galton, '*Thus far shall thou go and no further*' is not correct. However, if we take it for granted, then even 'thus far' we can't go without the cooperation of environment.

If the environment cannot help us in growing beyond the limits determined by heredity, at least it gives us enormous assistance within those limits. How far can a rubber band be stretched depends upon the nature of the raw material used in it. It can be stretched to the maximum limit but stretching even up to this limit will depend upon the strength of the individual who pulls it and the favourable or unfavourable circumstances at the time of pulling.

Therefore, it is the duty of the teachers and parents to see that every child gets maximum opportunity for his development. It is true that nothing entirely foreign to one's nature can be acquired. From a tree of cactus, mangoes cannot be grwon. But to have fine mangoes out of the seed, which heredity has provided, we must be careful like a wise gardener who provides proper manure and water to his plants and cares for their well-being and safety as he can. Like him we teachers cannot arrange for the selected seeds and plantation. Heredity factor is out of our control. But environmental influences can be controlled to a great extent. With proper environment the native powers which may be dormant are awakened and stimulated to activity. Every child is able to explore his maximum abilities only when he is provided with appropriate opportunities for growth and development.

SUMMARY

Heredity refers to a biological mechanism as a result of which a child receives the traits and characteristics of his ancestors and race through the transmission of particular genes to him by his immediate parents at the time of his conception in the womb of his mother.

Dissimilarities between the child and his immediate parents may arise on account of the fact that the child may inherit some or the other characteristics of his ancestors (not necessarily present in the parents) through the inherited genes.

Twins are born when two children are conceived by the mother at the same time. *Identical twins* have exactly the same set of genes and therefore possess same characteristics and are definitely of the same sex. **Fraternal twins** have different combination of chromosomes and genes and are therefore sure to differ in many traits. In addition they may belong to the same or opposite sex.

Many theories have been propagated for explaining the mechanism and outcomes of the hereditary endowments. *Theory of continuity of Germ plasm* was propagated by Weisman. According to him, there are two types of cells in the human body named as somatic and germ cells countable towards the heredity endowments. These germ cells are formed through germ plasm which is subject to transmission from one generation to another in a continuation process. The immediate parents being the trustee of the age-old hereditary germ plasm of their ancestors pass them to their offsprings. In such a transfer, there is no transmission of ancestral acquired traits. It is only the inherited traits in the form of ancestral stock of germ plasm that are transmitted from one generation to another. *Galton's Biometry Theory* holds that not only the immediate parents but all their ancestors contribute their shares of hereditary endowments to the child in a diminished order. *Mendel's theory of heredity* (propagated by Gregor Mendel on the basis of his experiments on two varieties of peas, one tall and other short) brought out two principles namely the principle of dominance (out of the two traits dominant and recessive, the dominant one has more chances for being inherited) and principle of segregation (the basic traits always try to retain their individuality and thus recessive traits may appear in successive generation). The other two theories put forward by Darwin and Lamark tries to throw light on the mechanism and consequences of the process of evolution in the transmission of the modified and acquired traits. Darwin came with his new ideas like "*Struggle for existence*", "*Survival of the fittest.*" and *"process of natural selection"* in the process of acquiring and transmitting the adapted traits to the coming generation. Lamark, on the other hand, emphasized the role of an inward urge of a species to adjust itself to the changed environment. These changes, variations or acquired traits are then transmitted to the offspring through the mechanism of heredity.

The theories of heredity have given birth to certain specific principles and laws known as Laws of heredity like law of similarity (like begets like), Law of variation (one may vary or differ from their parents), and Law of regression emphasizing an inherent tendency of moving towards the mean or average for the transmission of traits from one generation to another.

The forces of environment begin to play their role in the growth and development of an individual right from the time of the conception of the child in the womb of the mother. The child is exposed to the influence of such internal environmental forces first in the womb of the mother and later on by so many external environmental factors categorized as physical and socio-cultural factors.

Whether heredity or environment plays a decisive role in the growth and development of the individual has been a subject of wide controversy. Both hereditarians and environmentalists (supported by their observations and experiments) have forwarded their claim of supremacy in this direction. However, nothing is truer than the clear assertion that both are essential for the growth and development of the personality of a child. Their relationship is like that of seed and soil. While heredity provides the base and starting point, environment provides the favourable conditions for the growth and development of one's personality to the maximum extent possible. However, as a teacher we can hardly exercise any control over the herediatarian endowments of our students. Therefore, all our efforts should always be concentrated on giving them appropriate and favoural conditions for their growth and development as properly as possible for us.

References and Suggested Readings

Bhatia, H.R., *Elements of Educational Psychology*, Orient Longman, 1968, Calcutta.

Boring, E.C., Langfield, H.S. and Weld, H.P. (Eds.), *Foundations of Psychology*, (Ind. ed.), John Wiley, New York, 1961.

Crow, L.D. and Crow, Alice, *Child Psychology*, Reprint, Barney Noble, New York, 1969.

———, *Child Psychology*, 3rd Indian Reprint, Eurasia Publishing House, New York, 1973.

Douglas, O.B. and Holland, B.F., *Fundamentals of Educational Psychology*, Macmillan, New York, 1947.

Garrett, H.E., *General Psychology*, Indian Reprint, Eurasia Publishing House, New Delhi, 1968.

McDougall, William, *An Outline of Psychology*, Methuen & Co., London, 1949.

McIver, R.M. and Page, C.H., *Society: An Introductory Analysis*, Macmillan, London, 1949.

Pasricha, Prem, *Educational Psychology*, University Publishers, Delhi, 1963.

Sorenson, Herbert, *Psychology in Education*, McGraw-Hill, New York, 1948.

Stern, C., *Principles of Human Genetics*, W.H. Freeman, San Francisco, 1973.

Woodworth, R.S. and Marquis, D.G., *Psychology*, Henry Holt, New York, 1948.

5

Human Growth and Development—Stages and Dimensions

CHAPTER COMPOSITION

INTRODUCTION

The sole aim of education is to bring an all-round development in the personality of the student. Educational psychology, being a science and technology of education, should help in the realization of this aim. As you may be aware, human life starts from a single fertilized cell. The constant interaction with the environment results in the growth and development of the innate capacities, abilities and potentialities of the child. The task of formal as well as informal education is to help him in this path of growth and development. Therefore, it is imperative that the individuals, supposed to be connected with the task of helping the child to grow and develop satisfactorily, must be acquainted with the nature of growth and development.

It is only with a knowledge of growth and development of the learner at each stage of his life that it is possible for the teachers to render proper guidance, arrange learning situations and plan instructional programmes for bringing desirable harmonious development in their personalities. In the following pages, we would try to understand the process of growth and development with its various aspects.

MEANING OF GROWTH AND DEVELOPMENT

Mostly, these two terms are used interchangeably and taken as synonymous terms. Both relate to the measurement of changes occured in an individual after conception in the womb of the mother. Change is the law of nature. An individual, from being a fertilized egg turns into a full-fledged human adult. In this turnover process, he undergoes a cycle of changes brought about by the process of growth and development in various dimensions—physical, mental, social, emotional and so on. Therefore, in the wider sense, both the terms growth and development can be used for any change brought about by maturation and learning (formal as well as informal education), and essentially is the product of both heredity and environment.

However, in the strict sense of terminology, these two terms have different meanings that can be put in the followng ways.

S. No.	*Growth*	*Development*
1.	The term 'growth' is used in purely physical sense. It generally refers to an increase in size, length, height and weight. Changes in the quantitative aspects come into the domain of growth.	Development implies overall changes in shape, form or structure resulting in the improved working or functioning. It indicates the changes in the quality or character rather than in quantitative aspects.
2.	Growth is one of the parts of developmental process. In strict sense, development in its quantitative aspect is termed as growth.	Development is a wider and comprehensive term. It refers to the overall changes in an individual. Growth is one of its parts.
3.	Growth may be referred to describe the changes, which take place in particular aspects of the body and behaviour of an organism.	Development describes the changes in the organism as a whole and does not list the changes in parts.
4.	Growth does not continue throughout life. It stops once maturity is attained.	Development is a continuous process. It goes from womb to tomb. It does not end with the attainment of maturity. The changes, however small they may be, continue throughout the life span of an individual.
5.	The changes produced by growth are the subject of measurement. They may be quantified and are observable in nature.	Development, as said earlier, implies improvement in functioning and behaviour and hence brings qualitative changes, which are difficult to be measured direclty. They are assessed through keen observation in behavioural situations.
6.	Growth may or may not bring development. A child may grow (in terms of weight) by becoming fat but this growth may not bring any functional improvement (qualitative change) or development.	Development is also possible without growth as we see in the cases of some children who do not gain in terms of height, weight or size but they do experience functional improvement or development in physical, social, emotional or intellectual aspects.

Hence, observed in minute details, both growth and development show differentiation. But in wider and practical sense, both terms are used to denote the changes in an organism's physical as well as functional behaviour. These changes which cover physical, emotional, intellectual and social aspects of a human life have been roughly divided into four major classes by Mrs. Hurlock (1956, pp. 2-3).

(i) Changes in size

(ii) Changes in proportion

(iii) Disappearance of old features

(iv) Acquisition of new features.

All these types of changes have qualitative as well as quantitative aspects and hence generally, growth and development go hand in hand. And it is in this sense that the two terms are to be used collectively. Both, when taken together, explain the total changes—functional as well as constitutional with in the body and behaviour of an individual with the lapse of time after the conception. In the following pages, these terms will be used in synonymious sense for convenience.

STAGES OF GROWTH AND DEVELOPMENT

For human beings, life starts from a fertilized ovum in the womb of the mother. Not only before birth, but also many years after that, child is a helpless organism unless he is helped by the continuous process of growth and development and attains maturity. When one attains maturity, one is ceased to be called an adolescent and becomes an adult member of the society. He is supposed to play a responsible role in the society. Before being called as adolescent, he is called a child or an infant. All these names—infant, child, adolescent and adult etc.—are linked with various stages of growth and development through which the child passes during his lifespan.

There are certain common development or practical characteristics belonging to each stage. A human being shows peculiar quantitative and qualitative changes in his body and behaviour with the help of which we can say at what particular age an individual belongs to which definite stages of his life.

If we also include the pre-birth period, the lifespan of a human being can be divided conveniently into the following stages:

Name of the stage	*Period and approximate age*
1. Pre-natal (Pre-birth) stage	From conception to birth.
2. Stage of Infancy	From birth to two years.
3. Childhood stage	From 3 to 12 years or in strict sense, till the onset of puberty.
4. Adolescent stage	From the onset of puberty to the age of maturity (generally from 13 to 19 years)
5. Adulthood	From 20 years and beyond or in strict sense from the age of attaining maturity till death.

I do not claim absolute rigidity in the above classification in terms of either the division of lifespan into the above-mentioned stages or the duration of the period mentioned against them. There are certainly vast individual differences and so we should not imagine that every child will necessarily have each stage according to the period indicated above.

Since from the angle of school education, the first and the last stage serve no useful purpose, in the text, therefore, we will confine our attention to the remaining three stages of development. For discussing these stages of development, let us first analyse the various aspects of growth and development at each stage.

VARIOUS ASPECTS OF GROWTH AND DEVELOPMENT

If we use the term growth and development synonymously, the major aspects or areas, in which a human child undergoes complete development, can be described as follows:

Physical Development

The physical development of an individual includes the development of his internal as well as external organs.

Intellectual or Mental Development

It includes the development of intellectual powers like the power of reasoning and thinking, imagination, concentration, creativity, sensation, perception, memory, association, discrimination and generalization.

Emotional Development

Under this aspect, right from the development of the basic instinct, the evolution of various emotions takes place and also the emotional behaviour is developed to the point of emotional maturity.

Moral or Character Development

Moral or Character development includes the evolution of moral sense and development of the character. The individual develops his ethical and moral codes.

Social Development

Initially a child is selfish and antisocial. Gradually he develops into a social being by learning to behave according to the rules and norms of his society and makes adjustment according to it.

Language Development

It includes the learning of the language for communications and the development of various skills and abilities for the effective use of language.

PRINCIPLES OF GROWTH AND DEVELOPMENT

The changes brought about in an individual by the process of growth and development tend to follow some well-defined principles. These are known as principles of growth and development. These principles are being described below:

Principle of continuity: Development follows continuity. It goes from womb to tomb and never ceases. An individual starting his life from a tiny cell develops his body, mind and other aspects of his personality through a continuous stream of development in these various dimensions.

Rate of growth and development is not uniform: Although development follows continuity, yet the rate of growth and development is not steady and uniform at all times. It proceeds more rapidly in the early years of life but slows down in the later years of childhood. Again at the dawn of puberty, there is a sudden rise in the speed of growth and development but it is not maintained for long. Therefore, at no stage the rate of growth and development shows steadiness. It rather takes place by fits and starts.

Principle of individual differences: According to this principle there exists wide individual differences among children with respect to their growth and development in various dimensions. Each child grows at his own unique pace.

Uniformity of Pattern: Although development does not proceed at a uniform rate and shows marked individual differences, yet it follows a definite sequence or pattern and is somewhat uniform in the offsprings of a species. For example, the motor development and language development in all children seems to follow a definite sequence.

Development proceeds from general to specific responses: In all phases of a child's development, general activity precedes specific activity. His responses are of a general sort before they become specific. For example, the child waves his arms in general, random movements before he is capable of so specific response as reaching. Similarly, when a newborn infant cries, the whole of the body is involved. With growth, the crying is limited to the vocal cords, eyes etc. In language development, the child learns general words before specific. He uses the word daddy in greeting many men and it is only afterwards that he uses it for his father alone.

Principle of integration: While it is true that development proceeds from general to specific or from whole to parts, it is also seen that specific responses or part movements are combined in the later process of learning or development "Development," as Kuppuswamy (1971) observes, *"thus involves a movement from the whole to the parts and from the parts to the whole"*. It is the integration of whole and its part as well as of the specific and general responses that make a child develop satisfactorily in the various dimensions of his growth and development.

Principle of interrelation: The growth and development in various dimensions like physical, mental, social etc. are interrelated and interdependent. Growth and development in any one dimension affects the growth and development of the child in other dimensions as well. For example, children with above average intelligence are generally found to possess above average physical and social development. The lack of growth in one dimension diminishes the bright possibility in other dimensions. That is why, a child having poor physical development also tend to regress in emotional, social and intellectual development.

Development is predictable: With the help of the rate of growth and development of a child it is possible for us to predict the range within which his mature development is going to fall. For example, X-rays of the bones of the wrist of a child will tell approximately what his ultimate size will be. Similarly, the knowledge of the present mental ability of a child will help in predicting his ultimate mental development.

Principle of developmental direction: Kuppuswamy (1971), throwing light on this principle points out two specific facts concerning the direction of development. He says that development is "cephalic-caudal as well as proximodistal".

By cephalic-caudal development he means that development proceeds in the direction of the longitudinal axis (Head to foot). First, the child gains control over his head and arms and then on his legs so that he can stand.

According to the proximodistal tendency of the development, it proceeds from the centre to the periphery. In the beginning child exhibits its control over the large fundamental muscles but afterwards due to growth and development of smaller muscles he can exhibit more movements that are refined. For example, control over fingers comes after the control over the arm and the hand.

Development is spiral and not linear: The child does not proceed straightly on the path of development with a constant or steady pace. Actually he makes advancement during a particular period but takes rest in the following period to consolidate his development. In advancing further, therefore, he turns back and then moves forward again like a spiral (Fig. 5.1).

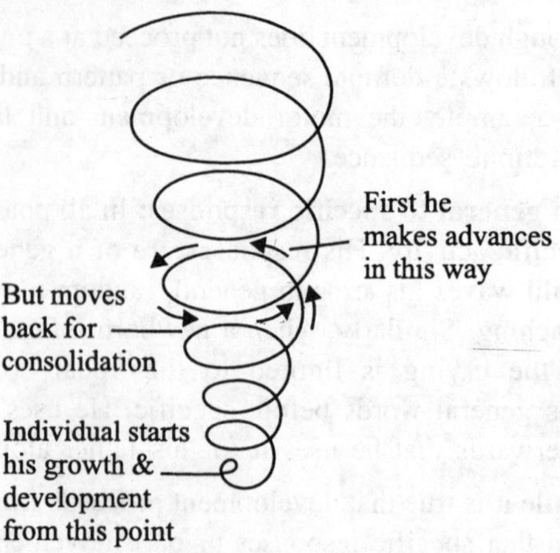

Fig. 5.1 Development is spiral.

Growth and development is a joint product of both heredity and environment: Child at any stage of his growth and development is a joint product of both heredity and environment. The forces of heredity and environment directly or indirectly influence his growth and development in any dimension at all times.

Education Implications of the Principles of Growth and Development

The above mentioned principles of growth and development carry wide educational meaning for the children, parents and the teachers. It can be explained as follows:

1. Knowledge of the principles of growth and development tells us that there are wide individual differences among children with respect to their rate of growth and development. Therefore, we must pay attention to their individual pattern and growth rate while planning the course for their education and development.
2. This knowledge helps us to know what to expect and when to expect from an individual child with respect to his physical, mental, social development, etc. at different stages of development. The correct knowledge of the growth trend of a child helps the parents and teacher not to under or overestimate the future competency or expectancy of their child.
3. It helps us to know the direction as well as the general pattern of development. It guides us to locate the degree of abnormality in our children and students and to take likewise remedial steps. The knowledge that development starts from whole to parts and then from parts to whole helps us to plan the learning procedure and set the learning methods accordingly.
4. Principles of interrelation and interdependence of the various aspects of growth and development help us to aim for the harmonious growth and development of the personality of the child and warn us against developing a particular aspect at the cost of another.
5. The knowledge of the uniformity of pattern with respect to growth and development makes it possible for the parents and teachers to plan ahead of time for the changes that will take place in their children. Children will also get benefitted if they can be acquainted with these changes beforehand.

6. The knowledge that heredity and environment both play a joint role in the process of growth and development helps us to pay sufficient attention over the environmental conditions in the upbringing of the children.

In this way, the knowledge of the principles of growth and development helps much in the well-being of the youngsters.

SUMMARY

Life of an individual starts with his conception in the womb of his mother. Starting from a fertilized egg (like a germinating seed) he develops into a full-fledged being (like a mature plant or tree) with the help of a process named as growth and development. The terms growth and development responsible for making such changes are often used interchangably and regarded as synonymous terms. However, they differ in some aspects and are capable of conveying different meanings.

The term 'development' carries a wider and more comprehensive meaning than the term 'growth' as it stands for the overall changes occuring in both the quantitative as well as qualitative aspects of one's personality. The term growth on the other hand, carries a quite limited and narrower meaning as it confines itself only with the changes in the quantitative aspect like increase in size, length, height and weight and expansion of vocabulary etc. In additon it does not continue throughout one's life. It stops when maturity has been attained while development is a continuous process and a complex one also as the changes brought about development are quite complex in terms of their actual assessment and measurement.

The journey of one's life from conception till death as a result of both the processes of growth and development is divided into certain specific stages referred to as the stages of growth and development namely, infancy, childhood, adolescence, adulthood and old age. Each of these stages chronologically extends over a rather definite periods in years exhibiting somewhat definite and typical behavioural characteristic in all dimensions of behavioural and personality make up.

The major aspects or areas which witness the quantitative as well as qualitative changes in an individual as a result of the processes of growth and development can be seen in the dimensions of one's personality like physical, mental, social, emotional, moral and language.

The changes brought out in the individual by the process of growth and development tend to follow some well defined principles like Principle of Continuity, uniformity of the rate of growth and development, the principle of individual differences, uniformity of pattern, proceeding from general to specific responses, principle of integration, principle of interrelation, predictability of development, principle of developmental direction, spiral nature of development and its evolution as a joint product of both heredity and environment.

The knowledge of these principles of growth and development may prove quite useful to parents and teachers for ensuring the harmonious growth and development of the personalities of their children. For example, the correct knowledge of the growth trend of the child may help them in not under or overestimating the expectancy from their child. Similarly, the knowledge of the principle of individual differences may remind them to plan the education and care for their children in view of their wide individual differences.

References and Suggested Readings

Carmichael, L. (Ed.), *Manual of Child Psychology*, John Wiley, New York, 1946.

Crow, L.D. and Crow, Alice, *Educational Psychology*, Eurasia Publishing House, New Delhi, 1973.

Hurlock, E.B., *Child Development*, *Asian Students,* 3rd ed., McGraw-Hill, Tokyo, 1956.

Kuppuswamy, B., *An Introduction and Social Psychology*, Asia Publishing House, Bombay, 1971.

Levin, H.J., *Psychology: A Biographical Approach*, McGraw-Hill, New York, 1978.

Mangal, S.K., *Advanced Educational Psychology*, Prentice-Hall of India, New Delhi, 2002.

6

Physical Growth and Development

CHAPTER COMPOSITION

MEANING OF PHYSICAL GROWTH AND DEVELOPMENT

'Physical growth and development' refers to a process which brings bodily and physiological changes—internal as well as external—in an organism from the conception till his death. Generally these changes take place in the following dimensions:

(i) **In his gross physical structure or physique:** It involves changes in terms of height, weight, body proportions and general physical appearance.

(ii) **In his internal organs:** It involves changes in the functioning of glands, nervous system and other body systems—circulatory, respiratory, digestive, muscular, lymphatic and reproductive.

The process of physical growth and development plays a significant role in the proper adjustment and progress of an organism. In the beginning, an infant is quite helpless. It depends upon its parents and other members of the family for the satisfaction of his bodily needs. As a result of the changes brought by physical growth and development, the baby's body organs become adaptable to his increasing body needs and gradually he is developed into a mature adult.

GENERAL PATTERN OF THE HUMAN PHYSICAL GROWTH AND DEVELOPMENT

Although there are wide individual differences among the human beings and it is not possible to describe a perfect general pattern of the growth and development, yet physical growth and development seems to follow, to some extent, a general pattern which can help us to think about some definite structural changes in the case of normal children at each stage of their growth and development.

Below we have tried to summarize this general pattern of growth and development along with definite structural changes.

Increase in Height and Weight

On an average, at birth a baby measures about 45-47 cm in height and between 3 and 4 kg. in weight, boys being slightly taller and heavier. During the first two years, there is rapid increase in both the height and the weight. There is a steady and slower growth from the third year till the onset of puberty. By the age of five, the height of the child becomes almost double and he weighs almost five times of his birth weight. During the period of adolescence, we again find a sudden increase in both height and weight. Girls reach puberty about a year or two earlier than boys. Therefore, between the age 12 to 14 they are found slightly taller and heavier than boys. But they are again surpassed by the boys. By the end of adolescence, young men are generally higher and heavier than the young women. Generally both men and women attain their maximum height and weight upto the end of adolescence. However, there are lot of variations in weight as it is more susceptible to environmental influences. Therefore, it is no surprise to note the sudden increase or decrease in weight in later years even after attaining maturity.

Weight of the brain increases rapidly in the early years of life. By the time the child atains the age of four, his brain would have gained almost 80 per cent of its final weight, another 10 per cent being added by the time he completes his eight years. By the 20th year, the brain gains almost all its weight.

Table 6.1 Increase in height and weight with age

Age	*Height (in cm)*		*Average Weight (in kg)*	
	Girls	*Boys*	*Girls*	*Boys*
Below 3 months	55.0	56.2	4.2	4.5
3 months	60.9	62.7	5.6	6.7
6 months	64.4	64.9	6.2	6.9
9 months	66.7	69.5	6.6	7.4
1 year	72.5	73.9	7.8	8.4
2 years	80.1	81.6	9.6	10.1
3 years	87.2	88.8	11.2	11.8
4 years	94.5	96.0	12.9	13.5
5 years	101.4	102.1	14.5	14.8
6 years	107.4	108.5	16.0	16.3
7 years	112.8	113.9	17.6	18.0
8 years	118.2	119.8	19.4	19.7
9 years	122.9	123.7	21.3	21.5
10 years	128.4	124.4	23.6	23.5
11 years	133.6	133.4	26.4	25.9
12 years	139.6	138.3	29.8	28.5
13 years	143.9	144.6	33.3	32.1
14 years	147.5	150.1	36.8	35.7
15 years	149.6	155.5	38.8	39.6
16 years	151.0	159.5	41.4	43.2
17 years	151.5	161.4	42.4	45.7
18 years	151.7	163.1	42.4	47.4
19 years	151.7	163.4	42.4	48.1

(Source — Growth and Development of Indian infants and children, Technical Report series No. 18, Indian Council of Medical Research, 1972.)

Changes in Body Proportions

A child not only grows in size but also shows a marked change in the proportion of the different parts of the body. For example, the head constitutes about one-fourth the height of the body at birth, its size being relatively much larger than the arms and legs. As the child grows older, the proportion of the head decreases and by the end of adolescence it becomes one eighth of the body. In addition to head, the other body parts, legs, arms, torso etc. also show change in proportions as the child requires them more and more in his adaptation to coming life.

Anatomical Growth and Development

The bones of a child are not only smaller in size than the bones of an adult, but they also differ in the composition. The child's bones contain, relatively, a larger amount of water and smaller quantity of mineral matter than those of the adult. They are softer and more blood flows through them than through the bones of an adult. This accounts for their greater reliability. But it also increases the chances of bones deformities and infection.

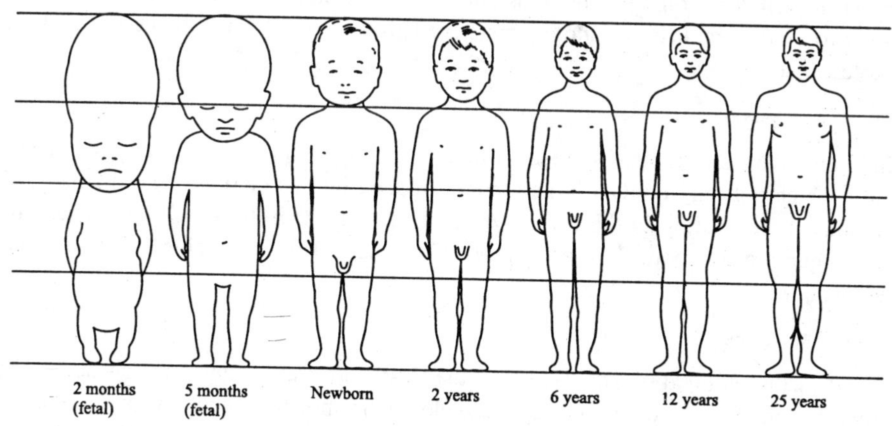

Fig. 6.1 Changes in body proportion from birth to 25 years.

As regards the development of teeth, it has been found that most of the children acquire their milk teeth by the time they are two years of age. Near the end of the fifth year, permanent teeth begin to appear the growth of which takes a long time. The last four of the permanent teeth, the wisdom teeth, develop between the age of 17 and 25, if they appear at all. Girls usually show more advanced teeth growth than the boys except in the case of wisdom teeth, where boys are usually ahead of the girls.

Growth and Development of Internal Organs

Once a child is born, his internal organs body undergo constant development. As a result the child's body systems show desirable change in order to satisfy the growing needs. Below we consider the growth and development of these internal organs.

Nervous System

It shows rapid growth during the prenatal period and the first four years after birth. Before birth the development consists primarily of increase in the number and size of nerve cells. Because no new cells are formed after birth, therefore the development in the first four years consists of the development of immature cells present at birth. After the age of 4, the growth of the nervous system proceeds at a relatively slow rate.

Muscular System

Muscular system also shows a remarkable development, although no new muscle fibres develop after birth. The muscles of a child are more delicate and less firmly attached to the bones than the adult muscles. However, gradually the muscles change in shape, size and composition and become firmer and stronger.

Circulatory and Respiratory Systems

Lungs as well as heart are very small in early childhood but gradually they grow in volume as well as in weight and reach their maximum by the end of adolescence. They also show desirable improvement in their functioning. The veins and arteries do not follow the same growth pattern as that of the heart and lungs. Prior to adolescence, they grow rapidly, whereas they show little growth during adolescence.

Digestive System

Young children have small tubular shaped stomach in comparison with the bag like shape stomach of the adults which not only holds a large amount of food but also empties more slowly. Therefore children require more feeding in the earlier years of their life than they will need later. In addition to the greater quantity of food, they need food with essential energy value for their rapid growth and development.

Lymphatic System

It is involved in the elimination of waste and the destruction of bacteria in the body. From birth onward, this system shows the sign of rapid development until it reaches to its maximum between the age of 11 and 12 years, when the death rate is about the lowest. After 12 years it decreases rapidly.

Reproductive System

The development of sex organs shows a peculiar trend in contrast with the overall growth and developmental pattern. Their rate of development is very slow during early childhood but picks up its speed as the child advances towards adolescence and becomes almost developed by the end of adolescence.

A close observation of the above-mentioned pattern can reveal the following important facts regarding the general trend of physical growth and development:

1. It is very rapid from birth to the age of two or three years.
2. Then, it continues at a diminished rate till the beginning of adolescence.
3. The first three years of adolescence are marked as the years of rapid growth and development.
4. This is followed by a period of slow growth and development to the time of maturity.

FACTORS AFFECTING PHYSICAL GROWTH AND DEVELOPMENT

The physical growth and development of an individual is conditioned by both heredity and environment. Some of the important heredity and environmental factors which influence the process of physical growth and development are:

1. The traits and characteristics inherited at the time of conception
2. Single birth or multiple births.
3. The physical as well as mental health of the mother during pregnancy.
4. Nutrition received by the embryo within the womb of the mother.
5. Normal or abnormal delivery.
6. Conditions and care at the time of delivery.
7. Lookafter of the baby and its mother.
8. Nutrition received by the child after birth.
9. Presence or absence of physical defects.
10. The living conditions—physical, social and cultural.
11. The opportunities of recreation, self expression, play and exercise.
12. Presence or absence of illness and diseases.
13. Emotional and social adjustment of the child.
14. Adequate or inadequate rest and sleep.
15. Proper or improper medical care.

Educational Significance of Physical Growth and Development

All the aspects of growth and development—physical, intellectual, emotional, social, moral etc.—are closely interlinked. The growth and development of any one of these aspects affects the growth and development of the other. Physical growth and development is not an exception. Certainly, it influences the development in other directions. For example, growth and development of the nervous system influences the growth and development of intellectual powers. Emotional and social adjustment is also linked with physical growth and development. While the children having normal physical growth and development are accepted by their age group, the physical deviates—who are very small, very large, too fat or too thin etc.—remain isolated. They are often nicknamed, ridiculed and denied participation in the play and recreational activities enjoyed by their age associates. It brings serious maladjustment and personality problems. A young child is intelligent enough to become aware of the fact that he differs in appearance and physical abilities from other children. His attitude towards self is injured and self confidence is shaken. In this case, he either becomes shy and timid or becomes aggressive in order to compensate for his inferiority feelings.

Moreover, on the balanced growth and development of the internal as well as external organs depends the balanced functioning of the body systems. The functioning of the body systems decides the interest, attitude and the total behaviour of all individual. For example glands and their functioning affect his emotional behaviour to a great extent. Similarly his anatomical development, the development of circulatory, respiratory systems, etc. give the person the required abilities for participating in various motor activities.

Hence, physical development influences the total make-up of an individual and thus needs a very careful attention. It can help the teachers to achieve one of the most important aims of the educational process—to bring an all-round balanced development in the personality of the child. Therefore the knowledge of the process of physical growth and development is very essential for a teacher. Specifically it can serve him in the following ways:

1. He can be aware of the physical deviates, their psychology and problem of adjustment. Consequently he can help them in their social and emotional adjustment as well as in school learning.
2. Children are the backbone of a nation's strength. Their health and proper physical development is an asset to the progress of the country. Our schools have to play decisive role in the task of physical welfare of the children. The teacher with the knowledge of physical growth and developmental process can render valuable help in this direction.
3. Needs, desires, interests, attitudes and in a way the over all behaviour of an individual is controlled, to a great extent, by his physical growth and development. Therefore at a particular age level, what would be the expected behaviour of the child of that age group can be estimated through the physical growth and developmental pattern. For example, with the study of the trend of the physical development in adolescence, one can be aware of their growing physical, emotional and social needs. Accordingly, adolescents can be helped by the teacher in the adjustment to their rapid development and changes.
4. Study of the pattern of physical growth and development helps us in knowing what can be expected normally from the children of a particular age level. In turn it can help us to arrange school programmes like curricular and co-curricular experiences, methods and techniques of teaching, time-table, text-books, aid material, seating arrangement and learning environment etc.

In this way we can see that the knowledge of process of physical growth and development helps the teacher in the realization of his objectives. By its knowledge, he not only becomes equipped for setting his programmes according to the needs of his students but can also help in improving their health and attaining proper physical strength and abilities.

SUMMARY

Physical growth and development refers to the process responsible for bringing bodily and physiological changes—internal as well as external—in an organism from the time of conception till his death.

In spite of wide individual differences, the process of human physical growth and development may be seen to exhibit a somewhat general pattern characterized as (i) Uniformity in the increase of height and weight with the growing age (till the end of adolescence) (ii) Change in body proportions (iii) Uniformity in Anatimical growth and development (iv) Uniformity in growth and development of internal organs like nervous, muscular, circulatory digestive, lymphatic and reproductive systems.

In a general way, the process of physical growth and development is quite rapid from birth to the age of two or three years. After then it continues at diminised rate till the beginning of adolescence. As soon as the child enters the adolescence era, his first three years are marked as the years of rapid growth and development. It is then followed by a period of slow growth and development to the time of maturity.

Factors affecting the physical growth and development of an individual begin to play their role right from his conception till death. The traits and characteristics transmitted through genes, the internal environmental forces affecting the growth and development after birth etc. may be named some of the such factors.

The knowledge of the process of the physical growth and development may help the teacher well in the realization of his objectives—an all-round development of the personality of children. By caring for their physical growth and development, he may help them to grow and develop not only in physical aspect but also in the other aspects of their personality make up like intellectual, emotional; social, moral etc. (as all these aspects of one's personality are closely inter-linked). Moreover study of the pattern of physical growth and development may help in knowing what can be expected normally from the children at a particular age level. It may help them in the planning and organization of curricular and co-curricular experiences for the education and welfare of the children.

References and Suggested Readings

Carmichael, L. (Ed.), *Mannual of Child Psychology*, John Wiley, New York, 1946

Harlock, E.B., *Child Psychology*, McGraw-Hill, Tokyo, 1959.

Indian Council of Medical Research, *Growth and Development of Infants and Children, Technical Report*, revision 19, 1972.

Marry, F.K. and Marray, R.V., *From Infancy to Adolescence,* Harper & Brothers, New York, 1940.

7

Cognitive or Mental Development

CHAPTER COMPOSITION

MEANING OF COGNITIVE OR MENTAL DEVELOPMENT

In the previous chapter, we have seen how the mechanism of physical growth and development brings desirable changes in the internal as well as external body organs of an individual in order to increase his physical skills and strength. This development enables him to do physical work and play games he could not when younger. Similarly, a child at the time of his birth or in early childhood cannot be expected to perform such tasks that require high mental abilities. As he advances in his age, his mental abilities and capacities gradually are developed and he is able to solve the problems he could not when younger. *The growth and development of the mental abilities and capacities which helps an individual to adjust his behaviour to the everchanging environmental conditions or to enable him to accomplish a task that needs complex cognitive abilities is referred to as mental or cognitive development.*

Actually, the process of mental growth and development is responsible for the development of an individual's all cognitive, mental or intellectual abilities like sensation, perception, imagination, memory, reasoning, understanding, intelligence, generalization, interpretation, language ability, conceptual ability, problem-solving ability and decision-making ability. These abilities are interrelated and never develop in isolation. Therefore, mental development of an individual at any stage of his development includes the overall development of these abilities.

VARIOUS AREAS OR ASPECTS OF MENTAL DEVELOPMENT

As said above, mental or intellectual development takes into consideration the development of various mental abilities and capacities. How these abilities grow and develop from birth onwards is an interesting as well as a useful thing to know. Though the development in the areas of various abilities proceeds simultaneously and is continuous, yet the studies have revealed possibility of the differences in the rate of overall mental development at various ages. Similarly, it has also been noted that there is a personality of greater growth and development in one aspect or area of mental activity than in other at one or the other stage of life.

As far as the general characteristics or trends of mental growth and development at various stages are concerned, we will discuss it in Chapter 12 of this text. However, in the following pages we will try to discuss the changes and development in some of the important mental abilities or aspects of mental power of a small child as he grows older and older.

Sensation and Perception

Both sensation and perception are considered important aspects of one's mental development. Sensations are elementary impressions gathered by sense organs. When these impressions are interpreted and some definite meanings are attached to them, they take the form of perception.

In the beginning, a child lacks in sensation as well as in perception. His sense organs are not developed. As a result, he cannot discriminate between things and understand their meanings. Focusing the eye towards the lamp, bright coloured objects, etc. can be said to be the beginning of an infant's perceptual growth. Later on, he distinguishes people from objects and then familiar people from strangers and in this way his environment gradually becomes differentiated into perceived objects. These perceived objects later on become associated with a verbal sound that he can recognize when heard.

When he becomes able to use his sense organs, he becomes increasingly conscious of the things around him and begins to ask a series of questions such as why, what and who. At this point he has a poor perception of space, time, form, movement and distance. For example, due to lack of perception of the size of distant objects, the train, when viewed from a distance, may appear to him as a toy train.

But gradually, his ability of perception gets developed. As the individual passes through the years of his adolescence, the sensory acquity reaches almost to its peak and perceptual pattern become most organised and refined. His perceptions now become more definite, rich and detailed. They are now beginning to be influenced by his beliefs, opinions, ideas etc., besides his needs, interests and mental sets. They now need not necessarily be associated with concrete objects.

Concept Formation

Acquiring conception is another important aspect of the child's mental development. A concept is the generalized meaning that is attached to an object or idea. It is the result of one's perceptual experiences and involves both discrimination and generalization.

Discrimination begins early in life. Sometimes, the child tries to generalise his perceptual experiences and thus begins to acquire concepts. Experience is a great factor in concept formation. In early childhood, the concrete experiences in the form of actual objects help the child in the formation of concepts. He tries to develop various concepts from direct experiences.

In the later period, vicarious experiences offered by reading, watching movies, attending lectures, etc., also provide the base for concept formation. In the later years, not only new concepts are formed, the old concepts may also get a new shape. They may be broadened, developed or the wrong concepts can be altogether abandoned. Normally during development concepts go from abstract to concrete to vague to clear and from inexact to definite, depending on the type of experiences one receives as one grows older.

In this way, the concepts of the child in the beginning are characterized by vagueness, indefiniteness and inadequacy. For example, the child has very poor time concepts. As Crow and Crow put it, *"Time as such means little to the young child. He cannot distinguish among 'today', 'tomorrow' and 'next week' except as they represent words rather than actual duration of time."* (1969, p. 73)

Development of Language

Development of language adds to the mental growth and development of an individual. The growth and development in speech, vocabulary, length of response are some of the important aspects of language development.

At birth, the child can only utter some crying sounds. By the age of one and a little later, he may learn to speak a few words. After that spoken vocabulary increases rapidly. Much of the speech pattern that the child learns is the result of imitation of others in the environment. During the course of learning to speak, it is possible that certain speech disorders like omissions, stuttering, stammering, etc. may develop. Therefore the parents as well as the teachers of small children must remain very cautious about this.

The vocabulary of children in the beginning is too limited. There is continuous increase in the size of one's vocabulary during childhood. Later on as the result of environmental needs and opportunities in learning, the vocabulary develops. Maintenance of the past and addition of new words in one's vocabulary may continue even till the period of old age depending upon one's reading habit and interests.

In addition to the change in vocabulary and speech, the pattern of giving responses also changes with age. In the early childhood the child's responses are characterized by the one-word response. Also, generally, he uses more nouns than other forms of language. Later, he gradually begins to use descriptive words like adjectives and adverbs and his responses include a large variety of words and almost every form of sentence structure.

Development of Memory

Memory is also an important aspect of mental development. At birth, there is little memory; but, gradually with maturation and experiences memory increases. The developmental schedule, as discussed by Hurlock and Schwartz, indicates that *"memory of an impressionistic kind appears in the first half of the year and instances of true rememberance appear by the end of the first year. During the first year memory is only aroused by sensory stimuli. With the learning of speech the child is able to remember ideally by the end of the second year. During the first and second years, the memory is stronger for persons and objects than for situation. During early childhood, from 3 to 6 years, situations become significant factors in the child's memory. Also the emotional quality of the impressions influence memory. By 2 years the child can recount the story heard a few days ago and he can also give information about past experiences."* (Kuppuswamy, 1964, p. 98).

Therefore, a child shows signs of memory from early childhood. The memory which the child possesses in his young age, is generally a rote memory. He enjoys repetition and seldom uses logic and insight in memorizing a thing. During later childhood and adolescence, the memory tends to function more logically and a selection process of remembering and forgetting begins to operate. In the later years of childhood, memory tends to decrease. But the age from which the downfall begins, is difficult to say with certainty. It varies from individual to individual and generally besides the age and health, the situation and stimuli which are associated with a particular kind of memory significantly effects its rememberance or forgetting.

Development of Problem-Solving Ability

Problem-solving ability is an important constituent of mental development. An individual needs this type of ability in discovering the solution of the problems. Therefore problem-solving ability depends upon the development of thinking and reasoning. Thinking and reasoning powers begin to grow as early as two and a half or three years. However, reasoning at this stage is confined to concrete and personal things from the child's immediate environment. A younger child deals more easily with the concrete than with the abstract. We cannot expect him to solve complicated problems which require abstract thinking and more developed reasoning. But gradually, he shows an increase in the ability to deal with abstract as he grows older. He begins to compare and evaluate ideas and solve problems through the utilization of verbal symbols and imaginary concepts.

It can be drawn from this discussion that in the beginning, children should be provided with simple realistic problems depending on concrete situation, and related to their own experiences and environment so that they can solve them with insight and understanding. As they grow older, more complicated problems requiring abstract thinking and widened experiences may be given to them. In this way children should gradually be made to increase their problem-solving ability.

In addition to these aspects, the other aspects of mental growth and development include attention, imagination, decision making and ability of interpretation etc. Like other aspects they also change, grow and mature with the increase in age due to maturation and learning.

FACTORS AFFECTING MENTAL GROWTH AND DEVELOPMENT

Mental growth and development is controlled by both hereditary and environmental factors. An individual's mental abilities, at any age of his life, are the products of his heredity and environment. For a child what he gets from his ancentral stock through his immediate parents at the time of conception in terms of mental traits or characteristics and mental apparatus is in fact a valuable asset to his future mental growth and development. But the environment which he gets afterwards for the development of these innate mental abilities is no less significant. The social and cultural experiences, learning opportunities and education which he avails for the developmental process as he advances in age, contribute significantly towards his mental growth and development.

In fact, maturation and learning are responsible for controlling the process of mental growth and development. Maturation helps in achieving physical growth and development which in turn affects the process of mental growth and development. Brain and the nervous system play a significant role in this direction. At birth, the brain and the nerves that lead to it are not fully developed. They grow and develop rapidly after birth and get matured in due course. As the nervous system advances toward maturity, the mental powers of the child also go on developing. Therefore, organic growth of the nervous system is the basic factor in mental development.

Learning in the form of experiences and education helps the developmental process and in fact intensifies it to reach its optimum level. It is said to play the same part as exercises play in developing physical skills and power as Sorenson puts it — *"A child's legs, arms and body are made stronger by healthful play. We can deduce that the mind with its organic counter-part, the nervous system, improves and becomes better equipped because of use and exercise in the form of reading, calculating, memorizing, speaking, imagining and other mental activities."* (1948, p.32).

CESSATION OF MENTAL GROWTH

At what age does the increase in mental growth cease is a controversial question. Mental growth is a complex process. There is no universal pattern of mental growth for all individuals. Neither is the pattern same for all mental functions or abilities. Therefore it is difficult to tell the age at which mental growth, with all its aspects, will cease to grow. Actually, the age of cessation of mental growth varies with different individuals and with different mental functions or abilities.

Psychologists have tried to give various ages ranging from 13 to the early 20s or even a much later age after which there is no further mental growth. The variation in the results is due to the fact they have worked on different groups and used different tests of mental ability. Despite such differences in opinion, Sorenson has tried to arrive at some conclusion regarding the age of cessation of mental growth. He writes :

"It is probably safe to conclude that a person reaches his maximum mental level at about the age of twenty or perhaps a little before or a little after twenty. It is true that on the average there is only a little mental growth during the late teens— nevertheless this small amount may be very important." (1948, p.44)

Therefore, the age of cessation of mental growth can be estimated as 20 or little before or a little after 20. But now the question again arises : Does the development of mental capacity or power also cease with the cessation of mental growth at the age of about 20?

In this connection, latest researches have shown that development in mental power and capacity does not necessarily stop with the cessation of mental growth. In most of the cases, the mental power or capacity reaches its maximum in the mid 30s. But whatever changes after the natural mental growth occur in the mental abilities of capacities, are definitely the result of learning, experience and education. After attaining their maximum height, mental capacity declines gradually but can be maintained effectively even in the old age by those who keep their minds alert and active.

MENTAL DEVELOPMENT AND EDUCATION

The knowledge of the trend of mental growth and the subsequent changes in the various mental abilities is of great use for teachers. Briefly, we can summarise this utility as follows:

1. It can help them in the selection of curricular and co-curricular experiences at various age levels.
2. It can also help them to arrange learning situations, decide methods and techniques of teaching and the nature of the aid material for the illustration of their teaching.
3. It can also help them to bring appropriate books suiting to the intellectual growth and development of children at different age levels.
4. It makes them conscious that a particular type of work or activity which needs some or the other developed mental abilities, needs to be introduced when the age of acquiring that approaches. We must not be too hasty to give him a particular piece of knowledge to train him in a particular act if the mental abilities required for that knowledge or act have not been acquired by the child. Definitely, in such cases, we should wait for the ripe stage.
5. If they understand the pattern of mental growth, they can lead their students to acquire their maximum mental capacity and power. Such teachers can impart training in problem solving

and creative expression. Also they can develop their logical understanding and take them to intelligent learning in place of mechanical fumbling and parrot-like cramming. Their ability of using language, perception and ability to interpret and generalization can also be developed through the natural course of their mental growth and development pattern.

In this way, a teacher can lead his students to acquire their maximum mental capacities and powers and help them to use these intelligently and judiciously for their own welfare as well as that of the society.

SUMMARY

Mental growth and development refers to a process responsible for the development of an individual in all cognitive, mental or intellectual abilities (interrelated to each other) like sensation, perception, imagination, memory, reasoning, understanding, generalization, interpretation, language ability, conceptional ability, problem-solving ability and decision-making ability, etc. All these aspects of mental growth and development change, grow and mature with the increase in the age of the child due to maturation and learning.

In fact maturation and learning are responsible for controlling the process of mental growth and development. Maturation helps in achieving physical growth and development specifically in terms of the organic growth of the nervous system which in turn helps in one's mental development. Learning in the form of experiences and education helps the mental developmental process to reach to its optimum level.

There is neither a universal pattern of mental growth for all individuals nor is the pattern same for all mental abilities. However, it can be seen that there is a cessation of mental growth in all individuals with respect to one or the other mental abilities. Latest researchers have concluded that the age of cessation of mental growth can be estimated as 20 or little before or little after 20. However, with such cessation of mental growth, development in mental power and capacity is not necessarily stopped.

The knowledge of the trend of mental growth and development and the resulting changes in the various types of mental abilities may prove quite useful for the teacher to plan and organise his teaching-learning material, teaching-learning situations and environment as to ensure for the maximum growth and development of the mental abilities of his students for their own as well as social welfare.

References and Suggested Readings

Carmichael, L. (Ed.), *Mannual of Child Psychology*, John Wiley, New York, 1946.

Crow., L.D. and Crow, Alice, *Child Psychology*, (Reprint), Barney & Noble, New York, 1969.

Harlock and Schewartz, quoted by Kuppuswamy, B., *Advanced Educational Psychology*, Delhi, University Publication, 1964.

Marry, F.K. and Marray, R.V., *From Infancy to Adolescence*, Harper & Brothers, New York, 1940.

Sorenron, Herbert, *Psychology in Education*, McGraw-Hill, New York, 1948.

8

Emotional Development and Emotional Intelligence

CHAPTER COMPOSITION

- Introduction
- What are Emotions?
- Nature and Characteristics of Emotions
- Kinds of Emotions
- Physiological or Bodily Changes Accompanying Emotions
- Emotional Development during Different Stages of Development
- Emotionality of Childhood vs Adulthood
- Factors Influencing Emotional Development
- Methods for Training of Emotions
- Role of Teachers in Proper Emotional Development of Children
- Emotional Quotient (E.Q.) and Emotional Intelligence
- Summary
- References and Suggested Readings

INTRODUCTION

Our emotions play quite a significant role in guiding and directing our behaviour. Many a time they are seen to dominate our behaviour in such a way that we have no solution other than behaving as per their wish. On the other hand, if a person has no emotional current in him then he becomes crippled in terms of living his life in a normal way. Hence, emotions play a key role in providing a particular direction to our behaviour and thus shaping our personality according to their development. In this chapter, we would like to throw light on the emotional aspect of our behaviour.

WHAT ARE EMOTIONS?

Etymologically, the word emotion is derived from the latin word 'emovere' which means 'to stir up' or 'to excite'. Therefore, emotion may be understood as an agitated or excited state of our mind and body. Taking clue from such derivation, various psychologists have tried to provide the definition of the term 'emotion' in their own ways. Let us reproduce a few of such definitions.

- **Woodworth**, *"Emotion is a 'moved' or 'stirred-up' state of an organism. It is a stirred-up state of feeling, that is the way it appears to the individual himself. It is a disturbed muscular and glandular activity, that is the way it appears to an external observer."* (1945, p. 410).
- **Crow and Crow**, *"Emotion is an affective experience that accompanies generalised inner adjustment and mental and physiological stirred-up states in the individual and that shows itself in his overt behaviour."* (1973, p. 83).
- **Charles G. Morris**, *"Emotion is a complex affective experience that involves diffuse physiological changes and can be expressed overtly in characteristic behaviour patterns."* (1979, p. 386).
- **McDougall** (1949) Considering instinct as an inate tendency, he maintains that emotion is an affective experience that one undergoes during an instinctive excitement. For example, when a child preceives a bull coming towards him (cognition) he experiences an affective experience in the form of the arousal of accompanied emotion of fear and consequently tries to run away (conative aspect of one's behaviour). McDougall discovered 14 basic instincts and concluded that each and every emotion, whatever it may be, is the product of some instinctive behaviour.

These instincts with their associated emotions can be listed as:

S. No.	*Instinct*	*Emotion accompanying it*
1.	Flight or escape	Fear
2.	Pugnacity or combat	Anger
3.	Repulsion	Disgust
4.	Curiosity	Wonder
5.	Parental	Tender emotion, Love
6.	Appeal	Distress
7.	Construction	Feeling of creativeness
8.	Acquisition	Feeling of ownership
9.	Gregariousness	Feeling of loveliness
10.	Sex, Mating	Lust
11.	Self-assertion	Positive self-feeling or Elation
12.	Submission	Negative self-feeling
13.	Food-seeking	Appetite
14.	Laughter	Amusement

Thus, whatever may be the terminology used by all these different writers and psychologists, their definitions tend to describe *emotions as some sort of feelings or affective experiences which are characterised by some physiological changes that generally lead them to perform some or the other type of behavioural acts.*

NATURE AND CHARACTERISTICS OF EMOTIONS

From the definitions and discussion above, we may be able to conclude following things about the nature and characteristics of emotions.

1. **Emotional experiences are associated with instincts or biological drives.** When the basic need is satisfied or challenged (the satisfaction is in danger), the emotions play their part.
2. **Emotions are the product of perception.** The perception of a proper stimulus (object or situation) is needed to start an emotional experience. Organic changes within the body (favourable or unfavourable) may then intensify the emotional experiences.
3. **The core of an emotion is feeling.** Actually every emotional experience, whatever it may be, involves feelings—matter of the heart. Feelings and emotions both are affective experiences. There is only the difference of degrees. After perceiving a thing or a situation, feelings like pleasure or displeasure can be aroused. There may be some intensity or degree of strength in these feelings. When the feelings are so strong that they are able to disturb the mind and excite an individual to act immediately—they are turned into emotions. Therefore, the urge to do or act (conative aspect) is the most important emotional experience.
4. **Emotions bring physiological changes.** Every emotional experience involves many physical and physiological changes in an organism. Some of the changes which express themselves in overt behaviour are easily observable. Examples of such changes are—bulge of the eyes, flush of the face, flow of tears, pulse rate, beating of the heart, choke in the voice, fleeing from the situation or attack on the emotion arousing stimulus. In addition to these easily observable changes, there are internal physiological changes as well. Examples of such changes are changes in the circulation of blood, impact on digestive system and changes in the functioning of some glands like adrenal glands etc.

These changes become so specific and distinguishable in human beings that a simple glimpse can enable us to detect a particular emotional experience in an individual and we can see whether he is in anger or scared.

In addition to the above characteristics, emotions have some more specific features that need to be menioned. These are:

(i) Emotions exist in every living organism.

(ii) They are present at all stages of development and can be aroused in young as well as in old.

(iii) Emotions are extremely individualistic and they differ from person to person.

(iv) Same emotion can be aroused by a number of different stimuli—objects or situations.

(v) Emotions rise abruptly but die down slowly. An emotion once aroused tends to persist and leaves behind emotional mood.

(vi) Emotions have the quality of displacement. The anger aroused on account of one stimulus gets transferred to other situation. The anger on account of the rebuking by boss is transferred in beating the children at home.

(vii) One emotion can give birth to a number of likewise emotions.

(viii) There is a negative correlation between the upsurge of emotions and intelligence. While reasoning and sharp intellect provide a careful check on the sudden upsurge of emotions, under emotional experiences, the reasoning and thinking powers are decreased.

KINDS OF EMOTIONS

If we try to analyse the impact of various emotional experiences upon the well-being of an individual, we can come to the conclusion that emotions have both positive as well as negative effects. Whether an emotion will prove to be helpful or harmful to an individual depends upon the following factors :

(i) Frequency and intensity of emotional experience.

(ii) Situation, occasion and nature of the stimulus which arouses the emotion.

(iii) Kind of emotional experience or emotions.

The last factor—the kind of emotional experience—counts much in this direction. Emotions, in general, can be categorized in two kinds—Positive and Negative emotions.

Unpleasant emotions like fear, anger, jealously which are harmful to an individual's development are termed as negative emotions while pleasant emotions like affection (love), amusement, curiosity, joy and happiness which are very helpful and essential in the normal development of an individual are termed as positive emotions.

By their nature of positiveness and negativeness, it should not be assumed that all the positive emotions are always good and the negative emotions are bad. While weighing their impact, other factors like the frequency and intensity, situations and the nature of stimuli should also be considered. Excess of everything is bad. Emotions with too much intensity and frequency, whether positive or negative, bring harmful effects. On the other hand, the so called negative emotions are also very essential for the human welfare. The emotion of fear prepares an individual to face the danger ahead. A child who has no emotion of fear is sure to get injured because he has not learnt to save himself against a possible danger.

PHYSIOLOGICAL OR BODILY CHANGES ACCOMPANYING EMOTIONS

When we are in the waves of positive or negative emotions, our behaviour is totally controlled and directed by that emotion. During this period, various types of internal or external changes occur in our body which may be briefly summarised as below:

Internal Bodily Changes

The internal structure and functioning of our body is very much influenced and affected by the ongoing emotional experience. Some of these bodily and physiological changes may be judged through outward observation or simple instruments but for others we often have to make use of sophisticated special instruments like galvanic skin reflex instrument, electro encephalograph (EEG), syphygmomanometer (blood pressure checking instrument) and polygraph (lie detector) etc. Some of these internal bodily changes can be mentioned as below :

1. Functioning of our heart is affected by emotional experience. Generally the heart beat increases under the states of agitation and excitement provided by the emotion.
2. Blood circulation system is very much affected by the emotional experiences. Generally it increases but in some cases of fear, anxiety and shock it may also go down deeply.
3. Rate of respiration and breathing is deeply affected by an emotional experience. Generally it increases but in some cases of excessive fear, happiness, shocks and excitements it may go down to the extent of becoming absent.
4. Digestive system is adversely affected by emotions. Experimental studies have concluded that under the current of emotions, our stomatch and intestines work quite slowly and sometimes become inactive. The secretion of the digestive glands including saliva is also

sufficiently decreased resulting in the malfunctioning and inactivity on the part of our digestive system. This is why extremely emotionally charged individuals are mostly found to suffer from the malfunctioning of their digestive system.

5. Emotions bring changes in the chemical composition of our blood like (i) increase in the amount of adrenin; (ii) increase in the amount of sugar level; (iii) changes in the number and proportion of the red corpuscles.
6. There is a change in the temperature of the body. At the time of intense excitement, it generally goes down.
7. There are significant changes in the secretion of the duct and ductless glands. The flow of these secretions in the form of saliva, tears, sweat etc. may also be easily identified through external observation.
8. There are significant changes in the electrical or galvanic skin responses. There is a decrease in the case of emotions like distress, disgust and anger which results into sweating or perspiration. On the other hand, there is increase in the case of emotions like fear, love, wonder, etc. which results in the goosebumbs, a condition in which hair or the skin rises.
9. Muscles of our body are hardened and get tensed during an emotional current. It may bring destabilization and unequilibrium to our body functioning. The twisting and hardening of the muscles of the stomach, arms, legs and neck etc. may be easily detected from external observation.
10. The functioning of the brain is also adversely affected during intense emotional currents. The sensory and perceptual processes are also influenced through these emotional experiences. Quite often, the emotions play a dominant role by almost making our brains inactive and ineffective making us behave in an improper and delinquent way.

External or Observable Bodily Changes

Apart from the covert changes mentioned above, there are many such overt changes in our body during the current of the emotions that can be detected through simple observation without the need of any special instrument. These may be of the following nature.

Changes in Facial Expression

Face, to some extent, is said to be the index of human behaviour. It equally applies to our emotional behaviour. Under the influence of an emotional current, there are significant changes in our facial expression that can be identified through simple external observation. By looking at one's facial expression, we can judge one's intended emotion and term it as anger, laughter, fear, disgust, contempt, love, happiness or surprise. The basis for the correlation between facial expressions and emotions may be discovered both in one's innate dispositons and socio-cultural environment. While the way of expressing emotions may vary from culture to culture, it may also represent innate responses to particular situations like jumping at the time of hearing a sudden noise and baring teeth at the time of anger.

Behavioural expressions in the form of facial expressions and non-verbal communications, however, cannot be understood as sufficiently objective, reliable and valid instrument for the identification and measurement of one's emotions. One can hide one's feelings in the garb of an apparent mask of false facial expressions and other non-verbal communications and thus may make the task of identification difficult and most unreliable.

CHANGES IN BODY POSTURES

Besides the changes in facial expression, there are significant changes in one's body postures during emotional experiences. For example when one is angry, besides the redness of his face, his bodily postures and movements may also tell the same story. He may begin to walk fast, push and pull his hands and feet, take a fighting posture, utter nonsensible words, etc. In this way, his whole body and its movements through their various forms and postures may provide identification of a particular type of emotional behaviour. That is why when one is trembling or trying to hide or run away in a bid to save one's life, we say that one is in the grip of some fear. Similar identification may also be made in the case of other emotions like love, delight, disgust, wonder or distress etc.

However, there lies less objectivity and reliability in the identification of the emotions through one's body postures. One may be able to hide one's emotional fealings by exhibiting different types of body postures other than those expected for the display of one's actual feelings. Apart from this, there lies another difficulty in the identification of emotional behaviour on the basis of the observed body postures and movements simply on account of the fact that many of the emotions have similarities in terms of the observable body postures and movements.

CHANGES IN VOICE OR VOCAL EXPRESSION

There are significant changes in one's voice or vocal expression during an emotional current. Laughing, weeping, speaking in loud voice with an unusually high pitch, crying, talking slowly with some hesitation, feeling difficulty in speaking, uttering abusive language, speaking in a very sweet and affectionate manner, whistling, murmuring, humming, etc. demonstrate our various emotions. That is why when we listen to the dialogues of the various actors in a play or programmes on the radio and television broadcasting we can very well say that at this particular time one is displaying the emotion of anger, fear, disgust, love or lust etc. However, it is also not a reliable method for the identification of one's emotional experience simply on the ground that many of the emotional expressions may demonstrate similarities in terms of the voice or vocal expressions. Besides this, there may be individual differences with regard to the vocal expression of a particular emotional behaviour. In such cases, therefore, no general conception for the vocal expression of an emotion, may come to our help and hence we may remain undecided or take wrong decision about one's emotional behaviour.

EMOTIONAL DEVELOPMENT DURING DIFFERENT STAGES OF DEVELOPMENT

Development, in general, applies to the changes brought about with the passage of time. Emotional development in this respect reflects the following changes:

- There is a gradual birth of different emotions in an individual since his birth.
- There are changes in the conditions or nature of the stimuli that arouse child's emotions.
- There are changes in the manners in which a child expresses his emotions.

In the light of these changes, we will try to discuss the process of emotional development during different developmental stages.

Emotional Development during Infancy

1. Right from the time of his birth, the infant cries and his bodily movements seem to give evidence of the presence of emotional element in him.What are the specific emotions, if any, he experiences at this stage is a difficult question to be answered.

2. Truly speaking, as Mrs. Hurlock puts it, *"At birth and shortly afterwards the first sign of emotional behaviour is general excitement to strong stimulation. There are no indications of clearcut, definite emotional patterns that can be recognised and identified as specific emotional states."* (1959, p. 216).

   Thus, it is the stage of an undifferentiated excitement to any stimulus.
3. The stage of undifferentiated excitement is over in a very short time, when the general excitement becomes differentiated into simple responses that suggest pleasure and displeasure. Stimuli like sudden loud noise, wet, cold or hot objects applied to the baby's skin, feeling hungry and uncomfortable etc. bring unpleasant responses. The stimuli like sucking, patting, and warmth etc. bring pleasant responses.
4. The differentiation of general excitement into pleasant and unpleasant responses takes the following pattern according to Spitz:

   "During the first two months, pleasure and displeasure come in response to 'physical' stimulation. By the third month, pleasure is aroused by 'psychological' stimulation as shown in the baby's smile in response to human face. Slightly later displeasure can be aroused by psychological as well as physical stimuli as may be seen in the baby's reaction to being left alone." (Hulock, E.B., 1959, p. 217)
5. As said above, before the age of 6 months, the emotional behaviour is expressed through pleasant and unpleasant responses, that is, there are only two emotions (distress and delight) up to this stage. When the infant completes his six months, the negative emotions take the lead and gradually in the coming months, fear, disgust, anger, jealousy all are distinguishable. Between the 10th and 12th months the positive emotions like elation, love, sympathy, enjoyment all enter in the field. Up to 2 years, as the study of Bridges conducted in 1931 shows almost all the emotions, positive as well as negative, take their shape and become quite distinguishable.
6. There is continuous variation in the manifestation of emotions during infancy. In the earlier months it is very difficult to distinguish on the basis of facial expression and bodily positions. Only the mothers can determine the reasons behind her child's crying and yelling. Later on they gradually become distinguishable. Moreover in the earlier months of infancy, child reacts more violently to emotionally disturbing situations, but as an infant approaches childhood, his crying, yelling and the vigorous movements of the body parts become less and less violent. Gradually with increasing age there is an increase in linguistic responses and a decrease in motor responses.

Emotional Development during Childhood

As said above, almost all the emotions make themselves distinguishable by the beginning of childhood. Therefore, emotional development after the stage of infancy, concerns itself only to the changes in the nature of situations or stimuli arousing emotions and the changes in the expression of emotional experiences. We find the following changes in a child during childhood:

1. In infancy, the child is only concerned with his own well-being. Therefore, the emotions are generally aroused by the conditions which are related with his immediate well-being. But as he grows, his world grows larger and he has to respond to a variety of stimuli. During childhood, peer group relationship and school atmosphere and other environmental factors influence his emotional behaviour. His emotions get linked with the new experiences and interests and his emotional behaviour gets linked with the new stimuli. At the same time,

he does not react to various old stimuli. For example, he does not show anger at being dressed or bathed, nor does he show any fear of strangers.

2. There is a remarkable change in the expression of emotional behaviour. In infancy his behaviour is usually dominated by too much intensity and is usually expressed through motor responses like crying, yelling etc. But in childhood and specially in later childhood, the child tries to express his behaviour through reasonable means and is the result of many factors. In childhood, the child is in a position to express his feelings through language. Secondly, he becomes social and realises that it may not be desirable or proper for him to show his emotions at all times. Thirdly, his intellect begins to play a proper role in exercising check over emotional outbursts.

Thus, the child advances towards emotional stability and control and during the later period of his childhood, demonstrates an appreciable degree of control over his emotions.

Emotional Development during Adolescence

The emotional balance is once again disturbed in adolescence. An individual once again experiences the violent and intensive current of emotional experiences. With regard to emotional experiences, this is the period of intensive storm and stress. At no stage this emotional energy is as strong and dangerous as in adolescence. It is very difficult for an adolescent to exercise control over his emotions. The sudden functioning of sexual glands and tremendous increase in physical energy makes him restless. Moreover, adolescents are not consistent in their emotions. Emotions during this stage fluctuate very frequently and quickly. It makes them moody. In a very short span of time they could switch between being happy and extremely sad. So there is too much uncertainty in the nature of their emotional state.

At this stage, there is a strong need for training of emotions and proper channelization of emotional energy. The Hadow report has emphasized this need in the following words :

"There is a tide which begins to rise in the veins of youth at the age of eleven or twelve. It is called by the name of adolescence. If that tide can be taken at the flood, and a new voyage begun in the strength and along the flow of its current, we think that it will move on to fortune." (Ross J.S., 1951, p.153).

Emotional Development in Adulthood

Emotional development reaches its maximum in adulthood. During this stage, generally, all individuals attain emotional maturity. Let us try to understand what is meant by emotional maturity.

Meaning of emotional maturity

In brief, a person can be called emotionally mature if he is able to display his emotions in an appropriate degree with reasonable control. An emotionally mature person will possess the following characteristics:

(1) Almost all the emotions can be distinctly seen in him and their pattern of expression can be easily recognised.

(2) Manifestation of emotions is very much refined. Usually he expresses his emotions in a socially desirable way.

(3) He is able to exercise control over his emotions. Sudden inappropriate emotional outbursts are rarely found in him. He is able to hide his feelings and check his emotional tide.

(4) The person no more hangs in mere idealism, but he actually perceives the things in their real perspective. He is not a daydreamer and does not possess the desire to run away from realities.

(5) The intellectual powers like thinking, reasoning etc. are properly exercised by him in making any decision. He is more guided by his intellect than his emotions.

(6) He does not posses the habit of rationalization *i.e.* he never gives arguments in defence of his undesirable or improper conduct. Also he never puts the responsibility of his own mistakes on others. He is always honest in his behaviour.

(7) He possesses an adequate self-concept and self respect. He never likes to do the things or to show such behaviour as can injure his self respect and is adverse to his self-concept.

(8) He is not confined to himself. He thinks for others and is keen to maintain social relationships. He never engages himself in such a behaviour which is antisocial and can result in the social conflicts and blockage of social relationships.

(9) He has the courage to exercise his emotions at a proper time in a proper place. If there is a danger to his self respect or if an innocent person is attacked, he can rise to the occasion by exercising his emotion of anger. But if he commits a mistake and is rebuked by his boss, he is equally able to check his emotion of anger. Mature emotional behaviour is characterised by greater stability. Person having such maturity shows no sudden shift from one emotion to another.

As a conclusion regarding the meaning of emotional maturity, I would like to quote Arthur T. Jersild. He is of the opinion that emotional maturity *should not* involve only simple restriction and control. According to him, it is a very narrow view of emotional maturity. He writes, "*An adequate description of emotional maturity must take account of the full scope of the individual's capacity and powers, and of his ability to use and enjoy them. In its broadest sense emotional maturity means the degree to which the person has realized his potential for richness of living and has developed his capacity to enjoy things, to relate himself to others, to love and to laugh: his capacity for whole-hearted sorrow when an occasion for grief arises... and his capacity to show fear when there is occasion to be frightened, without feeling a need to use a false mask of courage.*" (Skinner, C.E., 1968, p. 281).

EMOTIONALITY OF CHILDHOOD Vs ADULTHOOD

The emotional experiences during childhood differ markedly from those of the adulthood. This difference can be easily seen through some of the following distinguished characteristics :

Intensity

Children's emotions are characterized by too much intensity. There are sudden outbursts of emotions among children. If a child weeps, he weeps bitterly. In anger, he loses control over himself. But an adult's emotional experiences are not so intense. Volcano-like sudden emotional outbursts are seldom observed in adults.

Briefness

Children's emotional experiences are very brief. Their emotions last for a short time and these end all of a sudden. However, in adults the emotions play their part for a long time and in the end, make their existence drawn over a period of time in the form of 'mood'.

Transitoriness

Children's emotions are transitory in character which means there is a rapid shift from one emotion to another. We find that for a weeping child, a piece of chocolate is enough to shift his emotion from distress to delight. Similarly, we find a quick shift in his emotion from delight to distress. Similarly we find a rapid shift from anger to smile, from laughter to tears or from jealously to affection. Contrary to this, emotions of adults do not shift so rapidly. They are marked by a greater degree of stability.

Frequency

On the average, the number of emotional experiences experienced by a child during a day is significantly greater than those experienced by a normal adult. A child undergoes different currents of emotional streams during a period of time, sometimes a specific emotion being repeated a number of times. But as the child grows older, he learns to make adjustments and tries to meet situation by reactions other than the emotional ones, hence resulting in a gradual decrease in the frequency of emotional responses.

Detection of Emotionality

The emotional state of a child is easily detectable. He is very innocent and does not know the art of hiding his feelings and emotions. The behavioural symptoms like speech difficulties, frequent crying, restlessness, nail-biting and thumb sucking etc. give indications of his emotionality. Adults, on the other hand, are generally able to hide their feelings and emotions. Therefore, in their case, it is difficult for others to know how they feel and detect their emotionality.

Differences in the Emotional Expression

An infant is quite unable to exercise control over his violent emotional outbursts. Emotions at this stage are expressed through motor responses. As the child grows, the way of emotional expression gets modified. This modification goes on till the attainment of maturity in adulthood. A mature adult seldom engages himself in the motor activity during emotional stress. He learns to exercise control over his emotions and expresses them in a refined and socially approved way. The emotional expression either in the form of motor responses or in a socially unacceptable way is labelled as 'childish'. The emotional response of an adult is always guided by his intellect while in the child, the intensity of feelings rules over the reasoning and thinking power. The adults are able to keep their emotions reserved for a future expression but in childhood it is a difficult task.

FACTORS INFLUENCING EMOTIONAL DEVELOPMENT

The emotional development of a child rests on many factors. Six of the important ones are given below:

Health and Physical Development

Physical development and health has a positive correlation with emotional development. Any deficiency on physical front — internal or external — creates emotional problems. Children, weak in somatic structure or suffering from illness, are more emotionally upset and unstable than those with better health. The normal functioning of the glands is very important for the balanced emotional development. Any abnormal increase or decrease in their power of secretion creates obstacles in the proper emotional development.

Intelligence

Intelligence, as the ability to make adaptation, has a significant correlation with the emotional adjustment and suitability of a child. Meltzer (1937) concluded that —

"There is less emotional control, on the average, among those of the lower intellectual levels than among children of the same age who are bright." (Hurlock, E.B., 1959, p. 254).

An intelligent person, with his reasoning and thinking powers, exercises control according to the situation and make proper use of his emotions. At every stage, the child's intellectual power guides and controls his emotional development.

Family Atmosphere and Relationships

Emotional development is significantly influenced by the family atmosphere and relationships. The emotional behaviour of the parents and elder members and the cordial atmosphere prevalent at home develops positive emotions among the children, while conflicts, fights and tensions in family relationships give birth to negative emotions. Also the treatment given to a child by parents and the members of the family influences his emotional development. The order of birth (whether the first or the youngest child), the size of the family, the socio-economic status of the family, the parental attitude (negleted, pampered or over-protected child) — all are decisive factors in the emotional upbringing of the child.

School Atmosphere and Teachers

School life plays an important role in the emotional development of children. The healthy conducive atmosphere of the school always results in the balanced emotional development of children. All such things like the physical facilities provided in the school, the methods of teaching, the organisation of cocurricular activities and social life in the school, the relationship among the staff members and the head of the institution, attitude of teachers towards the students and the self-example of the teacher's emotional behaviour influence the emotional development of children.

Social Development and Peer-Group Relationship

Social development of children is closely linked to their emotional development. The more social is the child, the more emotionally adjustable he will prove. Socially rejected or maladjusted children always face difficult emotional problems. The maintenance of proper social relationships and acquisition of social virtues are the effective means for bringing essential modification in the emotional behaviour of the child. The proper social development can only bring desirable and socially approved emotional development in children.

Neighbourhood, the Community and the Society

The other social agencies like neighbourhood, the community and society, of which an individual is the member, also exert significant influence upon his emotional set-up. He picks up so many traits of his emotional behaviour from these surroundings. A brave community is sure to produce fearless and courageous children. The society where the elder members unnecessarily exhibit emotional outburst of anger leads the youngers to such negative development. Similarly, so many good or bad things related to emotional behaviour of an individual can be acquired due to the impact of neighbourhood and the society.

In this way, the factors influencing the emotional development of an individual can be labelled into two categories— In the first category there are personal factors like his physical, physiological, mental and social development. In the second category there are social factors like parents, family, school, neighbourhood, community and the society. Both these factors exert a significant influence upon the emotional development of the child. While taking care of the proper emotional development of a child, parents as well as the teachers should keep in view all the factors belonging to both the categories.

METHODS FOR TRAINING OF EMOTIONS

Emotions in their crude form are harmful to the individual and the society. One of the major objectives of any good scheme of education is to train and modifiy the emotions for the welfare of the individual and that of the society. The various methods employed for this purpose are:

1. Repression or Inhibition.
2. Industriousness or mental occupation.
3. Redirection and sublimation.
4. Catharsis.

Repression or Inhibition

Here the undesirable emotional behaviour of the child is checked by imposing restrictions and giving punishment. No outlet or opportunity is provided to the child for the emotional expression. Rules and regulations are very strictly observed and the child is always required to express his emotions in socially desirable ways. Actually it is a negative method of exercising control over the emotions and is in no way helpful for the healthy emotional development.

Industriousness or Mental Occupation

Another method for exercising desirable control over emotions is to keep oneself busy in some constructive activities. Empty mind is said to be a devil's workshop. Therefore, it is essential to have provision for co-curricular and leisure activities for the balanced emotional development of the children.

Redirection and Sublimation

The direction of flow of emotional energy is changed through the process of redirection and sublimation from an undesirable goal to a socially desirable one. In both these processes, there is only a difference of degrees. While, in redirection there is no change in the nature of the emotion and only the direction of the flow is changed, in sublimation, there is modification of original instincts or emotions. Sublimation changes the very form of the emotion.

As far as the method of controlling the emotions is concerned, redirection serves the best purpose. Unlike repression or inhibition, it does not have negative effect on the personality development of the children. It does not destroy the emotion, but only brings desirable changes in the mode of its expression. If a child is very aggressive and displays emotion of anger frequently, his emotion of anger can be diverted towards the enemies of the country and the devils of the society. In this way, his energy can be utilized in the defence of the country and for the weaker members of the society. Similarly, the sublimation of love in the cases of Tulsidas and Kalidas presents clear example of the role of sublimation in changing the emotional set-up of an individual.

Catharsis

In this method, desirable channels are provided for the release of the emotional energy. In some way or the other, the individual is provided with the opportunity of self-expression so that the pent up emotions get appropriate outlet. Under the clouds of emotions, tensions are created in the minds of the individuals. By providing a proper outlet for emotional expression, the tensions can be removed and one is made to feel better and lighter. Listening patiently to the verbal expression of an individual under emotion is the simplest catharsis process. The opportunity for self expression in the form of co-curricular activities, participation in festivals and fairs and rituals of the society—all provide means for the catharsis of emotional energy.

ROLE OF TEACHERS IN PROPER EMOTIONAL DEVELOPMENT OF CHILDREN

Role of Education and specially that of teachers in bringing balanced emotional development in children deserves special mention. The emotional development of the children are influenced and controlled by many factors. These factors have been mentioned earlier. Let us analyse the part played by the teachers in bringing balanced emotional development of children in the light of these factors.

(1) Emotional development, as said earlier, depends upon physical and physiological development. Therefore, every care is to be taken for the proper physical development of children. Children should be made to learn the ways of healthy living. With due cooperation from the parents and the state authorities, children need to be cared for proper nourishment. The parents should be made aware of the physical weaknesses, deformities and illnesses of their children and necessary provision for the treatment should be made in schools or state hospitals.

(2) Home atmosphere exercises a good amount of influence over the emotional character of children. Therefore, teachers should seek active cooperation of the parents in making the atmosphere of the homes suitable for proper emotional development. Parents and the elder members of the family should exhibit better examples of emotional expression before their children. They should try to develop healthy attitude towards their children and in no way spoil them by their own modes of behaviour. The teacher should try to know the causes of emotional maladjustment of children and find out how far home atmosphere and parents are responsible for this. Accordingly, he should take suitable steps for the proper emotional development of the children.

(3) The teachers in school, with the active cooperation of the authorities, should take care of the following things:

(i) There should be an adequate provision for various co-curricular activities for the full expression and outlet of emotional energies of the children.

(ii) Instructional methodology and curriculum should be dynamic, progressive and child-centred.

(iii) Children should get desired love and sympathy from the teachers. Their individuality should be respected and individual differences recognized. The teacher should see that the basic emotional needs of the children are satisfied in the classroom or school.

(iv) With the help of positive methods of controlling and training the emotions, the emotional tension present in the minds of the children should be removed and the creation of undesirable complexes avoided.

(v) Moral and religious training should form a part of the school programme. High ideas of life and moral principles should be made the guiding factors of the children's lives.

(vi) Emotions are caught, they are not taught. Therefore, teachers should refrain from any act or behaviour which can bring undesirable influence on the emotional development of the children. They must put their own example before the children for the refined emotional expressions and behaviour.

(vii) Proper care should be taken for the balanced social development of the children. Each child should get due recognition in his group and in no case he should feel isolated or rejected by his peer group and classmates.

(viii) Teachers need to understand when behaviour is normal and when it is a symptom of something wrong. The causes for emotional deviation should be sought and in case the behaviour is expressively immature, services of a skilled guidance personnel should be obtained.

(ix) Teachers should recognize the place of emotion in the learning process. Balanced emotional feelings can serve as a tonic to the body and can make the learning an active and exciting experience. Therefore, teachers should make the child emotionally involved in his work.

EMOTIONAL QUOTIENT (E.Q.) AND EMOTIONAL INTELLIGENCE

Emotional Quotient represents a relative measure of one's emotional intelligence potential in the same way as intelligence quotient (I.Q.) does for the measurement of one's intellectual potential.

We know that one's intelligence is an innate as well as an acquired intellectual potential. Every child is born with some intellectual potential which grows and develops on account of maturity and experiences. Similary, one is also born with some innate emotional intelligence potential in terms of one's level of emotional sensitivity, emotional memory, emotional processing and emotional learning ability. This potential (unlike intelligence) is liable to be developed or damaged as a result of one's life experiences. See the difference here between the development pattern of innate emotional intelligence and general intelligence as a result of maturity and experiences.

While general intelligence is generally not subjected to the decline or damage with life experiences (it always picks up the rising trend), the emotional intelligence can be either developed or damaged depending upon the type of environmental experiences one gets in one's future life. More specifically, if a child starts with a certain level of innate mathematical abilities, he has almost no chance of getting his potential lowered through training or experiences. Since no teacher, parent or television programme persuades him to learn 2 + 2 = 5 or 3. Thus, there are enough chances that unhealthy environmental influences or lessons taught by the parents, teachers and other models may lead to the declining or damaging of one's innate or previously held level of emotional intelligence.

Thus, what is referred to by one's emotional intelligence at a particular lifetime is that level of one's emotional intelligence which is with him at that time as a result of the ongoing emotional lessons or life experiences.

The level or potential of one's emotional intelligence is relatively measured through some tests or life situations resulting into one's emotional quotient (E.Q.), a relative measure of one's emotional intelligence potential. Consequently, the term emotional quotient (E.Q.), may be defined as under:

Emotional Quotient is a relative measure of one's emotional intelligence potential held by him at a particular period of his life.

Emotional Intelligence—Meaning and Definition

Emotional intelligence, like general intelligence, is the product of one's heredity and its interaction with his environmental forces. Until recently, we have been led to believe tht a person's general intelligence measured as I.Q. or intelligence quotient is the greatest predictor of success in any walk of life—academic, social, vocational or professional. Consequently, the I.Q. scores are often made into use for the selection, classification and promotion of the individuals in various programmes, courses and job placements. However, researches and experiments conducted in the 90s onwards have tried to challenge such over-dominance of intelligence and its measure I.Q. by replacing it with the concept of emotional intelligence and its measure emotional quotient (E.Q.). These have revealed that a person's emotional intelligence measured through his E.Q. may be a greater predictor of success than his or her I.Q.

Historically speaking, the term emotional intelligence was introduced in 1990 by two American University professors Dr. John Mayer and Dr. Peter Salovey in their attempt to develop a scientific measure for knowing the differences between people's ability in the areas of emotions. However, the credit for popularizing the concept of emotional intelligence goes to another American psychologist Daniel Goleman through his book *Emotional Intelligence : Why It Can Matter More Than I.Q.*, published in 1995.

Let us now consider the views and definitions of the term emotional intelligence given by eminent psychologists and researchers in the field.

1. Although the term emotional intelligence has been defined in many best sellers including Dr. Daniel Goleman's 1995 book "Emotional Intelligence" in a number of ways—comprising many personality traits such as empathy, motivation, persistence, warmth and social skills—yet the most accepted and scientific explanation of the term emotional intelligence may be found in the following definition given by John D. Mayer and Peter Salovey in their 1997 book "Emotional Development and Emotional Intelligence":

"Emotional intelligence may be defined as the capacity to reason with emotion in four areas: to perceive emotion, to integrate it in thought, to understand it and to manage it."

Let us now try to analyse the viewpoint of this definition.

- According to this definition, every one of us may be found to have varying capacities and abilities with regard to one's dealing with emotions. Depending upon the nature of this ability, he or she may be said to be more or less emotionally intelligent in comparison to others in the group.
- A person will be termed emotionally intelligent in proportion to his ability to:
  - — identify and preceive the various types of emotions in others (through face reading, body language and voice tone etc.);

— being aware of his own feelings and emotions;
— incorporate or integrate the preceived emotions in his thought. (such as using his emotions feelings in analysing, problem solving, decision making etc.);
— have proper understanding about the nature, intensity and outcomes of the emotions;
— exercise proper control and regulation over the expression and use of emotions in dealing with his self and others in view of promoting harmony, prosperity and peace.

2. For further clarification and explanation of the terms emotional intelligence and emotionally intelligent person, we would like to quote here Mr. Yetta Lautenschlager, a NIP teaching fellow of Hamden, Connecticut, U.S.A. He writes :

"To be emotionally intelligent, I submit that you must become proficient in the Four A's of emotional intelligence i.e. Awareness, Acceptance, Attitude and Action. Awareness means knowing what you are feeling when you are feeling it. Acceptance means believing that emotions are biological process taking place in the body and the brain that is not always rational. It means being able to feel an emotion without judging it. Attitudes are beliefs that are attached to emotion. There are times when the emotion follows an attitude, or is colored by an attitude. Unless the attitude is challenged, the emotion will continue to be felt in the same direction. Action is the behaviour you take based on emotion and attitude."

The above viewpoints of Yetta Lautenschlager clearly emphasizes that for developing as an emotionally intelligent individual, one must develop the ability of (i) emotional awareness (knowing the feelings of the self and the others), (ii) cognitive realization that emotional expression may be irrational or unhealthy and hence, one should be cautious in utilising his emotions into action, (iii) having a fresh look or formation of desired attitude for the proper utilization of emotional feelings, (iv) resulting ultimately into proper behaviour for the progress of the self in proper tune of the others.

Based upon these contemporary viewpoints about the concept of emotional intelligence, we may understand one's emotional intelligence *as a unitary ability (related to but independent of standard intelligence) helpful in knowing, feeling and judging emotions in close cooperation with one's thinking process for behaving in a proper way in the ultimate realization of the happiness and welfare of the self in tune with others.*

Significance and Importance of Knowing about One's Emotional Intelligence (E.I.)

The knowledge about one's emotional intelligence in terms of his emotional quotient has a wider educational and social implications for the welfare of the individual and the society. This fact has now been recognized and given practical shape and implications all round the globe. The credit of giving due publicity and acquainting the world population with the importance and significance of emotional intelligence goes to the famous American psychologist Dr. Daniel Goleman through his bestsellers like *Emotional Intelligence — Why it can matter more than I.Q.* and *Working with Emotional Intelligence,* etc. He has brought to the forefront the following points regarding the importance of emotional intelligence and its measure through his writings.

- Emotional intelligence is as powerful, and at times more powerful than I.Q. While I.Q. contributes only about 20% to succcess in life, the other forces contribute the rest. We can infer that emotional intelligence, luck and social class are among those other factors.
- Unlike I.Q., emotional intelligence may be the best predictor of success in life. Emotionally intelligent people are more likely to succeed in everything they undertake in their lives.

- Unlike what is claimed about I.Q., we can teach and improve in children and any individual some crucial emotional competencies paving the way for increasing their emotional intelligence and thus making their lives healthier, more enjoyable and successful in the coming days.
- The concept of emotional intelligence is to be applauded, not because it is totally new but because it captures on one compelling term the essence of what our children or all of us need to know for being productive and happy.
- I.Q. and even Standard Achievement Test (SAT) scores do not predict who will be successful in life. Even school success can be predicted more by emotional and social measures (e.g. being self-assured and interested, following directions, turning to teachers for help and expressing needs while getting along with other colleagues) than by academic ability.
- In working situations also, emotional intelligence helps more than one's intellectual potential in terms of one's I.Q. or even professional skills and competencies. A professionally competent person having poor emotional intelligence may suffer on account of his inability to deal with his self or in getting along properly with others.
- One's emotional intelligence helps him much in all the spheres of life through its various constituents or components namely knowledge of one's emotions (self awareness), managing the emotions, motivating oneself, recognizing emotions in others (empathy) and handling relationships. The achievement of the end results in terms of better handling of mutual relationships is quite essential and significant in one's life. It can only be possible through one's potential of emotional intelligence and its proper development.

The viewpoints and ideas propagated by Daniel Goleman have brought a revolution in the field of child caring, home, school and work place management. It has also provided sufficient support to the guidance and counselling services including physical and mental health programmes. Although these may seem a bit exaggeration in the tall claim that emotional intelligence is a sure guarantee for unqualified advantage in life, yet there is no denying of the fact that one's emotional make-up counts quite substantially towards one's ability to deal successfully with other people and with one's own feelings. Since these qualities count significantly towards one's success in one's area of achievement, it may help one to step in for the required success. Most of the problems in our life whether childhood or adolescent problems, home and family problems, work situation problems or political, regional or international problems are the result of the mishandling of the involved sentiments, feelings and emotions of the individuals concerned, group of individuals, society and the nations. If proper education, opportunities and efforts are made for the training of emotions and development of proper emotional intelligence potential among the people right from their childhood, then it will surely help in bringing mutual emotional understanding, empathy accompanied with right actions and behaviour on the part of the individuals and groups for leading a better life with peace and cooperation.

To progress and let others progress and to live and let others live are thus the ultimate goals of any education or training provided for developing one's potential of emotional intelligence. Let us now consider such measures to be adopted for the welfare of the youngsters and emotionally affected individuals.

How to help in the proper development of emotional intelligence?

The following measures may prove helpful in this direction:

- Try to help yourself and the youngsters develop the ability to correctly perceive feelings both in oneself and others.
- Try to give up the misgivings and misperception of the feelings in others. It leads to a hostile attribution bias. Remember that love always begets love, while suspicion, hatredness and aggressions are rewarded likewise.
- In all situations, self awareness of the feelings and emotions is most important. Try to teach the children and help yourself to know what you are feeling when you are feeling it at a particular time.
- For understanding others and their feelings, develop the qualities of a good listener. People who have a high E.Q. (emotional quotient) also have a high score on empathy and empathy comes through effective listening.
- Try to do away with the wrong notion that thought is most appropriate when not clouded by emotions. Try to learn the integration of thoughts and emotions, heart and mind for the appropriate behaviour at the right time. Therefore, do not try to supress emotions (as every feeling has its value and significance) but to strike a balance between rational thoughts and emotions.
- Teach the children and yourself that all emotions are healthy (because emotions are what unite the heart, mind and the body). Anger, fear, sadness, the so called negative emotions are as healthy as peace, courage and joy. The important thing is to learn the art of expressing one's feelings or emotions in a desirable way at a desirable time in a desirable amount. In this connection, have this remark of the Great Greek Philosopher Aristotle as a guideline.

"Anyone can become angry—that is easy. But to be angry with the right person, to the right degree, at the right time, for the right purpose, and in the right way—that is not easy."

- Try to practice and teach the children the art of managing the feelings and emotions as adequately as possible. This is especially important for the distressing emotions of fear, pain, anger, etc.
- Don't allow the emotions and feelings to develop as hindrance and obstacles in your path. Use them us a motivating agent or force for achieving your goal.
- Teach yourself and your children the lessons of empathy, *i.e.* developing a sense of what someone else is feeling.
- Have measures for the proper development of social skills for better communication and interpersonal relationship with others. Don't break the communication channel and express your feelings with an equal sense of attending and listening to other's feelings for the better management of relationships.
- Try to provide more time and efforts for developing not just cognitive professional skills but also affective skills for the development of emotional intelligence.
- Last but not the least is to provide yourself as a model or companion for maintaining proper emotional bonds. If you have developed yourself as an emotionally intelligent individual, you may inspire or lead others to become so. However, it is not essential to be perfect or complete for guiding others as parents, teachers or bosses. One just needs to see what others need, and be there for meeting their needs.

The Measurement of Emotional Intelligence

For the measurement of one's intelligence, we make use of one or the other intelligence test (verbal or non-verbal). Similarly for the measurement of one's emotional intelligence we can make use of such measures called emotional intelligence tests or scales. These tests and measures are not available easily and in sufficient numbers like intelligence tests standardized for measuring intelligence of the varying population of the human beings. A few of such well known measures of emotional intelligence may be cited as under.

1. **Mayer Emotional Intelligence Scale (MEIS)** constructed and standardized by Dr. John Mayer of the University of New Hampshire, U.S.A.
2. **Mayer, Salovey and Caruso Emotional Intelligence Test (MSCEIT)** constructed and standardized by Dr. John Mayer, Dr. Peter Salovey and Dr. David Caruso of U.S.A.
3. **Bar-On Emotional Quotient Inventory (EQ-i)** constructed and standardized by Dr. Reuven Bar-On and published by Multi-Health Systems; U.S.A. for the first time in 1996. This test covers five areas: intrapersonal, interpersonal, adaptability, stress management and general mood.
4. **Mangal Emotional Intelligences Inventory (MEII)** constructed and standardized by S.K. Mangal (author) and Shubhra Mangal. It has been published by National Psychological Corporation, Agra. It covers four areas—Intra-personal awareness, Inter-personal awareness, Intra-personal management and Inter-personal management.

In addition to these well standardized measures, we may also come across some emotional intelligence measures which have a limited value or somewhat meant just for a fun or amusement. However, these may provide vital clue of what is expected from an emotionally intelligent person in an arbitrary assumed emotional situation. The sample items of such tests are reproduced here for providing an idea of such measures.

Test Items of a Scale Type Measure

1. I find myself using my feelings to help make big decisions in my life.

O	O	O	O	O
Always	Usually	Sometimes	Rarely	Never

2. People don't have to tell me what they feel__________I sense it.

O	O	O	O	O
Always	Usually	Sometimes	Rarely	Never

3. I have trouble handling conflicts and emotional upsets in relationship.

O	O	O	O	O
Always	Usually	Sometimes	Rarely	Never

Test Items of a Multiple Choice Type Measure

Item No. 1

Situation : You are hanging out with a group of friends and one of your friends starts to make negative comments about a friend who is not there.

Your response:

- You add a few negative comments about the friend who is not there.
- You say nothing at the moment and later you privately talk about your feelings to your friend who made the comment.

- You tell your friend that you don't feel comfortable talking about people who are not there, and change the subject.
- You keep quiet and beat yourself up for not saying anything to stop it.

Item No. 2

Situation : Your best friend has recently broken up with someone and is taking it hard.

Your response:

- You take him or her out for a wild night on the town to get his or her mind off the breakup.
- You start to worry about your own relationship and if you might get dumped.
- You bash your friend's mate and tell your friend that he or she is better off alone.
- You ask your friend what you can do to help him or her get through this.

SUMMARY

Emotions are some sort of feelings or afffective experiences which are characterized by some physiological changes that generally lead them to perform some or the other types of behavioural acts.

A particular type of emotion has distinguished characteristics like (i) its association with some basic instincts or drives, (ii) aroused as a result of perception (iii) intensity of feelings (iv) accompanied with the specific physiological changes (v) its sudden rise but slow death, (vi) displaying the quality of displacement *i.e.* transferred to other situation or target etc.

Emotions in general can be categorized into two kinds — positive or pleasant emotions like love, amusement, curiosity, etc. and negative and unpleasant emotions like fear, anger, jealously, etc.

Emotions are always accompanied with some distinctive physiological or bodily internal and external changes. Examples of such internal changes—increase in heart beat, decrease in blood pressure, increase and decrease in the rate of respiration and breathing, malfunctioning of the digestive system, change in the body temperature, chemical composition of the blood, and secretion of the duct and ductless glants, hardening and tensing of muscles of the body and changes in the electrical or galvalic skin responses. Among the external changes (detected only through simple observation) are changes in facial expression, body postures and voice or vocal expressions.

The process of emotional development in an individual during different developmental stages is mainly characterized by the changes like (i) gradual birth of differnet emotions since birth (ii) changes in the conditions or nature of stimuli that arouse the emotions and (iii) changes in the manner in which emotions are expressed.

Emotional experiences during childhood differ markedly from those of the adulthood mainly in terms of (i) Intensity (ii) Briefness (iii) Transitoriness (iv) Frequencies (v) Detection and (vi) Differences in the emotional expression.

Emotions development of the children may be influenced by so many factors like his health and physical development, intelligence, family atmosphere and relationships, school atmosphere and teachers, social development and peer group relationships, neighbourhood, the community and the society etc.

The welfare of the individual and society lies in the proper emotional functioning. For this purpose, there is a need of proper training and modification of the emotions. The various methods employed for this purpose may be named as (i) Repression or Inhibition (ii) Industriousness or mental occcupation (iii) Redirection and Sublimation and (iv) Catharis.

Teachers can play a big role in bringing balanced emotional development of children by taking due notice of their physical development, providing guidance to them and their parents, by providing exemplary behaviour, by providing outlet for the emotional energies of the children through proper curricular and co-curricular experiences and so on.

We may understand one's emotional intelligence as a unitary ability (related to but independent of standard intelligence) helpful in knowing, feelings and judging emotions in close cooperation with one's thinking process for behaving in the most proper and desirable way. The potential of one's emotional intelligence is measured through a relative measure known as Emotional Quotient (E.Q.) much in the same way as general intelligence is messured through Intelligence Quotient (I.Q.).

In view of the so wide significance of the emotional intelligence from the individual as well as social angles, it becomes quite necessary to make earnest efforts for its proper development right from early childhood. Awareness of the feelings and emotions in the self and others as well as their proper management is in fact a key for the proper progress and development of emotional intelligence among the children. From time to time, we must also have some proper measures for the assessment of the potentiality of emotional intelligence in terms of their E.Q. It can be done through some proper well standardized emotional intelligence tests or scales like Mayer Emotional Intelligence Scale (MEIS), Mayer, Salovey and Caruso Emotional Intelligence Test (MSCEIT) and Bar-on Emotional Quotient Inventory (EQ-I) developed in USA. In India too we have such standarized emotional intelligence tests like Mangal's Emotional Intelligence Test, published by National Psychological Corporation, Agra.

References and Suggested Readings

Arnold, M.B., *Emiton and Personality* (2 Vols.), Columbia University Press, New York, 1960.

Bar-on, Reuven, *The Emotional Quotient Inventory (EQ-i)*, A Test of emotional intelligence, Multi-Health Systems, Toronto, 1996.

Cannon, W.B., *Bodily Changes in Pain, Hunger, Fear and Rage,* 2nd ed., Appleton-Century-Crofts, New York, 1929.

Crow, L.D. and Crow, A., *Educational Psychology,* 3rd Indian reprint, Eurasia Publishing House, New Delhi, 1973.

Darwin, C., *The Expression of the Emotions in Man and Animals*, reprint, Chicago University Press, Chicago, 1965.

Delgado, J.M.R., *Physical Control of the Mind: Towards a Psycho-civilized Society,* Harper & Row, New York, 1969.

Drever, J., *Instinct in Man*, Cambridge University Press, Cambridge, 1917.

Goleman, Daniel, *Emotional Intelligence: Why it can matter more than IQ*, Bantam Books, New York, 1995.

———, Daniel, *Working with Emotional Intelligence*, Bantam Books, New York, 1998.

James, William, *Psychology: Brief Course*, Collier Macmillan, London, 1969.

Jersild, A.T., *In Essentials of Educational Psychology*, Skinner, C.E. (Ed.) , Prenticee-Hall Inc., 1968.

Lindsley, D.B., *Emotion* in S.S. Stevans (Ed.), *Hand Book of Experimental Psychology*, John Wiley, New York, 1951.

Mayer, John D., and Salovey, Peter, "Emotional Intelligence and the Construction and Regulation of Feelings, *Applied & Prevention Psychology*, **4**(3), 197–208.

McDougall, William, *An Introduction to Social Psychology,* 28th ed., Methuen, London, 1946.

———, *An Outline of Psychology*, 13th ed., Methuen, London, 1949.

Morris, Charles G., *Psychology*, 3rd ed., Englewood Cliffs, Prentice-Hall, New Jersey, 1979.

Salovey, Peter and Mayer, John D, *Emotional Intelligence, Imagination, Cognition and Personality*, **9**, 185-211.

Schachter, S. and Singer, J.E., "Cognitive, Social and Physiological Determinants of Emotional State," *Psychological Review*, **69**, 369–399, 1962.

Schachter, S., *Emotion, Obesity and Crime*, Academic Press, New York, 1971.

Selye, H., *The Stress of Life*, McGraw-Hill, New York, 1956.

Young, P.T., *Emotion in Man and Animal*, 2nd ed., Krieger, Huntington, New York, 1973.

Wood, J., *How Do You Feel*? Prentice-Hall, Englewood Cliffs, New Jersey, 1974.

Woodworth, R.S., *Psychology*, Methuen, London, 1945.

9

Social Development

CHAPTER COMPOSITION

WHAT IS SOCIAL DEVELOPMENT?

Human beings possess a unique characteristics which separates them from animals. Their behaviour is social. Society to them is as essential as food. They believe in the maintenance of social relationships and try to adjust with others. But this does not mean that the child is born with such social behaviour and social qualities. Like other aspects of growth and development, he develops the necessary social characteristics in him. *The process of the development of such qualities which brings desirable changes in his social behaviour is referred to as social development or socialization of the child.* Social development occupies very important place in the overall process of growth and development. We cannot even describe an individual a person if he has not passed through the process of social development or socialization.

Let us try to analyse this further. What does this term social development (also described as socialization) mean? Various thinkers have tried to define it. Some of the definitions are given below.

- **Sorenson:** *"By social growth and development we mean increasing ability to get along well with oneself and others."* (1948, p. 50)

  Thus Sorenson explains that during the process of social development there is a progress in the social abilities or skills of an individual. With these increasing abilities he tries to bring improvement in the maintenance of social relationships. He tries to mould his behaviour and seek adjustment and harmony with others.

- **Freeman and Showel:** *"Social development is the process of learning to confirm to group standards, mores and traditions are becoming imbued with a sense of oneness, inter-communication and co-operation."* (Hurlock, E.B., 1959, p. 257)

  The definition lays stress on the following:—

  (i) Social development refers to the process by which a person acquires the necessary knowledge, skills and disposition that makes him an acceptable member in his own group.
  (ii) It develops group loyalty and encourages mutual dependence, co-operation and cohesiveness.
  (iii) It is the process which helps an individual to behave in accordance with social traditions and mores and thus makes him able to adjust in his social environment.

- **Hurlock:** *"Social development means the attaining of maturity in social relationships."* (1959, p. 257)

  This brief definition carries a wide meaning. It asserts that as in the case of emotional development, the goal is to attain emotional maturity, similarly in the case of social development, the goal should be the attainment of social maturity. An individual should have all the opportunities to modify or improve his social behaviour so that he may be able to maintain proper social relationships and can adjust himself to his social environment.

- **Garrett:** *"Socialization or social development is the process whereby the biological individual is converted into a human person."* (1968, p. 555).

  This definition is based upon the distinction between the term 'individual' and 'person'. We cannot name each and every body as person. The person always possesses some personality. The personality is the product of social interaction between him and his social environment. Socialization and social development—the process of social interaction—helps the individuals to attain essential personality characteristics.

In the light of all these views, we can come to the conclusion that social development or socialization is a process which:

(i) Begins with the infant's first contact with other people and continues throughout his life,
(ii) Is the net result of the constant interaction with his social environment,
(iii) Helps in learning and acquiring various social qualities and characteristics, and
(iv) With the result of learning helps the individual become adjusted to his social environment and maintain proper social relationships.

DEVELOPMENT OF SOCIAL BEHAVIOUR AT DIFFERENT STAGES OF DEVELOPMENT

Social Development in Infancy

The behaviour of a human infant is not social at birth. He is extremely self-centered and is only concerned with the satisfaction of his physical need. He does not even distinguish between people and inanimate objects.

Social behaviour is said to be taking its birth when the infant first communicates with the adults for the satisfaction of his needs. Therefore, normally the baby's first social contacts are with an adult. Mrs. Hurlock in her book 'Child Psychology' has beautifully explained the process of social development during the first two years of a child as a result of the contact with adults. Below we give the summary of her findings.

Social development of infants as a result of contact with other adults

Duration of age	*Pattern of social behaviour*
During the first month	Cannot differentiate between the human voices and other noises.
Second month	Recognises the sounds of human beings and gives smiles to the person.
Third month	Recognises its mother and feels unhappy on separation.
Fourth month	Shows selective attention to the human face and feels happy in company.
Fifth month	Reacts differently to smiling and scolding and distinguishes between friendly and angry voices.
Sixth month	Recognises familiar persons with a smile and shows definite expressions of fear of strangers.
Eighth and ninth month	Attempts to imitate the speech, simple acts and gestures observed in others.
Between the tenth and twelfth month	Plays with his image and even kisses it as if it were other persons.
At twelfth month	Can refrain from doing things in response to 'no-no' or some other form of request.
At second year	Can cooperate with adults in a number of routine activities and becomes an active member of the family.

With regard to an infant's social reactions to another infant or child, it has been observed that his early behaviour is egocentric and selfish. He cannot share his toys with others. He wants to have all things for himself and does not tolerate any external interference. From the 13th to the 18th month, the young child's interest shifts from play materials to the playmates. There is a decrease in fighting for toys and increase in cooperative use of them. Up to 3 years, he learns to divide and share his possession with others and to cooperate with them. Children of this age are now in a position to engage themselves in the cooperative and organized plays activities. Up to 7 years or so, children seek companionship regardless of sex of the other children. Usually the boys and girls play together at this stage.

Like emotions, the early stage of social behaviour during infancy is characterized by negative social characteristics. Imitation, timidity, shyness, rivalry and desire for possession dominate the first two years of development. Between 2 to 6 years, both negative and positive aspects of social behaviour are seen. Negativism, rivalry, quarreling, teasing and bullying, cooperation, sympathy and social approval are some of the new social behaviours which are learned at this stage.

Social Development during Childhood

As we have seen that during the period 2 to 6 years, a child progresses from being relatively unsocial to becoming a distinctly socialized individual. He learns to share, cooperate and do things with others. But the circle of his social contacts is limited at this stage. Therefore, we cannot expect much from him regarding his social development.

With the entrance in childhood, most of the children begin to go to school. The area of their social contacts is now widened. We note the following changes in the social behaviour of a child:

1. This period is marked by greater degree of social awareness. There is a great expansion of child's social world. Most of the important types of social behaviour, necessary to adjustment with others, begin to develop at this stage.
2. He tries to seek independence from his parents and other elders and spends less time with them. In actual sense, he now drives no enjoyment from them. Thus interest in playmates of his own age gets increased.
3. He becomes an active member of a 'peer group' and this group gradually replaces the family group in its influence over his behaviour and attitudes. The members of such a group are almost of the same age. They believe in group loyalty and thus try to conform to the rules and values maintained by their group.
4. We find a sort of segregation among boys and girls of this age. They form their groups among members of their own sex because of a definite and clear differentiation between their habits, interests and attitudes etc.
5. The interests and values of the peer group often clashes with the interests and values of the teachers and parents. The child at this age is caught between the two. On one hand, he aspires for the social values of his own group; on the other hand, he is equally anxious to win the love and affection of his parents as well as teachers. Therefore, a proper balance between these two influencing forces—peer group, parents and teachers—is essential. If neglected by either side, he may develop a maladjusted and antisocial personality.
6. Till the end of the stage of childhood, i.e. 11th or 12th year, the child enters the peek of "gang age" with increasing loyalties towards his own gang and conflicts with other gangs, parents and teachers. The gang life develops many good and bad social qualities in a child.

Social Development during Adolescence

Adolescence is the period of rapid change and adjustments and holds a greater significance in the social sphere. The social development of this age is marked by the following characteristics:

1. Adolescence is marked with too much sex consciousness, sexual development and the accompanying attraction for opposite sex. Boys and girls of this age try to attract and hold the attraction of each other through their style of dress, manner of talking and other forms of social behaviour. They also try to seek friendship and even sexual relationships. Therefore, the social behaviour pattern during adolescence is almost dominated by sexual needs and desires.
2. During this stage, group loyalty becomes very much pronounced. Like childhood, it does not confine itself to the gang only but extends to the school, community, province and the nation. Martyrs and patriots are the product of this age. Cooperation reaches its peak during this period and the individuals are in a mood to sacrifice their own interests for the greater cause of the group, society and the nation.
3. Adolescence is also marked with an increase in friendly relationships. The nature of friendship maintained at this stage differs much from that of the childhood. While the childhood friends are generally chosen from the neighbourhood or class, in adolescence

there is no such bar of distance. Adolescents tend to choose friends of their own age, mental level and from the same socio-economic group to which their own family belongs. Their friendships are based on their common interests, hobbies and skills or the satisfaction of their mutual needs and subsequently tend to last longer than the friendships made in early childhood. It sometimes cements life-long relationships.

4. Adolescence is a period of intense emotions. Emotional behaviour dominates the social characteristics and qualities of adolescents. An adolescent is highly sensitive, idealist and social reformer by nature. He feels strongly for the weak and suffers. He is always ready to do some sort of social and community service. From time to time, he exhibits his desire for bringing reforms in the social set-up and is highly critical of social evils and injustice.
5. Their areas of specific interests and social contacts get widened during adolescence. Besides individual characteristics, culture, socio-economic status of the family, sex education—all effect their social interest and contacts. We find too much diversity in the adolescents regarding their interests and sociability. While some are highly extrovert and sociable, others like to remain aloof and shirk from social contacts and participations.

In the end, we can say that adolescence is a period of maximum social awareness, increasing social relationships and intimate friendships. During this age the individual is provided with wide area of interests and opportunities for making social adjustment and learning so many social qualities. During this period, an individual prepares himself to play the role of an adult in his social life. By the end of this stage, the social behaviour of the child becomes almost matured.

SOCIAL MATURITY

As we have seen earlier, the aim of social development is to gain social maturity. A child while passing through various stages from his very birth strives to attain it. Let us see what does the term social maturity indicate or what *characteristics* are supposed to be present in a socially mature individual?

1. A socially mature individual likes to mix up with people. He is capable of making and keeping friendships.
2. He is not self-centered. He is always ready to sacrifice his interests for the greater cause of groups, society and the nation. While demanding and asserting for his rights, he always cares for the social obligations.
3. He possesses the ability of sharing and shouldering the social responsibilities. He is prepared to play the role of a leader or of a staunch follower as the situation demands from him.
4. He is able to make proper decision and take suitable action at the time of any social crisis, problem or situation in which his help is needed.
5. He is very cooperative. He believes in maintaining relationships and working with others. He does not do anything that hurts the feeling of others. He possesses social virtues like the feeling of sympathy, kindness, courtesy and cheerfulness. He believes in justice, equality and fraternity and never does anything to disrupt the cohesiveness and unity of the social structure.

Actually, he is imbued with all the important social qualities like patience, respect for others' opinions, kindness and sympathy, cooperation, courtesy and politeness, cheerfulness, self-confidence, self-control, sentiment of self-regard, respect for the opposite sex, religions and culture etc.

6. The area of his social interests and participation is very wide. He possesses refined tastes and adequate social etiquettes.
7. His social behaviour conforms to the norms, mores, social codes and ethics. He never engages himself in any sort of activities or behaviour which is anti-social and looked down upon by the society.
8. He possesses a strong desire to serve the cause of the society. He is critical of the evils and malpractices in the society and tries to bring desirable reforms.
9. He possesses a greater degree of adaptability and adjustability. He can make himself adjusted easily to the varying needs of the society and social circumstances.

FACTORS AFFECTING SOCIAL DEVELOPMENT

How to help a child in the task of his social development is a relevant question at this stage. In this task, the individual in addition to his own physical, mental and emotional development is helped by various social agencies. All these factors—personal and environmental—work together in influencing the social development of the child. What are these factors and how they influence the pattern of social development have been discussed below:

Personal Factors

1. **Bodily structure and health:** Development of social behaviour is influenced by the physique and health which one possesses. A healthy child with a normal physique develops self-confidence and a sense of self-respect. He has the strength and ability to adjust in the challenging social situations. He is always cheerful and cooperative. He is able to mix with the people and maintains proper social relationships. A child suffering from an illness or having poor health or any physical deformities and defects develops the feeling of inferiority and feels difficulty in social adjustment. Therefore, proper care should be taken for the balanced physical development of the children.
2. **Intelligence:** *Intelligence* is defined as the ability to make and take the right decision at a right time and the ability to adapt or adjust to new situations. These qualities are very essential for effective social behaviour. The more intelligent a person is, the more adjustable and social he will prove to be.
3. **Emotional development:** *Emotional development* of a child bears a positive correlation with social development. Emotional adjustability and maturity is one of the very important elements of social maturity. Those who can express their emotions in a proper degree at a proper time are found to possess a healthy social personality. Emotionally maladjusted personalities possess poor social qualities. Therefore, due care should be taken for the training of the emotions of the child so that he may not feel any obstacles in the path of his social development.

Environmental Factors

1. **Family environment:** Family is named as the most important primary agency for the socialization of a child. The home atmosphere and the family relationships exercise much

influence upon his social development. A child learns the first lesson of social qualities from his parents. Consciously or unconsciously, he imitates the behaviour of his parents and other members of the family and thus picks up many good or bad social characteristics which stay with him till the end of his life. The size of the family, relationships within the family, attitude of the parents and family members, socio-economic status and position of the family in the society, traditions, culture, values and the ideals of the family—all influence the social development of the child.

A family, which provides healthy social atmosphere and where basic needs of children are satisfied, produces socially balanced personalities whereas those houses where the family relationships are under strain and the elders possess negative social characteristics, the child is not brought up properly and consequently he produces socially undesirable and negative behaviour. Therefore it is essential to seek active cooperation of the parents in providing suitable atmosphere at home for the proper social development of the children.

2. **School environment:** Social development in children is greatly influenced by the social environment and functioning of the schools. The human relationships maintained by the school, the kinds of programmes and activities performed, its traditions, values and principles, the social qualities and behaviour of the teachers and schoolmates—all influence the social development of the child. A school, having a healthy social and democratic atmosphere, inculcates many social virtues among the students while poor and unhealthy atmosphere at the school and negative social behavioural characteristics of the teachers and schoolmates cast a bad influence on the social behaviour of the child. Therefore, teachers as well as the authorities should try their level best to make the school environment as healthy as possible for the proper social development of the children. They must produce good examples of social virtues and democratic living before children and through curricular and co-curricular activities, proper methods of instruction and personal contact, should help children in their proper social development.

3. **Peer-group relationship and gang influence:** The playmates, school or classmates also influence the social development of a child. He picks up the habits and social qualities of his companions. A good company helps him to learn good qualities while a bad company provides all opportunities to spoil him and turn him into an anti-social person. On the positive side, through peer group relationships and gang influence he learns to cooperate, lead and follow, think for a common cause and adjust in the challenging social situations. It inculcates the sense of loyalty, sympathetic attitude and the willingness to obey social rules and regulations in him.

   Parents, teachers and other responsible members of the society should remain very careful to see that a child gets a healthy company. Negative influence of the peer group and the gang in the form of an unsocial behaviour should be checked. A child should be accepted by his peer group. He should get proper environment and opportunities to mix with his peers.

4. **Community and neighbourhood:** As a child grows older, he comes in contact with the social circle of his neighbourhood and the community to which he belongs. The social interests, habits and characteristics of the neighbours, unconsciously and consciously, influence the social behaviour of the child. Every community and society is characterized by its unique cultural pattern, social mores, traditions and social characteristics. The child, as a member of the community and the society, picks up these things which go in shaping his social behaviour and influence his social development.

5. **Religious institutions and clubs:** The social agencies like temple, church, social clubs etc., also influence the social development of the child. These places serve as a meeting ground for the members of the society and help in developing social contacts and relationships. The social behaviour of an individual is greatly influenced by the traditions, values, ideals and social characteristics maintained by these institutions.
6. **Information and entertainment agencies:** Agencies like Newspapers, magazines, radio, cinema, television, etc., also exercise their influence on the social development of the children. Such sources constantly inform the readers, listeners and others about the changes in the social structure, customs, traditions and values and thus bring desirable changes in the social behaviour of the individuals. The mass entertainment agencies like radio, cinema, television etc. play a vital role in moulding and shaping the behaviour of the members of the society. The impact of these agencies in social life can very well be recognized. What a hero or heroine does on the screen is at once imitated. The values of life, style of living, traditions and cultural pattern of the society—all undergo a drastic change by the impact of these modern mass agencies.

These agencies should not be allowed to functions unchecked. Society or the government should exercise a desirable control and check upon the functioning of these agencies so that no undesirable and anti-social influence is left over the masses. Directly or indirectly, these agencies should be made an important means for the assimilation of the social and democratic virtues among the citizens.

SUMMARY

Social development refers to a process as a result of which a child acquires various social qualities and characteristics through his constant interaction with his social environment. It helps him for his adjustment in the social environment by maintaining proper social relationships.

The process of social development begins with an infant's first contact with other people and continues throughout his life. The early stage of social behaviour during infancy is characterized by negative social characteristics like shyness, rivalry, desire for possession, imitation etc. Later on, in early childhood positive aspects of social behaviour like co-operation, sympathy and social approval etc. begin to take their roots. During later childhood, a child begins to acquire distinctive social qualities with the widening of his area of social contact. In his further journey towards social development, adolescence provides him valuable opportunities for the acquisition of maximum social awareness, increasing social relationships and intimate friendships. By the end of this stage, the social behaviour of the child becomes almost matured.

Social development aims at helping a child attain social maturity. A socially mature individual proves a valuable asset to himself (by being properly adjusted in his social world through the maintenance of proper social relationships) and to the society (by becoming conscious of his social obligations).

Both personal as well as environmental factors work side by side in the process of social development of a child. Among the personal factors we can include bodily structure and health, intelligence and emotional development. Environmental factors include factors like family environment, school environment, peer group relationships and gang influence, community and neighbourhood, religious institutions, clubs, information and entertainment agencies as a potent means for shaping and moulding the social behaviour a child.

References and Suggested Readings

Carmichael, L. (Ed.), *Manual of Child Psychology*, John Wiley, New York, 1946.

Crow, L.D. and Crow, Alice, *Child Psychology,* reprint, Barney & Noble, New York, 1969.

Freeman and Showel, quoted by Hurlock, E.B., *Child Psychology*, Asian student 3rd ed., McGraw-Hill, Tokyo, 1959.

Garrett, H.E., *General Psychology*, 2nd ed., Eurasia Publishing House, New Delhi, 1968.

Hurlock, E.B., *Child Psychology*, Asian student 3rd ed., McGraw-Hill, Tokyo, 1959.

Marry, F.K. and Marry, R.V., *From Infancy to Adolescence*, Harper, & Brothers, New York, 1940.

Sorenson, Herbert, *Psychology in Education*, McGraw-Hill, New York, 1948.

10

Spiritual Development (Development of Character)

CHAPTER COMPOSITION

- Meaning of the Term Spiritual Development
- Spiritual Development Needs the Development of Character
- Role of Education in Character Development
- Summary
- References and Suggested Readings

MEANING OF THE TERM SPIRITUAL DEVELOPMENT

In simple words, the term '*spiritual development*' stands for the development of spirituality, which lies within a child since the time of birth. The use of this term in this way is an ample proof that every child is endowed with the essence of spirituality much the same way as he is endowed with the potentialities for the development of his body and mind in terms of his physical and mental development. Now here question may arise as to what does one mean by spirituality?

Actually speaking we all are created by the God, the greater soul and in this sense we are all part of the greater soul carrying sparks of the divine nature in ourselves. These sparks of divine nature are nothing but the essence of spirituality lying well within ourselves. Therefore each one of us is born with a divine nature. A child, therefore, shares His image, but as part of this creation, is subject to natural laws. God the almighty has created us for his own purposes, i.e. to share with Him forever the joys of relation with Himself and His creation. As a result the task regarding the development of spirituality in human beings is solely aimed at maintaining their relationship with God and his entire creation. One must realize that he is the constituent or part and parcel of his creator, the God and therefore is essentially divine in nature. One must also realize that not only the human beings, but whatever exists on this earth is entirely His creation, therefore, he must try to serve the interest of His creation. In a true sense, such type of self realization on the part of the human beings is the ultimate objective to be realized through the process of spiritual development.

With the help of above discussion, we can now try to define spiritual development in the following words—

Spiritual development means the development of spirituality well lying within the individual to the extent of making one realize and share his relationship with the creator, the God and His creation.

SPIRITUAL DEVELOPMENT NEEDS THE DEVELOPMENT OF CHARACTER

The task of spiritual development as said earlier needs the proper development/nourishment of the spirituality lying within one's self. Now, question may arise as to how should we proceed or what path should be followed for the development of spirituality. One must attain self realization, but what are the means for achieving this end? All lies in one's actions and behaviours and it is these actions or behaviours that may lead one to achieve his aim. In behavioural language, we term it as one's character. In case we aim for the proper development of the character of human beings we are sure to get him quite close to his desired spiritual development. It is in this sense both the terms spiritual development and character development may mean one and the same thing. If one has a strong character, one is supposed to attain his maximum in terms of spiritual development and vice versa. Thus the process of the development of spirituality may be directly linked with the process of the development of one's character. Therefore, in this text, we will discuss the process of one's spiritual development in terms of the process of one's character development. Let us begin by getting acquainted with the true concept of the terms character and character formation.

What is Character?

Various authors have tried to explain the meaning of the term 'character' in their own ways. Some of these meanings are given below:

Samuel Smiles

"Character is the bundle of habits." (Pathak, 1973, p. 153)

Boenheim

"When we talk of a strong character we mean strength of will." (1946, p. 35)

McDoutall

"The units of character are the sentiments and thus asserts that character is the system or organization of sentiments." (1949, p. 417)

Dumvile

"Character is the sum of all the tendencies which an individual possesses." (1938, p. 311)

Let us analyse these definitions.

1. The viewpoint that character is the sum total of habits is wrong. The term 'habit' denotes the repetition of similar actions in similar circumstances. As a result habits are mechanical and automatic ways of behaving in certain definite situations while the human life is seldom so automatic and mechanical. We cannot take the character as the mere bundle of habits. It is more than that. The good habits may form an integral part of one's character but they cannot impart any such strength to a person as may help him always in shaping his character.

2. In the second definition, the will has been designated as character. *Will* is the power that leads a man to decision. The power of taking proper decision at a proper time is an important element of one's character. Stronger the will of a person is, sounder is his character. But character is not limited to will power, it is more than that.
3. McDougall believes that character is the system or organization of sentiments. Let us see what he means by this.

MEANING OF SENTIMENT

First of all we should make ourselves clear about the meaning of the term sentiment. Sentiment as a term has been defined by *Valentine* in the following words:

"A sentiment is more or less a permanent and organized system of emotional tendencies and impulses centered about some object or person." (1965, p. 156)

Therefore in the formation of sentiments, many emotions concerning the same object, idea or individual combine to form a permanent structure. It is altogether an acquired disposition, a product of development and environment. A person has so many emotions—pleasure, love, lust (sexuality) and the feeling of ownership—centered around his wife. All these emotions may organize themselves into a permanent structure and as a result, the person develops a sentiment for his wife.

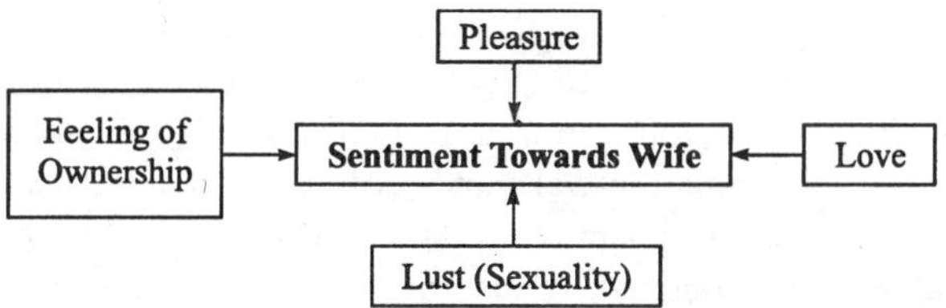

Fig. 10.1 Formation of a sentiment

Difference between sentiment and emotion. Sentiments are not merely a collection of emotions. Emotions are temporary but sentiments are more or less permanent. In emotions, no judgment is involved but in the formation of sentiments the intellect has a definite role to play.

A person's character is judged through the kinds of his sentiments and their organization.

Some Important Sentiments. Some of the important sentiments can be named as:

(i) Patriotic sentiment
(ii) Moral sentiment
(iii) Religious sentiment
(iv) Social sentiment
(v) Intellectual sentiment
(vi) Aesthetic sentiment
(vii) Self regarding sentiment.

Among these, *self regarding sentiment* is regarded as the highest and is known as the master sentiment. Through this sentiment, a person develops an adequate idea of self and his philosophy of life. All our attitudes and reactions to social and moral set-up are governed and approved by this master sentiment. In our thinking like—*"I am an honest man, I should not accept bribe or I am a college lecturer, I should not eat on the road side."* The sentiment of self-regard plays its part and decides our modes of behaviour or traits of character.

In the character of a person we find a compact organization of a number of his sentiments. As long as the individual's sentiments are scattered and lack organization and system, he is not supposed to possess a character. Moreover, the master sentiment plays a dominant role as it rules over all the other sentiments. Therefore, it is proper to define the character as the system or organization of sentiments directed by the supreme or master sentiment—the sentiment of self-regard.

The fourth definition seems to possess a comprehensive view as it suggests that character is the sum total of all the tendencies—innate as well as acquired—which an individual possess. It takes into consideration the following:

(i) In the first place, there are instincts which are inborn and innate. They provide the native mental capital for a person at the time of birth in order to start his life.

(ii) With increasing age and experience, instinctive behaviour is replaced by habit formation. At this stage habits mechanize the behaviour of an individual. But as they are mechanical in nature they have no power to control or manipulate the behaviour pattern.

(iii) Instincts give birth to emotions and these emotions play an important part in the personality or character development. The various emotions centered around an object or idea often combine themselves to form a composite group or organisation. When this organisation or structure takes a permanent structure in the mind of an individual, he develops a sentiment regarding that particular object or idea.

(iv) In the last stage the various sentiments are combined so as to form a system or organization. The equilibrium of this system is maintained by the intellect and the master sentiment.

This system of properly organized sentiments, which is known as the *character* of an individual, is completely an acquired disposition. In actual sense the character formation of an individual can be compared with a building whose foundation is in the form of (refined) instincts. The emotions can be taken as the bricks for building the walls and roofs of the sentiments. The sentiment of self-regard is the cement or the adhesive material. In this way character like building consists of the foundation materials and the other constructive materials and is thus defined as the sum total of what an individual possess.

In *conclusion*, we can quote Ross who said that *"character is just the organized self."* (1951, p. 129) Instincts, emotions, habits, temperament, will and sentiments—all are the constituents of character. The organization of these constituents into one in the form of a permanent mental structure is taken as the character of an individual. Therefore the study of one's character needs complete understanding of one's habits, motivation, will, sentiments, intellect, self image and many other factors affecting his total personality. A person's behaviour in the social situation is governed by his character. Therefore, *character in its essence can be defined as an organized and stable mental structure of an individual which determines his social behaviour.*

Levels or Stages of Character Development

Psychologists have tried to lay down their views about the course of moral or character development among children. The most notable among them has been Lowrence Kohlberg, a Harvard University psychologist. He concluded through his researches that there exists some universal stages or levels in the development of moral values among the children, namely, pre moral level (4 to 10 years), conventional morality level (10 to 13 years) and self-accepted moral principles level (age 13 to later adulthood)—Kohlberg, 1976.

In such classification, level one signifies absence of morality in true sense, level two indicates the development of moral sense more or less controlled by conventions, rules and regulations of the society and the level three marks the highest level of the attainment of true morality. In a bid to have more clarification with regard to the development of morality among children, we have divided the course of moral or character development into five levels or stages as described and demonstrated as below:

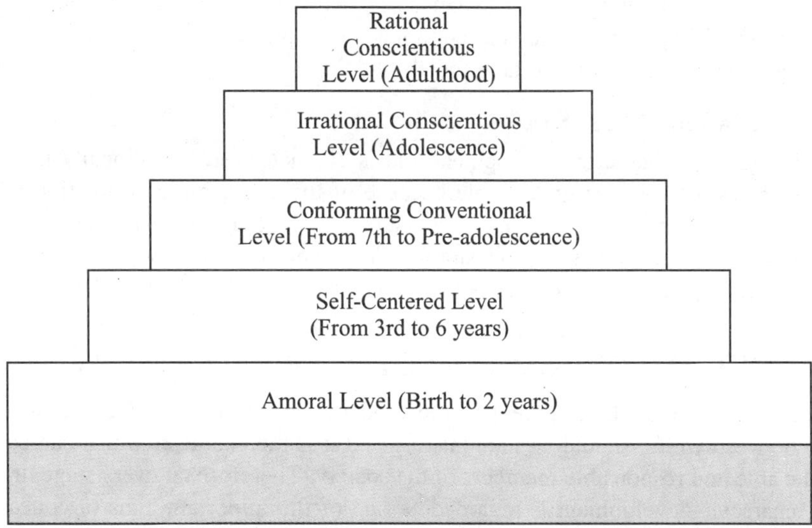

Fig. 10.2 Levels of character formation.

AMORAL STAGE

This state lasts from birth to two years. During this stage, the performer does not know or realize that his choice has good or bad effect on others or affects the welfare of others, e.g. plucking flower from a neighbour's garden. Wants are the sole motivation for a newly born infant who has no concept of good or bad, has no emotional control, cries at the time of every need without bothering if the cry disturbs others.

SELF-CENTERED STAGE

It lasts from 2 to 6 years. Durings this stage the person gratifies his own needs and wishes without caring about the effects of his act on others. His action might interferes with the happiness of others though he may not desire to violate the rules. The choice in this case is selfish and if fixation takes place, the person may develop miserly and selfish habits, and become source of trouble to himself and others. The selfish choices are reduced by socialization. Selfish choices may also sometimes be seen in case of men of character.

CONFORMING, CONVENTIONAL STAGE

The child in his early life is at this stage. The person may do as the Romans do even when his behaviour harms others. A person may not copy as it results in punishment. Many good citizens follow conventional pattern of behaviour to avoid bad consequences by breaking the norms.

IRRATIONAL CONSCIENTIOUS STAGE

The internal self-criticism which is responsible for making a person dissatisfied with some conduct even though that conduct will satisfy his external goals is called conscience. It can be compared with the concept of **Super-ego** as given by Sigmund Freud.

When a person acts in the light of the values held emotionally rather than rationally, e.g. speaks the truth irrationally, he is said to exhibit irrational conscientious behaviour. He will always speak the truth even if he were to be hanged for it.

Some people opine that since we attach topmost important to value, we should consider it the best form of character whereas others believe that people not able to tell gracious social lies will find it most difficult, rather impossible, to get along with the world. No doubt many irrational conformers have good adjustment with the community in spite of the fact that rigid truthfulness proves an obstacle or hindrance in certain social situations.

Rational Conscientious Stage

It is the highest stage of character development and is characterized by rationally not emotionally sticking to the values, e.g. war is undesirable because of the undesirable destruction of life which accompanies it. But destruction of life may not matter much to a person because war is a means to prevent oppression which again is undesirable. We commonly observe that if two values are important for a person, he may reconcile both of them or subordinate one value to the other.

ROLE OF EDUCATION IN CHARACTER DEVELOPMENT

The importance of character development in the field of education can never be underestimated. Education, to be worthwhile, should be man making and it is the character which can equip persons to be men—the able and responsible members of the society. Therefore, at every stage, in any system of education, character development is regarded as one of the important aims of education. Let us see how education can bring desirable development in the character of the children or in which way can schools and teachers help the youngsters in character formation. In general, the following techniques and provisions can prove as valuable guidelines in the task of character development:

(1) **Proper training of instincts and emotions.** Instincts form the rockbottom of a character. Therefore, the first step in the formation of character is the sublimation and modification of instincts. The emotions, which control the behaviour of an individual, take their energy from different instincts. In fact, instincts and emotions give birth to many elements of one's character. Nature of instinctive and emotional behaviour contributes much to the character development. Therefore, proper care should be taken to modify and sublimate the instinctive impulses and emotions along socially desirable channels. For instance, the crude instinct of combat and emotion of anger after sublimation can be channelised into patriotic and philanthropic deals and thus may help in character formation.

(2) **Training of will power.** Proper care should be taken for the development of a strong will power among the children. Firm determination and power of taking right decision at a right time are the products of will power and these two qualities are very essential for the development of a strong character. There is a perfect correlation between will and the character. There are so many undesirable and negative things which we do and consider them bad but due to weakness of our will cannot do away with them. A man of strong will can free himself from these harmful factors and remove the obstacles in the path of his character development.

(3) **Organization of good habits.** Habits also form a path of the character. Therefore, due care should be taken to develop healthy habits among the children through proper conditioning. Wrong habits need to be get eliminated through de-conditioning.

(4) **Development of worthy ideals.** What a person does and how he will behave in a particular situation depends much on his aims of life and the ideals for which he strives. In other words, the character of a person can be judged through his values and ideals. Higher the ideals and goals in life, stronger is the character of a person. Therefore, children should be

made to develop worthy ideals, higher values and noble aims in life so that they can imbibe good virtues.

(5) Organization and development of proper sentiments. Character is referred to as the system or organization of sentiments. Therefore, every care should be taken to develop a well organized stable system of healthy sentiments among the children. First of all due consideration should be paid for developing right types of sentiments like sentiment of patriotism, moral sentiment, social sentiment, intellectual sentiment, aesthetic sentiment and self-regarding sentiment. Later on all these positive like wise sentiments should be well organized with the help of the master sentiment, i.e. self-regarding sentiment. The strength of one's character always depends upon the sentiment of self-regard. Therefore, children must be helped to develop a strong sense of self respect and a sentiment of self-regard. In developing this very important sentiment, the following points should be kept in mind:

(i) Due respect must be shown for the individuality of the child.

(ii) The child should be given reasonable freedom in day-to-day work.

(iii) He must be encouraged to do his work independently and every care should be taken to build his self-confidence.

(iv) He must get proper love and affection coupled with an adequate sense of security.

(v) He must be helped to share and play a role of responsible individual in his school and social life.

(6) The role of suggestion. Suggestion occupies an important place in the formation and development of a character. Children are very sensitive to suggestion. Therefore, help of suggestion should be taken in character formation. But as far as possible, positive suggestion should be given to the children for bringing desirable improvement in their behaviour. This can be achieved through stories and the life sketches of great men and women. Teachers and parents may provide the living examples. After stepping in for character development, the children should be assured that they are making satisfactory progress. Auto-suggestion can also bring very good results at this stage. The feeling, that he is improving day-by-day and acquiring good habits and characteristics can immediately help the child to become a man of character.

(7) The rolc of imitation. Child is imitative by nature. He imitates what he sees and hears. To him his parents, elders and the teachers are ideals. He imitates them consciously and unconsciously. Hence it is essential that the teachers, parents and other elder members of the society place ideal examples of their own conduct and character. Every care should be taken by the parents and teachers that nothing undesirable is imitated by the children. They must be provided with healthy and inspiring atmosphere both inside the school and at their homes. It should be ensured that they do not fall prey to bad company and unhealthy society.

(8) Role of reward and punishment. Punishment and reward both occupy an important place in the development of character. In the modern age of democratic values and applied psychology, the role of punishment in character formation is decried. It is said that it creates complexes in the mind of the students and does more harm than good. The main function of punishment is negative as it can only check wrong things, but it certainly cannot develop the desired attitude.

Undoubtedly, there is some truth in these observations but we cannot completely give up the punishment in our educational system. Sometimes punishment appears to be the only tool to curb the undesirable activities. But as far as possible, punishment should be resorted to only when other measures fail. Most of the time-positive measures like rewards, praise, appreciation and other methods for the due incentive and encouragement should be applied.

(9) Role of moral instructions and religious education. No one can question the utility of moral and religious education as an instrument for character formation. In one form or the other, provision should be made for its inclusion in a sound system of education. Religious education in a secular state like India creates some doubts in the mind. Such type of education need not be based upon some narrow rigid sectarian feelings. In fact it should emphasize the lofty moral and human values and keep itself away from the rituals of the various religions. It should teach the children to pay respect to all the religions and men of character irrespective of caste, colour and creed.

The moral values may be inculcated in the children by suggestions through short stories like the stories from Panchtantra and Hitopdesh, Ramayana and the Mahabharata. Biographies and autobiographies of the great men may also serve the purpose. Prayer assembly, talks on morality and other programmes of co-curricular activities can also be made use of for the moral and religious instruction.

(10) Proper socialization of the child. Social development and character development bear a positive correlation. A socially developed child always behave according to the norms and values of the society and therefore is more conscious of his character. Therefore, every care should be taken for the proper social development of the child. He must be helped in the inculcation of desirable social virtues and maintenance of essential social relations with his peers and other members of the society.

(11) Proper mental development of the child. Character formation is also linked with the proper mental development of the child. Intellect plays a vital role in the organisation of the elements of character. How a person will behave in a particular situation and face the realities of life depends much upon his intellectual powers like reasoning, thinking, imagination, memory and concentration etc.

(12) Role of school, family and society. Environment plays a vital role in the development of character. Right from the birth or from the time of conception, the environmental forces begin to influence the behaviour of the child. Parents and the family is the first social institution where the foundation stone of the child's character is laid down. Outside the family, the neighbourhood, community and social forces influence the conduct of the child. When he goes to school, the school atmosphere, along with the teachers and schoolmates, cast its influence on the character of the child. Therefore, it is essential that all these social forces join their hands in the task of the children's character formation. The social environment as a whole must be so suggestive and inspiring that the children can pick up the habits and characteristics essential for proper character development.

In fact, character formation is a gigantic task. Without the active cooperation of all the persons—children, parents, teachers and all the important social agencies—it is hard to achieve some fruitful results in this direction. We have to exploit all the resources at our command and strive hard with all the methods and techniques in our possession. The observation made by Skinner and Harriman reminds us of the same. In their words—

"There is no curriculum or method that will produce character by magic. On the contrary, every experience in the home, at church, on the playground or at school presents an opportunity for character development." (1937, p. 261)

Character formation, in its true sense, is an all-round development and needs an all round effort. To pay attention to the over all aspects, it is needed that a programme of character formation should be chalked out and implemented with the hearty cooperation of all the involved partners.

SUMMARY

Spiritual development stands for the development of spirituality lying well within the individual to the extent of making one realize and share his relationship with the creator, the God and His creation. However, the path leading to such self-realization or spiritual development rightly passes through one's character building. In another words, the process of the development of spirituality is directly linked with the process of the development of one's character. This means that for attaining spiritual development one should take care of his character building.

The term 'character' stands for an organized self. Instincts, emotions, habits, temperament, will and sentiments — all are the constituents of character. The organization of these constitutes into one in the form of a permanent mental structure (capable of guiding one's social behaviour) is taken as a character of an individual.

Character formation or development in children passes through some specific age-linked stages or levels, named as Amoral stage (birth to 2 years), Self-centered stage (from 3 to 6 years) conforming, conventional stage (7 to early adolescence), Irrational conscientious stage (adolescence) and Rational conscientious stage (adulthood). In this way starting from the negation of maturity and sociability a mature person reaches the highest level of character development when he acts rationally and not merely emotionally sticking to the conventions and values.

Children can be properly helped in the task of character building by following a number of techniques and provisions like (i) proper training of their instincts, emotions and will power; (ii) developing healthy and desirable habits, as well as ideals of life; (iii) helping them in the organization and development of proper sentiments, like sentiment of patriotism, social sentiment, aesthetic sentiment and self regarding sentiment etc.; (iv) applying the behaviour modification techniques like suggestion, imitation, reward and punishment, moral instructions, religious education and socialization of the child; (v) caring for the proper physical, mental and emotional development of the child; (vi) seeking proper involvement of parents, family members, school and society in the character building of the child.

References and Suggested Readings

Boenheim, Curt, *Introduction to Present day Psychology*, Staples Press, London, 1946.

Cumville, Benjamin, *The Fundamental of Psychology,* 3rd ed., University Tutorial Press, London, 1938.

McDugall, Willaim, *An Outline of Psychology*, 13th ed., Methuen, London, 1949.

Ross, J.S., *Ground Work of Educational Psychology*, George G. Harrap Co., London, 1951.

Samuals Smiles, quoted by Pathak, P.D., *Educational Psychology*, Vinod Pustak Mandir, Agra, 1973.

Skenner C.E. and Harriman, P.L. (Eds.), *Child Psychology*, 6th print, Macmillan, New York, 1937.

Valentine, C.W., *Psychology and Its Bearing on Education*, English Language Book Society & Methuen, London, 1965.

11

Stage Specific Characteristics and Developmental Tasks

CHAPTER COMPOSITION

INTRODUCTION

Infancy and childhood are infact the most formative periods of one's life. They are also quite important from the angle of providing meaningful education to the youngsters for their adequate harmonious development and preparation as a grown up individual. However, every stage of human development is a unique stage with regard to its stage specific characteristic. This is equally true for all the developmental stages—infancy, childhood and adolescence. Consequently, we have to plan the developmental education of the youngsters well in tune with their age and stage-specific developmental characteristics. Accordingly in the present chapter we are going to discuss the special features of the developmental trend as well as needed developmental tasks during the first two educational stages—infancy and childhood while the same for the adolescence will be discussed in the subsequent chapter.

THE STAGE OF INFANCY AND EARLY CHILDHOOD

The special features of the developmental trend and behaviour pattern at this stage (up to 5 years) are as under:

1. **Rapid growth and development:** It is the period of rapid growth and development. Inner as well as outer organs develop rapidly at this stage. There is a rapid growth in terms of

height, weight and size. There is also rapid development of emotions and almost all the emotions are developed in the child during this stage. This stage is marked by intensive motor activity and restlessness.

2. **Dependence:** At this stage, a child depends upon his mother, father and other family members for the satisfaction of his basic needs. He is a helpless creature and can move and function only with the help of others. Even for the emotional satisfaction, he depends upon others. He expects that everybody around him should love him and give him his entire affection and attention. He wants to love and to be loved and in exchange he totally depends on the mercy of others. Hence a child at this stage is dependent but as he moves into the later years of his infantile behaviour, he slowly proceeds towards independence.
3. **Self-assertion:** Although the child is helpless and depends upon others for the satisfaction of his needs, he is quite self-assertive. He tries to dominate his superiors and elders. His wishes must be fulfilled. He thinks he is always right and all around him should obey him. He is the prince although without a crown and tries to assert himself all the time in all the situations.
4. **Period of make-believe and fantasy:** Here, children live in the world of their own creation. This is a period of rich but baseless imagination. As in this stage the child has limited potentialities and aspires more than what he can actually get in actual life, he compensates this in fantasy and make-believe.
5. **Selfish and unsocial:** At this stage the child is almost completely ego-centric and selfish. He does not want to share his toys or give any of his possessions to anyone else. He wants to have all the things, even love, admiration and affection reserved for him. He does not care for the social and moral codes and principles and places his self interest at the premium.
6. **Emotionally unstable:** It is the period of violent emotional experiences. Emotions at this stage are marked by intensity, frequency and instability. They are spontaneous and the infant is hardly able to exercise control over them. He is not capable of hiding his feelings and in this way, the emotional expression of the infant is generally in the overt form.
7. **Characteristics of mental development:**
   - (i) **Developing curiosity and questioning attitude:** At this stage the child is very curious about the things around him. The world and the environment is new for him. He is full of questions like what is this, why does it happens or not happen etc. His queries are virtually endless. Answers do not interest him as much as asking question.
   - (ii) **Intellectually not developed:** A child at this initial stage is very immature in intelligence. He lacks in reasoning and abstract understanding. He can think only in concrete terms and is not developed in abstract reasoning and thinking. The powers of observation, perception, concentration, etc. are also not developed.
   - (iii) **Rote memory:** The child, though not much developed intellectually, has a very good memory. However, this memorization is without reasoning and is purely a rote memory. He can cram and reproduce the matter easily.

(iv) **Creativity:** This period is also characterized by the tendency of creative impulse in the child. He develops a creative attitude and often engages himself in making or collecting many things. He tries to draw satisfaction realizing that he can make, construct and perform the activities like his elders.

(v) **Time concept not developed:** For a child at this stage, the divisions of time such as yesterday, today, tomorrow, month, year etc. are meaningless as he has not yet developed the concept of time.

8. **Sexual development:** Although the sex organs at this stage are not developed, the sex tendency is in a continuous stage of development. The findings of psychoanalysists like Freud and others have clearly shown that the sexual life of a child at this stage is as rich as that of an adolescent. He passes through three stages of sexual development—stage of self-love, homosexual and heterosexual. At the initial stage, the child derives pleasure from his own body by sucking his thumb or touching the sex organs. Later on, he seeks satisfaction of his sex impulse outside and develops sentiments of love for the mother or father depending upon his sex. Finally the child develops heterosexual tendency and in this respect a male child gets attached to the mother and the female child to the father.

THE STAGE OF CHILDHOOD: MAIN CHARACTERISTICS

When a child completes his five years and steps into the school-going age, the period of childhood starts. It continues till the onset of puberty. During this period, significant changes in the sphere of physical, intellectual, emotional and social aspects take place. The main characteristics of development during this stage can be named as follows:

1. **Period of slow and steady growth:** While infancy is the period of rapid and intensive growth, the stage of childhood is characterized as the period of slow, steady and uniform growth. Development rate, although continuous and uniform, is very slow at this stage.
2. **Independence:** An infant seeks help in every sort of work even if he is able to do it independently, whereas a child at this stage desires independence. By acquiring experiences and developing physically, intellectually and socially he tries to adjust in his environment. In fact at this stage he feels more at home with the world and takes satisfaction in doing his work with his own efforts. He becomes increasingly independent of his parents whom he considers merely convenient persons to provide food and shelter.
3. **Emotional stability and control:** Childhood in the emotional aspect is the period of stability and control. Intense emotional outbursts which usually find their expression in motor activity and physical form during infancy are rarely repeated at this stage. The child learns to hide his feelings, he can exercise control over his emotions and express them in appropriate and socially approved ways. His emotional behaviour is not guided by instinctive cause but has an appropriate rational behind it.
4. **Developing social tendency:** In contrast to an infant who is egocentric, the child at this stage develops social tendencies and picks up many social virtues. He likes to play in a

group and shares his toys with others. Feelings of mutual cooperation, team spirit and group loyalties are developed among children of this stage. This period of childhood is often named as gang-age as the child of this age is always a member of some group and develops a very strong sentiment for the group. He is so loyal to his group that sometimes he does not even mind the displeasure of his parents and teachers.

5. **Realistic attitude:** Child at this stage begins to accept and appreciate the hard realities of life. He no longer remains in his own world of make-believe, fantasy and fairy-tales. He now becomes a perfect realist from being an imaginative idealist. He begins to take a close interest in the world of realities and tries to adapt himself to the real environment.

6. **Formation of sentiments and complexes:** Infancy is the age of innocence. A child at this stage is used to neither hiding his feeling nor checking his emotions. Therefore, no complexes are formed at this stage whereas childhood stage gives birth to many complexes due to inhibition, repression, and so on. At the stage of infancy, emotional behaviour does not turn itself into a permanent structure for giving birth to sentiments. But at this stage of childhood, emotional behaviour gets structured into sentiments. Various sentiments like religious, moral, patriotic and aesthetic sentiments begin to develop at this stage. The formation of each sentiment leads towards character development.

7. **Sexual development:** With regard to sexual development, this stage is called 'latency period.' Sexual energy, generally, at this stage remains dormant but emerges with great force at the end of this stage. The sexual behaviour of the children at this stage is characterized by the development of an attitude of antagonism and indifference towards the opposite sex. While at the infancy stage boys and girls play together, a child likes to play with the members of his own sex. Due to their varied interests, children gradually develop a general attitude of antagonism towards the opposite sex. As a result of this antagonistic in family gatherings, boys and girls of this age are barely civil to one another. Sex antagonism is more pronounced in boys than in the case of girls. They do not want anything that resembles a girl. In the case of girls, the attitude of antagonism generally takes the form of indifference. They try to ignore the boys in place of tormenting, teasing and interfering with their games.

8. **Intellectual development:** This stage is the period of intellectual advancement. The rate of intellectual development is quite rapid at this stage which resembles the rate of physical growth at infancy. At this stage, the child acquires new experiences and tries to adapt himself to his environment and prepares himself to solve the problems. His power of reasoning, thinking, observation, concentration, perception, imagination etc. are developed. He cannot very well go with abstract thinking. He develops the concept of length, time and distance and learns to express himself in various ways.

9. **Development of interest and aptitudes:** In childhood, the child's field of interests widens and he shows special aptitudes, likings and disliking towards various things and work. The children of this age are usually extrovert and very fond of excursions and visits. They develop interest in reading various types of books. Radio, television drama and movies hold a strong appeal for them. They are interested in everything which is mysterious and romantic. Wide differences in the interest pattern can be seen among boys and girls. Boys are interested in the activities requiring fearlessness, courage and adventures while girls are inclined towards the activities requiring tenderness, softness and other feminine characteristics.

MEANING OF THE TERM DEVELOPMENTAL TASKS

The terms and concept regarding developmental tasks were first introduced by Robert Havinghurst of the University of Chicago, USA by a definition given below:

Havighurst, R.J.

"Developmental task is one which arises at a certain period in the life of the individual, successful accomplishment of which leads to his happiness and success with later tasks, while failure leads to unhappiness and difficulty with later tasks.", 1972

A close analysis of the above definition may lead us to conclude the meaning of the term developmental tasks as under :-

(i) Development task is essentially linked with the development and developmental period (from birth till the expiry of the adolescence) of an individual.

(ii) Developmental tasks are age-specific and essentially linked with the developmental stages of one's life.

(iii) An individual at a particular age or stage of his growth and development is expected to perform certain tasks (performing certain types of conative, cognitive and affective behaviour) quite specific to his age and stage of development.

(iv) Adjustment with the self and the environment depends upon the extent to which one in capable of performing these age-specific and stage-related developmental tasks.

(v) In case one is successful in accomplishing the related developmental tasks (specific to his age and developmental period), he feels happy at his present and is expected to perform future tasks successfully in his later life. Failure, on the other hand, makes his present life miserable and puts a question mark on his ability to perform future tasks successfully in his later life.

(vi) Key to happiness and adjustment thus lies in the proper identification of developmental tasks and learning the ways and means of their successful accomplishment during the related developmental periods of one's life.

After having some acquaintance with the meaning and nature of the developmental tasks, the questions can now be raised regarding—(i) The identification and naming of the developmental tasks; (ii) The sources contributing towards the upsurge of the developmental tasks at a particular age and development period; (iii) Critical ages at which the society expects its members to master the developmental tasks of that age; (iv) Purposes and goals of such tasks; (v) Role of the cultural and social pattern regarding expectation of certain developmental tasks from its growing youngsters; and (vi) Specific tasks associated with the stages of developmental period.

Let us think over all such issues.

Identifying and Naming the Development Tasks

Developmental tasks are related with the changes in behaviour belonging to its all three domains namely conative, cognitive and affective. What a developing child is expected to do, think and feel at a particular age or stage of one's developmental period for his adequate adjustment in one's social and cultural environment can then work as a base for the identification and naming of various developmental tasks at a particular age or stage of one's life. Since there lies a number of activities or tasks belonging to these three behavioural domains that can be expected to be executed by the growing children of developmental period, the list for the identification and naming of the developmental task will naturally be too lengthy and exhaustive. However, for illustration purpose let us try to mention the name of the developmental tasks needed to be performed by the growing children as below:

(i) **Conative developmental tasks:** Crawling, sitting, standing, walking, riding, jumping, running, throwing, catching, controlling elimination of bodily wastes, combing, dressing, eating, biting, stretching, stopping, drinking, kneeling, holding, leaning, smashing, balancing, identification by touching, seeing, smelling or hearing, writing, handling the instruments, dancing, dining, driving, knitting, playing a musical organ, teasing, posing, handling of the technologically advanced instruments etc.

(ii) **Cognitive developmental tasks:** Recognizing, recalling, reproducing, selecting, listing, measuring, counting, reading, underlining, classifying, distinguishing, explaining, justifying, interpreting, choosing, modifying, illustrating, comparing, analyzing, synthesizing, concluding, contrasting, arguing, generalizing, associating, criticizing, evaluating, summarizing, verifying, reporting, supporting, predicting, using, solving, relating, etc.

(iii) **Affective developmental tasks:** Accepting, attaining, showing specific interests attitudes and aptitudes for things, ideas, processes and persons, demonstrating particular or generalized habits of thinking, feeling and actions, demonstrating a particular level of social and emotional maturity, sex behaviour, personal and social adjustment and moral sense, etc.

Sources Contributing towards the Upsurge of Development Tasks

Development tasks specific to an age and stage of development may be necessitated and brought in existence on account of the following factors:

(i) **Maturation:** As the child matures, *i.e.* grows in age, he definitely needs to perform certain tasks so as to adjust himself according to the changing needs of his growing age. Examples of such tasks are learning to crawl, stand, walk, dress, etc.

(ii) **Adjustment to the physical, social and cultural environment:** Many developmental tasks are necessitated on account of seeking proper adjustment to one's physical, social and cultural environment. Sometimes physical environment puts pressure on a growing child to learn proper ways and means of adjusting according to the condition prevailing in one's physical environment. Hilly, desert or coastal areas demand specific activities and ways of living from the growing children and as a result it generates some typical development tasks for them. Similar is the case with the needs and pressures put up by one's social and cultural environment for learning the execution of specific development tasks suiting to one's age and developmental stage. One needs to learn the use of special devices like telephone, mobile, Internet, or read, write and speak a particular language, learn specific social and cultural behaviour, etc. according to the demands of one's social and cultural environment at a particular age or stage of one's life.

(iii) **Adjustment to one's self:** Many developmental tasks are necessitated on account of seeking harmonious relationships or adjustment to one's self. Sometimes one needs to fulfill the demands of his own desires, basic interests, liking and disliking, philosophy of life, values and aspirations, somatic structure and cognitive and emotional characteristics. Aspiring to study a particular course of instruction and choosing a particular course or profession are examples of such demands needed for the adjustment of one's self. Accordingly, an individual is forced to include the related tasks in the list of developmental tasks suiting to his growing age like trying to get entry into a specific academic and professional course or preparing oneself for the entry in the desired profession and vocation.

In this way, developmental tasks are mostly generated naturally on account of maturation or the pressures put on the individual for getting adjusted to one's self and his environment.

Critical Ages and Developmental Tasks

As emphasized earlier, developmental tasks are quite age and developmental stage specific. Hence particular type of developmental tasks need to be carried out at a particular age and developmental stage level. The age spans during which the growing children are expected to perform a certain type of developmental task in a particular society and cultural group are termed as *critical ages* and *periods of the life*. These critical ages and periods of life present quite a ripe stage in terms of maturation and learning experiences gained from one's environment for performing the developmental tasks relevant to the critical ages and periods of life. As a result, we can't expect a growing child to perform a certain type of developmental task unless he or she has not reached the required stage of maturation and development, *i.e.* entered in the period of the relevant critical age. Further, we can't also expect from a more mature child or adult to perform certain developmental tasks after the expiry of the critical age period, *i.e.* learning gymnastic skills etc.

Purposes and Goals of Developmental Tasks

It is well in the interest of the growing children, parents and teachers that they are acquainted with the nature of the developmental tasks needed to be performed by the children at a specific age and developmental period of the life. The purposes and objectives realized through such knowledge may prove fruitful in the following way:

- It may provide the norms and expectations of a particular society or cultural group from its growing children in terms of the general behaviour pattern (demonstrable through conative, cognitive and affective tasks) during the various ages and developmental periods of life.
- It may help in setting the minds and attitudes of the children for making desirable attempts to learn the execution of the developmental tasks relevant to different developmental periods of their life.
- It may provide proper guidelines to teachers and parents to help youngsters in their adequate growth and development by providing richer experiences for the execution of the developmental tasks related to the critical ages and stages of their lives.
- It may help the society or a cultural group to develop its own set of developmental tasks needed to be performed at one or the other stage of development by their children in view of the changes of future developmental course of that very society and cultural group.
- The knowledge of developmental tasks specific to critical ages may help the children, teacher and parents to plan their obligation and duties well in advance in view of the targets lying ahead in terms of the required expected stage of maturity and experiences gained for executing the tasks. What is expected at present and what lies ahead in terms of the level

of developmental tasks to be performed by the growing children, the knowledge of such aspects may prove a boon to the education and development planner, besides being a source of self motivator to the youngsters themselves.

Role of Cultural and Social Patterns in Developmental Tasks

The developmental tasks, besides being age-specific, are also said to be influenced by the nature of the life patterns prevalent in a social and cultural group. That is why we can't expect our youngsters to perform developmental tasks performed by the English, American, Japanese or African children. For example, in our social and cultural set-up children acquire puberty at quite an early age in comparison to the children of European nations. It will definitely affect the expectation from them in term of the developmental tasks selected to their sex behaviour, emotional and social maturity etc. Similarly, there may be many types of social and cultural behaviour patterns, mental make-up, etc. that may be expected from the children of the developed countries and fast moving societies in a sharp contrast to the children belonging to developing and deprived social segments. Such differences may essentially force to adopt somewhat different approaches in planning the developmental tasks relevant to specific periods of life. In reality it does happen and thereby we may clearly observe that the list of developmental tasks needed to be performed by the growing children at the specific ages and periods of their life varies from culture to culture and society to society.

Developmental Tasks of the Various Stages of Development

The developmental period, as we know in the human beings ranges from birth to the attainment of maturity, *i.e.* expiry of the adolescence period. The significant stages of development during this period may be named as the stages of infancy, childhood and adolescence. Let us try to know something about the nature of development tasks needed to be performed by the youngsters during the above mentioned three development stages of our life.

Development Tasks of Infancy (up to two years)

- Learning to crawl, stand, walk, run, climb, jump, throw etc.
- Learning to drink and take solid food
- Learning to talk
- Learning to acquire physiological stability
- Learning to control elimination of bodily wastes
- Learning to explore the physical environment surrounding him
- Learning to play with toys
- Learning to accomplish the skill of tri-cycling
- Learning to pay attention towards the things, persons and events
- Learning to recognize and identify things and persons
- Forming simple concepts of social and physical reality
- Learning to recite poems and stories
- Learning to imitate the behaviour and actions of others
- Learning to acquire almost all the positive and negative emotions in his behaviour expression

- Learning to shift his attention from the play material to his playing mates
- Learning to take interest in the company of his age mates and other growing children
- Learning to relate oneself emotionally to parents, sibling and others.

Development Tasks of Early Childhood (from 3 to 5 years)

- Learning to acquire competencies in motor skills like walking, jumping, climbing, sliding, tri-cycling, hopping, galloping, skipping, throwing, bouncing and catching
- Learning to acquire simple basics in language skills like speaking, listening, reading and writing
- Learning sex differences and sex modesty
- Learning to distinguish between right and wrong and developing a conscience
- Learning to develop right concepts related to social and physical reality
- Learning to remain away from the parental fold and enjoy the companionship of other children
- Learning to give up the 'I' feeling and develop the 'we' feeling
- Learning to acquire the ability to sense similarities and dissimilarities and compare and contrast things
- Learning to control overt expression of emotions.

Development Tasks of Later Childhood (from 6 to 12 years)

- Learning motor and physical skills necessary for playing different indoor and outdoor games
- Learning to get along with age-mates
- Learning to appropriate sex roles
- Building wholesome attitudes towards oneself as a growing organism
- Developing necessary skills in language and communication, computation, sketching and drawing etc.
- Developing interest, attitudes, liking and dislikings towards things, persons and ideas
- Developing concrete and abstract concepts regarding things, persons, ideas and processes
- Development of conscience, morality and scale of values
- Development of the capacity to reason, think and problem solving
- Development of loyalty towards the group.

Development Tasks of Adolescence (from 13 to 18 years)

- Development of abilities, motor and physical skills for playing difficult, complex and hard indoor and outdoor games
- Development of abilities, motor and physical capacities for performing mental tasks and physical capacities for performing mental tasks and physical labour
- Development of mental and cognitive abilities to perform difficult mental tasks and operations
- Development of all types of concept—requiring concrete or abstract operations
- Learning to accept one's physique and satisfaction with one's appearance
- Learning to play a masculine or feminine role

- Learning to develop new relations with age mates of both the sexes
- Learning to acquire maturity in sex behaviour
- Development of sentiments towards things, persons, places and values
- Learning to acquire civic sense, social responsibilities and ways of democratic living
- Learning to build a sense of belonging to one's social group, culture, community and nation
- Learning to adjust with a sense of self-sacrifice and martyrs like feelings for the cause of society, religion, nation and humanity
- Gaining vocational awareness and getting ready for entering into higher academic or professional courses of study
- Gaining competencies and skills for meeting the needs of specific interests and aptitudes
- Striving to gain desired height on the mental, emotional and social maturity scales
- Preparing for playing the roles of a mature adult in future life.

In this way, every society and cultural group has a list of general and specific developmental task specifically associated with ages and developmental periods of life. It expects the youngsters belonging to the developmental age to successfully execute these tasks for their proper adjustment with themselves and their physical, social and cultural environment. Similar schemes of developmental tasks expected from the adult and older generations may also be planned for serving the individual and social interests and seeking proper harmony with their selfs and the environment resulting happiness in the personal and social lives.

Role of Teacher in Facilitating Development

We need all-round growth and development of the personality of the child. He must seek his harmonious growth and development in all the aspects or dimensions of growth and development, *i.e.* social, mental, emotional, moral or spiritual. Since it is the child who is to develop in all the dimensions the will for the development and the desired attempts for doing so should invariably be initiated and carried out by the child himself. The role of the teacher in this task can only be limited to a guide and facilitator for helping and providing facilities for the development and nourishment of the child's potentialities. Now the question arises as to what should a teacher do to play his role as a facilitator for the desired development of his students in all the required dimension or aspects of their personalities. In brief we can summarize his activities in this regard as below:

1. **Diagnosing the potentialities:** He must try to study and investigate the potentialities of his students and then decide to provide them due guidance and incentives for the development of their potentialities. True diagnosis of the strength, and weaknesses of the students is essential for facilitating them in their proper development.
2. **Helping in setting proper goals:** In the light of the diagnosed potentialities and achievement motivation of his students, he must help his students in setting realistic goals and objectives for their striving. These should neither be too high nor too low but a little realistic for avoiding unnecessary failures and frustrations.
3. **Arranging needed facilities for their adequate development:** The teacher should take care of all types of men-material facilities helpful in the adequate development of his students in all the dimensions of their personality. In the shape of physical, academic/curricular,

co-curricular, activities as well as formal-informal, direct and indirect experiences, in short, whatever is useful and needed for their multi-dimensional growth and development the students, should be helped by the teacher for proper access to the maximum extent possible.

4. **Provide his own example for their proper development:** It is a well known saying that example is always better than precept. There lies much substance in this saying. Whatever a teacher wants to see in his students, he must try to provide a model for such expectation for his students. He may take the help of the glorious men of the past as role models but his own exemplary behaviour and actions will surely find no match as a role model for his students. Therefore, as far as possible, he should provide his own example for the proper development of his students.
5. **Due incentive and reinforcement:** He must try to accept his students with their strengths as well as limitations. Whenever they try for development in one field or the other, they must be properly watched and given due reinforcement at the needed hours. He should never ridicule or make them feel small for their mistakes, but provide remedial steps and useful suggestion for overcoming their mistakes. Words of praises and steps of reinforcement may do wonders in facilitating them in the proper advancement of the developmental tasks.
6. **Teacher must have a proper knowledge of developmental psychology:** Teacher, while playing a role of facilitator in the development of his students, should have adequate knowledge of developmental psychology. What type of development is normal for the student of a particular age? What type of developmental tasks are expected from him? What facilities or development conditions should be provided for a child of a particular age for his growth and development in one or the other dimension? Such type of questions should be properly answered by the teacher for playing the role of a good facilitator.

In this way, a wise teacher should always plan and execute his ways of behaviour and resources in a proper way to provide due facilities and environmental conditions for the proper development of his students in all the dimensions of growth and development.

SUMMARY

Every stage of human development is characterized with some unique characteristics named as stage specific characteristics. For example the stage specific characteristics of the stage of infancy and early childhood (up to five years) may be named as (i) the period of rapid growth and development, (ii) Child's dependence on others, (iii) Self-assertive nature of child, (iv) Children living in the world of make believe and fantasy, (v) Child's selfish and unsocial behaviour (vi) Emotional instability (vii) Lacking in terms of intellectual and sexual development. Similarly the childhood (6 to the beginning of adolescence) stage may be distinctly marked with the stage-specific characteristics like (i) Period of slow and steady growth (ii) Independence (iii) Emotional stability and control (iv) Development of social tendency (v) Adoption of realistic attitude (vi) Formation of sentiments and complexes (vii) Developmental progress in terms of intellect, interests and aptitudes (viii) Development of indifference and antagonism towards the opposite sex.

Quite specific to one's age and stage of development, an individual is supposed to perform certain tasks often named as developmental tasks. The adjustment with the self and the environment depends upon one's capacity to properly perform these age and stage related developmental tasks. It is, therefore, the duty of the parents and teachers to get acquainted with the nature of developmental task for helping their children in the proper execution of their tasks at each of their developmental stage.

Developmental tasks belonging to all the three domains of behaviour may be classified into three broad categories namely conative developmental tasks, cognitive developmental tasks and affective developmental tasks (related to doing, thinking and feeling aspects of one's behaviour).

Developmental tasks specific to an age and stage of development are mostly necessitated and brought into existence naturally on account of maturation or the pressures put on the individual for getting adjusted to one's self and his environment.

The age spans during which the growing children are expected to perform a certain type of developmental task in a particular society and cultural group are termed as critical ages and periods of the life. Children for their own and social welfare are necessarily directed to perform the needed development tasks within the boundary of these critical ages/periods.

The developmental tasks, besides being age-specific, are also culture specific as these are known to be greatly influenced by the nature of the life pattern prevailing in a social and cultural group. That is why every society and cultural group has its own list of general and specific developmental tasks specifically associated with ages and developmental periods of life. After such specification, it then expects the youngsters (from infancy to the end of adolescence) to execute these tasks properly for their adequate adjustment.

The teacher has to play a substantial role in helping the children in their proper growth and development. For this purpose, he must first try to acquaint himself what is needed by children at each of their developmental ages and stages. Then he should properly study and diagnose the potentiality of individual child and strive for providing needed facilities, examples, incentives and reinforcement for the proper development of the potentialities of the child well in tune with the needs of critical ages.

References and Suggested Readings

Crow, L.D. and Crow, Alice, *Child Psychology,* Reprint, Barney & Noble, New York, 1969.

Havighurst, R.J., *Developmental Task and Education,* 3rd ed., David Mckay, New York, 1972.

Hurlock, E.B., *Child Psychology*, Asian student 3rd ed., McGraw-Hill, Tokyo, 1959.

Marry, F.K. and Marry, R.V., *From Infancy to Adolescence*, Harper & Brothers, New York, 1940.

Skinner C.E. and Harriman, P.L. (Eds.), *Child Psychology,* 6th print, Macmillan, New York, 1937.

12

Growth and Development during Adolescence

CHAPTER COMPOSITION

INTRODUCTION

The word 'adolescence' comes from the Latin verb 'adolescere' which means 'to grow'. So, the essence of the word *adolescence* is growth and it is in this sense that adolescence represents a period of intensive growth and change in nearly all aspects of a child's physical, mental, social and emotional life. It is a very crucial period of one's life. The growth achieved, the experiences gained, responsibilities felt and the relationships developed at this stage destine the complete future of an individual.

WHO IS AN ADOLESCENT?

When does this crucial period start and end in one's life? Who should be labeled as an adolescent? These are some pertinent questions which should be answered at this stage.

Technically speaking, a child is described as an adolescent when he achieves puberty, *i.e.,* when he has become sexually mature to the point where he is able to reproduce his kind. He ceases to be an adolescent when he has acquired maturity to play the role of an adult in his society or culture. *Maturity*, as the term used here, does not mean mere physical maturity, it also implies mental, emotional and social maturity.

It is very difficult to point out the exact range of the adolescence period in terms of chronological years. Achieving puberty and becoming mature cannot be bound to a universal span or period. Therefore, the range of adolescence not only differs from country to country but also varies from community to community and from individual to individual. Generally, girls become sexually as well as socially mature at an early age. The standard of living, early or late marriage, health and climate, cultural traditions and environment, attitude towards sex, role expected from the child at different ages are some of the other factors which control the dawn of puberty and attainment of maturity by human beings.

Compared to western countries, the period of adolescence starts early in our country as Indian children achieve puberty earlier because of favourable climate and cultural factors. Also it ends early due to early attainment of maturity whereas in the West—"*the adolescence extends roughly from 13 years of age till 21 for girls and 15 till 21 for boys*", (Harriman, 1946, p.3). In India, it usually ranges from 13 to 19 among boys and from 11 to 17 years among girls.

The above classifications of the range of the period of adolescence are not rigid. There are wide individual differences. However, with a view of a rough estimate for universal applicability, adolescents, also referred to as teenagers, are individuals having chronological age between 13 to 19 years.

SIGNIFICANCE OF THE STUDY OF ADOLESCENCE

You may be curious to know why such special emphasis is being laid on the study of adolescence in your syllabus. How is it so important for a secondary teacher training course? In what way is it going to be useful to you in dealing with your students? Let us try to seek answers to these questions which are more or less related to the significance of the study of adolescence to you as a secondary school teacher.

The reason for confining your syllabus to the study of adolescence lies in the fact that you are being prepared as a teacher of secondary or at the most higher secondary classes to teach the students ranging in the age group 11 to 18 years. This mean, you are supposed to deal with the adolescents and therefore you need to be familiar with the development pattern of these children along with their specific needs, characteristics and problems. In the pages to follow in the chapter, we are going to discuss these issues. This knowledge will definitely help you in dealing with your adolescent students, especially in the following ways:

1. You would know that adolescence is a period of intensive growth and development with respect to children's physical, cognitive, social, emotional and sexual aspects of their personality. Normally what should be expected from the children in terms of their growth and development under various aspects of their personality will be known to you and it should be able to help your students to achieve their maximum in terms of their growth and development.

2. Adolescence is said to be a stage of great stresses and strains. Children of this age are quite perplexed and worried about their somatic variations and sudden changes in their total appearance, behaviour and others' attitude towards them. They are worried about the sudden changes in their sex behaviour, sex related physiological and psychological problems and so on. The study of adolescence will enable you to understand the stresses and strains of this age and devise means for helping them pass through the turbulence.
3. Adolescents are said to be quite touchy, moody and sensitive. They are very conscious about their self-respect. The study of their behaviour and characteristics will enable you to deal with them properly.
4. Adolescence is the age of action laced with varied interest and tastes. It is the age of poets, writers, scientists, creative artists and martyrs. You shuld be able to recognize the abilities and talents of your students, give them proper opportunity for the nourishment of their interests and abilities so that the tremendous energy of this age may get a constructive channel.

In this way, the study of adolescence will definitely help you in dealing with your adolescent students with a clear-cut objective of helping in their all-round growth and development.

PATTERN OF GROWTH AND DEVELOPMENT DURING ADOLESCENCE

As said earlier, the human growth and development takes a spiral form and not linear. Therefore, within the alternate stages of life, we find a sort of repetition and resemblance of characteristics. The old adults are often found to behave like children. In adolescence also, we find a sort of repetition and recapitulation of what has been done during infancy. The observation of Ross reflects the above idea when he says, "*Adolescence is best regarded as a recapitulation of the first period of life,* as a second turn of the spiral development (1951, p. 146). Like infancy, adolescence is the period of too much disturbance or as Stanley Hall regard it "*a period of great stress and strain, storm and strife.*"

Let us see how far these observations are true. The adolescence's growth and developmental pattern, along with the peculiar characteristics of this age, can help us in understanding our adolescents. In the following lines, we will make an attempt in this direction:

Physical Growth and Development

During adolescence, the physical growth and development reaches its peak and human body finds its final shape. The maximum limit with regard to increase in size, weight and height is achieved. Bones and muscles increase to the greatest possible extent leading to a great increase in our activities. The growth and function of all other outer and inner organs also reach its maximum and almost all the glands become extremely active at this stage.

There is a growth of hair under arms and around genital organs. Boys and girls develop the characteristic features of their respective sexes. There is roundness of breasts and hips among the girls and growth of beard and moustaches among the boys. There is a distinct change in voice among the two sexes. While the girls' voice acquires shrillness and becomes sweet, the boys' voice deepens and becomes harsher. The girls begin to menstruate monthly during this period and the boys have nocturnal emissions (discharge of semen during sleep) accompanied by erotic dreams. In this way physiologically boys and girls attain all the male and female characteristics respectively during this age and are ready to be called men and women or gentlemen and ladies. The typical physical changes during this age may be studied through the given figure 12.1.

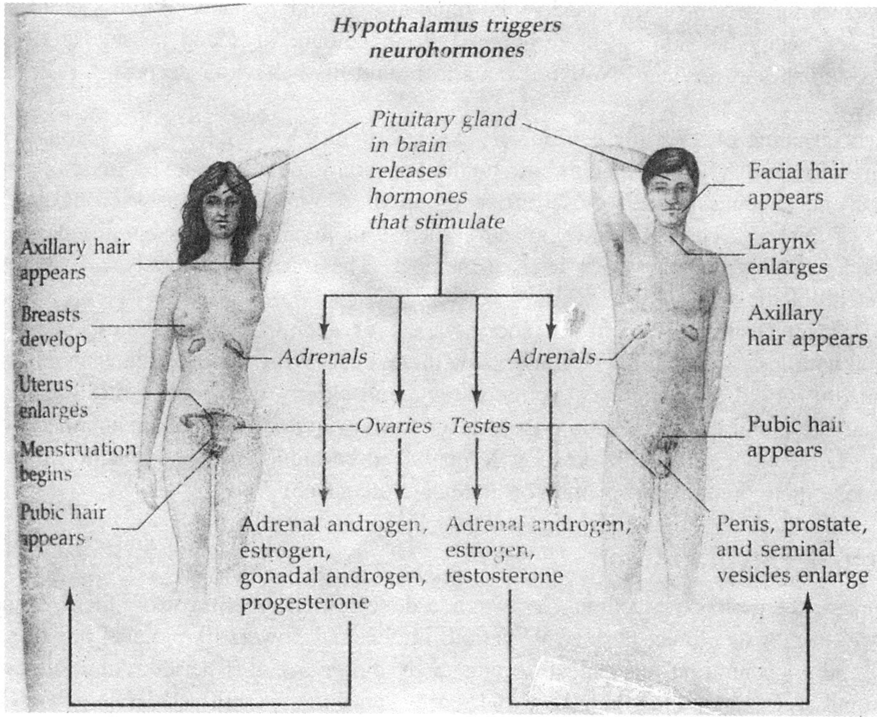

Fig. 12.1 The typical physical changes in boys and girls during adolescence.

Emotional Development

Emotional development reaches its maximum during adolescence. It is the period of heightening of all emotions like anxiety, fear, love, anger, etc. Once again like an infant, an individual experiences emotional instability and intensity during adolescence. The physical growth and development being maximum, the strength of the boys gives them the opportunity for maximum motor activity. Therefore, in the matters of emotional expression and experiences, adolescence provides the highest peak. At no stage is the child so restless and emotionally perturbed and touchy as in adolescence. He is too sensitive, inflammable and moody. In the words of Ross: "*the adolescent lives an intensely emotional life, in which we can see once more the rhythm of positive and negative phases of behaviour in his constant alternation between intense excitement and deep depression*". (1951, p. 147). That is why the period is often designated as a period of stresses and strains.

Thus, as Ross clarifies, adolescents are not consistent in their emotional expressions. Their emotions fluctuate very frequently and the current of emotional flow is also very intense. It is very difficult to put check on the emotions during the peak of adolescence. In fact, during adolescence emotions take their roots into sentiments. Self-consciousness, self-respect and personal pride soars. Group loyalty and sentiments of love etc. are developed making an adolescent sentimental and passionate. What he feels, he feels very strongly and when he reacts, he reacts vigorously.

Social Development

Adolescence is the period of increased social relationships and contacts. While a child cares very little for the society, an adolescent develops a good amount of social sense. He ceases to be egocentric, selfish and unsocial. Now he wants to mould his behaviour according to the norms of the society.

The social circle of an adolescent is very wide. Contrary to childhood, he becomes interested in the opposite sex. The friendships are no longer nominal. He believes in making intimate friendships and attaches himself closely to a group. Peer group relationship controls the social behaviour of this age. The child develops strong sense of loyalty towards his group. He wants to be accepted by the group of which he is a member. The rejection is costly as it creates many adjustment problems.

Another significant change in the social aspect of a child during adolescence lies in his relationship with his parents and the family. Now there is a craving for independence. He wants that his personality should be recognized by the parents and elderly members of the family. He must not be treated as a child. He gives more importance to the values and beliefs maintained by his peer group than to the advice of his parents. There may even be hidden or open rebellion if the parents try to impose their opinion and values on their adolescent children.

Intellectual Development

Adolescence is the period of maximum growth and development with regard to mental functioning. Intelligence reaches its climax during this period. Intellectual powers like logical thinking, abstract reasoning and concentration are almost developed by the end of this period. An adolescent learns to reason and seeks answer to 'how' and 'why' of everything scientifically. His power of critical thinking and observation is much developed. He does not try to follow the beaten track. He is critical of almost everything. He develops a fine imagination. Writers, artists, poets, philosophers, and inventors are all born in this period. Improper channelization of imagination and dissatisfied needs may turn an adolescent to daydreaming. Therefore, to great care is to be taken for properly cultivating their power of imagination.

Hero worship is most prominent in this period. Adolescents generally love adventures, wandering, fairly tales and develop interest in reading such books. Their area of interest is actually widened. Adolescence is the age of action. According to the difference in tastes and temperaments, nearly all the adolescents have some or the other hobbies and strong likes and dislikes for the world of nature, man and things.

Moral and Religious Development

With the development of social and civic sense, children during the period learn to behave according to the norms of their society and culture. Also the 'group' sense makes them follow some moral or ethical code. It prepares a stage of proper moral development. The formation of strong sentiments during this period intensifies the process of moral development. The character by which we know a person in his life to a great extent is the product of the experiences gained, complexes formed and sentiments made during this age.

The impact of religion and religious practices is also felt for the first time at this age in one's life. An adolescent tries to talk about God and religion. He often engages himself in the discourse about philosophical concepts like soul, Brahma, the meaning of life, the question of death etc.

Sexual Development

Sexual development reaches its peak during adolescence. An adolescent is sexually mature. In fact, the whole personality structure and behaviour of an adolescent is dominated by sex. During adolescence, the sexual development, like infancy, is divided in three stages as described below:

Stage of auto-erotism or self-love

At this stage, young boys and girls fall in love with themselves. They try to derive pleasure with their own bodies. Self-decoration and spending time before mirror is their common practice. Self-enjoyment by indulging in masturbation is also prevalent at this stage.

Stage of homo-sexuality

At this age boys and girls are attracted towards the members of their own sex and seek gratification from each other's body by grouping in two or three at one time.

Hetero-sexual stage

At this age boys and girls are seen attracted towards each other. They are keen to make friendship or even establish sexual relationship with the members of the opposite sex.

SPECIAL CHARACTERISTICS OF ADOLESCENCE

With Reference to the Needs and Problems of Adolescence

After arming ourselves with a little knowledge about the growth and developmental pattern during adolescene, it is worthwhile to point out some of the special characteristics of this stage. Adolescence, often termed as the age of storm and stress, has many a conflicting situation and problem of adjustment which need a careful study. Let us think over the origin of such problems and try to analyze the specific needs and demands of adolescents.

Perplexity with regard to somatic variation

Every adolescent has more or less the difficult task of adjusting to 'somatic variation' which may occur during or after puberty. As said earlier, during the period of adolescence maximum physiological changes take place. These rapid changes create problems for the adolescents in the following ways:

(a) Menstruation creates worries among girls and gives rise to many fears and anxieties. Similarly, the discharge of semen during nocturnal emission among boys horrifies them. They become quite perturbed about this penomenon. These particular physiological changes bring many complexes in the minds of the children. These changes make them introvert and secretive.

(b) There are always individual differences among human beings and so one cannot deny the possible differences with regard to bodily development, looks and appearance among the adolescents. An adolescent with his nearly developed body is constantly making comparisons between himself and his contemporaries. Differences are almost certain to cause him some anxiety, particularly regarding height, weight, fatness, thinness, facial blemishness, largeness or smallness of hips and breasts in girls and of genitals in boys.

For both boys and girls, appearance and bodily condition, which is not in keeping with what is considered the norm, will cause some anxiety. Girls want to look feminine and attractive to boys. Boys want to look manly to gain prestige among other boys and particularly from girls. To be reasonably satisfied with one's physical appearance, thus becomes an important task for an adolescent. He needs to become accustomed to new bodily changes. Any deviation from the norms and standards of the peer group can produce complexes in the mind and make him maladjusted.

INTENSIFICATION OF SELF-AWARENESS

Self-consciousness is extremely developed in adolescence. There is a strong desire in an adolescent that his or her bodily changes should be noticed by the elders as well as by the members of his own age group. Adolescence can be described as an age of self-decoration. Boys and girls pay more attention to their dresses, make-up, manner of talking, walking, eating etc. In fact, there is a craving for recognition in adolescents. Every adolescent desires that he or she should be the center of attraction for the opposite sex and his abilities, intelligence, and capabilities should be recognized by the peer group and elders. Moreover, adolescents are very sensitive, touchy and inflammable. They aim to maintain at any cost their concept of themselves and whenever possible to enhance their status among their peers. An attack on their phenomenal self invites strong reactions and behavioural problems. It makes an adolescent either aggressive or withdrawn depending upon the circumstances.

INTENSIFICATION OF SEX-CONSCIOUSNESS

Sex-consciousness becomes too intense at this stage. Most of the adolescents' problems are concerned with the sudden functioning of their glands, secretion of sex hormones and the awakening of the strong sex instinct.

Firstly, menstruation and ejaculation through natural occurrences at puberty give a shock to most of the adolescents. Afterwards every adolescent feels a sort of strong sensation in the sex organs. This motivates him to seek satisfaction through masturbation and homosexual relations. In the third stage of their sexual development, adolescents are attracted to the opposite sex. Sex sensation combined with curiosity about sex draws the members of the two opposite sex nearer and nearer. This nearness is sometimes developed into relationships and creates many problems and complexes for the future.

These activities create many worries and complexes in the minds of the adolescents. They become perturbed and develop a sense of guilt. In most of such cases, they opine that by acquiring these habits they have ruined their lives and they will now remain unfit for future sexual life.

INDEPENDENCE V/S DEPENDENCE

An adolescent is on the boundary line of childhood and adulthood. So, he is typically a person who needs security, guidance and protection like a child and independent views, maturity of opinion and self-support like an adult. He is still immature. His abilities and capacities are still in the process of growth and development. He depends for the satisfaction of his so many needs—physical, emotional etc. — on his parents and elders. The emotional instability of his behaviour and difficulty in coming in terms with the somatic changes makes him quite restless and often insecure.

He needs security and complete freedom from unnecessary worries and anxiety at this stage and in some way he is again in search of mother's lap and father's affection. Also, his intense love for thrill and adventure, coupled with his uncontrolled emotions, needs to be guided, and his unbridled flow of energy should be checked.

On the other hand, as his social circle is widening, he tries to emancipate himself from the care and look after of his parents and elders. He thinks himself a mature and full-fledged adult. He reacts strongly when the parents and the elders still consider him a child. He tries to assert or show that he is now a mature person and not a child. His opinion should now be given weightage. He has every right to give suggestions and directions in family matters. He can very well manage his own affairs and the elders should not interfere unnecessarily. He begins to feel ashamed and embarrassed about the protection and care shown by the parents.

It is not only the adolescent who suffers from the duality in his behaviour, but even the parents are not clear about the roles of their child at this age. Sometimes, they expect him to behave as an adult and at other times, they treat him like a child. Therefore, the poor adolescent is caught between the role of a child and an adult. He possesses a strange mix of the needs of dependence and independence which creates conflicting situations and problems for him.

PEER-GROUP RELATIONSHIP

Peer group relationship plays a substantial role in the life of an adolescent. He drifts away from his parents and elders and spends much of his time with the members of his peer group. He values the ideals of the group and develops a sense of loyalty towards it. He is now directed by the standard and norms of his peer group and pays least attention to the desires and advice of his parents and elders. He is more concerned with gaining prestige and recognition in the eyes of his peers. Every child at this stage wants that he should be fully accepted by his peers. Nothing can be more devastating to adolescent than to be rejected by his age mates. There is sure to exist a difference in the opinions, views, liking and disliking of the elders and adolescents. It is here that the difficulty arises. The adolescents find themselves the victims of the conflicting demands of social and cultural norms of adults and their peer group and they often become confused and perplexed with regard to any decision making.

IDEALISM V/S REALISM

A typical feature of adolescents lies in their interest in ideals. They desire to help in the creation of an ideal society. They are very critical of the existing circumstances, happenings, and think of bringing reform. They often engage themselves in questions like—Where is the world going? What is the meaning of our life? Where is God? What is humanity? Why are there so many sufferings and inequalities? In this way, they try place themselves on a superior level by searching some lofty aims and ideals and want a set of moral principles they can understand as well as some guiding principles by which they can operate.

But in this search of idealism an adolescent moves away from realism. In fact, lack of experience makes him somewhat unrealistic. He tends to accept the impossible. When this is not attainable, he becomes quite disturbed and unreasonable. Many of the adolescents grow up into problem youths. Some of them become pessimistic and believe in destroying whatever comes in way of realizing their dreams. Some turn withdrawal and begin daydreaming. They begin to live in their own make-believe world of imagination, and fairy-tales and thus have possibility to turn into maladjusted personalities.

VOCATIONAL CHOICE AND NEED OF SELF-SUPPORT

An adolescent's strong desire is to achieve self-sufficiency and become independent like an adult member of the society. Also, the life ahead demands from him that he should prepare himself for the future vocation which he wants to adopt. Therefore, the period of adolescence requires from the individuals to take a decision about their vocations. Vocational decision is an important one for an adolescent and he often finds himself not quite up to the mark in making a right choice.

Emotional instability, lack of experience and maturity prove as obstacles in making the right choice. Moreover, his interests, aptitudes and abilities are still in the process of making. This uncertainty about the interests and abilities makes him quite puzzled. Therefore, adolescents want proper guidance and advice with regard to their interests, aptitudes and vocational choices.

If we try to make a close analysis, we can find that adolescence is like a crossroad, which provides an equal opportunity to the adolescents to choose and proceed in wrong as well as the right direction. It has every chance of turning adolescents into maladjusted personalities, the chief cause of which is the frustration of needs and conflict of motives. At the adolescent age, there emerges new physical, social and emotional needs. With regard to physical needs the adolescent needs to become accustomed to new bodily changes and desires to have others notice the changes.

In the social aspect, he has a strong need for the belongingness to a peer group. Emotionally, he needs to be loved, accepted and admired. He needs security, freedom from anxiety and recognition of self. He is striving for independence from parental control and is struggling to make the active sexual instincts and urges satisfied or sublimated within the norms of the society and culture.

All this demands proper direction and guidance to the adolescents. The educational process, parental care, efforts of the teachers and the environmental conditions—all should be designed so as to bring proper growth and development of the adolescents and channelization of their energies into proper direction.

Special Characteristics with Reference to Aspirations, Attitudes and Self Concepts

Special characteristics with regard to their desires and aspirations

As a living being, all of us have our own desires and aspirations experienced at all ages and stages of our lives. There is a significant deviation in the nature and degree of these desires and aspirations with respect to the individual as well as stages and spans of human life. The desires, wishes and aspirations of an infant, child, adolescent or adult thus will naturally differ, not only in its shape or size, but also in terms of motivation and anxiety felt for their fulfillment. Let us discuss the types of desire and aspirations generally felt by our adolescent boys and girls. We can summarize them as below:

(i) To become quite handsome or beautiful or to look more masculine or feminine in the eyes of others, especially the member of opposite sex.

(ii) Desire and aspiration to love and to be loved by the parents, family members, teachers, peers and companions.

(iii) Aspiration of becoming the center of attraction and object of admiration and praise.

(iv) Aspiration of becoming economically independent.

(v) Aspiration of getting admission in a prized or self-interesting academic and professional course or vocation and profession.

(vi) Aspiration of getting a good life partner for leading a happy married life.

(vii) Aspiration of becoming a big personality by having name and fame in the area of one's choice *i.e.* a political, social, business, literary, art and culture or sports etc.

(viii) Aspiration of devoting time and energy for saving others, including country, religion and a particular section of the society.

(ix) Aspiration of becoming a leader, reformer or detector for the eradication of social evils, inequalities, miseries, corruption and all that is liked by them.

(x) Aspiration of living the life of the role models of their likings and choices.
(xi) Aspiration of making their parents, teachers and other elders understand their points of view and having the freedom to lead their lives in their own ways.
(xii) Aspiration of taking decisions themselves, leading others and making others agree to their likings or actions.
(xiii) Aspiration of being accepted by their social groups, peers, classmates, parents and other members of the society.
(xiv) Desire and aspiration for pleasure and sexual enjoyments.

Special Characteristics with Regard to the Attitudes of Adolescents

Attitude is one of the important attributes of human behaviour. Most of the time, our behaviour is very coloured and affected with the type of attitude—positive, negative or indifferent—we have towards a thing (ideas, person or object). It is equally true with our adolescents. Their attitudes almost colour and shape their personality and behaviour and make them behave like true adolescents. Let us here mention some special characters regarding the pattern of attitudes generally exhibited by adolescents in their behaviour.

1. **Attitude towards their somatic structure and physical appearance:** Adolescents have a big surprise for themselves in the form of sudden changes in their physical growth and development, somatic structure and physical appearance. Generally they possess an attitude of love and admiration for their physical appearance and physical makeup. That is why, they spent a lot of time in dressing up and decorating and enjoy admiring themselves in the mirrors. However, in some cases, they may develop negative attitude and feel dissatisfied with their somatic structure and physical appearance simply on account of the remarks passed by others or developing inferiority feelings by comparing their physique and appearance with their peers and companions.
2. **Attitude regarding independence:** Generally all adolescents have a strong desire and develop an attitude of independence by asserting their release from the earlier accepted dependence on the parents and other adults. At times, they are seen to be on loggerheads with their parents, teachers and elders simply for demonstrating their strong developed attitude of independence.
3. **Attitude towards sex:** There is a sudden awakening of sex interests and awareness towards opposite sex among the boys and girls as they approach the adolescence period. They feel a strong sense of attraction and crave to develop intimacy and even have physical sexual relationship with the opposite members of the sex. As a result, they may develop soft feelings and attitude of love and admiration for a member of the opposite sex. In some cases, however, they may develop negative attitude on account of their bitter experiences with the opposite members of the sex or may learn to behave negatively on account of improper social influences.
4. **Attitude related to idealism:** Adolescence is the age of action. An adolescent boy or girl is a reformist, and seeks change by nature. Accordingly, we may see adolescents exhibiting an attitude of selfless idealists. They may have this inner urge to serve others, help the needy, bring a change in the life of the suffering and deprived ones, work for the removal of inequalities, tensions, conflicts, corruption, nepotism and other sorry state of affairs from this earth.

5. **Attitude related to hero worship:** Adolescents can be easily drifted under emotional current. Their love and admire for somebody is at its peak and so an attitude of hero worship can be generally found in adolescent boys and girls. They have a role model, a hero or heroine from their own areas of interest, to whom they are too emotionally attached. Such attitude forces them to initiate good or bad action behaviour of their role models and moulds and shapes their personality accordingly.
6. **Attitude regarding group loyalty:** Adolescents are quite faithful to the group to which they belong. Their personal identity is almost merged with the behaviour of the group. They try to think, act and feel as the member of their group (generally the peer group) think, act and feel. They remain almost loyal to their groups and exhibit such loyalty towards their group in their attitudes and action. This group loyalty linked attitude is further generalized to exhibit loyalty towards one's family, neighbourhood, religion, state and country as much so as they are ready to make any sacrifice for serving the cause of these wider groups.
7. **Attitude towards religion and morality:** During adolescents, feelings and emotions can take their roots in the shape of sentiments. The character formation, thus may take its proper shape in adolescents. So, we may now see a perfectly positive or negative attitude of the adolescent boys and girls towards religion and morality depending upon the learning from their environment.

Special Characteristics with Regard to Self Concept of the Adolescents

Concept about the self is termed as one's self-concept. It reflects the image, considerations or judgments about one's abilities and limitations usually held by an individual not only for projecting himself before others but also for estimating his self in his own eyes. It is in this context that the term self-concept has been defined by the famous psychologist. H.J. Eysenck (1971) in the following words:

> *"The totality of attitudes, judgement and values of an individual relating to his behaviour, abilities and qualities may be referred to as his self concept."*

In this way, what one thinks of himself may be referred to as his concept about his self. Like the development of other concepts about people, idea, objects and places, the formation of self concept is also the result of the interaction of his self with the environment surrounding him. Such interaction loaded with past and present experiences may make an adolescent have a judgmental value related to his potentialities, his strengths and weaknesses, personality traits and behaviour pattern etc. Actually this is his judgment about his self drawn from his own experiences and interaction with his environment. Therefore, the past of an adolescent related with his infancy and childhood intermingled with his present experiences become a deciding factor for a particular type of self concept. Thereby we may notice significant differences among the adolescent boys and girls depending upon their individualities, social and cultural background and varying experiences. However, adolescents, in general may be found to exhibit some typical characteristics with regard to their self concepts. For illustration let us here mention two of these typical characteristics.

(i) **Identity crisis:** Adolescents most often struggle in identifying their selves. With regard to the concept of their self, they may come across with a crisis known as identity crisis. A sense of identity is defined as a sense or knowledge of how one's own personality traits, values and beliefs fit together in defining who he is. At a cross road of the childhood dependence and emerging need of adolescent independence, the adolescent like somehow gets confused about their identity. They often put such questions to themselves who am I? what am I capable of? What do others actually think of me, etc. The all-round growth and development resulting in the enhanced physical and cognitive abilities, strengthened emotional flow, widened social interests make them overconfident of their strengths and capabilities, but the judgment of themselves thrust upon by the elders may again force them to underestimate their potentialities. It happens so because in the eyes of the parents, teachers and elders they are still the growing children needing their protection and dependence. However, most of the adolescents successfully come out of this identity crisis either through their own struggling or as a result of proper guidance and counseling on the part of parents, elders and teachers. It ultimately helps them to develop a proper concept of themselves by getting rid of the felt identity crises.

(ii) **Love for the phenomenon self and development of self esteem:** Adolescents have a lot of care and love for their phenomenon self. As a result they develop a strong sense and feeling regarding their self esteem. Actually the consciousness and awareness about their self makes them appraise their strengths and weaknesses and this appraisal, in turn, may result into the development of a sense of self-esteem. In case they perceive that their strengths outweigh their weaknesses, their level of self-esteem may go higher. Contrarily when their self-concept indicates that their weaknesses outweigh their strengths, they may go down in terms of self-esteem. Thus the identification and views held by them in terms of their self-concept may be able to help them ride on the horses of enthusiasm or fall in the valley of despair, in accordance with the levels of their self-esteem.

However, whatever may be the level of their self-esteem, every adolescent tries to defend his phenomenon self and self respect at any cost. On this front he shows lot of sensitivity and may get annoyed by a simple remark or incident causing damage to his self concept, self-regard or self-respect. That is why, teachers, parents and elders are always advised not to do or say anything that may hit the self-respect, self-regard or self concept of the adolescents.

DIFFERENCES IN THE TRENDS OF GROWTH AND DEVELOPMENT OF BOYS AND GIRLS AT ADOLESCENCE

Differences in the trends of growth and development of boys and girls can be listed as under:

(i) Girls reach puberty about a year or two earlier than boys. Consequently, growth spurt occurs earlier in girls than in boys. Therefore, between the age 12 to 14 they are found to be taller and heavier than boys. But they are again surpassed by the boys. By the end of adolescence, the young men are generally taller and heavier than the young women.

(ii) Boys and girls develop the characters and features and of their respective sexes. There is roundness of the breasts and hips and thinness of the waistline among the girls and growth of facial hair and the development of larger muscles in the upper body among the boys. There are distinct changes in the voice among the two sexes. While a girl's voice acquires shrillness and becomes sweet, the boy's voice deepens and becomes harsher. Regarding primary sex characteristics, development in girls involves the development of ovaries, uterus and vagina, and the beginning of menstrual periods. Meanwhile in boys, it brings with it the growth of the scrotum, testes and penis and the ability to produce sperm. There is also occasional discharge of semen during sleep accompanied by erotic dreams among boys.

(iii) In the matter of physical strength and stamina, adolescent boys, in general, show marked superiority over adolescent girls.

(iv) Like physical growth and development, girls demonstrate more intelligent behaviour in the early adolescent years than the boys. However, in the field of abstract thinking boys are usually seen ahead of the girls. However, there seems no much significant difference in the intellectual functioning of adolescent boys and girls and it can never be stated that adolescent girls are inferior to adolescent boys in intellectual functioning or vice versa.

(v) In moral development also, there seems no significant difference in the trend of growth and development of adolescent boys and girls except that girls are more likely found to focus on the needs of others, to be concerned about social relations, and to take other points of view into account whereas boys tend to deal more narrowly with rules and moral issues and focus on individual rights and self fulfillment.

(vi) In the areas of interests and liking, there seems some observable difference among boys and girls. Boys take interest in the activities and play which are considered to be more masculine and involve more physical strength and stamina. Girls take interest and prefer light games and exercises. They exhibit wider areas of interests than the boys. They are more inclined to literature, fine arts and aesthetic activities. They show more inclination towards reading romantic novels, poems, literature, etc. and take interest in self-decoration as well as beautification of their home, schools and surroundings. On the other hand, boys exhibit more interest in outside activities, outdoor games and difficult adventurous risky tasks.

(vii) There seems difference in the emotional make-up of the adolescent boys and girls. In comparison to boys, girls in our culture are found to be more sensitive, emotional and sentimental. Kindness, sympathy, tolerance and other tender feelings are more intensely shown by the girls than the boys.

(viii) In our culture, outward manifestation of their sex feelings are usually prevalent in boys than the girls. Although girls are attracted to boys, they do not make it public as boys do.

(ix) Usually girls are found more expressive. It's rather difficult for them to hold a thing or idea with them. They are in the habit of expressing and disclosing it while the boys are more secretive and seclusive. May be this is why girls can release their tension easily through such expression than the boys.

However, the demonstration of such behaviour and trends of growth and development by the adolescent girls and boys cannot be taken as universal. It differs from culture to culture, place to place and situation to situation. With the change in attitude towards girls and improved rearing practices, the gulf regarding the developmental and personality characteristics between the boys and girls, is getting narrower day by day and now there is hardly any area left where girls cannot or have not surpassed the boys.

ROLE OF TEACHERS, PARENTS AND SCHOOL

The needs of the adolescents have to be satisfied and their problems realized in a proper way in order to help them in their proper growth and development. The task is serious and desires all dimensional efforts. Some of these efforts are mentioned below:

1. **To have the proper knowledge of adolescent's psychology:** Adolescence is the bridge between childhood and adulthood. The behaviour of an adolescent and his personality

needs a careful study. It is essential to have the knowledge of the adolescent's psychology in order to understand him. What are his specific needs? What types of changes take place during this period? What are the problems faced by the adolescent? How should they be treated? All this is essential to be known by the parents, teachers and administrators who have to deal with the adolescents.

2. **Providing suitable environment for proper growth:** We already know growth stops at the end of adolescence after attaining maturity. Adolescence is the stage where maximum growth takes place. To attain maximum during this stage, all that one can get with respect to physical and mental growth, suitable environment should be provided by the parents and teachers at home as well as in schools. Adolescents must be provided with balanced diet. Their eating habits should be properly checked upon. They must be taught about health, personal hygiene, cleanliness, various diseases and their prevention etc. to keep them fit for growing. Adequate provision for physical exercise and activities should be made in the school curriculum and necessary facilities should be provided.
3. **Rendering proper sex education:** Sex plays a very dominant role during adolescence. The rapid physiological changes, secretion of sex hormones, sudden awakening of sex instinct and urges—all necessitate the provision of adequate sex information and education for adolescents. The following things may help in this direction:
   - They should be helped in making adjustments with regard to their new bodily changes and somatic developments. Girls should know that flow of blood during menstruation is not a disease. It is a natural process which prepares them for becoming mothers. Similarly boys should be told that the occasional discharge of semen during sleep is not in any way harmful to them and should not be a cause of worry.
   - Their curiosity about sex also needs to be satisfied. For this purpose parents and teachers should provide adequate information on sex hygiene and physiology, the process of the birth of a baby, the hazards of immature and pre-marriage intercourse, etc. in a very frank, scientific, judicious and impersonal manner.
   - The sex instinct and urges also need to be cared properly. There should be proper sublimation of sex instinct and canalization of sexual energy. Forceful inhibition, taboos, and restrictions imposed in this direction bring disastrous results. With the provision of wide field of interests, a network of co-curricular activities and social situations, boys and girls should be given a chance to know and get along to work with each other. This will remove their many misconceptions about each other and will lead to their healthy adjustments.
4. **Proper dealing with adolescents:** Recent researches in the field of adolescents' psychology have revealed that adults, parents, elders and teachers and their unreasonable ways and points of view are the real problems of adolescence. They are in the habit of criticizing the adolescents and always impose their authority and assert their likings and dislikings. They forget that there is a generation gap between them and the adolescents. In dealing with them, parents and teachers should realize that the demands of their peer group are more important than their own expectations.

   Secondly, among adolescents, there is a craving for recognition and they also try to maintain their self-prestige and status among their peers. They assert that they are now mature individuals. Their opinions should be valued and they should be given a patient hearing. Therefore, it is badly needed on the part of the teachers as well as parents that they stop treating them as children and give them due recognition. Their opinions should be invited and they should be given opportunities for free expression. They must refrain from activities damaging the pupil's self-concept. The adolescents must not feel that they are insulted and their phenomenal self has been attacked unnecessarily. The teachers and parents should stop murmuring and blindly criticizing the attitudes and actions of the adolescents. Youths are more in need of models than critics. The elders must give a deep consideration to adolescent's needs and problems. It is futile to punish their misbehaviour.

5. **Training of emotions and satisfaction of emotional needs:** The age of adolescence is marked by lot of intensity, force, instability and immaturity of emotions. The adolescent youths are highly inflammable and restless. Their emotions can be aroused with slight provocation. The political parties and opportunist leaders can easily fool them and use them in destroying national property. Therefore, there is a strong need of emotional education to the adolescents. Their emotions should be properly trained and emotional energies should be diverted towards constructive ends.

   Moreover, adolescents suffer from certain emotional needs. They have a strong desire to love and to be loved. They need to be accepted by their agemates and every adolescent aspires that he should be admired and praised. He wants that he should be given freedom to proceed in his own way and adopt his own style of life but on the other hand, he needs protection, shelter and affection from parents, elders and teachers. He becomes disturbed if he is not provided proper security and freedom from anxiety. The parents and teachers should take care of these needs of the adolescents. They must be given what they need in terms of their emotional requirements.

6. **To take care of the special interests of the adolescents:** Adolescence is the age of wide interests and aptitudes. There are wide individual differences among the adolescents with regard to their special interests and aptitudes. Great care should be taken to locate their special interests and aptitudes. According to their interests and aptitudes, they should be provided with learning experiences and opportunities for participation in co-curricular activities. The curriculum should provide an open choice for various subjects and activities according to the tastes and temperaments of the adolescents.

   Their curiosity, wandering and adventurous tendencies should be taken care of by activities like excursion, N.C.C. mountaineering, scientific exploration etc. The love for humanity and ideals should be utilized in rendering social services and community services in the neighbourhood and distressed areas. In brief, adolescents should be provided with useful activities according to their interests so that they are constantly busy and their mind is preoccupied with healthy and constructive ideas.

7. **Providing religious and moral education:** One of the causes of increasing restlessness, indiscipline, dishonesty and aimlessness among the youth of India is that there is no proper provision of religious and moral education in our system of education. Ours is a secular state and therefore the doubts are expressed on the erroneous grounds. Actually the roots and the goals of all the religions are one and the same. If we try to do away with the rituals, the essence of all the religions is morality. Therefore, it is education of morality and character formation that should be provided by religious education and every school, home and other social agency can work in this direction. The parents, teachers, social workers and administrators should join hands in creating suitable atmosphere and offering opportunities of practicing moral qualities.

8. **Provision for vocational education:** There is a strong desire of achieving independence in adolescents. Economic factors obstruct their way. Therefore, they are worried about acquiring self-sufficiency on the economic front. What occupation should they choose, how can they earn their livelihood are some questions, the answers of which they try to seek. Here arises the need of proper vocational guidance and vocational education for them. The youth of today is bewildered and aimless because of the indefiniteness of his vocation. The education imparted to him does not provide jobs and occupations. Therefore, the strong need of today is to provide job-oriented and vocation-based practical education for the adolescents. The government, society, parents and teachers should make their efforts in this direction.
9. **Arranging guidance services:** Lack of guidance creates aimlessness, indefiniteness and restlessness among the adolescents. Adolescents have their problems which need careful attention and proper solution. They are at the crossroads of life. A slight mistake can lead them on the wrong path. Therefore, it is the utmost duty of the state, society and school to provide proper guidance services to the students as well as to their parents. Guidance services should be organized in a proper form both inside and the outside the schools. There should be well trained guidance workers and personnel. As far as possible, individual guidance should be provided.

The list of suggestions regarding the solution of the adolescents' problem and the satisfaction of their needs cannot be called complete with the above-mentioned few points. The task is gigantic and requires strenuous efforts from all directions. Moreover, it is difficult to prescribe some common rule or formula for the direction and guidance of adolescents with respect to their problems and needs. It is not a mass phenomenon. In actual sense, there are no problem adolescents. Therefore, the focus of guidance is always the individual and not the problem. Every adolescent is to be studied carefully as he requires special guidance and help for the solution of his problems and satisfaction of his needs.

SUMMARY

In his journey of growth and development, a child is entitled to be called as an adolescent when he attains puberty (ability to reproduce his kind) and he ceases to be an adolescent when he has acquired maturity (in terms of physical, mental, social and emotional aspects) to play the role of an adult in his society or culture. However, in day-to-day functioning, adolescents can be referred to as teenagers—individuals having chronological age between 13 to 19 years.

In most of the syllabi of the secondary schools teacher preparation courses, we always find one or the other topic in relation to the study of adolescence. It is simply because that secondary school teacher have to deal with adolescent students (studying in the secondary or higher secondary classes) ranging in the age group from 11 to 18 years. For their proper growth and development as well as desirable behaviour modification, it is utmost essential to get acquainted with the needed adolescent psychology, the nature needs and problems of their growth and development and so on.

As a consequence of the process of growth and development carried out in the period of adolescence, a child tries to attain his maximum in terms of the physical, mental, social, emotional, moral and sexual development. This is why it is termed as the period of intensive as well as maximum growth and development. However, such sudden growth and development on a large scale may generate specific types of problem and adjustment needs for the developing adolescents so much so as to designate their period of adolescence as "period of great storm and stress".

Adolescents like infants and children possess many age-specific and stage-specific needs, characteristics and problems like (i) Perplexity with regard to somatic variation or adjustment with new bodily charges. (ii) Intensification of self-awareness and sex consciousness (iii) Conflicting demands of social and cultural norms of adults and their peer group (iv) Caught between the role of a child and an adult in taking decisions about independence v/s dependence, idealism v/s realism, vocational choice and self support etc.

The stage specific characteristics of adolescents are also very much reflected clearly in their various personality/behavioural traits like desires and aspirations, attitudes and self concept. Here the adolescents differ not only in the shape, dimension and magnitude of these traits with respect to the infants and children or adults but also exhibit markedly difference in terms of the motivation and anxiety felt for their fulfillment.

Adolescent boys and girls may exhibit significant differences in their respective growth and development. They develop the characteristic features of their respective sizes, physical and stamina, specific attitudes, interests aesthetic sense, emotional make-up etc. suiting to their gender needs.

Adolescent is the age of action. However, adolescents may find themselves many times on the cross road on account of their age specific characteristics, needs and problems felt by them for the proper growth and development of their personality. It is the duty of the parents, teachers, school authorities and members of the society to join their hands for providing best means & opportunities not only for realizing the felt needs of the adolescents but also for the maximum development of their potentialities in the interest of their self and the society.

References and Suggested Readings

Carmichael, L.(Ed.), *Manual of Child Psychology*, John Wiley, New York, 1946

Crow, L.D. and Crow, Alice, *Child Psychology* (Reprint), Barney & Noble, New York, 1969.

Harriman, P.L. (Ed.), *Encyclopaedia of Psychology*, Phil Lib., New York, 1946, Student 3rd ed., McGraw-Hill, Tokyo, 1959.

Hurlock, E.B., *Child Psychology*, McGraw-Hill, Tokyo, 1959.

Kuppuswami, B. (Ed.), *Advanced Educational Psychology*, University Publications, Jalandhar, 1963.

Marry, F.K. and Marry, R.V., *From Infancy to Adolescence*, Harper & Brothers, New York, 1940.

Paplia, D.E. and Olds, S.W., *Psychology*, McGraw-Hill, New York, 1987.

Ross, J.S., *Ground Work of Educational Psychology*, George G. Harrap, London, 1951.

13

Maturation and Training

CHAPTER COMPOSITION

MEANING OF THE TERM 'MATURATION'

Maturation, in fact, is a natural process. It is the growth which takes place within an individual. The maturational changes are the result of unfolding and ripening of inherited traits and are relatively independent of activity, practice or experience. Biggie and Hunt (1968) clarify these ideas in the following words:

> *"Maturation is a developmental process within which a person, from time to time manifests different traits, the blue prints for which have been carried in his cells from the time of his conception."*

In this way, maturation involves changes that are associated with normal growth.

EFFECT OF MATURATION ON GROWTH AND DEVELOPMENT

1. As one grows in age, he or she is naturally bound to be accompanied with some changes in his body, mind and behaviour purely because of the phenomenon of maturation. This is more clear and revealing in the case of lower species like birds and animals. Let us have a look at examples from around us. A bird conceives and as a result lays eggs in its nest.

If we observe, we find that after a few days, there are signs of life in those eggs. A little later young chicks come out from the eggs, jumping here and there, being fed by the parent birds but still unable to fly. However one day, we find that they have grown enough and developed the capacity to fly like the other grown-up birds.

2. Similarly, we observe in the case of tadpoles that as a result of maturation, *i.e.* natural process of growth and development, there is definitely a major change in their behaviour. They are able to swim and after sometime they begin to jump like an adult frog. What is observed in terms of their growth and development here can be purely attributed to the process of maturation. It is also true in the case of the young ones of animals. No training or experience is received by them in the beginning for growing and developing their abilities to walk and run like their adult parents. A baby deer is able to run quite fast just after its birth. How does it manage to eat grass and drink water, is just the result of the process of maturation as there is no such attempt of providing any formal experience or training to it by the parents or the other members of the species for the performance of such behaviour.

   In this way, we can have enough evidence from the surrounding nature that explains the role of maturation in bringing desired growth and development in the behaviour and functioning of the small babies of insects, birds and animals.

3. In the case of human beings also, we may observe and notice the impact of maturation on the growth and development of the youngsters from their very birth in almost all the aspects and dimensions of their personality as illustrated below:
   - With the passage of the time they grow and develop physically in their height, weight and body proportions and functioning of the internal and external organs. The process of maturation thus helps them in acquiring physical maturity and thus they turn into fully physically mature adults at the expiry of the period of adolescence.
   - Same is true with the other dimensions of their personality as well. They grow and develop as mentally, socially, emotionally, morally and aesthetically mature personality at the time of acquiring adulthood. The process of maturation, *i.e.* an act of the natural growth and development helps them well in this task. However, the question here may arise as to whether the growth and development acquired in the case of human babies for turning them into a fully matured personality in terms of the mental, social, emotional, moral and ethical standards is purely a function of the process of maturation or environmental influences, including training, or a combination of both.
   - Definitely here the last one is the appropriate answer and as such it may be easily concluded that growth and development in the case of human beings for gaining maturity is a combined function of the process of maturation and learning. How does it become a combined function may be well illustrated through a number of instances described as follows:

     (i) A child is not able to speak or utter words correctly until he reaches a certain stage or age in maturation. We can't expect a baby of 6 months to speak and utter words correctly even if he belongs to a very high hereditary stock (like the parents are too rich and scholarly in the linguistic capacity, say Ph.D. in language) or is being constantly inspired and formally trained in speech. He has to grow and develop in the linguistic capacity in accordance with the maturation level he needs for doing so. In the natural process, he will learn to utter with the maturation of his vocal chords and other similar physical and mental functioning required for learning correct language. At the same time, it is also true that we can't rule out the impact of favourable or unfavourable environmental influences, including schooling, formal or informal training, for acquiring proper and excellent linguistic ability.

A child at any stage of his schooling or life does not learn the language or develop his language ability just because he attains that stage. Definitely, the language is taught to him. The language which he learns is the one he hears and more specifically the one he gets through specific training. As a result, what a child acquires in terms of his language development at any stage of his life is a joint product of the natural process of growth and development, *i.e.* maturation and the environment influences including training.

(ii) What is true for language development is also true for the development of other mental functioning. The development of mental facilities like thinking, reasoning, problem solving, decision making, analyzing, synthesizing discriminating, drawing inferences all need maturation as well as planned experiences and training on the part of the youngsters. Normally, we can't expect a child of tender age to be too logical, consistent, methodological in his approach and systematic in thinking and abstraction. He has to wait before he acquires the ability of abstraction, *i.e.* a certain stage of maturation, for developing his mental faculties for being capable of performing mental tasks requiring power of abstraction, creative, imagination, innovation and novelty.

(iii) In case of emotional development also, we can observe a similar phenomenon. A child develops in terms of emotional maturity on account of the process of maturation helped and influenced by the environmental influences. It is true that a child has to be a child in terms of his emotional behaviour. We can't expect him to behave like a grown-up adult. There is definitely an age characteristic emotional behaviour. That is why we can observe a definite pattern of emotional behaviour at each stage of maturation, *i.e.* infancy, childhood, pre-adolescence, adolescence, adulthood and old age. However, how one behaves and why one behaves under the influence of a particular emotion depends heavily on the impact of the environmental influences or feedback one gets from his formal or informal surroundings. The same is true for social, moral, religious or aesthetic standards and aesthetic sense from the individuals belonging to different stages of their maturation.

(iv) Surely age is a great factor. One learns and picks up so many things related to these aspects as he or she grows in age. Take the case of sexual development, a distinctly visible area showing the impact of maturation. As one grows in age, he or she is sure to pick up many things and practices related to sexual activities even without any prior experiences of formal training. Attraction towards opposite sex, to feel the necessity of the satisfaction of sexual urge are thus the peculiar developments that are bound to emerge as and when a child reaches the adolescence stage. However, his attitude and practices towards sex may now be coloured or influenced side by side by the exposures, experiences or formal/informal training he receives for doing so.

Thus from the above discussion, it may be clear that growth and development in the various aspects and dimensions of the personality of an individual is very much helped and influenced by the process of maturation. As one grows in one's age he is helped by the process of maturation for being grown and developed into a full-fledged matured personality. However, how much maturity in the deeds and kinds is shown by an individual again depends upon the quality of experiences, environmental influences, formal or informal training, education etc. received by an individual for this purpose.

MEANING OF THE TERM 'TRAINING'

Maturation as we have seen earlier allows an organism including human beings to grow and develop in quite a natural way with the passage of time, *i.e.* growth in age. However, this growth and development can't be termed as an organized, systematized or planned enterprise. In case we need a particular type of growth and development suitable to our needs and requirement, we have to put up some pulls and pushes, checks and restrains, incentives and examples for moulding and shaping the current of growth and development in our desired direction and dimension. It is here that we feel the need of providing some planned and organized formal experiences to the growing and developing human being so as to help him develop into a personality of our choice. It is the sole objective of any training programme. We train an animal in the circus to act as we wish and we train a pilot to fly the airplane for carrying passengers or doing any public, domestic or defence services as per the requirement. The training you are receiving for becoming a competent and efficient teacher is also serving the same purpose. You are being exposed to many informal and formal experiences, opportunities and practices which may help you to acquire certain necessary skills, teacher like behaviour and personality traits etc. so that you ultimately grow and develop into a figure capable of adopting teaching as a profession. Judging in this way, any training programme may be seen to involve the following attributes in its objectives and functioning.

- Behavioural changes we are aiming at on account of the training imparted to the individuals.
- Chalking out the training programme in terms of theoretical knowledge and practical experiences.
- Ways and means of implementing the chalked training programme and putting it into action.
- Evaluation of the results of training in terms of the realization of the set objectives, *i.e.* behavioural changes or types of growth and development expected from an individual after being trained.
- Modification in the objectives, plan and procedure of training or any remedial provisions for removing the shortcomings, weaknesses etc. in the light of the feedback of the evaluation.

Going through the steps suggested above we can be able to provide well thought, structured and formal experiences, opportunities and practices to the individuals for bringing desired growth and development in their personality dimensions.

EFFECT OF TRAINING ON GROWTH AND DEVELOPMENT

A training programme as discussed above may help an individual or a group of individuals to seek or attain the desired directions and dimensions in terms of growth and development in one or the other aspect of one's life. Such effect of training of one's growth and development may be visualized as under:

1. Physical training and exercises help much in the growth and development of one's physical abilities and capabilities. One can reach the height and dimensions of one's expectations in terms of his physical growth and development because of a planned and disciplined training.
2. Mental abilities and capacities can be fully developed through the mental and intellectual exercises and training. One can undergo a training programme for developing his language ability. As a result, he may develop into a linguistic giant, a literary figure, a good orator, translator, writer, poet, debater, journalist and likewise. Similarly, one can develop his thinking and reasoning power, numerical ability, computation ability, problem solving ability, power of drawing inferences and drawing conclusions, etc. with the help of planned exercises, opportunities and practices provided under a well thought programme.
3. Emotional development in the desired direction may also be well carried out through training programmes. Through well training strategies of catharsis, sublimation, redirection, refocusing, examples and illustration, modeling and other therapeutic measures, individuals may be helped to develop into an appropriate emotionally mature personality by getting rid of the undesirable emotional behaviour. Now such measures are also available that can help an individual to develop his emotional intelligence for equipping him to live his life to a fuller extent.
4. Training may also help an individual or group of individuals to develop socially and remain socially adjusted to the full extent in the society to which they belong. The habits, attitudes, manners, etiquettes, ways of living and behaving in a particular social group, community or society can be well learned through one or the other formal or informal training opportunities provided by the parents, school authorities or members of the society.
5. The development of morality or ethical sense can be learned through the formal or informal attempts of a training program. One can learn through situational happenings, observational learning or planned moral lessons delivered through an organized training schedule. The environment of a training institute may be so planned and organized as to provide a living example for imbibing many good habits, attitudes and practices related to desired moral values. As a result, one can grow and develop into a honest, sincere, punctual, hardworking, disciplinarian and law abiding peaceful citizen.
6. The development of aesthetic sense of ability may also become a function of training. One can be trained as a lover of nature, a seeker of *Satyam, Shivam* and *Sundram*, an artist of very refined and developed taste, temperament and creative talent, a person of such attitude and ability who finds harmony in disharmony, turning the earth into a piece of heaven.

In this way, training programme has enough strength to drift an individual or group of individuals to desired direction and dimensions of the growth and development related to its personal or professional life. Professionally one can grow and achieve the desired height through well-organized training schedules as well as his own will power and capacities. Therefore, in a nut-shell, it can be easily concluded that training helps an individual to grow and develop in many ways.

RELATIONSHIP BETWEEN MATURATION AND TRAINING

Maturation and training, as we have realized through the above discussion, serve the same purpose, *i.e.* helping an individual in his growth and development. Therefore, should we consider them as one and the same thing? Certainly not, they differ a lot in their nature and processes as may be evident from the following discussion.

Maturation is a natural process of bringing growth and development. A child is grown and developed in many aspects of his personality quite naturally as a result of the process of maturation, *i.e.* increase in his age span. No type of training, schooling or experiences is required for the results achieved through maturation. Here modifications or changes in behaviour are acquired by simply growing in age. As a result we can conclude that if a behaviour sequence matures (growth and development occur) through regular stages (with the growth in age) irrespective of intervening practices or training, the growth and development should be considered to be developed through maturation and not through training or learning.

Training, on the other hand, provides worthwhile experience, environmental influences, practice and exercises for inducing desired changes in one's behaviour leading to one's growth and development in one or the other aspect or dimension of one's personality. Sometimes, we may get success in inducing desired changes in one's behaviour irrespective of his or her level or stage of maturation. But most of the time, especially in human beings, the processes and products of training are found to have essential links with the stage and status of maturation. For example, to teach or train a child in a skill may require a particular stage of maturation. He may not learn to speak or acquire a specific linguistic ability unless he is appropriately matured to do so. Similarly, the learning of gymnastic skills or floor exercises requires that one must try to receive training for this purpose at an early age of his life. If the right stage of maturation for such training is missed, then it becomes quite difficult for developing such abilities at the later stage of life. Similarly, it is futile to talk to children about many things related to their emotional, social, moral and aesthetic development unless they have reached a ripe stage of learning and developing in these areas.

As a conclusion, it seems that maturation and training irrespective of being good competitors in ensuring changes in one's behaviour join hands with each other resulting in the overall growth and development in one or the other field or dimension of one's personality. Hence, their relationship is supplementary and complimentary to each other rather than contradictory or competitive. As a result, we as teachers and parents must remain cautious while making provisions for the growth and development of our children at the specific stages of their age span. The effects of maturation as well as training at one or the other stage of life must be well coordinated and integrated for achieving desired results with respect to their growth and development. On one hand, where it is useless to train them for the capabilities for which they have not attached the desired stage and status or maturation, on the other, it will also be a cardinal educational error to miss the appropriate time for providing specific training to develop the desired ability and capacity in a particular area. Therefore, we must always remember the proverb 'hit the iron when it is hot' which provides appropriate training at the right time of maturation for achieving desired success in the matter of the growth and development of the children.

SUMMARY

Maturation refers to a developmental process which brings specific changes in a developing organism mainly associated with his normal growth. These changes are the results of unfolding and ripening of one's inherited traits and are therefore, relatively independent of activity, practice or experience.

As a clear-cut example of the effect of maturation (the process of natural growth) on the growth and development of the organisms, we can cite the growing behaviour of species like birds and animals. The offsprings of the birds may come out from the eggs of their mother, begin to jump and fly like the other grown-up birds without receiving any experience or training for this purpose. The same is true with a baby dear who is able to run quite fast just after its birth and also with a tadpole who can swim and jump like an adult frog without being trained to do so.

In the case of human beings also, maturation brings significant changes leading to the attainment of maturity in terms of the growth and development of the various aspects of their personality. However, impact of maturation in their cases are not so clearly defined as observed in the cases of lower species. It is why growth and development in human beings for gaining maturity is always considered as a combined function of the process of their maturation and learning or training.

Training or learning provides worthwhile experiences, environmental influences, practice and exercise for inducing desired changes in one's behaviour leading to one's growth and development in one of the other aspect of one's personality. These changes brought out in one's behaviour are totally acquired and are the result of one's interaction with his environment. These are not so simple and natural as those induced through maturation.

The processes of maturation and training linked with one's inherited and acquired behaviour may thus apparently look like good competitors in ensuring changes in one's behaviour for the desired growth and development in one or the other aspect of one's personality. On the contrary, their relationship is supplementary and complimentary to each other rather than being contradictory or competitive. Therefore it is essential to coordinate and integrate the effects of maturation as well as training at one or the other stage of life for achieving the desired results in the process of growth and development. For example, a child should be made learn to speak or acquire specific linguistic ability after getting properly matured to do so. In case the child has become mature for acquiring a specific skill, *e.g.* learning of gymnastic skills, then we must not miss the right time for providing training in the acquisition of that skill. Therefore the principle of providing appropriate training at the right time of maturation should always be followed in the matter of the desired growth and development of children.

References and Suggested Readings

Biggie, M.L. and Hung, M.P., *Psychological Foundations of Education*, Harper & Row, New York, 1968.

Crow, L.D. and Crow, Alice, *Educational Psychology*, Eursaia Publishing House, New Delhi, 1973.

Hilgard, E.R. and Bower, G.H., *Theories of Learning*, 4th ed., Prentice-Hall, Englewood Cliffs, New Jersey,1975.

Hulse, S.H., Deese, J., and Egenth, H., *The Psychology of Learning*, 4th ed., McGraw-Hill, New York, 1975.

Kingsly, H.L. and Garry, R., *The Nature and Conditions of Learning*, 2nd ed., Prentice-Hall, Englewood Cliffs, New Jersey, 1957.

Levin, M.J., *Psychology—A biographical approach*, McGraw-Hill, New York, 1978.

14

Individual Differences

CHAPTER COMPOSITION

MEANING OF THE TERM 'INDIVIDUAL DIFFERENCES'

There seems to be no end to the variations, deviations and differences present among the creations of the Almighty in the form of living or non-living. We can see different types of soils, rocks, stones around us on this very earth. The quality and characteristics of the water we drink varies from place to place and region to region. Besides non-living, such variations and differences are equally prevalent among the living beings as well. We can see uncountable number of varieties among plants, insects, birds and animals on the earth. Some are named as fruits, some as vegetables, some as pulses or some as grains depending upon their common or varying characteristics. It is true that there are some characteristics common or otherwise, that help in grouping a class of objects or living beings in one category or species and thereby also separating them from others. It helps us in differentiating and distinguishing a particular type of living or non-living being from others. As a result, we can confidently say that this particular bird is a crow and this is a parrot or a peacock.

However, with such classification or grouping, it should not be assumed that members of the same species are all alike in all aspects. Apparently all cows, buffaloes, parrots and peacocks may seem to be alike on account of their common resemblance as well as qualities and characteristics peculiar to their species. However, a cow is not the same as anothers. In spite of having all the common qualities and characteristics unique to its species, all cows differ from one another in so many aspects.

As a conclusion, it must be clearly understood that whatever lies around us in the form of non-living or living being differ from each other in so many aspects. These differences and variations become more intense and remarkable as we draw closer to human beings as one of the ultimate creation of the Almighty in the history of evolution. We as human beings quite distinctly differ in size, shape, appearance, speed of reaction and innumerable other aspects of our personality make-up and behaviour. Among us, some are healthy and jolly while others are weak and irritable. Some are blue-eyed and black haired while others have black eyes and gray hair. Some are known as girls or women while others are termed as boys or men. Some learn quickly and others slowly, some remember well while others forget, some respond quickly and others slowly. In this way, no one among us is just same as another. The sons and daughters of the same parents or even identical twins are not exactly similar to each other. Every one of us is a typical human being in oneself.

Though alike in some aspects, we are definitely different in so many ways. We, in spite of belonging to a common species known as human beings, have our own individuality which contributes towards the variance and differences found in us. It is these differences that are entitled as "individual differences" in the languages of sociology and psychology. It is a very simple and practicable meaning of the term "Individual differences". However, let us try to know something more about it in order to build up a definition. For this purpose, let us begin with the citation of two different explanations given for this term in the "Dictionary of Education" by Carter B. Good. (1959, p. 172).

1. Individual differences stand for "the variations or deviations among individuals in regard to a single characteristic or a number of characteristics."
2. Individual differences stand for "those differences which in their totality, distinguish one individual from another."

The above two dictionary meanings of the term individual differences, now can help us in building a workable definition with reference to our discussion earlier in this chapter:

> *The differences among individuals, that distinguish or separate them from one another and make one as an unique individual in oneself, may be termed as individual differences.*

TYPES OR VARIETIES OF INDIVIDUAL DIFFERENCES

Whatever physical or physiological differences among the human beings, they may be generally grouped or classified in two broad categories, namely (i) physical or physiological differences and (ii) psychological differences. While physical or physiological differences among us are related with the differences created on account of the differences or variations in terms of physical or physiological make-up of our bodies, psychological make-up or conditions generate differences among us in terms of varying intellectual potentialities, interests, attitudes, aptitudes, emotional, social and moral development etc.

These two broad classifications of individual differences may give birth to a number of sub-categories like below:

- Differences related to physical growth and development.
- Differences related to mental growth and development.
- Differences related to motor skills and abilities.
- Differences related to socialization and social development.
- Differences related to morality and character development.
- Differences related to aesthetic sense and artistic ability.
- Differences related to diversified interests and aptitudes.
- Differences in attitudes, beliefs and opinions.
- Differences with regard to value system and self-concept.
- Differences with regard to levels of aspiration, study habits and achievements.
- Differences with regard to acquisition of psychomotor skills.
- Differences with regard to status of maturation and learning performance.
- Differences with regard to overall development of the personality.

Out of the individual differences listed above, let us discuss a few important ones.

Differences in Interests

Interest is the central force that drives the whole machinery of the teaching-learning process. The things in which a learner has its interest are attended well, learned properly, retained for a long time and made use of at the proper time. The reverse is also true. If one is not interested in one or the other aspect of learning, all the attempts of making him learn will serve no purpose. On similar lines, the term 'interest' has been defined by Crow and Crow (1973) as:

"Interest may refer to the motivating force that implies us to attend to a person, a thing, or an activity" (p. 248). Like for serving our own individual interests, we are always inclined towards some persons, things or activities while not caring or attending to others at one or the other time. In other words, our areas of interest show wide choices and diversities. We are interested in some and not in others and it is due to this that we can observe wide individual differences related to interests among the human beings. Just sit in the drawing room of a family and you will notice the diversity of interests when the members of the family begin to quarrel over watching one or the other television channel. Those interested in sports, particularly in cricket, will force others to see the match while those interested in serials, movies, antakshri, cartoon, music would insist on watching the programme of their choice. The same is true with the studies and classroom learning. A child may be interested in one or the other subject, topic or a particular sub area of the subject, an activity or experience while the other may have different choices depending on his outlooks, desires, motives, drives and basic needs. Thus as a teacher, you must always realize that there exists great variation among the individuals in relation to specific tastes and interests. This is why while some of your students take so much interest in meeting people, attending social functions, picnics and excursions, others feel happy in solitude, avoid social gatherings and are interested in meditation or enjoy the company of books.

Differences in Attitudes

Attitudes is one of the important attributes of our behaviour. Our behaviour to a great extent depends on our attitude towards a thing idea, person or object that exists in our environment. As a matter of definition, we may here reproduce a definition given by Sorenson (1977).

> *"An attitude is a particular feeling about something. It, therefore involves a tendency to behave in a certain way in situations which involves that some thing, whether person, idea or object. It is partially rational and partially emotional and is acquired, not inherent in an individual."* (p. 349).

A particular feeling about something that makes our attitude towards that very thing is almost an individual phenomenon. We always behave in a certain way when needed to respond to a particular thing, person, idea or object depending on the nature of our own attitude—positive, negative or indifferent formed towards that thing. Here we may show commonalties as a member of a group, class, community, religion or sect. For example, Hindus as a whole may have a certain type of attitude towards Muslims. As Indians, we may have a certain type of attitude towards Pakistanis, Chinese, Russians and Americans depending upon our own feelings generated through our past experiences. However, it is not essential that we all should exercise a same sense of attitude. We may have diversities in unity or commonalities. Some of us may have a positive attitude and strong liking while others may have negative attitude, strong disliking, resentment, hatred or feeling of enmity towards a particular community, religion or nation. This is equally true in our classroom situations. Some of our pupils may have positive attitude and strong liking for the study of a particular subject, area of activity, place, idea and person, while others may show a negative attitude and strong disliking depending upon their own experiences, *i.e.* interaction of their self with their environment. A wise teacher should observe the nature of attitude possessed by the individual pupils towards the things, persons, idea, activities or objects and then try to exploit this characteristic for the attainment of teaching-learning objectives. In case there is no right formation of the desirable attitudes, then he should try to provide a reconstructed desirable experience for bringing desired changes in their attitudes.

Differences in Aptitudes

We may find a strange pattern of similarities and dissimilarities, commonalties and differences among individuals with regard to their possession of different types of aptitudes. An aptitude, in a simple way, may be considered a special ability or specific capacity besides the general intellectual ability which helps an individual to acquire a required degree of proficiency or achievement in a particular field. We may here reproduce definition of the term 'aptitude' given by Freeman (1971). *"An aptitude is a combination of characteristics indicative of an individual's capacity to acquire (with training) some specific knowledge, skill or set of organized responses, such as the ability to speak a language, to become a musician, to do mechanical work."* (p. 431).

In this way, by taking note of one's present abilities and capacities we may come to know that one has an aptitude for learning or becoming successful in a particular area after getting opportunities for learning or training in that area. Like, we may observe that while one has mechanical aptitude, others have musical, clerical, scientific, legal, medical, and other professional scholastic or artistic aptitudes. There may lie commonalties with regard to the possession of one or the other type of aptitudes, *i.e.* a group of students seeking admission to a particular course of instruction or professional study may be found to have a high degree of aptitude for that course or profession. Within themselves, we may find a distinct range of diversities and variations when we take notice of the evaluation records of the aptitude tests. Some of them may be found to have very high aptitude compared to average or low aptitudes possessed by others. Similarly we may also find that while many of them do well in a particular aptitude test, they show a little or almost no aptitude for other subjects, activities or areas. Hence, it is observed that while one gets success after entering and getting required training in one area, the other makes little or no progress. It is, therefore, essential that we pay due regard to the differences or variations existing in individual students with regard to the aptitudes possessed by them for guiding them about their educational and vocational choices. It will automatically help in avoiding the possible failure or disaster by placing the round pegs into square holes and square pegs into round holes.

Differences in Values

We have different values—-materialistic, social, moral or spiritual—depending upon our own philosophy of life, environmental situations and circumstances. Here we may come across certain commonalities and wide variation among human beings with respect to possession of varieties of values like economic, political, physiological, psychological or social and moral values. Simply said we may associate our values with our needs—physical, physiological, psychological, social and spiritual. We always value a thing because we need it. Accordingly we are materialistic in our values because of our need to satisfy our materialistic desires. As soon as we are saturated or reasonably satisfied with the realization of our material needs, we may seek the realization of spiritual needs or search for inner peace, social integration and other essential psychological or human values. In this way, our needs decide our perception and value for a thing—object, idea and person.

Needs of the human beings are generally classified as physical or physiological, social and psychological. Based on the satisfaction of such needs, values are generally classified as physical and material values, psychological values, social and moral values, human and spiritual values and so on. Human and spiritual values are said to be universal irrespective of any society, culture or region. These are said to be more refined and higher values on the ladder of the values held by human beings in comparison to the social and psychological values lying in the middle and physical and material values at the bottom.

With all such differences in the nature of the values held by human beings, we come across a wide degree of variations among individuals. Some are materialistic while others give weightage to the social, cultural, moral, spiritual or human values in their life at one occasion or the other. Students are no exception. They also exhibit a wide degree of variations with regard to the nature and amount of the personality traits and behaviour pattern reflecting their adherence to one or the other value system. Now it is our duty as a patron or wellwisher to help them in imbibing proper desirable values for the betterment of themselves as well as of the society, nation and the world brotherhood at large.

Differences in Level of Aspirations

To achieve or acquire something, the most essential requirement is to have an aspiration for its achievement. One can't achieve without aspiring for it. Aspiration is thus the key for wish fulfilment, progress and success in life. Everybody wants to achieve one or the other thing in life and therefore, it is quite appropriate to generalize that everyone of us has the urge of aspiration irrespective of its magnitude and nature. In other words, while we all as human beings are endowed with an inner urge of aspiration, we differ with regard to its level. While many of us demonstrate a very high level of aspiration for achieving things in their lives, a good large number is also found to have a very low level of aspiration for achieving or avoiding failure.

However, to maintain a certain level with respect to one's aspiration for achieving a thing is a must for getting success in the attainment of that very thing. The magnitude of that level needs to be balanced with one's potential. In other words, the level of aspiration must be set in tune with one's potential, *i.e.* abilities and capacities for the attainment of a thing. A level of aspiration more than one's potential may cause frustration to the individual. A student, hardly capable of clearing examination, thus is likely to get frustrated if he sets his level of aspiration to the point of seeing his name in the merit list of the board. On the other hand, to set one's level of aspiration quite below one's potential is equally dangerous, frustrating and improper. If one does not know about his potential or is in the habit of underestimating oneself, he is likely to miss many things in his life for which he was quite competent and capable. On realization or feeling the pain of not achieving an achievable thing, one is sure to get frustrated and maladjusted to his self and the environment. Therefore where it is quite common for the students to differ in terms of their level of aspiration for achieving one or the other thing, it is the duty of teachers, parents and guidance personnel to help them set their level of aspiration neither too high nor too low but well in tune with their levels of potential.

Differences in Self-concept

As a child grows and develops in age, he is sure to develop his ability of concept formation about the things and events available in his environment. Besides the formation of concepts about the things other than his self, he is sure to form a concept about his self. Such concept about the self is termed as one's self-concept. It reflects the images, considerations or judgment about one's abilities and limitations usually held by an individual not only for projecting himself before others but also for estimating his self in his own eyes. It is in this context that the term self-concept has been defined by the famous psychologist H.J. Eysenk (1971) in the following words.

> *"The totality of attitudes, judgement and values of an individual relating to his behaviour, abilities and qualities may be referred to as his self-concept."*

Thus, what one thinks of himself may be referred to as his concept about his self. Most often formation of such a concept (as happens in the case of his concept about other things-people, ideas, objects and places) is the result of the interaction of his self with the surrounding environment. Such interaction loaded with past and present experiences may make him have judgemental values related to his potentialities, his strength and weaknesses, personality traits and behaviour patterns etc. This is his judgement about his self drawn from his own experiences and results. However, erroneously in most of the cases the individual, instead of making judgement about self, tries to accept others' judgement about him for the formation of his self-concept. Commenting on such aspect Hurlock (1959) writes *"The child's concept of himself as a person is nothing but a mirror image of what he believes significant people in his life thinking of him."* For example while being called naughty, liar, creative, genius, coward, handsome or ugly he may form the same concept about his own self for behaving in his life. It is this that should be avoided in the interest of the welfare of the children. Slowly, and slowly, they must be made to form proper and real concept about their 'self' so that they may be helped in their progress and development by maximizing their potentials after getting rid of evils and negative things detrimental to their progress. It is in the context that we must realize that every pupil may differ from others with respect to this self-concept, *i.e.* image of the self maintained by him. His individuality in this regard must be well-recognized and accordingly he should be helped to strengthen, reshape or reorient his concept about his self for the cause of his total welfare and progress.

Differences in Study Habits

Children and even we adults are found to have wide variations in terms of our study habits. As grown-up and mature individuals we may have no study habit or may exhibit great variations in terms of study habits. We may be habitual of studying a particular thing of our interest, show great variations in terms of the time devoted, purpose served by the study and the method, mode and medium employed for our study. The same is true with the students studying in a particular class. Apart from some sense of commonalties in the matter of one or the other aspect or attribute of their study habits, they are bound to differ and have wide variations in terms of study habits as listed as follows:

- They differ in terms of attitudes, belief and opinion about studying one or the other thing.
- They differ in terms of their interest and aptitudes for studying one or the other thing.
- They differ in their methods and mode employed for studying different things.
- They differ in their approaches and objectives served by studying different things.
- They differ in terms of the time devoted and attempts made for studying different things.
- They differ with respect to proper use of the results of their study in one or the other areas related to their academic, professional and future life.

As a result of the above cited differences, you may find your students exhibiting wide differences and variation related to their study habits. Some are slow while others are fast in studying the content or subject matter of their syllabi. Some grasp and understand well what they study while others don't. Some are used to studying well at a particular time in a particular manner and in a particular environment while others have their own variations in this respect. Some study well in isolation while others need company for doing so. Some study at night, others prefer to rise early for their studies. Some need no help, guidance or direction for their studies while others need constant help, motivation and supervision for doing so. In this way, learners in any group demonstrate a wide diversity and variations related to their specific study habits.

Differences in Achievements

Individuals may be seen to differ in terms of their achievements in one or the other areas of the subject of study, professional courses, occupations and other various aspects of life. Some are seen to excel in one field or the other while lagging behind in the rest, others may exhibit dominance in almost all the fields or failure everywhere at each occasion. In this way, we can observe various types of variations and diversities among human beings with regard to their achievements in life. The same also holds true for the children studying a particular course-academic or professional. We may find that a particular student excels in the study of one or more curricular areas, while remains average or shows very poor performance in others. In the achievement tests, internal or external, one may score the highest, may register himself in the merit list or get good division while others of the same class studying along with him exhibit low performance getting second of third division or even failing in the class. In this way, we come across too many diversities and variations even among the students of the same section and school taught by the same teacher in the same environment. In day-to-day classroom teaching, we may also notice variation among the learners while asking them to respond to the type of experiences given to them, providing answers to the questions put in the class, supervising the classroom drill work, home assignments and project activities. All this may safely help us to conclude that there lies wide diversity and difference among the learners' achievements in any learning situation belonging to any learning environment.

Differences in Psychomotor Skills

Individuals are found to differ with regard to development and acquisition of one or more types of skills. These difference are very much observable right from an early age in children. Some are very quick, efficient and methodical in performing skilled tasks like jumping, running, skipping, hopping, galloping, climbing, dancing, swimming, reading, writing, drawing, catering, copying, drawing, handling laboratory equipment and working tools, experimenting, computing, surveying, measuring, sketching, stitching, sewing, cooking, washing, dry-cleaning, etc. However, others may not be so efficient and competent and be quite unfamiliar or fail in performing these skilled tasks. All these psychomotor skills are quite helpful for the proper all-round growth and development of the personality of a child. Not only the physical but mental, social, moral, ethical and aesthetic development is properly linked with the development of psychomotor abilities and skills. Academic as well as professional development is also quite dependent on the proper development and efficient functioning of the skills. Any deficiency in terms of improper way of learning a particular skill or its inadequate development may hamper the growth and development of the child making him backward or even a problem child. It is well illustrated in the case of children with poor handwriting, defective language skills, inadequate geometric and mathematical skills, poor sketching and drawing skills, poor reading and compositions skills, poor comprehension skills and problem solving skills, etc. A wise teacher should carefully diagnose the strengths and weaknesses of the students with regard to the development of the various psychomotor skills and accordingly plan for their best use or provide remedial measure for their proper and adequate development.

Distribution of Individual Differences

It might be clear now that we all differ from one another in one way or the other in so many aspects. However, at this point the question may emerge as to how much are we likely to differ, what should be the range or limitations of the difference existing among us? Do these variations or differences follow some pattern? How these differences are distributed over a large number of population? Let us seek answers for such questions.

Answer to all such questions lies in the fact that distribution of almost all the things in nature follow the pattern of a normal curve. Height, weight, beauty, wealth, intelligence and similar other attributes of our personality are distributed in our population in a normal way. Let us discuss what does this normal distribution mean. For this, let us take simple practical instances from our day-to-day life. We find that most of us are quite average in terms of the possession of the attributes of our personality. As a result you will find that majority of us possess average weight, height, wealth, beauty and intelligence etc. There are very few who are too fat or too thin. Similarly while we seldom come across beauties like Noor Jahan, Padmavati or Cleopetra, we also rarely find extremely ugly figures. Mostly there are normal or average beautiful figures all around us. This is equally applicable to the distribution of intelligence. Most of us have normal intelligence with IQ ranging between 90 and 100. Person having IQs more than 140 or 150 (Genius) as well as possessing IQs less than 60 or 40 (Imbeciles) are rarely found.

In this way, it can be easily concluded that most of us or majority of us are average or normal in terms of the possession of all the attributes of our personality. How many of us are above or below averages in a given population can be understood with the help of a distribution pattern shown by normal curve. Let us try to draw such a normal curve on the basis of a hypothetical data related with the distribution of the achievement scores (as attribute of the personality) over a given population of the examinees.

To obtain a large sample of population of the examinees, let us approach the Board of School Examination, Haryana or Delhi for the record of the last year XII class annual examination arranged serially according to their roll numbers. Out of this huge data we can randomly select the total marks scores of 10,000 students for our study. Let us now calculate the average score or mean value of the sample. For this purpose, we will add individual total marks of these 10,000 students and then divide it by 10,000 for getting mean or average score value for the sample. If we try to analyze the total marks earned by this population of 10,000, we will find that majority of them have either earned the mean average score or lie quite near to this value. There are very few who have earned distinction marks or got very low marks. In case we try to plot the total marks (scores) earned by these 10,000 students on a sheet of graph paper by taking scores on X-axis and no. of students earning these scores (frequencies) on Y-axis, we can have a bell-shaped curve like below (shown

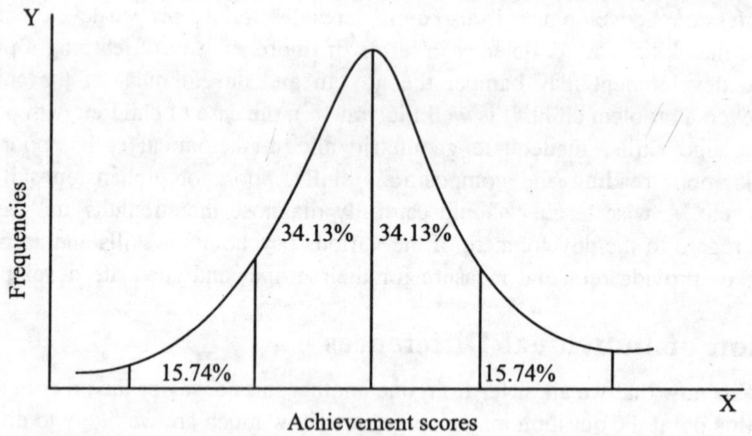

Fig. 14.1 The distribution of achievement scores in a population of examinees.

in figure 14.1).

Let us analyze the pattern of distribution of achievement scores in the population of examinees.

1. As revealed by this curve, we can locate the majority, 34.13% + 34.13%, *i.e.* 68.26% of the students either getting marks equal to the mean average value or lying quite near to this value. This sub-population of 6826 out of 10,000 thus can be declared as normal, *i.e.* the students who possess normal or average academic achievement abilities.
2. The curve shows that there are 15.74% of the students who have earned more marks than the average. This 15.74% sub-population of the students, *i.e.* 1574 out of 10,000, is named as above average in terms of their academic achievements. A similar percentage, *i.e.* 15.74% of the students also lie on the other side of the mean value. It shows that there are 15.74% students *i.e.* 1574 out of 10,000, who have got less marks than the average value. These students are named as below average or sub-normal in respect to their academic

achievement in class XII final examination.

3. The normal curve thus can portrait the pattern of distribution of an attribute in a given population. Here it has demonstrated that out of 10,000, the majority 68.26%, *i.e.* 6826 out of 10,000 consists of averages. There are only 15.74%, *i.e.* 1574 out of 10,000 who are below average and a similar percentage 15.74%, *i.e.*, 1574 out of 10,000 are labeled as above average.

As a consequence, we may easily conclude that individual differences among us always follow the pattern of a normal curve.

It is true that we do differ from each other and no two people are alike. However, majority of us, *i.e.* 68.26% are quite average, which means they possess average typical value in terms of the possession of personality attributes. A very few of us deviate too much from this average value, depending on which we are termed as quite above or below than the averages or normal.

Divisions as such referred above in the form of averages, below averages, above averages etc. help us in discovering some sort of commonalities emerging out of so much diversity and variation in individual differences. It may further help in the task of ability grouping, homogeneous grouping etc. for tailoring the need of individualized instructions.

CAUSES OF INDIVIDUAL DIFFERENCES

Whatever differences in the individuals seem to exist can be clearly attributed to the varieties in hereditary endowment or environmental stimulation or both.

Firstly, it can be observed that people belong to different heredity stock and are thus bound to differ in native endowments and characteristics. These native endowments, abilities and capacities provided by heredity decide the path of the progress and development of an individual. In a way heredity provides the limits of one's growth and development in various dimensions and aspects of one's personality and thus variations in hereditary characteristics cause differences among individuals. Heredity, not only contributes directly towards the differences in individuals with respect to the colour of the skin, eyes and shape, composition and working of various internal as well as external bodily organs, but also makes contributions indirectly by creating differences in the individuals in relation to sex, intelligence and other specific abilities.

Secondly, if we try to consider environmental influences and stimulation experienced by the individuals right from their conceptions in the wombs of their mothers, we can come to the conclusion that no two individuals in the universe get exactly the same environment. Definitely there happens to be a difference with respect to the stimulation received by the individuals from their respective internal as well as external environments.

The differences in environmental stimulation and influences in the womb of the mother, varying conditions at the time of the birth and nutrition as well as care received by the infants at the early age, differences in the amount and nature of schooling, socio-economic status of the family, race, caste and nationality, education of the parents, peer group relationships and so many other physical, emotional, mental or social environmental stimulation bring lot of differences in the personality characteristics and behaviour patterns of individuals.

In this way, heredity and environment both seem to be contributing towards the individual differences. Similarly as we have discussed in chapter four of this text, nothing can be said about the relative importance of these two factors in connection with the creation of individual differences. Hence, it is difficult to say whether heredity or environment is responsible for the differences between Ram and Shyam or Gita and Sita. Unless they are identical twins (with different names) they have a different heredity and some of the differences between them are attributable to this. They certainly have somewhat different environment even if living in the same home or reading in the same school and enjoying same privileges and getting similar nourishment and educational facilities. Any part of the difference—physical and psychological—is thus attributable to the differences in their environments.

Consequently, the difference between different individuals is normally attributable to both heredity and environment and thus, we should always keep in mind the hereditary characteristics and traits of the individuals as well as the physical, social and psychological stimulation they receive from their peculiar environments in looking towards the cause of differences between them.

Educational Implications of Individual Differences

The notion that individuals differ in various abilities, capacities and personality characteristics is in fact responsible for bringing individual tendencies in education. It has helped the teachers to realize the following facts:

1. In any group there are individuals who deviate from the norms of the group. Along with the average, the presence of very superior and extremely dull is equally possible in a class.
2. Every teacher should try to have the desired knowledge of the abilities, capacities, interests, attitudes, aptitudes and other personality traits of his pupils and in the light of this knowledge should render individual guidance to children for the maximum utilization of their potentialities.
3. It is wrong to expect uniformity in gaining proficiency or success in a particular field from a group of students. On account of their subnormal intelligence, previous background, lack of proper interest, aptitude and attitude etc, some students lag behind in one or the other area of achievement.
4. All students cannot be benefited by a particular method of instruction and a uniform and rigid curriculum.

ROLE OF SCHOOLS IN MEETING THE INDIVIDUAL DIFFERENCES

Realization of such above mentioned facts makes us think that we must have some provision for the wide individual differences among our pupils in our schools. Emphasizing this need, Crow and Crow write, "*Since we supposedly are teaching individuals, not groups of individuals, it is the function of the school within its budgetary personnel and curricular limitations to provide adequate schooling for every learner no matter how much he differs from every other learner.*" (1973, p. 215).

How we can accomplish this task is a pertinent question to be asked at this stage. In fact, to provide adequate schooling or learning experiences for every learner according to his individuality is not a simple task. However, the following suggestions can prove helpful for the teacher in this direction.

Proper Knowledge of the Individual's Potentialities

The first step in making provision for the individual differences is to know about the abilities, capacities, interests, aptitudes and other personality traits of individual pupils. For this purpose, help from intelligence tests, cumulative record card, interest inventories, attitude scales, aptitude tests and measures for assessing personality traits should be taken.

Ability Grouping

In the light of the results derived from various tests for knowing individual differences in terms of individual potentialities in various dimensions, the students in a class or area of activity can be divided into homogeneous groups. Such division can prove beneficial in adjusting instruction to varying individual differences.

Adjusting the Curriculum

To meet the requirements of varying individual differences among pupils, the curriculum should be as flexible and differentiated as possible. It should have the provision for a number of diversified courses and co-curricular experiences so that the pupils may get opportunity to study and work in the areas of their own interests and abilities. It should provide adjustment suiting the local requirements and potentialities of the students in different groups.

Adjusting the Methods of Teaching

To make provision for the varying individual differences, adjustment with regard to the adaptation of methods of teaching is also most essential. Every teacher should be somewhat free to formulate his own plan and strategy and adopt instructional procedure which he finds most suited to the particular types of pupils under him. He should try to follow a different procedure or method of instruction suiting the requirements of varying ability groups of his pupils.

Adopting Special Programmes or Methods for Individualizing Instruction

Schools may also adopt special programmes or methods of teaching like Dalton plan, the Winnetka plan, the Project Method or use programmed learning material for enabling the students to learn with their own individual pace.

Other Measures of Individualizing Instructions

For the purpose of individualizing instruction a few practicable measures can also prove beneficial.

(i) The size of the class or section should be as small as possible.

(ii) The teacher should try to pay individual attention to the group under instruction.

(iii) The teacher should keep in view the individual differences of his students while engaging them in drill or practice work in classroom or assigning home-task.

(iv) In case ability grouping is not possible and more specifically under the prevalent system of class teaching, special coaching and guidance programme for both the dull and the gifted children is most helpful.

In this way, the problem of individual differences needs a multi-dimensional attack for its proper solution. The teacher, school authorities, parents and Government as well as voluntary agencies—all should come on a common platform to meet the individual requirements of children who possess tremendous individual differences.

SUMMARY

There lie wide individual differences among the human beings. As a matter of definition, these can be referred to as the differences among individuals that distinguish or separate them from one another and make one as an unique individual to oneself.

Individual differences among human beings may be grouped in two broad categories, one related with the physical or physiological make-up of our bodies and the other related with the psychological make-up consisting of one's intelligence, interests, attitudes, aptitudes, emotional, social and moral development etc.

Distribution of all types of these individual differences among human beings follow the pattern of a normal curve. This meaning that majority among us consists of averages or are normal in terms of the possession of all the attributes of our personality. Only a few of us deviate too much from this average value for being designated as exceptional.

Causes of individual differences found in human beings may be attributed to their hereditary endowment as well as to the environmental stimulation. However, their impact and role in creating such individual differences is so interwoven and intermingled that it is quite reasonable to conclude that both hereditary and environmental forces are responsible for generating as well as perpetuating all these differences.

The knowledge and understanding gained about the nature and causes of individual differences among children may provide valuable help to the parents and teachers for planning and organizing the educational experience of their children according to their individuality. Psychology of individual differences has in fact revolutionized the field of education by individualizing the whole process of education in the true interest of the welfare of the individual child. Accordingly the efforts in terms of ability grouping, adjusting the curriculum, methods of teaching and environmental situation according to the individual differences, adopting special programmes, methods or other measures for individualized instruction are taking their roots in every new schemes and innovations in education.

References and Suggested Readings

Bingham, W.V.D., *Aptitude and Aptitude Testing*, Harper & Brothers, New York, 1937.

Crow, L.D. and Crow, Alice, *Educational Psychology,* 3rd Indian reprint, Eurasia Publishing House, New Delhi, 1973.

Eysenck, H.J., *The Structure of Human Personality*, Methuen, New York, 1971.

Freeman, F.S., *Theory and Practice of Psychological Testing*, 3rd Indian ed., Oxford & IBH, Bombay, 1971

Good, Carter, V., *Dictionary of Education*, McGraw-Hill, New York, 1959.

Hurlock, E.B., *Child Psychology*, McGraw-Hill, Asian Student 3rd ed., Tokyo, 1959.

Slain, R.E., *Educational Psychology*, Prentice-Hall, New Jersey, 1991.

Sorenson, Herbert, *Psychology in Education*, McGraw-Hill, New York, 1977.

15

Learning—Concept, Nature and Domains

CHAPTER COMPOSITION

CONCEPT OF LEARNING

In the process of education, *learning* occupies the central place. Whatever exists in our educational set-up is meant for the learning of the learners, *i.e.* students. Therefore it is quite essential for you as would-be teachers to be acquainted with the concept of the term 'learning'. Let us analyse the concept of the term by:

(i) knowing about its meaning and definitions; and

(ii) knowing about the process of learning

Meaning and Definitions of the Term Learning

Learning situations are the most natural and common in life and everyone of us is learning one thing or the other although he may not necessarily be aware of it. An individual starts learning immediately after his birth. While playing with a burning matchstick, a child burns himself and withdraws. Next time when he sees a burning matchstick, he takes no time in withdrawing himself from it. He learns to avoid not only the burning matchstick but all the burning things. When this happens we say that the child has learned that if he touches a flame, he will be burnt.

In this way, the behaviour of an individual is changed through direct or indirect experiences. This change in behaviour brought about by experience is commonly known as 'learning'. This is a very simple explanation of the term 'learning'. But a complete understanding of the term needs more clarification and exact definition. Some well-known definitions of the term 'learning' are given below

Gardner Murphy
The term learning covers every modification in behaviour to meet environment requirements." (1968, p. 205).

Henry P. Smith
"Learning is the acquisition of new behaviour or the strengthening or weakening of old behaviour as the result of experience." (1962, p. 260).

Woodworth
"Any activity can be called learning so far as it develops the individual (in any respect, good or bad) and makes him alter behaviour and experiences different from what that would otherwise have been." (1945, p. 288).

Kingsley and Garry
"Learning is the process by which behaviour (in the broader sense) is organized or changed through practice or training." (1957, p. 12).

Robinson and Horrocks
"Learning is an episode in which a motivated individual attempts to adapt his behaviour so as to succeed in a situation which he perceives as requiring action to attain a goal." (1967, p. 232).

Crow and Crow
"Learning is the acquisition of habits, knowledge and attitude. It involves new ways of doing things and it operates in an individual's attempts to overcome obstacles or to adjust to new situation. It represents progressive changes in behaviour. It enables him to satisfy interests to attain goals." (1973, p. 255).

Hilgard
"Learning is the process by which an activity originates or is changed through reacting to an encountered situation, provided that the characteristics of the change in activity cannot be explained on the basis of native response, tendencies, maturation, or temporary states of the organism (e.g., fatigue of drugs, etc.)," (1958, p. 3).

An overview of these above definitions may clearly reveal that learning may be termed as *a process or its outcome in which necessary changes in the behaviour of the learner are brought through experiences—direct or indirect*. Here it has also been emphasized that although changes in behaviour are also brought out by the factors other than experience yet all such changes in behaviour are not associated with the process and product of learning. In this connection special mention can be made about Hilgard's definition. Let us reconsider this definition now.
On the basis of Hilgard's definition of learning, the factors responsible for bringing changes in our behaviour can be divided into following three forces:

- Factors or forces that bring permanent or enduring changes in our behaviour, *e.g.* categories.
- Factors or forces that bring temporary changes in our behaviour like mental or physical fatigue, illness, drugs or intoxicating objects, medicines, sleeplessness, emotions like anger, fear etc.

- Factors or forces that bring relatively enduring or permanent changes (the changes lying between the temporary and permanent status—neither too temporary nor too permanent) in our behaviour, *e.g.* training, practice and experiences etc.

Let us now analysis the type of changes brought out by these three category of factors or forces in our behaviour. First let us consider the effect of maturation.

Learning and Maturation

These two phenomena are so interrelated that sometimes it becomes difficult to say as to which of the behavioural changes are the results of learning and which are the consequences of maturation. For the clear differentiation let us try to make distinction between these two terms.

Maturation, in fact, is a natural process. It is the growth which takes place within the individual. The maturational changes are the results of unfolding and ripening of inherited traits and the relatively independent of activity, practice or experience. Biggie and Hunt clarify these ideas in the following words-

> *"Maturation is a developmental process within which a person, from time to time manifests different traits, the 'blue prints' for which have been carried in his cells from the time of his conception."* (1968).

In this way maturation involves changes that are associated with normal growth.

Learning, on the other hand, is a change in a living individual which is not heralded by his genetic inheritance. It is a process which takes place as a result of stimuli from outside. The changes in the behaviour, in the process of learning, are always produced through some activity, training or experiences.

Maturation is learning's chief competitor as a modifier of behaviour. The distinction can be made on the following grounds:

If a behaviour sequence matures (develops) through regular stages, irrespective of intervening practices or training, the behaviour is said to be developed through maturation and not through learning. If training procedures do not speed up or modify the behaviour, such procedures are not casually important and the changes do not classify as learning.

On this ground, the relatively pure cases like the swimming of tadpoles and the flying of birds can be attributed primarily to maturation. But in most of the activities of human beings, it is difficult to decide whether these activities result from maturation or learning. The simplest example is the language development of the child. A child does not learn to talk until he reaches a certain stage or age in maturation, but it is also equally true that he does not learn the language just because he attains that stage. The language is taught to him. The language, which he learns, is that which he hears.

Therefore, the two processes—maturation and learning—are closely related to each other. Maturation helps in the process of learning. Learning can only take place if the stage for that type of learning has been achieved through the process of maturation. If a teacher understands the complexity of the changes that are going on as the result of both processes and the interaction between the two, he would not go astray in his teaching. The reverse will be harmful. For example, forcing a child to attempt to learn certain speech patterns, before a certain maturation has occurred, can disrupt the normal development of speech in the child and do damages. On the other hand, failure to provide specific training in speech at an appropriate time may be a cardinal educational error.

FACTORS ASSOCIATED WITH THE TEMPORARY CHANGES IN BEHAVIOUR

Let us now think over the second category of factors responsible for bringing temporary changes in behaviour. Fatigue, illness, medicine, and intoxicating objects, fear, anger etc. cause serious and quite effective changes in one's behaviour. A person who was quite normal when leaving home in the morning may seem quite fussy and irritable after returning home in the evening. This change in his behaviour is the result of his mental and physical fatigue. However, the change is quite temporary as the behaviour may again turn into normal after some rest or refreshment. The same is true with the behavioural changes introduced on account of taking drugs, alcohol and other intoxicating items. The behaviour becomes normal as soon as one gets rid of the intoxication influences. Similarly, under emotional current one may drift away from his normal behaviour but as soon as one comes to his senses, he realizes his outburst and irrational behaviour and begins to behave as usual. In this way, the changes introduced in our behaviour on account of the factors failing in the second category are quite transitory and temporary. The changes in behaviour automatically vanish as soon as the impact of the factors or forces responsible for introducing such changes come to an end. (You may very well equate these changes in behaviour to the type of changes called physical changes known to you as a student of physical sciences like change of ice into water, lightening of an electric bulb, etc.) On the other hand, the changes brought about by maturation are quite permanent like chemical changes e.g. burning of the piece of a paper, conversion of milk into curd, etc.

RELATIVELY PERMANENT CHANGES THROUGH EXPERIENCE AND TRAINING

The third category of changes in behaviour are neither too temporary (as brought about by the factors like fatigue, illness, alcohol etc.) nor too permanent (as brought about by maturation). They somewhat lie between these two and therefore may be treated as relatively permanent or enduring changes in one's behaviour. The factors or forces responsible for bringing such changes are named as experiences—direct or indirect—involving training, practice, and formal as well as informal education attempts. Only such type of relatively permanent changes in our behaviour brought about through experience may be associated with the process and product of learning. Their characteristics of being neither too permanent nor too temporary is a boon to the system of education. Imagine if the results of our learning, *i.e.* changes in behaviour might have been too temporary, then the strenuous efforts for making the students learn, remember and utilize the results of learning would have been too futile. Being temporary and transitory changes, all that was learnt by a child could have vanished in no time. Similarly the introduction of too permanent changes in one's behaviour through learning would have been quite an unpleasant experience as a student's learning to pronounce PUT as pat might become a lifelong mistake. The done could never be undone and thus picking up of the bad habits on account of any learning might have ruined the future of ill-fated learners. In this way it is quite a welcome sign that changes introduced only through experience are termed as learning.

In this way, if we attempt to analyse the nature of changes introduced in our behaviour with reference to the factors responsible for such changes, a proper definition of the term learning may be evolved in the following words.

Learning is a process of bringing relatively enduring or permanent changes in behaviour through experience or training.

PROCESS OF LEARNING

Learning is a process and not a product. This process has continuity and is carried out in various steps. While summing up these steps, Smith gives the following definition—

> *"In short, the learning process involves a motive or drive, an attractive goal and a block to the attainment of the goal. All these are essential."* (1962, p. 262)

Let us try to examine Smith's statement. The first step in the process of learning is motive or drive. Motive is the dynamic force that energizes behaviour and compels a child to act. Every individual has to take care of the satisfaction of his basic motives and needs. As long as our present behaviour, knowledge, skill and performance are adequate to satisfy all our needs, we do not feel any need to change our behaviour or acquire new knowledge and skills. It is this requirement that initiates a learner to learn something.

Motives and needs of the learner demand their satisfaction. When the need of a learner is strong enough, he is compelled to strive for its satisfaction. For this purpose, he has to set definite goals and aims for achievement. Definiteness of the aim and setting of the goal helps in making the learning purposeful and interesting. The goal attracts us to learn.

Then comes the third step in the process of learning which is equally essential as the previous ones. It is in terms of some obstacle or block or barrier that keeps us from attaining that goal (Fig. 15.1). If we face no difficulty in attaining our goal, we need not bring any change in our present behaviour, stock of knowledge and skills. This means that we do not need to learn. Hence, the block or problem is an essential step in the learning process. We try to change or modify our behaviour only when there is a need to do so to reach the goals that our unsatisfied motives create.

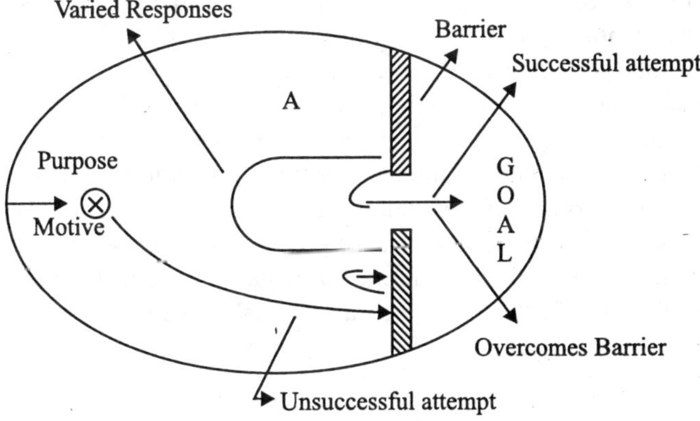

Fig. 15.1 Elements in the process of learning.

Let us clear the above views by taking an example. Suppose, you wish to be included in your college Hockey team and that appeals to many of your psychological needs. You want the esteem of your colleagues and your teachers. You are also motivated by the interesting experiences that you may enjoy. But you are blocked by your lack of skill in dodging, tackling and handling the ball. These obstacles and blocks in the path of goal achievement will set you work on your deficiency and acquire essential skill through sufficient practice and coaching.

By these steps, Smith has tried to consider the problem as to why we learn and has emphasized the role of motivation, needs and goals in the process of learning.

But the process of learning remains incomplete with just these three elements—motives, goals and blocks—which Smith has suggested. It is rather a preparatory stage for learning than being the stage for actual learning. With these three steps, strong desire and essential readiness is produced in the child for learning something. It is very essential for any scheme of learning. The child's readiness and his positive attitude towards learning is to be ascertained before beginning the learning programmes. There are many factors that contribute towards the learning readiness. Those worth mentioning are his physical and mental maturity, previously acquired knowledge and skills and his ability in goal setting. With the help of all these factors, teachers or parents should try to fix an appropriate level of aspiration for the child so that he may proceed properly on the path of learning.

The next steps in the process of learning, after the preparatory stage, are concerned with the task of actual learning by the learner. One of such important steps is the learning situation. The learning situation provides opportunity for learning. The quality, speed and effectiveness of learning depends much upon the kind of learning situation and environment available to the learner. Healthy and favourable learning environment brings satisfactory results in learning while poor and unfavourable learning environment proves an obstacle in the path of learning.

In a particular learning environment, when the learner strives to learn something, the process of learning involves constant interaction. According to Udai Pareek *"Interaction is the process of responding to a situation and getting feedback from it—satisfaction or thwarting of the needs. Learning results from such interaction."* (Kuppuswamy, B. 1964, p. 112).

In fact, when a child strives to learn something in order to achieve his desired goal, he is very curious to know the results of his striving. On this path when he acquires some new knowledge and skills or brings changes in his behaviour, he is desirous to know, whether or not, with these changes he will be able to cherish the desired end. If he finds that all that has been learned so far is useful and feels satisfied with his progress, he is sure to gain speed in the path of his learning. Moreover, the learning process has continuity in its flow. What has been learnt so far on in the path of learning works as a running capital and base for further learning.

Learning at a particular moment in a learning environment brings essential changes in the behaviour of an individual. These changes later on become part and parcel of the learning behaviour. These learned acts are retained for a longer time, depending upon the nature of the learner and effectiveness of the learning process and used in similar situations when the need and opportunity arise. Therefore, the process of learning does not end with the acquisition of certain knowledge, skill and changes in behaviour in one particular situation. It is a never ending process. The change once acquired or the learning once accomplished gets its fixation in other like-wise situations. It stands for its modification and thus always seems in a process of continuous change and development.

CHARACTERISTICS OF ACQUIRED BEHAVIOUR OR LEARNING

The changes brought about in our behaviour through learning by all means are accounted as acquired phenomenon. Learning in this way can't be attributed to some or the other hereditary influences. It is earned and acquired by us like other attributes of our personality and that is why learning of all types is given a common name, *i.e.* acquired behaviour. It has its special nature and characteristics, a glimpse of which you may find through the following description.

1. **Learning is the change in behaviour:** Learning in its any form or shape is always associated with some change in the learner's behaviour. That is why learning is always

directed or aimed at bringing changes in the learner's behaviour. However, these changes should always be desirable ones as the undesirable changes, if allowed to occur can prove detrimental to the welfare of the learner as well as to the society.

2. **Change in behaviour is relatively enduring or permanent:** Change in behaviour caused by learning is neither too permanent (as caused through maturation) nor too temporary (as caused by the factors like fatigue, illness etc.). They lie between these two states and are usually referred to as relatively permanent changes implying that although frequent or unwanted changes in the learned behaviour can't take place, yet the needed changes can be introduced like getting rid of the bad habits or unlearning a wrong method of doing things etc.
3. **Learning is a continuous life long process:** Learning though not inherited, can begin right from the conception of the child. The environment available in the womb of the mother may work as a facilitator for such learning. We have *Abhimanyu* as an example who learned the art of *Chakravueh Bhedan* from his father *Arjuna* in the womb of his mother *Shubhadra*. After birth, the process of learning picks up speed with the constant interaction and stimulation received from the physical, social and cultural environmental forces and it does not stop till one's death. Regarding its continuity we have enough evidence that one activity leads to another and the individual engages himself to learn more and more. Every day new problems are faced, new situation are created and the individual has to face these situations and bring essential changes in his behaviour. Thus it is a never ending process and so referred to as process which goes from womb to womb.
4. **Learning is a universal process:** We, the living creatures on this earth, have the abilities and capabilities for learning irrespective of the nature of our species, caste, colour, sex, geographical location or some other such individual differences. Therefore, myths like members of the upper castes especially Brahmins have more ability of learning than the members belonging to the lower castes and untouchables, women have inferior learning capacity than men, or the blacks possess sub-normal capacities for learning in comparison to whites, etc. have no substantial ground. The truth remains that every living being on earth has been favoured by the nature to possess the capacity to learn according to the species specific characteristics and environment as well as opportunities available for learning.
5. **Learning is purposive and goal-directed:** All learning is goal-directed. It is the definiteness of the aim and clear understanding of the purpose which makes an individual immediately learn the techniques of performing a particular task. It is the purpose or goal which determines what he sees in the learning situations and how he acts there in. Therefore, the purpose or goal is the pivot around which the entire system of learning revolves. In cases where there is no purpose, there would hardly be any learning.
6. **Learning involves reconstruction of experiences:** We learn something at a particular stage and it is stored in our learning experiences store in the form of past experience or learning for the learning of a future task. However, what has been learnt by us at a particular occasion always remains in the state of modification in the light of new or richer experiences gained by us in this respect. As a result old learning is replaced by new learning and our previous experiences are restructured and reorganized to give birth to a new structure composed of the reconstructed experiences. It is therefore education, *i.e.* the process of learning, that is often referred to as the process of continuous reconstruction of experiences.

7. **Learning is the product of activity and environment:** The basic condition of the emergence of any learning essentially lies in one's responding activity to the stimuli belonging to one's environment. In case the child is not willing to respond to the stimuli present in his learning environment, he can't be persuaded to proceed on the path of his learning journey. More the learner will respond actively to the stimuli present in his learning environment, the more progress will he be able to make in terms of his learning outcomes. Therefore, the key to successful learning in any teaching learning-process always lies in the active responding of the learner to the stimuli present or the activities going on in the teaching-learning environment.
8. **Learning is transferable from one situation to another:** Learning has a special characteristic of being transferred from one learning situation to another having positive as well as negative effect. In its positive transfer, learning in one situation helps the learning in another situation but in the case of negative transfer, we may observe the adverse effect when learning in one situation hinders or obstructs the path of learning in another situation.
9. **Learning does not necessarily imply improvement:** Learning is often considered a process of improvement with practice or training. This means that all types of learning helps the child in the path of his process towards desired ends or results. But this is not always true. A child learns so many things in the classroom that do not help him at all in achieving his goal. Habits like idleness, disrespect towards authority, truancy, developing poor handwriting and defective pronunciation and exposition are among these. Therefore, it should be known clearly that learning does not necessarily imply improvement (with respect to the achievement of an end).
10. **Learning does not necessarily imply development in right direction:** In a similar way, while defining learning as a process of development, the word development should never be confined to mean 'progress in right direction to achieve certain ends or results'. Hence as Woodworth clarifies in his definition, as a result of learning, the pattern of development is free to move in either direction—positive or negative. It is no guarantee that an individual will always pick up good knowledge, desirable habits, interest and attitudes. He has equal chances to be drifted to the debit side of the human personality.
11. **Learning helps in bringing desirable changes in behaviour:** Learning is the process of bringing changes in behaviour. It can help in introducing desired changes in the behaviour of the learner in all its three domains, *i.e.* cognitive, conative and affective.
12. **Learning helps in the attainment of teaching-learning objectives:** The teaching-learning objectives and teaching-learning situation can be effectively reached through the help of learning and consequently children can be made to acquire essential knowledge, skills, applications, attitudes and interests etc.
13. **Learning helps in the proper growth and development:** Learning helps in reaching to one's maximum in terms of growth and development under their various dimensions, namely physical, mental (cognitive) emotional, social, moral, aesthetic and language.
14. **Learning helps in the balanced development of personality:** Our educational efforts are directed to bring an all-round development in the personality of the child. The process of learning results in bringing such an all-round development of the personality.

15. **Learning helps in proper adjustment:** Adjustment is the key to success in life. Learning helps the individual to seek adjustment with his self and environment.
16. **Learning helps in the realization of the goals of life:** Every man has his own philosophy and style of life and he strives to achieve the goals of his life. Learning process helps the individual to realize these goals.
17. **Learning is a very comprehensive process, possessing a wide scope:** The world of learning is considered to limit itself in the narrow walls of the activities concerning intellectual and motor efficiency. It is often thought of as the acquisition of some knowledge and skills, memorization of certain facts and principles, development of reasoning and thinking power etc. These are some of the learning activities which formally go on inside the classroom or in any arranged learning situation. But learning is not only limited to these activities. It is a very comprehensive process that covers nearly all the aspects of the human personality. Its scope touches aspects like the formation of habits, development of interests, attitudes, a sense of appreciation and critical observation, acquisition of beliefs, perfection of values and ideals and setting of the goals and purposes.

Therefore, learning as a whole, is not confined to the formal classroom learning activities. Life presents enormous opportunities to learn and learning activities are so many that it is difficult to limit them in any specific categories. How one eats, drinks, dresses, what are his specific hobbies, interests, attitudes, beliefs and aspirations, how he strives and what ideals and values he aims at, what is his concept of himself etc., all are examples of learned and acquired behviour. And the scope of learning definitely embraces all these aspects into its domain.

DOMAINS OF LEARNING

Learning as already emphasized, is always designed to bring desired changes in the behaviour of the learner. These changes in the behaviour of a learner are brought about in all the aspects and domains of his behaviour. Let us try to know about the meaning and types of the domains of one's behaviour.

The term behaviour carries a wide meaning in its scope and application. While emphasizing this truth, Woodworth (1993) writes-

> *"Any manifestation of life is activity and behaviour is a collective name for these activities."*

Hence, scope of the term 'behaviour' can be safely extended to any type of activity that we as human beings resort to at one or the other time in our life situations. From the moment our life starts to its end, we are always doing one or the other type of activity in life situations. Even if you are sitting or lying idle, you would be wrong in saying that you are doing nothing. Even at that particular moment, you would have been indulged in one activity or the other.

One is always engaged in some or the other activity, *i.e.* either doing something or thinking or feeling about something. These "doing", "thinking" and "feeling" aspects of our behaviour may thus constitute the different domains of our behaviour.

In the language of psychology and education, these three different aspects or domains of behaviour are known as—conative, cognitive and affective domains of our behaviour. Since learning absolutely stands for bringing changes in one's behaviour, it implies that with the help of the learning performed by a learner at one or the other time, it is sure to result in bringing changes in one and/or the other domains of his behaviour.

From the discussion so far, we may easily conclude that Domains of learning are nothing but the domains of our behaviour which are subjected to some or the other changes as a result of our one or the other type of learning at a particular time. Consequently we may classify the domains of our learning into the following three types.

1. Conative Domain of learning
2. Cognitive Domain of learning
3. Affective Domain of learning

Let us have a brief description on these domains of learning.

Conative Domain of Learning

The learning related with this domain is expected to bring changes in one's conative behaviour. It is characterized by "doing" aspect of our behaviour. Therefore, changes brought about by performing activities like walking, talking, running, jumping, dancing, bending, moulding, eating, drinking, sewing, knitting, smelling, chewing, touching, throwing, holding, seeing, hearing, watching, grinding etc. (performed through our actions as well as sense organs—*Karmendriyana* and *Gyanendriyana*) may fall in the conative domain of one's learning. Learning related to this domain of behaviour usually results in the acquisition of necessary skills for the adequate physical and motor development as well as seeking adjustment to one's environment and ways of living.

Cognitive Domain of Learning

The learning related with this domain is expected to bring changes in one's cognitive behaviour. It is characterized by 'thinking' aspect of one's behaviour. Therefore, changes brought about in performing activities like thinking, reasoning, imagining, analyzing, synthesizing, concluding, generalizing, estimating, interpreting, memorizing, elaborating, summarizing, explaining, illustrating, etc. may fall in the cognitive domains of one's learning. The learning related to this domain of behaviour usually results in the acquisition of intellectual competencies and academic abilities leading to one's mental and intellectual development and harmonious adjustment with one's self and the environment.

Affective Domain of Learning

The learning related with this domain is expected to bring changes in one's affective behaviour. It is characterized by "feeling" aspect of one's behaviour. Therefore, changes brought about by performing activities like feeling happy and sad, angry and cool, expressing one's emotions in a desired way, exhibiting one's preferences, likes and dislikes, attitudes and interests, holding values and ideas etc. may fall in the affective domains of one's learning. The learning related to this domain of behaviour usually results in the acquisition of social skills, emotional maturity, moral and character development and makes an individual a right human being.

In this way, domains of learning categorized as conative, cognitive and affective, stand for the different aspects or components of one's behaviour in which desired behavioural changes are planned through a system of education. In the classroom or school situations, deliberate attempts are usually made for bringing desired changes in these domain of learning for the realization of stipulated teaching-learning or educational objectives.

SUMMARY

Learning refers to a process of bringing changes in behaviour through experience or teaching. However, all types of changes in our behaviour are not necessarily caused by learning. Maturation (the natural process of growth and development) causes changes quite independent of any experience, practice or learning. Similarly the changes produced by some factors like fatigue, illness, medicine, intoxicating objects, fear, anger etc. also do not cause such serious and enduring changes in behaviour. The changes associated with our direct and indirect experiences and formal attempts of practice and teaching can only result in quite stable and enduring changes in our behaviour and that is why such type of changes are likely to be associated with the processes and product of learning.

The process of learning is carried out in the stages namely preparatory stage involving learning readiness, active stage involving the task of actual learning and the feedback stage necessary for the continuity of the cycle of learning. However, the process of learning does not end in one cycle. It is a never ending process that needs to be carried out for bringing changes in one's behaviour in facing never ending changes and situation of one's life.

Learning can't be attributed to any hereditary influences. It is by all means an acquired behaviour earned by us through our experiences and teaching. The other distinctive feature of learning include (i) its ability to bring relatively permanent changes in behaviour (ii) its being a continuous and universal life long process (iii) its being purposive and goal-directed (iv) transfer ability from one situation to another (v) not always necessarily associated with improvement or development in right direction (vi) planned learning attempts are always directed to bring desirable behaviour changes and balanced development of the personality etc.

Changes in the behaviour of the learner can be brought out in all the aspects and domain of his behaviour. In general the domains of one's behaviour are usually categorized and labeled as cognitive, conative and affective domains of behaviour. Cognitive domain of one's behaviour is characterized by 'thinking' aspect and conative, by 'doing' aspect and affective by 'feeling' aspect. In bringing changes through any planned process of learning we have to take care of the desirable changes in all the three domains of child's behaviour.

References and Suggested Readings

Biggie, M.L. and Hung, M.P., *Psychological Foundations of Education*, Harper & Row, New York, 1968.

Crow, L.D. and Crow, Alice, *Educational Psychology*, Eurasia Publishing House, New Delhi, 1973.

Hilgard, E.R. and Bower, G.H., *Theories of Learning*, 2nd ed., Prentice-Hall, Englewood Cliffs, New Jersey, 1957.

Kuppuswami, B., *Advanced Educational Psychology*, University Publication, Delhi, 1964.

Murphy, Gardner, *An Introduction to Psychology*, Oxford & IBH, New Delhi, 1968.

Pressey, Robinson and Horrocks, *Psychology in Education*, 2nd ed., Universal Book Stall, Delhi, 1967.

Smith H.P., *Psychology in Teaching*, Prentice-Hall, Englewood Cliffs, New Jersey, 1962

Woodworth, R.S., *Psychology*, Methuen, London, 1945.

16

Factors Influencing Learning

CHAPTER COMPOSITION

INTRODUCTION

In the preceding chapter, we have tried to understand the concept and nature of learning, so we are now able to conclude that learning brings relatively permanent or enduring changes in our behaviour, quite distinctive to the changes brought about through maturation and factors like fatigue and illness. It is also made known to us that learning behaviour is by all means an acquired behaviour. Whatever we learn, we learn through experiences gained in our environment. Learning in no way can be said to be a gift or contribution from our hereditary stock. It is always regarded as a coefficient of friction between our self and the environment. It is, therefore, the environment that is supposed to influence and shape our learning. The contribution of the mechanism of motivation is also nowhere less than the actual efforts and attempts made by a learner in learning a thing. This motivation is also influenced by so many environmental factors like the process and product of teacher-learning process. In this chapter, we would be discussing the various factors that may be held responsible for affecting one's learning related to one or the other type of teaching-learning process.

FACTORS INFLUENCING LEARNING

Learning as you have studied earlier can be defined as a process of bringing relatively enduring changes in the behaviour of the learner through experience and learning. An analysis of this definition may reveal that the learning process related with a particular teaching-learning situation is mainly centered around the two things, namely—

(i) the learner whose behaviour is to be modified.

(ii) the type of experience and training available for the modification in the learner's behaviour.

Therefore, the success or failure in the task of learning in a particular teaching-learning situation or environment mainly involves two types of factors, one related with the learner and other with the prevailing learning environment. Therefore, the differences observed in the results of learning or performances exhibited by a group of learners may be surely attributed to the differences present in the learner's themselves or within their learning environment. Consequently the factors influencing learning may be broadly classified as personal (learner related) and environmental (learning facilities and situations) related. The environmental related factors, then can be further categorized as teacher related, content related and process related (sources available to the learners for their learning). As a result the factors influencing learning may be categorized as below :

A. Learner Related Factors

B. Teacher Related Factors

C. Content Related Factors

D. Process Related Factors

Let us discuss now these four types of factors one by one—

Learner Related Factors

The learner is the key figure in any learning task. He has to learn to bring desired modification in his behaviour. How will he learn or what will he achieve through a particular learning act depends heavily on his own characteristics and way of learning. Such things or factors associated with him can be described as below—

1. Learner's physical and mental health: Learning is greatly affected by the learner's physical and mental health maintained by him particularly at the time of learning. A simple headache or stomach ache can play a havoc with the process and products of learning. Children who did not keep up with satisfactory physical health have to suffer adversely in terms of the gain in learning. Similarly, the mental state and health of the learner at the time of learning become potent factor in deciding the outcome of the learning. A tense, emotionally and mentally disturbed learner cannot be expected to show satisfactory results in learning.

2. Basic potential of the learner: The results achieved by the learner through a process of learning depend heavily upon his basic potential to undergo such learning. Such potential may consist of the following things.

- Learner's innate abilities and capacities for learning a thing.
- Learner's basic potential in terms of general intelligence and specific knowledge, understanding and skills related to particular learning area.
- Learner's basic interests, aptitudes and attitudes related to the learning of a particular thing or area.

3. Level of aspiration and achievement motivation: Learning is greatly influenced by the level of aspiration and nature of achievement motivation possessed by the learner. How can we expect from a learner to achieve a thing for which he has no aspiration? One has to maintain the level of his aspiration and achievement motivation to a reasonable level neither too high causing frustration for non-achievement nor too low so as not to try for things for which he is quite capable. In this way, one's level of aspiration and achievement motivation works significantly towards gains in learning.

4. Goals of life: The philosophy and immediate as well as ultimate goals of one's life affect the process and products of learning. His mode and ways of looking towards the things, his inclination towards the learning in a particular area and patience and persistence maintained for continuing his learning, despite the heavy odds, all depend upon his goals and philosophy of life.

5. Readiness and will power: Learner's readiness and power to learn is a great deciding factor in the results of learning. No power on earth can make a learner learn if he is not ready to learn. Contrarily, if he has a will to learn something then, he will himself find the way for effective learning.

Teacher Related Factors

If the learner stands at one end of the on-going teaching-learning process as one of the pole then inevitably, it is the teacher who is entrusted to act as the other pole for the desired flow of the teaching-learning activities in the classroom. He is the person who has to play the role of friend, philosopher and guide for initiating, interacting as well as concluding all the activities pertaining to the classroom journey traveled along with the students of the class. Hence, teacher related factors are bound to play significant role in shaping and directing the teaching-learning process of a classroom or work situation. Let us here briefly summarize the role of such teacher related factors in the teaching-learning process.

1. Mastery over the subject matter: A teacher should know the art and skill of teaching so that the students are able to realize the stipulated teaching-learning objective in a particular teaching-learning situation. He may know his subject well but for sharing, communicating and interacting various experience related to the learning of the subject, he needs specific teaching skills, art and sciences of his teaching profession. The proficiency and deficiency possessed by a teacher in this regard are quite responsible for turning the teaching-learning process into a big success or a failure.

2. Personality traits and behaviour of the teacher: A teacher as a leader has to lead his students in the teaching-learning process through the magnetic influence and incredible impression left on the minds of the students on the basis of his personality traits and behaviour. He is a role model for his students. His actions, behaviour pattern and personality traits carry a great meaning to his students for being imitated and brought into practice. Therefore, much of the task regarding desirable behaviour modification, an essential target meant for any teaching-learning act, is very much influenced by the types of personality traits and behaviour pattern demonstrated by the teacher in his action and behaviour in the classroom and work situations. Moreover, how he behaves with his students during the various types of activities and interactions carried out in the teaching-learning process also prove a decisive factor in finalizing the teacher learning outcomes.

3. Level of adjustment and mental health of the teacher: How adjusted a teacher feels in his personal and professional life and the state and level of mental health maintained by the teacher carries much weight in influencing his behaviour and effectiveness needed for the effective control and management of the teaching-learning process. A teacher possessing poor mental health and lack of adjustment in his personal and professional life may prove total failure in the realization of teaching-learning objectives, whereas a teacher possessing good mental health and adjustment may prove an ideal image to his students and boon to the effectiveness of the teaching-learning process.

4. Type of discipline and interaction maintained by the teacher: A teacher who is a good disciplinarian (democratic and persuasive) and believe in providing due interactive roles to his students in the teaching-learning process brings more positive and better teaching-learning outcomes in comparison to the teachers who are poor in terms of maintaining discipline (autocratic or lethargic) and are in the habit of providing unidirectional flow of communication by discouraging any initiative and interaction from his students.

Content Related Factors

In a teaching-learning process, one thing that is shared most between the learner and the teacher is the contents of the subject matter. Desired instructional objectives and educational aims can be effectively achieved only on the basis of the quality of these contents or learning experiences shared during the process of teaching-learning. Poor contents lead to poor teaching and inadequate or sometimes no learning while contents rich in the desired learning experiences suited to the nature, interest and ability of the learner always pay rich dividend in terms of the realization of set teaching-learning objectives. In brief the factors related to contents influencing teaching-learning may be broadly divided into three main categories named and discussed as below.

1. Nature of the contents or leaning experiences: Teaching-learning process is influenced by the nature of the contents, subject matter or learning experiences shared in the process. Whether the nature of the content material or learning experience provided in a teaching-learning process is formal or informal, incidental or organized, direct or indirect, proves quite a potent factor in influencing the process and products of teaching-learning.

2. Selection of the contents or learning experiences: Proper attention, time and energy employed for the desired selection of the contents or learning experiences best suited for the realization of the teaching-learning objectives in a particular teaching-learning situation always proves decisive in influencing the process and products of teaching-learning. Therefore, it is always advisable to select content material or the learning experiences on the basis of the desired principles like principle of child centeredness, principle of activity, criterion of activity, age, grade and experiences of the learners etc.

3. Organization of the contents or learning experiences: Selected contents or learning experiences need better organization for the effective sharing among the learners and teacher. A better organization will be more convenient and provide strength to the learners and teacher for the better realization of the stipulated teaching-learning objectives. Therefore, the methods like logical v/s psychological, spiral v/s concentric, criterion of difficulty level, correlation etc. should be properly employed for the effective organization of the contents or learning experiences.

Process Related Factors

Teaching-learning output can always be better realized in terms of the stipulated teaching-learning objectives if the factors related to the process of teaching-learning are better planned, organized and executed in a proper way. Such process related factors have been explained as under:

1. Methodology adopted for teaching-learning experiences: In teaching-learning, much depends upon the methods, techniques and approaches employed for the teaching and learning of the selected contents and learning experiences. Let us weigh the truth of this statement from various angles.

(a) Linking of the new learning with the past: The quality of the result in teaching-learning depends much on the abilities of the teacher and the learner to link the present new learning with the past experiences of the learner. Past experience help the learner to assimilate and understand the new learning by providing success as well as cementing force for this purpose.

(b) Correlating the learning in one area to the other: Correlation facilitates the task of teaching-learning as it allows maximum transfer of training or learning from one area to another. Accordingly, one can expect good results in learning if learning experiences are given in view of seeking correlation—(i) among the different subjects or areas, (ii) within the branches or experiences or experiences of the same area and (iii) with the real life happenings and situations.

(c) Utilization of maximum number of senses: Senses are said to be the gateway of knowledge and consequently the results in teaching-learning are very much influenced by the nature and type of the utilization of one's senses for the acquisition of learning experiences. A learner who learns through the utilization of his maximum senses like sense of sight, hearing, touch, smell, tastes and also tries to learn by doing the things himself always reach at an advantageous point.

(d) Provision of drill work, revision and practice: Review and practice always brings good results in the achievements of student's learning. A learner who makes use of sufficient drill work, practice work, revision and review of his learning can be expected to harvest a good yield in terms of its good retention, reproduction and utilization at the proper time.

(e) Provision of proper feedback and reinforcement: The teaching-learning yields are much dependent upon the nature and quality of the feedback and reinforcement provided to the learner in his learning task. One must be acquainted with the progress of his learning in terms of his strengths and weaknesses and remedial action, if needed, may be taken at the proper time. The knowledge of the results and progress may work well for providing immediate reinforcement to the learner. In addition, the learning process can be suitably designed if we take due care for the planning of proper reinforcement technique in the shape of approval of the learning response. Nodding of the head, smiling, saying good-bye, etc. bring a magic in terms of learner's interest and achievement.

(f) The selection of the suitable learning methods and teaching: There are sufficient methods and a number of good techniques available for the teaching and learning of different subjects and areas of experiences. The results in teaching-learning are always influenced by the nature and quality of the methods and techniques employed for the teaching and learning of a particular content, subject matter or learning experiences like those given below—

(i) Whether or not methods and techniques are helpful in learning at memory, understanding or reflective level?

(ii) Whether or not these are teacher-dominated, learner-centered or allow useful teacher-pupil interaction?

(iii) Is it possible to proceed on the path of self learning through them?

2. Teaching-learning environment and resources: The learner is helped by the available resources and environment available for bringing desirable changes in his behaviour. How effectively will such changes be introduced in his behaviour depend much of the equality and management of these resources. Such things and factors affecting teaching-learning process may be listed as below—

(a) The socio-emotional climate available in the institution in the shape of teacher-pupil relationships, pupil-pupil relationships and school-staff relationships etc.
(b) The availability of appropriate learning material and facilities in terms of teaching-learning aids, textbooks, library and laboratory facilities, project work, etc.
(c) The proper conducive environment and learning situations like those given below—
    (i) Proper seating arrangement
    (ii) Calm and peaceful environment
    (iii) Management and control of the factors leading to distraction
    (iv) Cooperative and competitive group situations
    (v) Congenial learning environment at home
    (vi) Provision of proper change, rest and recreation
    (vii) Provision of opportunity for creativity and self-expression

In this way the process and products of teaching-learning are said to be influenced by the personal factors associated with the learner and teachers and the external factors (like type of content material and their proper delivery to the learner) lying within the teaching-learning environment.

SUMMARY

Learning activities are quite independent of learner's hereditary stock. The environmental forces and factors go in a variety of ways to shape the processes and products of learning. In fact learning in all its means and shapes is always regarded as a coefficient of friction between the self of the learner and the teaching-learning environment. This is why the factors influencing one's learning may be categorized as learner related factors, teacher related factors, content related factors and process related factors.

In the process of learning much depends on the learner. How well will he learn thus depends upon so many learner's related factors like his physical and mental health, basic potential, level of aspiration and achievement motivation, goals of life and his readiness and will power for the learning.

Teacher is always a key figure in any teaching-learning process and all his attempts are almost directed in helping the learners in his learning. How will he be helpful in the task depends upon the factors like his mastery over the subject matter, art and skills of teaching, personality traits and behaviour, his level of adjustment and mental health and type of discipline and interaction he can be able to maintain etc.

Apart from the learner and teacher (dependent and independent variables in a teaching-learning process) the role of intervening variables involving mainly the contents as well as the process related factors can never be underestimated. In content related factors we can mainly include factors like the nature of the contents or learning experiences and the selection as well as organization of these learning experiences. The process related factors, on the other hand, are related with the processing of selected and organized learning experiences in the hands of both the teacher as well as the learner and may thus be grouped into two distinct categories i.e. factors related with the methodology adopted for teaching and learning, and factors associated with the type and nature of the teaching-learning environment and resources.

References and Suggested Readings

Biggie, Morris, L, *Learning Theories for Teachers,* Universal Book Stall, Delhi, (Indian Reprint), 1967.

Biggie, M.L. and Hung, M.P., *Psychological Foundations of Education*, Harper & Row, New York, 1968.

Crow, L.D. and Crow, Alice, *Educational Psychology*, Eurasia Publishing House, New Delhi, 1973.

Skinner, B.F., *The Technology of Teaching,* Appleton-Century Crafts, New York, 1968.

Smith H.P., *Psychology in Teaching*, Prentice-Hall, Englewood Cliffs, New Jersey, 1962.

17

Theories of Learning

CHAPTER COMPOSITION

INTRODUCTION

What goes in the process of learning? How do we learn? How does a child learn to solve mathematical problems? How does a girl learn to cook food or sew clothes? There are so many questions, the answer to which needs a thorough explanation of the phenomenon of learning. Psychologists have conducted experiments to throw light on the phenomenon of learning and as a result have developed various learning theories. Each theory with its systematic body of knowledge explains the nature and process of learning. These theories represent broad principles and techniques of learning. The set of rules and the laws of learning, having wide applicability, are drawn from these theories. Also, these theories put forth various methods of learning and suggest the teacher and learner to take proper steps for the effective learning.

Modern leaning theories may be broadly classified into two types, namely—

(A) Stimulus responses-associationist type of theories.

(B) Gestalt field or field cognition type of theories.

The former interpret learning in terms of the change in behaviour of the learner brought about by the association of the response to a series of stimuli. The chief exponents of this type of theories are—Edward, L. Thorndike (1874-1949); John B. Watson (1878-1958), Evan Petrovich Pavlov (1949-1935) and Burrhus Frederic Skinner (1904). While the ideas and system propagated by Thorndike is called 'Connectionism', the system presented by Watson and Pavlov is known as 'classical conditioning' and the system given by Skinner is called 'operant conditioning'.

The second type of theories look at learning as the change in the field consisting of the learner and his environment and the learner's perception of the field. These theories emphasize the role of purpose, insight and understanding in the process of learning. The chief exponents of this type of theories are Max-Wertheimer (1880-1943); Wolfgang Kohler (1887-1967), Kurt Koffka (1886-1941) and Kurt Lewin (1890-1947).

As a result of modernization due to computer technology and humanistic trends in education, a new theoretical approach has also evolved on the horizon of theories of learning giving birth to several information processing and humanistic theories.

All these theories belonging to one or the other type represent the viewpoints held by their propagators about the nature and process of learning. None of these theories is said to be complete in all aspects for explaining the phenomenon of learning. Each one of them gives a partial description. For example, one theory is good in explaining the learning process in one situation while the others hold equally good in other different situations. Therefore, it is essential to have a working knowledge of some important theories. Below, we try to analyse some of the most important theories. These are:

1. Thorndike's connectionism or Trial and Error learning
2. Watson's & Pavlov's classical conditioning
3. Skinner's operant conditioning
4. Kohler's Insight Theory
5. Lewin's Field Theory
6. Information Processing Theories
7. Roger's Experiential Learning
8. Maslow's Humanistic Theory

THORNDIKE'S CONNECTIONISM OR TRIAL AND ERROR LEARNING

Thorndike propagated the theory with the help of his experiments performed on chickens, rats and cats. Pierre Flooure (1794-1857) had proposed that conclusions drawn from animal experimentation should be equally applicable to man. This proposition started the chain of experimentation in the field of learning with animals. Thorndike selected chickens, rats and cats for experimentation. He placed them under different learning situations and studied them carefully. With the help of these experiments, he tried to evolve certain laws and propagated his theory of connectionism or trial and error learning. It is interesting to study the type of experiments he performed with these animals. For illustration, below we narrate one of his experiment.

He put a hungry cat in a puzzle box. There was only one door for exit which could be opened by correctly manipulating a latch. A fish was placed outside the box. The smell of the fish worked as a strong motive for the hungry cat to come out of the box. As a result, the cat made every possible effort to come out of the box (see Fig. 17.1).

The situation is described by Thorndike (1911) himself as—*"It tries to squeeze through any opening and claws at everything it reaches"*. In this way, it made a number of random movements. In one of the random movements, by chance the latch was manipulated. The cat came out and got its reward responses. In due course, the cat was able to open the door without any error or in other words, learned the way of opening the door.

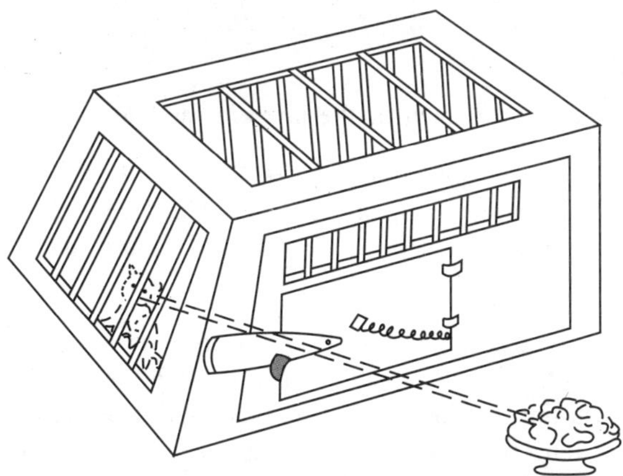

Fig. 17.1 Thorndike's cat is trying to come out of the box.

Thorndike named the learning of his experimental cat as "Trial and Error Learning". He maintained that learning is nothing but the stamping in of the correct responses and stamping out of the incorrect responses though trial and error. In trying for the correct solution, the cat made so many vain attempts. It committed errors and errors before getting success. On subsequent trials, it tried to avoid the erroneous ways and repeat the correct ways of manipulating the latch.

Thorndike called it *"Learning by selecting and connecting"* as it provides an opportunity for the selection of the proper responses and connect or associate them with adequate stimuli. In this reference, Thorndike has written—*"Learning is connecting. The mind is man's connection system"* (1931, p. 122).

As a result, learning is caused by the formation of connection in the nervous system between stimuli and responses. There is a definite association between sense impression and impulses to action. This association can be known as a bond or connection. Since it is these bonds or connection, which become strengthened or weakened in the making and breaking of habits, Thorndike's system is sometimes called "bond psychology" or simply "connectionism".

Thorndike propounded the following laws of learning on the basis of his theory :-

The Law of Readiness

The statement runs as under

> *When any conduction unit is ready to conduct, for it to do so is satisfying. When any condition unit is not in readiness to conduct, for it to conduct is annoying. When any condition unit is in readiness to conduct, for it not to do so is annoying.*

This law is indicative of the learner's state to participate in the learning process. Readiness, according to Thorndike, is preparation for action. It is very essential for learning. If a child is ready to learn he learns more quickly, effectively and with greater satisfaction than if he is not ready to learn. It warns us not to make the child learn till he is ready and also not to miss any opportunity of providing learning experience if the child is already prepared to learn. The right movements concerning the learning situation and the learner's state of mind should be very well-recognized and maximum use of this knowledge should be made by the teacher. He should also attempt to motivate his students by arousing their attention, interest and curiosity.

The Law of Effect

In the words of Thorndike, the statement of the law runs as under:

> *When a modifiable connection between situation and response is made and accompanied or followed by a satisfying state of affairs, that connection's strength is increased. When made and accompanied or followed by an annoying state of affairs, its strength is decreased.*

In simple words, it means that learning takes place properly when it results in satisfaction and the learner derives pleasure out of it. In the situation when the child meets failure or is dissatisfied, the progress on the path of learning is blocked. All the pleasant experiences have a lasting influence and are remembered for a long time, while the unpleasant ones are soon forgotten. Therefore, the satisfaction or dissatisfaction, pleasure or displeasure obtained as a result of some learning ensure the degree of effectiveness of that learning.

In other words, this law emphasizes the role of rewards and punishment in the process of learning. Getting reward as a result of some learning motivates and encourages the child to proceed on the same path with more intensity and enthusiasm while punishment of any sort discourages him and creates distaste and repulsion towards that learning.

THE LAW OF EXERCISE

The law of exercise has two sub-parts—law of use and law of disuse which may be defined as:

LAW OF USE

When a modifiable connection is made between a situation and response that connection's strength is, other things being equal, increased.

LAW OF DISUSE

When a modifiable connection is not made between a situation and response, during a length of time, that connection's strength is decreased.

Thus, law of use refers to the strengthening of connection with practice while the law of disuse refers to the weakening of connection or forgetting when the practice is discontinued. In brief, it can be said that the law of exercise as a whole emphasizes the need of repetition, practice and drill work in the process of learning.

Revised Second and Third Laws

In the later years of his life, Thorndike changed his stand on the laws of exercise and effect.

He experimented upon a blindfolded man who was asked to draw a line of 3 inches in length. Mere repetition did not bring any change or improvement. So, he concluded that practice without rewarding the response was meaningless, which follows that in the process of learning, connections get strengthened by being rewarded and not by just occurring.

Regarding the law of effect, he concluded that rewards and punishment were not equal and opposite in effect. Though rewards strengthen the connection considerably, punishment does not weaken the connection to the same degree. The intensity and speed of reward in casting influence upon learning is greater than that of punishment. It also brings healthy and desirable improvement in the personality of the child. In this way, he began to give more importance to rewards and praise in place of punishment and blame.

All these three laws—law of readiness, law of effect and law of exercise—have a wide field of application in the teaching-learning process. These laws imply the truth of the well-known proverbs and maxims like "You can lead a horse to water but you cannot make him drink," or "Nothing succeeds like success," or "Practice makes a man perfect."

Some More Laws of Learning Given By Thorndike

(i) **Law of multiple response or varied reactions:** The law implies that when an individual is confronted with a new situation, he responds in a variety of ways before arriving at the correct response.

(ii) **Law of attitude:** Learning is guided by a total attitude or 'set' of the organism. The learner performs the task properly if he has developed a healthy attitude towards the task.

(iii) **Law of analogy:** An individual responds to a new situation on the basis of the responses made by him in similar situations in the past. He makes responses by comparison or analogy.

(iv) **Law of associative shifting:** The law states: "*We can get any response from the learner of which he is capable, associated with any situation to which he is sensitive.*"

In other words, any response, which is possible, can be linked with any stimulus. Thorndike clarified his stand through one of his experiments in which he demonstrated how a cat can be trained to stand up at command. He explained that first of all, a bit of fish is dangled before the cat while you say "Stand up". After enough trials, there will be a stage when you would not need the help of the fish. The verbal signal or command will alone evoke the response. The idea put through this law gave birth to a new theory of learning known as the Theory of Conditioning.

Educational Implications of Thorndike's Theory and His Various Laws of Learning

Thorndike's theory of trial and error has enough educational significance. It tries to explain the process of learning carefully on the basis of actual experiments performed. Not only the animals but human learning also, to a great extent, follow the path of trial and error. A child while confronted with a mathematical problem tries many possibilities of its solution before he arrives at the correct one. Even the discoveries and inventions in the various fields of knowledge are the results of the trial and error process.

For example, let us take the discovery made by Archimedes that is today a well-known principle. He was confronted with a problem given by his emperor. There was a *Drive* that he would be beheaded if he could not get the solution of the problem. There was a *Block*, as he could not think of any solution. The problem was difficult. He went on experimenting and made a number of attempts (trials) to find the solution. One day while taking his bath, he got *Chance success* in one of his attempts that led to the formulation of the law of floating bodies.

However, excessive use of the trial and error method, without caring for the development of understanding should not be encouraged in any circumstances. We cannot reduce human learning as mechanical and blindfolded as advocated by this theory. It must be supported by reason, understanding and insight. Trials and practice coupled with insight will make the process of learning more effective than either of the methods adopted alone.

As far as the Thorndike's laws of learning are concerned, it goes without saying that Thorndike has done a valuable service to the field of learning and teaching by providing these laws. These laws imply the following things in general:

1. In the process of teaching and learning, the main task of the teacher is to see what things he wants his students to remember or forget. After this, he must try to strengthen the bonds or connections between the stimuli and responses of those things, which are to be remembered, through repetition, drill and reward. For forgetting, the connections should be weakened through disuse and annoying results.
2. The child must be made ready to learn. His interest, attitude and mental preparation is essential for the smooth sailing in the teaching-learning process.
3. It is also emphasized that past experiences and learning give an adequate base for new learning. Therefore, the teacher should try to make use of the previous knowledge and experiences of the students. The child must also be encouraged to see similarities and dissimilarities between the different kinds of responses to stimuli and with the help of comparison and contrast should try to apply the learning of something in one situation to other similar situations.
4. The child should be encouraged to do his work independently. He must try the various solutions of the problem before arriving at a correct one. But every care should be taken to see that he does not waste his time and energy. He should not be allowed to repeat his mistakes and proceed blindly without using his reasoning and thinking powers and utilizing the past experiences.

In short, Thorndike's theory and laws of learning have contributed a lot to the educational theory and practice. It has made learning purposeful and goal-directed and has brought motivation in the forefront. It has also given impetus to the work of practice, drill and repetition and realized the psychological importance of rewards and praise in the process of teaching and learning.

WATSON & PAVLOV'S CLASSICAL CONDITIONING

After performing various experiments on subjects like dogs, rats and cats, psychologists like Watson and Pavlov gave birth to a new theory of learning known as Conditioned Response Theory or simply as Learning by Conditioning. To understand 'conditioning' and what implies this theory, it is desirable to have an idea of the type of experiments performed by these psychologists.

Experiment by Pavlov: In one of the experiments, Pavlov kept a dog hungry for a night and then tied him on to the experimental table which was fitted with certain mechanically controlled devices as shown in Fig. 17.2. The dog was made comfortable and distractions were excluded as far as possible. The observer kept himself hidden from the view of the dog but was able to view the experiment by means of a set of mirrors. Arrangement was made to give food to the dog through automatic devices. According to the arrangement, every time the food was presented before the dog, a bell also rang. When the food was put before the dog and the bell was rung, there was automatic secretion of saliva from the dog's mouth. The activity of presenting the food accompanied with ringing of bell was repeated several times and the amount of saliva secreted measured.

Fig. 17.2 Diagramatic view of the experiment conducted by Pavlov.

After several trials, the dog was given no food but the bell was rung. In this case also, the amount of saliva secreted was recorded and measured. It was found that even in the absence of food (the neutral stimulus), the ringing of the bell (an artificial stimulus) caused the dog to secrete the saliva (natural response).

On the basis of such experiments, Pavlov considered learning as a habit formation based on the principle of association and substitution. It is simply a stimulus-response type of learning where in place of a natural stimulus like food, water, sexual contact etc, artificial stimulus like sound of the bell, sight of light of a definite colour etc. can evoke a natural response. When both the artificial or neutral stimulus (ringing of the bell) and natural stimulus (food) are brought together, several times, the dog becomes habituated or conditioned to respond to this situation. There becomes perfect association between the types of stimuli presented together. As a result, after some time natural stimulus can be substituted or replaced by an artificial stimulus and this artificial stimulus is able to evoke the natural response.

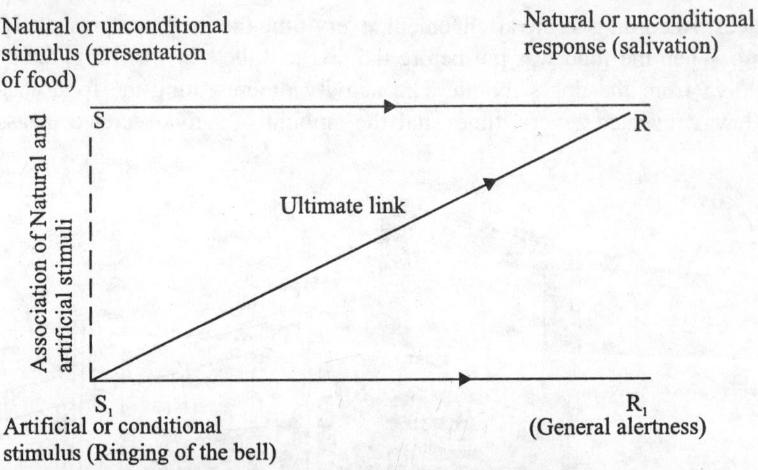

Fig. 17.3 Diagrammatic presentation of the Pavlov's experiment.

In this experiment, the dog learned to salivate at the sound of the bell. This kind of learning was named as Learning by conditioning.

Another experiment: In one of the experiments done by Watson, the subject was a human baby of 11 months. The baby named Albert was given a rabbit to play with. The baby liked it very much and was pleased to touch its fur. He carefully watched the pleasant responses of the baby. After some time in the course of the experiment, as soon as the baby touched the rabbit a loud noise was produced to frighten the baby. The baby was frightened. Every time he tried to touch the rabbit, the loud noise was produced and he gave fear response. After some time he began to fear the rabbit, even if no loud noise accompanied it. In this way, he learned to fear the rabbit through conditioning.

From these experiments, Watson, Pavlov and other concluded that all types of learning can be explained through the process of conditioning. What is this process, can be understood through the following conclusion:

It is a learning process whereby an artificial stimulus is able to behave like a natural stimulus when both natural and artificial stimuli are presented together. In this kind of learning, association plays a great role since the individual responds to an artificial stimulus because he associates it with the natural stimulus.

The conditioning theory of learning put forward by Watson and Pavlov actually involves the conditioning of the respondent behaviour through a process of stimulus association and substitution. Here the responses of the learner become so much conditioned—behaving in the same way or responding similarly to a similar situation—that he does not care for the natural stimuli for evoking the related natural response. As a result the new substituted stimulus behaves like original stimulus and is able to evoke the desired response.

Educational Implications of the Theory of Conditioning

The phenomenon of conditioning does not limit itself to such laboratory experiments only. The day-to-day learning at home, school etc. consists of plenty of examples where a child learns through conditioning.

Fear, love and hatred towards different subjects are created through conditioning. A mathematics teacher, with his defective methods of teaching or improper behaviour, may be disliked by students or by a particular student. If he, without caring to know the basic reason, always rebukes and punishes the child while assessing his assignments, the child gradually begins to fear home assignments of any sort. He also develops a distaste and hatred towards the subject mathematics.

On the contrary, sympathetic treatment given by a teacher and his interesting and effective methodology can have a desirable impact on the students through the process of conditioning. They would develop a positive attitude towards the subject and love their teacher as well as the subject taught by him.

The use of audio-visual aids in the teaching-learning process involves the conditioning theory in making the students learn so many things. The child gets an idea of a particular object or phenomenon through these aids. For example, the teacher shows him the picture of a cat, along with the written word 'cat'. The teacher speak out 'cat' with the picture of the cat and sound of the word.

In developing desirable habits, interests, attitudes, sense of appreciation in the children, the conditioning process may help the teachers and parents a lot. Not only it helps in the development of proper behaviour in them, but is also helpful in removing so many bad habits like unhealthy attitudes, superstition, fear and phobias, through de-conditioning. A child who fears a particular object can be made to seek pleasure from it. Another child who thinks it dangerous if a cat crosses his way can be made to give up his belief. In this way, the conditioning theory throws light on many aspects of learning and helps the teacher and the parents in their task.

SKINNER'S OPERANT CONDITIONING

Although classified and included in the category of conditioning, operant conditioning differs a lot from the classical conditioning advocated by Pavlov and Watson. The most outstanding difference lies in the order related with the initiation and response, i.e. stimulus response mechanism. In classical conditioning the organism is passive. It must wait for something to happen for responding. The presence of a stimulus for evoking a response is essential. The behaviour cannot be emitted in the absence of a cause. The child expresses fear only when he hears a loud noise, the dog waits for food to arrive before salivating. In each of these instances, the subject has no control over the happening. He is made to behave in response to the stimulus situations. Thus the behaviour is said to be initiated by the environment, the organism simply responds.

Skinner opposed the "no stimulus, no response" mechanism in the evolution of behaviour. He argued that in practical situations, we cannot always wait for things to happen in the environment. Men is not a victim of the environment. He may often manipulate the things in the environment with his own initiative. Therefore, it is not always essential that there is some known stimuli or cause for evoking a response. Quite often, most of our responses can not be attributed to a known stimulus. The organism itself initiates the behaviour. A dog, a child, or an individual "does" something, "behaves" in some manner, it "operates" on the environment and in turn, the environment responds to the activity. How the environment responds to the activity, rewarding or not, largely determines whether the behaviour will be repeated, maintained or avoided.

A question may arise as to where Skinner got the clue for such ideas. Definitely, it was from the studies and observations of an earlier psychologist named Edward Lee Thorndike. Through his experiments, for propagating his famous trial and error theory of learning, Thorndike concluded that the rewards of a response (like getting food by the cat after a chance success through randomized movements) leads to repetition of an act and the strengthening of S-R associations. These conclusions made Skinner begin a series of experiments to find the consequences of the rewards in repeating and maintaining behaviour. Based on the findings of his experiments, he concluded that "behaviour is shaped and maintained by its consequences. It is operated by the organism and maintained by its result." The occurrence of such behaviour was named as operant behaviour and the process of learning that plays the part in learning such behaviour was named by him as operant conditioning.

For understanding what Skinner propagated through his theory of operant conditioning, let us try to build a base by defining and explaining some of the concepts used by him for bringing out his theory.

Respondent and Operant Behaviour

As we have seen, the earlier theories of learning assumed the existence of a known stimulus as a necessary pre-requisite for evoking a response. Skinner, first time, got the idea that most of the responses could not be attributed to a known stimuli. He defined two types of responses – the one 'elicited' by known stimuli which he called as 'Respondent behaviour' and the other 'emitted' by the unknown stimuli which he called as 'Operant behaviour'. Examples of respondent behaviour may include all reflexes such as jerking one's hands when jabbed with a pin and the papillary constriction on account of bright light or salivation in the presence of food.

In the respondent behaviour, the stimulus preceding the response is responsible for causing the behaviour. On the other hand, in the operant behaviour the stimulus causing such behaviour is unknown and it is not important to know the cause of the behaviour. Here it is not the stimulus but the consequences of the behaviour which are more important and hence the operant behaviour is controlled by the strength of its consequences instead of stimuli. Examples of such behaviour may include the behaviour like moving one's hand, arms or legs arbitrarily, a child abandoning one toy in favour of the other, eating a meal, writing a letter, standing up and walking about and similar other everyday activities.

Operant

Skinner considers an operant as a set of acts that constitutes an organism's doing something, e.g. raising its head, walking about, pushing a lever, etc.

Reinforcer and Reinforcement

The concept of reinforcement is identical to the presentation of a reward. A reinforcer is the stimulus whose presentation or removal increases the probability of the recurrence of a response. Skinner thinks of two kinds of reinforcer—positive and negative.

A positive reinforcer is any stimulus the introduction or presentation of which increases the likelihood of a particular behaviour. Food, water, sexual contact, etc., are classified as positive reinforces. A negative reinforcer is any stimulus the removal or withdrawal of which increases the likelihood of a particular behaviour. Electric shock, a loud noise, etc, are said to be negative reinforcers.

The schedules of reinforcement

Skinner put forward the idea of planning of Schedules of reinforcement of conditioning the operant behaviour of the organism. The important schedules are as under:

Continuous Reinforcement Schedule: It is a hundred per cent reinforcement schedule where provision is made to reinforce or reward every correct response of the organism during acquisition of learning. For example, a student may be rewarded for every correct answer he gives to the questions or problems put by his teacher.

Fixed Interval Reinforcement Schedule: In this schedule the organism is rewarded for a response made only after a set interval of time, e.g. every 3 or every 5 minutes. The many times he has given correct response during this fixed interval of time does not matter; it is only on the expiry of the fixed interval, that he is presented with some reinforcement.

Fixed Ratio Reinforcement Schedule: In this schedule, the reinforcement is given after a fixed number of response. A rat, for example, might be given a pallet of food after a certain number of lever presses. A student may be properly rewarded after answering a fixed number of questions, say 3 or 5. Fixed ratio schedule is used in some factories, and by employers of casual workers or labourer where salary is paid on a piecework basis, number of garments sewn and number of baskets of fruit packed.

Variable Reinforcement Schedule: When reinforcement is given at varying intervals of time or after a varying number or responses, it is called a variable reinforcement schedule. In this case reinforcement is intermittent or irregular. The individual does not know when he is going to be rewarded and consequently he remains motivated throughout the learning process in the wait of reinforcement. The most common example of such schedule in human behaviour is the reinforcement operation schedules of gambling devices. Here rewards are unpredictable and keep the players well-motivated through occasional returns.

Conclusion about the various Reinforcement Schedules

Reinforcement and its schedules play a key role in the conditioning of operant behaviour and acquisition of a learning. While a continuous reinforcement schedule increases the response rate, the discontinuation or reinforcement may result in the extinction of that response or behaviour. Continuous reinforcement schedule thus yields least resistance to extinction and the lowest response rate during learning. Therefore, learning of a response takes place quickly if every correct response is rewarded, but it is easily forgotten when the reinforcement is stopped. If reinforcement is given after a varying number of correct responses or at varying intervals of time, the response is remarkably resistant to extinction. However, the fixed interval reinforcement schedules are found to provide the lowest yield in terms of performance as the individual may soon learn to respond correctly only when the time or turn of reinforcement arrives. Similarly, he may lose interest in getting reinforcement after a fixed interval or fixed number of correct responses. Weighing all these properly, Skinner suggests to begin with 100 per cent schedule, practice the fixed interval or fixed ratio schedule and finally arrive at the variable reinforcement schedule for better results in learning or training.

Defining Operant Conditioning

Operant conditioning refers to a *kind of learning process whereby a response is made more probable or more frequent by reinforcement.* It helps in the learning of operant behaviour, the behaviour that is not necessarily associated with a known stimuli.

Distinction between Classical and Operant Conditioning

Classical or respondent conditioning is based on respondent behaviour. Specifically, it deals with responses that invariably follow a specific stimulus and are thus elicited e.g., blinking at bright light, jumping at an electric shock, salivation to the test of food, and so forth. In this, greater importance is attached to the stimulus for eliciting the desired response. Hence, it is also called S type conditioning.

On the other hand, operant conditioning helps in conditioning or learning of operant behaviour—behaviour that is emitted (rather than elicited). The organism seems to initiate operant behaviour on his own without a single, explicit, proceeding stimulus. In this type of learning, much emphasis is placed on the response rather than the stimulus causing the response. That is why, it is also named as type R conditioning. In type S conditioning, the problem for the trainer or teacher is in selecting appropriate stimuli for evoking desired response. On the other hand in R type conditioning, out of many responses which an organism is capable of giving, the problem for the trainer or teacher is to evoke only the appropriate responses and then fix them properly with the help of suitable reinforcement.

The difference between these two types of conditioning may thus be summarized as follows:

Classical respondent conditioning	*Operant conditioning*
1. It helps in the learning of respondent behaviour.	1. It helps in the learning of operant behaviour.
2. It is called type S conditioning to emphasize the importance of the stimulus in eliciting desired response.	2. It is called type R conditioning because of the emphasis on the response.
3. In this type of conditioning, beginning is made with the help of specific stimulus that brings certain responses.	3. Here beginning is made with the responses as they occur "naturally" or unnaturally shaping them into existence.
4. Here strength of conditioning is usually determined by the magnitude of the conditioned response *i.e.* the amount of saliva (as in the case of classical experiment of Pavlov with dog).	4. Here strength of conditioning is shown by the response *i.e.* the rate with which an operant response occurs as a result of some reinforcement.

SKINNER'S EXPERIMENTS REGARDING OPERANT CONDITIONING

B.F. Skinner conducted a series of experiments with animals. For his experiments with rats, he designed a special apparatus known as Skinner's Box. It was a much modified form of the puzzle box used by Thorndike for his experiments with cats. The darkened soundproof box mainly consists of a grid floor, a system of light or sound produced at the time of delivering a pallet of food in the food cup, a lever and a food cup. It is arranged such that when a rat (hungry or thirsty) presses the lever, the feeder mechanism is activated, a light or a special sound is produced and a small pellet of food (or small drops of water) is released into the food cup. To record the observations of the experiment, the lever is connected with a recording system that produces a graphical tracing of the lever pressings against the length of time the rat is in the box (Fig. 17.4).

Skinner, in one of his initial experiments, placed a hungry rat in the above described box. In this experiment pressing the bar in a certain way by the rat could result in the production of a click sound and emergence of a food pellet. The click sound acted as a cue or signal indicating to the rat that if it responded by going to the food cup, it would be rewarded. The rat was rewarded for each proper pressing of the lever. The lever press response having been rewarded, the rat repeated it and when it was rewarded again, it further increased the probability of the repetition of the lever press response and so it continued. In this way, ultimately the rat learned the art of pressing the lever as desired by the experimenter.

Fig. 17.4 A rat in a Skinner box.

In his experiments with pigeons, Skinner made use of another specific apparatus called the 'pigeon's box' (Fig. 17.5). In this experiment if the pigeon pecked at a lighted plastic key mounted on the wall at head high, it was consequently rewarded with grain.

Fig. 17.5 A pigeon in an operant conditioning box.

With the help of such experiments, Skinner put forward his theory of operant conditioning for learning not only the simple responses like pressing the lever but also for learning the most difficult and complex series of responses.

Mechanism of Operant Conditioning

Operant conditioning as emphasized earlier is correlated with operant behaviour. An operant is a set of acts that constitutes an organism's doing something. Hence, the process in operant conditioning may start with the responses as they occur naturally or at random. In case they do not occur naturally, then attempts may be made for shaping them into existence. How it can be done will be explained later on in this chapter under the heading "Shaping".

Once a response (as desired by the trainer, experimenter or teacher) occurs, it is reinforced through a suitable reinforcer (primary or secondary, positive or negative). In due course, this response gets conditioned by constantly reinforcing it. In Skinner's experiment, a pellet of food worked as a positive primary reinforcer for the hungry rat. He got the reinforcement after emitting a certain response (pressing of the lever as desired by the experimenter). The secondary reinforcement may also produce the results same as brought about by the primary reinforcement. It is a sort of neutral stimulus which acquires the reinforcing properties (rewarding value) after getting paired or associated with a primary reinforcer (e.g., food or water). The clicking of a sound and lighting of a bulb in Skinner's experiment may work as secondary reinforcement if they are paired with the appearance of a pellet of food.

The important thing in the mechanism of operant conditioning is the emission of a desired response and its proper management through suitable reinforcement. Here, the organism is to respond in such a way so as to produce the reinforcing stimulus. The subsequent reinforcement gradually conditions the organism to emit the desired response and thus learn the desired act.

SHAPING

There are situations, especially in case of the acquisition of complex behaviour and learning of difficult skills, etc., where there may arise very remote chances of occurrence. In such cases, waiting for an organism to behave in specific way at random (the natural occurrence) may take a lifetime. For example, the chances of a pigeon dancing in a specific way are extremely remote. The same holds true for a child learning a foreign language or even table manners. In these situations, where the desired responses do not occur at random (or naturally), efforts are made for eliciting the appropriate responses. It is done by building a chain of responses through a step-by-step process called "shaping."

In one of his experiments for shaping the behaviour of a pigeon—to teach it to walk in a figure eight—Skinner watched its activity and gave it a small amount of grain (reward) for simply turning in proper direction. At first the pigeon got his reward for simply turning its head in the right direction, then for taking a step in the right direction, then for making the correct turn, and so on, until it had learned to do a complete figure eight.

Shaping in this way, may be used as a successful technique for making individuals learn difficult and complex behaviour and also for introducing desirable modifications in the behaviour. Behaviour modification technique and aversive therapy used in treating the problem behaviour and abnormality have come into existence through the use of shaping of behaviour mechanism.

Implications of the Theory of Operant Conditioning

Theory of operant conditioning has revolutionized the field of training or learning by bringing forward the following practical ideas and implications:

1. A response or a behaviour is not necessarily dependent (contingent) upon a specific known stimulus. It is more correct to consider that a behaviour or response is dependent upon its

consequences. Therefore, for training an organism to learn a particular behaviour or response, he may be initiated to respond in such a way so as to produce the reinforcing stimulus. His behaviour should be rewarded and in turn, he should again act in such a way that he is rewarded and so on. Therefore, the learning or training process and environment must be designed such that it creates minimum frustration and maximum satisfaction to a learner to provide him proper reinforcement for the desired training or learning.

2. The principle of operant conditioning may be successfully applied in the task of behaviour modification. We have to find something which is rewarding for the individual whose behaviour we wish to modify, wait until the desire behaviour occurs and immediately reward him when it happens. When this is done, the rate with which the desired response occurs goes up. When the behaviour occurs for a next time, it is again rewarded, and the rate of responding goes up further. Continuing in the same way, we will induce the individual to learn the desired behaviour.
3. The task of the development of human personality can be successfully manipulated through operant conditioning. According to Skinner, *"We are what we have been rewarded for being. What we call personality is nothing more than consistent behaviour patterns that summarize our reinforcement history. We learn to speak English, for example, because we have been rewarded for approximating the sounds of the English language in our early home environment. If we happened to be brought up in a Japanese or a Russian home, we would learn to speak Japanese or Russian because when we approximately sound in that language, we would have been attended to or rewarded in some other way".* (Hergenhahn, 1976, p. 87).
4. The theory of operant conditioning does not attribute motivation to internal processes within an organism. It takes for granted the consequences of a behaviour or response as a source of motivation to further occurrence of that behaviour. Food is reinforcing to a rat or a pigeon. Knowledge of correct response is reinforcing to a learner. Secondary reinforcers also prove very important sources of motivation for a learner. Verbal praise, positive facial expressions of the trainer or teacher, feeling of success, scores, grades, prizes, medals and the opportunity to do the work of one's liking, all constitute good motivator. In this way operant conditioning provides an external approach to motivation.
5. Operant conditioning lays stress on the importance of schedules in the process of reinforcement of behaviour. Therefore, in trying to train or learn behaviour, great care is to be taken for the proper planning of the schedules of reinforcement.
6. This theory advocates the avoidance of punishment for unlearning the undesirable behaviour and for shaping the desirable behaviour. Punishment proves ineffective in the long run. It appears that punishment simply suppresses behaviour and when the threat of punishment is removed, behaviour returns to its original level. Therefore, operant conditioning experiments suggested rewarding the appropriate behaviour and ignoring the inappropriate behaviour for its gradual extinction.
7. In its most effective application, theory of operant conditioning has contributed a lot towards the development of teaching machines and programmed learning. The theory of operant conditioning has led us to think that learning proceeds most effectively if—
   (i) The learning material is so designed that it creates less opportunities for facing failure and more opportunities for gaining success
   (ii) the learner is given rapid feedback regarding the accuracy in his learning, and
   (iii) the learner is able to learn at his own pace.

These principles originating from operant conditioning have revolutionized the training and learning programmes. As a result, mechanical learning in the form of teaching machines and computer-assisted instructions have replaced the usual classroom instructions.

KOHLER'S INSIGHT THEORY

The learning theory named as "Learning by Insight" is the contribution of Gestalt Psychologists. *Gestalt Psychology* began with the work of German psychologists who were studying the nature of perception. Wertheimer is generally considered to be the Gestalt Psychology's founding father. Wertheimer, Kohler, Koffka and Lewin—all four of these men, originally German, eventually settled in America—are the leaders of what is historically *Gestalt Psychology.*

"Gestalt" is a German noun for which there is no English word equivalent so the term was carried over in English psychological literature. The nearest English translation of Gestalt is *'configuration'* or more simply *'an organized whole'* in contrast to a collection or parts. Gestalt psychologists consider the process of learning as a gestalt—an organized whole. A thing cannot be understood by the study of its constituent parts but only by the study of it as a totality—is a basic idea behind this theory.

In practical sense, Gestalt Psychology is primarily concerned with the nature of perception. According to it, an individual perceives the thing as a whole while the behaviourists and Stimulus-Response theorists define perception in such a way as to make it analogous with taking photographs. They think that sensation comes prior to meaning and consider these two acts as separate. But the Gestalt psychologists do not separate sensation of an object from its meaning. They are of the opinion that unless a person sees some meaning in an object he will pay little or no attention to it. Furthermore, to a Gestalt psychologist, the meaning of sensation or perception is always related to the total situation. According to them, perception always involves a problem of organization. A thing is perceived as a relationship within a field which includes the thing, the viewer and complex background incorporating the viewer's purposes and previous experience.

Gestalt psychologists tried to interpret learning as a purposive, exploratory and creative enterprise instead of trial and error or simple stimulus-response mechanism. Learner, while learning, always perceives the situation as a whole and after seeing and evaluating the different relationships intelligently takes a proper decision. He always responds in terms of proper relationship rather than specific stimulus. Gestalt Psychology used the term 'insight' to describe the perception of the whole situation by the learner and of his intelligence in responding to the proper relationships. Kohler, first of all, used this term (insight) to describe the learning of his apes. Kohler conducted many experiments on chimpanzees and brought out a book 'Mentality of Apes' in 1925 which was the result of his experiments, conducted during the period 1913-17 on the Canary Island. These experiments, show learning by insight. Some of them are given below:

(i) In one experiment, Kohler put a chimpanzee Sultan inside a cage and a banana was hung from the roof of the cage. A box was placed inside the cage. The chimpanzee tried to reach the banana by jumping but could not succeed. Suddenly, he got an idea and used the box as a jumping platform by placing it just below the hanging banana.

(ii) In other experiment, Kohler made this problem more difficult. Now it required two or three boxes to reach the banana. Moreover, the placing of one box over the other required different specific arrangements.

(iii) In a more complicated experiment, banana was placed outside the cage of the chimpanzee. Two sticks, one larger than the other, were placed inside the cage. One was hollow at one end so that the other stick could be thrust into it to form a longer stick. The banana was so kept that it could not be picked up by one of the sticks (Fig. 17.6).

The chimpanzee first tried these sticks one after the other but failed. Suddenly, he got a bright idea. The animal joined the two sticks together and reached the banana. In these experiments, Kohler used many different chimpanzees. Sultan, who was the most intelligent of Kohler's chimpanzees, could solve all the problems. Other chimpanzees could solve the problems only when they saw Sultan solving them.

With such experiments, Kohler concluded that in the solution of problems, his apes did not resort to blind trial and error mechanism. They solved their problems intelligently. Kohler used the term 'Insight' to describe the learning of his apes.

Fig. 17.6 Kohler's experiment on chimpanzee Sultan (Learning to assemble a long stick from two shorter ones).

Insight involves the following criteria:

(a) The situation as a whole is perceived by the learner.

(b) The learner tries to see and judge the relationship between various factors involved in the situation.

(c) As a result, the learner is helped in the sudden grasping of the solution of the problem.

On similar line, other experiments were also conducted by the Gestalt psychologists. All the experiments have shown that at some stage there is a new organization of the perceptual field resulting in sudden discovery of the solution. Therefore, learning according to them is re-structuring the field of perception through insight. As a whole, insight depends upon the following factors:

(a) Experience: Past experiences help in the insightful solution of the problems. A child cannot solve the problems of modern mathematics unless he is well-acquainted with its symbolic languages.

(b) **Intelligence:** Insightful solution depends upon the basic intelligence of the learner. More intelligent an individual is, greater will be his insight.

(c) **Learning situation:** How insightfully the organism will react, depends upon the situation in which he has to act. Some situations are more favourable than others for insightful solution. As a common observation, insight occurs when the learning situation is so arranged that all the necessary aspects are open for observation.

(d) **Initial efforts:** Insightful learning has to pass through the process of trial and error. But this stage does not last long. These initial efforts, in the form of simple trial and error mechanism, open the way for insightful learning.

(e) **Repetition and Generalization:** After having an insightful solution of a particular type of problem, the organism tries to repeat it in another situation, demanding similar type of solution. The way found in one situation helps him to react insightfully in the other identical situations.

Educational Implication of the Theory of Insightful Learning

This theory brings the following important facts into limelight:

1. The whole is greater than the parts and, therefore, the situation should be viewed as a whole.
2. The use of blind fumbling and mechanical trial and error should be minimized. The learner should try to see relevant relationships and act intelligently.
3. The purpose or motive plays the central role in the learning process.

Based on the appeal of this theory, teachers are required to pay attention to the following aspects:

- Subject-matter (learning material) should be presented in Gestalt form. While teaching the topic, parts of a flowering plant or flower, it should not be started by presenting the different parts. Initially the plant or flower as a whole should be presented before them and later on the parts should be emphasized. The problem of mathematics requiring solution should be presented as a whole and after grasping it as a whole, it should be tried for the solution.
- In the organization of the syllabus and planning of the curriculum, the Gestalt principle should be given due consideration. A particular subject should not be treated as the mere collection of isolated facts or topics. It should be closely integrated into a whole. Similarly, the curriculum, comprising different subjects and activities, should reflect unity and cohesiveness.
- This theory has brought 'motivation' in the forefront by assigning purpose and motive, the central role in learning process. The child should be motivated by arousing his interest and curiosity and he should be well acquainted with the specific aims and purpose of his learning.
- The greater contribution of the insight theory of learning is that it has made learning an intelligent task requiring mental abilities instead of blind fumbling and automatic responses to specific stimuli. It has called a halt to age-old mechanical memorization, drill and practice work which lack in basic understanding and use of thinking, reasoning and creative mental powers.

LEWIN'S FIELD THEORY OF LEARNING

Kurt Lewin born in 1890 was a German psychologist who eventually settled in USA and worked as professor at the Stanford University and University of IOWA. He is most renowned for his development of the field theory based on his doctoral dissertation. It was propounded by him in the year 1917.

In simple words, the field theory propagated by him proposes that human behaviour *is the function of both the persons and the environment expressed in symbolic term;* B = f (P.E.) *'Lewin'* in his own terminology symbolized 'P' for a psychological person (note not just the biological organism) and 'E' for his psychological environment (not the physical and social environment as exists) and 'f' for the field or life space denoting the interaction of the psychological person with his psychological environment.

His system of describing human behaviour and learning is based mainly on three key concepts and terms

(i) Life space,
(ii) Vectors and Valences, and
(iii) Topology

Let us try to know first about these terms and their concepts.

Life Space

The life space of person is also known as the psychological field. According to Lewin's basic behaviour formula, i.e. B = f (P.E.), the psychological field or life space (f) is nothing but the result of the interaction between a psychological person (P) and his psychological environment (E).

Let us make it more clear by considering what is meant by the terms psychological person and psychological environment here. Psychological person as Lewin advocates should not be considered (under no circumstances) a person identical with a biological organism. A person is neither limited to a mind or body nor a mind and body. He is in fact a conscious self. It is why a person in his life space represents complete human being in a given situation. It represents his psychological self expressed as "I" or "me". He could not be seen in isolation of his psychological environment simply because it is only his environment and its psychological perception that helps him in the emergence and evolution of his self throughout his life. Diagrammatically a psychological person (P) is always represented as point P moving about in his life space, affected by pulls and pushes and overcoming the barriers in the way of reaching his goal.

Psychological environment

Ordinarily we mean by one's environment everything external to him in physical and social context that may affect his learning, development or behaviour at one or the other time. Lewin tried to assert that one's psychological environment should not be taken as identical with that of his physical and social environment. It is not one's physical and social environment but rather its perception that matters much to an individual for behaving in a particular situation. Therefore, perceived situation and the psychological meanings derived by the person out of the available physical and social environment (affecting him psychologically) must be taken as his psychological environment at a particular moment in a given situation.

Now we can attempt to understand one's life space or psychological field.

A psychological person now interacts with psychological environment for the formation of his psychological field or life space at a particular moment in a given environmental situation related to his life. In a life space a person and his environment are in the constant stage of mutual interaction and mutual independence. One can't exist and function without the other. A life space is surrounded by a foreign hull–the aspects of the physical and social environment which, to that person at that particular moment, are not psychological, i.e. not included in his psychological environment. However, as and when this aspect of the physical and social environment previously termed as foreign hull, becomes the subject of his psychological environment and the psychological person begins to interact with it, it becomes a part and parcel of his life space. The foreign hull is very much a part of one's physical and social environment but as long as it does not become a subject of interaction with the psychological person, it can't be included into one's life space. For example, there is definitely a snake in the corner of a room. It is observable by the one studying the particular person but for the person being studied at the moment this snake does not exist. It may lie in the boundaries or foreign hull of his life space but at the present moment it is not there in his life space. As and when the situation changes it may emerge into his perception by coming out through the boundaries of foreign hull and then becomes a part of his life space. Therefore, in a nut shell one's life space at a particular moment may be termed *the space in which one lives psychologically at that moment involving one's own perception and depicting one's own view point.* It includes each and every object, person or idea with which one is concerned at a given time in relation to his goal, and the incentives and barriers one faces for reaching the goal (see Fig. 17.7).

Therefore, perception is the key concept and core element in the definition and understanding of one's life space. How does one react to his environment or his self interacts with the perceived environment constitutes his life space at a particular moment. The life space of an individual with all its characteristics as advocated by Lewin can be represented by Fig. 17.7.

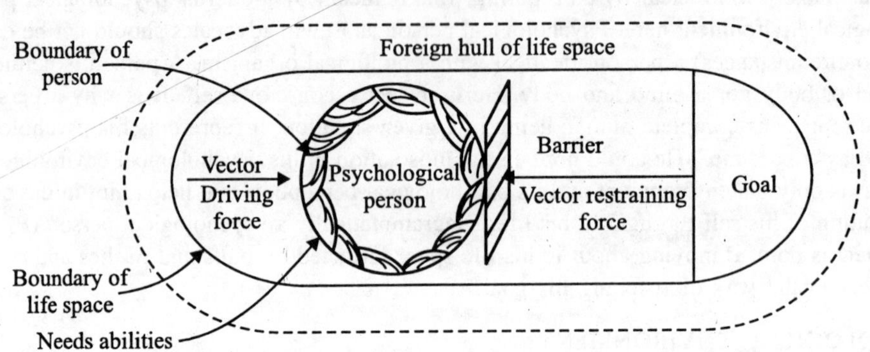

Fig. 17.7 Life space of an individual according to Lewin.

Let us now try to analyze the above diagram depicting one's life space at a particular moment in a given situation.

(i) A psychological person with his needs and abilities has been shown by a centrally closed circular figure.

(ii) He has in his life space his self, his psychological environment, driving forces and restraining force (on account of the barrier) for attaining his goal.

(iii) Foreign hull of his life space just lies outside the boundary of his life space in a concentric order.

(iv) One's life space, including his foreign hull, may provide base for his behaviour, learning and developmental pattern at a particular moment in a given situation.

Vectors and Valences

The term 'vectors' and 'valences' were borrowed by Lewin from mechanics and physics. He used the term vector is his field theory for representing a force capable of influencing movement towards or away from the goal. In case there is only one vector (force) then the movement must be in the direction of the vector but if there are two or more vectors (forces) simultaneously acting in different directions (some pulling and some pushing) then the resultant vector arising out of the vectors in action will decide the direction as well as the magnitude of the movement towards or away from the goal. The outcome of the vectors (driving or restraining forces) are thus able to predict dynamics of a relation—What is happening or is likely to happen in term of the likewise changes introduced in one's life space at a particular time in a given situation?

With regard to the concept of valences it can be said that Lewin used two types of valences—positive (+ve) and negative (–ve) for describing their power of attraction and repulsion. According to him, when a person is attracted by a goal or a region of his life space, that goal or region is said to have a positive valence. On the other hand if he is repelled, the goal or region of the life space possesses a negative valence. Consequently, the person is likely to be pulled along or pushed away by the positive or negative valence inherent in the region of his life space or goal.

Topology

The term topology was borrowed by Lewin from the field of mathematics. In mathematics, this concept is employed to describe the relative position of geometrical figures in a space using terms like inside, outside and boundary. In this way, topologically things may be described as next to, inside or outside one another instead of their usual description in terms of length, breadth, thickness, area and volume etc. It is why topology makes no difference between a circle, an ellipse, a regular or irregular polygon with any number of sides.

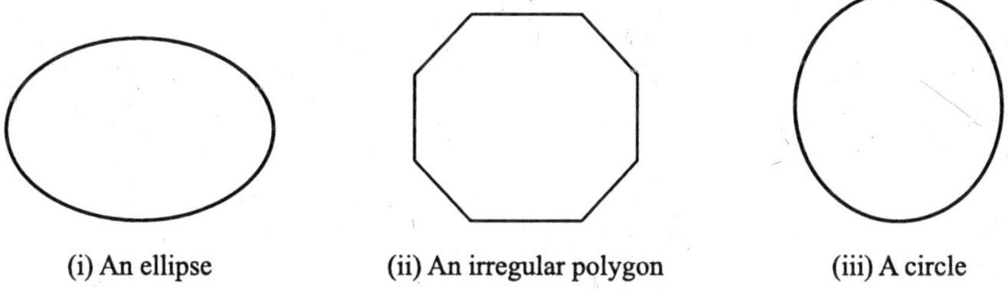

Fig. 17.8 Topologically equivalent figures.

Topologically, there lies no difference among figures (boundary area) drawn above. Their topological equivalence may be well demonstrated through an experiment.

Take a rubber or an elastic band, dip it in a red or blue ink or colour. Now it stretch in the shape of an ellipse, regular or irregular polygon, circle or any geometrical shape you like and place it on the paper for getting various shapes and designs. The figures you will have on paper, will all be considered topologically equivalent to one another (These have been obtained by the same rubber band on being stretched in different ways). Lewin made the best possible use of the above topological concept for representing the structure of life space in such a way as to define the range of possible perceptions and actions. This he achieved by showing the arrangement of functional parts of the life space as several regions and their boundaries and then their restructuring through the equivalent topological figures (product of the various vectors and valences in varying psychological situations).

How does Lewin's Field Theory Explain Learning and its Outcomes?

After getting acquainted with the key concepts used in Lewin's field psychology, let us now study what is conveyed by it for explaining the mechanism of learning and its outcomes. Learning, in its simplest meaning, is known as the change in one's behaviour. The elicitation of behaviour is, however, explained by the field theory in the following way.

According to the field theory, a person in a given situation always lives in his life space. His perception about his life space provides a cognitive structure to his life space. As a result of this cognitive structuring he, at a particular moment and situation, is well aware of his needs, the goal, attraction for attaining the goal and the barrier to attain the goal etc. The perception of situation, i.e. cognition of one's life space in a particular situation at a particular moment, may give birth to a psychological tension in relation to the realization of the felt needs, i.e. attainment of the desired goal. There are two alternatives for the release of his tension either through reaching a goal or through restructuring one's life space, i.e. learning to see things differently (bring change in one's goal or methods of reaching goal). It may be well seen that it is the latter development that makes one to bring changes in the behaviour leading to the process of learning in given situation.

Let us illustrate this point with an example. Suppose a bright and ambitious student in a given situation at a particular time period has an ambition to become an IAS officer. He organizes his life space to attain this goal. He does not get success. Now there lies two alternatives for the release of his tension. He can either repeat the attempt without bringing any change in his life space or reconstruct the life space for attaining the desired end. This reconstruction of the life space may also involve two different channels. One is to bring change in one's method of attempts, ways of studying, preparing and striving to become an IAS officer and the other is to bring changes in the nature of the goal substituting the higher goal with some other attainable goal, i.e. striving for being selected to state cadre like provincial civil services (PCS) or becoming lecturer in a university or a college. In fact such reconstruction of life space is the essence of one's learning process. Learning starts at the moment one feels the need of bringing some changes in his life space and engages oneself in bringing such changes.

So, learning is the cognitive structure (development of new insight or change in the old views) of one's life space needed for achieving a particular goal or needs of an individual at a particular time in a given situation.

Elaborating further, the field theory emphasizes that the changes in cognitive structure (resulting in the processes and products of learning) are generally of three types—differentiation, generalization and restructurization.

Differentiation. This helps in responding to different environments of stimuli in different ways. In the language of psychology, it refers to a process in which regions of one's life space are subdivided into smaller but distinct areas and regions in the life space of the smaller children. As they grow up with the help of learning, these unstructured vague and undefined regions or areas of life space become cognitively structured and thus more distinct and specific. The child can then discriminate and distinguish one thing from the other, i.e. eatable from non eatable, realities from the unrealities of his present environment, past and future, and so on.

Generalization. It is another product that arises gradually from his learning. As a definition, it is referred in psychology as a process of deriving valid conclusions through categorization of sub regions into a unified region of one's life space. When a child learns that bananas, apples, oranges, mangoes are fruits and petrol, diesel, electricity, liquefied or compressed natural gases are the sources of energy, he is said to reach generalization as a result of his learning.

Restructurization. Learning is a never-ending process. Therefore, according to Lewin, the regions and sub-regions of the life space of an individual always remain in a state of continuous organization and reorganization. An individual, therefore, not only differentiates and generalizes his life space into new regions but also remains engaged in restructuring and reorganizing these regions of his life space so as to provide them new meaning for the better understanding of himself and his environment.

Finally as a result of the process of differentiation, generalization and restructurization of the regions of his life space, one may be able to enjoy the fruits of his learning in terms of habit formations, development of thinking and reasoning power, memorization, problem solving ability and intelligence for the benefits of himself and the environment.

In explaining the process and product of one's learning, Lewin field theory has adopted its own terminology and language, let us have a brief discussion on them as below:

1. **Motivation and learning:** Lewin's field theory of learning attaches much significance to motivation in the process of learning. It takes motivation as attraction towards a goal and clarifies its strength through a relative role of valences, the level of aspiration, needs and aroused tension by concluding that the study of ones motivation determines the result of one's learning.
2. **Development of problem solving ability:** In problem solving, learning behaviour, problematic situations faced by an individual represents an unstructured region of his life space. The need of solving the problem generates tension and this tension can be resolved by working for the structuring of his life space, or in other words, reorganization of the field of perception to devise a new insight and understanding to solve the given problem. When this is done, the problem gets solved and the method of solving similar problems can thus be learnt.
3. **Habit Formation:** In the learning of the habit one uses his insight, i.e. the organization and structuring of his life space. He gives a meaning to an event, a sub region of his life space by fully knowing what action will lead to what results in a particular situation. This is the basis of habit formation.
4. **Learning and intelligent behaviour:** By defining all learning as essentially a process of developing cognitive structure or insights, field theory provides great significance to learning for the development of intelligent behaviour. The clarity about the purpose and goal has a greater value for one's learning. It is further enhanced through one's insight, i.e. learning new ways of responding and behaving. The clarity of purpose and using insight thus become the forerunner of one's intelligent behaviour. Accordingly Lewin advocates an intelligent behaviour as that behaviour in which one has the purpose followed by the essential insight for achieving the purpose.

SALIENT FEATURES

Curt Lewin theory of learning is named as cognitive field theory of learning. It differs from other theories like behaviouristic and psychoanalytical theories of learning. Its main distinguished features may be summarized as follows:

- Lewin's field theory does not believe that human learning is pushed and pulled by mechanical forces either of stimuli and reinforcement (as advocated by behaviourists) or of unconscious instructional impulses (as advocated by psychoanalysts).
- This theory represents a realistic (as opposed to an absolutistic or mechanistic) way of viewing the learner and his learning process. Like S.R. associationists and psychoanalysists, it does not consider the learner as a biological organism who learns some or the other thing lying at present in his environment. Rather it has a strong belief that nothing is perceivable or conceivable as a thing in itself and therefore everything needs to be perceived or conceived in relation to other things lying in one's perceptional field.
- In the field of psychology, the learner is termed as a psychological person instead of being considered as a biological organism. He has a definite purpose, a goal for his behaviour and learning. He does not reach his goal through a series of machine-like events/stimulus response chain reaction or through banking upon his past experiences/habits etc, nor is he driven by his instinctive actions and unconscious motivation, etc. He definitely acts purposeful by bringing desirable changes in the cognitive structure of his life space, i.e. using needed insight for perceiving the things in their right perceptive and choosing the right available alternative for reaching the goal.
- Reality in the language of field psychology is not defined in absolute terms as happens in the case of S.R. theorists and scientists. Here reality is one that is perceived by the person himself in relation to his environment at a particular time in a given situation. He perceives the things in his own ways and the meaning given to things through his own perception is the reality concerning these things. Therefore, the situations or environment, internal as well as external conditions, have a great significance in the teaching-learning process as they can make a psychological person to perceive the learning field in one or the other ways depending upon the inherent needs, incentives and barriers for reaching the objectives of learning and getting desired success.
- The term 'behaviour' has a unique meaning in the field psychology. Here it is described, not in physical term (as done by behaviourists and psychologists), but in terms of what exists at a particular moment in a particular situation for the psychological person whose behaviour is under study.
- While S.R. theorists and psychoanalysists tried to make generalized predictions about the learning and behaviour on the lines of what leads to what, Lewin concentrated on the prediction of behaviour of individual persons in their specific life spaces. According to him every learner has his own life space consisting of himself and his psychological environment, including foreign hull, the organization or reorganization of this life space, resulting in his learning or behaving in a particular way at a particular time. Since every learner has his own life space, his own ways of perception, i.e. interaction with the environment depending upon his own needs, values and behaviour for realizing the goal and his own individuality as a psychological person, it is not feasible to have generalized prediction about the terms and conditions for learning and behaving in a particular way, in a particular teaching-learning situation.

Educational Implications

The salient features so described and the understanding gained till this stage about Lewin's field theory may help us to draw the following educational implications for the teaching-learning process of our classrooms.

1. Every learner should be treated as a psychological person instead of a biological organism, having his unique life space at a particular time in a particular teaching-learning situation. In the light of his knowledge, a teacher should try to acquaint himself with the individuality of every child. The needs, interests, attitudes, aptitudes, abilities and capacities of the learner should, therefore, be known to the teacher in order to understand the dynamicity of their life space and accordingly they should be helped in developing desired cognitive strengths or insight for better learning and development.
2. For the proper organization and restructuring of life space (with the use of proper insight), the learner should be well acquainted with the purpose and goal of their learning attempts in a particular teaching-learning situation. The goal should be made as attractive as possible and the barriers in reaching the goal should be so handled that it ensures proper success in the teaching-learning process. Both the teacher and the learners should remain motivated in their respective acts of teaching and learning for achieving desired outcomes.
3. Students should be helped in developing proper insight and understanding of the things, processes and events related to a particular teaching-learning situation. The repetition without understanding and banking upon the past experiences instead of developing new insights in understanding and creating new things should be discouraged.
4. The teaching-learning environment is to be structured such that it provides maximum help to the learners in relation to their own life space and teaching-learning goals. The negative factors and unfavourable elements posing barriers in reaching the goals should be properly controlled so as to help in getting desired result in a teaching-learning situation.
5. A favourable group dynamics always facilitates the teaching-learning process. The teacher should, therefore, try to seek harmony through a smooth common intersection of the life space of individuals (learners and teacher) engaged in the process of teaching and learning. Each must have a proper understanding of the others. The ego clashes should be avoided as far as possible and every care should be taken to meet the individual choices and tastes within the group dynamics of a particular teaching-learning situation.
6. For the better learning and development, the learners should be helped and trained in bringing desired changes in their cognitive structures by learning the art of differentiation, generalization and restructurization of the regions and sub regions of their life space. Gradually they should be helped in acquiring various concepts and using them in their future learning and development.
7. A learner can be better understood by studying the structure of his space operative in a particular teaching-learning situation (in relation to his needs and abilities and barriers, boundary and foreign hull of his life space and goal). It can help the teacher to develop an accurate idea of what actually is going on in the minds-life spaces of the children in the class. There may be significant variations. For example in a particular teaching-learning situation some students may have the teacher and classroom activities in the center of their life spaces and everything else lying in their room and outside environment in the foreign hull of their life spaces. Definitely, these students will be getting maximum benefits out of the classroom teaching-learning activities. Some of the students of the class may have

teacher and the classroom activities in their life spaces while a few may not have anything belonging to classroom activities in their life spaces. They may be wandering outside while keeping their bodies in the classroom. Seeing such variations in the structures of the life spaces of the students of the class, a teacher has to be very cautious about the dynamicity and functioning of the life spaces of the students, then and only then he can be a better manager of the ongoing teaching-learning situation.

INFORMATION PROCESSING THEORIES OF LEARNING

Information processing theories of learning represent the group of theories that make use of the concept of information processing for explaining the mechanism of learning. Let us, therefore, try to understand the meaning and concept of information processing for gaining insight in the nature of these theories.

What is Information Processing?

Simply put, information processing stands for an act of processing the information, i.e. to analyze, employ or make use of information for gaining some knowledge or experience. In the words of Joyce and Weil—*"Information processing refers to the ways people handle stimuli from the environment, organize data, sense problems, generate concepts and solutions to problems, and employ verbal and non-verbal symbols."* (1972, p. 9)

In this way information processing deals with the ways and means an information (sensory input or data) is handled by an individual for deriving desired meaning for its further use. Consequently, the handling or processing of the information may help an individual in gaining new experiences and insight for the solution of felt problems or modification of his ways of behaving.

Information Processing Theories

The way people process the available information (resulting in gaining new experiences or bringing modification in their behaviour), may give birth to significant theories of learning. This very assumption has led to the formulation and establishment of some well known learning theories termed as information processing theories of learning. The key question answered by all these information processing theories of learning is: "Cognitively, what process are occurring in a person's brain when they are presented with a learning situation." Consequently they throw light on the mechanism how the human brain senses, processes and recalls information. The working of our brain, in terms of information processing, may be easily equated to the working of computers. Like computers, the information processing in human brain may find its expression in the mechanism of input, processing and output. The brain receives sensory impulses from the environment and decides to process this input as warranted. Processing depends on the nature and complexity of the data as perceived by the learner. The way, information is received, processed and recalled by the learner then decides the outcomes of his learning.

For gaining some idea about the nature and functioning of information processing theories of learning, we would be discussing here some of the popular theories and models of instruction developed by the eminent psychologists. In such description, we may easily notice a significant trend that all these Information processing theorists approach learning primarily through a study of memory and so you can find due mention of the terms related to the process of memorization like temporary memory, short term memory, long term memory, recall, retrieval, etc. Let us begin with the description of these theories one by one.

Three Stage Information Processing Theory

This theory is the outcome of the ideas propagated by Atkinson and Shiffrin (1968, 1971). According to this theory, *learning* is the outcome of the processing of the information carried out by human brain at the following three stages.

(i) Sensory registry (ii) Short term memory and (iii) Long term memory.

1. The process of learning or memorization thus starts with the interaction of one's sense organs with one's environment. The sensory information is first picked up by one or more sense organs, then it travels through the nervous system and reaches the brain for its interpretation. The sensory information stays in the nervous system (just to register its presence) briefly about a second or two, giving brain the time for its interpretation. After being registered in the sensory register, it can be responded immediately or may be transferred to the short term memory. Usually it depends upon the nature of sensory information and its interpretation by the brain. The brain may interpret it as useless or of little significance and thus may order for its disappearance from the sensory register or it may be ordered for its monitoring at a low attention level. As an example of such type of information processing at the sensory registry level, we can cite the driving of our car while carrying on a conversation. Here we can monitor and respond to driving conditions without transferring the information to short term memory.
2. The information not processed or vanished at the level of sensory registry then travels to short term memory (STM) of our brain. It may automatically stay for up to 20 seconds here. However, it can be retained as long as an individual wants it in his short term memory through rehearsal or repetition. *Short term memory* is equivalent to one's working memory. It is here that the information is duly processed by the brain for its proper interpretation, assimilation and responding. There are usually three means employed for the information processing or handling of cognitive tasks in STM. These are:
   (i) Encoding the information in chunks.
   (ii) Breaking the information into sub parts and then processing them one at a time.
   (iii) Practicing skills until they are automatic.
3. The information unprocessed at the short term memory stage, is then transferred to the long term memory (LTM). LTM is believed to have unlimited capacity and duration. It is used for storing and procession of sensory information on a permanent basis. The stored as well as organized information in the *long term memory* (LTM) in the coded form is transferred back to the short term memory where it is decoded and employed for response as desired and ordered by our brain.

Levels of Processing Theory

This theory of information processing has been put up by Craik and Lokhart (1972) as an alternative to the above discussed information processing theory postulating three stages—sensory, working and long term memory for the processing of information. The main ideas lying within this theory may be summarized as below:

- Memory is of only one kind rather than of three types namely, sensory, short term and long term.
- Ability to learn or remember is dependent on how deeply information is processed by us.

- Levels of such processing may range from very shallow to very deep.
- The greater the depth of processing, the better can the material be learned or remembered. For example, information that involves strong visual images or many associations with existing knowledge will be processed at a deeper level. Similarly information that suits our interests or serves our purposes well will receive more processing than other stimuli events.
- The things that are meaningful to us are processed quite deeply in comparison to the meaningless or less meaningful stimuli and are consequently learnt or remembered well.
- Processing of information at different levels is carried out quite unconsciously and automatically unless we attend it to that level. For example, we are usually not aware of the sensory properties of stimuli, or what we have in own working memory, unless we are asked to specifically identify such information. From this it follows that there is hardly any place for the mechanism of attention in the processing of information. It may thus be taken as an interruption in processing of information rather than a cognitive process in its own right.

Miller's Information Processing Theory

This theory has been put forward by George A. Miller as an extension of the earlier approaches of cognitive psychologists expressing learning primarily in terms of the study of the process of memorization. The main ideas behind his theory may be summarized as below:

(i) Information processing helps in acquiring new experiences and learning new ways of behaving.

(ii) Students learn better when they are actively processing, storing and retrieving information.

(iii) Information processing helps the students build desirable cognitive structures (structuring of the subject matter) for the proper comprehension and understanding.

(iv) Successful encoding is essential for the proper processing of the received sensory information or data. Working memory (STM) also processes the information for being transferred to Long Term Memory (LTM) by encoding the information. Therefore, meaningful encoding is a must for the desired task of information processing.

(v) Miller (1956) presented the concept of "Chunking" for the meaningful organization or encoding of the subject matter at all levels of cognitive processing. Classical example of chunks is the ability to remember long sequences of binary numbers because they can be encoded into decimal form. For example the sequence 10100 01001 11001 101 1010 could easily be remembered as 20 9 25 5 10. Of course this would only work for someone who can convert binary to decimal numbers (i.e. the chunks are meaningful).

(vi) We can expand the capacity of a person holding information in his short term memory by utilizing the concept of chunking. It can hold 5—9 chunks of information (seven plus or minus two). Therefore information should always be organized in the form of chunks (meaningful units) for its better processing and fruitful learning outcomes.

(vii) The second useful concept regarding that of the information processing (other than chunking) propagated by Miller is concerned with his acceptance of the computer as a model of human learning. Like the computer, the human mind takes in information, performs operations on it to change its forms and content, stores and locates it and generate responses to it. Thus information processing, according to Miller, involves (i) gathering and representing information, i.e. encoding, (ii) holding information, i.e. retention and (iii) getting at the information when needed, i.e. retrieval.

(viii) The third useful concept emphasized in Miller's information processing theory is known by the term TOTE (Test Operate Test Exit). By introducing this concept, Miller et. al. (1960) suggested that TOTE should replace the stimulus response mechanism as the basic unit of behaviour. In a TOTE unit, a goal is tested to see if it has been achieved through the mechanism of information processing. If not, an operation is performed to achieve the goal, this cycle of test-operate is repeated until the goal is eventually achieved or abandoned. By adopting this technique, an individual may be capable of finding the solution of his problem or learning the desired way of achieving his goal.

Dual Coding Theory of Information Processing

This theory has been proposed by A. Paivio as an attempt to give equal weightage in the processing of verbal and non-verbal information in the task of learning. On account of its emphasis on the dual functionality of the verbal and non-verbal information, the theory has been named as *Dual coding* theory. Initiating his theory Paivio (1986) writes: "*Human cognition is unique in that it has become specialized for dealing simultaneously with language and with non-verbal objects and events. Moreover, the language system is peculiar in that it deals directly with linguistic input and output (in the form of speech or writing) while at the same time serving a symbolic function with respect to non-verbal objects, events, and behaviours. Any representational theory must accommodate this dual functionality.*" (p. 53).

The chief characteristics and main ideas lying behind the dual coding theory of information processing may be summarized as below:

1. According to this theory, there are three types of processing namely representational, referential and associative. A given task may require any or all the three kinds of processing narrated as below:
   (i) In representational information processing, there remains a direct activation of verbal and non-verbal representation.
   (ii) In referential information processing, there remains an activation of the verbal system by the non-verbal system or vice-versa.
   (iii) In associative information processing, there remains an activation of representation within the same verbal or non-verbal system.
2. The theory is based on the assumption that there lies two cognitive subsystems recognized as below.
   - The one of these subsystems is specialized for the representation and processing of non-verbal objects or events. (i.e. imagery).
   - The other subsystem is specialized for dealing with language.
3. Based on the above referred two cognitive subsystems, Paivio in his theory postulated two different types of representational units (Similar to "Chunks" as described by Miller) as mentioned below.
   (i) Representational units named as '*imagens*' for mental images (non-verbal information).
   (ii) Representation units named as '*logogens*' for verbal entities (verbal information).
4. According to Paivio while logogens are organized in terms of associations and hierarchies, the imagens are organized in terms of part-whole relationships.

5. By following the above mentioned systems and pattern of organization, the information (verbal and non-verbal) is processed appropriately by the individual learner for the desired learning outcomes.

EDUCATIONAL IMPLICATION OF THE THEORIES OF INFORMATION PROCESSING

All the theories of information processing described above may be said to have the following educational implications.

1. The information (verbal or non-verbal) should be organized in terms of meaningful units for its better processing and fruitful learning outcomes.
2. Students should be helped in focusing on the most important details and separating less vital information.
3. Students should be helped in making connection between new information and what they already know.
4. As far as it is adequate and possible, students should be provided for repetition and review of information.
5. The learning material experiences (Instruction) should be organized in a clear, systematic and organized way.
6. We must always focus on meaning and not the memorization of information on the part of students.

ROGER'S EXPERIENTIAL LEARNING

In his search of the basic nature of learning, Rogers tried to distinguish two types of learning—cognitive and experiential. He termed *cognitive learning* as meaningless in itself unless it is subjected to some use. Such learning is knowledge-based and thus may include the learning of vocabulary, multiplication tables, mathematical formulae, historical events and geographical facts. The *experiential learning*, on the other hand, is quite vital to one's progress and welfare. It is associated with the application of the acquired knowledge such as learning about engines in order to repair a car, learning psychological principles and methods in order to help the children get rid of bad habits. Thus experimental learning is learner centered. That is to say, it cares for the needs and wants of the learner, Carl Rogers has tried to enumerate these qualities of experiential learning in the following ways:

1. Experimental learning is characterized by *personal involvement* of the learner.
2. It is *self-initiated*. The learner willingly takes initiative to engage in such type of learning.
3. It is characterized by *self-evaluation*. The learner himself is interested in evaluating the results and outcomes of such learning by applying it to the realization of learning objectives, i.e. he wants to test his knowledge of repairing an electrical gadget by actually doing the repair.
4. It leaves a *pervasive effect* on the learner. Whatever is learned through this method can be made into use when and where he needs.

Rogers, as a humanist, believed in the strength and potentialities of human beings. According to him, all human beings have a natural inclination for learning and a desire to grow and progress. The role of the teacher and the parents is thus to help their children in their inherent desire for personal change and growth. Teacher as well as the parents have to care for and facilitate such learning which helps the children to grow and develop according to their requirements. The attempts of the teachers and the parents in realizing the objectives of experiential learning may, thus include the following provisions:

1. Arranging a favourable and positive climate for learning.
2. Helping the learner or learners to have clear-cut objectives and purpose of his/her learning.
3. Organizing the learning resources and making them available to the learners.
4. Balancing intellectual and emotional components of learning.
5. Sharing feelings and thoughts with learners in a democratic way.

Thus, the primary responsibility of a teacher lies well in his sincerity as a helper, a guide and a facilitator in the ongoing teaching-learning process. He is not there to provide mere information or demonstrate his skills in any area of information or fact-finding. Through many tools and materials and his own characteristic ways, a teacher, while following the doctrine of experiential learning, has to play the role of a learning facilitator. For realizing this objective as Rogers points out, a learner must at least take care of the basic conditions that facilitate learning. According to him, learning is well facilitated when:

1. *threat* to the self of the learner is minimum;
2. learning resources and climate are in favour of the learner;
3. the learner participates completely in the learning process and has control over its nature and direction;
4. it is primarily based on direct confrontation with practical, social, personal or research areas;
5. self-evaluation is the principal method of assessing progress or success; and
6. the learner realizes the importance of learning and develops an openness as well as willingness to learn.

Thus, experiential learning is, in fact, a learner-centered enterprise. Here the learner is the key figure in the ongoing teaching-learning process. The role of a teacher is to facilitate such learning. The primary responsibility of learning and change in the behaviour of the learner for his personal and social development lies with him. However, he is to be properly helped, guided and kept on the proper track by the teacher as and when the need arises. The main thing is to help the learner realize the importance and significance of the learning task. If we can make him see the profit or gain of the learning task, we can very well realize the objectives of learning. Therefore, according to Rogers, learning must be linked with the motives, goals and ideals of the learners. Accordingly, for a learner who is interested in becoming rich, learning of the subject and topics like economics, investment, financing, banking etc., may be of great importance. Decidedly he will take more interest in learning the topics and subjects that are helpful in realizing his motives and ambitions, as compared to other students of his class who have significantly less interest in money matters.

So, it can be easily concluded that Carl Rogers, through his theory of experiential learning, advocates a humanistic and learner-centered approach to be adopted in classrooms by the teachers, with the sole purposes of making the learning process more humane and suitable to the needs and interest of the learners, and turning it into more significant and purposeful events from the angles of their personal and social growth and development by emphasizing more on application than on theory alone.

MASLOW'S HUMANISTIC THEORY OF LEARNING

Humanistic theories of learning have been propagated by the psychologists belonging to the school of humanism. The school is particularly associated with Carl Rogers and Abraham Maslow

(Psychologists), John Halt (Child Education) and Macolm Knowles (Adult Education). Abraham Maslow coined the term "the third force" to describe the humanistic approach to emphasize how it differed from the psycho-dynamic and behaviourist approaches that dominated psychology for quite a long time. Humanism thus in fact was a reaction against overly mechanistic and dehumanizing approaches prevalent in psychology. It called for a halt of the prevailing practice of treating people as objects and rationalism and made them feel as human beings by paying due concern to their self. It paved the way for the reaffirmation of the affective and subjective world by providing due place for personal freedom, individual choices, motivation and feelings.

As a consequence, humanistic approach was adopted for throwing light on the nature and mechanism of learning. Why do human beings learn, thus was now explained through the humanistic theories of learning brought forward by humanistic psychologists. Perhaps the most significant and persuasive explanation of humanistic orientation to learning came from the two famous psychologists named Carl Rogers and Abraham Maslow. Here in this text we would be concentrating our efforts on the humanistic theory of learning brought forward by Abraham Maslow (as an illustration of humanistic orientation to learning).

Humanistic theory of learning propagated by Abraham Maslow owes its origin to his most famous concept of hierarchy of needs. While proposing this well known concept, Abraham Maslow in 1954 stated that human needs tend to arrange themselves in hierarchies of prepotency. In other words, the appearance of one need generally depends on the satisfaction of the others. They are closely related to each other and may be arranged from the lowest to the highest development of the personality. He proposed five sets of basic needs that can be arranged in a definite hierarchical order for understanding human motivation to learning and striving as shown in Figure 17.9.

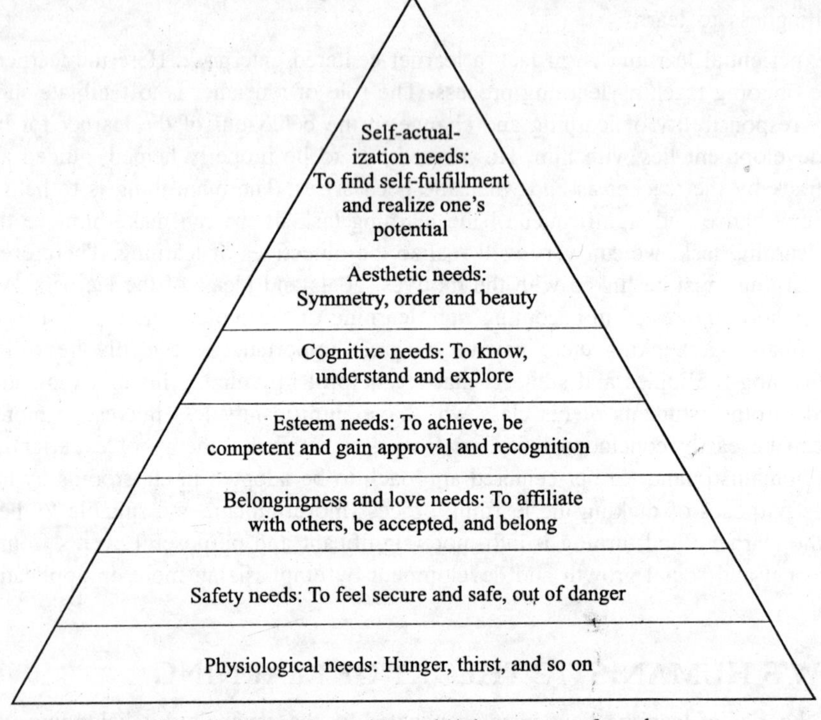

Fig. 17.9 Maslow's hierarchical structure of needs.

The needs shown in the above hierarchical structure may be briefly described levelwise as under.

- Level one: *Psychological needs* such as hunger, thirst, sex, sleep, relaxation and bodily integrity must be satisfied before the next level comes into play.
- Level two: *Safety needs* call for a predictable and orderly world. If these are not satisfied, people will look to organize their worlds to provide for the greatest degree of safety and security. If satisfied, people will come under the force of level three.
- Level three: *Belongingness and love needs* involve the desire for being affiliated, accepted, loved and getting affection from others especially by those who matters most in one's life.
- Level four: *Self-esteem needs* involve the desire for strength, achievement, adequacy, mastery and competence. They also involve confidence, independence, reputation and prestige.
- Level five: *Self-actualization* is the full use and expression of talents, capacities and potentialities.

By putting the human needs in a hierarchical structure, Maslow then tried to explain the mechanism of learning by concentrating on the problem of why and how do we learn? He argued that needs determine the perception. One feels the need of learning or striving because he needs to satisfy his one or the other needs. In the process of satisfaction of his needs, he may come across or go through various experiences that may persuade or force him to bring desired changes in his behaviour, i.e. causing him to learn one or the other ways of behaving or struggling for the satisfaction of his needs.

So, *learning,* according to Maslow, may be termed as *a process of bringing desired changes in the behaviour of an individual for helping him to satisfy his one or the other needs depending upon his individuality and interaction with his environment.*

The nature and quality of the learning thus depends upon the nature and quality of the needs being satisfied and the resultant changes brought about in the behaviour of the individual. In the satisfaction of lower order needs, one may thus learn and acquire those behaviour that tend to satisfy his lower order needs, while the satisfaction of the higher order needs like belongingness and love, esteem and self actualization may help him to imbibe and inculcate higher order values and qualities for the complete and overall development of his personality.

Maslow's theory of learning thus concentrates on the satisfaction of the needs of a learner, i.e. his natural desire and motivation to learn. It follows from this that Maslow's humanistic learning theory lays more importance on the learner than the subject or the teacher. It has helped in the development of individual tendencies and individualization of education by aiming to develop the self concept and self esteem of the individual child for actualizing his total self.

In this way, the theory ultimately aims to help a child in his desired self-actualization. Maslow considers it the supreme aim of human life and thus emphasizes that a learning process, in any system of education, must always be directed to achieve its ultimate aim, i.e. to help the child in his self actualization. In the words of Maslow *"A musician must make music, an artist must paint, a poet must write poetry, if he is to be ultimately at peace with himself. What a man can be, he must be. He must be true to his own nature. This need we may call self actualization"*. This is why in Maslow's theory, learning is always aimed and learning process is always designed for helping the child to become true to himself by developing himself according to his own nature, i.e. the self which he wants to be actualized.

Educational Implications

The humanistic theory of learning forwarded by Maslow may be attributed with the following educational implications.

1. In providing learning experiences, the children should be treated as human beings and not as a machine or objects for being run or moulded according to the wishes of the mechanists, i.e. the teacher.
2. Self is always great and hence due consideration should always be provided for the development and actualization of the self of the individual child. Therefore, due care should always be taken for the development of personal values like:
   - *Development of self concept:* Child must know himself and as far as possible feel good about himself.
   - *Self expression:* Child must be able to express himself fully in the manner he likes.
   - *Self actualization:* Child must progress towards the pinnacle of self development which Maslow terms as self actualization.
3. A child's learning behaviour must be guided through intrinsic motives, i.e. the satisfaction of his inner felt needs. A child learns better when his learning behaviour is inwardly driven and derives his reward from the sense of achievement or satisfaction after getting his one or the other needs satisfied through the outcomes of his learning.
4. Child should never be given positive reinforcement, such as praise, or punishment in the form of criticism. Both praise and blame were rejected by Maslow simply on account of adverse effects in the proper development of the children. Children may get addicted to praise or any positive reinforcement and thereby may put their efforts only for receiving such positive reinforcements from their teachers instead of striving properly for their actualization/development.
5. Children should be moved towards self government, self regulations and autonomy simply for the reason that informal control and self discipline proves much better than the control by external means and forces.
6. Teacher must pay due respect to the self of the children. They must help the children in the development of their self esteem. It would be important for an individual child to feel good about himself (high self esteem) and to feel that he can set and achieve appropriate goals (the satisfaction of his lower as well as higher order needs).
7. Education must be made child-centered by giving the child a unique position according to his nature, i.e. the self. He must be made to feel responsible for his education and own his learning. The role of the teacher in any process of learning must be that of a good facilitator and not a disseminator of knowledge and therefore participatory and discovery methods should be followed instead of traditional didacticism (i.e. learn parrot fashion every thing teacher says).
8. Humanistic touch should be essentially given to the processes of education and learning. The learning environment and the behaviour of the teacher must be quite humane to the children. It should cater to the satisfaction of children's basic needs more particularly for the children's affective (or emotional) needs. The children should be made to feel positive about themselves.
9. Development of human potential and higher values of life should always be paid due consideration in any scheme of education and learning. This attainment of material goals

(satisfaction of lower order needs) should not be over emphasized. The development of the values and qualities essential for the satisfaction of the need of belongingness and love, self esteem and self actualization etc., should always be aimed at and given due recognition as the higher goals of human learning and education.

SUMMARY

Theories of learning represent broad principles and techniques of learning, throwing light on the mechanism of how we learn. Most of these can be broadly classified as Stimulus-Response associationist type theories and Gestalt field or field cognition type of theories. In the remaining ones, we can chiefly notice—Information processing theories, Experiential and Humanistic theories —that can count substantial towards understanding the mechanism of human learning.

Theory of trial and error learning or connectionism put up by L.N. Thorndike emphasize that in learning we make some attempts or trials. Errors are obvious in such attempts. However, in making frantic efforts we learn to make right responses by omitting the incorrect ones and thus ultimately learn to take desired responses without committing any error. Thorndike's theory also paved the way for the propagation of certain laws of learning like the law of readiness (implying that if one is ready to learn, he can learn), law of exercise (emphasizing the need of practice, drill and repetition) and law of effect (the fate of learning is decided by the effect or consequences of learning).

Classical conditioning is best associated with the names of a Russian psychologist Ivan Pavlov and American behaviourist J.B. Watson. Pavlov, through a series of experiments with dogs, successfully demonstrated that an artificial stimulus (like bell) in association with a natural stimulus (like food) becomes strong enough to produce salivation (natural response to food) even when not accompanied by food. Pavlov described it as the conditioning of the dog resulting in its learning to get food with the ringing of the bell. Watson also tried to demonstrate such type of conditioning by inducing fear in an eleven-month-old baby named Albert.

Operant conditioning, propagated by Skinner, does not believe in stimulus response trigger like behaviour initiating mechanism. Skinner asserted that the presence of a stimulus for evoking a response is not essential. In most of our learning situations, our behaviour is shaped and maintained by its consequences. It is operated by the organism itself and maintained by its results. The occurrence of such behaviour was named as operant behaviour and the process of learning resulting in such type of behaviour was named as operant conditioning by Skinner. Reinforcement (any thing that increases the chances of the repetition of a behaviour) is an essential attribute of this type of conditioning. The success of the learning achieved through operant conditioning mainly depends on the right choice of reinforcement and its schedules. Emitting of a desired response is properly managed through suitable reinforcement schedules for its properly maintenance and desired shaping. The techniques of operant conditioning have proved quite useful in the field of learning and education in the tasks and programmes like behaviour modification, programmed learning and computer-assisted instructions.

Insightful learning as a theory of learning evolved out of the attempts of Gestalt psychologists. However, the main initiation in this direction was taken by Kohler. He, for the first time, used the term "insight" for describing the learning of his apes. Through his number of experiments, Kohler concluded that an individual while learning a way to solve his problem does not resort to blind trial and error mechanism rather he reacts intelligently by using his insight, i.e. perceiving the situation in a gestalt form (as a whole), evaluating all the possibilities of finding solution in the given confronting situation and then arriving at an insightful solution.

Lewin's field theory, propagated by Kurt Lewin, considers learning as a process of perceptual organization or reorganization of one's life space or field (the space in which one moves psychologically as a person and not biologically as an organism). In doing so, he definitely acts purposefully by bringing desirable changes in the cognitive structure of his life space, i.e. using needed insight for perceiving things in the right manner and choosing the right alternative for reaching the goal.

Information processing theories try to throw light on the mechanism, how the human brain senses, processes and recalls information and thus equate the information processing of our brain with the working of a computer (involving its three aspects—input, processing and output). *The three stages Information processing theory* propagated by Atkinson and Shiffrin considers learning as the outcome of the information processing carried out by human brain at the subsequent three stages namely—sensory registry, short term memory and long term memory. *Levels of processing theory* propagated by Craik and Lokhart postulated three stages—sensory, working and long term memory for the processing of information. *Miller's Information Processing theory* put forward by George A Miller, while accepting computer as a model of human learning, emphasizes on (i) gathering and representing information, i.e. encoding in the form of chunks (ii) holding information, i.e. retention and (iii) getting at the information when needed, i.e. retrieval. After going through these three stages of information processing, a goal is tested to see if it has been achieved or not. If not, an operation (involving three stages) is performed to achieve the goal and this cycle of test-operate is repeated till the goal is achieved. *Dual Coding Theory of Information Processing* proposed by A. Paivio attempts to provide equal weightage to verbal and non-verbal information processing in the task of learning. Accordingly this theory maintains that there lies two cognitive subsystems namely 'imagery' for the representation and processing of non-verbal objects or events and 'logogens' for dealing with verbal entities. In learning we must take care of these two subsystems properly.

Experiential learning propagated by Rogers tried to emphasize on the application of knowledge instead of a mere knowledge-acquiring learning known as cognitive learning. The application of knowledge is more significant from the viewpoints of a learner than merely the acquisition of knowledge. Experiential learning is designated as learner-centered and is more famous for its humanistic touch among the theories of learning.

Humanistic theory of learning propagated by Abraham Maslow owes its origin to his most famous concept of hierarchy of needs. According to him the needs of human being may be arranged from the lowest to the highest development of the personality. They are closely related to each other and the appearance of one need generally depends on the satisfaction of the others. Learning, according to him, may be termed as a process of bringing needed behavioural change in the pursuit of the satisfaction of one or the other needs of individual depending upon his individuality and interaction with his environment. This is why through its humanistic approach, this theory of learning is always aimed to arrange the learning process in a way to help a child become true to himself by developing him according to his own nature.

References and Suggested Readings

Alkinson R.G. and Shiffrin, R.H., *Human Memory: A proposed system and its control process* in K.W. Spence and J.T. Spence (Eds), The Psychology of Learning and Motivation—Advances in Research and Theory, Vol. 2, Academic Press, New York, 1968.

Crow, L.D. and Crow Alice, *Educational Psychology*, Harcourt Braceworld, New York, 1938.

Craik, F.I.M. and Lokhart, R.S., *Levels of Processing: A framework for memory,* Research Journal of Verbal Learning and Verbal Behaviour, Vol. II, 671–684, 1972.

Hergenhanhn, B.R., *An Introduction to Theories of Learning*, Prentice-Hall, Englewood Cliffs, New Jersey, 1975.

Joyce, Bruce and Weil, Marsha, *Models of Teaching*, Prentice Hall, Englewood Cliffs, New Jersey, 1972.

Levin, M.J., *Psychology—A biographical approach*, McGraw-Hill, New York, 1978.

Mangal, S.K., *Advanced Educational Psychology*, 2nd ed., Prentice-Hall, New Delhi, 2002.

Maslow, A., *Motivation and Personality*, Harper & Row, New York, 1954.

Miller, G.A., "The magic number seven plus or minus two, some limits on our capacity for processing information," *Psychological Review*, **63**, 81–97, 1956.

Miller, G.A., Gialanter, E. and Pribram, K.H., *Plans and Structure of Behaviour*, Holt Rinehart and Winston, New York, 1960.

Pavlov, J.P., *Conditional Reflexes*, Oxford Clarendon Press, 1927.

Reynolds, G.S., *A Primer of Operant Conditioning,* 2nd ed., Scott, Forman, Glenview, Illionis, 1975.

Rogers, C.R., *Freedom to Learn*, Merril, Columbus, OH, 1969.

Skinner, B.F., *The Behaviour of Organism*, Appleton-Century Crofts, New York, 1938.

Thorndike, E.L., *Animal Intelligence*, Macmillan, New York, 1911.

Throndike, E.L., *Human Learning*, Cornell University, New York, 1931.

Watson, J.B., *Psychology from the Stand-point of a Behaviourist*, Lippincott, Philadelphia, 1919.

Woodward, R.S. and Marquis, *Psychology*, Henry Holt, New York, 1948.

18

Transfer of Learning or Training

CHAPTER COMPOSITION

- What is Transfer of Learning or Training?
- Types of Transfer
- How to Achieve Maximum Positive Transfer?
- Summary
- References and Suggested Readings

WHAT IS TRANSFER OF LEARNING OR TRAINING?

We learn many things and perform many tasks in our lives. Sometimes when we learn or perform a new task, we find that it has been influenced by some of our previous learning or training. The learning of addition and subtraction helps the child learn multiplication and division. Learning of mathematics helps him in solving the numerical problems in physics. Similarly if one has learned to play tennis, one finds it easier to learn playing ping-pong or badminton. Thus, learning or training in one situation influences our learning or performance in some other situation. This influence is usually referred to as the carry over of learning from one task to another. The learning or skill acquired in one task is transferred or carried over to other tasks. Not only the learning of the tricks of a trade or the knowledge and skill acquired in a particular school subject is transferred to other situations, but also the habits, interests and attitudes get transferred and try to influence the activities of the individual in future. Crow and Crow express it in the following words:

> *The carry-over of habits of thinking, feeling, or working, of knowledge or of skills, from one learning area to another usually is referred to as the transfer of training.....* (1973, p. 323)

Sorenson also takes the same stand when he explains the meaning of transfer in the following words:

> *Transfer refers to the transfer of knowledge, training and habits acquired in one situation to another situation.* (1948, p. 387)

In this way, we can define transfer as a process by which some influence is exercised over our new learning or performance by our previous learning or training.

TYPES OF TRANSFER

There is no guarantee that learning in one situation or one field will always help the learning in another situation or field. Sometimes the learning of one task creates difficulty in performing or learning another task. Having learned to pronounce BUT correctly, the child finds it difficult to pronounce PUT correctly. In this way, transfer of training or learning also involves the possibilities of negative and adverse effects besides the positive and favourable ones. Consequently, transfer is said to have the following three forms:

(i) Positive transfer,

(ii) Negative transfer,

(iii) Zero transfer.

Transfer is said to be positive when something previously learned benefits performance or learning in a new situation. Similarly, when something previously learned hinders performance or learning in a new situation, we call it negative transfer. In case the previous learning makes no difference at all to the performance or learning in a new situation, there is said to be zero transfer from the previous situation to the new one.

Sometimes, it is also possible that previous learning may partly help and partly interfere with the performance or learning in a new situation. In learning to play a game of tennis, for example, a person learns many things that are likely to be transferred in learning to play baseball. Promptness in starting, keen observations of the position of one's opponents and movement of the ball and one's attention on the game rather than on the spectators are some of the positive transfer effects. But there may be some negative transfer effects also. A baseball comes at a faster speed than a tennis ball. The style of using the baseball bat is also different from that of the tennis racket. A similar thing may also be said about the influence of one's mother tongue on the subsequent learning of some other language. In this case also, we have positive as well as negative transfer effects.

It should be clear from the above discussion that on account of its transfer value, a particular learning is able to exercise positive as well as negative effects on some subsequent learning. Therefore, it is necessity for a learner to realize the transfer value of the learning in a particular subject. On one hand, he has to reduce as much as possible the negative transfer effects of one learning and on the other, he has to make attempts for getting maximum advantage by securing positive transfer efforts. In order to do this, he has to know what is it that introduces the element of transfer from one situation to another. How does the transfer take place from one situation to another? Psychologists, from time to time, have tried to find out the answer to this question. As a result of their experimentation and thinking, various theories have come up. Some of the important theories (explaining transfer of training) are mentioned below.

Theories of Mental Discipline (Faculty theory)

It is the oldest of all the transfer theories. This theory believes that the mind is composed of many independent faculties like memory, attention, imagination, reasoning and judgment etc. These faculties, according to this theory, are nothing but the 'muscles of the mind' and like muscle of the body, they can be strengthened or improved through exercise (practice and use). Such properly strengthened or improved faculties later on function automatically in all the situations and areas in which they are involved. For example, if the memory of a person is strengthened or improved to a great extent through the memorization of long and difficult passages, then it can prove useful in memorizing dates, names, formula, figures and in fact anything and everything that involves memory. In the same way, propagators of the theory claim that reasoning and imaginative powers developed through the study of geometrical propositions can be used in solving various problems in life that demand a good deal of reasoning and imagination.

Mental discipline as an educational doctrine and as the basis for transfer of training was first seriously challenged by William James. He wanted to see whether daily training in the memorization of poetry of one author would affect the learning of a slightly different poetry of another author. For this experiment he acted as a subject for himself. He memorized 158 lines from Victor Hugo's 'Satyr' in 131 5/6 minutes spread over eight days. He then worked for about 20 minutes daily memorizing all of the first book of Milton 'Paradise Lost'. This required 38 days. After this period of memory training, he returned to the 'Satyr' and memorized 158 additional lines. But now he could do so in 151 ½ minutes as against 131 5/6 minutes in the first instance. James, therefore, concluded that memory was not affected by training as claimed by the faculty theory.

Similar experiments were performed by many psychologists to test the validity and reliability of the faculty theory. Worth mentioning are the experiments conducted by Dr. Sleight and Briggs. The findings of all these experiments have gone against the mental discipline or faculty theory. Therefore, nowadays it stands almost rejected.

Theory of Identical Elements

The chief propounder of the theory of identical elements in transfer of training was Thorndike. Later on Woodworth supported this theory and used the word 'components' in place of elements. Therefore, the theory is also called 'Theory of Identical Components'.

This theory maintains that the transfer from one situation to another is possible to the extent that there are common or identical elements in the situation. For example, there is a possibility of transfer from the field of mathematics to the field of physics to the extent that there are some common elements like symbols, formulae, equations, numerical calculations etc. In a similar way, transfer takes place from typing to playing a piano to the extent that such skills as eye-finger co-ordination are identical to both the activities. Thus, similarity in the two situations with regard to the common elements of content, skill, attitude, method, aims, habits, interest etc., facilitate the process of transfer.

Theory of Generalization

The theory of generalization as an explanation of transfer of training or learning has been put forth by Charles Judd. This theory advocates the transfer of generalizations in the new situations in place of identical elements as suggested by Thorndike. As a result of certain experiences, the individual reaches some conclusion or generalization. This conclusion or generalization can be applied by him in the coming new situations. Thus generalization is nothing but a principle, law or rule that can be easily transferred to other situations.

According to this theory as Crow and Crow put it. *"The developing of special skills, the mastery of specific facts, the achieving of particular habits or attitudes in one situation have little transfer value unless the skills, facts, habits are systematized and related to situations in which they can be utilized."* (1973, p. 319)

Therefore, this theory, in order to achieve the maximum transfer of learning or training, insists on systematic organization and generalization of experiences.

Judd's experiments: Judd conducted a dart throwing experiment to test the transfer value of generalization. He took (after matching them in terms of intelligence) two groups of children of fifth and sixth grades. He called one group as an experimental group and the other as control group. The purpose of experiment was to study the effect of instruction in the principle of refraction of light upon the ability of boys to throw darts at target placed 12" under water. The experimental group was given a full theoretical explanation of refraction and the other group was left to work without any theoretical training. Both the groups were then asked to throw darts to hit a target placed 12" under water. Both the groups did not do well irrespective of the fact that the experimental group had a theoretical understanding of the phenomenon of refraction. Mere theoretical understanding of refraction could not help the experimental group to have better performance than the control group. Again the situation was changed. The target was placed 4" under water. This time, the experimental group showed much better performance than the control group. Both the groups had an equal chance of practice but while the control group could not make use of its earlier experience, the experimental group derived maximum benefit from it. The understanding of the principle of refraction (theoretically as well as practically) helped them to hit the underwater targets that appeared a little raised than their actual position.

On the basis of his experiment, Judd concluded that it is the generalization of the general understanding of some relationship (a rule or a law) that is usually transferred from the earlier situation to the later one. Similarly the day-to-day generalized experiences of a child like—"In touching the fire, we get burnt", or "green apples are sour in taste"—always get transferred to the coming new situations.

Therefore, one is largely benefited by the systematic and organized generalization of experiences and in this way, this theory lays stress on the generalization of specific experiences and formulation of some rules or principles so that they may be transferred from one situation to another.

Theory of Ideals

This theory was put forward by W.C. Bagley. He tried to explain mechanism of transfer in terms of ideals. He asserted that generalizations are more likely to transfer if they are regarded as ideals of some value as desirable. There are two experiments on transfer of neatness that support Bagley's assertion.

In the first experiment, the experimenter emphasized neatness in the preparation of arithmetic papers by pupils in the third grade. Nothing was said about neatness in the rest of the school subjects. Language and spelling papers were then compared with arithmetic papers for improvement in neatness. While the arithmetic paper showed clear proof of neatness, the language and spelling paper rather showed a decrease in neatness. It was concluded that specific training in neatness in one area did not transfer to other areas.

In the other experiment, the experimenter insisted on neatness in all papers, and the children were told about the advantage of neatness in other respects of life inside and outside the school. In this way, great effort was made to develop an ideal of neatness. The result showed an overall improvement in neatness in all the subjects. The conclusion was that ideals do transfer.

In this way, the theory of ideals emphasizes that the ideals like love for wisdom, thirst for knowledge, tolerance for difference of opinion, spirit of enquiry etc. are transferable from one situation to another and therefore, every attempt should be made to develop desirable ideals among the children.

All the above theories seem to hold divergent opinion regarding the explanation to transfer from one situation to another. But in general, these differences are probably more apparent than real. All these theories are complementary and not contradictory. In one way or the other, each one of them tries to explain the mechanism of transfer. By synthesizing the points of view of all these theories, we can place ourselves in a position to know how transfer or learning or training takes place from one situation to another.

HOW TO ACHIEVE MAXIMUM POSITIVE TRANSFER?

The problem of transfer of training occupies significant place in the process of education. It brings economy and effectiveness in the learning process. By realizing transfer, what one learns or experiences in some previous situation can be either utilized for the learning in the new situations or applied to the solution of the day-to-day problems. Therefore, a wise learner should try to secure maximum transfer so that he may be benefited properly from his earlier experiences and training.

The following suggestions can help in this direction

1. What is being learned at present should be linked with what has already been learnt in the past. What one already knows should form the base for one's present learning. In this way, one should try to take advantage of the past experiences of learning by seeking its proper transfer.
2. While engaging in learning, the learner should try to integrate theoretical studies with the practical experiences.
3. The learner should always keep in mind the principle of correlated learning. What he is trying to learn should be properly correlated with his life experiences, environmental surroundings and other areas of study and knowledge.
4. Identical components between the two learning situations should be properly identified by the leaner. Afterwards he should try to see the relationship between them. With the knowledge of such relationship, he should try to transfer learning from one situation to another.
5. The leaner should avoid rote learning. He must develop the habit of learning through proper understanding and insight in view of his past experiences and present understanding.
6. He must try to take the help of multimedia and sensory aids for the proper understanding and gaining of the required knowledge and skills.
7. As far as possible, the learner should try to learn through his own efforts. He must make use of logical thinking for knowing and discovering the things by himself.
8. The learner should try to seek unity in diversity by searching for the commonness and harmony among the different subjects and learning experiences. He should never hesitate to utilize the learning of one field in the learning of other fields.

9. Instead of learning discrete and isolated facts the learner should concentrate on the learning of the principles, generalization and rules. He should try to discover formulae, rules and principles on the basis of his experiences and then give sufficient time for their utilization and practice.
10. The learner in all the situations should be fully convinced about the importance and value of the transfer of learning or training. He may take the help of his teacher, elders and other experts for learning the art of transfer. As far as possible, he should try to imbibe an attitude of transferability so much so that he remains engaged in making conscious and deliberate efforts for the transfer of his learning and experiences from one situation to another.
11. Ideals as we have seen, possess a great transfer value. Therefore, the learner should try to imbibe desirable attitudes and ideals for the things he wants to transfer from one situation to another, or more specifically to their specific life activities.
12. Learner should try to gain proper knowledge and insight for making distinction between positive and negative transfer of his learning or training. As far as possible, he should seek the maximum positive transfer of his learning or training by saving himself from the ill effects of the negative transfer.

In this way, if one keeps in his view some of the above points, one may be able to get advantage of the mechanism of the transfer of learning and training for illuminating his path of learning.

SUMMARY

Transfer of learning or training refers to a process by which learning or training in one situation is transferred or carried over to other situation. Such transfer is generally categorized into three distinct types — positive, negative and zero. It is said to be positive or negative when learning in one situation helps or hinders the learning in other situations. It is said to be zero when it neither helps nor hinders. Apart from these three general types of transfer, there may be a fourth probability that learning in one situation may partly help and partly hinder the learning in another situation, i.e. learning of a foreign language under the influence of one's national language or mother tongue.

Theories of Transfer of learning or training aim to throw light on the mechanism of transfer of learning, i.e. how does the transfer take place from one situation to another. Theory of mental discipline (Faculty theory) advocates that the faculties of one's mind like memory, attention, reasoning etc, can be trained and strengthened like the muscles of our body for being utilized automatically in the other learning or training situations.

Theory of Identical elements or component propagated by Thondike and Wordworth maintains that the transfer from one situation to another is possible to the extent that there are common or identical elements or components involved in these situations.

Theory of generalization put forth by Charles Judd asserts that transfer do take place in the form of generalizations (conclusions derived through experiences or experiments) instead of the isolated facts related to the identical situation. That is why we usually find that laws, principles or rules once established and understood by a learner may help him a lot in their application and further learning in other likewise situations.

Theory of Ideals put forward by W. C. Bagley asserts that only the ideals and not the common elements or the generalization get transferred from one learning situation to another. It, therefore, suggests that one should first concentrate on building desirable attitudes and ideals about a theory or idea for seeking its transfer from one situation to another.

The findings of the theories of transfer of learning or training can be properly summed up and utilized for seeking maximum positive transfer from one learning situation to another. In the task of seeking such transfer, thus a learner may be properly helped if he keeps in his mind the principle of correlation, integration of the acquired experiences, generalization of the facts and principles and accepting generalization in the form of ideals etc. However much depends upon the determination, will power and sincere efforts of the learners for making him successful in achieving such transfer.

References and Suggested Readings

Crow, L.D. and Crow, Alice, *Educational Psychology*, 3rd Indian reprint, Eurasia Publishing House, New Delhi, 1973.

Ellis, Henry, *Transfer of Learning*, Macmillan, New York, 1965.

Horton D.L., and Turnage, T.W., *Human Learning*, Prentice-Hall, Englewood Cliffs, New Jersey, 1976.

Hulse, S.H., Deese, J. and Egeth, H., *The Psychology of Learning*, 4th ed., McGraw-Hill, New York, 1975.

Kingsley, H.L. and Garry, R., *The Nature and Conditions of Learning*, 2nd ed., Prentice-Hall, Englewood Cliffs, New Jersey, 1957.

Peterson, L.R., *Learning Scott Foresman*, Glenview, Illinois, 1975.

Sorenson, Herbert, *Psychology in Education*, McGraw-Hill, New York, 1948.

Stephens, J.M., *Hand Book of Classroom Learning*, Holt, New York, 1965.

Throndike, E.L., *Human Learning*, Cornell University, New York, 1931.

Woodward, R.S., *Psychology*, Methuen, London, 1945.

19

Motivational Aspect of Behaviour

CHAPTER COMPOSITION

CONCEPT OF MOTIVATION

A small bird collects the material to build its nest in the upper corner of our drawing room. We try to remove it as soon as we see it. The bird, however, again brings the small pieces of straw, leaves etc., and gets back to building its nest. What makes it work so hard? Why did it learn to build the nest? Similarly, we see a student slogging day and night during exams days or a boy constantly trying to learn cycling even after getting many cuts and bruises. What makes them engage in one or the other type of learning and continue their effort even after facing many handicaps and obstacles?

Answers to such questions related to the why of learning lie in a keyword 'Motivation'. The bird, which is building its nest; the student, who is studying hard; and the boy, who is learning to cycle—all do so because of the 'motivation'. They learn because they are motivated to learn. They act because they are persuaded to act in order to satisfy their basic needs and attain the desired goals. There is something that energizes or compel them to act and behave in a specified way. The question arises as to what is it that pushes and pulls an individual to move or act in a specified manner to attain the desired objectives. In psychology, it is named as motive. A motive drives our behaviour in the same way as a motor vehicle is driven by the fuel in its tank. There are a number of motives in our social life that are responsible for energizing and motivating our behaviour. These motives can be broadly classified into two categories as—Primary motives, and Secondary motives.

Primary Motives

These are linked with the basic primary needs associated with the biological or physiological well being of an individual. That is why these motives are often named as biological or physiological motives. The motives ensure the preservation of life for an individual and his race. Examples of such motives are hunger, thirst, sex, avoidance of pain, elimination of body wastes, sleep and rest. The primary motives are universal motives; they are found in all living organisms—human or non-human in one form or the other. They serve the basic physiological need of an organism. They are inborn and innate.

Secondary Motives

Secondary motives are linked with one's socio-psychological needs and hence are named as the psychological or social motives. They are acquired like other forms of learned behaviour in the course of seeking satisfaction to our socio-psychological needs. As examples of these motives we may name achievement motive, self actualization motive, security motive, application motive, affiliation motive etc.

At any occasion when a primary or secondary motive is attached with one's action or behaviour, then his behaviour patterns get dominated by such motive. His behaviour is then termed as motivated behaviour forcing and compelling the individual to behave in a particular way at the command of the involved motive.

Such motivated behaviour of an individual possesses the following characteristics.

1. A motive works as a source or energizer for pushing and pulling the motivated behaviour.
2. It is in fact aimed at the satisfaction of one or the other basic need.
3. One's behaviour can be properly initiated and its continuity properly assured in the shape of his motivated behaviour.
4. Motivated behaviour is quite selective. It tries to respond to the environmental stimuli strictly in view of the satisfaction of the desired needs linked with the motivated behaviour.
5. Motivated behaviour has dynamicity and flexibility in its nature. In the course of behaving, if there is some alteration in the nature of the further requirements or satisfaction of the need, it may bring change in one's motives of behaving. As a result, the shape or direction of the motivating behaviour may altogether be changed as per the demands of the new situation.
6. Motivated behaviour is goal directed. The individual is totally engaged in the realization of the goals of his motivated behaviour. The realization of one's goal may further put him in the cycle of motivated behaviour as he may feel the necessity of the realization of his further needs in the path of his progress or cycle of his life.

7. Motivated behaviour helps us in seeking equilibrium between our needs and their satisfaction. It lies between one's need and its satisfaction. Since the key to our adjustment lies in the satisfaction of our needs, the motivated behaviour proves an important tool and means for making ourselves adjusted and integrated.

From what we have discussed above, we can now derive a workable definition of the term 'motivation' or 'motivated behaviour' in the following way;

> *Motivation as a process or behaviour refers to reinforced, selective and goal-directed behaviour initiated and energized by a motive which aims to maintain balance and equilibrium of the person in relation to his environment by keeping his basic needs satisfied.*

The Motivational Cycle

Motivation, as we have discussed earlier stands for the state of an organism which involves the existence of a need that moves or drives him from within towards a goal for the satisfaction of the desired need.

As visualized from the Fig. 19.1, the motivation or motivation behaviour functions in a continuous flow in the shape of a cycle named as motivational cycle and can be explained as follows:

1. The behaviour is initiated on account of some inherent need. Thereby, the first stage or the starting point of the motivation cycle is the birth of a desire, want or need in an individual. This desire, want or need makes an individual think about the ways and means of its satisfaction. He may now become quite anxious and perturbed for the satisfaction of his desire or need, such that the stage of his mind and body become a germinating point for the birth of a drive or motive.

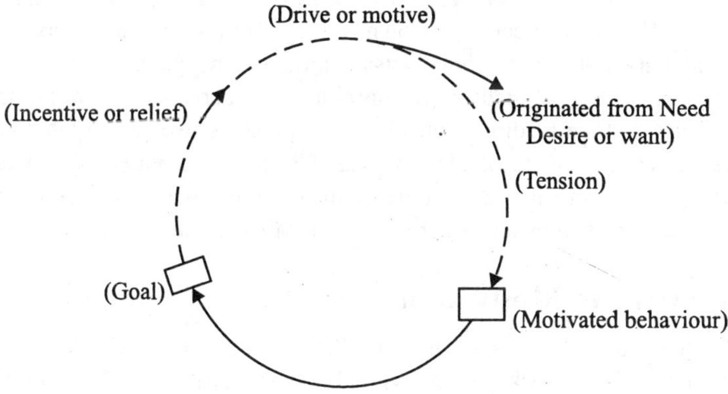

Fig. 19.1 The motivational cycle.

2. The drive or motive so produced on account of the felt need or desire now becomes a driver, persuader and energizer of one's behaviour. It initiates one's behaviour to a goal-directed path, provides sufficient inputs for the continuation of such behaviour till the goal in terms

of the realization of the desired need, desire or want is not attained. Thus in the end, the organism is able to reach the desired goal and get relief from the anxiety and tension with the satisfaction of his need and motive.

3. However, what one gets from the satisfaction of his felt need or desire through his motivated behaviour provides a temporary halt to his behavioural activities. The journey is not at all completely stopped but in fact advances further with a new zeal and enthusiasm for the realization of some other needs and desires. Satisfaction of a need through a motivated behaviour reinforces one's behaviour to work for the realization of another goal, i.e. satisfaction of other needs or desires accompanied with new motives. In this way, one's motivated behaviour gives birth to the next motivated behaviour in the shape of a motivational cycle. Originated from the felt needs, energized and directed by one's motives, reinforced by the progress in the satisfaction of the need or other external reinforcement, the motivation behaviour thus helps in the satisfaction of one's needs or motives. It further energizes an individual to remain in the cycle of motivation by creating new desires, ambitions and needs, the satisfaction of which further requires a set of motivation behaviour and motivation cycle.

KINDS OF MOTIVATION

The motivation can be broadly classified into two kinds :

1. Natural Motivation or Intrinsic Motivation.
2. Unnatural Motivation or Extrinsic Motivation.

Natural Motivation or Intrinsic Motivation

This type of the motivation is directly linked with the natural instincts, urges and impulses of the organism. The individual, who is intrinsically or naturally motivated, performs an act because he finds interest within the activity. He is engaged in learning something because he derives pleasure in learning that thing. The activity carries its own reward and the individual takes genuine interest in performing the activity not due to some outside motives and goals.

When a student tries to solve a mathematical problem and derives pleasure in the task of solving it or tries to read poetry and the reading itself gives him pleasure, we can say that he is intrinsically motivated. In these cases the source of pleasure lies within the activities. He solves the problems or reads the poetry for its own sake. Such type of motivation has real values in the learning task as it creates spontaneous attention and interest and sustains it throughout.

Unnatural or Extrinsic Motivation

In such motivation, the source of pleasure does not lie within the task. Such kind of motivation has no functional relationships to the task. The individual does or learns something not for its own sake, but as a means of obtaining desired goals or getting some external reward. Working for a better grade or honour, learning a skill to earn the livelihood, receiving praise and blame, rewards and punishment etc. all belong to this category.

In comparison to Extrinsic motivation, Intrinsic motivation, as a source of spontaneous inspiration and stimulation, brings better results in the teaching-learning process. Therefore, it is always better to make use of intrinsic motivation, whenever possible. But in case it is not appropriate to make use of intrinsic motivation, the use of extrinsic motivation should not be suspended.

Depending upon the learning situation and the nature of the task, the choice for providing appropriate motivation should be made by the teacher so that the learner may take profound interest in the learning activity.

NEEDS, DRIVES AND INCENTIVES

While discussing the process of motivation through a motivation cycle, we have used the terms needs, drives and incentives, etc. All these concepts need a necessary explanation for knowing about their true nature and role in the process of motivation. Let us briefly discuss all of them.

Needs

MEANING OF THE TERM 'NEED'

We make use of the term 'need' in our day-to-day life in many ways. When we desire or wish to have food, we say that we are in need of the food. We need water for quenching our thirst, sex objects for the satisfaction of our sex needs, companions and friends in the hours of loneliness and loneliness or rest after being tired from the busy schedule. We have a craving for being loved or to love and also keep struggling for some status, recognition and appreciation for our work and duties. In this way, the term 'need' is very often used as synonymous with the terms 'want' and 'desire'. We are always in a state of anxiety, eagerness and temptation for fulfilling our desires or wants. In fact these desires or wants (psychologically named as needs) prompt or persuade us to behave in a specific way.

We may have a workable definition of the term 'need' in the following way:

Need refers to a condition or state of our mind that prompts or persuades us to act or behave in a specific way.

WHAT ARE THE BASIC NEEDS?

There is no end to our desires or wants in our life. As a result it is difficult to number our individual needs. However, there are needs that are quite essential for an individual in terms of his staying alive, maintaining proper physical and mental health, leading a social life and getting well in terms of personality development etc. Such essential needs are referred to as an individual's basic needs. These basic needs for their proper understanding may be broadly classified into the following two categories.

A. Physiological or Biological Needs

B. Socio-psychological Needs.

Physiological or Biological Needs. All our bodily or organic needs fall into this category. They may be further categorized as under:

In this first category of biological needs are the need for oxygen, water and food. These needs are most fundamental for our survival and existence. Without them, we can hardly survive.

In the chain of our survival and existence, the other category of the biological needs include:

(a) Need for rest when tired.
(b) Need for being active when rested.
(c) Need for sleep when deprived of it for long.
(d) Need for regular elimination of waste products from the body.

(e) Need for having an even internal body temperature.

(f) Need for protection from the threats of physical environment like hazards of weather, natural calamities, wild animals etc.

In the third category of biological needs, we can place the need for satisfaction of sex urge or desire to seek sex experiences. Although sex urge is not essential for the survival of an individual, it is the strongest human urge in the satisfaction of which lies his proper growth, development, adjustment and well-being. Moreover, the satisfaction of this need and normal sex behaviour are more essential for a happy family life and the continuity and survival of the human species.

In the last category of biological needs, we have needs that are associated with the demands of our senses. These sensory needs include the need for physical contact, sensory stimulation and stimulus variability and manipulation. Although we may not die if deprived of these needs, they are supposed to be quite essential for our general welfare and optimal growth.

Socio-psychological Needs. Under this category, we can list all those needs that are associated with the socio-cultural environment of an individual. They are acquired through social learning. Although such needs are not linked with the survival of the organism or species, their deprivation may lead to a psychological stage seriously affecting his survival and welfare. These needs for the sake of clarity may be classified as follows:

1. *Need for freedom or gaining independence:* An individual possesses a craving for independence. Nature has created us free and independent as individuals and requires us to remain so. Therefore, all human beings have an urge to remain free and independent.
2. *Need for security:* Every one of us needs to feel secure not only to save ourselves from the physical dangers but also from socio-psychological angles. One needs desirable emotional, social and economical security for his well-being.
3. *Need for love and affection:* Every one of us, irrespective of age, caste, colour and creed, has a strong desire to love and be loved. Depending upon one's age and circumstances, it may vary in kind and nature, but a sort of emotional craving for the satisfaction of this need is exhibited universally by all living organisms.
4. *Need to achieve:* Every human being has a strong desire to achieve some or the other things like money, fame, reputation, degree, merit, position, medals, good life partner, spiritual attainment, etc., not only for raising his status in the eyes of others but also for the satisfaction he draws from his own accomplishment.
5. *Need for recognition or social approval:* Each one of us has an inherent desire for gaining recognition, appreciation and esteem in the eyes of others. An artist may thus desire to be known for his art, a young woman may desire to be appreciated for her beauty, good manners or house-keeping by fellow human beings, especially the members of the group to which she belongs. A student may show this desire in surpassing other students of his class and thus gaining required social status, prestige or approval from his fellow students, teachers and parents.
6. *Need for social company:* Man is referred to as a social animal in the sense that he has a strong urge to be with his own kind and maintain social relations with them. The real strength of this need can be felt by those individuals who are faced with social rejection or solitary confinement.

7. *Need for self-assertion* : Every one of us has an inherent desire to get an opportunity to rule or dominate others. It may vary in intensity from person to person but it is surely exhibited by all of us in one or the other situation irrespective of age, strength and status. Some may show it to their juniors, servants, life partner or children while others may exhibit it towards their pet animals, birds and even inanimate things like dolls or pictures. This need of asserting oneself gives birth to an important motive called power motive that works as a strong determiner of one's personality and behaviour.
8. *Need for self-expression or self-actualization*: We all have an inherent craving for the expression of our self and actualization of our own potentialities. An individual may have a hidden poet, musician or painter in his self and thus may have a strong desire to get his talent exhibited or nurtured. So, one wants to get adequate opportunities for the expression and development of his potentialities and subsequently he strives for it and is not happy until he gets opportunities for such expression and self-actualization.

HIERARCHY OF NEEDS

We have tried to mention the basic needs of the human beings which are quite essential for proper living. Which of these needs are superior to others, which one falls in the list of priority in our life, these are some of the questions that remain unanswered at this stage. Abraham Maslow, the famous psychologist tried to answer such questions by providing a hierarchical structure of the human needs in the way shown in Fig. 19.2.

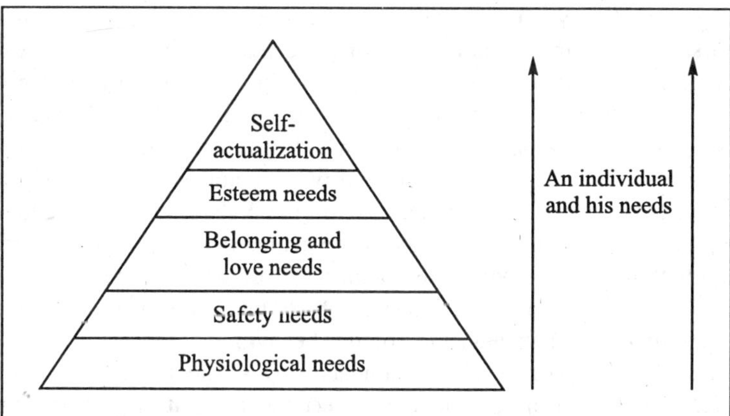

Fig. 19.2 Maslow's hierarchical structure of needs.

As is evident from the figure, in the hierarchy of needs first comes the needs related to one's survival (like the need for water, food, sleep etc.) and species-specific survival (like need for sex). It is the base and starting point. In the beginning, one has to struggle for the satisfaction of these needs. After their satisfaction, one moves to the next higher order of needs, i.e. safety needs. When one feels secure and is satisfied with the physiological needs, one can think for the satisfaction of the next higher order of needs, i.e. love and need for affection. After meeting the demands of these three levels of needs, one aspires for getting respect and gaining importance in the eyes of the others. After the satisfaction of one's esteem needs, one reaches the top of the hierarchy of needs, i.e. self-actualization needs. These needs, according to Maslow, are the very fine and superior needs, exclusively distinctive to the human beings for gracing one as an individual and a person. Here, through these needs one gets an opportunity to make one's internal as external self. One expresses one's self through the satisfaction of such needs. As a result one may bring out, through one's creation or expression, the painter, poet, scientist, musician, dancer etc, hidden in one's inner self.

Through such hierarchical structure of needs, Maslow has emphasized that as one grows and develops as a human being, he advances through the satisfaction of these needs in the order as provided in the structure. Also at any point or age of his life, an individual is confronted to satisfy his needs in the order as specified in the structure. One who is hungry can't be expected to think of showering love and affection or aspiring for status. The satisfaction of lower order needs paves the way for attending to the next higher order needs. The cycle of one's growth and development is not completed unless one is able to satisfy the top order needs, i.e. self-actualization needs.

The structure of needs as suggested by Maslow, generally fits well for most of the people. However, there may be exceptions when one does not care for the satisfaction of lower order needs and makes frantic efforts for the realization of the higher order needs. The biographies of many saints, national heroes, martyrs, inventors and discoverers, poets, writers and composers may reveal this fact that one can reach the top order in the satisfaction of his needs without caring much for the satisfaction of his lower order needs.

Drives

A need gives rise to a drive which may be defined as *an aroused reaction tendency or a stage of heightened tension that sets up activities in an individual and sustains them for increasing his general activity level.* The existence of a need moves or drives the individual from within and directs his activities to a goal that may bring about the satisfaction of the need. The strength of a drive depends upon the strength of the stimulus involving the related need.

Drives of any nature are divided into two categories. In the first category, we have *biological* or *primary drives* such as hunger, thirst, escape from pain and sex drive. In the second category, we have *socio-psychological* or *secondary drives* such as fear or anxiety, desire for approval, striving for achievement, aggression and dependence. These drives are not related to our physiological needs and, therefore, do not arise on account of imbalances in the body's internal functioning. They arise from the socio-psychological needs and are said to be acquired through social learning as a result of one's interaction with his socio-cultural environment. These drives move an individual to act for the satisfaction of his socio-psychological needs which in turn proves as a reinforcer of the behaviour for the continuity and maintenance of the behaviour.

Contrary to the socio-psychological or secondary drives, the biological drives are basically unlearned in nature. They arise from our biological needs as a result of an attempt to satisfy these needs.

Incentives

Needs and drives, as we have studied in the earlier pages, reveal and represent the inner state of an individual's behaviour. When there is a deficiency or shortage of water and food in our body, we feel the need for them. The need gives birth to thirst and hunger drives. But sometimes, it may happen that we feel the necessity of getting some eatables or drink in spite of the fact that our body does not require them. There is no shortage of water or food and hence there is no biological or physiological need that is to be gratified by our behaviour. In this case, such need is produced on account of our excessive liking for a particular type of food or drink or on account of its smell, taste and perception instead of its natural demand or necessity by our body. Such external factors, affecting our needs, are usually referred to as *incentives*. Not only our needs but drives—physiological and socio-psychological—are also influenced and guided by incentives. If one gets incentives in terms of the food of his choice and taste, he may be attracted and feel necessary of getting it more and more. The drive of hunger here gets a new source of energy and backing by such incentives.

As the examples of incentives, we may cite praise, appreciation, rewards, bonus, fulfillment of one's needs and getting the desired objectives.

Any type of incentive always works as a reinforcing agent as it adds more force to a new attached drive like adding fuel to the already ignited fire. As a result, the individual behaves with new zeal and enthusiasm for achieving his need-based objectives. For example, let us take the case of providing bonus to the workers of a factory. Here bonus is an incentive. It provides an additional back up and energy to the workers for doing hard or extra work to meet the production targets of the factory. It works as a reinforcing agent to activate their behaviour and creates an extra drive for bringing efficiency in their work. The same may be perceived in the case of any individual where we may find a tremendous change in his behaviour. For example, a piece of toffee, chocolate or ice-cream or a child toy may work as an incentive for a child to give more strength to his drive and as a result he may be further motivated to act or behave in a desirable way. Similarly a favourite food may provide an incentive for an individual to eat or a favourite movie may compel other individuals to go and see it. In this way needs and drives, whether primary or secondary, are greatly affected and directed by the incentives.

It is not essential for these incentives to remain external. The internal incentives, from within, also have the same effect of directing or influencing one's drive for the satisfaction of one or the other need. During the course of his activity, if one feels satisfied with his progress in work or gets success in achieving his objectives, he gets a lot of incentive from his own self providing fresh energy to put his heart and soul in the work.

Motives

In the search of the origin of a motivated behaviour, the psychologists, as we have already emphasized above, start from basic needs—biological or socio-psychological. A particular need gives rise to an activating force named drive that moves an individual to act or behave in a particular fashion at a particular time. Drives thus work as a basic activating force behind a behaviour. However, practically, in psychological as well as day-to-day language, we usually come across statements like: What was the motive behind this crime? What may be the motive of an individual to criticize or blame us? and so on. These statements clearly point out that motives work as a basic activating force behind a particular behaviour. It makes one think as to why the terms 'drive' and 'motive' (which carry the same meaning) are often employed interchangeably. However, psychologists, while explaining the mechanism of behaviour, have now started to concentrate on the term 'motive' instead of the old term 'drive'. For clarity, they have tried to define it in the following ways:

Fisher

A motive is an inclination or impulsion to action plus some degree of orientation or direction. (Quoted by Labh Singh and Tiwari, 1971, p. 72).

Rasen, Fox and Gregory

A motive may be defined as a readiness or disposition to respond in some ways and not others to a variety of situations. (1972, p. 41).

Caroll

A need gives rise to one or more motives. A motive is a rather specific process which has been learned. It is directed towards a goal. (1969, p. 21)

All these definitions lead us to generalize that:

1. Motive is an inner state of mind or an aroused feeling.
2. It is generated from basic needs or drives.
3. It compels an individual to respond by creating a kind of tension or urge to act.
4. It is a preparation for responding in some selective way to the satisfaction of the related need.
5. It is a goal-directed activity, pursued till the attainment of the goal.
6. A change in goal may bring changes in the nature and strength of the motive.
7. Attainment of a goal helps in the release of tension aroused by a specific motive.
8. Motive may be considered as a learned response or tendency and also an innate disposition.

Understood in this way, *a motive may be considered as an energetic force or tendency (learned or innate) working within the individual to compel, persuade or inspire him to act for the satisfaction of his basic needs or attainment of some specific purposes.*

HOMEOSTASIS

The term 'homeostasis' was coined by W.B. Cannon, a prominent Harvard University physiologist. On the basis of his experiments he concluded that our body system constantly works toward an optimum level of functioning, i.e. maintaining a normal state of balance between input and output. For example, when blood sugar level drops, the brain, glands, digestive organs and other parts of the body send out signals that activate a hunger drive or hunger motive and makes one hungry. After food has been consumed by the individual's body, it returns to a state of balance called homeostatic state. The regulating phenomenon or process that is required to maintain system equilibrium or balance of the body is known as homeostasis. During homeostasis, the body undergoes a constant change. For example, when the hot days set off or disturb the physical mechanism that lead to perspiring, a cooler environment helps the body to return to a homeostatic state.

The term 'homeostasis' used by Cannon with reference to body chemistry has now been broadened to include any behaviour that upsets the balance of an individual. The denial or failure in the satisfaction of any basic need may disturb the equilibrium or balance of an individual. This may give birth to a relevant drive or motive and compel an individual to behave in a specific way so that the felt need is satisfied and the balance is restored. For example, when an individual feels deprived of love after not being able to meet his need for affection, he gets disturbed. In other words, the balance of his psyche gets upset. Its restoration is needed for making the individual adjusts in relation to his environment. Thereby, a drive or motive arises making the individual behave for the satisfaction of his need for love and affection and thus ultimately restore the balance of his mental state. Similarly, a need and drive connected with visual stimulation may arise for the restoration of the disturbed mental state of a long-distance driver who gets bored with the sameness of the highway.

MEASUREMENT OF MOTIVATION

How much is one motivated for performing a particular type of task or behaviour? What is the motive behind his motivated behaviour? What type of motivation is guiding or directing one's behaviour at a particular time? These are the issues which are taken up through the measurement of motives. Generally the following four techniques or methods are employed for such measurement.

Observation Method

In this method or technique, the behaviour of an individual is observed under carefully controlled situations as well as naturalistic conditions. What is one's daily routine? What type of activities or behaviour are demonstrated by him during the course of his life activities? How do different types of motives guide and direct his behaviour? All such issues are answered on the basis of proper analysis of the data obtained through observation.

Experimental Method

In this method, measurement of the motivational process is carried out with the help of experiments or experimental studies. These experiments may be conducted on animals, birds as well as human beings.

In general, these may be of the following nature.

(i) As we know that the deficiency of a particular thing like food, water etc., makes an individual feel its desire, want or need. This need then gives birth to a subsequent drive or motive like hunger or thirst motive. This aroused motive then directs the behaviour of an individual towards the satisfaction of the felt needs. In this way, motivated behaviour is nothing but one's behaviour or attempts directed towards the satisfaction of the felt needs. Based on this ground, we can plan the experimental situations for measuring the intensity of a particular type of motivational behaviour. If an animal or individual is hungry or thirsty, he may be motivated to work in the desired way through the exploitation of this hunger or thirst motive. He can be made to work in any way we desire by assuring or providing him the meal or drink he needs for his survival or satisfaction. The manner in which he demonstrates his behaviour during the lack or deficiency of food or drink and also at the time of fulfilling his need may thus be utilized for the measurement of his motivational behaviour.

(ii) The performance and achievement level as well as the manner and style of one's behaviour may also be made a yard stick for the intensity, nature and quality of the motivational behaviour. We can have experimental studies to find out the effects of praise, rewards and other incentive on the ways of working and behaving, achievements and production etc. of the various working groups like students in a school and labourers on a working site.

Using Personally Measurement Techniques

The method and techniques used in the assessment of personality and behavioural characteristics may also be utilized in the assessment and measurement of the motivational behaviour. Interview, rating scales, questionnaires, inventories are some of the techniques with the help of which we can have a direct measurement or assessment of one's motivational behaviour. We can also utilize projective techniques like Rorschach ink blot test, TAT, CAT, sentence completion, picture composition, gaming techniques etc. for the indirect measurement or assessment of one's motivational behaviour.

Using Standardized Tests

Many of the standardized tests are now available with the psychological laboratories established in the schools and colleges for the measurement of different types of motivational behaviour. These are also available with the publishers and shopkeepers who especially deal with the educational and psychological tests and materials. We can utilize these sources for the needed experimentation and testing of the one or the other type of motivational behaviour. For example, if we want to measure the achievement motivational level of a group of students or a particular individual (or student) we can take the help of the standardized tests available for this purpose. Two of the easily available tests for this purpose are:

(i) CIE Achievement Motivation Test by Dr. N.K. Dutt and Dr. K.G. Rastogi.

(ii) Achievement Motivation Test by Dr. B.P. Bhargava.

The test material of such tests usually contains the items of the following nature:

I prefer...

A. Happy go lucky life to industrious life.
B. Accepting facts based on Logic to those based on authority.
C. Getting encouragement from my friends and elders.
D. Complex problems to simple problems.
E. The company of elders and experienced persons.

I believe that...

A. It is better to die than beg.
B. Freedom is better than repression.
C. It is better to be faithful than famous.
D. Love is more justice.
E. My future lies only in doing something significant.

With the responses of the subjects, one can have an idea of the relative level of their achievement motivation.

PRINCIPLES OF MOTIVATION

Motivation is the key word and essential requirement for the success of the teaching-learning process carried out in the classroom. Unfortunately there is no single magic formula or set of principles for motivating all students in every teaching-learning situation. Motivation is in fact an individual phenomenon. What is true for one learner may not suit the others in the same or other learning situation. However, on the basis of researches and experiences in the field of motivation psychology and pedagogy, the followings may be named as the general principles of motivation.

1. **Principle of readiness to learn:** Readiness to learn is an initial crucial step for motivating one to learn for which he is prepared mentally as well as physically. If a student is not ready to learn, he or she may not be reliable in following instructions and realizing the instructional objectives. Sometimes the student's readiness to learn comes with time and the teacher's role in such a situation is to create conditions and encourage its development.
2. **Principle of Capitalizing on the needs and motives:** Motivation is best carried out if it is based on the existing needs and motives of the learner. You, as a teacher, better know

that some of the needs your students may bring to the classroom are the need to learn something in order to complete a particular task or activity, the need to seek new experiences, the need to perfect skills, the need to overcome challenges, the need to become competent, the need to succeed and do well, the need to feel involved and to interact with other people etc. Satisfying such needs is rewarding in itself and such rewards bring more motivation than any grades or prizes.

3. **Principle of active participation in learning:** Good motivation requires active involvement on the part of the learners. Passivity dampens student's motivation and curiosity. Therefore as a teacher, pose questions. Don't tell your students something when you can ask them. Encourage students to suggest approaches to a problem or to guess the results of an experiment, lead a discussion in a small group, adopt collaborative learning and see the results. Your students will always remain motivated to learn.
4. **Principle of arousing and maintaining interest:** Interest is the key word and central figure in any process of motivation. One gets motivated and remains absorbed in a particular learning task depending upon the degree of arousal and maintaining interest in the task. Therefore, make the teaching-learning task as interesting as possible so as to motivate your students.
5. **Principle of capturing and sustaining attention:** Attention is the mother of interest and interest is the mother of motivation. Therefore, if you have to motivate the students for learning, you will have to catch hold the mother and particularly the grandmother first. Unless the learner does not attend the learning activity, how will he be attracted and motivated for its learning. Therefore, the initial task in getting the learner motivated is to capture his attention and then to hold or sustain it till it is needed to keep him motivated.
6. **Principle of clarity and definiteness of goal and purposes:** The learner is motivated to the extent he or she sees some purpose, values and advantages drawn from the learning. Similarly, if one is definite about the goals and objectives of his learning, he can go straight ahead on the path of his learning without any confusion and ambiguity. He can be more attentive, take more interest and show more zeal and enthusiasm towards the learning of the things that are clear to him in nature and outcomes.
7. **Principle of proper organization of the instructional material:** Learner's interest and motivation very much depend upon the quality of the instructional material and its proper organization. If the learners realize that the instructional material possesses many of the new and knowledgeable things and in fact serve their purpose and needs in so many ways naturally, they will be more attracted and inclined for their learning format. Similarly the best organized material making the information more meaningful and relevant will automatically make them more motivated to learn the things of that instruction material. This is why the teachers who take the pain in planning and preparing their lessons and organizing instructional material in a proper way make way with their students in motivating them towards their classroom teaching.
8. **Principle of employing proper methods and devices:** Much depends upon the art of teaching. A good teacher, by adopting suitable proper methods, may motivate his students for a successful journey of teaching and learning inside or outside the classroom. The choice of proper methods, including aid material, devices and modern technology, may thus work as a good motivating agent.

9. **Principle of creating an open and positive environment:** The autocratic functioning, breeding of the conformity and passivity, denial of the freedom to ask and respond, irrelevant rebuking and reproofing of the student etc. prove quite detrimental to the enthusiasm and initiatives of the learners. It is better to say good bye to all these negative elements and introduce an open and positive teaching-learning environment for the student's motivation.
10. **Principle of change and variety:** Introduction of change and variety proves a big factor in motivating the learner in any teaching-learning situation. It brings novelty, newness, curiosity, adventurism and other likewise things in a routine or the otherwise boring and fatigued environment of learning situation. Therefore it is always advisable to introduce change and variety in terms of the instructional material, methods, devices teaching-learning situations etc. for keeping the students motivated.
11. **Principle of providing proper feedback:** The learner should know about the progress of his learning as frequently and immediately as possible. It helps in maintaining his interest and motivation further in the ongoing teaching-learning process. The knowledge of the progress in attaining the prior set goals motivates the student in directing his activities with more energy and enthusiasm towards the goal by offering continuous opportunities to experience success.
12. **Principle of providing incentives and reinforcement:** A behaviour gets reinforced through a proper schedule of appropriate reinforcer including incentives. It is also true of the learning behaviour. However, the decision in a particular teaching-learning situation rests on the teacher for the employment of one or the other reinforcer and incentive. Sometimes the learner may be motivated through a few words of praise or non verbal behaviour like smiling or nodding of the head, other times he may need recognition in terms of grades, medals or prizes.
13. **Principle of resorting to internal motivation:** It is an acceptable fact that internal motivation is more long-lasting and more self-directive than the external motivation. It is also true that some individuals, particularly children of certain ages and some adults, have little capacity for internal motivation and must be guided and reinforced constantly through external rewards and incentives. In such cases, the beginning may be made through these means of external motivation. However, caution should always be exercised in using external rewards as to use them only when they are absolutely necessary. Ultimately one should learn to get motivation from the internal sources instead of the external rewards and incentives.
14. **Principle of ensuring success:** It is an underlying fact that success is more predictably motivating than failure. This is why the fear of getting failure or not getting desired success keeps the learners away from the learning situation. It is, therefore, quite essential that learning tasks and processes must follow the maxims like 'simple to complex' and 'concrete to abstract'. Learner should be presented with the learning matter and taught with the methods that suit their abilities and capacities. In this connection, it is always better to choose activities and methods of intermediate difficulty value rather than those are difficult (little likelihood of success) or easy (high probability of success) as the students feel little or no motivation for the things that are too difficult or too simple.
15. **Principle of maintaining mild level of anxieties:** When one is set to learn something for realizing one's needs or learning objectives in a particular teaching-learning situation, he

consciously or unconsciously suffers from some anxiety. It is this anxiety which initiates and rather prompts and forces him to remain motivated in the teaching-learning process. However, severe anxiety is incapacitating. It may adversely affect the working and behaviour of the learner. In such over-anxious moments, he may lose control of the learning activities and drift away from his learning goals. Therefore, it is the duty of the teacher to save the learners from severe anxiety-producing learning situation.

16. **Principle of affiliation and approval:** Both affiliation and approval are said to be strong motivators. This is why groups or corporate learning is considered to be better than individual or separate learning. One needs his affiliation to a class or a group for better learning, particularly in connection with comparing his abilities, opinion and emotions with others. Similarly, one needs the acceptance and approval of his learning behaviour (changes of opinions, beliefs, knowledge, skill etc.) from others. Therefore, a teacher should keep in view the principle of group behaviour and group dynamics for the proper motivation of his students in the teaching-learning process.

17. **Principle of good rapport between teacher and students:** The arousal of motivation and its maintenance in a teaching-learning process depends upon the existence and quality of rapport between the teacher and his students. The better rapport will automatically have better motivation while its absence will have negative impact in making the students attracted and engaged in the classroom activities.

18. **Principle of realistic expectation from the students:** Psychological and educational researchers have proved that the teachers' expectations have powerful effect on the student's performance. If your behaviour as a teacher shows that you expect your students to be motivated, hardworking and interested in the learning task, they are more likely to be so. In case, you have neither such expectations nor do you show them through your behaviour, then the student will hardly be motivated towards the teaching-learning process. There is one more thing you would need to take care of. As a teacher you must maintain a realistic level regarding your expectations from your students. Realistic in the sense that your standards might be high enough in motivating students to do their best but they should not be so high that students are frustrated in trying to meet them.

19. **Principle of avoiding intense competition among students:** Competition provides opportunities to motivate the students to work and excel. However, on the negative side it may produce anxiety and unhealthy rivalries among the students that can interfere with their learning. Therefore, as a teacher you must discourage your students from comparing themselves to one another, refrain from public criticisms of student's performance and from comments on activities that pit students against each other and as far as possible you should arrange the teaching-learning situation in such a way that they work co-operatively in groups rather than compete as individuals.

20. **Principle of setting good examples and models:** Students can be set on the path of motivated behaviour easily with the help of presenting good examples and models of appropriate behaviour before them. For this purpose they must be acquainted with the biographies and autobiographies of great men and scholars for imbibing their traits and ways of working. The help of multimedia may also be taken in this task. Similarly students should also be made aware of the good work done by the contemporaries particularly by their peers. The good work, ideas, knowledge and accomplishments of individual students, groups, classes or schools should be brought to the notice of the students so that they may

set these persons, events and situations as their role models for their motivation toward learning accomplishment and creation.

21. **Principle of efforts and enthusiasm of the teacher:** Last but not the least, motivation of the students depends much upon the motivation of the teacher, his abilities and capacities to teach and his sincerity and enthusiasm for fulfilling his obligations as a teacher. It is perfectly true. If you become bored or apathetic about your subject and teaching, so will your students. Therefore, never loose your heart and slacken your efforts. The necessary motivation and enthusiasm for motivating your student would then automatically emerge from your confidence and mastery over the content material and the genuine pleasure you feel about your teaching.

Techniques of Motivation in Classroom Situation

Motivation, as discussed earlier, occupies a central place in the teaching-learning process. It is, in fact, indispensable to learning. Every teacher, at one time or the other, is faced with the problem of motivating his students to learn. Therefore, it is essential to think of the ways and means for achieving motivation in the classroom situation. The principle of motivation described earlier may provide necessary guidelines for this purpose. However, in brief, we can discuss the following techniques in this regard.

1. **Child-centered approach:** It is the child who has to learn. The teacher only helps him to learn. Therefore, a teacher only helps him in learning whatever the child has to learn. But what the child has to learn, should be judged according to his ability, interest, capacity and previous experiences. Is he mature enough to understand the new material or do the assigned task? Does he possess necessary skills and abilities for doing the present task? Is he mentally prepared for the present learning? These are some of the questions that should be kept in mind while asking the child to learn something new or perform some assigned task. The learning material or experiences should always be assigned according to the needs, interests and abilities of the child.
2. **Linking the new learning with the past:** Experience is a great teacher. What has been learned or experienced in the past proves a good base for the present learning. The assigned task seems to be interesting, easy and within the capacity of an individual if it is properly related with a past experience. The child is easily motivated to learn the new material if he thinks that he knows all that is required as the base for the new learning. Therefore, it is the duty of the teacher to base his present teaching upon the previous learning experiences acquired by the pupil.
3. **Use of effective methods, aids and devices in teaching:** Whatever the subject-matter may be, a good teacher with his art of teaching can simulate the students for learning. Old dogmatic methods kill the initiative and interest of the learner while the progressive methods based on the psychological principles keep him motivated. The use of audio-visual aids and the service rendered by museum, library, places of visit etc., directly help the teachers in motivating his students. Therefore, a teacher should make use of the suitable methods, devices and aid-material in his teaching.
4. **Definiteness of the purpose and goals:** One cannot feel interested in a task if one is not aware of the purpose served by doing that. Definiteness of aims and the goals makes the learner interested and sets him to work in a desirable direction. The students must be acquainted well with the aims and objectives of studying a subject or topic. They must be

told the purpose of acquiring a new skill or experiences so that a clear perception of the goal may motivate them and bring required results.

5. **Knowledge of the results and progress.** Every learner wishes to know the result of his striving. When we engage ourselves in doing some task, it is natural to be curious about the progress made in that task. The knowledge that we are progressing satisfactorily gives us proper incentive. A child, who is attempting a mathematical problem under a particular topic, gets constant motivation if he is well-acquainted with his progress. Immediate knowledge of the results provides sufficient feedback to the learner. It does not only acquaint him with his success or failure but makes him able to plan his further attempts in reaching specific goals. Proper critical evaluation of the pupil's work in terms of specific defects, errors and good points etc., proves an effective incentive for the desirable improvement. Teachers should make provision for acquainting the students well with their progress. For this purpose, proper report-cards, graphs and charts should be maintained in the schools.

6. **Praise and Reproof:** Both praise and reproof are potent incentives. They can be safely used for the achievement of desired motivation in the classroom situations. Which one of these incentives will prove more effective depends upon the personality of the learner as well as of the person who gives them. In case of some individuals, both praise and reproof work well while others respond best to one or the other. Generally, those having feelings of inadequacy respond more favourably to praise, and those who are self-assured, work harder after criticism. The ways in which these incentives are given or repeated by the teacher, also count much. The essential condition for the effectiveness of these incentives is that they must either satisfy or threaten our security or one or more of our other motives. In this way, the teacher must try to recognize the nature of the students and consequently make use of the praise or reproof in motivating and inspiring them.

7. **Rewards and Punishment:** Rewards and punishment bring the same results as praise and reproof. Both of these are powerful incentives and try to influence the future conduct or learning of an organism favourably. While punishment as a negative motive is based on the fears of failure, losing prestige, insult on rejection, physical pain and so on; the reward as a positive motive seeks to influence conduct favourably by associating a pleasant feeling with the desired act.

   As far as possible, the use of punishment as a motivating agent should be avoided as it kills initiative, leadership resourcefulness and the spirit of free thinking and adventurous living. On the other hand, rewards like prizes, honours, certificates, medals etc. have psychological value and develop in the students creative abilities, spirit of emulation, self-confidence and self-respect and other democratic feelings.

   With this discussion, it should not be taken that punishment as a rule should be decried in all circumstances and never be given to anybody. In some cases, it brings more improvement than reward. On the other hand, indiscriminate and unqualified use of reward proves harmful as it sometimes tends to become an end in itself. For example, a student may strive hard to get the gold medal but in doing so he may be interested not in learning but in the medal. Therefore, the teacher should be very careful in using rewards or punishment as an incentive to motivate his students.

8. **Competition and Cooperation:** Competition as a source of motivation is universally recognized. Simply said, it indicates the desire to excel others. Nowadays we find too much

competition in all walks of life. In the field of education, this spirit can be turned into a powerful motivating force. We can create learning situations where the students of a class are engaged in a healthy competition. Competition may take one of the two forms—competition against another person or competition against one's own record. In the former form of competition, there lies a danger of developing undesirable habits in the individual as he may resort to unfair means to excel. The other form of competition stimulates the learner to compete with his own past record. It sets him on the path of self-learning and provides an intrinsic motivation. Therefore, the teacher should try to inculcate the feeling of self-improvement in the learner.

Competition, particularly, the group-competition may give birth to bitter criticism, improper rivalry, enmity and conflicts etc. To remove these bad effects, the remedy is often suggested in the form of cooperation. The cooperation as well as competition are used in combination. In this process, the members of a group may cooperate with other groups in competition with still other groups and so on. The type of cooperation and friendly competition develop team spirit, community feeling, thinking for a common cause, a sense of unity and other socially desirable habits. A wise teacher should try to make use of the competition based on co-operation and the feeling of 'we' and 'us'.

9. **Ego-involvement:** The ego consists of attitudes raising to the self. Everyone of us tries to maintain status and self-respect. We like those people, objects and situation who make us feel important and dislike those who make us feel inferior. Teachers, generally, are in the habit of ridiculing and snubbing their students. It is not the proper way of motivating them. Instead of using such means, the teacher should try to motivate his students by appealing to ego maximization. He should engage them in the activities which can appeal to his self-respect and raise his status among his classmates or peers.
10. **Development of proper attitude:** Attitude is defined as one's set to react in a given way in a particular situation. It is closely related to attention and interest. A child, who has developed a healthy attitude towards manual work, takes genuine interest in working with hands, while the other one who has developed a negative attitude towards it, shirks away. In this way, a favourable attitude helps the learner in setting of his mind or preparing him mentally for doing a particular task or learning something. Therefore, the teacher should try to develop proper attitude towards the desired act or learning.
11. **Appropriate learning situation and environment**: The situation and the environment, in which the learning is to be made by the learner, influences the learning process. A well-equipped, healthy classroom environment proves a motivating force. The child likes to read, write or listen to the teacher carefully if he finds favourable environment and appropriate learning situations. The suitability of the school building, the seating arrangements and other physical facilities available and affection he gets from his teachers, the mutual cooperation and help he gets from his classmates, the opportunity of participation in the school co-curricular activities etc. all influence and motivate the learning behaviour of the child. Therefore, efforts should be made to provide suitable learning situations and environment of effective learning.

SUMMARY

Motivation refers to a process in which an individual is compelled or energized to act or behave in a particular way at a particular time for accomplishing some specific goal or purpose in order to satisfy his one or the other basic need. The behaviour demonstrated by an individual as a result of the process of motivation is termed as motivational behaviour.

Motivational behaviour of an individual is found to function in a continuous flow of a cycle named motivational cycle. The first stage or the starting point of the motivational cycle is the birth of desire, want or need in the individual. The felt need or desire then becomes a germinating point for the birth of a drive or motive. The drive helps in the realization of the felt needs. But the satisfaction of one need may provide incentive and thus give birth to another similar or higher needs and in this way one may remain in the repeated cycle of such motivational behaviour for going ahead in the path of his progress.

Motivation may be broadly classified as Intrinsic and Extrinsic motivation. In Intrinsic motivation, the source of motivation lies within the task of activity itself. The individual gets motivated to do one or the other things on account of the satisfaction received by him in doing so in order to satisfy his natural instincts, urges and impulses. In extrinsic motivation, however, the source of pleasure does not lie within the task. Here one does not learn or do something for its own sake but does it as a means of getting some external reward i.e. working for a grade or honour instead of seeking joy in the activity itself.

The activating forces lying behind one's motivational behaviour may be named as needs, drives, incentives and motives. The needs that are quite essential for human beings are called basic needs and are classified as physiological (biological needs) and socio-psychological needs. These needs of human beings may be arranged in a hierarchical order. Abraham Maslow provided such structure by grouping the needs of human beings in five distinct categories like physiological needs, safety needs, love needs, esteem needs and self-actualization needs (arranging them from bottom to peak). These needs give birth to one or the other related drives which work as a driver for driving an individual from within to behave for the satisfaction of his needs. Hence drivers are responsible for activating an individual from within. However, the behaviour involving the satisfaction of our needs and drives are also affected by some external factors named as incentives like praise, appreciation, reward bonus. Incentives in fact work as a positive reinforcing agents for energizing one's behaviour.

The old term 'drive' responsible for initiating and energizing a particular behaviour has now been replaced by a more forceful term 'motive'. It is defined as an energetic force (learned or innate) working within the individual to persuade, compel or inspire him to act for the satisfaction of his needs or purposes. Like drives, these may be classified as physiological and socio-psychological motives. Hunger motives, thirst motives, achievement motives are some of the examples of these motives.

Homeostasis, a term coined by an American physiologist W.B. Cannon, was formerly used in reference to our body chemistry as a process essential for maintaining system equilibrium or balance of the body. In reference to motivational behaviour, its use has now been extended for bringing balance in the psyche or adjustment process of the human beings. The birth of a desire or need may upset the psychological balance of an individual. The upsurge of an appropriate drive or motive accompanied by due incentive, then may provide proper energy for him to work for the satisfaction of his need leading towards the restoration of his upset balance.

The techniques or methods like observation method, experimental method and using personality measurement technique and standardized tests may be utilized for the measurement of motivational behaviour. Among these the use of standardized tests, however, provide quite a handy and reliable technique. The specialized motivational behaviour like one's level of achievement motivation can also be measured through such available standardized measures.

Motivation is an important key to learning. We can follow some general principles for motivating the students in the teaching-learning process. Some of these may be named as principle of readiness to learn, active participation, arousing and maintaining interest, definiteness of goal and purposes, capitalizing on their needs and motives, principles related to the adoption of proper methods of teaching, selection and organization of the subject matter, providing timely and appropriate feedback etc.

Apart from the principle of motivation, a number of special motivational techniques may be required for being used in a classroom situation. These may include the adoption of a child-centered approach, linking the new learning with the past, use of effective methods, aids and devices, definiteness of the purposes and goals, knowledge of the result and progress, and judicious use of the techniques named as praise and reproof, reward and punishment, competition and cooperation, attempts for the development of proper attitude and ego involvement and caring for the betterment of the available learning situation and environment etc.

References and Suggested Readings

Arkes, H.R. and Garske, J.P., *Psychological Theories of Motivation*, Monterey Calif, Brooks/Cole, 1977.

Atkinson, J.W. and Feather, N.T. (Eds.), *Theory of Achievement Motivation*, John Wiley, New York, 1966.

Brown, J.S., *The Motivation of Behaviour*, McGraw-Hill, New York, 1961.

Caroll, H.A., *Mental Hygiene—The Dynamics of Adjustment*, Englewood Cliffs, Prentice-Hall, New Jersey, 1969.

Fisher, V.E., "An Introduction in Abnormal Psychology" cited by Labh Singh and G.P. Tiwari in *Essentials of Abnormal Psychology*, Vinod Pustak Mandir, Agra, 1971.

Hokason, J.E., *The Physiological Bases of Motivation*, John Wiley, New York, 1969.

Irving Sarnoff, "Personality Dynamics and Development" cited by Mangal S.K. in *Educational Psychology* (4th ed.) Prakash Brothers, Ludhiana, 1983.

Maslow, A., *Motivation and Personality*, Harper & Row, New York, 1954.

McClelland, D.C., Atkinson, J.W., Clark R.A. and Lowell, E.C., *The Achievement Motive*, Appleton, New York, 1953.

McDougall, W., *Social Psychology*, John Luice, Boston, 1921.

Petri, H.L., Motivation: *Theory and Research*, 2nd ed., Bolment C.A. Wardsworth, 1985.

Rosen, E., Fox, Ronald and Gregory, Ean, *Abnormal Psychology*, 3rd ed., Saunders, Philadephia, 1972.

Stain, R.E., *Educational Psychology*, 3rd ed., Prentice-Hall, Englewood Cliffs, New Jersey, 1986.

Stacey, C.L. and De Martino, M.E. (Eds.), *Understanding Human Motivation,* Rev. ed., Howard Allen, Cleveland, 1963.

Stipek, D.J., *Motivation to Learn from Theory to Practice*, Prentice-Hall, Englewood Cliff, New Jersey, 1988.

Valley, F.P., *Motivation Theories and Issues*, Califf, Brooks/Cole, Monterey, 1975.

Weiner, B., *Human Motivation*, Holt Renehart & Winston, New York, 1980.

20

Memory

CHAPTER COMPOSITION

WHAT IS MEMORY?

Learning plays a significant role in all the walks of human life. All our attempts in the field of education are directed to make the pupil learn properly. But if we just learn to recall in a desirable way in a particular situation without being able to repeat that successfully on subsequent occasions, learning is of no avail. This means that for an effective learning, it is essential that we should be able to preserve our past experience and learning and make use of them whenever needed. In the psychological world this ability of retention and repeating is known as '*Memory*'.

Many times we use the word "remembering" in place of 'memorization'. Both these terms carry the same meaning. Woodworth also tries to label them as synonymous terms when he writes:

> *In defining memory, we should first repeat what has been said before, that this noun is properly a verb. The real fact is remembering.* (1945, p. 324).

However, in the present chapter, we would like to use a single term 'memory' by considering memory and remembering as one and the same thing.

The Process of Memorization

Our minds possess a special ability by virtue of which every experience or learning leaves behind memory images or traces that are conserved in the form of '*engrams*'. Thus what is learned leaves its after-effect which is conserved in the form of engrams composed of memory traces. This preservation of the memory traces by our central nervous system or brain is known as retaining of the learned or experienced act. How long can we retain depends upon the strength and quality of the memory traces. When we try to recollect or repeat our past experiences or learning we make use of the memory traces. If we are successful in reviving our memory traces, our memory is said to be a good one. But if somehow or the other, the memory traces have died out and we are unable to reproduce or make use of our past experiences and learning, it is said that we are not able to retain what has been learned or we have forgotten.

In this way for remembering or memorization, learning is the primary condition. If there is no learning there would be no remembering. Secondly, we should see that these learning experiences are retained properly in the form of mental impressions or images so that they can be revived when the need arises. The third and the fourth stages in the process of memorization or remembering can be named as Recognition and Recall. Recognition is much easier and simpler a psychological process than recall. What is the difference between these two terms can be explained by the following example:

Suppose, Mr. Jai Kishan has been your classmate. You have spent a good time with him. The old experiences have been retained in the form of memory traces. Now if you are told only the name of the gentleman and you can recollect all that you had experienced in his company and can describe his personality, it is said that you have been able to recall your past experience. In this case memory traces are said to be retained in a proper form. But if the memory traces are very weak and therefore, retention is poor, then recall (perfect revival of the past experiences) may not be possible.

In such cases, 'recognition' is possible. Recognition is nothing but the awareness of an object or situation as having been known to the person. Here the presence of the already experienced object or thing makes the task of recollection easy. In the above example, the photographs or the actual presence of Jai Kishan may facilitate the task of recollecting past experiences.

With the above discussion, it can be easily concluded that the process of memorization or remembering begins with learning or experiencing something and ends with its revival and reproduction. Therefore, memory is said to involve the four stages *i.e.* learning or experiencing something, its retention and finally its recognition and recall.

Encoding, Storage and Retrieval

The above four stages (Learning, Retention, Recognition & Recall) related with our memory process have been given a new shape nowadays. These have been replaced by three distinct stages named as—

1. Encoding
2. Storage
3. Retrieval

Encoding refers to a process to translate or convert the sensory information (the thing of the environment we want to have in our memory) into such a coded form that can be easily stored and reproduced at the time of our need. The process of encoding as we can visualize resembles the stage of learning described earlier for the process of memorization. During the process of learning, we try to encode the learned material or acquired experiences according to our own ability, style, experience, training or capacity. Every bit of this information can thus be transformed in the form of engrams and codes for the storage and its further retrieval. When we have proper encoding of the learned material, the results in terms of its storage and retrieval in proportion are always better. One can opt for any form, method or technique for choosing a particular code for any type of the information to be coded in one's memory like figure, symbol, word, sentence, incidence etc.

The storage is concerned with the power of retention. What is available in the form of engrams or encoded message is kept safe by this storage so that it can be revived at the time of the need.

Retrieval is concerned with the revival or reproduction of the stored encoded messages or memory engrams into their original form. Here the coded message undergoes a process of decoding and as a result we can reproduce the things in the form they were experienced or learnt by us during the process of learning or experiencing.

Defining Memory

After some knowledge of the process of memorization or remembering, it is worthwhile to be acquainted with the definition of the term 'memory' given by different psychologists. Some of these definitions are:

Stout
Memory is the ideal revival so far as ideal revival is merely reproductive... This productive aspect of ideal revival requires the object of past experiences to be reinstated as far as possible in the order and manner of their original occurrence. (1938, p. 521)

Woodworth and Marquis
Memory consists in remembering what has previously been learned. (1948, p. 542).

Ryburn
The power that we have to 'store' our experiences, and to bring them into the field of consciousness some time after the experiences have occurred, is termed memory. (1956, p. 220)

In this way, *memory is regarded as a special ability of our mind to conserve or store what has been previously learned or experienced for being recollected or reproduced after some time.* It must also be clearly understood that memory does not merely consist of reproducing or recollecting previous experiences or learning as most of us usually understand it. It is a complex process which involves all the four factors mentioned above namely, learning, retention, recall and recognition. Therefore, when we say that a person has a good memory we mean that he has an ability to learn something easily, retain it for a long time, recognize and recall it accurately with rapidity and lastly to make proper use of his previous learning or experiences. A good memory should be serviceable. We must be able to recognize, recall and recollect the relevant ideas, things, or persons at the proper time. Then and only then our learning and retention will be of any value and we would be making proper use of our power of memorization or remembering.

TYPES OF MEMORY

Psychologists have tried to classify memory into certain types according to their nature and purposes served. The broad classification consists of immediate memory, short-term memory and long-term memory. Let us see what we mean by these types:

Sensory or Immediate Memory

Immediate memory or *sensory memory is that memory which helps an individual to recall something immediately after having perceived it.* In such type of memory, retention time is extremely brief, generally from a fraction of a second to several seconds. Old sensory impressions disappear as they are 'erased" by new information.

Immediate memory is needed when we want to remember a thing only for a very short period of time. Like we enter the cinema hall and see the seat number given on our ticket. After occupying the seat, we forget the seat number. We look up a telephone number from the directory and remember it. But after making the call, we usually forget it. In all such cases, immediate memory is needed to help us learn a thing immediately with speed and accuracy, remembering it for a short time and forgetting it rapidly after use.

Short-Term Memory

As the name suggests, this type of memory is also temporary and short-lived like the immediate memory. Its impressions do not disappear or erase quickly like sparks of the lightning or waves of the sea as happens in the case of immediate memory. The distinction between these two types of memory can be properly understood through the comparison given in the table ahead.

Immediate Memory	*Short-term Memory*
1. The retention time is less than one second. In special circumstances, it can go up to two seconds for the visual stimuli and four to five seconds for the auditory stimulus.	1. Its duration is longer. The information temporarily stored up in short-term memory may endure as long as 30 seconds or so, even if the material is not being rehearsed.
2. The sensory impressions in the form of engrams in the brain disappear or decay in no time like the waves in the sea. Any type of rehearsal, practice or deliberations on the part of the learner can't help in their further retention.	2. The period of retention here can be extended to quite a longer duration as a result of the proper efforts and rehearsal by the learner.
3. Span of immediate memory is generally more than the short-term memory. One can have a retention of 11 to 16 items in one's immediate memory for at least half a second in the form of visual images and hearing echo etc.	3. The span of short-term memory is shorter than the immediate memory. Generally, five to nine items (the magical number, seven plus or minus two) can be held in short-term memory at one time. However, one can retain much information in one's short memory by special processes like chunking (grouping information through coding). As a result one can remember a phone number 143254376 by grouping under three heads; 143, 254, 376.

Immediate Memory	Short-term Memory
4. The sensory impressions retained in the immediate memory are either immediately erased or transferred to the short-term memory.	4. The sensory information stored in the short-term memory are lost in a short period if they are not subject to repetition or rehearsal. Proper deliberate attempts and rehearsals can help in transferring them into long-term memory.
5. The sensory information is preserved and retained in this type of memory in the form and shape as it was originally received.	5. The sensory information is subject to a process of encoding for being retained in short-term memory in the form of special visual and auditory impressions, symbols, signs, words etc.
6. Forgetting is quite rapid in the case of immediate memory. Here the sensory impressions have quite a temporary retention resulting in their rapid forgetting.	6. In this memory, there is natural as well as deliberate forgetting. Here one can deliberately erase the old impressions for making space for the new ones.

Long-Term Memory

As the name suggests, long-term memory has quite a durable or endless retention of the sensory impressions. That is why, it is also referred to as permanent memory. In addition to its long duration of retention, it has a seemingly limitless capacity to store information. In this way the span of retention is far greater than the short-term or immediate memory. The sensory impressions stored in long-term memory are subjected to very little or no decay and requires little, if any, rehearsal for their lengthy and effective retention. On account of its such nature and characteristics, it is the only memory that is our best friend and help us to remember a number of limitless things on a relatively permanent basis. Remembering our identifying data like our name, father's name, date of birth, date of marriage, etc. is the simplest example of our long-term memory. With the help of our long-term memory, we can store, retain and remember at record notice most of the things of our lives and can thus make things in our life quite easy.

The most important thing or attribute attached to the long-term memory is related with its uniqueness in encoding the received sensory information in a properly organized and systematic way. The codes are properly selected in relation to the meaning, patterns and other characteristics of the received sensory information. This coded language is quite methodical, carries in all its way a distinctive meaning, purposeful understanding for the individual to carry out its storage and timely revival.

The sensory impressions, encoded in the long-term memory are mainly of two types—Episodic and Semantic. As a result, long-term memory may be subdivided as Episodic and Semantic memory.

Episodic memory

It is connected with episodes and events, which may consist of personal events and experiences associated with one's life. For example, if an individual reads in a newspaper or becomes an eyewitness to the scene of a rail accident, he may retain all his sensory impressions about this event or episode in his memory known as episodic memory. Such retention will help him narrate all the details regarding this accident almost throughout his life. Equipped with such episodic memory, you may also feel well equipped in narrating to your friends all that you did, experienced, felt and enjoyed during an excursion. Thus, episodic memory is that type of permanent memory, which depends on retrieving the particular events or episodes experienced by a person through his indirect or direct experiences.

SEMANTIC MEMORY

On the other hand, it helps in storing as well as retrieving a collection of relationships between events or association of ideas. Here an episode or event as such is not stored in one's memory. What one infers or generalizes through such episode is usually registered in the semantic memory. A scooter rider should essentially wear a helmet; train accidents are the result of carelessness on the part of railway employees; drinking and driving should not be mixed—such well drawn inferences and conclusions can thus be made a part of one's semantic memory. It is your semantic memory that helps you in recalling the names of the capitals of the different countries, and the formulae for the computation of simple and compound interests and many of your chemical symbols and equations. Semantic memory is thus based on general knowledge coupled with meaningful interpretation, generalized rules, principles and formulae.

In this way, our long-term memory tries to encode our experiences and inferences in such an effective way that they can be stored properly in our brain in the form of engrams and encoded language with an objective of their safe retrieval at the time of the need. Here what we store is stored permanently. Normally it does not disappear or get erased from our memory. The proof of its such presence can be very well found in your own experiences. Many times, you forget a thing, try hard to remember it but do not get success. After some time, it may automatically come into your mind either through some association or as a result of incubation. It was very much permanently present in your memory. Had it not been so, how could you remember it afterwards? You may also realize it when you are unable to recall the answer of a question at the time of an examination or interview but it appears into your memory immediately after coming out from the examination or interview room.

After the above discussion on long-term memory, we are certainly in a position to separate it from our short-term memory. The two types of memory have been compared in the table below:

Short-term Memory	*Long-term Memory*
1. The duration is short. Generally it does not exceed 30 seconds.	1. The duration is quite long and enduring. It is not limited to some hours, days or years and thus may cover the entire life period of an individual.
2. The memory span is quite short and limited. Generally five to nine items can be held in one's short-term memory.	2. The span is quite wide and comprehensive. It has a seemingly limitless capacity to store any type of information.
3. There is no automatic rehearsal of the stored information in one's brain. So the memory traces are faded or erased very soon.	3. Here the memory traces undergo very little or almost no decay and requires little, if any, rehearsal for being permanently present in one's memory.
4. Encoding process is defective. No rules or principles are followed for the proper upkeeping of the collected sensory information. In fact, the encoding is performed quite haphazardly without any consideration of the organizational characteristics and principles.	4. Encoding process in the long-term memory is quite structured, planned and organized. Here encoding of the information is performed according to well-thought meaning, pattern and other organizational characteristics. In this way, the sensory information is stored in a proper way for keeping them safe and alive to the limitless period.

Short-term Memory	Long-term Memory
5. The things and material in one's short-term memory is quite short-lived. It disappears soon if not subjected (frequently and repeatedly) to adequate practice and rehearsal. So, this memory is characterized by a rapid rate of forgetting the learnt material.	5. Complete forgetfulness is almost absent in the long-term memory. The things and material learnt are permanently retained in the long-term memory stores. From there it never disappears. An individual may feel some difficulty in recollecting the things stored but by conscious or unconscious efforts, he always gets success in its desired retrieval.
6. The short-term memory can be transformed into a long-term memory in case one deliberately tries in this direction by properly practicising, revising and rehearsing the learned material or things.	6. There is no such transfer of the retained material or experiences in one's long-term memory to any other type of memory.
7. The disappearance or erasing of the memory traces in quite a little time, provides early opportunity for the arrival of the new sensory experiences by saying goodbye to the older ones. Thus process of receiving the new and erasing the old runs quite rapidly in the short-term memory.	7. Long-term memory does not show such speed of remembering the new and forgetting the old sensory experiences. Here forgetting is quite minimum or say quite negligible. In this case, one does not need to erase the old impressions for providing accommodation to the new ones.

MEASUREMENT OF MEMORY

The soundness or quality of one's memory can be judged on the basis of his power of retention or retentivity. How properly can one store and retain the learned things or materials in one's memory storage, may provide a base for the measurement of the ability and capacity of one's memory. In general, we make use of the following formula for the computation of such storage capacity of an individual. Amount of Retention = Amount Learnt – Amount Forgotten.

In this way if we want to test or measure one's memory, then we have to measure the storage capacity or retentivity of one's power of memorization. This can be done easily with the use of the above formula by subtracting the amount of material forgotten from the amount of the material originally learnt by an individual.

Measurement of Retention

What has been retained in one's memory out of the total originally learnt material provides a measure of one's retentive power. The following four methods are usually employed for the measurement of such retention.

METHOD OF RECALL

What is actually retained by the learner in his memory can be ascertained by testing his performance through reproduction or retrieval, *i.e.* in terms of recognition and recall. As a result he may either be asked to recognize or recall a previously learnt thing. Let us first concentrate on the method of recall.

In using the method of recall for using one's power of retention, we can ask an individual to reproduce the retained material in his memory through the process of recall (oral citation or written presentation). For example, a child may be asked to reproduce the retention of the spelling of ten words (remembered by him previously) by way of oral recitation or written presentation. This method of recall may take the following three shapes and designs designated as—(*i*) Free recall method, (*ii*) Probed recall method and (*iii*) Serial recall method.

In **Free recall method**, the learner is provided with a list of items (It can be read in an oral form or presented in a written form before him). After such proper presentation of the list, he may then be asked to recall (orally or in writing) in any order as many items as possible from the list he has seen or been told about. The list of the items employed in this method may contain meaningful words like RAT, CAP, TENT, PAINT or digits like 29, 57, 36, 71, 85 or even nonsense syllables like NAL, SOK, PAB, KAZ etc. In addition to the use of such lists, we may make use of other study material like a stanza of a prose or poetry composition, an incidence or a pictorial presentation. No matter what material is employed, the objective remains to test the power of retention, *i.e.* what one is capable of recalling out of the total material presented to him for his learning.

In **Probed recall**, the individual may be provided with a cue for helping him in the process of recall. For example, in a paired associate list like CORN-MUSIC, BOX-CAT, FOOD-BOOK etc., he may be asked to tell, what word appeared with BOX in the list seen by him. For the items of a serial list, this cue may be in the shape of the location of the item in the list *e.g.* what item was there at the top/bottom/middle of the list seen by him?

In **Serial recall**, the individual is asked to recall the items in exactly the same order as presented to him previously for his learning or memorization. The serial order reproduction of his retention is quite essential in such measurement. The mistakes in order may prove quite costly to him. For example, if one is able to recall 12 words correctly out of the 20, but out of these 12 he is wrong at four times in terming their serial recall, he may then be scored as 12 – 4 = 8 instead of 12.

Method of Recognition

In this method, we take the help of one's power of recognition to test one's power of retention. The things that he has seen, the material he has studied, are supposed to be present in his memory. How much of it lies there is tested by giving him opportunity to reproduce it by way of recognition. Generally there are two types of recognition tests that are employed for testing one's power of retention. These are named as simple recognition test and multiple-alternate recognition test.

In **simple recognition type test**, the individual may be presented with a photograph, picture, scene of a film or a real item to decide whether or not he has seen it before. He may also be presented with an audio tape, smell or taste experience to decide whether he has listened, smelled or tasted it ever before and if yes, he is asked to tell something about it through its recognition.

In a **multiple-alternate recognition test**, one has to recognize a particular person or item seen, heard or experienced before, out of the several pictures, voices or items presented to him. For example, he can be presented with 10 pictures or photographs. He may be asked to recognize a particular person, place or event out of the ten given pictures or photographs. He may be asked to recognize as many items as possible out of the given alternatives. The words, letters, symbols etc. can also be used for such recognition tests. In addition to this, some suitable multiple alternate objective type questions may also be constructed for testing the power of recognition like who among the following was the first prime minister of our country?

(a) Mahatma Gandhi
(b) Sardar Patel
(c) Jawaharlal Nehru
(d) Motilal Nehru

Saving Method

The saving method was first of all adopted by the famous psychologist Ebbinghaus in his experiments related with the study of memory. While making use of this method, the individuals under study are asked to learn or memorize fully a given study material (words, digits, pictures or events). The total time taken or the total number of repetitions or trials utilized for such memorization is then noted down by the experimenter. The individuals may then be given a period of rest or they may be engaged in some other subject or activities. Naturally during this period, they are sure to more or less forget the material. For relearning they are provided with trials. The individuals will differ in requiring more or less trials for such relearning and reproducing of the complete list. The number of trials or repetitions saved in the second learning (relearning) are then considered as a measure of the power of retention. If, for example, a subject had 10 trials to learn all the 12 nonsense syllables correctly in the first learning and took 7 trials to learn again in the second learning session he had a saving of 3 trials. His retention power will definitely be better than that of someone who needed 8 trials again or had only 2 saving, assuming of course, that he too had 10 trials in the first learning.

Reconstruction Method

As the name suggests, this method is concerned with the task of reconstruction or restructuring. This method may be employed as under:

To begin with, the subject is presented with certain learning materials in the form of letters, words, pictures, items, event or episode. The subject is then asked to memorize it fully in the way he intends to do so. For testing his power of retention, we can go ahead in the two different ways explained below:

- The subject is tested for his power of retention after a period of considerable gap since the time of his full memorization of the presented study material. It is assumed that he must have forgotten some things memorized earlier. However, as a substitute of his such forgetting, he may bring some new material in his reproduction by utilizing his creative and constructive abilities. How much new he has created or constructed in place of the old ones, may constitute a basis for the measurement of his power of retention or comparison with the other individuals.
- In the second approach the subject is first asked to memorize a given study material fully to his satisfaction. Afterwards the arrangement or order of the presented learning material is disturbed or some extra items or stimuli are mixed up. Now the subject is asked to re-arrange or reconstruct the stimuli or contents of the material in the same order or style as was originally learned by him. The number of items correctly rearranged is termed the retention score of the subject.

FACTORS INFLUENCING MEMORY

Various factors, internal as well as external, may be considered responsible for affecting, influencing and controlling one's memory and its process. In the internal factors, we may include all those things that lie within the individual and for these factors he is himself responsible in terms of the processes and products of memorization. These may be named as physical or mental health or state of his body and mind, his will power, the nature of his attitude, aptitude and interest regarding the learned material, his status regarding the growth and development in various personality dimensions like physical, mental, social, moral, emotional and aesthetic, etc. and his level of adjustment to his self and the environment and so on. Among the external factors, we may include all those factors lying outside the person in his environment that may influence the process and products of his memorization. In addition to all these internal and external factors influencing one's memory, there is a third type of factor or element that is specifically associated with the learning material. This factor generally falls in the following two types or categories.

A. Nature of the material to be memorized
B. Methods and techniques adopted for memorization

Nature of the Material to be Memorized

The nature of the material, which is to be learned or memorized, carries a lot of weight in influencing the process and products of memorization.

Regarding the nature of the learning material, two of its components or characteristics—its purposefulness and amount—are said to be a great deciding factor for the good or poor results of one's efforts towards memorization. Let us think over these attributes of the learning material.

Meaningfulness of the Material

What is useful, meaningful and suits the needs, motives and purposes of an individual can be learned properly, retained for a long time and may be reproduced easily when needed. It is true for all types of learning material and learners. There have been a number of studies to demonstrate that meaningful material can be effectively memorized in comparison to the meaningless or less meaningful material. The list of the meaningful words like RAT, CAP, TENT, PAINT etc. can be effectively memorized by a learner in place of the list of meaningless nonsense syllables like NAO, SOK, PAB, KAZ etc. Similarly in case of the paired associate lists, the list of the well-connected paired words like BANANA-FRUIT, CHANDIGARH-CAPITAL, MILK-COW etc. can be effectively memorized in comparison to the list of unrelated paired words like CORN-MUSIC, FOOD-BOOK, PIANO-WHEAT, etc. Similarly the material in the form of sentences, paragraphs or longer passages or skills in the form of any actions can only be effectively managed and memorized if they are meaningful and are supposed to carry some meaning to the learner. In such memorized material, what he does, he does it with his full interest, attention and capacities in his command and thus better results are always insured through the meaningfulness of the memorized material.

Amount of the Material

Success as the task of effective memorization depends to a great extent, upon the size and quantity of the material to be memorized. If the amount of material under memorization falls within the reasonable limit of the individual's memory, he is able to handle it properly, but in case it crosses one's reasonable limit, no satisfactory result is likely to be achieved. It has been experimentally proved that in comparison to the long list of words, or lengthy paragraphs or longer passages, whether meaningful or meaningless, used in the study of memory, the fewer or the shorter ones always prove effective to every type of learner in all learning situations. The greater the amount, the greater efforts in memorization it needs and the greater possibility of failure in terms of learning, retention and reproduction is caused. Therefore, it is always safer to have a convenient amount of the material for memorization at a particular sitting.

Methods and Techniques of Memorization

How much success one gets in keeping a thing in one's memory depends to a large extent, upon the quality of the methods or techniques employed by him in its memorization or learning. While the unpsychological poor and dogmatic methods of learning or memorization may cause disappointment in terms of their effective retention, the progressive and economical methods based on sound psychological footing produce better results. At present many such methods and techniques are available with us. We can choose one or the other method that suits our own requirements or learning situations. Let us have a view of these well-known economical and effective methods of memorization.

RECITATION METHOD

In this method, the learner first reads the matter once or twice and tries to recite and recall it without looking at the material. In this way, the recitation method provides continuous self-appraisal. Learner evaluates himself from time to time and notes the points that he has been unable to recall. On these points due attention can be paid and thus he is saved of unnecessarily repeating the already memorized material. Moreover, the recitation method is more stimulating than the continued re-reading of the same material. It helps in early detection of errors by paying close attention.

WHOLE AND PART METHODS

There are two methods of memorizing a thing. For example take a poem. One is to read the poem again and again from the beginning till the end as a whole. This is called whole method of memorization. In the other method—part method—the poem is divided into parts and each part is memorized separately.

Both these methods have advantages as well as disadvantages. Which of the two would prove suitable and economical depends upon the prevailing conditions and the nature of the thing to be memorized. The whole method is found better than the part method in case of memorizing a thing requiring less time, say, a short poem; while the part method proves more advantageous if the poem is a longer one. In some cases a combination of these two methods has been found most suitable. In this combined method, the learner starts initially by the whole method and tries to locate the areas of difficulty. These difficult portions are attended through part method. After that the subject once again comes to the whole method and is able to remember it successfully.

SPACE AND UNSPACED METHODS. (METHODS OF DISTRIBUTED AND MASSED PRACTICE)

In the spaced or distributed practice method of memorization, the subject is not required to memorize the assigned material in one continuous sitting. After memorizing for some time, some rest is provided and in this way the principle of 'work and rest' is followed in this method. For example, if one has to memorize a piece of poetry by this method, in the beginning he will be advised to go on repeating it. After some time he will be given some rest. Again he will memorize it and take rest. In this way with repeated intervals of work and rest he will be able to gain mastery over the assigned piece.

On the other hand, in unspaced or massed practice method of memorization the subject has to memorize the assigned material in one sitting without any interval or rest. Hence in this method, the memorization work is done continuously without interruption till it is mastered.

Many experimental studies have been done to assess the relative values of these two methods. Although short lessons have been preferred without any interval, in general the results have been in favour of spaced method. It has been observed that instead of working continuously without taking rest, it is better to distribute the hours of work in some sittings and introduce the periods of rest in between these sittings. This helps in removing the monotony caused by long periods of study. The chief advantage of the spaced method over unspaced method lies in the fact that less number of trials (repetitions) are required for learning the same material as compared to the unspaced method. On account of such economy in the number of trials, the subject is saved from the unnecessary fatigue that may be caused by a large number of trials and continuous sitting. Moreover, the subject gets a fresh start after a period of rest and thus his interest can be maintained in the task.

Which one of these above methods and techniques of learning or memorization is best or superior to others, is quite a ticklish question. Actually all these methods work well in quite an economical way for yielding effective results in their own spheres and working conditions. However, none of them can be thought as all-rounder, *i.e.* effective in all the learning situations. Moreover, the economy and effectiveness in terms of memorization and retention depends more on the nature of the learner and learning material rather than on the methods of learning. In addition, there may be many other things related with the situations and environments available at the time of learning, which facilitate or interfere with the processes and products of memorization. It is quite difficult to mention all such factors at this juncture in this text. However, we would definitely try to point out some well tried methods and techniques that may prove quite helpful in the task of effective memorization.

MEASURES AND TECHNIQUES FOR EFFECTIVE MEMORISATION

The following techniques and measures may be adopted for obtaining better results in the process of memorization (learning, retention and its reproduction).

1. **Will and determination.** There must be firm determination or strong will to learn, retain and reproduce for achieving the desired success in memorization. Where there is a will there is a way. Materials read, heard or seen without intention or mood are difficult to be remembered at later times.
2. **Interest and attention.** Interest as well as close attention are essential for effective learning and memorization. One who has no interest in what one learns, cannot give due attention to it and consequently will not be able to learn it. H.R. Bhatia emphasizes this fact in the following words :

   Interest is the mother of attention and attention is the mother of memory; if you would secure memory, you must first catch the mother and the grandmother. (1964, p. 94)

   Therefore, every care should be taken to create the desired interest in the material by making its purpose clear and linking it with one's natural instincts and urges. Again all the factors causing distraction should be reduced to the minimum so that full attention can be paid to the material in hand.
3. **Adopting proper methods of memorization.** There are so many economical methods of memorization but all are not suitable on all occasions for all individuals. Therefore, a judicious selection should be made in choosing a particular method in a given situation.
4. **To follow principle of Association.** It is always good to follow the principle of association in learning. A thing should never be learnt in a complete watertight compartment. Attempts should be made to connect it with one's previous learning on one hand and with so many related things on the other. Sometimes for association of ideas special techniques and devices are used that facilitate learning and recall. The letter VIBGYOR has proved to be effective in remembering the colours of the spectrum. Similarly, many associations may be formed so that the material can be learned and easily remembered.

5. **Grouping and Rhythm.** Grouping and Rhythm also facilitate learning and help in memorizing. For example, a telephone number 567345234 can be easily memorized and recalled if we group it as 567 345 234.

   Similarly, rhythm also proves as an aid in learning and memorizing. Children learn effectively the multiplication tables in the sing-song fashion. The arrangement of the material in the form of a verse with rhythm and rhyme is found very useful in this direction. As an illustration the following verse is worth quoting:
   Thirty days has September, April, June, and November
   All the rest have thirty-one, Excepting February alone.
   To which they twenty-eight assign, Till leap year gives it twenty-nine.
6. **Utilizing as many senses as possible.** Senses are said to be the gateways of knowledge and it has also been found that the things are better learned and remembered when presented through more than one senses. Therefore, attempts should be made to take the help of audio-visual aid material and receive impressions through as many senses as possible.
7. **Arranging better learning situations.** Environmental forces also affect the learning process. Therefore, due care should be taken to arrange better learning situation and environment. A calm and quiet atmosphere and simulating environment proved an effective aid to learning.
8. **Internal factors within the learner.** Besides the external factors there are things within the learner that affect his learning and reproduction. His physical and mental health and emotional state of mind at the time of learning as well as reproduction counts a lot in memory. Therefore, due attention should be given to the improvement of students' health—physical as well as mental. His emotions should also be trained and emotional tensions removed as far as possible.
9. **Provision for change and proper rest.** Adequate provision for change of work, rest and sleep should be made as it helps in removing fatigue and monotony. A fresh mind is necessarily able to learn more and retain it for a longer time than a tired and dull one.
10. **Repetition and practice.** Last but not the least is the repetition and continuous practice that adds to effective memorization. An intelligent repetition with full understanding, always helps in making the learning effective and enduring. The things repeated and practiced frequently are remembered for a long time. Therefore, due care should be taken for drill work, practice and review etc in the process of memorization and learning.

SUMMARY

Memory refers to a special ability of our mind to conserve or store what has been previously learned or experienced for recollection or reproduction after sometime. In this way, (i) learning, (ii) retention and (iii) recollection or reproduction, may form the essential ingredients or stages of the process of memorization. In the modern psychology these stages have been given new names like encoding, storage and retrieval.

Memory may be broadly classified into certain types in view of their nature and purpose served like sensory or immediate memory, short-term memory and long-term memory. Sensory or Immediate memory refers to that memory which helps in recalling something immediately after its perception. It has an extremely brief retention or span, *i.e.* from a fraction of second to a few seconds. Short-term memory is also temporary, though not nearly as short-lived as immediate memory. It may have its time of retention up to 30 seconds or so and may be further extended through rehearsals. Long-term memory on the other hand has an almost limitless capacity to store as well as retain one's sensory impressions. The sensory impression stored or encoded in the long-term memory are of two types—Episodic (connected with episodes and events) and Semantic (inferences or generalization reached out of the episodes and events).

The quality of one's memory can be judged on the basis of his power of retention which, in turn, may be computed by using the formula: Amount of retention = Amount learnt – Amount forgotten. Usually the methods like method of recall, method of recognition, saving method and reconstruction method are used for the measurement of such retention.

Various factors, internal and external, may be considered responsible for influencing and controlling one's memory and its process. In the internal factors, we may include all those things that lie within the individual like his health, will power and interest. In the external factors, we may include those factors lying outside the person, *i.e.* in his environment. In addition to all those internal and external factors, there may be a third type of factors affecting one's memory, specifically those that are associated with the nature of the material to be memorized and methods and techniques adopted for memorization.

Measures and techniques for effective memorization (helpful in better learning, retention and its reproduction) may be named as the learner's will and determination, interest and attention, adopting proper methods of memorization, to follow principle of association, grouping and rhythm, utilizing as many senses as possible, arranging better learning situations, provision for change and rest, repetition and practice and taking control of the internal factors associated with the learner etc.

References and Suggested Readings

Adams, J.A., *Learning and Memory: An Introduction*, Dorsey Press, Homewood, Illinois, 1976.

Bartlett, F.C., *Remembering: A Study in Experimental and Social Psychology,* Cambridge, New York, 1932.

Bhatia, H.R., *Elements of Educational Psychology*, 3rd Indian reprint, Orient Longman, Calcutta, 1968.

Cermak, L.S., *Human Memory—Research and Theory*, Ronald Press, New York, 1972.

Collins, M. and James, Drever, (Eds.), *Experimental Psychology*, Methuen, London, 1930.

Deese, J. and Hulse, S.H., *The Psychology of Learning*, 3rd ed., McGraw-Hill, New York, 1967.

Ebbinghaus, H., *On Memory*, Dover, New York, 1964.

Highee, K.L., *Your Memory: How it Works and How to Improve it*, Prentice Hall, Englewood Cliffs, New Jersey, 1977.

Hunter, Ian M.R., *Memory*, Penguin Books, London, 1964.

Klatsky, R.L., *Human Memory*, Freeman, San Francisco, 1976.

Ryburn, W.M., *Introduction to Educational Psychology*, Reprint, Oxford University Press, London, 1956.

Skinner, B.F., *Verbal Behaviour*, Appleton Century, Crofts, New York, 1957.

Stout, G.E., *A Manual of Psychology*, University Tutorial Press, London, 1938.

Wickelgren, W.A., *Learning and Memory*, Prentice-Hall, Englewood Cliffs, New Jersey, 1977.

Woodworth, R.S. and Marquis, D.G., *Psychology*, Henry Holt, New York, 1948.

21

Forgetting

CHAPTER COMPOSITION

INTRODUCTION

Forgetting and remembering are the two facets of the same coin. Both have equal importance in one's life. Generally we are very much worried about remembering but give little importance to forgetting. But forgetting is of no less importance. It is an essential aspect of the learning process. One must be able to forget the incorrect responses in order to acquire correct ones. Unimportant, improper or irrelevant things should always be forgotten in order to make room for the learning of the essential and relevant ones. Moreover, we have hundreds and thousands of experiences and kinds of learning everyday in our lives. To remember all these without forgetting will be a difficult task.

Therefore, actually forgetting is a boon to us. Had the nature not gifted us with the ability of forgetting, our life would have been miserable. On the other hand, unusual, unreasonable and excessive forgetfulness also causes great harm to us. It needs careful checking and control. Here comes the necessity of knowing about the mechanism of forgetting. The root causes behind it must be discovered and attempts should be made to do away with unusual habits, intervening factors and faulty methods of remembering. In the following pages, we will try to look in this direction.

MEANING AND DEFINITIONS OF FORGETTING

As an excuse, we often hear people say, "Excuse me, I have really forgotten it". A student complaints and repents over forgetting the material he remembered. A housewife feels ashamed of when she forgets to add salt in the cooked vegetable. Therefore, in general, the term forgetting seems to be a part of our day-to-day speech. But in order to be more specific and scientific in our approach, let us study some of the definitions given by eminent writers.

Munn

Forgetting is the loss, permanent or temporary, of the ability to recall or recognize something learned earlier. (1967, p. 425)

Drever

Forgetting means failure at any time to recall an experience, when attempting to do so, or to perform an action previously learned. (1952. p. 99)

Bhatia

Forgetting is the failure of the individual to revive in consciousness an idea or group of ideas without the help of the original stimulus. (1968, p. 203)

In all these definitions, forgetting is termed as failure. Let us see how it is termed as the failure of an individual.

The power of long retention or better storage and rapid reproduction or retrieval (recall and recognition) makes a good memory. It counts towards the success of an individual in the task of learning or memorizing. Forgetting, on the other hand, counts towards the failure. "I have forgotten", implies "I have failed to retain or to be able to recall what was learned or experienced by me earlier." In this way forgetting is just the opposite of remembering and essentially a failure in the ability of reproducing.

CURVE OF FORGETTING

What is the curve of forgetting? Forgetting increases with the lapse of time, or in other words, retention diminishes with time. If we plot the rate of retention or the rate of forgetting on a graph paper, we can get what we call the retention curve or the curve of forgetting. In this way the *curve obtained on the graph paper by plotting the amount of forgotten as a function of time is named as curve of forgetting.*

Ebbinghaus' Curve of Forgetting

The studies made by the psychologist Ebbinghaus (1885) present the earliest systematic work in studying the phenomenon of forgetting. He himself worked as a subject for the studies and described his results by sketching a *curve of forgetting*.

He memorized a list of nonsense syllables and then tested himself at intervals from 20 minutes to a month to see how much of the list did he remember. The results in terms of the percentage of material forgotten with the lapse of time were found in the following order:

Time elapsed	*Amount forgotten*
20 minutes	47%
One day	66%
Two days	72%
Six days	75%
Thirty-one days	79%

He tried to plot the above data on a graph paper as shown in Fig. 21.1.

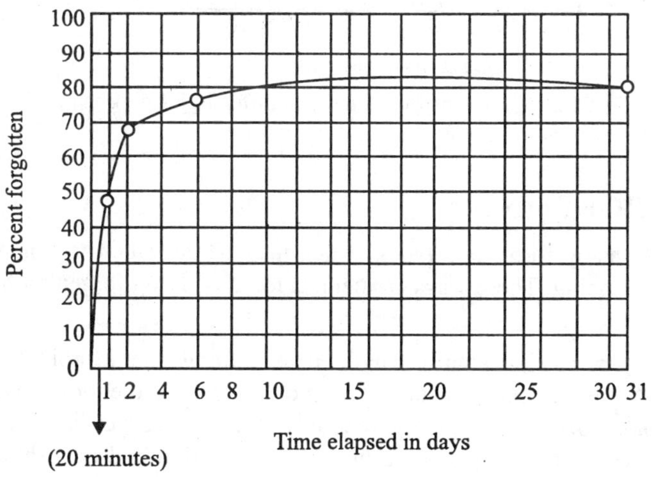

Fig. 21.1 Ebbinghaus's curve of forgetting.

The curve obtained by plotting the amount forgotten as a function of time was named by him as the *curve of forgetting*. Through his experimental data and the presentation in the form of the above curve of forgetting, Ebbinghaus concluded that:

(i) the amount of learnt material forgotten depends upon the time lapsed after learning, and

(ii) the rate of learning is very rapid at first and then gradually diminishes proportionally as the interval lengthens.

Different Kinds of Forgetting Curves

The shape and size of the forgetting curves depend upon so many factors like the nature of the learner, learned material, conditions at the time of learning and recall, methods of learning or memorizing etc. Therefore, we get quite different retention or forgetting curves even for the same learner if there are variations in the factors like nature of the material to be learned, methods of learning and changes in the inner or outer conditions at the time of learning or recall. It has been experimentally proved that there is more retention or less forgetting with meaningful learning material (words like cat, map, dog etc.) in comparison to the meaningless ones (nonsense syllables like nof, cem, hdl, etc.).

The curves of forgetting given below in the Fig. 21.2 may well illustrate the findings of such experiments.

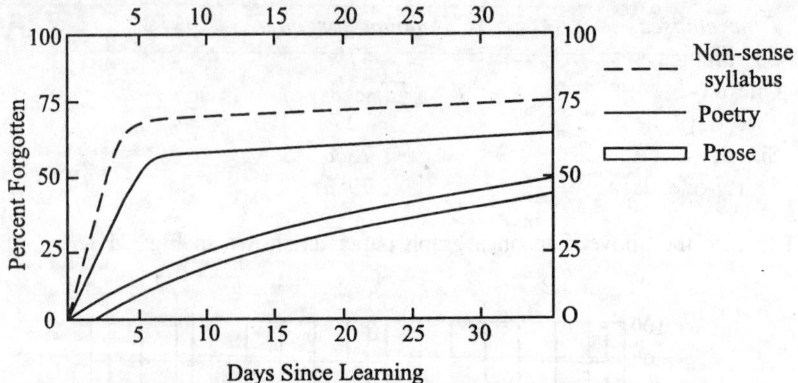

Fig. 21.2 Curves of forgetting with different learning materials.

TYPES OF FORGETTING

Forgetting may have many forms and types, which may be described in a number of ways based on its nature and functioning. These ways or attempts for classifying forgetting have been mentioned below:

1. In one way, it may be simply classified as Natural and Morbid forgetting. In *natural forgetting*, forgetting occurs with the lapse on the part of the individual whereas in *morbid or abnormal forgetting,* one deliberately tries to forget something. This type of forgetfulness, as Freud explains, results from repression and is wishful as one happens to forget the things which one does not wish to remember.
2. According to an other view, forgetting may be classified as general or specific. In *general forgetfulness,* one suffers a total loss in recalling some previous learning while in *specific forgetfulness*, the individual forgets only one or the other specific part of his earlier learning.
3. Still another view related to the cause of forgetting, classifies forgetfulness as physical or psychological. In case one loses one's memory on account of the factors of age, diseases, biological malfunctioning of the brain and nervous system, accidents, consumption or liquor or other intoxicating materials, etc., it is said to be *physical* or *organic forgetting*. But in case loss of memory occurs due to psychological factors like stress, anxiety, conflicts, temper provocation, lack of interest, aversion, apathy, repression or similar other emotional and psychic difficulties, the resulting forgetfulness is termed as *psychological* forgetfulness.

THEORIES OF FORGETTING

All our attempts are directed to retain and remember a learnt thing for a considerable period of time to utilize it at some later stage according to our needs. In this way, everybody is in need of a good memory—better retention and timely reproduction. However, it does not always happen in the way we desire. All of us universally get affected by the mechanism of forgetting. Why do we forget? It is not a simple task to answer this question. It has been a subject of extensive research and investigation on the part of psychologists. As a result, they have come out with some explanations named as theories of forgetting. Let us have a view of some of these main theories.

The Memory Traces Decay Theory

This theory is also named as 'Natural Decay Theory' or 'Theory of Disuse'. This theory considers forgetting as quite a natural and universal phenomenon. It advocates that every one of us is bound to forget some or the other thing stored in our memory simply on account of the lapse of time. The cause of such natural forgetting can be explained through a process known as decay of the memory trace. It says that learning results in neurological changes leaving certain types of memory traces or engrams in the brain. With the passage of time through disuse, these memory traces of learning impressions get weaker and weaker and finally fade away. It leads us to conclude that the older an experience, the weaker its memory and as time passes, the amount of forgetting goes on increasing.

Famous psychologist Ebbinghaus tried to provide experimental evidences for his trace decay theory. He conducted a series of experiments for demonstrating the effects of such forgetting and placed his findings in the form of his famous forgetting curves. We have already discussed these curves in this chapter. With all such attempts, he tried to calculate that amount of our forgetting depends upon the lapse of time.

This view point has now been greatly criticized. It is now felt that it is not just the passage of time that determines how much we forget but also it is what happens during this time. There is active or abnormal forgetting also. The theory of disuse is a failure in explaining this type of forgetting. Therefore, we should look for some other causes for forgetfulness.

The Interference Theory

The second major theory of forgetting which provides quite a reasonable explanation for forgetting is known as 'interference theory' or 'interference of association theory'. Blaming the mechanism of interference as a reason for our forgetting, famous psychologist and author C.T. Morgan writes, *"We forget because in large part associations interfere with one another."* (1961, p. 241)

It means we forget something because what we have learned previously interferes with the remembering of what we learn afterwards.

The interfering effects of associations can work both ways forward and backward. The psychological terms used for these types of interference are 'Retroactive Inhibition' and 'Proactive Inhibition'. In *Retroactive inhibition,* later learning or activity somehow works backward to interfere or inhibit memories of earlier learning. *Proactive inhibition* is just the reverse of retroactive inhibition. Here what we have learned previously interferes with the memory of what we learn afterwards.

In both the cases, it can be easily seen that similar experiences when they follow each other produce more interferences than dissimilar experiences. In this case all experiences are so intermingled that a state of utter confusion prevails in the mind of an individual and consequently he faces difficulty in retention and recall.

Interference theory as a whole has been proved quite successful in providing adequate explanation for natural and normal forgetting for both the short-term and long-term memory. However, for explaining the cases of abnormal or morbid forgetting, we should search for some other explanation.

Repression or Motivated Forgetting Theory

The explanation for the abnormal or morbid forgetting may be given with the help of the repression theory put forward by Freud's psychoanalytic school of psychology. *Repression*, according to this school, is a mental function that safeguards the mind from the impact of painful experiences. As a result of this function, we actually push the unpleasant and painful memories into the unconscious and thus try to avoid at least consciously the conflicts that bother us. This kind of forgetfulness is well motivated and intentional. We usually intend to see ourselves—and to some extent, the world around us—as quite pleasant and reasonable. The memories that are in harmony with this view are acceptable to us, but those that oppose it are often pushed out and this explains why our forgetting like attention, is selective. Thus as a result of repression, we forget the things that we do not want to remember. We forget about our dearest relatives and friends who are dead and gone. We forget to attend a marriage party which we did not want to attend. Similarly, most of us tend to forget the names of the people we do not like. In such forgetting, we can come across some serious mental cases. People under a heavy emotional shock are seen to forget even their names, homes, wives and children.

Apart from causing abnormal forgetting, an impaired emotional behaviour of an individual also plays its part in disrupting his normal memory process. For example, a sudden rise of emotions in excess may completely block the process of recall. When one is taken over by emotions like fear, anger or love, one may forget all one has experienced, learned or thought beforehand. During these emotions one becomes so self-conscious that one's thinking is paralyzed. That is why a child fails to recall the answer to a question in the presence of a teacher whom he fears very much. Similarly, many of us cannot do well before the interview board or in an examination due to interview or test phobia. An actor, orator or musician may also fail miserably in his performance on the stage as he becomes panicky and forgets his prepared dialogue, speech or art.

The Theory of Storage Failure

This latest view holds responsible the failure in terms of proper storage of the learnt material in one's memory. We forget because the way we had stored something in our memory was quite defective and unsatisfactory. As a result, we sometimes have nothing in terms of its storage in our memory or even if it lies there, we are unable to locate and reproduce it neither by recognition nor by recall. This explanation is quite relevant to the memory storage performed at all levels of our memorization.

Let us begin with the sensory memory, *i.e.* the first initial level of the storage of our sensory experiences or impressions about a thing, object, idea or event. These memory traces, in the form of sensory impressions, can be stored properly in one's memory storage only when these are received quite properly and vividly by the receptors of our sense organs for being stored in our brain. For one reason or the other, the sensory impressions remain poor in their quality and strength, they leave a very poor or diminished impression in terms of memory traces in our brain. In such cases, their storage in one's memory remains quite poor, unsatisfactory and temporary. As a result, their retention as well as reproduction in a proper form always remain questionable.

Let us further talk about our short-term memory. We know that the information and impressions related to sensory stage of our memory travel further in our short-term memory. The journey from sensory memory to short-term memory may witness one or the other following things.

(i) The information stock of the sensory memory may be so huge that it goes beyond the capacity of the short-term memory to provide accommodation for its storage. In such circumstances when there is no storage of one or the other sensory information or memory trace in the short-term memory store, then how can we expect their retrieval at one or the other stage.

(ii) In the other case, it may be possible that the information and impressions lying in one's sensory memory may not be welcomed by our short-term memory on account of their insignificance or our indifference and hostility towards them. In such cases, there happens to be no entry of the sensory impression or experiences in our short-term memory and consequently no retention or retrieval of them ever becomes possible.

The sensory information or impressions or memory traces then further travel from short-term memory store to long-term memory store. Here only those information or impressions that are quite meaningful or rehearsed properly make way to the long-term memory store. The remaining ones are faded or vanished in the journey. The long-term memory storage has a large capacity to hold a large infinite volume of the sensory impression, experiences or memory traces. On account of the infinite capacity of holding information and impressions for a limitless period, it becomes too crowded to store things in the long-term memory store. It needs a lot of systematic planning, proper organization and arrangement of the stored information. In the absence of such careful planning and proper organization, it becomes difficult to locate and reproduce an information or memory trace lying in the store of the long-term memory. In the course of collection or storage of almost an infinite number of information or memory traces, it may also be possible that some of these may lie quite beneath the collected heap or bundle of layers of the stored information.

In such a situation, the retrieval of such information or memory traces may become quite difficult at one or the other occasion. When we fail to remember or reproduce an information or memory trace at the time of our need, it is essentially counted towards our forgetfulness. May be the thing lies in the long-term memory storage, but its presence is unhelpful, when it cannot be used by its retrieval or representation. In this way, improper, inadequate and defective planning and organization of the sensory information or memory traces in the memory storages may become a potent cause of its forgetting.

In the above pages, we have given a brief account of the four important theories of forgetting. Each of these theories provide an explanation for our forgetting. All are right in their own perspectives, but none of them is able to provide a full account or explanation for all the types of forgetting. Hence when we are in a need to know about the causes of the forgetting behaviour, we must take help from the findings of all these theories. Sometimes, a single theory may help in this direction but it is always better to have a synthesized picture of all the viewpoints and explanations given by all the known theories of forgetting. In all such situations, we must learn a lesson from the practical implication of these theories and try to avoid all such things that add to our unwelcome natural or morbid forgetting.

SUMMARY

Forgetting means failure in retention and reproduction of the things that have been previously learned. Depending upon its nature and intensity, it may be classified as natural or morbid (abnormal), general or specific, and physical or psychological.

A psychologist Ebbinghaus is known for presenting the results of his studies about the phenomenon of forgetting through some special curves termed as curves of forgetting. He obtained these curves on the graph papers by plotting the percentage of the material forgotten against the time elapsed. With a proper analysis of these curves he was able to conclude that (i) forgetting depends upon the time lapsed after learning (ii) rate of forgetting is rapid at first and then gradually diminishes and (iii) there is less forgetting with meaningful learning material in comparison to meaningless.

Theories of forgetting tries to explain the causes of our forgetting. *The memory traces decay theory* holds that we forget in a natural way on account of the decay of the memory traces with the lapse of time. *The interference theory* put forward by famous psychologist C.T. Morgan holds that we forget something because of the interference of other things. Such interferences can work both ways, forward and backward. When earlier learning interferes with the later learning, we term it 'Proactive inhibition' and when later learning somehow works backward to interfere or inhibit memories of earlier learning, it is named as 'Retroactive inhibition'. *The theory of repression* put forward by the school of psychoanalysis is held to be more useful in providing explanation for our morbid (abnormal) forgetting. According to this theory, we repress or push out those things in our unconscious, we don't want to remember and as a result, we don't have any memory of such things. *The theory of storage failure*—the latest theory in the theories of forgetting holds that we fail to remember a thing at the later stage only because of our failure in terms of its proper storage.

References and Suggested Readings

Adams, J.A., *Learning and Memory: An Introduction*, Dorsey Press, Homewood, Illinois, 1976.

Bhatia, H.R., *Elements of Educational Psychology,* 3rd Indian reprint, Orient Longman, Calcutta, 1968.

Cermak, L.S., *Human Memory—Research and Theory*, Ronald Press, New York, 1972.

Drever, James, *A Dictionary of Psychology,* Penguin Books, Middlesex, 1952.

Ebbinghaus, H., *On Memory*, Dover, New York, 1964.

Hunter, Ian M.R., *Memory*, Penguin Books, London, 1964.

Klatsky, R.L., *Human Memory*, Freeman, San Francisco, 1976.

Munn, N.L., *An Introduction to Psychology*, 2nd ed., Oxford & IBH, Delhi, 1967.

Wickelgren, W.A., *Learning and Memory*, Prentice-Hall, Englewood Cliffs, New Jersey, 1977.

Woodworth, R.S., and Marquis, D.G., *Psychology*, 5th ed., Henry Holt, New York, 1948.

22

Intelligence—Concept, Theories and Measurement

CHAPTER COMPOSITION

INTRODUCTION

In contrast to animals, man is considered to be endowed with certain cognitive abilities that make him a rational being. He can reason, discriminate, understand, adjust and face new situations. He is definitely superior to animals in all such aspects of behaviour. But human beings themselves are not alike. There are wide individual differences. A teacher easily discovers these differences among his pupils. Some learn with a good speed while others remain lingering for long. There are some who need only one demonstration for handling the tools properly while for others even the repeated individual guidance brings no fruitful result.

What is it that causes one individual to be more effective in his response to a particular situation than another. No doubt, interest, attitude, desired knowledge and skill etc., count towards this achievement. But still there is something that contributes significantly towards these varying differences. In psychology, it is termed as 'Intelligence'. In ancient India, our great *rishis* named it '*Viveka*'.

CONCEPT AND MEANING

Since time immemorial, attempts have been made to understand the meaning and concept of intelligence. Let us be acquainted with the concept and meaning of intelligence by throwing light on the following aspects:

A. Meaning and definition of intelligence.

B. Some established facts about intelligence.

C. Misconception about intelligence.

Meaning and Definitions of Intelligence

As discussed earlier, in our day-to-day conversation an individual is said to be intelligent in proportion to his success in general life situations. What is this intelligence that contributes towards such success, is a question that has been attempted by psychologists in different ways resulting in so many varied definitions. Below we give some of these important definitions.

Woodworth and Marquis

Intelligence means intellect put to use. It is the use of intellectual abilities for handling a situation or accomplishing any task. (1948, p. 33)

Stern

Intelligence is a general capacity of an individual consciously to adjust his thinking to new requirements. It is general mental adaptability to new problems and conditions of life. (1914, p. 3)

Terman

An individual is intelligent in proportion as he is able to carry on abstract thinking. (1921).

Wagnon

Intelligence is the capacity to learn and adjust to relatively new and changing conditions. (1937, p. 401)

David Wechsler

Intelligence is the aggregate or global capacity of an individual to act purposeful to think rationally, and to deal effectively with his environment. (1944, p. 3)

ANALYSIS OF THESE DEFINITIONS

Above we have given some definitions, more of such definitions can further be cited. All these definitions when taken separately, give an incomplete picture because they partly emphasize that intelligence is the ability—

(i) to learn,

(ii) to deal with abstraction,

(iii) to make adjustment or to adapt to new situations.

The definition given by Wechsler seems to combine all the three viewpoints but this definition too has come under criticism due to difference of opinion among psychologists. Several attempts have been made to reach at some general agreement but in vain. However, British psychologists are said to have reached some measures or agreement regarding a suitable definition of intelligence.

To them intelligence consists of the ability—

(i) to see relevant relationships between objects or ideas; and

(ii) to apply these relationships to novel situations.

It leads to the conclusion that intelligent behaviour can be divided into two categories—theoretical and practical, abstract and concrete. The theoretical operations make an individual capable to face and solve the actual life problems and make adjustment to the environmental situations. If we try to analyze the factor which determines the success of an individual's activities, we can by all means say that cognitive or mental abilities have a dominant role to play in the success or failure. "Intelligence," as Rex and Margeret Knight have put it, *"is the factor that is common to all mental abilities"* (1952, p. 124) and therefore, the judgement about intelligence can ever be taken with the evaluation of the task one performs, how he reacts and responds to a situation. In this way, if we try to come to the practical ground, we can define intelligence as follows:

Intelligence consists of an individual's those mental or cognitive abilities which help him in solving his actual life-problems and leading a happy and well-contented life.

Some Established Facts about Intelligence

1. **The relation of intelligence with nature and nurture:** There have been a number of attempts on the part of psychologists to weigh the relative importance of nature and nurture. The conclusion of their studies reveals that intelligence is the product of heredity and environment. Both are necessary for the intellectual growth of an individual and neither can be considered more important than the other.

2. **Distribution of intelligence:** There are individual differences with regard to the distribution of intelligence in nature like wealth, health etc. This distribution is governed by a definite principle that states "The majority of the people are average, a few very bright and a few very dull."

3. **Growth of intelligence:** As a child grows in age, so does his intelligence as shown by intelligence tests. Now the questions arises as to at what age does this growth cease? The age of cessation of mental growth varies from individual to individual. However, in majority of cases, intelligence reaches its maximum somewhat at the age of 16 or 20 in an individual. After that the vertical growth of intelligence ceases. But the horizontal growth—accumulation of knowledge and acquisition of skills—continues throughout the life span of an individual.

4. **Intelligence and Sex differences:** Various studies have been concluded to find out if women are less intelligent than men and vice versa. The result of these researches have been either ways. In some of the cases, no significant difference has been found. Therefore, it is proper to think that difference in sex does not contribute towards the difference in intelligence.

5. **Intelligence and racial or cultural differences:** Whether a particular race, caste, or cultural group is superior to other in intelligence — the hypothesis has been examined by many research workers. In U.S.A., it has been a burning problem for centuries. The results of earlier studies, which considers the whites to be a superior race in comparison to the Negroes, have been questioned. Now it has been established that intelligence is not the birth right of a particular race or group. The 'bright' and the 'dull' can be found in any race, caste or cultural group and the differences that are found can be explained in terms of environment influences.

Misconception about Intelligence

There are a number of misconceptions prevalent about the nature and concept of intelligence. For the clarification let us be clear about what is not meant by intelligence.

(i) Intelligence is not knowledge though acquisition of knowledge depends, to a great extent, on intelligence and vice versa.

(ii) Intelligence is not memory. A very intelligent person may have a dull memory and vice versa.

(iii) Intelligence is not guarantee against abnormal behaviour, backwardness and delinquency in spite of the fact that it is one of the major factors contributing towards achievement, adjustment and character formation.

THEORIES OF INTELLIGENCE

With the help of definitions, we can be able to understand how intelligence operates or what type of behaviour makes an individual intelligent or unintelligent. But it does not explain the structure of intelligence or in other words, the different components or elements of intelligence. The theories of intelligence propagated by psychologists from time to time have tried to answer this question. These theories can be grouped under two heads, namely, factor theories and cognitive theories. However, in this text we will limit our discussion to factor theories.

Factor Theories of Intelligence

Let us try to discuss some of these theories below:

UNITARY THEORY OR MONARCHIC THEORY

This theory holds that intelligence consists of one factor—a fund of intellectual competency—which is universal for all the activities of an individual.

A man who has vigour can move so much to east as to the west. Similarly if one has the fund of intelligence, he can utilize it in any area of his life and can be as successful in one area as in the other depending upon his fund. However, in actual life situations, the ideas propagated by this theory do not fit well. We find that the children who are bright in mathematics may, despite serious interest and hard work, be not so good in civics. A student very good in conducting science experiments does not find himself equally competent in learning languages. This makes us conclude that there is nothing like one single unitary factor in intelligence. Therefore, the unitary theory stands rejected.

ANARCHIC THEORY OR MULTIFACTOR THEORY

The main propagator of this theory was E.L. Thorndike. As the name suggests, this theory considers intelligence a combination of numerous separate elements or factors, each one being a minute element of one ability. So, there is no such thing as general intelligence (a single factor) and there are only many highly independent specific abilities which go into different tasks.

Monarchic and Anarchic theories thus hold the two extremes. Just as we cannot assume good intelligence to be a guarantee of success in all the fields of human life, we cannot also say with certain specific type of abilities, one will be successful in a particular area and completely unsuccessful in the other. As Gardner Murphy puts it, *"There is a certain positive relationship between brightness in one field and brightness in another and so on."* (1968, p. 358). This brings us to the conclusion that there should be a common factor running through all tasks. The failure to explain such phenomena gave birth to another theory named Spearman's two factor theory.

SPEARMAN'S TWO FACTOR THEORY

This theory was advocated by Spearman. According to him every different intellectual activity involves a general factor 'g' which is shared with all the intellectual activities and a specific factor 's' which it shares with none (Fig. 22.1).

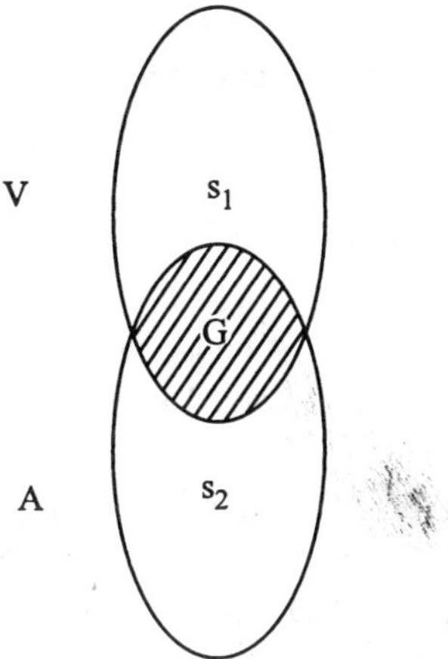

Fig. 22.1 Spearman's two factor theory.

In this way, he suggested that there is something which might be called 'general intelligence', a sort of general mental energy, running through all the different tasks but in addition to this general factor, there are specific abilities, which make an individual able to deal with particular kinds of problems. For example, an individual's performance in Hindi is partly due to his general intelligence and partly some kind of specific ability in language which he might possess, *i.e.* $g+s_1$; or in mathematics his performance would be due to $g+s_2$; or in drawing it will be due to $g+s_3$; and so on and so forth. The factor g (in lesser or greater degree) will enter in all specific activities. The total ability or intelligence of such an individual (symbolized as A) thus will be expressed by the following equation schedule:

$$G + s_1 + s_2 + s_3 + \cdots = A.$$

This two factor theory of Spearman has been criticized on various grounds, some of which have been listed below:

(i) Spearman said that there are only two factors expressing intelligence but as we have seen there are not only two but several factors (g s_1, s_2, s_3, ... etc.) expressing it.

(ii) According to Spearman, each task requires some specific ability. This view was not proper as it implied that there was nothing common in the tasks except a general factor and professions such as those of nursing, compounders and doctors could not be put in one group. In fact the factor s_1, s_2, s_3, s_4...........etc. are not mutually exclusive. They overlap and give birth to certain common factors.

This idea of overlapping and grouping has been responsible for the origin of a new theory called Group Factor theory.

THURSTONE'S GROUP FACTOR THEORY

For the factors not common to all the intellectual abilities but common to certain activities comprising a group, the term 'group factor' was suggested. Prominent among the propagators of this theory is L.L. Thurstone. While working on a test of primary mental abilities, he came to the conclusion that certain mental operations have a primary factor in common which gives them psychological and functional unity and differentiates them from other mental operations. These mental operations constitute a group factor. So, there are a number of groups of mental abilities each of which has its own primary factor. Thurstone and his associates have differentiated nine such factors. These are:

(i) Verbal factor (V): concerns with comprehension of verbal relations, word and ideas.

(ii) Spatial factor (S): is involved in any task in which the subject manipulates an object imaginatively in space.

(iii) Numerical factor (N): concerns with the ability to do numerical calculations, rapidly and accurately.

(iv) Memory factor (M): involves the ability to memorize quickly.

(v) Word Fluency Factor (W): is involved whenever the subject is asked to think of isolated words at a rapid rate.

(vi) Inductive reasoning factor (RI): concerns with the ability to generalize through specific examples.

(vii) Deductive reasoning factor (RD): concerns with the ability to make use of generalized result.

(viii) Perceptual factor (P): concerns with the ability to perceive objects accurately.

(ix) Problem-solving ability factor (PS): concerns with the ability to solve problems independently.

The weakest link in the group factor theory was that it discarded the concept of common factor. However, it did not take Thurstone too long to realize his mistake and reveal a general factor in addition to group factors.

G.H. THOMSON'S SAMPLING THEORY

This theory was propagated by G.H. Thomson, a brilliant psychologist. According to the theory, mind is made up of many independent bonds or elements. Any specific test or school activity sample some of these bonds. It is possible that two or more tests sample and utilize the same bonds. In such cases, general common factor can be said to exist among them. It is also possible that some other tests sample different bonds, then the tests have nothing in common and each is specific.

This theory seems to combine various theoretical viewpoints as:

(i) It appears to be similar to Thorndike's multifactor theory except that it concedes to the practical usefulness of a concept like 'g'.

(ii) At the same time Thomson seems to maintain that the concept of group factor (G) is of equal usefulness.

VERNON'S HIERARCHICAL THEORY

P.E. Vernon, a British psychologist, has propagated a theory of intelligence by suggesting hierarchical structure for the organization of human intelligence (See below figure 22.2).

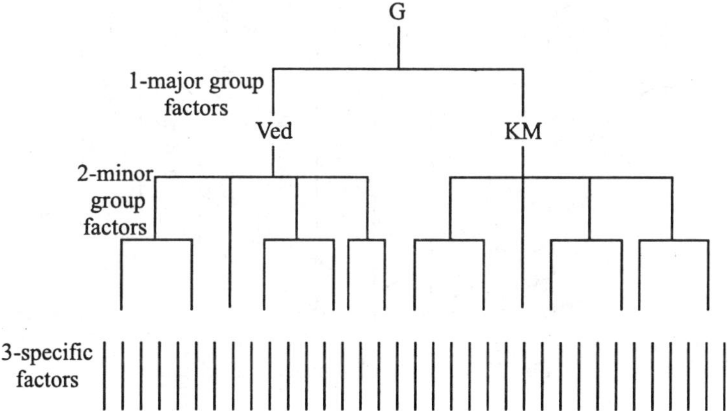

Fig. 22.2 Vernon's hierarchical structure of human intelligence.

Thus, according to Vernon, intellectual abilities or factors of intelligence lie in hierarchical order. On top we have G, a general type of major factor representing the overall intelligence of an individual. Under G, there lie two prominent group factors namely Ved (concerning with the verbal, numerical and educational abilities) and KM (connected with practical, mechanical, spatial and physical abilities). These two major factors may be divided into minor group factors and these minor factors in turn may be further sub-divided into various specific factors related with minute specific mental abilities.

GUILFORD'S THEORY INVOLVING A MODEL OF INTELLECT

J.P. Guilford and his associates have developed a model of intellect on the basis of the factor analysis of several tests employed for testing intelligence of human beings. They have come to the conclusion that any mental process or intellectual activity of the human being can be described in terms of three basic dimensions or parameters known as operation (the act of thinking or way of processing the information); contents (the terms in which we think or the type of information involved); and products (the ideas we come up with, i.e. the fruits of a thinking). Each of these parameters—operations, contents and products—may be further subdivided into some specific factors or elements. As a result, operations may be subdivided into 5 specific factors, contents into 5 and products into 6. The interaction of these three parameters, according to Guilford, thus results into the $5 \times 5 \times 6 = 150$ different elements or factors in one's intelligence. In a figural form, these

150 factors or independent abilities of the human beings along with the basic parameters and their divisions can be represented through a model named as Guilford's Model of Intellect or Intelligence (See figure 22.3).

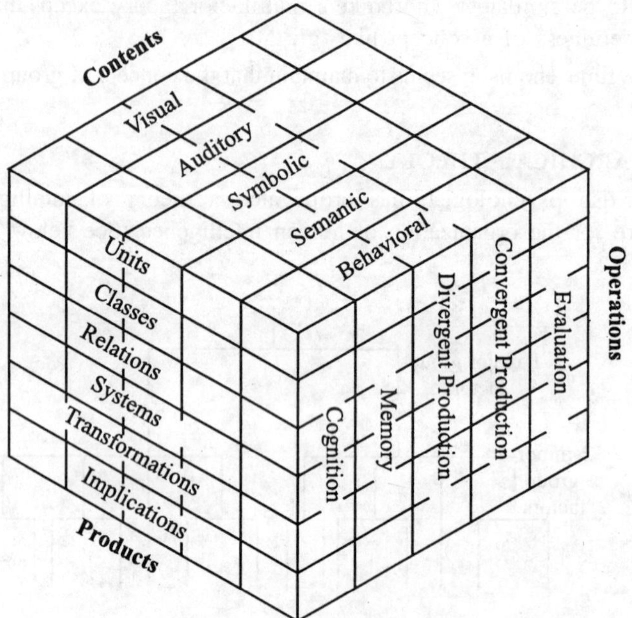

Fig. 22.3 Guilford's model of intellect.

This model proposes that intelligence consists of 150 independent abilities that result from the interaction of five types of contents, five types of operations and six types of products. Guilford, 1982.

What is implied by these contents, operations and products can be understood through the following brief description.

Contents (The type of Information involved).

- **Figural (visual)**—The properties of stimuli we can experience through visual senses e.g. colour, size, shape, texture and other visual characters of figure.
- **Figural (Auditory)**—The properties of stimuli we can experience through the auditory senses, e.g. voice and sound.
- **Symbolic**—Numbers, letters, symbols, designs.
- **Semantic**—The meaning of words, ideas.
- **Behavioural**—The actions and expressions of people.

Operations (The way of Processing information).

- **Cognition**—Recognizing and discovering.
- **Memory**—Retaining and recalling the contents of thought.
- **Divergent production**—Producing a variety of ideas or solutions to a problem.

- **Convergent production**—Producing a single best solution to a problem.
- **Evaluation**—Taking decision about the nature of the intellectual contents or gathered information whether it is positive or negative, good or bad etc.

Products (The results obtained through Operations).

- **Units**—Individual pieces of information limited in size, e.g. a single number, letter or word.
- **Classes**—Groups of units information related to each other on the basis of some common characteristics involving a higher order concept (e.g. men + women = people).
- **Relations**—A connection between concepts.
- **Systems**—An ordering or classification of relations.
- **Transformation**—Altering or restructuring intellectual contents.
- **Implications**—Making inferences from separate pieces of information.

In this way, according to Guilford's model of intellect, there are 150 factors operating in one's intelligence. Each one of these factors has a trigram symbol, i.e. at least one factor from each category of three parameters has to be present in any specific intellectual activity or mental task.

Let us illustrate this basic fact with an example. Suppose a child is asked to find out the day of the week on a particular date with the help of a calendar. In the execution of this mental task, he will need mental operations like convergent thinking, memory and cognition. For carrying out these operations, he has to make use of the contents. In this particular case, he will make use of semantics, i.e. reading and understanding of the printed words and figures indicating days and dates of a particular month in the calendar. By carrying out mental operations with the help of contents he will finally arrive at the products. The day of the week to which the date in question refers, represents the factor known as "relations". He may further transform and apply this knowledge to identify the days for contiguous dates or vice versa.

Conclusion about the Factor's Theory of Intelligence

Each of the seven theories of intelligence described above attempts to provide a structure of intelligence in terms of its constituents or factors. These theories exhibit wide variations in terms of the numbers of factor that they consider important. The range of all such factors also varies from 1 (Unitary theory) to 150 (Guilford's Intellect Model). However, for understanding what goes on inside one's intelligence we must try to build an eclectic view by incorporating the essence of all the workable theories of intelligence. Consequently, any intellectual activity or mental task may be said to involve the following three kinds of basic factors (arranged in the order as suggested by Vernon or in the form of the model suggested by Guilford).

1. General factor g (Common to all tasks)
2. Specific factors s_1, s_2, etc. (Specific to the tasks)
3. Group factor G (Common to the task belonging to a specific group)

MEASUREMENT OF INTELLIGENCE

We are only familiar with that intelligence of an individual which is manifested by him on an intelligence test or tests. Psychologists have devised many such tests for the measurement of intelligence.

Classification of Intelligence Tests

1. As far as the administrative point of view is concerned the intelligence tests can be classified into two broad categories namely—
   (a) **Individual tests:** In which only one individual is tested at a time.
   (b) **Group tests:** In which a group of individuals is tested at a time.
2. Another way of classifying the intelligence tests is based on the form of the test. Accordingly there are two types of tests:
   (a) **Verbal or Language tests:** These tests make use of language. Here the instructions are given in words (either in written or oral form or both). Individuals are required to use language as well as paper and pencil for giving the responses. The test content of these tests is loaded with verbal material.
   (b) **Non-Verbal and Non-Language tests:** These tests involve such activities in which the use of language is not necessary. The use of language is eliminated from test content and response except in giving directions.

The typical examples of such non-verbal tests are Performance Tests. The principal characteristics of these tests are given below:

(i) Test contents of these tests are in the form of material objects.
(ii) What an individual has to do is indicated by the tester either through oral instructions or by pantomime or signs.
(iii) Individual's responses depend upon what he does or performs than by what he says or writes.
(iv) Generally these tests are individual tests. As Dr. Pillai observes. *"These cannot be used as group tests, chiefly because it is necessary to supervise the individual testee at work and give him necessary direction."* (1972, p. 265).

If we try to have a final picture of all the types of tests in intelligence we will have to keep in view both the ways of classifying them as mentioned above. All these types of intelligence tests can be represented diagrammatically as in Fig. 22.4.

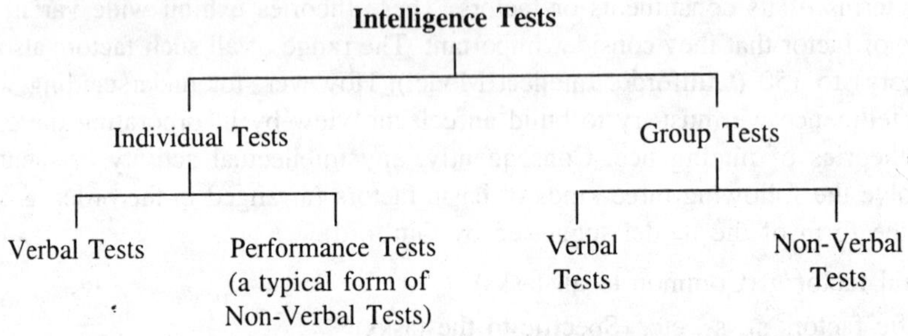

Fig. 22.4 Classification of intelligence tests.

Now we will discuss these types one by one.

Individual Verbal Tests

The tests involving the use of language and administered to an individual at a time belong to this category. As an example of such tests we can refer to **Stanford-Binet Scale**. It is the revised form of the Binet-Simon test. Actually, French psychologist Alfred Binet is said to be the father of intelligence test construction movement. He, along with Theodore Simon, prepared a test in as early as 1905, comprising 30 items (arranged in order of increasing difficulty) graded for different levels. The test included items like:

At age 3—Point out the nose, eyes and mouth.

At age 7—Tell what is missing in the unfinished picture.

In 1931, the first American revision of this test was published by Terman at Stanford university and in 1937 another revision was carried on with the help of Maud A. Merril. This as well as 1960's revision is called Stanford-Binet Scale and widely used as an individual intelligence test.

The tests in this scale are grouped in age levels, extending from age 2 to 22 years. The tasks to be performed by the subjects in these various tests range from simple manipulation to abstract reasoning.

Binet Tests have been adopted in India too. The first such attempt was made by Dr. C.H. Rice in 1922 when he published his "Hindustani Binet Performance Point Scale." This was an adaptation of the Binet test along with some performance tests. The State Manovigyan Shala of Uttar Pradesh has made a Hindi version of Stanford Binet test. This test is divided into several age-groups and named as *'Budhi Pariksha Anooshilan'*.

The other common Verbal Individual Intelligence test (used in India) is *Samanya Budhi Pariksha* (Pt. 1 and 2). This test is an Indian adaptation of the well-known test of William Stephenson. It has been prepared by State Bureau of Educational and Vocational Guidance, Gwalior (M.P.).

Individual Performance Tests

As said earlier, the complete non-verbal or non-language tests of intelligence for testing an individual at a time come into this classification. In these the contents and responses are in the form of performance and language is not used at all. In these tests the items which require responses in terms of motor activities are included. Generally the activities, on which the performance of an individual is tested, are of the following types:

- **(i) Block building or cube construction.** Here the subject is asked to make a structure or design by means of blocks or cubes supplied to him. The examples of the tests involving such type of activities are Merril Palmer Block Building, Koh's Block Design Test, Alexander's Pass-along Test etc.
- **(ii) To fit the block in the holes.** Test material of such types provides numerous blocks and a board in which there are holes corresponding to these blocks. The subject has to fit the blocks in these corresponding holes (in the board). Examples are Seguin Form Board Test and Goddard Form Board Test.
- **(iii) Tracing a maze.** Test material consists of a series of mazes of increasing difficulty, each printed on a separate sheet. The subject is required to trace with pencil the path from entrance to exit. Porteus Maze Test is an example involving such type of activities.
- **(iv) Picture arrangement or picture completion.** In picture arrangement test, the task is to arrange in series the given picture whereas in picture competition test, the subject is required to complete the pictures with the help of given pieces cut out of each picture. The Healy pictorial completion test is a good example of such test which provides a good estimate of the intelligence of the subject without making use of language.

As seen above, these tests try to emphasize upon one or the other types of performance. Instead of using one or two tests a group of performance test, organized either into a scale or battery, may be used for a comprehensive picture of an individual's mental ability. Some of the popular known scales are:

(i) The Pinter Patterson Scale.
(ii) The Arthur Point Scale.
(iii) Alexander's Battery of Performance Tests.

In India too, attempts for constructing such batteries have been made. Dr. Chander Mohan Bhatia's work in this regard deserves special mention. He has developed a battery of performance tests known as **'Bhatia's Battery of Performance Tests'**. It contains the following five sub-tests:

(i) Koh's Block Design Test.
(ii) Alexander's Pass-along Test.
(iii) Pattern Drawing Test.
(iv) Immediate memory test for digits (with an alternative form suitable for illiterates).
(v) Picture Construction Test.

The last three tests in this battery have been constructed by Mr. Bhatia himself while the former two have been borrowed.

WECHSLER BELLEVUE INTELLIGENCE SCALE

This scale is available in two forms. While the WISC form is used for children, the WAIS form is for adults. It is an individual test that has a unique quality of being named as verbal and performance scale simultaneously.

The scale consists of eleven sub-tests—six sub-tests make up a verbal scale and five performance scale. These tests are listed below in the order in which they are administered.

Verbal Scale:

1. Test of General information.
2. Test of General comprehension.
3. Test of Arithmetic reasoning,
4. Test of distinction between similarities.
5. Test of Digit span.
6. Test of vocabulary

Performance Scale:

7. Digit symbol test.
8. Picture completion test.
9. Block Design test.
10. Picture arrangement test.
11. Object assembly test.

The scores on these sub-tests are added to get an idea of an individual's intelligence.

Group Verbal Intelligence Tests

The tests, which necessitate the use of language and are applied to a group of individuals at a time, come under this category. Some of the earlier tests belonging to this category are:

(i) Army Alpha Test (developed in World War)

(ii) Army General Classification Test (developed in second World War)

Today we have a large number of group verbal tests. In India too, attempts have been made to construct such tests. Some of the popular tests of this nature are—

1. C.I.E. verbal Group Test of Intelligence (Hindi) constructed by Prof. Uday Shankar.
2. The Group Test of General Mental Ability (*Samuhik Mansik Yogyata Pariksha*) constructed by Dr. J.S. Jalota (Hindi).
3. Group test of Intelligence, prepared by Bureau of Psychology, Allahabad (Hindi).
4. Prayag Mehta's Group Intelligence Test (*Samuhik Budhi Pariksha*, Hindi). This test has been published by Mansayan, Delhi.
5. General Mental Abilities Test prepared by Dr. P.S. Hundal of Punjab University (Panjabi).
6. Group verbal intelligence test prepared by Dr. P. Gopala Pillai of the Kerala University (Malayalam).
7. *Samuhic Budhi Pariksha* (Hindi), prepared by Sh. P.L. Shrimali, Vidya Bhavan G.S. Teacher College, Udaipur.
8. *Samuhic Budhi Ki Jaanch* (Hindi), prepared by Shri M.S. Mohsin, Educational and Vocational Guidance Bureau, Patna, Bihar.

The Group Non-Verbal Intelligence Tests

These tests do not necessitate the use of language and are applicable to a group of individuals at a given time.

The difference between performance test (used for an individual) and non-verbal tests (used for a group) is in the degree as far as their non-verbal nature is concerned. The performance tests require the manipulation of concrete objects or materials supplied in the test by the subject. Responses are purely motor in character and seldom require the use of paper and pencil by the testee, (except in cases like Maze Test etc.) where as the test material used for group testing, is provided in booklet and requires the use of pencil by the testee.

Still in these tests, material does not contain words or numerical figures. It contains pictures, diagrams and geometrical figures etc. printed in a booklet. The subject is required to do such activities so as to fill in some empty spaces, draw some simple figures to point out similarities and dissimilarities etc. So, although the subject uses paper and pencil, he does not need to know words or numerical figures. What he has to do is explained clearly by the examiner usually through clear demonstrations so as to make the least possible use of language.

The examples of such type of tests are:

(i) **Army Beta Test.** It was developed during World War I, in U.S.A. for testing the intelligence of those soldiers who were either illiterate or were not used to English language.

(ii) **Chicago Non-verbal Test.** This non-verbal test has proved most useful for young children aged between 12 and 13 years.

(iii) **Raven's Progressive matrices Test.** This test was developed in the U.K. It is a very popular non-verbal group test of intelligence. The test has been designed to evaluate the subjects ability—

(a) to see relationship between geometric figures or designs.

(b) to perceive the structure of the design in order to select appropriate part for the competition of each pattern.

(iv) **C.I.E. Non-Verbal Group Test of Intelligence.** Originally prepared by J.W. Jenkins, the test is printed by C.I.E. for adaptation into Hindi medium schools. The test contains such terms as instructed in Fig. 22.5.

नीचे प्रत्येक पंक्ति में बाईं ओर तीन आकार दिये गये हैं जो एक जैसे हैं दाईं ओर 5 आकार दिये हैं। इनमें से वह आकार ढूँढो जो बाईं ओर दिए हुए तीन आकारों में से सबसे अधिक मिलता-जुलता हो उसके नीचे रेखा खींच दो।

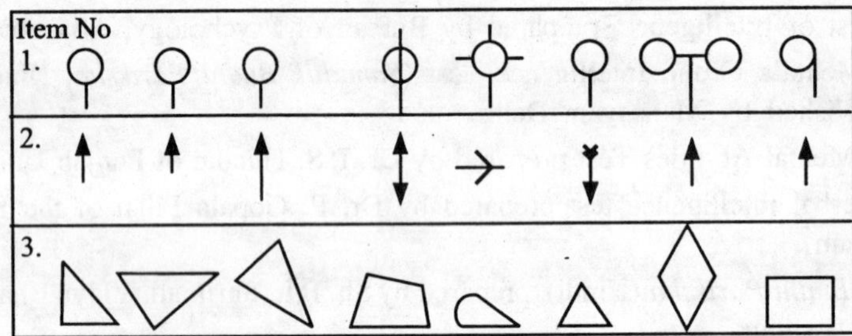

Fig. 22.5 An item from C.I.E. non-verbal group test of intelligence.

Individual and group tests have their advantages as well as disadvantages. We can compare them on the following lines:

Individual Tests	*Group Tests*
1. With these tests, only one individual is tested at a time. They cannot be administered to a group and this makes them costly in terms of time, labour and money.	1. These tests have two-fold advantage. In addition to their applicability in testing a group of individual at a time, they can also be administered to the individuals separately. Testing of so many individuals at a time gives them the advantage of saving time, money and labour.
2. Individual tests have the unique advantage of being used for children as well as adults.	2. Group tests cannot be given to young children below 9 to 10 years of age.
3. As the examiner has a close contact with the subject, he can take into account all personal and emotional factors and like-wise have all those additional pieces of information which may prove useful for the interpretation of an individual's test scores.	3. The examiner does not have a desirable contact with the subject. He cannot detect and rectify influence of such factors as ill health, mood, poor social background or practice and coaching that might have been given to a subject for boosting his score. What the examiner gets at all is the numerical score and nothing of additional information as obtained in individual tests.
4. Individual tests are not as objective and standardized as group tests. Their administration require well-trained and competent examiners.	4. Group tests are more objective and standardized in comparison to individual tests. The manuals and instruction provided with these tests make their administration, scoring and interpretation so easy that a need of such trained personnel is seldom felt.

VERBAL TESTS VS NON-VERBAL AND PERFORMANCE TESTS

What led to the construction of non-verbal and performance test when verbal tests were there for testing the intelligence, is a relevant question to be asked. Verbal tests, as already said, laid emphasis on linguistic ability. They were loaded with verbal material words and numericals. Hence those with linguistic superiority were always on the advantageous side in comparison to those having language weakness. To do away with such flaws, non-verbal and performance tests were put to use. In brief, the advantage of these tests over verbal tests are as under:

1. Performance tests are useful for those who have language handicap due to one or more of the following reasons:
   - (i) They may belong to the foreign language speaking groups.
   - (ii) They may be illiterates, not knowing how to read and write.
   - (iii) They may have difficulties in reading, writing and listening due to defects in their sense organs (deaf, dumb etc.)
   - (iv) They may be younger children who are not yet able to read and write well.
   - (v) They may be mentally retarded or mentally deficient children and therefore, very slow in grasping and responding to the verbal items.
   - (vi) They may belong to unprivileged class or strata of the society and hence may have had limited education opportunities.
2. Verbal test belonging to one region contains the material which has a direct relationship with the language or culture of that region or country. Non-verbal and performance tests are more or less language and culture-free and hence can be used for cross-cultural and linguistic study of intelligence.
3. They can prove useful in the efforts to determine aptitude and promise in shop work, mechanical jobs and so on.

LIMITATIONS OF NON-VERBAL AND PERFORMANCE TESTS

1. They may not be able to predict scholastic success in schools as do the verbal tests simply because school work itself is predominantly verbal.
2. They, specially the performance tests, are very costly and pose difficulty in being transported from one place to another.
3. They are more susceptible to practice-effects and chance successes are more frequent than in the case of verbal tests. Therefore, they are less reliable than verbal tests.
4. These tests are limited in their range of mental functioning tested since they do not require much use of the ability to make abstractions and deal with concepts. They are thus not able to differentiate among above-average individuals.

Thus these are the merits and limitations of the tests. In fact, the testing of mental ability is a comprehensive task and cannot be solely left either to the verbal or performance tests. For taking a reliable view of a person's intellectual ability, following things should be kept in mind:

- (i) Performance test should be taken as a supplement to verbal tests and vice versa.
- (ii) No single test or tests are suitable for this purpose. There should be an attack from many angles.

How to Test the Intelligence with an Intelligence Test?

So far, we have discussed the problem of measuring intelligence theoretically. To deal with such a practical problem is in fact a difficult task. Below we shall illustrate the process with the help of a group verbal test. We take the Group General Mental ability test constructed by Dr. S. Jalota for this purpose.

THE TEST

This is a verbal group test of mental ability for Hindi knowing school-age children. The test material is devided in four parts:

(a) **Test Booklet.** In the test booklet the direction for attempting the items of the test are written. There are 100 questions (on each page 20) in this test which require verbal ability for answering. Some specimen questions are given below:

(1) तट का अर्थ (1) गंगा (2) किनारा (3) बांध (4) पर

(2) 19, 17, 15, 13, 11, 9 इन संख्याओं के क्रम के अनुसार आगे की एक संख्या उत्तर पत्र पर लिखो।

All these questions are to be answered in 20 minutes.

(b) **Answer Sheet.** These are not re-usable. They are supplied to test the intelligence of the students of a group.

(c) Scoring key for evaluating the answers.

(d) Test manual (for direction and table of conversion)

PROCEDURE

The group under examination is made to sit comfortably. They are provided with answer sheets and test booklets. The task is completed in the following steps—

(i) They are instructed not to write anything on the test booklet.

(ii) On their respective answer sheets, they have to write a brief introduction about themselves like name, class, school, father's name, date of birth and age in years, months and days.

(iii) Again, they are directed to read the instructions on the beginning of the test booklet carefully. The examiner also tries to explain to them.

(iv) Now they are asked to answer the questions. Students are supervised properly so as to check the cases of cheating etc. They are supposed to finish their work within 20 minutes.

(v) After collecting the answersheets, the scoring is done with the help of an answer key. The total raw score of each testee is thus calculated.

(vi) With the help of table provided in the manual, the raw scores of these individuals are converted into their mental ages.

(vii) Chronological ages are known with the help of the date of birth supplied by the subjects.

(viii) Finally, by dividing the mental ages with their chronological ages and multiplying the quotient with 100, the I.Q. of the subjects can be known.

How Good can Intelligence be Measured?

Measurement of intelligence is not possible in the same way as we measure a piece of cloth or the temperature of our body. Why is it not possible can be understood through the following discussion:

1. **Nature of the thing we want to measure:** Intelligence is not a thing. It is only an idea, an abstraction. Therefore, its measurement is not possible like the measurement of a piece of cloth, wood or land etc.

2. **Nature of the instrument or the scale by which intelligence is measured:** In measuring a piece of cloth we use scales made up of absolute units. For measuring temperature of the body we use thermometers having degrees as units of measurement. In such measurement, we use scales made up of absolute units and the instruments give somewhat reliable and valid results. But in case of intelligence measurement we don't have such scales. Here, as Griffith observes "the standard of measurement is the group of performance." (1933, p. 138)

Therefore, when we measure intelligence of an individual with the help of an intelligence test we try to interpret the resulting score in the light of norms established (group performance) by the author of the test. In this way, one's intelligence is determined relatively to the classified group to which he belongs. So, while in the case of a piece of cloth absolute measurement is possible, in case of intelligence measurement we have relative measurement.

With the difference in the nature of measuring instruments, we can observe that while measuring a piece of cloth or body temperature, it is quite convenient to use the relevant measuring instruments for providing reliable and valid measures intelligence tests can not be used in such a way. In addition of giving a relative measurement of one's intelligence, the administration as well as interpretation of these tests require sufficient competency, skill and labour on the part of the examiner.

In this way, we can see the measurement of intelligence is not such a simple, definite, reliable and valid task as the measurement of a piece of cloth or the temperature of a body.

CONCEPT OF MENTAL AGE (M.A.) AND INTELLIGENCE QUOTIENT (I.Q.)

As we have already used the term 'mental age' and 'I.Q.' in the interpretation of intelligence test results, it is worth knowing something about them as well.

Mental age. The term mental age was first used by Binet. Its concept can be clarified with the help of the following example.

Suppose there is a test comprising 100 questions (like Jalota's test) and the majority of the subjects, whose age is 13 years 6 months, answer successfully 48 questions, then an individual who earns a score, 48, regardless of his chronological age, will be said to have a mental age of 13 years 6 months.

Intelligence Quotient (I.Q.) This term was initiated by the German psychologist William Stern and put into wide practice by Terman. It appeared to Stern that if a child was 6 years old (chronologically), but could do what an 8 years old normally does he would be 8/6 or 1.33 as bright as the average. And in this way, he made the ratio M.A./C.A., measure of the rate of mental development of an individual. The ratio was given the name of Intelligence Quotient (I.Q.). To do away with the decimal point, the ratio was a gain multiplied by 100 and thus the formula to calculate I.Q. is:

$$\text{I.Q.} = \frac{\text{Mental Age (M.A.)}}{\text{Chronological Age (C.A.)}} \times 100 \text{ (as used in Standard Binet Scale)}$$

or,

$$\text{I.Q.} = \frac{\text{Attained or actual score}}{\text{Expected mean score for age}} \times 100 \text{ (as used by Weschsler)}$$

Classification of I.Q.

By making use of the formula of I.Q. by Stem, Terman tried to classify the individuals into certain specific categories on the basis of the data collected through the administration of his intelligence tests for terming them average, below average and above average as given below:

I.Q.	*Level of Intelligence*
140 and above	Gifted or Genius
120–140	Very Superior
110–120	Superior
90–110	Normal or Average
75–90	Border Line and Dull
50–75	Morons
25–50	Imbeciles
Below 25	Idiots

However, as far as the classification based on the intelligence tests suitable to the Indian conditions is concerned, the following one presented by professor Uday Shankar may work well.

I.Q.	*Level of Intelligence*
140 and above	Genius
125–140	Very Superior
110–125	Superior
90–110	Average
75–90	Border Line and Dull
50–75	Morons or Feeble minded
25–50	Imbeciles
Below 25	Idiots

The Constancy of I.Q.

As mentioned earlier, intelligence grows till the age of 16 or 18 years, but I.Q. for most of the individuals remains constant. Primarily I.Q. provides a ratio for knowing how bright an individual is as compared with others of his own age.

Actually, it is an index which is independent not only of the particular score that an individual makes on a particular scale but also of the particular age at which he happens to make it. It is thus a measure which acquaints us with the relative brightness of intellectual possibilities of an individual more or less permanently (see Fig. 22.6).

It is true that an individual grows in intelligence but the whole group (the other individuals of his own age) also grows at the same rate. Thus I.Q., a measure of defining relative brightness or intellectual possibilities of an individual, remains practically constant. Under ordinary circumstances (accident or disease exempted), an individual's I.Q. is supposed to remain constant throughout his life or at least throughout the age limits covered by the scale. This property of I.Q. is referred to as constancy of I.Q. by psychologists.

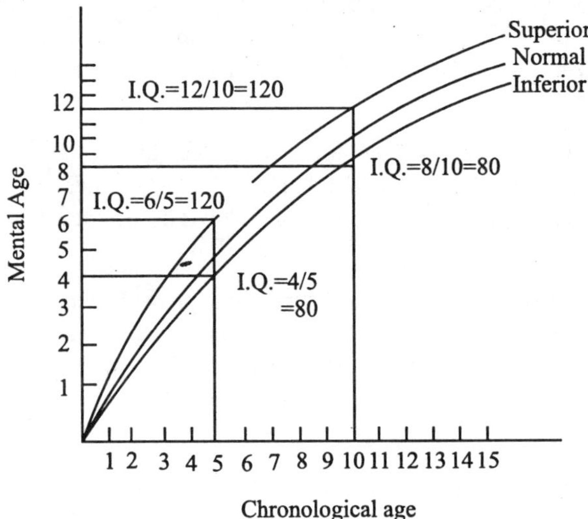

Fig. 22.6 Hypothetical growth curves which give a constant I.Q. (From H.E. Garrett's and M.R. Shneck, 1933)

Uses and Limitations of Intelligence Tests

Intelligence tests have their advantage as well as drawbacks. Below we list them one by one.

Uses of Intelligence Tests

1. For the purpose of selection. Intelligence tests are often used for the purpose of making selection of the suitable candidates for activities like—

(i) admission in a particular course of instruction.
(ii) deciding the cases of scholarships.
(iii) choosing candidates for assigning some specific responsibilities.
(iv) selecting candidates for participation in various co-curricular activities etc.

2. For the purpose of classification. Intelligence tests help the teacher classify the students as bright, dull or average and put them in homogeneous groups in order to bring efficiency in the teaching-learning process.

3. For the purpose of promotion. Intelligence tests can prove as one of the useful instruments in promoting the individuals not only in educational fields but in all other occupational and social situations where one studies to go higher on the ladder.

4. For knowing one's potentiality. Intelligence tests help in revealing the potentialities of an individual and thus make possible the predication of one's success in a particular field. The knowledge of such potentiality helps the teacher in the following ways :

(i) ***Giving guidance.*** Teacher or a guidance personal can give guidance to the pupils in the selection of various courses of instruction and occupations.

(ii) ***Helps in learning process.*** Teacher can plan teaching-learning activities with the help of this knowledge. *"Results of intelligence tests"* as Crow and Crow write, *"can help a teacher to discover what the child can learn and how quickly he can learn as well as the teaching methods that should be applied and the learning content that should be utilized to guide the learner to use his mental potentialities to their utmost."* (1973, p. 160)

(iii) ***To establish a proper level of aspiration.*** As Sawrey and Telford write. *"One of the most important ends served by intelligence testing is that of the assisting of the individual to establish a level of aspiration that is realistic in terms of intellectual potential."* (1964, p. 484).

5. For diagnostic purpose. Exceptional children like gifted, backward and the mentally retarded children can be detected with the help of intelligence tests. Moreover, the intelligence tests help in the diagnosis of the root causes of problematic behaviour of the child and likewise suggest possible remedies.

6. Helps in Research work. Intelligence testing has proved very useful in psychological, sociological and educational research. For example, in deciding the relative role of heredity and environment in the process of growth and development, research workers have made much use of intelligence testing.

Limitations of Intelligence Tests

Intelligence tests have given birth to many problems due to their limitations and shortcomings. We can list them as follows:

1. Intelligence tests and students. Intelligence tests label some students as superior and the others as inferiors. This type of knowledge creates many problems. Children who are slightly dull are still intelligent enough to realize through the results of the intelligence tests that they are slow to learn. It makes them disappointed and causes inferiority feelings and ultimately mars their future. On the other hand, students with a slight more I.Q. may become overconfident. There is every possibility that these students may not then give serious attention to their work. Also the consciousness of their superiority may result in misbehaviour on their part and can turn them into problem children.

2. Intelligence tests and teacher. Teachers, after knowing the I.Q. of the child, make a permanent opinion about the child's potentialities and abilities. They try to see him through his I.Q. They leave no attempt to discourage or create overconfidence in the students according to the level of their intelligence announced by their tests. Moreover, knowledge of the intelligence of the pupils for a teacher may result in slackness on his part. He may put the entire responsibility of a pupil's failure on his inferior intelligence and not care for a bright pupil thinking that he would be able to learn on his own. In this way, the knowledge of intelligence supplied by these may bring disastrous results to the teacher.

3. Given birth to Segregation and conflicts. Intelligence test results have been misused to uphold the theory of royal blood, segregation and sectarian outlook. In U.S.A., it has led to a conflict between the Negro and the white populations. The conflict, in actual sense, is the result of misconception about the predictive value of these tests and their correlation with hereditary factors. In defence, we can put forward the following points:

(a) No intelligence tests, including the most refined performance tests, can be claimed to be completely free of practice or coaching effects and independent of cultural, social, racial and other environment factors. Hence, they cannot be claimed as a measure of initial mental abilities and capacities of the individual and therefore it is quite unfair to deny or uphold the right of admission or job opportunities to the people on the basis of these tests. Now the contemporary researches in this direction have proved that intelligence tests results always favour healthy environmental conditions like improved sanitation, family atmosphere, education of parents, cultural background, socio-economic conditions and better education opportunities etc.

(b) In fact, intelligence test helps in knowing very little about the total make-up of the child's potentialities. Only cognitive (mental actions) domain can be said to be touched by these tests. They leave many important aspects like interests, attitudes, motives etc. Hence they cannot be relied as the predictor of the future success of an individual.

(c) *"The results of all such tests,"* as Crow and Crow put it, *"may be effected by many factors inherent in the testing conditions, the child's background of experience and other favourable or unfavourable elements. Hence, no administrator, teacher or student of education should accept test results as the only measure of an individual's ability to learn."* (1973, p. 60)

In this way, it is not proper to give undue weightage to intelligence tests. They should not be accepted as the only measure of an individual's degree of ability to learn. They should not be made an instrument of creating complexes among the students and misunderstanding among the teachers. In a nut-shell, the result of these must be interpreted and used intelligently. They should be taken as the means and not the end in themselves.

SUMMARY

Intelligence may be considered as a sort of mental energy, an aggregate or global mental capacity of an individual for helping him in coping with his environment in terms of adaptation and dealing with novel situations as effectively as possible. It has many established facts regarding its nature like—(i) the distribution of intelligence in the population follows the properties of the normal distribution, (ii) It is a joint product of heredity and environment (iii) Differences in sex, race or culture do not create differences in intelligence etc.

Theories of intelligence try to explain the structural composition of our intelligence by pointing out specifically its different components or factors. *Unitary theory*, the oldest theory in this regard, for example holds that intelligence consists of only one single factor, i.e. simply a fund of intellectual competency which is universal for all the activities of the individual. Quite contrary to this, *multifactor theory* insists that one's intelligence consists of numerous separate elements or factors, each one being a minute part or component of an intellectual activity. *Spearman's two factor theory* asserts that there are two types of factors working in one's intelligence namely, the general intelligence (common to all the different cognitive tasks) and specific intelligence (quite specific to a specific task).

The group factor theory advocates that our intellectual activities can be categorized into certain specific groups and each of these groups is governed by a special type of intelligence component known as a group factor. Thurstone and his associates (the main propagator of the theory) have pointed out 9 such group factors as the constituents of one's intelligence. *Thomson's sampling theory* tries to provide an eclectic approach by giving place to general intelligence 'g', specific intelligence 's' and group factor 'G' in one's intelligence. *Vernon's hierarchical theory* put forward a hierarchical structure for explaining the structural composition of one's intelligence in the shape of factor 'G' representing an overall intelligence of an individual branching into two major group factors and various specific factors. *Gulford's theory* put forward by J.P. Guilford and his associates lay down a model of intellect involving three interrelated basic parameters — operations, contents and products for explaining the structural composition of human intelligence.

Measurement of intelligence is not possible in the same way as we measure a piece of cloth or the body temperature. However, it can be well assessed with the help of some or the other intelligence tests categorized as individual and group tests involving the use of verbal and non-verbal test material. In individual tests, we test one individual at a time but in group tests a group of individuals can be tested at a given time. In all these individual as well as group tests, we either try to make use of the verbal material, i.e. language, or non-verbal material for testing the intellectual level of our students. Performance tests are a typical example of such non-verbal (language-free) tests where we try to test the intelligence of a student on the basis of his performance in some intellectual tasks.

The concept of mental age and I.Q. is put into use for interpreting the raw scores earned on an intelligence test. The term 'mental age' coined by Binet stands for the mental level of a child against the level which is normal for the majority of children of his age. For the computation of I.Q., we make use of the formula I.Q. = Mental age / Chronological age multiplied by 100.

The data collected after administration of the intelligence tests have helped the psychologists to classify individuals into certain specific categories of average, below average and above average intelligence. It has helped us in the diagnosis and identification of gifted, backward and mentally sub-normal children among a particular group or population.

The results derived on the basis of I.Q. measurement have revealed one of its unique characteristics named as "the constancy of I.Q.". It postulates that I.Q., a measure of defining relative brightness or the intellectual possibilities of an individual, remain practically constant throughout his life or at least throughout the age limits covered by the scale (test utilized for measuring one's I.Q.).

Intelligence tests have their advantages as well as drawbacks. These can be properly utilized for the purpose of selection, classification, promotion, diagnosis and assessment of one's potentiality, besides being used in the task of guidance, counseling and research work. However, the results of these tests can also be misused by the students in perpetuating a number of complexes (inferiority or superiority), fears and disappointment etc. They may also colour the viewpoints of the teachers towards their students and give birth to many types of segregations and conflicts in the society.

References and Suggested Readings

Binnet, A. and Simon, T., *The Development of Intelligence in Children,* Williams & Wilkins, Baltimore, 1916.

Crow, L.D. and Crow, Alice, *Educational Psychology,* Eurasia Publishing House, New Delhi, 1973.

Garrett, H.E. and Shoneck, M.R., *Psychological Tests, Methods and Results*, Part II, Harper & Brothers, New York, 1933.

Griffith, J.H., *The Psychology of Human Behaviour*, George Allen, London, 1933.

Guilford, J.P., *The Nature of Human Intelligence*, McGraw-Hill, New York, 1967.

Jensen, A.R., *Bias in Mental Testing*, Free Press, New York, 1980.

Knight, Rex and Knight, Margaret, *A Modern Introduction to Psychology*, University Tutorial Press, London, 1952.

Murphy, Gardner, *An Introduction to Psychology*, Oxford & IBH, New Delhi, 1968.

Pillai, N.P., Pillai K.S. and Nair, K.S., *Psychological Foundation of Education*, Kala Niketan, Trivandrum, 1972.

Sawrey, J.H. and Telford, C., *Educational Psychology*, 2nd ed., Prentice-Hall, New York, 1964.

Stern W, *Psychological Methods of Testing Intelligence,* Warwick and York Inc, 1964 Baltimore, 1914.

Stoddard, G.D., *The Meaning of Intelligence*, Macmillan, New York, 1943.

Terman, L.M. and Merrill, M.A., *Measuring Intelligence*, Hougton Mifflin, Boston, 1937.

Thompson, G.H., *The Factorial Analysis of Human Ability*, University Press, London, 1939.

Thurston, L.L., *Primary Mental abilities*, University of Chicago Press, Chicago, 1938.

Vernon, P.E., *The Structure of Human Ability*, Methuen, London, 1950.

Wagnon, M.J. (Ed.), *Readings in Educational Psychology*, Houghton Mifflin, New York, 1937.

Wechsler, D., *The Measurement of Adult Intelligence,* Williams & Wilkins, New York, 1944.

Woodworth, R.S., and Marquis, D.G., *Psychology*, Henry Holt, New York, 1948.

23

Creativity

CHAPTER COMPOSITION

INTRODUCTION

The Almighty God, the creator of the universe, is the supreme mind who possesses the finest creative abilities. He has created all of us and all that is revealed in nature. We are elevated to be called His creation. According to our Indian philosophy, we all are constituents of the supreme power as the rays of the sun are the constituents of their creator—sun. Therefore, every one of us ought to possess creative abilities. But every one of us is a unique creation, thereby the degree of possession of creative ability is not uniform. Some of us are found to possess high creative talents and these are the people who move the world ahead by their discoveries and inventions in the fields of art, literature, science, business, teaching and other fields of human accomplishments. They are responsible for coming up with new ideas and bringing about social and cultural changes.

Gandhi, Lincoln, Bhabha, Newton, Shakespeare, Bertrand Russel, Leonardo da Vinci were such creative individuals who left their marks in their respective fields. Certainly, they were endowed with creative abilities but the role of environment in terms of education, training and opportunities cannot be ignored. Good education, proper care and provision of opportunities for creative expressions inspire, stimulate and sharpen the creative mind and herein the parents, society and teachers come into picture. They are required to help the children in nourishing and utilizing their creative abilities to the maximum degree. Therefore, educational process—formal or informal—should be aimed at developing creative abilities among children. It needs to acquaint the teachers and parents with the actual meaning of creativity, the knowledge of the creative process, and ways and means of developing creativity. In the following pages, we shall try to know something about these aspects.

CONCEPT OF CREATIVITY

The real nature and concept of creativity may be properly explained by emphasizing on its following aspects.

— Its meaning (including attempts of its defining)

— Its nature and characteristics.

Meaning and Definition of Creativity

The term 'creativity' or 'creative process' has been defined by some eminent scholars in the following different ways:

Stagner and Karwoski

Creativity implies the production of a 'totally or partially' novel identity. (Crow and Crow, 1973, p. 314)

Drevdahl

Creativity is the capacity of a person to produce compositions, products or ideas which are essentially new or novel and previously unknown to the producer. (1956, p. 22)

Wilson, Guilford and Christensen

The creative process is any process by which something new is produced—an idea or an object including a new form or arrangement of old elements. The new creation must contribute to the solution of some problem. (Dutt, N.K., 1974, p. 208)

Skinner

Creative thinking means that the predictions and/or inferences for the individual are new, original, ingenious, unusual. The creative thinker is one who explores new areas and makes new observations, new predictions, new inferences. (1968, p. 529)

If we try to analyze the above definitions we would find that the creation or discovery of something new is the central element in all these definitions. Therefore, we can easily conclude that *creativity is the capacity or ability of an individual to create, discover or produce a new idea or object including the re-arrangement or reshaping of what is already known to him.*

Nature and Characteristics of Creativity

On the basis of the above mentioned definitions as well as the findings of various other scholars, the nature and characteristics of creativity or creative expression can be summarized as follows:

1. Creativity is universal. Everyone of us possesses creative capacity to some degree.
2. Although creative abilities are natural endowments, they are capable of being nourished and nurtured by training or education.

3. Through creative expression, something new or novel is produced. But novelty or newness does not necessarily imply to produce a totally new idea or an object which has never been experienced or produced earlier. To make the fresh and noble combination for the given separate elements or to reshape or rearrange the already known facts or principles or to bring a slight reform and modification in the previously known techniques, are as much the acts of creative expression as the discovery of a new element in chemistry or a new formula in mathematics. The only precaution for naming an expression as creative is that it should not be a mere repetition or reproduction of what has already been experienced or learned by an individual.
4. Any creative expression is the source of joy and satisfaction for the creator. The creator says what he sees or feels in his own way. There is perfect individuality in one's creative expression. He expresses himself, to a great extent, through his creation. It is his own way of looking at things; persons or events and therefore, it is not essential that a creative work may arouse the same feeling or give same satisfaction as experienced by the creator himself.
5. The creator is the person who is able to make ego-involved statements like, "It is my creation', 'I have solved this problem.' 'It is my ideas,' etc. In creative expressions there is complete ego involvement.
6. Creative thinking cannot be a closed thinking. It must have complete freedom for the multiplicity of responses, choices and lines of action. By traveling on the routine, beaten track, one cannot be able to create but can only reproduce or repeat.
7. The field of creative expression is very wide. It covers all the aspects of human accomplishments like scientific inventions and discoveries, composition of poems, writing of stories and drama and good performance in the fields of dance, music, painting, sculpture, political and social leadership, business, teaching and other professions. Our day-to-day life activities also need creativity. Therefore, in a nutshell, life as a whole present enormous opportunities for creative expression.

The question as to what different cognitive factors constitute creativity has been a subject of excessive experiment, action and research. J.P. Guilford, Torrance, Drevadahl and others have tried to identify the important components of creativity. As a result, ideational fluency, originality, flexibility, divergent thinking, persistence, self-confidence, sensitiveness, ability to see relationships and make associations are some of the factors that are found favourable for creative output.

DIFFERENCE BETWEEN CREATIVITY AND INTELLIGENCE

Intelligence and creativity should not be considered as one and the same process. Differences between the two can be summarized as follows:

(i) It has been established that convergent thinking is the basis of intelligence whereas divergent thinking forms the basis of creativity. In convergent thinking, an individual has the tendency to find out the one most appropriate idea or response whereas divergent thinking allows as many responses as possible. Therefore, while in intelligence tests (usually requiring one correct response) convergent thinking is being tested, creativity emphasizes more on testing divergent thinking.

(ii) It has been observed that highly creative persons usually possess intelligence to a high degree but it is not essential for an intelligent person to be creative. One may possess high intelligence without having creative abilities. On the other hand, an adequate level of intelligence is a necessary condition for being creative. A mentally retarded person cannot be expected to be creative.

(iii) In intelligence testing, the speed and accuracy of the cognitive behaviour is emphasized while in creative tests novelty, flexibility and originality are given more weightage.

CREATIVITY IN CHILDREN

Identification of Creative Children

The term 'creativity' cannot be used synonymously with giftedness. Therefore, we should not make a mistake of considering every gifted child as a creative child. Creativity in its all shapes and forms is the highest expression of giftedness that may or may not be found in a particular gifted child. The problem then lies in the identification of the creative children.

Creative behaviour and expression, like other behaviour patterns, possesses its basic components in the form of cognitive, conative and affective behaviour. Consequently, we can label a child creative to the extent to which he is able to demonstrate creative aspect in his thinking, feeling and doing behaviour. For such labeling, we may employ two different approaches:

(i) making use of tests of creativity, and

(ii) making use of non-testing devices observation, interview, rating scale, personality inventory, check-list etc.

Let us discuss these approaches one by one.

CREATIVITY TESTS

As we make use of intelligence tests to label a child as intelligent, we have the use of creativity tests for labeling a child as creative. There are so many tests available in India and abroad for this purpose. We are mentioning a few of these tests below.

- **Tests Standardized Abroad**
  1. Minnesota tests of creative thinking
  2. Guilford's Divergent Thinking Instrument
  3. Remote Associate Test
  4. Wallach and Kogan Creativity Instrument
  5. A.C. Tests of Creative Ability
  6. Torrance Tests of Creative Thinking
- **Tests Standardized in India**
  1. Baquer Mehdi's Tests of Creative Thinking—Hindi and English.
  2. Passi's Tests of Creativity.
  3. Sharma's Divergent Production Abilities Test.
  4. Saxena's Tests of Creativity.

As pointed out earlier, creativity is a complex blend of a number of abilities and traits. Therefore, in all the creative tests, attempts are always made for the assessment of these abilities and traits with the help of verbal and non-verbal test items. The factors or dimensions commonly measured through these tests are fluency, flexibility, originality, divergent thinking and elaboration.

Let us now illustrate the measurement of creativity components with the help of two creativity tests—one standardized abroad and the other in India.

Torrance Tests of Creative Thinking. It is a set of two tests—one verbal and the other non-verbal. It has been developed by the famous American psychologist E. Paul Torrance and can be employed to test the creativity of the children from Kindergarten to graduation.

For testing the creativity through non-verbal and verbal performance, Torrance has thus developed figural form A and B and verbal form A and B (Forms B are the equivalent alternatives of the forms A).

The figural form (Non verbal testing device). The activities required in this test are of the non-verbal nature. The subject has to perform certain non-verbal activities, i.e. draw or make something as a response to the test items. This test has three sub-tests as described below:

(i) **Figure or picture completion test.** In this sub-test, there are some incomplete figures. The subject is asked to complete these figures in whatever way he desires.

(ii) **Picture or figural construction test.** In this sub-test, the subject in provided with a piece of coloured paper cut in a curved shape and asked to think of a figure or picture of which this piece or paper may be a part.

(iii) **Parallel lines test :** In this sub-test, there are several pairs of straight lines. The subject is required to draw as many objects or pictures by using such pair.

The verbal forms (used as a verbal testing device). Through the items of the sub-tests of this form, the subject is required to provide written responses. There are six sub-tests incorporating activities of the following nature.

(i) **Asking type:** Here the subject is encouraged to reveal his ability to perceive all things that are not normally perceived by others.

(ii) **Guess cause and guess consequences type:** Here the subject is encouraged to reveal his ability to formulate hypotheses concerning cause and effect, *i.e.* what is behind the situation in the picture and what its consequence may be.

(iii) **Product Improvement Type:** The subjects are asked to suggest ways and means to improve a toy, a machine or such other products.

(iv) **Unusual Uses Type:** These are meant to test the divergence about the ways of using a product. Here the subjects have to tell about as many unusual uses as they can point out to use a product.

(v) **Unusual Questions Type:** Here for a particular object or verbal description, the subjects are required to ask as many unusual questions as they can.

(vi) **Just Suppose Type:** The subjects are required to predict outcomes of unusual situations.

The responses of the subject are scored in all the sub-test items of both the forms (figural and verbal) and then his total score is computed for providing an estimate of his overall creative potential.

Baquer Mehdi's Tests of Creativity. This test has been developed by Dr. Baquer Mehdi. It has been published by National Psychological Corporation, Agra. There are four verbal and three non-verbal sub-tests under this. This verbal form has the following four sub-tests:

1. Consequence Test (duration 12 minutes). In this test, the subject is asked to think of as many consequences as possible for situations like—

1. What would happen if we could fly like a bird?
2. What would have happened if your school had wheels?
3. What would happen if you do not have any need for food?

2. Unusual uses test (duration 15 minutes). It includes test items like—Write as many novel, interesting and unusual uses for objects like a piece of stone, a wooden stick, water.

3. New relationship test (duration 15 minutes). It has the test items like below.

Think of as many relationships between the following pairs of words, as possible. (*i*) Tree, house (*ii*) Chair, ladder (*iii*) Air, water

4. Product improvement test (duration 6 minutes). It consists of test items like below.

You have a toy horse. Now think of as many new things or features that can make it more useful and interesting.

Non-verbal Sub-tests: The three sub-tests of this category are of the following types :

(i) Picture construction test (duration 20 minutes). It contains test items like below.

In Fig. 23.1, there are two geometrical figures—a semi-circle and a rhombus. Construct and elaborate pictures using each figure as an integral part. For each picture give a separate title.

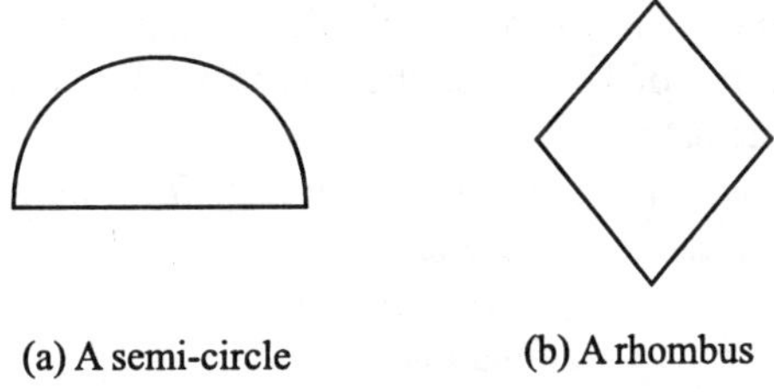

Fig. 23.1 Picture construction test.

(ii) Line figure completion test (duration 15 minutes). Below in Fig. 23.2, there are 10 incomplete line drawings. You have to draw meaningful and interesting pictures using each of them. Also give an appropriate title for each of your creation.

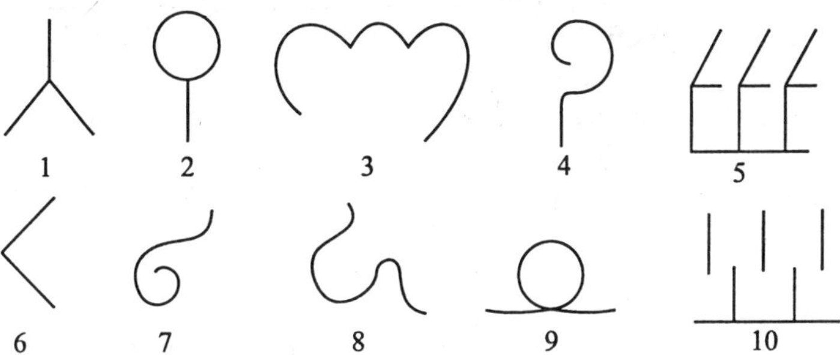

Fig. 23.2 Line figure completion test.

(iii) Picture construction test (duration 10 minutes). Here there are seven triangles and seven ellipses. Construct different meaningful and interesting pictures by using these figures in multiple associations.

In all such creativity tests as illustrated above, the verbal and non-verbal activities are evaluated in terms of related creative abilities like fluency, originality, flexibility and elaboration. A high score on this creative test increases the probability of declaring the subject as creative. However, such declaration may need further support from the results of the assessment made through some other testing devices.

USE OF NON-TESTING DEVICES

The creative aspect of a child can also be assessed through some non-testing devices like Natural observation method, Situational techniques, Rating scale, Check list, Interview, Personality inventories, Interest inventories, Attitude scales, Aptitude test, Value schedules, and Projective techniques, and so on. These devices help in the revelation of those personality traits and behavioural characteristics that are supposed to be present in a creative child. Some of these traits or characteristics, as identified by the research workers in the field of creativity, are mentioned below.

Personality and Behavioural Characteristics of a Creative Child

1. Demonstrates originality in ideas and actions.
2. Is more adaptable as well as adventurous.
3. Possesses good memory and broad knowledge background.
4. Possesses a high degree of keenness, attentiveness, alertness and power of concentration.
5. Is very curious about nature.
6. Possesses little tolerance for boredom but greater for ambiguity and discomfort.
7. Possesses foresightedness in abundance.
8. Has the capacity to take independent decisions.
9. Shows interest in vague and ambiguous ideas.
10. Enjoys a reputation of having strange and silly ideas.
11. Shows preferences to complexity, incompleteness, asymmetry and open mindedness.
12. Possesses a high degree of sensitivity towards problems.
13. Can express his ideas as fluently as possible.
14. Shows flexibility in his thinking, feeling and doing behaviour.
15. Demonstrates the ability to transfer learning or training from one situation to another.
16. Demonstrates very rich imagination characterized as 'creative imagination'.
17. Is divergent and diversified in his thinking that is convergent and stereotyped.
18. Possesses ability to elaborate, i.e. to work out the details of a plan, idea or outline.
19. Is not frightened by the unknown, the mysterious and the puzzling and on the contrary is often attracted towards it.
20. Welcomes novelty of designs or new solution to a problem, gets enthused and suggests other ideas.
21. Demonstrates the ability to experience self as creative and the originator of one's act and takes pride in one's own creation.
22. Has more of him available for use and employment in creative purposes rather than wasting his time and energy protecting him against his self.
23. Possesses high aesthetic values and good aesthetic judgement.

24. Possesses a high degree of the feeling of self-respect and is self-disciplined, sensitive and intolerant towards injustice. On account of these qualities, is often misunderstood and evaluated disobedient, rebellious and mischief monger.
25. Demonstrates human playfulness, lack of rigidity and relaxation in his behaviour and products.
26. Is always alive to his obligations.
27. Possesses the ability to accept tentativeness and ability to tolerate and integrate the opposites.
28. Has a richer fantasy life and greater involvement in daydreaming.
29. Shows different brain patterns than the less creative, especially during creative activity.
30. Pays respect to others' opinions and welcomes disagreement to his own suggestions.
31. Is always found to be more spontaneous and expressive.

Methods of Developing Creativity among Children

Creativity, as a natural endowment, needs stimulation and nourishment. Most of the creative talent, if not given proper training, education and opportunities for creative expression, results in wastage. Moreover, creativity, as we have emphasized earlier, is universal. It is not the monopoly of a few geniuses only. Every one of us, to a certain degree, possesses creative abilities. In a democratic set up like ours, it is not only the geniuses who are needed to create, manifest and produce. Others, whether mediocre or below average, are also required to think constructively and creatively.

Therefore, it becomes essential for the teachers as well as parents to realize the need of providing proper environment and creating conditions for complete growth and development of the creative abilities of children. The problem is vital, but there is a solution. It lies in the proper stimulation and nurturing of the abilities that seem related to develop creativity. Originality, flexibility, ideational fluency, divergent thinking, self confidence, persistence, sensitiveness, ability to see relationship and make associations etc. are some of the abilities that are attached to creative output. The following few suggestions can work satisfactorily in the stimulation and nourishment of these abilities:

Freedom to respond

Most often we, teachers and parents, expect a routine type fixed response from our children and thus kill the very creative spark by breeding conformity and passivity. Therefore, we should allow adequate freedom to our children in responding to a situation. They should be encouraged to think about as many ideas as they may for the solution of a problem. Also we must let them have their own way when they strongly need a particular sort of novel expression.

Opportunity for ego involvement

The feelings like "It is my creation", "I have solved it", give much satisfaction to children. Actually, they can only be expected to put their determined efforts in creative activities when their ego is involved, i.e. when they feel that a particular creative work stands on account of their efforts. Therefore, we should provide opportunities for children to derive satisfaction from being a cause.

Encouraging originality and flexibility

Originality on the part of children in any form should be encouraged. Constant submission to the facts, unadulterated copying, passive reception, rote-memorization discourage creative expression and therefore, it should be checked as far as possible. In solving a problem or learning a task if they need to change their methods of learning or solving the problem, they should essentially be encouraged to do it. Adequate training can also be given by making them answer the problems like: How would you dig the earth if you don't have a spade? Or how would you draw an angle if you do not have proper instrument for drawing it? Or how would you cross a river if there is no bridge over it?

Removal of Hesitation and Fear

Most of the time (particularly in countries like ours where there is too much inferiority complex) there is a great hesitation mixed with a sense of inferiority and fear in taking initiative for a creative expression. We, generally, listen to the comments like "I know what I mean, but cannot write or speak before others." The causes of such hesitation and fear should be discovered and removed as far as possible. The teachers and parents should persuade such children to say or write something, anything, no matter how crude it may be.

Providing Appropriate Opportunities and Atmosphere for Creative Expression

A healthy favourable atmosphere for creative thinking, and expression is an essential condition for the stimulation and nourishment of creativity among children. There is a need to balance the rate of learning with its application, the passive receptivity with challenging productivity, and the stable certainty with risk and adventure. There is a need for sympathetic atmosphere in schools as well as at homes. For providing opportunities for creative expression, we can make use of the cocurricular activities in schools. Our social festivals, religious and social get-togethers, exhibitions etc. can also provide the opportunity for creative expression. A regular classwork can be arranged in such a way as to stimulate and develop creative thinking among children.

Developing Healthy Habits among Children

Industriousness, persistence, reliance and self-confidence are some of the qualities that are helpful in creative output. Therefore, children should be helped to imbibe these qualities. Moreover, they should be made to stand against the criticism of their creative expression. They should be made to feel that whatever they create is unique and it expresses what they desired to express.

Using the Creative Resources of the Community

Children should be made to visit the centers of creativity for scientific and industrial creative works. It can stimulate and inspire them for doing some creative work. Occasionally, creative artists, scientists and creative persons from other fields may also be invited to schools. It can be helpful in enhancing the span of the knowledge of our children and kindle the spark of creativity among them.

Avoidance of Blocks to Creative Thinking

The factors like conservatism, faulty methods of teaching, unsympathetic treatment, fixed and rigid habits of work, anxiety and frustration, high standards of achievement for low levels of work, overemphasis on school marks, authoritarian attitudes of teachers and parents etc. are known to be detrimental towards fostering creativity among children. Therefore, as far as possible parents and teachers should try to avoid such factors in upbringing and educating the children.

Proper Organization of the Curriculum

Learning experiences in the form of curriculum should be so designed that it fosters creativity among children. For this purpose we should organize the school curriculum primarily on the basis of concepts rather than facts. It should also cater to the individual needs of the students rather than to the generalized needs of every student. It should also follow the general philosophy that truth is something to be sought for rather than some thing to be revealed. It should be quite flexible and have provision for studying and doing something without the threat of evaluation. In a nut shell, the curriculum should reflect what is desired from the creative children in terms of fluency, flexibility, originality, divergent thinking, inventiveness and elaboration etc.

REFORM IN THE EVALUATION SYSTEM

Our education system is totally examination-ridden. Therefore, for making efforts to nurture creativity we must have suitable reforms in our evaluation system. The emphasis on rote memory, fixed and rigid single responses, and convergent thinking etc, which kill the creativity of the children, should be abandoned and a proper system of evaluation for encouraging complete and balanced experiences in developing their creative behaviour should be adopted.

USE OF SPECIAL TECHNIQUES FOR FOSTERING CREATIVITY

Researchers in the field of creativity have suggested some special techniques and methods for fostering creativity among children. A few of these are mentioned below:

BRAINSTORMING

Brainstorming is a strategy or technique for allowing a group to explore ideas without judgement or censure. In actual practice children may be asked to sit in a group for solving a problem and attacking it without any inhibition from many angles, in fact literally storming it by a number of possible ideas and solutions. To start with, the students may be provided with a focus, i.e. a particular problem like 'Students Unrest', 'Growing unemployment in India', 'How to check truancy in our school', 'What to do for improving school library services' and so on. The students are then asked to suggest ideas as rapidly as possible by observing the following norms:

(i) All ideas to be encouraged and appreciated, therefore, no criticism be allowed during the brainstorming session.

(ii) Students are encouraged to make their ideas as unusual as possible and suggest as many ideas as they can.

(iii) They are encouraged not only to put together separate ideas but also to suggest ideas that may be built on ideas already given by the fellow students.

(iv) No evaluation or comment of any sort should be made until the session is over. After the expiry of the session, all the ideas received (preferably written on the blackboard) should be discussed in a very free, frank and desirable environment and the most meaningful ideas should be accepted for the solution of the problem in hand.

USE OF TEACHING MODELS

Some of the teaching models developed by educationists may prove quite beneficial in developing creativity among children. For example, Bruner's Concept Attainment Model helps in developing creativity in children for the attainment of various concepts. Similarly, Suchman's Inquiry Training Model is very helpful in developing creativity among children besides imparting training in the acquisition of scientific inquiry skills.

USE OF PLAY WAY, PROBLEM SOLVING AND QUIZ

Gaming techniques, in a play way spirit, help the children in the development of creative aspects. These techniques provide valuable learning experience in a very relaxed, untimed and evaluative situation. The stimulus material used in such techniques is both verbal as well as non verbal. For illustration in verbal transaction of ideas, the following types of questions may be addressed to the children:

(i) Name all the round things you can think of.
(ii) Tell all the different ways you could use a knife.
(iii) Tell all the ways in which a cat and a dog are alike.

In non-verbal transactions, children may be asked to build a cube, construct or complete a picture, draw and build patterns, interpret the patterns of drawing and sketches, and build or construct anything out of the raw material given to them.

PROVIDING THE SELF-EXAMPLE AND IDEALS

There is a truth in the saying that 'Self example is better than precept.' Children are very imitative. The teachers and parents, who themselves travel on the beaten track and do not show any originality by taking the risk of being wrong or never experience an excitement of creating a novel act, fail to cultivate creativity among their children. Therefore, the teachers and parents must try to develop the habit of creative thinking among themselves. They should believe in change, novelty and originality, and experience the creative process themselves. Their teaching, their mode of behaviour must reflect their love for creativity. Then and only then can they inspire children for being creative.

SUMMARY

Creativity of an individual reflects one of his unique cognitive abilities or the capacity of his mind to create, discover or produce a new idea or object including the re-arrangement or reshaping of what is already known to him. It is both innate as well as acquired and a process as well as a product. It is also known for many of its specific features like open mindedness, ego involvement etc on the part of the creative person, the wideness of the field of creative expression and inner joy and satisfaction reached as a result of such expression. As a result of its such characteristics it has been found that creativity and intelligence can not travel side by side.

Psychologists have identified certain important components or factors of creativity. The main constituents of creativity thus emerged maybe named as ideational fluency, originality, flexibility, divergent thinking, persistence, self-confidence, sensitiveness, ability to see relationships and make associations. These characteristics so identified can be made into use of constructing a creative measure instrument for the identification of creativity.

For the identification of creative children we may employ two different approaches (i) making use of creativity tests like Torrance tests of creative thinking, Passi's test of creativity etc., and (ii) making use of non-testing devices like observation, interview, rating scale, personality inventory, check list etc. The test items of most of the creative tests (verbal as well as non-verbal) are highly loaded with the type of activities which are helpful in the assessment of the qualities like originality, fluency, flexibility, divergent thinking, and elaboration etc. (the typical features of one's creative expression). In making use of non-testing devices for the identification of creative children the help is generally taken from some well known distinguished characteristics found in the creative behaviour of the children.

Appropriate attempts can be made for the stimulation and nurturing of the creativity among children. Some of these measures may be named as (i) providing freedom to the children to respond with due involvement of their ego, (ii) encouraging their originality and flexibility, (iii) removal of their hesitation and fear for the new and novel, (iv) providing opportunities for creative expressions, (v) developing healthy habits for nurturing creativity, (vi) removal of blocks to creative thinking, (vii) Utilizing the creative resources of the community, (viii) taking care of the curriculum and methods of teaching for developing creativity, (ix) bringing suitable reform in the evaluation system, (x) using special techniques like brainstorming, problem solving and quiz and above all, (xi) providing self examples by the teachers, parents and elders for the development of creativity among children.

References and Suggested Readings

Arieti, S., *Creativity: The Magic Synthesis*, Basic Books, New York, 1976.

Drevdahl, J.E., *Factors of Importance for Creativity*, J. Ed. Psy. Vol. 12, 1956.

Getzels, J.W. and Jackson, P.W., *Creativity and Intelligence*, John Wiley, New York, 1962.

Mehdi, Baquer, *Verbal and Non-Verbal Tests of Creative Thinking*, National Psychological Corporation, Agra, 1989.

Skinner, C.E. (Ed)., *Essential of Educational Psychology*, Prentice-Hall, New York, 1968.

Stagner, R. and Karwoski, T.F., Quoted by L.D. Crow and Alice Crow, *Educational Psychology*, Eurasia Publishing House, New Delhi, 1973.

Torrance, E.P. and Myers, R.E., *Creative Learning and Teaching*, Dodd, Mead, New York, 1970.

Wilson R.C., Guilford, J.P. and Christensen, P.R., Quoted by N.K. Dutt, *Psychological Foundations of Education*, Daoba House, Delhi, 1974.

24

Aptitude—Concept and Measurement

CHAPTER COMPOSITION

- Meaning and Nature of Aptitudes
- How Aptitude Differs from Ability and Achievement?
- Difference between Intelligence and Aptitudes
- Difference between Aptitude and Interest
- Classification of Aptitudes
- Measurement of Aptitudes
- Summary
- References and Suggested Readings

MEANING AND NATURE OF APTITUDES

It is an observable fact that people differ from one another and within themselves in their performance in one or the other field of human activity such as leadership, music, art, mechanical work, teaching etc. Ramesh goes to a commercial institute in order to learn typing and shorthand. He progresses rapidly with his typing and shorthand and gets a diploma in due course. Later on, when he is offered a stenographer-cum-typist's job he carries it out satisfactorily. Suresh, although not in any way inferior to the former in general intelligence takes admission to this institute but progresses very slowly and even after getting diploma proves an inefficient typist as well as stenographer. Similarly, Radha gains from musical training while Sunita despite similar training, makes little or no progress.

So, in many spheres of everyday life, we come across individuals who under similar circumstances outperform others in acquiring certain knowledge or skills and prove more suitable and efficient in certain jobs. Such persons are said to possess certain specific abilities other than intelligence, which help them in achieving success in some specific occupations or activities.

Therefore in a simple way, aptitude may be considered a special ability or a specific capacity besides the general intellectual ability which helps an individual to acquire a required degree of proficiency or achievement in a specific field. However, for having a clear understanding of the term 'aptitude', let us consider the following definitions given by different scholars:

Bingham
Aptitude refers to those qualities characterizing person's ways of behaviour which serve to indicate how well he can learn to meet and solve certain specific kinds of problems. (1937, p. 21)

Traxler
Aptitude is a condition, a quality or a set of qualities in an individual which is indicative of the probable extent to which he will be able to acquire under suitable training, some knowledge, skill or composite of knowledge, understanding and skill, such as ability to contribute to art or music, mechanical ability, mathematical ability or to read and speak a foreign language. (1957, p. 49)

Freeman
An aptitude is a combination of characteristics indicative of an individual's capacity to acquire (with training) some specific knowledge, skill, or set of organized responses, such as the ability to speak a language, to become a musician, to do mechanical work. (1971, p. 431)

All these definitions reveal the predictive nature of aptitudes. When we say that Ram or Radha has an aptitude for teaching, we mean that he or she has the capacity or ability to acquire proficiency in teaching under appropriate conditions.

Similarly, when we say Mohan has an aptitude for music we mean that his present condition or ability reveals that if he is to learn music, he will succeed in this line. In this way the knowledge of aptitude helps us in predicting the future success of an individual, under suitable training or experience, in a particular area of activity.

Nature of Aptitudes

Are aptitudes inherited or acquired? Like so many other personality traits or characteristics, it is difficult to say that aptitude is an absolute product of heredity or environment. Certain aspects of many aptitudes may be inborn. For example, a person showing musical aptitude may have a musical throat and a person showing aptitude for typing or watch repairing may have long and dexterous hands. But this is one side of the picture. It is also equally possible that the person's aptitude for music is the result of his living in the company of good musicians or his aptitude for typing work may be due to his father or mother who happens to be a typist.

Therefore, it is safer to conclude that the aptitude of an individual at a particular moment is in all probability dependent upon both heredity and environment.

HOW APTITUDE DIFFERS FROM ABILITY AND ACHIEVEMENT?

Aptitude and present ability do not mean the same thing. You may have no present ability to drive a car but you may have a high aptitude for driving which means that your chances of becoming a successful driver are good provided you receive proper training. So, while aptitude has future reference and tries to predict the degree of attainment or success of an individual in an area or activity after adequate training; ability concerns itself only with the present condition, the potentiality or capability which one possesses at the present moment irrespective of his past and does not try to make any estimate of one's future success or failure.

Contrary to the forward-looking nature of aptitude and present-oriented characteristic of ability, achievement is past-oriented. It looks at the past and indicates what an individual has learned or acquired in a particular field.

But by this differentiation it should not be concluded that we can measure an individual's future accomplishment in any area of activity with the help of aptitude measurements. Aptitude tests, in all their forms, measure only the present ability or capacity of an individual which can be exploited for making prediction about his future attainments.

DIFFERENCE BETWEEN INTELLIGENCE AND APTITUDES

Intelligence tests as they exist usually test the general mental ability of an individual but aptitudes, as we have discussed, are concerned with specific abilities. Therefore, while with the knowledge of intelligence of an individual we can predict his success in a number of situations involving mental function or activity, the knowledge of aptitudes, acquaints us with those specific abilities and capacities of an individual which give an indication of his ability or capacity to succeed in a special field or activity. Therefore, in predicting achievement in some particular job, training, course or specialized instruction we need to know more about one's aptitudes (specific abilities) rather than of his intelligence or general ability.

DIFFERENCE BETWEEN APTITUDE AND INTEREST

To get desirable success in a given activity, a person must have both an aptitude for activity and an interest in it. Therefore, interest and aptitude usually go hand in hand. But by this co-ordination, we should never mean that interests and aptitudes are one and the same thing. A person may be interested in a particular activity, job or training but may or may not have aptitude for that. In such cases, the interest shown in a particular occupation or course of study is often the result of some other temptation or persuasion like ambition of the parents, probability of getting a job, provision of stipend or financial help, the prestige associated with the work rather than the personal aptitude. Similarly, a person may have long and dexterous fingers and can show a good performance on a mechanical aptitude test. Yet he may show little or no interest in becoming a watch maker. Therefore, a guidance or selection programme must give due weightage to the measurement of aptitude as well as of interest. Both are essential for the prediction of the success of an individual in a given activity—job or course of instruction.

CLASSIFICATION OF APTITUDES

Any manifestation of life is activity. We can manifest ourselves in too many ways and forms. Therefore, there is no end for our manifestation and as a result, the list of the activities which may be undertaken by the human beings is limitless. One may have aptitude for one activity and the other may demonstrate an aptitude in something else. In other words, we can say as the number of activities that can be undertaken by the human beings are limitless, so is the number of aptitudes. In this sense, it is quite impossible to have a fixed classification of human aptitudes. However, for the sake of their measurement and application in the field of education and professions, we have made an attempt to classify them as under:

Sensory Aptitudes

In this category, we can include all those aptitudes that are related to the sensory capacities and abilities of children. One may have aptitude in the tasks involving the use of his sense of hearing, other may have aptitude in the tasks using the use of the sight, smell, taste or touch. Here depending upon their present ability regarding a particular sensory capacity, we can have an idea of their future success in the area of professions where the use of such sensory ability or capacity is most demanded. Thus, in this category of sensory aptitudes, we can include the aptitudes related to the sensory abilities of the children.

Mechanical Aptitudes

Some persons have a specific bent of mind for the tasks related to the use of mechanical abilities and thus demonstrate aptitudes for all tasks and jobs that require the use of mechanical abilities. When we test their present abilities we can easily infer that a particular individual will be successful as a carpenter (provided he is given due opportunities, training etc.). In other case, we find that one can be a good mechanic looking after the repair of vehicles, engines and machines etc. Someone may have aptitude for the use and innovations in instrumentization and other sophisticated appliances etc. In this way, human beings can have different mechanical aptitudes varying in their nature and sophistication. All such aptitudes are grouped in the category of mechanical aptitude. The range of such mechanical aptitude may extend from the manipulation and use of needles to the know how of repairing and flying an aeroplane.

Artistic Aptitudes

All the aptitudes related to the expression of artistic abilities and capacities are included in this category. These activities are mostly related to the effective domain of human behaviour. The aesthetic sense is exhibited in such activities. All that is beautiful and the things that are to be appreciated belong to the demonstration of such aptitude. Generally the following types of aptitudes are kept in this category of artistic aptitude.

1. Musical aptitude
2. Aptitude for dance
3. Aptitude for graphic art
4. Aptitude for photography
5. Poetic aptitude
6. Aptitude for acting
7. Debating aptitude
8. Writing aptitude
9. Aptitude for designing, etc.

Professional Aptitudes

The aptitudes related to the activities of various professions and occupations are included in the category. These aptitudes are able to help in predicting the future success of an individual in the field or profession related to these aptitudes. For example, if one has the aptitude for teaching, we can say that he or she will be a successful teacher provided he or she gets appropriate opportunities and training for doing so. The examples of the aptitudes included in this category are as under:

1. Clerical Aptitude
2. Legal Aptitude

3. Teaching Aptitude
4. Pilot Aptitude
5. Navigation Aptitude
6. Banking Aptitude
7. Military Aptitude

Scholastic Aptitudes

The aptitudes of the scholastic and academic nature are included in this category. These aptitudes demonstrate and predict the future success of an individual in the learning of a particular subject or course in the capacity of a student. The examples of such aptitudes are as under:

1. Scientific Aptitude
2. Engineering Aptitude
3. Medical Aptitude
4. Commercial Aptitude
5. Sports Aptitude
6. Linguistic Aptitude

MEASUREMENT OF APTITUDES

Like intelligence tests, various aptitude tests have been devised to measure aptitudes of the individuals in various specific fields or activities. Generally, these tests can be classified into the following types according to the specific nature of the aptitude tested by them:

1. Mechanical Aptitude tests.
2. Musical Aptitude tests.
3. Art judgement test.
4. Professional Aptitudes tests, i.e. tests to measure the aptitudes for professions like teaching, clerical, medical, legal, engineering, salesmanship, research work, etc.
5. Scholastic aptitude tests, i.e. tests to measure the aptitudes for different courses of instruction.

In the following pages we will throw light on some of these above mentioned aptitude tests.

Mechanical Aptitude Tests

Like intelligence, mechanical aptitude is also made up of many components. Freeman explains it as—

'The capacity designed by the term 'mechanical aptitude' is not a single, unitary function. It is a combination of sensory and motor capacities plus perception of spatial relations, the capacity to acquire information about mechanical matters and the capacity to comprehend mechanical relationships.' (1971, p. 44)

Therefore, mechanical aptitude tests try to test the above mentioned qualities and capacities of an individual in order to know his mechanical aptitude. Some of the well-known mechanical aptitude tests are—

(i) Minnesota Mechanical Assembly Test.
(ii) Minnesota Spatial Relations Test.
(iii) The Revised Minnesota Power Form Board (1948)
(iv) Stenquist Mechanical Aptitude Tests (Part I and II)
(v) L.J.O.s' Rourke's Mechanical Aptitude Test (Part I and II)
(vi) Bennet Tests of Mechanical comprehension.
(vii) S.R.A. Mechanical Aptitude Test.
(viii) A battery of Mechanical Aptitude Tests (Hindi) prepared by Mano-Vigyanshala, Allahabad.

Usually these tests contain the items of the following nature:

(a) Asking the subject to put together the parts of mechanical devices.
(b) Asking to replace cut-outs of various shapes in their correct holes in the board.
(c) Requiring the ability to solve problems in geometric terms.
(d) Asking questions concerning the basic information about tools and their uses.
(e) Questions relating to the comprehension of physical and mechanical principles.

As an illustration, Bennet Mechanical comprehension test Form AA has 60 items in pictorial form. They present mechanical problems arranged in order of difficulty and involve comprehension of mechanical principles found in ordinary situations. Two items of this test are presented in Figs. 24.1 and 24.2 for illustration.

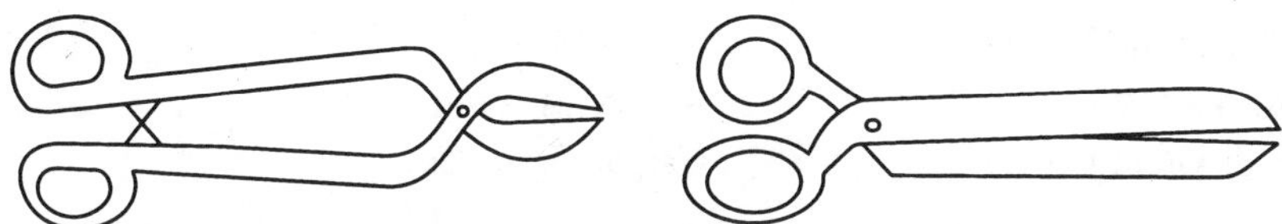

Fig. 24.1 Which would be the better shears for cutting metal?

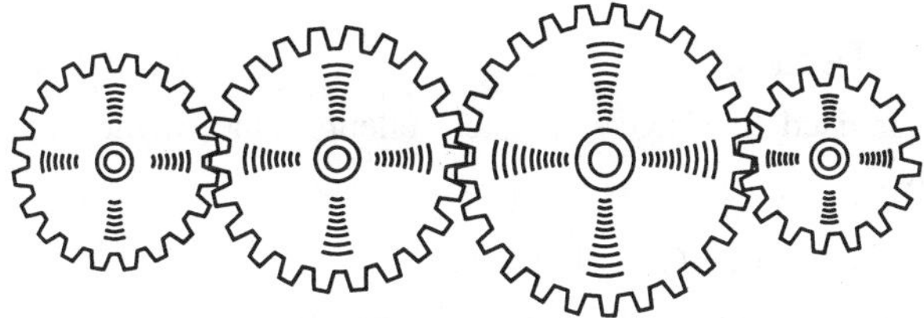

Fig. 24.2 Which gear will make the most turns in a minute?

Clerical Aptitude Tests

Like mechanical, clerical aptitude is also a composite function. According to Bingham (1973), it involves several specific abilities like—

(a) **Perceptual ability.** Ability to perceive words and numbers with speed and accuracy.

(b) **Intellectual ability.** Ability to grasp the meaning of words and symbols.

(c) **Motor ability.** Ability to use various types of machines and tools like typewriter, duplicator, cyclostyle machine; punching machine etc.

Some of the popular clerical aptitude tests are—

(i) Detroit Clerical Aptitude Examination.
(ii) Minnesota vocational test for clerical workers.
(iii) The Clerical ability Test prepared by the deptt. of psychology, University of Mysore, Mysore.
(iv) Clerical Aptitude Test Battery (English and Hindi), Bureau of Edu. And Voc. Guidance, Patna (Bihar).
(v) Test of Clerical Aptitude prepared by the Parsee Panchayat Guidance Bureau 209, Hornby Road, Bombay-1.

SPECIMEN ITEM FOR A CLERICAL APTITUDE

Samples done correctly of pairs of numbers. (Mark which one is correct)

	79542	...	79524
	5794367	✓	5794367

Samples done correctly of pairs of names. (Mark which one is correct)

	John C. Linder	...	John C. Lender
	Investor's Syndicate	✓	Investor's Syndicate

Now try the samples below and mark accordingly

(i)	66273894	...	66273284
	527384578	...	527384578
(ii)	New York World	...	New York World.
	Cargil Grain Co.	...	Cargal Grain Co.

This is a test for speed and accuracy. Work as fast as you can without making mistakes. Do not turn the page until you are told to.

(Reproduced from General Psychology by H.E. Garrett, 1968, p. 477)

Musical Aptitude Tests

These tests have been devised to discover musical talents. One of the important musical aptitude tests is described below:

SEASHORE MEASURE OF MUSICAL TALENT

It takes into consideration the following musical components:

(a) discrimination of pitch.
(b) discrimination of intensity or loudness.
(c) discrimination of time interval.
(d) discrimination of timbre.
(e) Judgement of rhythm.
(f) Tonal memory.

Test items in this battery are presented on phonograph records. The subject sits, listens and attempts to discriminate. He is required to mark his responses on an answer form supplied by the examiner. The instructions in these tests are of the following nature:

"You will hear two tones which differ in pitch. You are to judge whether the second is higher or lower than the first. If the second is higher, record H: if lower, record L."

Aptitude for Graphic Art

These tests are devised to discover the talent for graphic art. The two important tests of this nature—

1. The Meier Art Judgement Test.
2. Horne Art Aptitude Inventory.

In Meier Art Judgment Test, there are 100 pairs of representational pictures in black and white. One such pair have been illustrated below. (Fig. 24.3)

Fig. 24.3 Art Judgement Test (In this pair the subject is required to select the original and aesthetically superior work on the basis of the shapes of the pots).

One member of each pair is an acknowledged art master piece while the other is a slight distortion of the master piece. It is usually altered from the original so as to violate some important principles of art. Testees are informed about the aspect that has been altered and are asked to choose from each pair the one that is better—more pleasing, more artistic, more satisfying. For example, in the above given illustration, the examinees are required to select the original and aesthetically superior work on the basis of the shapes of the pots. The number of correct responses is taken as a measure of art judgement or aptitude for graphic art.

Another important test of measuring aptitude for graphic art is the Horne Art Aptitude Inventory. It requires from the subject to produce sketches from given patterns of lines and figures. The created sketches of the subject are then evaluated according to the standard given by the author of this test.

Tests of Scholastic and Professional Attitudes

For helping in the proper selection of students for the studies of specific courses or professions like engineering, medicine, law, business management, Teaching etc., various specific aptitude tests have been designed. Some of these tests are—

(i) Stanford Scientific Aptitude Test by D.L. Zyve.

(ii) Science Aptitude Test (after Higher Sec. Stage); N.I.E. Delhi.
(iii) Moss Scholastic Aptitude Test for Medical Students.
(iv) Ferguson and Stoddard's Law Aptitude Examination.
(v) Tale Legal Aptitude Test.
(vi) Pre-Engineering Ability Test. *(Education Testing Service, U.S.A.)*
(vii) Minnesota Engineering Analogical Test.
(viii) Coxe-Orleans Prognosis Test of Teaching Ability.
(ix) Teaching Aptitude Test by Jai Prakash and R.P. Shrivastava, University of Saugar (M.P.).
(x) Shah's Teaching Aptitude Test.
(xi) Teaching Aptitude Test by Moss, F.A. & others. George Washington University Press.

Now we should lay a little more emphasis on the teaching Aptitude test as it is directly concerned with Teacher Training Programme. Such tests can prove very useful in the selection of trainees for a professional course of teacher-training. There is a great dearth of some reliable and valid measure of teaching aptitude. The attempt made by Mr. Shah is a good beginning in this direction.

Utility of Aptitude Tests

Aptitude tests have a wide area of application. Firstly, they are the backbone of the guidance services. The results of these tests enable us to locate, with a reasonable degree of certainty, the fields of activity in which an individual is most or least likely to be successful. Therefore, these tests are found to be very useful in guiding the youngsters in the selection of special courses of instruction, fields of activities and vocations.

Secondly, they can be safely used for the purpose of educational and vocational selection. They help us in making scientific selection of the candidates for the various educational and professional courses as well as for the specialized jobs as Munn puts it, *"The chief value of aptitude testing is, in fact, that it enables us to pick out from those who do not yet have the ability to perform certain skills, those who, with a reasonable amount of training, will be most likely to acquire the skills in question and acquire them to desirable level of proficiency."*(1967, p. 117).

Therefore, aptitude tests properly anticipate the future potentialities or capacities of an individual (irrespective of the fact whether he possesses those future capacities before the training or not) and thereby, help us in making selection of those individuals who are best fitted for a particular profession and course of instruction or those who are likely to be more benefited by pre-professional training or experiences.

In this way any reasonable guidance and counseling programme or the entrance examination to specialized, academic and professional courses or the selection procedure for specialized jobs is required to give a proper weightage to Aptitude testing. Aptitude testing, when combined with the other information received through Interest Inventory, Personality tests, Intelligence tests and cumulative record etc. can greatly help in avoiding the huge wastage of human as well as material resources by placing the individuals to their proper places and lines of work.

SUMMARY

An Aptitude related to a particular area or activity refers to certain combination of specific capacities or abilities of an individual which may help us in predicting his future success in that area or activity under appropriate conditions. For example if Mohan has teaching aptitude, it will mean that he has the potential or capacity to acquire proficiency in teaching under appropriate conditions.

Aptitude of an individual at a particular moment is always a function of his heredity as well as that of his environment. We can't equate one's aptitude with one's ability and achievement. The ability concerns itself only with the present condition (what one possesses at present in terms of potential for doing a thing). The achievement looks at the past and indicates what an individual learned or acquired in a particular field. Aptitude, contrary to the present-oriented nature of the ability and past-oriented nature of the achievement is future-oriented (carrying strength for predicting one's success in a field).

Intelligence tests measure the intellectual or cognitive potential of an individual but are hardly appropriate in predicting success of an individual in some particular job, training or specialized instruction, the task that can be properly performed through aptitude tests.

Although both interest and aptitude are essential for getting desirable success in a field, yet these are not one and the same things. Both can function independently, which means that presence of one is not at all essential for the perpetuation of the other.

Aptitudes may be broadly classified as sensory, mechanical, artistic and scholastic aptitudes. All these types of aptitudes can be measured with the help of the suitably designed as well as standardized aptitude tests like we measure intelligence through intelligence tests.

Aptitude tests have a wide area of applications for candidates in choosing special courses of instructions, training, fields of activities and vocations according to their ability and potentialities. These are helpful in providing useful guidance and counseling to the students for planning their educational and vocational career as well as equipping the authorities with the instruments of making proper selection and placing the students/candidates at proper places.

References and Suggested Readings

Bingham, W.V.D., *Aptitudes and Aptitude Testing*, Harper & Brothers, New York, 1973.

Garrett, H.E., *General Psychology*, Indian ed., Eurasia Publishing House, New Delhi, 1968.

Freeman, F.S., *Theory and Practice of Psychological Testing*, 3rd Ind. ed., Oxford & IBH, Bombay, 1971.

Munn, N.L., *Introduction to Psychology*, Indian ed., Oxford & IBH, Delhi, 1967.

Traxler, A.E., *Techniques of Guidance*, Revised ed., Harper & Brothers, New York, 1957.

25

Attitude—Concept and Measurement

CHAPTER COMPOSITION

INTRODUCTION

The main aim of education is to modify the behaviour of a child according to the needs and expectancy of the society. Behaviour is composed of many attributes. One of these important attributes is attitude. One's behaviour, to a great extent, depends upon one's attitude towards the things—idea, person, or object—in his environment. The entire personality and development of a child is influenced by the nature of his attitudes. Learning of a subject and acquisition of habits, interests and other psychophysical dispositions are all affected by his attitudes. Therefore, it is important for a teacher to understand the meaning and nature of attitudes, the factors responsible for their formation and development and techniques of their measurement. In this chapter, we will try to understand the above aspects.

DEFINITION AND MEANING OF ATTITUDE

Various authors have defined attitude in the following ways:

Travers

An attitude is a readiness to respond in such a way that behaviour is given a certain direction. (1973, p. 337)

Meckeachie and Doyle

We define an attitude as an organization of concepts, beliefs, habits and motives associated with a particular object. (1966, p. 560)

Sorenson

An attitude is a particular feeling about something. It therefore involves a tendency to behave in a certain way in situations which involve that something, whether person, idea or object. It is partially rational and partially emotional and is acquired, not inherent, in an individual. (1977, p. 349)

Whilttaker

An attitude is a predisposition or readiness to respond in a pre-determined manner to relevant stimuli. (1970, p. 591)

According to the first definition, attitude is responsible for behaving in a particular and a definite way. If one keeps a positive and favourable attitude towards an object, he will be attracted towards it, he will admire it and try to achieve it. On the other hand, if one has negative or unfavourable attitude, one will try to avoid it and even feel hostile towards it. For example, a person having positive attitude towards democracy will respond positively to democratic practices and institutions and negatively to authoritarian procedures. His behaviour will speak about his attitude.

The second definition takes into account all the concepts, beliefs, habits and motives associated with the object. The concepts and beliefs associated with an attitude are often referred to as the cognitive component of attitude, the habit as the action component, and the motives as the affective component. In this way all that one thinks, feels and the way one reacts expresses one's attitude towards an object. For example, the formation of favourable or unfaourable attitude towards a political party is the result of his thinking and feeling towards that party and it would be exhibited overtly through some ace tendencies like heated discussion with associates or strangers, casting a vote in favour of the party candidate or doing active party work during the election campaign.

The third definition explains why an individual behaves in a certain way when he is needed to respond to a particular object for which he has developed a positive or negative attitude. He has an almost definite set of feelings, likes or dislikes for that object and they partly stand on rational and partly on emotional footing. But in all the cases, they are acquired and learned through varying experiences. One's attitude towards one's religion is an acquired tendency or disposition. He is not born with enthusiasm or apathy towards a particular religion. He has developed a sort of attachment or favourable feeling towards his religion due to his own experiences since his early childhood. His feeling is partly rational and partly emotional. He may be able to give very good reasons for advocating and appreciating his religion but their basis is partly beneath conscious reasoning.

The last definition accepts attitude as a predisposition or tendency to behave in a particular and definite way to a particular situation. One's attitude decides one's response to a particular stimulus. For example, in responding to all stimuli related with the congress party one has a predisposition or tendency to act in a certain way if one has developed an attitude towards that party.

In this way attitudes are to a great extent responsible for a particular behaviour of a person towards an object, idea or a person. But by this, it should not be concluded that one's behaviour is an absolute function of one's attitude. Behaviour by all means is a function of both characteristics of the behaving person and the situations in which he behaves. Hence a person may hold strong attitude and yet under certain circumstances, may behave in quite contradiction to those attitudes.

In this way, one's behaviour towards an object related to a particular attitude cannot be safely predicted through that attitude but it can be safely said that it makes the individual respond in a particular way to a particular stimulus.

Therefore, we may understand attitude *as a determining acquired tendency which prepares a person to behave in a certain way towards a specific object or a class of objects subject to the conditions prevailing in the environment.*

NATURE OR CHARACTERISTICS OF ATTITUDES

We defined attitudes as predispositions or determining tendencies to respond in a specified manner. Now the question arises: Should all the predispositions like habits, interests, traits and physiological motives be classified as attitudes? The answer is no. For a more clear distinction, an attitude should meet the following six criteria:

Attitudes have a Subject-Object Relationship

Attitudes always involve the relation of an individual with specific objects, persons, groups, institutions and values or norms related to his environment.

Attitudes are Learned

Attitudes, as pointed out earlier, are learned and acquired dispositions. They are not innate and inherent in an individual. Consequently they may be differentiated from physiological motives. Hunger, for example, is an unlearned physiological motive, while preference for a particular food, an acquired tendency, is classified as an attitude. Again, while almost any suitable member of the opposite sex may satisfy a man's sexual need, when the need becomes attached to a particular person, the attachment (acquired) becomes an attitude.

Attitudes are Re-actively Enduring States of Readiness

Attitudes represent the state of readiness to respond to a certain stimulus. Physiological motives also do the same. But in their case like hunger and sexual tension, the states of readiness disappear for a period when they are gratified. Attitudes, on the other hand, are relatively enduring states of readiness. Consequently, a wife may hold affective attraction to her husband even after the sexual tension has been resolved.

Attitudes have Motivational-affective Characteristics

Attitudes have definite motivational characteristics. Other dispositions like habit of writing with right hand do not have any motivational or affective quality; but attitudes towards one's family, nation, religion or other sacred and hallowed institutions have definite motivational affective characteristics.

Attitudes are as Numerous and Varied as the Stimuli to which They Respond

We may have a number of attitudes depending upon the number of stimuli to which we respond. Attitude is an implicit response, therefore it stands to be varied with the number and variety of the responses which the individual makes. The change in environment and the situations further bring variety in the expression of these attitudes. Therefore, it is correct to say that attitudes are as numerous as the object towards which they are directed and the situations in which they are expressed.

Attitudes Range from Strongly Positive to Strongly Negative

Attitudes involve direction as well as magnitude. When a person shows some tendency to approach an object he is said to have positive attitude towards it but when he shows tendency to avoid the object, his attitude is described as negative. These positive or negative attitudes may involve intense feelings and vary from the large negative values to increasingly positive.

FORMATION OF ATTITUDES

Attitudes are learned or acquired dispositions. How are they formed, has been a question for investigation to the psychologists. Based on the opinion of Allport, Stagner has suggested that attitudes are formed under one of the following four conditions:

- **Integration of experiences.** The accumulation and integration of a number of related experiences about an object gives birth to an attitude towards that object. Attitudes of Hindus towards Muslims or vice versa has been formed in this way.
- **Differentiation of experiences.** When new experiences are acquired, they are differentiated or segregated from the already acquired experiences. This segregation or differentiation may tend to make certain attitudes more specific.
- **Trauma of dramatic experience.** Attitudes are formed with greater speed and intensity on account of sudden unusual, shocking and painful experiences. A shopkeeper whose shop has been burnt down by the striking students may develop intensely negative attitude towards all students.
- **Adaptation of the available attitudes.** A large number of attitudes are acquired in a readymade fashion by simply following suggestions or examples of friends, teachers, parents or adopting the mores and traditions of the community or society. Negative attitude of the children of Tamil Nadu towards Hindi has been formed through the process of adoption, rather than as a result of first hand experience.

Factors Influencing the Formation or Development of Attitudes

Attitude is unquestionably an acquired disposition and therefore conditioned by learning or acquisition of experiences. Heredity factor does not play any role in the formation or development of attitudes. Environmental force helps an individual to form and develop various attitudes. An attitude at any stage is essentially a product of the interaction of one's self with one's environment. Therefore the factors influencing the formation and development of attitudes can be divided into two parts as follows:

A. Factors within the individual himself.

B. Factors within the individual's environment.

Factors Within the Individual

All individuals do not respond similarly to the same situations. The effect of environmental stimuli in acquiring some predispositions is very much conditioned by the growth and development pattern of an individual child. Let us try to emphasize these developmental factors.

1. **Physical growth and Development.** In the development of attitude, physical growth and development plays a significant role. Poor physical health, low vitality and undeveloped somatic structure is responsible for poor emotional and social adjustment and poor social adjustment inevitably exercises an important effect on the formation of attitudes in many different directions. A crippled and undersized girl of fifteen years is unlikely to form the same attitudes as those formed by another girl of fifteen who is tall, well proportioned and charming for her age. Even the colour of the skin, weight of the body or bio-chemical changes in the body tissues and fluids, for example sex hormones, have a vital effect on the development of attitudes through its connection with social adjustment.
2. **Intellectual Development.** Development of attitudes is conditioned by the growth of intelligence. The components of intelligence like memory, understanding, thinking and reasoning play a significant part in attitude formation as they help in gaining perceptual experience. Due to his limited intellectual capacities, a young child is incapable of forming attitudes about remote or complex abstract things. His attitudes are always of a particular kind that are related to his own immediate problems and experiences. With the growth of intellectual capacities, an intelligent adult is capable of having more abstract and generalized attitudes.
3. **Emotional Development.** Emotional development also affects the formation of attitudes. Emotions play a dominant role in overt or covert behaviour manifestation and behaviour is related to attitudes. As the child develops with age and growth the capacity for varied emotional experiences and attitudes is gradually developed. Emotional maturity helps in social adjustment and in seeking social approval. In turn it makes an individual to develop numerous attitudes through his direct or indirect experiences.
4. **Social Development.** Attitudes are rarely individual affairs. Social interaction and group processes are the key to attitude formation at any stage of human development. Children having poor social adjustment are more likely to have antisocial attitudes and are less likely to be influenced by groups while forming attitudes. Children with healthy social adjustment easily pick up social attitudes from their respective groups.
5. **Ethical and moral Development.** Each individual develops certain ideals, values and concept of the self in which he takes pride. For enhancing his feelings of self-esteem, one tries to develop those attitudes that suit his values and ideals. A student who values historical events or objects will have a favourable attitude towards the subject of history. A man who thinks that God is one will not have unfavourable attitude towards the persons belonging to the religion other than his own.

Factors Within the Individual's Environment

Besides the individual variations shown by their various personality characteristics on account of the pattern of their growth and development, attitudes are largely borrowed from the groups within one's environment to which one owes one's stronger allegiance. It has now been firmly established that environmental forces, in the shape of the social groups, institutions and community, cast a strong influence on shaping the beliefs and attitudes of an individual. Let us try to understand a few important environment factors.

1. **Home and family.** In attitude formation, home and family environment plays a leading role. A child by identifying himself with his parents and other members of the family picks up their attitudes. The family more or less defines for the child the expected roles which he must play in various situations and thus initiates the formation of specific attitudes. A healthy family environment and positive attitudes of the parents and other family members bring desirable impact on children in picking up desirable attitudes while negative parental attitudes, for example of hostility and rejection, lead them to imbibe ascendant and aggressive attitudes. Similarly, many antisocial attitudes are said to be the product of the faulty upbringing and uncongenial environment at home and in the family.
2. **Social Environment.** While the family and home environment plays its role in the formation of early attitude, contact with the people in neighbourhood, school, community and society and mores and traditions of the community, to which one belongs, cast strong influence in reshaping early attitudes and acquisitions of many more new attitudes. As a child grows older and has wider social contacts, he is influenced by many social institutions and groups and as a result he tries to pick up attitudes of those groups for which he has stronger allegiance or that suits his own nature and motives.

In schools, factors like teachers and their behaviour, classmates or schoolmates and their behaviour, the teaching methods, curriculum, general tone and discipline of the institution all contribute towards attitude formation.

The religious groups, social clubs or constitution where one learns or earns has a definite set of emotional and intellectual environment as a result of which members of the group pick up characteristic attitudes of the group and, in this way, social groups play a leading role in attitude formation.

Mass media in the form of newspapers, radio and television, moving pictures, propaganda literature and advertisement also play a key role in shaping and reshaping the attitudes. Individuals tend to identify themselves with the views expressed through these agencies. Thereby heroes and heroines on screens and in radio programmes, attractive figures shown in the advertisements and slogans of a popular leader prove potent sources for the formation of attitudes.

MEASUREMENT OF ATTITUDES

We have defined attitudes as implicit responses or predispositions to objects, persons, ideas, values or situations in the social surroundings. Thereby they are essentially covert tendencies. If we want to measure them, there must be some means to draw them out or make them manifested in the form of overt behaviours. This can be done in the following two ways:

1. **Direct Methods.** Measuring the verbal report of the attitude.
2. **Indirect Method.** Interpretation of the attitude from the unsaturated or indirect responses. Let us discuss these methods.

Direct Methods for Measurement of Attitude

In this method, opinion of an individual about a particular subject in the form of a verbal report is collected and based on this, his attitude towards the subject is estimated. Generally the following devices are used for the purpose.

(i) Asking the individual directly how he feels about a subject. (questioning and interview techniques)

(ii) Asking to mark those statements from a list with which he is in agreement. (Check list etc.)

(iii) To indicate his degree of agreement or disagreement with a series of statements dealing with the same subject. (Attitude scales)

The last mentioned devices known as attitude scales, are most widely used for the measurement of attitudes. Generally the following two types of scales are popular.

THURSTONE'S ATTITUDE SCALES

These are also known as equal-appearing intervals scales. In constructing such scales, a large number of statements representing a variety of opinions on a subject are collected. These statements are then given to a number of judges who are asked to sort the statements in two categories—say from "very favourable" to "very unfavourable". Whenever the judges disagree significantly over an item, it is rejected. The finished scale then consists of the remaining statements or items that represent clearly defined opinions on the subject. Each of these final statements is then assigned a scale value based on the median scale position given by the judges. If half the judges, for example, had assigned a particular statement to position 4 or lower and half had assigned it to position 5 or higher, the scale value assigned to the statement could be 4.5. Some of the statements from the Thurston's scale for measuring attitude toward the church with the scale value of each statement are shown below:

Items	*Scale value*
I believe the church is the greatest institution in America today	0.2
I believe church membership is almost essential to living life at its best	1.5
I believe in what the church teaches, but with mental reservations	4.5
I believe in religion but I seldom go to church	5.4
I do not receive any benefit from attending church service but I think it helps some people	5.7
I think the church is a parasite on society	1.0

In administering the scale, individuals are asked to check all the statements with which they agree. For each individual, then a scale position is computed as the average of the scale values of all the items he has checked.

LIKERT ATTITUDE SCALE

This scale is more popular than Thurstone's scale. It employs a larger number of items than Thurston's scale and discards the methods of scaling by several judges. In constructing such a scale, a number of statements or items concerning a particular subject are collected. These items, each of which clearly represents either a favourable or unfavourable attitude, are then tested for internal consistency, i.e. to see all the statements or items are actually concerned with the same subject. The tested items constitute attitude scale. The individual is asked to indicate the degree of his agreement or disagreement with each item on a five-point scale. Thus for assessing attitude towards internationalism, the sample items such as follows are presented.

Encircle one of the symbols preceding each of the following statements. A stands for "Agree", S.A. stands for "Strongly Agree", D for "Disagree", S.D. for "Strongly Disagree" and I for "Undecided."

Response	*Items*
S.A., A, I, D, S.D.	We should be willing to fight for our country whether it is in the right or in the wrong.
S.A., A, I, D, S.D.	Our country should never declare war again under any circumstances.

For scoring the items, a value of 5 may be given to the responses indicating strong agreement, 4 for simple agreement, 3 for undecided, 2 for simple disagreement and 1 for strong disagreement. Thus each individual can be assigned a single quantitative score for the measurement of his attitude.

Indirect Method for Measurement of Attitudes

The process of inferring attitude directly from the verbal report or expressed opinion has many limitations. One may conceal one's real attitudes and may not really know what one feels and unable to know one's attitude about a situation in the abstract. Even overt behaviour is not always a true indication of one's attitude. When politicians cuddle babies their behaviour may not be a true expression of their attitude towards children.

To avoid this problem, it has been tried to make use of the measurement methods that are indirect or disguised in nature. In these methods the subjects are given opportunities to structure their own responses without letting them know the real purpose of the task. The projective techniques used for the assessment of personality are the good examples of these indirect methods. These techniques have been discussed in detail in the chapter elaborating on the measurement of personality. The essence of these techniques is that the subject expresses his covert tendencies while responding to unstructured stimuli. An intelligent interpretation of his responses may show his attitude towards a particular object or issue.

Now the question arises as to which of these two techniques—direct or indirect—should be used for measuring attitudes. Both of these are very good instruments and have their own values and limitations. Perhaps in my opinion, the best method or the procedure adopted for the measurement of attitudes is the one that combines the verbal report and the interpretive techniques. It will surely help us in getting an extensive and intensive measurement of attitudes covering their covert tendency and overt manifestation.

CHANGING OF ATTITUDES

Attitudes are by no means fixed and unchanging predispositions. They can change. The task of attitudinal changes is very much related to their formation. As discussed earlier, attitudes are formed through experiences—direct or indirect. Consequently they may be changed through acquisition of new experiences as Sorenson remarks, *"Such factors as social, experiences, propaganda, education and personal experience with different attitudes do make for modifications and shifts in people's predispositions toward objects, persons, ideas and situations in their environment."* (1977, p. 187).

What Can Teachers and Schools Do

Let us try to utilize the knowledge of attitude formation and change in our classroom teaching. The simple question is that can our school or classroom teaching be so equipped that it develops desirable social attitude among the pupils or what should be done to bring changes in the otherwise negative or undesirable attitudes of the pupil? Let us try to think about this problem.

Whether we have to develop an attitude or modify it we have to think about the different factors contributing towards its acquisition. In brief we have to proceed in the following way:

1. Attitude formation is conditioned by the growth and development of an individual in all the dimensions like physical, intellectual, emotional, social and ethical. Therefore, efforts should be made to bring an all-round harmonious development in the personality of the child.
2. Home and family establishes the formation of early attitudes. Parents and members of the family should be educated and given proper guidance so that they can help their children pick up positive and socially desirable attitudes and family environment.
3. Attitudes towards things are very largely conditioned by one's desire to preserve or enhance one's feeling of self-esteem. Therefore, self-respect of the students should always be given due consideration while adopting any programme for the development of attitudes. They should never be let down or made to feel that by adopting such opinions or attitudes, their status or self-esteem will be lowered.
4. It should be kept in mind that it is easier to develop positive attitudes than negative ones. It is, for example, probably more effective to develop a liking for honesty or democracy than to attempt to develop a dislike for dishonesty or autocracy.
5. The attitudes are never taught, they are caught through direct or indirect experiences. Therefore, teachers should not try to teach attitudes directly as facts may be taught. They should make use of indirect suggestions or provide experiences that will naturally tend to result in the desired attitude formation.
6. Social environment as we have seen plays a dominant role in attitude formation. Therefore, attempts should be made to control and modify environmental influences in such a way that desirable attitudes may be developed.
7. Attitudes are rarely individual affairs. Group-interaction plays a key role in attitude formation. Therefore, it should be utilized for the development of desirable attitudes. A teacher should utilize his class as a well organized group for the attitude development. He should try to develop group support for expression of particular attitudes. Group discussions, seminars, skit, drama, and other social or group activities may be chosen for developing and organizing group attitudes. The important thing is to develop the attitude of a group, the attitude of the members will naturally follow because the individual tends to accept whatever his group accepts and to reject whatever his group rejects.
8. The teacher should not go too far from the opinion and attitudes of his students. Otherwise it will naturally segregate him from the group and he will cease to be a leader. Wise and successful political leaders know this fact and therefore they always carry with them the mass of voters. Teachers also should take note that they direct their efforts towards the attainment of reasonable goals.
9. The teacher should bring desirable and essential changes in their methods of instructions for developing favourable attitude towards their subjects. They should also learn to change their own behaviour according to the needs of the situations. They should try to produce their own examples for the development of desirable attitudes.
10. The audio-visual aids and mass-media may be utilized for developing desirable attitudes among the pupils. The test books should be so written that they do not encourage negative or unfavourable attitudes, e.g. disliking for a particular religion, caste, creed, colour of a

country, liking or temptation for dishonesty, corruption, war and quarrelling etc. Similarly radio, television, films, newspapers and magazines etc. should be properly controlled for developing desirable attitudes.

In this way development of desirable attitudes or reshaping of undesirable attitudes is a gigantic task. It needs cooperation of all the forces of environment. Parents, members of the society, teachers, schools and government authorities all need to join hands in this task of desirable attitude formation among the young generation. First of all they should feel the necessity of right attitude formation and then try to bring changes in their own attitudes before planning to bring similar changes in the younger generation. In brief, the overall environment, the cultural pattern of the community and outlook of the whole group need modifications and change before similar changes can be brought in the attitude of an individual child or person.

SUMMARY

Attitudes may be taken as predispositions or determining acquired tendencies which prepare a person to behave in a certain way towards certain specific objects or class of objects, subject to the conditions prevailing in the environment.

Attitudes differ from other pre-disposition or determining tendencies like habits, interests, traits and physiological motives in so many ways on account of their typical features like having subject-object relationship, their being learned and acquired dispositions, relatively enduring states of readiness, motivational-affective characteristics, being numerous and varied as the stimuli to which they refer, and their being ranged from strongly positive to strongly negative etc.

Attitude as the learned or acquired dispositions are formed under one of the four conditions like integration of experiences, differentiation of experiences, trauma or dramatic experiences and the adoption of the available attitudes in one's environment.

Factors influencing the formation and development of attitudes can be divided into two groups (i) Factors within the individual himself (like his physical, intellectual, emotional, social and moral development and (ii) Factors within the individual's environment (like his home and family, social environment outside his family etc.)

Attitudes can be measured by adopting two different means namely direct and indirect methods of measuring attitudes. In the direct approach, opinion of an individual about a subject of attitude measurement in the form of verbal report is collected and then on this basis his attitude about the subject is estimated. We usually make use of questioning and interview techniques, check list and attitude scales for seeking such opinion of the individual. However, the use of attitude scales like Thurston's attitude scales and Likert attitude scales are frequently made for the measurement of various attitudes.

In the indirect method for measuring attitudes, individuals are given opportunities to structure their own responses without letting them know the real purpose of the task. The projective techniques used for the assessment of personality are the good examples of such indirect approach.

Joint efforts should be made by the teachers, parents, members of the society, schools and government authorities through awareness propaganda, mass appeal, group appeal, and self examples for inculcating desirable positive attitudes as well as modifying and restructuring the undesirable ones. The attitudes are never taught, they are caught through direct or indirect experiences. Therefore, we should always try to plan and build such healthy and desirable environment around our children so that they can take up healthy and desirable attitudes towards persons, objects, ideas etc. automatically as a result of their interactions with such environment.

References and Suggested Readings

Boring. E.C. Langfield, H.S. and Weld, H.P. (Eds.) *Foundation of Psychology*, 2nd ed., John Wiley, New York, 1961.

Kuppuswamy, B., *An Introduction to Social Psychology*, Asia Publishing House, Bombay, 1971.

McDougall, William, *Introduction to Social Psychology*, Methuen, London, 1946.

McKeachie, W.J. and Doyle, C.L., *Psychology*, Addison-Wesley, New York, 1966.

Sorenson, Herbert, *Psychology in Education*, 7th ed., Tata McGraw-Hill, New Delhi, 1977.

Travers, Robert, M.W., *Educational Psychology*, Macmillon, New York, 1973.

Wittakar, J.O., *Introduction to Psychology*, W.B. Saunders, International Students Edition, New York, 1970.

26

Attention

CHAPTER COMPOSITION

MEANING AND NATURE OF ATTENTION

We use the term 'attention' frequently in our day-to-day conversation. During lectures in the classroom, a teacher may call for student's attention to listen to what he says or to look at the blackboard. At a railway station or an airport, you may hear the announcement starting with "your attention please", before informing the passengers, about the schedules of the trains or flights. Thus in the ordinary sense, attention is considerd as a power, capacity or faculty of our mind that can be turned on or off at will or something in kind or form that can be lent to this or that situation. However, this notion as we will find out, is misconceived. Attention can never be considered as a force or some faculty of our mind. We must try to understand it in terms of an act, a process or a function. Therefore, the use of this term as a noun is misleading. It may be better understood as a verb defined as attending or a process involving the act of listening, looking at or concentrating on a topic, object or event for the attainment of desired ends. For a proper meaning of the term 'attention', let us take a look at a few definitions provided by eminent authorities on this subject.

Dumville

Attention is the concentration of consciousness upon one object rather than upon another. (1938, p. 315)

Ross

Attention is the process of getting an object or thought clearly before the mind. (1951, p. 170)

Morgon and Gilliland

Attention is being keenly alive to some specific factor in our environment. It is a preparatory adjustment for response. (1942, p. 128)

Sharma, R.N.

Attention can be defined as a process which compels the individual to select some particular stimulus according to his interest and attitude out of the multiplicity of stimuli present in the environment. (1967, p. 392)

Nature of 'Attention'

All these definitions point out the following important facts about the meaning and nature of the term 'attention'.

(i) **Attention is focusing of consciousness on a particular object.** We see a number of things in the environment at a particular time and are aware or conscious of many of them. For example, while perceiving the blackboard writing in the classroom, a student is aware of the presence of the charts hanging on the walls, the teacher, his activities and the activities of the students sitting beside him. But he is not aware of all these very clearly. At one moment he can be clearly aware only of this or that object or activity. He is clearly aware of the words and sentences written on the blackboard because his consciousness is focused on them.

Therefore, focusing of consciousness on a particular object, idea or activity enables to understand it and we become fully conscious or aware of it. Attention is the name given to this process of the focussing of consciousness or awareness that makes us become alive to one thing while excluding others. Hence it is proper to define attention as the process of the concentration of consciousness upon one object rather than another.

(ii) **Attention is constantly shifting.** When we are attending to an object at a particular moment, we are clearly aware or conscious of it as our consciousness is focused on it. But what happens to other objects and activities that are not in focus of our consciousness at that moment? Are we aware of them or not? Of course we are aware of many of them but as not clearly as in the case of focused object.

The reason for this lies in the division of the field of perception or consciousness at a particular moment. Consciousness at a particular moment may be divided into two parts, central and marginal. When our attention is on the blackboard and consciousness is focused on it, the other objects and activities in the classroom remain within the reach of marginal consciousness. This helps us in becoming partly conscious or aware of them. Both these fields of perception or consciousness are interchangeable. The object, which is at one moment within the focus of consciousness, can in another moment shift to the marginal consciousness or even beyond that. Therefore, it is proper to realize attention as a flexible and dynamic process. The subject of attention generally goes on changing but the object of attention remains the same on which the consciousness is centered.

(iii) **Attention is selective.** At any given moment, there are various stimuli in the environment of an individual which try to affect him. For example, there may be music coming from the radio, someone talking and noises coming from the street. Besides these stimuli affecting the same sense organ, there may be stimuli affecting us from other sense organs too. We may have a headache or might be feeling extremely cold or hot. All these things make a bid for our attention. We do not attend to all of them at a time and also do not respond indiscriminately to each one of them.

Our reaction is selective. Only those stimuli which suit our interests and attitudes are able to attract attention while the others are ignored. The stimulus, which is more important and useful than the others, is attended to at once whereas the less important and insignificant ones are attended to later on. Thus attention represents a narrow field and is always selective.

(iv) Attention is a state of preparedness or alertness. As pointed out earlier in the definition by Morgan and Gilliland, attention is considered as a process involving a preparatory adjustment for response. During this process, the organism tries to prepare or adjust himself to the stimulus situation. In other words, he goes into a process of physical, mental and emotional alertness or preparedness. His sense organs adjust themselves to receive the stimulus more effectively. We may see him turning his head, or fixing his eyes towards the object of attention. Besides this, the muscles of the body are also specially prepared to the object of attention or to engage in the activity that is the focus of attention. At this stage of preparedness, one may easily notice the state of tension in the muscles. We can find such familiar instances in the military command of 'Attention' and the athletic call of 'Ready'.

Attention does not only involve motor preparedness but also brings mental alertness or preparedness. One becomes mentally alert and tries to exercise one's mental powers as affectively as possible while paying attention to a task. Thus attention brings an all-round alertness and preparedness in the organism for accomplishing the task successfully.

After knowing the meaning and nature of the term 'attention', we can now define the term as

Attention may be considered as a process carried out through cognitive abilities and helped by emotional and conditional factors to select something out of the various stimuli present in one's environment and then bring it in the center of one's consciousness in order to perceive it clearly for deriving the desired ends.

TYPES OF ATTENTION

Various authors have classified attention in a variety of ways but the following classification given by Ross (1951, p. 175) seems to be more agreeable.

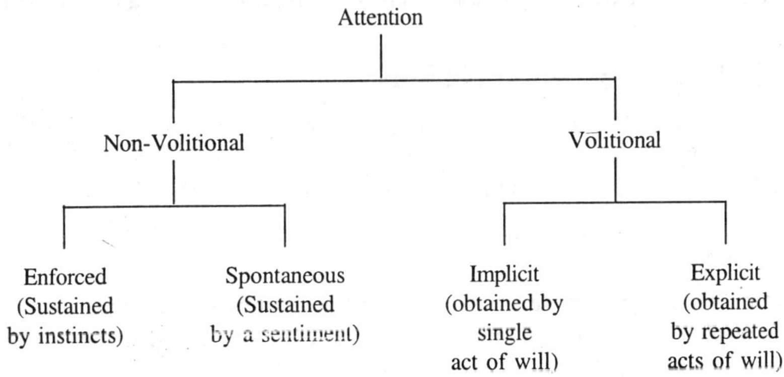

Non-volitional or Involuntary Attention

This type of attention is aroused without the play of the will. Here we attend to an object or an idea without making any conscious efforts on our part. Mother's attention towards her crying child, attention towards the members of the opposite sex, towards sudden loud noise, bright colours, etc., are examples of non-volitional attention.

Non-volitional attention as classified above can be aroused both by our instincts and our sentiments. The attention, which is aroused by the instincts, is called enforced non-volitional attention. A young man, when we make an appeal to his sex instinct or curiosity, becomes quite attentive in his task. The type of attention which he pays at this time can be called enforced non-volitional attention.

The other sub-type of non-volitional attention, aroused by the sentiments is called "spontaneous non-volitional" attention. It is the result of properly developed sentiments. We give somewhat automatic or spontaneous attention towards that object, idea, person around which our sentiments are formed.

Volitional or Voluntary Attention

Attention is volitional or voluntary when it calls forth the exercise of will. It demands conscious efforts on our part. It is least automatic and spontaneous and not given whole-heartedly like volitional attention. Usually in such a type of attention, we have a clear-cut goal before us and for its accomplishment we, with all our efforts, make ourselves attentive. Attention paid at the time of solving an assigned problem of mathematics, answering questions in an examination hall, consulting the railway time-table at the time of embarking on a railway journey are some of the examples of volitional attention.

Volitional attention is further sub-divided into two categories—Implicit Volitional attention and Explicit Volitional attention. While in the former, a single act of volition is sufficient to bring about attention, we need repeated acts of will to sustain it in the latter. When a child is assigned some mathematical sums in the classroom and he does not attend to them, he is warned by the teacher that he would be punished if he does not do his assigned work. This can make him exercise his will power, attend to the assigned task and finish it properly. Here a single act of will is responsible for arousing attention. Hence we can take it as an example of implicit volitional attention.

In explicit volitional attention, attention is obtained by repeated acts of will. One has to struggle hard for keeping oneself attentive. It requires a strong will-power, keen attention and strong motives for the accomplishment of the task. The attention paid during examination days for the required preparation against heavy odds and distraction, is a glaring example of such attention.

FACTORS AFFECTING ATTENTION

How properly and effectively are we able to pay attention to an object, idea, person or process depends upon so many factors. These factors may be broadly classified as External factors and Internal factors. Let us try to know about these factors or conditions affecting our attention in detail.

External Factors

External factors or conditions are generally those characteristics outside the situations or stimuli which make the strongest bid for capturing our attention. Let us examine these characteristics.

Nature of the stimulus

All types of stimuli are not able to bring the same degree of attention. A picture attracts attention more readily than words. Among the pictures, those of human beings invite more attention than those of animals or objects. Among the pictures of human beings, those of beautiful women or handsome men attract more attention. In this sense coloured pictures are more forceful than black and white ones. Thus an affective stimulus should always be chosen for capturing maximum attention.

Intensity and size of the stimulus

Compared to the weak stimulus, the intense stimulus attracts more attention of an individual. Our attention becomes easily directed to a loud sound, a bright light or a strong smell. Similarly a large object in the environment is more likely to catch our attention than a small object. A large building will be more readily attended to than a small one.

Contrast, change and variety

Change and variety strike attention more easily than the sameness and absence of change. If we are talking to our students the use of maps and charts suddenly attracts their attention. We do not notice the ticking on the wall but it arrests our attention as soon as it stops. Any change in the attention to which we have become adapted, immediately captures our attention. Actually the factor-contrast or change is highly responsible for capturing attention of the organism and contributes more than the intensity, size or nature of the stimulus. If all the LETTERS on this page were printed in capitals, the capitalized word in this sentence would have no greater attention getting value than any other word. It is the contrast or change which makes it more forceful.

Novelty also attracts attention. We are compelled to attend to anything that is novel. So it is always better to introduce the change or novelty for breaking monotony and securing attention.

Repetition of stimulus

Repetition is a factor of great importance in securing attention. We may ignore a stimulus at first instance but when it is repeated several times, it captures our attention. A misspelt word is more likely to be noticed if it occurs twice in the same paragraph than if it occurs only once. In the classroom also, the particular point on which the teacher tries to draw the attention of the students is raised again and again to get students' attention. During a lecture, the important aspects of the speech are often repeated so that the attention of the audience can be easily directed to the valuable points. But this practice of repetition should be carefully used. Too much repetition of stimulus may bring diminishing returns.

Movement of the stimulus

A moving stimulus catches our attention more quickly than a stimulus that does not move. In other words, we are more sensitive to objectives that move in our field of vision. Most of the advertisers make use of this fact and try to capture the attention of people through moving electric lights.

Internal Factors or Conditions

How much and in what way will a person attend to a stimulus depends not only upon the characteristics of that stimulus or the favourable environmental conditions but also upon his interest, motives, basic needs and urges. Every person likes to do or attend to those objects or activities that fulfils his own desires or motives and suits his own nature, interest and aptitude. Let us try to see the part played by these inner factors in securing attention of a person.

Interest

Interest is a very helpful factor in securing attention. We attend to objects in which we are interested and do not attend to those in which we have no interest. If we go to the market to buy a book, our attention will be captured more by bookshops than by cloth and shoe shops. A boy interested in hockey will be more attentive to watching a hockey match than the football or the volleyball matches played at the same time on the adjacent grounds. A wise teacher is able to secure the attention of his students if he tries to make his lesson interesting by connecting it with their basic needs, drives and interests.

Motives

The basic drives and urges of an individual are very important in securing his attention. Thirst, hunger, sex, curiosity, fear are some of the important motives that exercise definite influence upon attention. A hungry person is sure to notice the smell of cooking. The man who fears a snake will definitely attend to all things resembling a snake. Sex drive occupies a unique place among different drives. Even the most inattentive student in the class can be made to sit on the edge of his chair if the teacher announces that he is going to talk about the sex practices of American Hippies. Nowadays in the world of advertisement, sex is the drive that has been extremely exploited. We see girls sell such unrelated items as tyres, nuts, bolts and tractors.

Mental set-up

Besides our interests and motives, the mental set-up is an important factor for securing attention. Mental set-up means the tendency or bent of the whole mind. A person always attends to those objects towards which his mind has been set. A person waiting for the letter of his beloved can recognize her envelope among a huge pile of envelopes. Similarly, on the day of an examination, something remotely concerning the examination easily attracts the attention of the students. All this happens because concerned possess a definite bent of mind and consequently their attention is immediately directed towards the related objects.

Attitude

We are attracted towards a stimulus and attend to it in relation to the type of attitude, positive or negative, maintained by us towards that stimulus. In case we have negative attitude in the form of dislike, envy, jealously, disrespect, indifference etc., towards a stimulus we will certainly not pay any attention to it and in all such cases would like to avoid its company in physical as well as in mental terms. On the contrary, a stimulus for which we have positive attitude in terms of its liking, valuing, respecting, is always attended to in a proper and effective way.

Mental and physical state

The attention towards a stimulus also depends upon the relevant physical and mental states of the individual. His physical and mental health may also play a decisive role in this direction. Mental or physical fatigue may cause a great obstacle in the path of providing proper attention. On the contrary, when one is enjoying good physical and mental health, one may very carefully attend to a desired stimulus. In this way one should always remain fresh and energetic for paying proper attention to his desired stimulus.

Value and purposefulness of the stimulus

The thing which has some meaning, purpose and value attracts us more in comparison to those that are not so purposeful or valuable. Thus the intensity and strength of our attraction and attention towards a stimulus always rests on its purposefulness and valuability for us. The clarity of the meaning and purpose of the stimulus is thus an important factor in the process of paying attention towards it.

Prior experience and training

We have little or almost no hesitation in attending to or performing those tasks for which we have some prior information, experience or training. On the other hand, we often hesitate or avoid in paying attention to unfamiliar faces, places, things, ideas or ways of working and behaving. This means that familiarity and prior experience about a stimulus definitely affect one's attraction and attention towards that stimulus. Therefore, when one is asked to attend to a work, it should not be taken as a new difficult and typical work. The proper approach is that one should always be guided from known to the unknown. The process of catching one's attention thus should begin with the familiar stimulus and styles of work. Then gradually we may bring the unfamiliar and new ones into picture by mixing and relating them with the familiar stimulus and prior experiences.

Habits and temperament

Our habits and temperament play a significant role in getting attracted and paying attention towards a particular stimulus. An individual who is habitual of smoking or drinking will definitely be attracted and pay more attention to the places, people, situations and events that may be helpful in satisfying his habitual needs regarding smoking or drinking. A person who is habitual and temperamentally attracted towards cleanliness, morning walk, healthy intake, exercise, etc., will always attend to and perform such tasks and behaviour that may suit his habits and temperament for the stimulus to which one wants to react and attend to more and more in his personal and professional environment.

Instincts and emotions

Our instincts and emotions play quite a significant role in directing and shaping the attending behaviour. A mother's attention towards her weeping or crying child is the most glaring example of the role of the parental instinct in the attending behaviour. Similarly, the instincts of curiosity, constructiveness or creativeness, acquisition, gregariousness, flight, laughter, repulsion, sex etc. play quite a dominant role in capturing as well as sustaining one's attention towards the stimulus to which the satisfaction of our instinctive behaviour is linked. Similarly, our emotions like love, anger, fear, lust, disgust, and amusement also play a significant role in making us neglect or attend to particular stimuli in our environment.

Span of Attention

While defining attention, we have emphasized that in a strict psychological sense, only one object, idea, or fact can be the center of consciousness at one particular moment and consequently we can attend to only one thing at a time. However, it is found with some people that they can attend to more than one or even many tasks at the same time. While writing a letter they are seen answering the telephone, keeping track of the time from the wall clock and smilingly responding if somebody approaches. In other cases, immediately after entering a room or some hall, individuals are able to give a detailed account of the number of chairs and fans, persons present, the pictures hanging on the walls, the colour of the walls or curtains, and so on. In this way, people may possess the ability to grasp a number of objects or in other words, to attend to a number of stimuli in one brief presentation. This ability of an individual is evaluated in terms of the span of his attention which differs from person to person and even situation to situation in the same person. Therefore, *the term span of attention may be defined in terms of the quality, size or extent to which the perceptual field of an individual can be effectively organized in order to enable him to attend to a number of things in a given spell of short duration.*

Thus what one can perceive in terms of the number of objects or stimuli on account of a mere glimpse of the environment containing those objects or stimuli may be termed as one's span of attention.

Historically speaking, Sir William Hamilton was the first one to perform experiments on the span of attention in 1859. For his experiments he spread out marbles on the ground before his students and concluded that on an average, the span of visual attention is limited to 6-7 marbles, i.e. we are unable to see more than 6-7 marbles at a time. However, if these marble pieces are arranged in groups or units, we can attend to a great number of marbles. Further experiments were performed by psychologists like Jevons (1871), Cattell, Freeman (1916), Glanville and Dallen Back (1929), Woodworth and Shalsberg (1968). Proceeding on the lines of Hamilton, Mr. Jevons used seeds (in place of marbles) for studying the span of attention. He concluded on the basis of his studies that on an average, the span of visual attention is limited to 5-6 seeds. Later on, Cattell in 1986-87 conducted a series of experiments for studying the phenomenon of span of attention by using a simple machine type instrument known as Tachistroscope. Today in our school or college psychological laboratories, we make use of a little more advanced form—Falling door type Tachistroscope. Let us read a little about its operation.

The falling door type Tachistroscope usually consists of a wooden screen that has a window or hole in the middle. Digits, letters or small patterns written or printed on cards may be inserted in the apparatus for being seen through the hole or window. Its exposure is quite short (generally $1/10^{th}$ of a second) regulated by a movable falling shutter. The subject is shown the cards through the hole for the fixed exposure time. He may then be asked to record what he has perceived and the number of digits, letters, etc., correctly reproduced may then be considered as the measure of one's span of visual attention.

For the measurement of other sensory attention, different techniques may be employed. For example, the span of auditory attention may be measured by tapping a number of times and asking the subject how many taps he has heard.

The studies and experiments carried out by Cattell and other psychologists later have been able to derive the following conclusion about the nature and characteristics of the human span of attention.

- In case the time of exposure is 1/5 to 1/10 seconds then the span of attention for a normal adult is usually between 6 to 8 in terms of the perception of the dots, digits or letters. However, in the case of the children, it is between 4 to 5.
- In the case of perception of dots, letters or digits in groups, there is sufficient improvement and increase in one's span of attention.
- The span of attention related to the perception of simple and meaningful letters or words is always more than those related to the perception of difficult and meaningless letters or words.
- The span of attention related with the perception of familiar objects is always more than those related with the perception of the unfamiliar objects.
- Any increase in the intensity of the stimulus or time of exposure causes corresponding increase in one's span of attention.

- The practice provided in having experiences related to the perception of specific stimuli may enable the subject to gain in terms of his span of attention.
- The individuals are found to have more span of attention for the perception of those stimuli which have some purpose of value to them or cover their areas of interests.
- The favourable or unfavourable environment conditions, whether physical or psychological, play their effective role in influencing and affecting one's span or attention.

SUSTAINED ATTENTION

Mere capturing or attracting attention of the students is not enough. It is the beginning of a process and not the end. After capturing the attention, essential attempts should be made to hold it for a desirably long time. This needed task is named sustaining of attention. In the words of Woodworth *"To sustain attention is to concentrate one's activity continuously upon some object or happening or problem."* (1945, p. 48). Thus, in the case of sustained attention, there is no wandering. The individual's attention always remains on track and the activity proceeds systematically without any serious distraction.

To achieve the required objectives in a reasonable time, the habit of paying sustained attention is very helpful. One must be used to concentrate upon the activity that one is doing. The child who cannot keep his attention fixed for a reasonable period is sure to lag behind in his studies. An artist has to strive for sustained attention so that he can finish his desired piece of art. A writer, a poet, a musician all have to care for sustained attention. In holding the attention for long, there is a need of creating genuine interest of the subject in the task he is doing. All the internal as well as external factors of getting attention can be helpful in this task. Therefore, a wise teacher should make use of them for sustaining the attention of his students.

He must exploit their basic needs, instincts and motives and make them conscious of the desired objectives and purposes. He must bring desired modification in his methodology. Whenever needed, the factors of novelty, change and contract should be introduced, the use of effective devices and aids be called for and children should be given required freedom for encouraging their will. They must work with zeal and enthusiasm and not under pressure. All the factors, which create distraction and prove obstacles in the path of holding the attention long, should be removed. As far as possible, children should be made to work under most favourable environmental conditions and the causes which disturb them mentally and emotionally should be attended to carefully. Moreover, the will power of the students should be developed and they should be made to struggle hard for acquiring their set objectives and higher ideals.

DISTRACTION

What is Distraction?

When we are attending to a stimulus (object, person, place, idea or activity) for its perception, something may happen in the external environment as well as within ourselves that tend to intrude or divert our attention from that stimulus. This thing or event belonging to our environment thus interferes with the natural process of our attention. Thus the process that interferes with the natural process of paying attention towards a stimulus is known by the term 'distraction' and the things or events lying in the environment responsible for distraction are termed as distractors. Distractor as a psychological term has been defined by H.R. Bhatia in the following way.

"A distractor may be defined as any stimulus whose presence interferes with the process of attention or draws away attention from the object to which we wish to attend." (1968, p. 139).

How Attention is Distracted?

Let us think about the how and why of the process of distraction. Actually, when we are attending or paying attention to a particular stimulus, there are many other attractive or forceful stimuli (besides the attended one) in our external or internal environment. Each of these stimuli tries in its own ways for our attention. It is just like a big competition among all these stimuli for influencing and attracting our attention towards them. If the stimulus, which is being attended to, is quite meaningful, interesting, effective and forceful, it neutralizes the influences of the other intervening factors or distractors present in the environment. As a result we may be able to continue paying attention to our desired stimulus, despite wasting some of our energies in the task of fighting against the distractors. And in case any distractor or stimulus present in our environment makes its way, then we are forced to pay our attention to this new stimulus. This new stimulus may even belong to our internal environment like a headache, stomach ache, emotional disturbance, anxiety and mishappenings etc. Thus the stimuli that are responsible for distracting an attention can be mainly divided into two parts—external distracators and internal distractors.

Among the external or outside factors the more common and prominent are noise, music, improper lighting, uncomfortable seats, unfavourable temperature, inadequate ventilation, defective methods of teaching, improper use of teaching aids, defective voice of the teacher and his improper behaviour etc. These sources of distraction vary a lot. They affect the individual according to his own mental set-up and personality characteristics. The conditions that cause distraction to an individual may prove helpful in sustaining attention to others.

Therefore, the common notion that the external unusual environmental conditions always hinder the progress of the work is misleading. Some people are found to work better in a noisy environment. Many of us can concentrate better on studies while the radio is playing. Actually, the source of distraction lies more commonly in the individual himself than in the outside environmental conditions. Internal distractions such as emotional disturbances, ill-health, boredom, lack of motivation, feelings of fatigue or interesting thoughts unrelated to the matter in hand, have more effect than the everyday external distractors. If one is in normal health and does not suffer from any unusual mental worries and emotional disturbances, then no power on earth can distract his attention, provide he is determined to proceed on his course. Most of us are in the habit of offering lame excuses in the name of outside distraction, for our unwillingness and lack of determination.

But from this discussion, it should not be concluded that external factors distraction have little significance and should not be cared for at all. In the midst of external distraction, the individual has to struggle hard to overcome it. He has to put in greater energy to keep his mind focused. Surely and certainly, there should not be such mis-utilization of energy which otherwise can be saved for achieving higher aims. Therefore, great care should be taken to get away from all possible environmental causes of distraction. The working situations and environmental conditions should be so modified and adjusted that it provides adequate working facilities and a healthy congenial atmosphere for an individual whose attention in the work we wish to capture and sustain.

SUMMARY

One's attention may be considered as a process carried out through one's cognitive abilities and helped by his emotional and conational factors to select something out of the various stimuli present in one's environment and then bring it in the center of one's consciousness in order to have its clear perception for achieving the desired result.

Attention is closely related to interest and learning. We pay attention to the things in which we are interested and paying of our attention results in success in the task of learning. In fact attention helps us in seeking desired motive as well as mental preparedness for the execution of a task. In providing such attention, we remain quite selective which means that only those stimuli, which suit our interests and purposes, are able to attract our attention while the others are ignored and also at a particular time, we try to concentrate our consciousness on a particular object rather than another.

Attention may be broadly classified as volitional or voluntary (maintained by one's will power) and non-volitional or involuntary (without exercise of one's will). Volitional attention can be further classified as implicit volitional attention (obtained by a single act of will) and explicit volitional attention (obtained by repeated acts of will). Similarly, non-volitional attention can also be further divided into Enforced non-volitional attention (aroused by instincts) and Spontaneous non-volitional attention (aroused by the sentiments).

The factors affecting one's attention may be broadly classified as external factors and internal factors. Internal factors represent the factors lying within the individual like interest, motives, mind set attitude, mental and physical state, prior experience and training, habits and temperament and instincts and emotions etc. In external factors, we can include the factors associated with the stimuli in the environment like nature of the stimulus, intensity and size of the stimulus, contrast, change and variety, repetition of the stimulus and movement of the stimulus etc.

While paying attention, we can attend usually to only one thing at a time. However, there are people who can attend to more than one or even many tasks at the same time. This ability of these persons is evaluated in terms of the *span of their attention* which differs from person to person and even situation to situation in the same person. The span of one's attention can be experimentally studied with the help of an instrument known as Tachistroscope.

To obtain better results in the process of learning or execution of task, it is quite essential to hold one's attention for a desirable length of time without disruption. This needed activity on our part is known as *sustaining of attention*. One has to make serious and deliberate efforts to sustain attention by taking care of all the factors helpful in maintaining attention and eliminating or reducing the forces of distraction.

Distraction refers to the process that interferes with the natural process of paying attention towards a stimulus and the things or events lying in one's environment responsible for such distraction are termed as distractors. Distractors can be mainly divided into two parts — external distractors (like noise, improper lightening, uncomfortable seats, etc.) and internal distractors (like lack of motivations, emotional disturbances, ill health, boredom or fatigue etc.). For getting better results in the process of learning or performing any task, attempt should always be made for the elimination or reduction of the evil effects of such distractors.

References and Suggested Readings

Bhatia, H.R., *Elements of Education Psychology,* 3rd ed. reprint, Orient Longman, Calcutta, 1968.

Broadbent, D.E., *Perception and Communication*, Pergamon Press, Oxford, 1958.

Collins, Mary and Drever, James, *Experimental Psychology,* 3rd ed., Methuen, London, 1930.

Dumville, B., *The Fundamentals of Psychology*, 3rd ed., University Tutorial Press, London, 1938.

James, W., *Principles of Psychology* (Vol. II), Holt, New York, 1890.

Morgan, J.B. and Gilliland, A.R., *An Introduction to Psychology*, Macmillan, New York, 1942.

Ross, J.S., *Ground Work of Educational Psychology*, George G. Harrup, London, 1951.

Sharma, R.N., *Educational Psychology*, Rastogi Publication, Meerut, 1967.

Shanker, Udai, *Advanced Educational Psychology*, Oxonian Press, New Delhi, 1984.

White, Alan, R., *Attention*, Blackwell, Oxford, 1964.

Woodworth, R.S., *Psychology*, Methuen, London, 1945.

Woodworth, R.S. (Ed.), *Experimental Psychology*, Holt, New York, 1954.

27

Interest—Meaning, Nature and Measurement

CHAPTER COMPOSITION

MEANING AND DEFINITIONS OF INTEREST

Interest is the central force that drives the whole machinery of the teaching learning process. All our attempts are aimed at making our students interested in the learning experiences given to them. Interest as a driving force not only helps the children in acquiring certain learning experiences, but also colour and fashion their attitudes, aptitudes and other personality traits. It thus directs the course of their growth and development and individualizes their personalities. Visualization has such many-sided importance of interest and it is proper to know actually what they are. Many psychologists and thinkers have tried to explain the meaning of this term. Let us have a look at a few of these definitions.

Crow and Crow

Interest may refer to the motivating force that impels us to attend to a person, thing, or an activity or it may be the effective experience that has been stimulated by the activity itself. In other words, interest can be the cause of an activity and the result of participation in the activity. (1973, p. 248)

Ross

A thing that interests us is just something that concerns us or matters to us. (1951, p. 171)

Bhatia

Interest means making a difference. We are interested in objects because they make a difference to us, because they concern us. (1968, p. 130)

B.N. Jha

Interest is that enduring mental system which sustains, contains and continues the activity called attention. (1946, p. 247)

Thus 'interest' may be referred to as the key factor and a driving force that helps us in paying attention as well as remaining engaged in our so attended activities.

NATURE AND CHARACTERISTICS OF INTERESTS

The definitions given above and the studies and experiments carried out by various psychologists give enough ground to know more about the nature and characteristics of interests. We summarize them as under:

1. Our interests are very much linked with our wants, motives, drives and basic needs.
2. Interest is a great motivating force that persuades an individual to engage in a cognitive, conative or affective behaviour.
3. Interest and attention are closely related to each other. Commenting on their relationship, McDougall writes, *"Interest is latent attention; and attention is interest in action."* (1949, p. 277). This observation is true. Interest is the mother of attention. We attend to those objects in which we are interested and thus interest prepares us mentally to pay attention to an object, person or a thing. Attention always implies the activity, what we have in our mental structure in the form of an interest, that is given practical shape in the form of some activity, *i.e.* making one attend.
4. Interests are innate as well as acquired dispositions.
5. Interest is the personal meaning that a thing has for us. This meaning colours all the aspects of our vision. When interested in a thing, we interpret everything in line with the interest.
6. Pursuit of one's interest is always satisfying. It helps an individual realize the goals and aims set by him.
7. Interest helps in overcoming unusual or early arrival or frequent repetition of plateaus in learning. They also give enough strength to an individual to resist fatigue and avoid failure.
8. Interests and attitudes although have close similarity on the ground that both represent mental readiness or preparation for a particular behaviour pattern, yet there is a clear-cut distinction between the two. An individual usually likes the things in which he is interested and the thing that interests also seeks activity. Attitudes, on the other hand, may orient an individual either favourably or unfavourably towards certain objects, places or ideas. Also they are comparatively passive. A person may possess attitudes but may do nothing about them.

Interests are not permanent and fixed. They change as a result of maturation, learning and other internal as well as environmental conditions and factors.

WHY ARE WE INTERESTED IN SOME THINGS AND NOT IN OTHERS?

As a matter of fact, our innate or inborn tendencies are basically responsible for our peculiar interests. We are interested in the things that give satisfaction to our innate desires and urges. From the early childhood, it can be easily seen that instinctive drives (like curiosity, constructiveness, acquisition, self-assertion etc.) play a great role in making children interested in one thing or the other.

As one grows older, one's instinctive urges get developed and modified. Now in which manner and to which extent these urges develop depends upon many environmental factors. Environmental forces are responsible for giving a particular shape to the inborn or innate urges and basic drives. As a result, interests do not remain innate or inherited qualities, but change into acquired tendencies or characteristics.

Moreover, instinctive behaviour, as we grow older, gives birth to sentiments and complexes which in turn bring ideas and purposes in life. We begin to pay attention to things connected with our sentiments and complexes. Our attitudes, temperament and other personality traits also begin to influence our interest patterns. We strive for ideals and achieving some things in our lives. Such striving and struggle tries to give a new form to our interest patterns, as a result of which new interests are developed or acquired by us.

It is, therefore, not proper to consider interests purely as inborn or inherited characteristics. They are actually acquired dispositions or characteristics and the result of constant interaction between the instinctive behaviour of the organism and the peculiar environmental forces. Both internal or personal factors and external or environmental factors affect the interest patterns of an individual in the course of his growth and development. We can sum up these factors as below.

Personal Factors

(i) Physical health and physical development.
(ii) Mental health and mental development.
(iii) Social development.
(iv) Age and sex.
(v) Emotions, sentiments and complexes.
(vi) Wishes, ideals, motives and goals of life.
(vii) Attitudes.
(viii) Pattern of one's instinctive behaviour.

Environmental Factors

(i) Socio-Economic status of one's family.
(ii) Culture and social environment.
(iii) Education and training.
(iv) Opportunities available to him for exploring his potential interests.

GENERATING DESIRED INTERESTS IN LEARNING

The success of a teacher lies in his arousing and maintaining interest of his pupils. Therefore, most of their strenuous efforts are always directed in making their students interested in some or the other learning activities. All the factors involved in teaching-learning process, namely the learner, learning material, learning environment, learning methods and teacher, have to be controlled and designed in such a way that all of them may contribute significantly towards the maintenance of proper interest in a learning activity at a particular time. Therefore, the task requires a multi-dimensional attack. However, for the general guidance of teachers, the following points may prove fruitful:

1. **Setting proper aims and objectives:** Before teaching a lesson or engaging children in a learning activity, they should be told about the need and importance of learning that activity. The aims and objectives of teaching a particular lesson or unit should be clearly defined and the students should be made to set definite goals and purposes.
2. **Proper selection and organization of learning experiences:** The unsuitability of the content makes children disinterested in a particular lesson. Therefore, the teacher should select and organize the contents to be taught or the matter to be delivered in a suitable way by keeping in view all the psychological principles.
3. **Use of appropriate methods and teaching aids:** Most of the times, it is the teaching method that makes a particular learning interested or distasteful. The teacher should adopt efficient and effective methods of teaching lesson and use suitable audio-visual aids.
4. **Exploitation of various instincts of children:** The interests of children are controlled and guided by their instincts. Therefore, a wise teacher is the one who tries to exploit their basic drives like curiosity, constructiveness, acquisition, self-assertion and sex etc. for making his students interested in a learning activity.
5. **Make proper use of sentiments and ideals:** Sentiments and ideals also control and direct children's interests. Therefore, they should be harnessed for creating and maintaining interest.
6. **Arranging proper learning situations or environment:** Learning situation or environment plays a great role in making children interested or bored and tired. Therefore, the teacher should take care of the suitability of the learning environment. The classroom furniture, seating arrangement, lighting and ventilation, the scheduled time-table for learning a particular subject or activity, general atmosphere, physical and mental state of the pupils as well as the teacher, group-climate, etc.-all should be properly considered while making attempts for arousing and maintaining interest of the pupils in a learning activity.
7. **Teacher's personality and determination:** Teacher's personality and his determined bid to make the students interested in his teaching count much in this direction. A good teacher with his proper behaviour and personality traits can motivate, inspire and make the students almost lost in his teaching. Therefore, a teacher should try to imbibe the desirable personality traits and characteristics. He should bring honesty and sincerity in his thinking, doing and feeling and make the best possible efforts to take his students along with his teaching by making them interested in his teaching.

MEASUREMENT OF INTERESTS

After the above discussion, we may conclude that interest is a great motivating force and reservoir of one's inner potential capable of moulding and shaping one's behaviour and personality make-up in a particular direction. The measurement of one's interest in a related field may then help us in predicting his success in that field. Accordingly, we may provide educational and vocational guidance services to the students on the basis of the proper measurement of their educational and vocational interests. How this can be done may be a matter of your interest in the capacity of a teacher. This can be done properly by administrating the properly standardized educational or vocational interest tests or inventories. Such tests and inventories are very much available for the use of school and college students in India as well as abroad. For illustration purpose, we are going to discuss the process of the measurement of interests with the help of a standardized vocational interest test here.

The process of administration and reporting of a vocational interest test may be explained as follows:

Object

To know about the vocational interests of a subject through the administration of a vocational interest test.

Needed Test Material and Environmental Situations

(i) A copy of the vocational interest test construct and standardized by Dr. S.P. Kulshrestha which includes copy of the Vocational Interest Record and Test Manual.

(ii) A subject whose vocational interests are to be measured.

(iii) Maintenance of proper environment for the administration of the tests.

Identifying Data of the Subject

Name of the Subject	:	Deepti
Profession of the Father	:	Govt. Service
Monthly Income	:	Rs. 30,000
Belongs to Urban/Rural Area	:	Urban
Name of the School	:	DAV School, Rohtak
Class	:	XI
Age	:	18 years
Date	:	20-8-2002

Description of the Test Material

This vocational interest has been constructed and standardized by Dr. S.P. Kulshrestha. It has been published by National Psychological Corporation, Agra. The main objective of this test is to measure the vocational interests of the students in order to help them in making the right educational choices for entering into the professions of their interests.

Its test material can be properly understood through its division into:

(i) Vocational Interest Record, and

(ii) Test Manual.

Vocational Interest Record

It contains the instruction and test items covered in four pages. The top of the initial cover page contain columns for filling up the identifying data by the subject. It is followed by the necessary instructions regarding the test.

Material on second and third pages is so arranged that it helps the subject to express his interest or disinterest for 200 different vocations belonging to 10 main vocational areas. The material on the fourth page helps in recording the vocational interest choices of the subject and then drawing necessary interpretations and conclusions for the presentation of the test report.

Test Manual

It lies with the examiner. In this manual, Dr. Kulshrestha has discussed the needs and objectives of the construction of this test, the process of its construction and standardization, nature of the test material, instructions for the administration of the test, the procedure for scoring and interpreting the test, results etc. The proper reading of this manual is a must for the examiners for deriving proper benefits from the administration of the test.

Administration of the Test

The administration task was done in the following ways:

(i) The environmental situations was arranged so as to provide congenial environment for holding the test. The subject was made to sit comfortably and feel at home. A good rapport was established with her and she was told clearly about the objective of her testing.

(ii) The subject was then given a copy of the vocational interest record booklet (4 pages). She was asked to fill up the identifying data columns and read the instructions given on the front page. These instructions were also explained clearly to her by the examiner.

(iii) The subject was then asked to turn the page and mark as (√) or (×) for her liking or disliking of the different vocations mentioned on the second and third pages. When she marked all the 200 vocations, the test booklet was taken from her. She was clearly told that nothing was to be written on page 4 as it is meant for the examiner. While taking back the test booklet from her it was assured that she had responded to all the 200 items of the test.

Scoring of the Responses

Each of the responses marked as √ and × were scored as 1 and zero. In this test, each of the 10 main vocational areas have been named by the first letter of their Roman names, e.g. L has been used for the literature field. It has been further divided as L_1, and L_2. L_1 which represents the total sources of the responses given by the subject for her likings of the 10 literature-related vocational arranged vertically while L_2 stands for the total of her scores for her likings of the other 10 literature-related vocations arranged horizontally. In this way, there were 20 vocations belonging to the field of literature. Our subject marked (×) for all the vocations lying in the 10 vertical columns. Hence she earned her L_1 scores as zero. She repeated this with L_2 score by earning another zero. Thus her total scores $L_1 + L_2$ were zero and this score was written in front of the column L. Similar method was adopted for computing the total scores of other main vocational areas. Such scoring of the responses of our subject was tabulated as under:

S. No.	*Vocational Field*	*Vocations in Vertical Columns*	*Vocations in Horizontal Rows*	*Total*
1.	Literary	$L_1 = 0$	$L_2 = 0$	L = 0
2.	Scientific	$SC_1 = 2$	$SC_2 = 0$	SC = 2
3.	Executive	$E_1 = 7$	$E_2 = 8$	E = 15
4.	Commercial	$C_1 = 2$	$C_2 = 1$	C = 3
5.	Constructive	$Co_1 = 0$	$Co_2 = 0$	Co = 0
6	Artistic	$A_1 = 6$	$A_2 = 5$	A = 11
7.	Agriculture	$AG_1 = 0$	$AG_2 = 0$	AG = 0
8.	Persuasive	$P_1 = 1$	$P_2 = 3$	P = 4
9.	Social	$S_1 = 7$	$S_2 = 8$	S = 15
10.	Houshold	$H_1 = 1$	$H_2 = 1$	H = 2

INTERPRETATION OF THE TEST SCORES

The interpretation of the scores earned by our subject in 10 different vocational areas was done in two different ways. Firstly these scores were represented through a Profile (The space for such profile has been given). In this, the ten points representing the respective total scores earned in the 10 vocational areas were marked and then these 10 points were joined by the straight lines as shown in Figure 27.1.

Stan-nine	*Field of Interest*	*Raw Scores*	*L*	*SC*	*E*	*C*	*Co*	*A*	*AG*	*P*	*S*	*H*
IX	*High interest*	20	•	•	•	•	•	•	•	•	•	•
		19	•	•	•	•	•	•	•	•	•	•
		18	•	•	•	•	•	•	•	•	•	•
VIII	*Interest more than average*	17	•	•	•	•	•	•	•	•	•	•
VII		15	•	•	•	•	•	•	•	•	•	•
		15	•	•	•	•	•	•	•	•	•	•
		14	•	•	•	•	•	•	•	•	•	•
VI	*Average Interest*	14	•	•	•	•	•	•	•	•	•	•
V		12	•	•	•	•	•	•	•	•	•	•
IV		11	•	•	•	•	•	•	•	•	•	•
		10	•	•	•	•	•	•	•	•	•	•
		9	•	•	•	•	•	•	•	•	•	•
		8	•	•	•	•	•	•	•	•	•	•
		7	•	•	•	•	•	•	•	•	•	•
III	*Interest less than their average*	6	•	•	•	•	•	•	•	•	•	•
II		5	•	•	•	•	•	•	•	•	•	•
		4	•	•	•	•	•	•	•	•	•	•
I	*Low Interest*	3	•	•	•	•	•	•	•	•	•	•
		2	•	•	•	•	•	•	•	•	•	•
		1	•	•	•	•	•	•	•	•	•	•
		0	•	•	•	•	•	•	•	•	•	•

Fig. 27.1 Interest Profile of a subject

The above profile was then used for the required interpretation. The areas related to the various points of the profile were marked as the areas of high, average or low interests shown by our subject. Thus judging in this way, the areas (earning 13 as raw scores) related to executive and social fields were found to be the areas of main interests for our subject and the areas earning 0 as raw scores to literature, commerce and agriculture were the areas of the lowest interest.

The interpretation of the raw scores of our subject can also be made with the help of the stannine score marked from I to IX in the initial column of the profile.

By combining the results of both the interpretation, we can prepare the report of the test findings of our subject's vocational interests as follows:

General Report

1. Main Interest Area: Executive
2. Second area of Interest: Artistic
3. Third area of Interest: Persuasive
4. Lowest interest areas: (i) Literary, (ii) Commercial, and (iii) Agriculture

Specific Report

1. High Interest: Nil
2. Interest more than the average: Executive and Social
3. Average Interest: Artistic
4. Interest less than the average: Persuasive
5. Low Interest:

   (i) Literary, (ii) Scientific,
   (iii) Commercial, (iv) Constructive,
   (v) Agriculture, (vi) Household

CONCLUSIONS

The following conclusions can be drawn from the above two reports about the vocational interests of our subject.

1. Our subject Deepti has her main interests in executive and social areas. Demonstration of more than the average interest clearly indicates that she likes to become an executive. However, she has shown an equal interest in the social field, which means that she is interested in serving the social cause by her executive assignments.
2. Her second major interest area lies in the artistic field that reflects her hobbies and likings for artistic activities. She may adopt such artistic hobbies as a profession if she opts to do so in future.
3. Her third interest area is related to the agents like persuasive professions. She can motivate others to move in the direction she likes and this quality may prove very helpful in her socio-executive professions.
4. She has almost no interest in the professions related to literary, commercial, agriculture, scientific, constructive and household fields. Therefore, she is advised not to adopt these professions as her career.

SUMMARY

Interest may refer to as the key factor and a driving force that helps us in paying attention as well as remaining engaged in our attended activities. Most often our interests are the results of our wants, desires, motives, drives and basic needs. We attend a thing because we have interest in that thing. We do a task and will continue until we are interested in it. Our interest in a thing may be quite spontaneous or innate or it may be the result of our experiences related to that thing. However, pursuit of one's interest is always satisfying. It helps an individual realize his cherished goals. However, our interests are not always fixed or permanent. They may be abandoned or changed as a result of motivation and our interaction with our environment.

We are interested in some things and not in others both on account of our innate as well as acquired disposition. Both internal or personal factors (like wishes, ideals, motives, attitudes, emotions, sentiments and complexes as well as physical and mental health etc.) and external or environmental factors (like socio-economic status, education and training, cultural and social environmental and available circumstances in one's environment etc.) affect the interest patterns of an individual in the course of his growth and development.

Children may be made interested in a particular learning activity by taking care of the things like (i) setting the proper aim and objectives (ii) proper selection and organization of learning experiences, (iii) use of appropriate methods and teaching aids (iv) making use of various instincts, emotions, sentiments and ideals of the students. (v) Taking care of the learning situation or environment and (vi) Desirable behaviour and determination on the part of the teachers.

Observation of one's behaviour, while engaging one or the other activities, may provide sufficient clue about the degree of one's interest in those activities. However, a more reliable and valid measurement of one's interest may be made with the help of some standardized tests and inventories especially designed for the measurement of some particular type of interests like educational, vocational, literary, scientific, artistic and so on.

References and Suggested Readings

Bhatia, H.R., *Elements of Education Psychology*, 3rd ed., reprint, Orient Longman, Calcutta, 1968.

Crow, L.D. and Crow, Alice, *Educational Psychology*, 3rd Indian reprint, Eurasia Publishing House, New Delhi, 1973.

Jha, B.N., *Modern Educational Psychology,* rev. ed., Indian Press, Allahabad, 1946.

Kelly, W.A., *Educational Psychology,* 5th ed., Bruce Publishing House, Mil Wankee, 1956.

McDougall, William, *An Outline of Psychology*, 13th ed., Methuen, London, 1949.

Ross, J.S., *Ground Work of Educational Psychology*, George G. Harrup, London, 1951.

28

Habits—Meaning, Nature and Development

CHAPTER COMPOSITION

MEANING AND NATURE OF HABITS

One of my friends is employed in Delhi but he resides in Rohtak. He has to travel 180 km daily by bus besides his strenuous office duty. When asked how he manages the traveling and the work, he replied, "I have been doing this for the last 15 years, it has become my habit. Now I do not mind the daily journey though it mattered in the beginning." It is not a unique instance. We find a number of activities performed by others that seem easy and mechanical even though initially they were quite difficult and tiresome. Our walking, talking, dressing, eating, writing, smoking, typing, driving, swimming are all such acts. All these learned activities are commonly known by the term 'habit'. A number of attempts have been made to define the term 'habit' in a suitable way. Let us have a look at some of them.

Garrett

Habit is the name given to behaviour so often repeated as to be automatic. (1968, p. 282)

Sturt and Oakden

By strict definition, those acts are habitual which are performed with little or no thought and always in approximately the same way. (1948, p. 230)

Ryburn

A habitual action "is the result of many repetitions of the act in approximately the same way. It is done without conscious thought, performed smoothly and with the maximum speed required. (1956, p. 260)

These definitions point out that habits are the product of experiences and practice. Initially what we do, think or feel, may require a voluntary and deliberate attention and strenuous efforts on our part. But when this particular action is repeated several times almost in the same way under similar circumstances, one does not require voluntary attention and efforts and the action tends to become quite automatic like reflex-action. It is now termed as 'habitual action' and thus a habit is established.

Characteristics of Habit

In addition to the above discussion, the following characteristics of habitual behaviour may also throw light on the nature of habits.

1. **Acquired dispositions:** Habits are acquired dispositions. They are not innate and inherited.
2. **Uniformity:** Habitual actions are uniform actions. They are performed every time in the same way.
3. **Promptness:** Habitual actions are performed with promptness. The action is so quick and speedy that it resembles reflex action.
4. **Ease and facility:** Habitual actions are performed with great care and facility. In the beginning, one may feel difficulty in performing some task but once the habit is established, it is performed with great ease and facility.
5. **Accuracy:** Habit brings accuracy in action. We see an accountant adding columns of figures all day without a single mistake. Similarly a typist is able to type with great accuracy only due to his developed habit.
6. **Reducing the need of paying attention:** Habitual acts are performed with least or no attention. Women do knitting almost paying no attention to the work. Similarly a person playing a harmonium or violin places his fingers on the required string with no careful attention on his part.
7. **Diminishing fatigue:** Habit diminishes fatigue. Due to habit formation, the work that is too difficult and tiresome in the beginning becomes simple and spontaneous engagement for hours. The fact can be easily verified when we observe a bus driver driving on a long route for hours. Actually with the habit of driving, he learns to make the fewest and simplest movements and thus does not become the victim of fatigue easily.
8. **Resistance to modification:** Habitual actions possess a strong tendency of resisting any modification or change. Once a habit, good or bad, is formed, it is difficult to give it up or bring changes in its functioning. A habitual smoker or gambler finds it difficult to give up his habit of smoking or gambling. On the other hand, a man who is not accustomed to accepting bribe cannot accept bribe and thus change his habit.
9. **Nervous system is the base of habits:** The nervous system is the principal factor in the formation of habits. The role played by nervous system has been described beautifully by Ryburn, in the following words:

Nerves carry messages to and from the brain. When approximately the same message is taken to the brain, and the same answer comes back, for the same action to result, a kind of track is worn, so that the answer to the message carried to the brain becomes more and more automatic. It becomes more and more difficult for any other answer to come to the ingoing message than the one that has been given again and again in response to what is approximately the same message. Thus the basis of habit is this groove, as it were, which is born in the nerves. (1956, p. 260)

10. **Habits have a large field of operation:** Habits do not confine themselves to conative acts alone. We may have habits of good thoughts as well as of feelings.
11. **Habits are useful as well as harmful:** In general, habits are divided into two groups—good habits and bad habits. Good habits like speaking the truth, punctuality, proper habits of work etc. are considered useful for the welfare of the individual as well as of the society whereas bad habits like smoking, gambling, telling lies etc. are considered harmful to both the individual and the society.

HABITS, INSTINCTS AND REFLEX ACTIONS

Habits, instincts and reflex actions are many a times confused with one another as all of them are automatic and mechanical. They do not need any voluntary attention. They have similar characteristics marked by uniformity, accuracy, promptness, ease and facility. But there are so many points of difference which makes them quite different from one another. They are—

(i) Instincts as well as reflex actions are universal and are found in all the members of any species. However, habits are individual and specific.

(ii) Reflex actions are thoroughly mechanical. We sneeze almost in the same way as our remote ancestors did. They are incapable of any modification or change. But instinctive and habitual actions are capable of modification and change.

(iii) Instincts as well as reflex actions are innate and inborn while the habitual actions are acquired and learned.

(iv) Reflex actions are regarded as somatic or physiological phenomenon while the habitual and instinctive actions are considered physical or mental.

IMPORTANCE OF HABITS

Habits play an important role in one's life. If we analyze our day-to-day behaviour and activities, we would find that a major portion of them is dominated by our habits. Our acts like sleeping, walking, talking, reading, writing are nothing but the spontaneous, mechanical habitual actions. Through habit formation it is possible to do more than one thing at a time. Women knit, spin and cook while they talk. Thus, habit brings great economy in our life. As a result we can save our energy and time for more important things in life. Absence of habits hampers the progress of an individual as James William observes,

There is no miserable human being than one in whom nothing is habitual but indecision, and for whom the lighting of every cigar, the drinking of every cup, the time of rising and going to bed every day and the beginning of every bit of work are subjects of express volitional deliberations. Full half of the time of such a man goes to the deciding, or regretting, of matters which ought to be so ingrained in him as practically not to exist for his consciousness at all. (1969, p. 160)

A man is known by his habits as his personality is clothed in habits. All the personality traits—good or bad—are reflected through one's habits. Man infact is a creature of habits. He tends to become what he repeatedly practices. One who is habitual of gambling, smoking, eve-teasing, stealing etc. is sure to develop into a socially undesirable, unscrupulous person while the one who practices honesty, regularity, generosity, industriousness will become a useful and productive member of the society. Not only our actions but our interests, aptitudes, attitudes, beliefs, prejudices, opinions, faiths, feelings, emotions and sentiments are influenced and controlled by our habits. Therefore in short, what a man is, has been or will be is decided by his habits of thoughts, actions and feelings.

In the field of education too, habits exercise a strong impact. Good habits help in acquiring, learning and knowing many things with great ease and facility. A student who is habitual of concentrating on his studies for hours in school as well as at home is not easily overcome by fatigue. Similarly habits of efficient writing, thinking, making judgements, punctuality, regularity, neatness, cooperativeness, honesty—all help them in their proper adjustments as well as in acquiring and learning all the essential knowledge and skills in a short time with great facility.

Thus in all the walks of one's life and sphere of activities, habits tend to play a decisive role in making or marring one's present and future depending upon their nature—good or bad. While good habits are responsible for infusing in an individual what is good from social and moral angles, bad habits create obstacles in the path of his proper development, bring bad name to him and prove dangerous to the society.

It is, therefore, essential that proper care is taken to develop desirable habits of work, thought and feeling in children from the very beginning. They should not be allowed to pick up undesirable or bad habits. In case they are found to have developed any evil habit, they should be helped to get rid of them. In the following pages, we would try to pay attention on these aspects.

FORMATION OF DESIRABLE HABITS

The following general rules are found to be useful in the task of habit formation:

1. **To start at an early age:** The early years of childhood are very important from the point of view of habit formation. Younger age is marked with lot of plasticity and receptivity. It is the most impressionable or formative period of one's life. Most of our habits, good or bad, are the product of this age. Therefore, it is proper to keep an eye on the youngsters. They should be provided with congenial environment for developing proper habits. The inculcation of right habits in children should be started as early as possible so that they may be saved from picking up wrong habits and, modes of action, improper thoughts and feelings.

2. **Firm determination and initiative:** Firm determination and powerful initiative help much in the acquisition of desirable habits. It is a common saying that where there is a will there is a way. If you decide that you will get up early in the morning, decide it with all the firmness and launch the new habit with all the initiative of which you are capable. A public announcement of the pledge that you would get up early to attend the playground regularly from such and such date can prove a powerful initiative to start with. It provides a strong emotional stimulus and ego involvement and thus provides the most appropriate environment for launching the new habit.

3. **Setting up definite specification for the new habit:** It is of no use to declare that "From tomorrow I will be a good boy" or "I will work hard with my studies." Such vague resolutions do not materialize. If one really intends to study harder, he should chalk out a definite schedule of hours and subjects and stick to it.
4. **Seizing the very first opportunity to act:** It is of no use to make resolution after resolution and not put even a single one into action. It is not proper to wait for the future. Tomorrow never comes. When you determine to develop a habit, it is better not to postpone it for the next day and so on.
5. **Starting along the right track:** In an attempt to form a new habit, one should start in the right direction from the very first day. The initial mistakes cost very dearly. It is difficult to unlearn wrong practices and improper habits. Therefore early stages of habit formation must be watched out very carefully and every precaution should be taken to make the students learn the things rightly.
6. **Sufficient practice and repetition:** For habit formation, it is essential that action is repeated frequently in the same way under similar circumstances. Therefore, sufficient opportunities for practice and repetition should be provided to the students for the formation of desirable habits. It requires great patience on their part. They must be made to make persistent efforts in practicing a particular mode of behaviour (action, thought or feeling) until it is established into a habit.
7. **No exception in the persistent efforts:** It is not enough to get a right start along the right track in the formation of habits. In making persistent efforts for the repetition and practice of a particular mode of behaviour (which is established as a habit), it is kept in mind that no exceptions are made to it. Every exception to the habit permitted helps to defeat our purpose. If one tries to reach school in time, one can never do it by reaching in time for two days and then going late on the third day.
8. **Due appreciation and encouragement:** Pleasure-giving and satisfying behaviour or response tends to be repeated. Therefore, the good behaviour and conduct of the students should get proper appreciation and encouragement. Public praise and reward work as a great motivating force to children. They not only help in developing good habits among those who are rewarded but also stimulate others to pick up the desirable habit.

Breaking Bad Habits

Bad habits are harmful to the individual as well as to the society. Therefore, it is needless to say that they should not be allowed to grow. But as we usually find, evils and vices are more easily caught and spread than goodness and virtues, so the bad habits are also easily picked up. They are the blots on the personality of an individual. Therefore, every attempt should be made to get rid of them. The following suggestions can be found fruitful in breaking bad habits:

1. **Firm determination and strong will power:** First of all, one should realize the necessity of setting oneself free from the clutches of a bad habit. Moreover, one should have a firm determination to break it. Thus there is a need for strong will power so that the temptations are never allowed as even a single act of the repetition of a bad habit may throw the individual back on the starting point.

2. **Strong initiative with quick actions:** Bad habits are like powerful and dangerous enemy. Therefore, the initial attack should be well planned. One should leave nothing to chance. Public declarations and pledges help much in this direction as they give sufficient emotional strength to an individual. One who declares publically that one would not smoke from such and such date, receives an inner strength to give up his bad habit. But mere declaration and resolution do not suffice. They should be followed by actions.
3. **Use of voluntary practice:** Many improper habitual actions can be rectified by the use of voluntary practice. Incorrect spellings, mispronunciation, improper way of performing certain skilled work etc. can be corrected and improved by adopting and practicing the right way of performing these acts.
4. **Substitution of bad habits by the appropriate socially approved behaviour:** One of the convenient approaches in removing the bad habits is to replace them by socially desirable habits. These socially desirable habits gradually make the bad habits die their natural death. That is why a person who wishes to give up his habit of smoking is often advised to take cough drops or betel nuts, when the urge to smoke is strong. Similarly bad habits like telling lies, negligence, improper eating habits etc. can be replaced by truth telling, care and proper eating habits for neutralizing them in a course of time.
5. **To hit on the root causes of the bad habits:** The root causes of bad habits should be discovered and attempts should be made to remove these causes. If we try to analyze the genesis of bad habits, we can find that many habits are developed due to many a varying reasons. Sometimes they are formed due to certain complexes, inner conflicts or emotional disturbances. Nervous habits like nail biting, pen-chewing and nose picking belong to this category. No direct measure is useful in removing such habits. The emotional factor, which causes such habits, should be taken into consideration and children should be indirectly asked to give up such undesirable habits. Physical defects also sometimes lead to bad habits. Proper medical care and treatment in such cases should be arranged. Bad company and uncongenial atmosphere at home and the school also contribute in developing bad habits. In this way, bad habits are developed on account of many personal and environmental causes. The root of all such causes should be discovered and attempts should be made to remove them.

We can thus conclude that a teacher should try to seek active co-operation of the parents in digging out the root causes. It is the duty of the parents, elder members of the society and teachers to make their best attempts in providing good and congenial environment to children. They must not do what should not be done by the youngsters. Their own behaviour should be made a model for the inculcation of good habits among the children. It will help not only in checking the growth of bad habits but will also provide strong stimulation for the development of desirable habits among the youngsters.

SUMMARY

Habits are the product of experiences and practice. When a particular action of behaviour is repeated several times almost in the same way under similar circumstances, it tends to become quite automatic like reflex action. It is then termed as habitual action or behaviour and thus a habit is established. However, habitual actions differ significantly from the reflex action as well as instinctive actions on the grounds like (i) habits are acquired and learned while instinctive and reflex actions are innate and inborn and (ii) habits are individual and specific while instinctive and reflex actions are universal and found in all the members of any one species.

Habits play quite an important role in one's life. Reducing most of our acts and behaviour of the day-to-day life as automatic (requiring all most no attention and deliberate efforts), habits bring great economy in our lives by saving lot of our time and efforts. They are capable of providing a particular colour and shape to our personality. Actually what a man is, has been or will be is almost decided by his habits of thoughts, actions and feelings. Good and desirable habits of the students like concentration in studies, habits of efficient writing, reading and conversation etc. They may help them a lot in acquiring necessary knowledge, understanding and skills in many of the learning areas. Actually there is no area or sphere of activities in one's life where habits do not play a decisive role in making and marring one's present and future depending upon their desirability or undesirability from the individual as well as social perspectives. It is why the sincere and deliberate efforts are always needed in developing desirable habits as well as breaking bad habits among our children.

For the formation or development of desirable habits one can follow some general rules like (i) start at the early age (ii) make firm determination and initiative for the inculcation of desirable habits, (iii) set up definite specification for the new habit (iv) seize the very first opportunity to act (v) start along the right track (vi) have sufficient practice, drill and repetition (vii) allow no exception in the persistent efforts and (viii) provide proper reinforcement of a desirable habit or behaviour etc.

Habits, more particularly the bad ones, are quite resistant to desirable modification, i.e. once formed, it is quite difficult to give it up or bring changes in its functioning. However, deliberate attempts can be made in this direction by keeping in mind suggestions like (i) firm determination and strong will for giving up the bad habit (ii) strong initiative with quick action, (iii) use of voluntary practice (iv) substituting bad habits by the socially approved behaviour (v) hitting on the root causes of the bad habits, (vi) presentation of good models of desirable habits and behaviour and (vii) substitution of a poor environment with a healthy desirable environment (viii) providing due reinforcement for a slight change in one's bad behaviour etc.

References and Suggested Readings

Boring, E.C., Langfield, H.S. and Weld, H.P. (Eds.), *Foundation of Psychology*, Indian ed., John Wiley, New York, 1961.

Garrett, H.E, *General Psychology*, Eurasia Publishing House, New Delhi, 1968.

McDougall, William, *Introduction to Social Psychology*, Methuen, London, 1946.

Ryburn, W.M., *Introduction to Educational Psychology*, Oxford University Press, London, 1956 (Reprint).

Sturt, Mary and Oakden, E.C., *Modern Psychology and Education*, 2nd ed., reprint, Trench, Trubner & Co., London, 1948.

William, James, *Psychology: Briefer Course*, 4th print, Collier Macmillan, London, 1969.

29

Concept Formation

CHAPTER COMPOSITION

INTRODUCTION

Our environment is full of tremendously diverse things. It consists of an infinite number of living and non-living objects. Similarly we have limitless ideas, thoughts, principles, formulae, theories etc. related to various aspects of our life and the environment. In such an environment of tremendous diversity, we can adjust only if we have adequate power and ability to discriminate, classify and categorize the things around us (in view of their similarities and dissimilarities) in specific groups. Concept formation helps us a lot in this gigantic task of categorizing and classifying the environmental objects. Moreover, our concepts regarding people, objects, places, ideas or events provide the arms and legs to our symbolic and verbal behaviour. What we think, understand, reason and judge is to a great extent controlled by our concepts. Therefore, they are regarded as an important tool of our thoughts and expression. Judging their importance in our lives, we must try to pay due attention to their proper development from a very early age of our lives. In this chapter, we would like to concentrate on such efforts. For this purpose we would be focusing our attention on some of the important issues concerning this.

MEANING AND NATURE OF CONCEPTS

The term 'concept' has been defined in a number of ways by different scholars. Here we give some of these definitions.

Munn

A concept is a process which represents the similarities in otherwise diverse objects, situations, or events. (1967, p. 350)

Morgan

A concept is a process representing a common property of objects or events. (1961, p. 265)

Boring, Langfield and Weld

A concept is a 'general idea', an item in thinking that stands for a general class. (1961, p. 198)

Ross

Concepts are patterns, schemes or mental categories which enable us to interpret the objects of our thought, whether perceptual or imaginative. (1951, p. 202)

On the basis of the above given definitions, we can conclude that:

- Concept is a generalized idea about the things, persons or events. It stands for a general class and not for a particular object or event. It is a common name, given on the basis of similarities or commonness found in different objects, persons or events.
- It is a mental disposition that helps in understanding the meaning of the objects of our thinking.
- In one sense, it is the general mental image of the objects, events experienced or perceived earlier.

After analyzing all the above characteristics of concepts, we may easily conclude that a large portion of the words used and other symbolic expressions in our language represent concepts. The names horse, tree, dog, table, chair, represent our concept of things; father, mother, teacher, Indian, Russian, represent our concept of persons; honesty, truthfulness, cleanliness, redness, goodness represent our concepts of qualities and characteristics and small, big, high, low, equal, similar, congruent represent our concepts of relations. Similarly, we can have concepts of life, death, soul, God etc. Not only regarding the other things or persons but also regarding ourselves, we have the concepts of things, persons, qualities or characteristics, relations, events or to say for all what we can perceive or imagine in our thought process.

Our thinking about the things, persons or events carries two types of mental images or ideas. One is particular and the other is general. When we say "Mohan's horse", the word 'horse' refers to its particular meaning but when it is said that "Horse is a useful animal," it stands for general class, for all the horses in the universe. It is in the latter sense or meaning of the word horse (generalized meaning) that we use the term concept.

Similarly, concepts regarding tree, fruit, teacher, table etc., represent general idea about these objects. When we say tree, we refer to all types of trees—bamboo trees, mango trees, neem trees etc. All these trees do not resemble on many grounds. But in spite of the differences, they hold similarities on many points. Our concept of 'tree' is a mental image that brings to us the similarities or common properties of all the different trees we know. We will call a thing tree when it has some specific characteristics, the image of which we have already in our mind, on account of our previous experience, perception or rich imagination.

Concepts are very useful in recognizing, naming and identifying things. The common properties of similarities or patterns that are suggested by concepts help in this direction. When we say "It is a mango tree", we recognize or classify it on the basis of our concept about the tree. It also explains why we do not call it a neem or some other tree.

In every sphere of our life, we are very much helped by the identification, classification, categorization and naming of the objects, ideas or events provided by our acquired concepts. Had it not been possible to identity and categorize the things present in our environment, our lives would have been a complete chaos. There could have been an utter confusion on this earth in terms of maintaining any coordination, association and relationship among the infinite number of things and ideas lying then and there. In this way, concepts and their formation must always be regarded as a helping hand and boon to the cause of the individual and social welfare as well as progress.

TYPES OF CONCEPTS

The concepts, in view of their typical characteristics, nature, properties and utility etc. may be classified into three distinct types by one way or the other as discussed below:

Concrete and Abstract Concepts

Our concepts about the concrete things present in our environment are known as concrete concepts. These include all the concepts of the living or non-living things present in a concrete form (having their real existence) in our environment. On the other hand, abstract concepts are the concepts related to our generalized ideas about the abstract things or ideas prevalent in our surroundings. As examples of such abstract concepts, we may cite our concepts related to honesty, virtue and vices, good and evils, God, heaven etc.

Classical or Definite and Probabilistic Concepts

Some concepts prevalent in our environment may be quite old, traditionally transmitted from generation to generation. On account of their wide and lengthy use, these become almost fixed with respect to a certain section, culture or region of our society. The persons using such concepts are quite definite of their use in the process of communication. Example of such a classical and definite concept may be terms like widow, widower, bachelor, virgin and so on. All these concepts are quite old, classical and traditional in one's culture. One is quite definite about them. One will make their use in one's conversation for conveying definite sense in the related situations. For example he will name a women, widow who is a female and was married. But in case he has an improper concept of the term widow, he may use such terms as 'widow woman', 'married woman' or 'virgin' etc.

In contrast to such above concepts, there are many other concepts in our society that are not so common, classical, universal and definite. We have quite an indefinite and uncertain notion about making their use for a particular person, place, thing or idea. The attribute and characteristics accompanied with such concepts are not always true in all the circumstances. For example, let us take the concept of term '*Baniya*'. In defining this concept we may say that a *Baniya* is a person who belongs to the Vaish community, has more than enough interest in money matters and is quite a miser. In actual circumstance, it is not essential to have all these characteristics and attributes in the persons known as *Baniyas* in our society. One may definitely belong to the Vaish community, may also have interest in money matters but may or may not be a miser. Similarly one may not have born into the Vaish community but may possess the other two characteristics, i.e., having an established business and a quality of being a miser. In this way, nothing definite in the form of their typical characteristics and attributes is available in the case of other types of concepts. They are neither traditional and classical and nor do they have uniform and universal applicability. Their such indefinite use and application is thus responsible for naming them as probabilistic concepts.

Simple and Complex Concepts

Simple concepts are those concepts that may be defined by a single feature, attribute or property. Our concepts of the various colours like red, green, blue, yellow, black are the best examples of such simple concepts. The 'blue' at once communicates that it is a colour whose perception is blue. Its only attribute or feature of 'being perceived as blue' is quite enough for conveying all things related to its concept.

On the other hand, complex concepts are those concepts that are defined by two or more common properties, characteristics or attributes. Our concepts like blue shirt, red building, sources of energy, means of communication, mammals, birds, costly items etc. are some of the examples of such complex concepts. These complex concepts may be further sub-divided into the following three categories to further analyse their nature and characteristics. These are:

Conjuctive concepts

In the conjuctive concepts, we find two or more characteristics or features of an object quite connected or associated with each other. Their such connection or association provide a unique identification and meaning to the related concept. The concept of Red Fort provides a good illustration of the conjuctive concept. In this concept, there are at least three characteristics or attributes that are closely connected or associated with each other for its unique identification. These are (i) red representing its colour attribute, (ii) fort representing it as a form of building and (iii) its historical value as a Red Fort built by some Mughal Emperor in the capital Delhi. In the same way, we may consider the concepts like game of football, game of cricket, game of hockey as different examples of conjuctive concepts. Each one of them has its unique identification in terms of a number of well-connected attributes or features in the form of fixed number of players, size and characteristics of a special playing field, the rules of the game, playing equipments, etc.

Disjunctive concepts

Although there are several characteristics or attributes present in such concepts, it is not essential for them to maintain a connection or link between the conjuctive concepts. A single attribute or feature may appear in all the objects or items associated with such a concept for providing a unique similarity or commonness contributing in the formation of this concept.

Let us take the concept 'source of energy'. Petrol, kerosene oil, electricity, coal, atomic power, sun, wind and water are the examples of the sources of energy. They all have one common feature or property, *i.e.* the potential for generating energy. However, all of them have their own typical features and attributes which provides them their separate and unique identity. In the similar way, instruments like sitar, gitar, harmonium, flute etc., all have their own features and characteristics that may distinguish and separate them from one another. However, they have a single feature or attribute common to all of them, *i.e.* producing musical sound and that is why all of these instruments are associated with disjunctive concept 'musical instrument'. In order to provide some more examples of disjunctive concepts we can name the concepts of means of communication, means of transport, means of entertainment, mass-media, multimedia and so on.

RELATIONSHIP CONCEPTS

Relationship concepts are those concepts in which we find some special and unique relationship between their features or attributes. As a result, fat like elephant, a house with more doors than windows, a plot having three sides open, a family having more girls than boys, boys hostel, girls room, developed country, developing country, rich state, milky white, smaller than, greater than, taller than, etc. all may be termed as the examples of the relationship concepts.

CONCEPT FORMATION

It is interesting to know how concepts about various things or events are formed in our mind. Concepts, in general, are the results of our sensational and perceptual experiences. Senses are said to be the gateway of our knowledge. What is experienced through senses reaches in the form of mental images in our mind. These images or sensations are given meanings and the meaningful or objectified sensations become our perceptions about the things. Thus when a child perceives a white horse for the first time and is told that it is a horse, he tries to form an idea about it. In the beginning, the idea is very particular in nature and belongs to the perceived objects only. Later on, when he perceives a black or a brown horse he does not at once call it a horse. He again makes an enquiry and comes to know that this is a horse. He tries to compare the particular mental image or idea of the formerly perceived horse with the present images or ideas he is having at present, by perceiving black and brown horses.

In this way, he compares and contrasts the similarities or dissimilarities of his mental images or ideas related to all perceived horses. In spite of the differences in colour, appearance etc., they are found to possess many common properties or characteristics. Thus gradually he is able to discriminate the properties that several horses have in common. This is the stage of the formation of a generalized idea. He begins to use the word horse for a general class on the basis of the common properties found in different horses and now can easily recognize and name an animal as horse.

Therefore, the process of concept formation has three important phases—(i) Perception (experiences or learning), (ii) Abstraction, and (iii) Generalization.

Experiences or learning in any form is the starting point of the process of concept formation. Our perceptions or imaginary experiences, formal or informal learning, provide opportunities for getting mental images of the things, persons or events.

The mind analyses these images and synthesizes what is common to all, neglecting what is merely particular. This process of observing similarities and commonness is named as abstraction. After making such observation in the form of abstraction a number of times, the child is able to generalize or form a general idea about the common properties of some objects or events. On account of this generalization, he will develop a concept about these things or events.

Thus concept formation makes use of the inductive method. Here we proceed from particular to general. Particular things or events are first perceived. After proper comparison, the similarities and dissimilarities are recognized and the common elements are established. We try to discover such common elements in the other experienced or perceived objects or events, and if the common elements are found to be present in them, then we gradually try to derive conclusion or generalization out of all such experiences. Thus, finally we form a generalized idea or attach a general meaning to the object or events. So far, we have discussed the formation of concepts through direct experience. But direct experience is not the only way of acquiring concepts. There are times when we acquire concepts through indirect experience. Most of us, for example, have never seen a 'kangaroo' but we have a concept of a kangaroo. This concept has been acquired through seeing pictures or reading the description of the animal in books or magazines. The concepts regarding democracy, liberty, heaven and hell, all are formed through indirect learning.

Lastly, let us discuss one important fact regarding concept formation. In concept formation, we should always keep in mind that concepts are not static entities. With the acquisition of new experiences and learning, our concepts keep on changing. For example, if we take the concept regarding life and death we find that there is a gradual change in our stand. In early childhood, we attribute life to anything. The chair, table, doll or even walls are thought to be alive. Life is later attributed only to objects which move on their own volition. Now the bicycle is not considered alive as it does not move by itself. As the span of our knowledge expands, the concept also gets further refined. Gradually, we reach the stage when it is applied only to plants, birds, animals and human beings.

PROTOTYPE AND ITS SIGNIFICANCE IN CONCEPT FORMATION

Psychologists, on the basis of their experiments, have reached the conclusion that in the process of concept formation, we usually form a mental structure named as prototype in our mind for the objects to be identified through a particular concept. A particular object in turn may be included in a concept depending upon its degree of resemblance with the prototype. This mental structure (prototype) is nothing but a mental image or memory of some good example of that concept. For illustration, let us take the concept of 'bird'. It has a number of attributes and features for its proper definition (A bird is a living object that has feathers, wings, claws, reproduce through eggs and is able to fly, etc.). However, when we respond to a particular bird, (through its hearing, seeing or reading), there emerges a mental picture in our mind of a few particular birds (considered good and ideal examples of the concept 'bird') depending upon its degree of resemblance with the mental picture of the good examples. We at once call it a bird if it is near in its resemblance with our prototypes (mental picture of the good examples, pigeon, peacock, parrot for being included in the category). But in case there is some resemblance and some dissimilarities, then we have to strive hard for taking our decision with a clear-cut no or yes. In this way, a prototype may be an imaginary mental image or creation of some good examples of a concept which significantly helps in our task of concept formation about persons, places, objects, ideas and events related to our environment. Considering in this way a *prototype of a concept may be defined as a sudden mental image of a particular good example of that concept.*

In the above example of the concept 'bird', we have seen that there emerges a mental image or picture of some particular birds like pigeon, peacock, parrot etc. as soon as the word 'bird' is heard, seen or struck in our mind. Hence we can safely say that (particular examples of the concept bird) pigeon, peacock, parrot etc. are the prototypes of our concept about birds. Similarly, we can easily infer that mango tree, neem tree, coconut tree, peeple tree are the prototypes of the concept 'tree'. Whenever we think of concept 'tree', there will emerge a mental image of one or the other prototype (particular good examples of the concept 'tree') like mango, neem or coconut tree etc.

In this way, it is these prototypes of the concepts and not their several attributes or features that readily come to our help for identifying and categorizing a particular perceived object. Let us make it more clear through an example. We may have a few good or bad examples of the concept 'bird' in the following way.

1. A cuckoo is a bird
2. A bat is a bird
3. An aeroplane is a bird
4. A book is a bird
5. A crow is a bird

Let us discuss the validity of these above five statements.

Certainly we will be losing no time in telling that a cuckoo and a crow are birds. Similarly we will easily reject the book as a bird. However, we may feel a little difficulty in rejecting the claim that aeroplane is a bird. But the most difficult decision will be the selection or rejection of bats as birds.

You must have by now realized how your prototypes about the concept 'bird' are helpful in the task of identifying and categorizing the objects. On its basis you may take the decision of considering a particular object as an example or non-example of a known concept.

As a conclusion, therefore, attempts should be made to develop proper prototypes of the many concepts learned by us in our lives. As far as possible, we should remain away or get rid of the faulty concepts so that we may be saved of their ill consequences. The one thing that should always be remembered by us is that the key to proper communication lies in the hands of adequate and proper concept formation. Hence we should be quite conscious and careful in terms of its proper realization.

CONCEPT ATTAINMENT

How can we attain various types of concepts in our lives? Can we adopt some special techniques for the attainment of these concepts? These issues were made the subject of their investigation by J. Bruner and his associates (1967). The conclusions derived by them through their studies may be summarized as under:

1. We live in a very complex world filled with tremendously diverse things. It would have been impossible to adjust in it, if we had not been endowed with the capacity to discriminate, categorize things in groups and to form concepts.
2. A concept mainly consists of three elements (i) Examples (ii) Attributes and (iii) Values. Examples are instances of the concept. Some are positive and some are negative. In concept attainment, the negative and positive examples are tested and searched for their features. Each example can be described in terms of its basic characteristics called attributes and each attribute has an attribute value. For illustration, if the concept is "apple" then each fruit is an example. Here the pears and oranges are negative and the apples are positive examples. Thus colour may be an attribute and yellow or red may be attribute values.
3. For the attainment of the concepts, there must be some or the other concept well before us. If no concept is formed, then how can we talk about their attainment? Therefore, concept formation should always preceed the concept attainment. Concept formation is just an act of invention and discovery on our part. In concept attainment, we try to focus on the proper attainment of our discovered or formed concepts.
4. For the proper attainment of the concepts, we can make use of a few models or methods put forward by the researchers. A teacher in his laboratory or in his class can make use of such models for helping his subjects or pupils in the task or proper attainment of various concepts.

We may here mention the following two workable models, namely reception model or methods and selection model or method for the attainment of concepts.

Reception Model or Method

In this model or method, the experimenter puts before his subject a number of examples of a particular concept. Some of them are positive examples and the others are negative. By making use of the process of inductive thinking, the subject is then helped to reach some generalization about the true nature of the concept in hand. The generalized notion is then put to further verification through some more clear-cut examples of that concept for completing the task of concept attainment. In this way, reception model or method lays down the following four steps for helping the learner in the attainment of the desired concept. These are:

(i) Presentation of the examples
(ii) Analysis of the examples
(iii) Generalization
(iv) Verification or testing

Let us explain the use of this method through an illustration. As illustration we here take the attainment of the concept of proper noun. We can go ahead in this task by following the above-mentioned four stages or steps as under.

Presentation of the Examples

First of all, the subject is provided with the following positive and negative examples of the concept of proper noun.

Positive examples of the concept	Negative examples of the concept
(i) Delhi	Capital
(ii) Agra	City
(iii) Red Fort	Fort
(iv) Parliament House	House
(v) Tilak Nagar	Nagar
(vi) Swami Dayanand	Religious leader
(vii) Jagdish Chandra Bose	Scientist
(viii) Action Shoes	Shoes
(ix) Colgate Tooth paste	Tooth paste
(x) Dabar Red Tooth powder	Tooth powder

Analysis of the Examples

The positive and negative examples of the concept from (i) to (v) all are indicative and representative of the concept 'places'. While the negative examples like capital, city, fort, house and nagar are indicative of some general places, the positive examples on the left represent the particular places. Similarly the names of Swami Dayanand and Jagdish Chandra Bose at serial no. (vi) and (vii) represent the names of the particular religious leader or scientist. Similarly the names mentioned from serial no. (viii) to (x), in the left column are indicative of some special products in the general category of shoes, tooth paste and tooth powder.

The proper analysis of the positive and negative examples may thus lead the subject to reach the following conclusion or generalization about the concept 'proper noun'.

A proper noun denotes a particular or specific place, person or a thing as distinct from every other one.

Verification or testing of the attainment of concept: It may be carried out by putting some examples before the subjects.

(i) Indira Gandhi : The name of a particular person
Hence it is an example of proper noun.

(ii) Rohtak : The name of a particular place in the Haryana province.
Hence it is also an example of proper noun.

(iii) Usha Fan : The name of a particular fan (a thing or object)
Hence it is also an example of proper noun.

For distinction and discrimination some more negative examples of the concept proper noun may also be put before the subject and on the basis of such efforts, he may be helped in the proper attainment of 'proper noun concept'.

The Selection Model or Method

In this method of concept attainment, the subject is initially provided with a definition or generalized statement about the given concept. For the illustration of such definition, generalized rule or statement, a few proper examples (positive as well as negative) are placed before him. After that, a few more examples are given as a matter of further understanding about the given definition or rule and if necessary the definition or rule is modified in view of gaining proper insight about the given concept. Generally, the following steps are followed in going ahead with the method.

(a) Presentation of a definition or rule concerning the given concept.
(b) Presentation of examples for the illustration of the definition or rule.
(c) Analysis of examples.
(d) Verification or acceptance of the definition or rule or attempting for its re-definition.

Now we will illustrate the process of attainment of concept by following the above four steps.

Suppose we want to help a subject in the attainment of the concept 'mammals', we will proceed as under.

Presenting the Definition

The following definition of the mammals will be put up before the subject.

"Mammals are the living creatures who live on earth, their newborns are brought on this earth after they grow in the womb of the mother like human beings, and are nourished with milk that is sucked from the nipples of these mother mammals."

Presenting examples

For the illustration of the above definition, the following positive and negative examples will be presented before the subject.

	Positive examples	*Negative examples*
(i)	Dogs	Fish
(ii)	Cats	Frog
(iii)	Human beings	Turtles
(iv)	Rats	Birds
(v)	Sheep	Lizards
(vi)	Bats	Snakes
(vii)	Dolphin	Crocodiles

Analysis of the Examples

The subject will be asked to analyze the above positive and negative examples for the verification of the given definition. He can understand that the positive examples from (i) to (v) verify the validity of the given definition. The examples given in the right column represent those living creatures who produce their young ones through hatching eggs and do not possess any mammary glands for producing milk. There remains only two examples for consideration. These are bats and dolphins. Bats can fly like birds and lead life on the earth like animals. Dolphin is a well known creature of the water world.

Verification or Re-defining of the Definition

The subject is now made to realize to modify the given definition in the light of the controversial examples like bats, dolphins or whales. It can be re-defined as:

> *The mammals are the living creatures whose new born are brought on this earth after living in the wombs of their mother and they get nourishment from milk that they suck from the nipples of their mother.*

Similarly, the subject may again realize the need of bringing further modification in this newly defined definition. For this purpose, he may be presented with the examples of the following living creatures.

(i) Duckbill, and (ii) Spiny ant eater. In both these creatures, the newborn are produced through eggs. However, their females possess milk producing glands and the new borns are nourished through sucking of the milk from the nipples of the mothers.

Keeping in view these two latest examples, the definition of the concept mammals will be ultimately put as under;

> *The mammals are the living creatures whose females possess milk producing glands and also possess the characteristics of feeding their new borns by this milk through their nipples.*

In this way, the learners may be well helped by the experimenter or teacher in the task of their concept attainment by following the Reception or Selection models or methods.

SUMMARY

Our thinking about things, persons or events carries two types of mental images or ideals. One is particular and the other is general. When we say 'my horse' or 'his horse', the word 'horse' refers to its particular meaning but when we say that "horse is an useful animal", it stands for general class for all the horses in the universe. It is in the latter sense or meaning of the word horse (generalized meaning) that we use the term 'concept'. Known in this way, a concept may be defined as a generalized idea about a thing, person or event.

Concepts, in view of their typical characteristics, nature, properties and utility etc., can be classified into certain district types like concrete and abstract concepts, definite and probabilities concepts, simple and complex concepts etc.

The process of concept formation is carried out through induction method in three phases namely perception (experience or learning), abstraction and generalization. The starting is thus made by getting mental images of the things, persons or events through perception. The mind then analyses these images and comes out with what is common to all learning keeping aside what is merely particular. This process of observing similarities and commonness is named as abstraction. After going through such process of abstraction a number of times, one is able to generalize or form a general idea about the common properties of some objects or events. It is the generalization (by adopting inductive approach) that helps him form a concept about these things or events. However, the concept formation is a never-ending process. With the acquisition of new experiences and learning, our concepts keep on changing and so we may have newer or modified concepts out of our previously formed concepts.

A prototype of a concept may be defined as a sudden mental image of a particular good example of that concept. It is these prototypes of the concepts and not their several attributes or features that readily come to our help for identifying and categorizing a particular perceived object. For example the particular examples of the concept 'bird' like pigeon, peacock, parrot etc. are the prototypes of our concept about birds. As a result when we try to identify and label a perceived object as "bird", we are at once helped by the mental image or picture of some particular birds like pigeon, peacock, parrot etc. without taking into notice a number of common attributes and features of the birds like feathers, wings, claws, reproduction through eggs, ability to fly etc.

For developing needed concepts in the children, J. Bruner and his associates (as a result of their research findings), have suggested some special techniques in the shape of models for concept attainment. The mentionable are the reception model and the selection model. In the reception model or method, a child is helped in the attainment of the desired concept through inductive approach by following the four distinct steps namely presentation of the examples (positive as well as negative), analysis of the examples, generalization and verification or testing. In the selection model or method of concept attainment, a child is required to adopt deductive approach by following the four distinct steps namely, presentation of a definition or rule concerning the given concept, presentation of examples for the illustration of the definition or rule, analysis of examples and verification or acceptance of the definition or rule or attempting for its re-definition. We can thus help a child in the attainment of various concepts by adopting inductive and deductive approaches of the reception and selection models or methods of concept attainment.

References and Suggested Readings

Boring, E.C., Langfield, H.S., and Weld, H.P. (Eds.), *Foundations of Psychology*, Indian ed., John Wiley, New York, 1961.

Burner, Jerome, Goodnow, Jacqueline and Austin, George, *The Study of Thinking*, Science edition, Inc., New York, 1967.

Carmichael, L. (Ed.), *Manual of Child Psychology*, John Wiley, New York, 1946.

Hurlock, E.B., *Child Psychology*, McGraw-Hill, Tokyo, 1959.

Morgan, C.T., *Introduction to Psychology*, 2nd ed., McGraw-Hill, 1961.

Munn, N.L., *An Introduction to Psychology*, Indian Reprint, Oxford & IBH, New Delhi, 1967.

Murphy, Gardner, *An Introduction to Psychology*, 2nd ed., Indian reprint, Oxford & IBH, New Delhi, 1968.

Paplia, D.E. and Old, S.W., *Psychology*, McGraw-Hill, New York, 1987.

Ross, J.S., *Ground Work of Educational Psychology*, George G. Harrap & Co., London, 1951.

30

Psychology of Thinking, Reasoning and Problem-Solving

CHAPTER COMPOSITION

- Introduction
- What is Thinking?
- Nature of Thinking
- Tools or Instruments of Thinking
- Types or Kinds of Thinking
- Development of Effective and Correct Thinking
- Reasoning—Meaning and Definitions
- Types or Kinds of Reasoning
- Problem-Solving—Meaning and Nature
- Scientific Method of Problem-Solving
- Strategies of Problem-Solving
- Factors Affecting Problem-Solving
- Summary
- References and Suggested Readings

INTRODUCTION

Thinking is one of the important aspects of one's cognitive behaviour. Quite often, we hear comments like 'think before you act' or 'think before you feel'. Thus thinking provides the base on which not only our cognitive but also affective and conative behaviour depends. The poems and piece of art we enjoy, the scientific inventions we make use of and the ideas in a text book we receive are all the products of some thinking on the part of their authors and inventors. Moreover, we can be benefited by these valuable inventions and creations of art only when we make a judicious use of our thinking and reasoning powers. The development of thinking and reasoning powers not only helps in solving the numerous problems one faces in one's practical life but also in striving to solve the most typical social, cultural and scientific problems for the uplift of the society and humanity. That is why efforts in education are mainly concentrated in developing the problem-solving ability of children through their reasoning and thinking powers. In the following pages, we will try to know something about the process of our thinking and reasoning as well as the problem-solving behaviour from a psychological angle.

WHAT IS THINKING?

In our day-to-day speech, we label the term 'thinking' indiscriminately to different kinds of psychological activities. For example, when I say during an informal introduction that I am thinking of the days when I was a student at a college, I am using the term 'thinking' for a proper psychological term 'recollecting'. Similarly when a child says that he is thinking about the type of bungalow he would like to have for himself, he is simply imagining. Also when looking at a distant vague object one says 'I think it is taxi' it is nothing but a simple interpretation of one's perception.

When viewed from a close psychological angle, none of these above mentioned psychological activities – recollection, imagination, perception – is, in fact, thinking. Thinking, therefore, is not as simple a process as it is thought out to be. Various thinkers have tried to define it. Below we give some of these definitions.

Valentine
In strict psychological discussion, it is well to keep the thinking for an activity which consists essentially of a connected flow of ideas which are directed towards some end or purpose. (1965, p. 278)

Ross
Thinking is mental activity in its cognitive aspect or mental activity with regard to psychological objects. (1951, pp. 196–97)

Garrett
Thinking is behaviour which is often implicit and hidden and in which symbols (images, ideas, concepts) are ordinarily employed. (1968, p. 378)

Mohsin
Thinking is an implicit problem-solving behaviour. (1967, p. 117)

Gilmer
Thinking is a problem-solving process in which we use ideas or symbols in place of overt activity. (1970, p. 326)

Definitions like the above may be divided into two categories. In the first category, we have the definitions which maintain that thinking is a process of internal representation of external events (belonging to past, present or future). We may think about a thing or an event even when it is not actually manipulated or observed by us. In the second category, we may include the definitions which describe thinking in terms of problem-solving behaviour. The definitions falling in the second category are more concrete and function better than the first one because they do not rely on unobservable internal representations but rather define thinking as a problem-solving activity that can be readily studied and measured (Fantino & Reynolds, 1975, p. 166).

Actually, whatever the apparent differences, these two classes of definitions tell the same story. The internal representation helps in problem-solving behaviour and problem-solving behaviour provides evidence for the existence of internal representation. Therefore, what is representational may be used as functional and vice versa. The process of thinking and the product of thinking are both actually assessed by what we get as a result of thinking. The manner in which individuals think can always be inferred from their behaviour. Internal representation of mental exploration of the thing or events (the internal behaviour) should be made an essential aspect of the thinking process used in problem-solving behaviour. Therefore, in a workable definition of 'thinking', we must try to combine internal behaviour with the product of thinking (the aims or purposes of thinking). In such a case, we may define thinking as below:

Thinking refers to a pattern of behaviour in which we make use of internal representations (symbols, signs etc.) of the things and events for the solution of some specific purposeful problem.

NATURE OF THINKING

The meaning of the term 'thinking' as discussed in the preceding pages is further elucidated in the following lines:

(i) Thinking is essentially a cognitive activity.

(ii) It is always directed to achieve some end or purpose. In this sense, thinking differs from the aimless cognitive acts like daydreaming and imagination. In genuine thinking, we cannot let our thoughts wander without any definite end in mind.

(iii) Thinking is described as a problem-solving behaviour. From the beginning till the end, there is some problem around which the whole process of thinking revolves. Problems are said to arise when a fixed pattern of behaviour cannot satisfy one's felt needs. These problems give birth to thinking and thinking helps in finding out their solutions.

(iv) But every problem-solving behaviour is not thinking as Mohsin has emphasized in his definition. Thinking is only related to the inner cognitive behaviour. When we try to solve a problem by merely doing something in the situation, we are not thinking. Thinking demands the immediate suspension of one's overt or motor activities. It is an implicit activity that proceeds 'inside' the person. Its objective observation is not possible.

(v) In thinking, there is mental exploration instead of motor exploration. Suppose I need my key to unlock the room. I search my pockets where I keep it usually but I find that it is not there. Now if I simply run here and there, it is motor exploration. But instead of this tiresome trial and error overt exploration, if I sit down calmly and think where I might have put it, what I was doing where can I drop it and so on and so forth; it is mental exploration. In this way, in our solving of the problems, thinking serves the same purpose as we might otherwise do overtly in trial and error manner. It, therefore, economizes time and effort.

(vi) Thinking is a symbolic activity. In thinking, there is a mental solution of the problem, therefore there is no manipulation of the real object in thinking. Thinking makes use of symbols instead of objects and concrete experiences. For example, in designing the plan for the construction of a building, the engineer does not proceed with overt trial and error process. He actually uses mental images and various symbols (substitutes for objects, experiences and activities) in his thinking process.

On the basis of above discussion we can conclude that thinking is an inner cognitive process. It has a definite end or purpose. It is initiated to solve some difficulty or problem and ends in its solution. In the solution of the problems it does not resort to motor exploration but there is a mental manipulation of the objects, activities and experiences.

TOOLS OR INSTRUMENTS OF THINKING

The various elements involved in the thinking process may be summarized as under. In the process of thinking we usually rely on these four elements or tools.

Images

Very often images are used as an instrument of thinking. Images, as mind pictures, consist of personal experiences of objects, persons or scenes once actually seen, heard or felt. There are memory images formed through the recollection of past experiences. There are also visual, auditory and other sensory images formed through perception and imaginary images that do not stand for past perceptions. Thus images symbolize the actual objects, experiences and activities. In thinking, we usually manipulate the images instead of actual objects, experiences or activities.

Concepts

Another important tool of thinking is concept. A concept is a 'general idea' that stands for a general class and represents the common properties of all the objects or events of this general class. The concept formation or generalization economizes our effort in thinking. For example, when we listen to the word 'monkey' we are at once reminded not only about the nature and qualities of the monkey as a class but also our particular experiences and understanding about them emerge into our consciousness that stimulate our present thinking.

Symbols and Signs

Symbols and signs represent and stand as substitutes for actual subjects, experiences and activities. In this sense, they should not be confined to words and mathematical numerals and terms. Traffic lights, railway signals, school bells, badges, songs, flags and slogans all stand for the symbolic expression. Concepts also are usually represented in thinking by these symbols and signs. The word 'three' is a symbol for the concept of 'trinity' and 3 is another symbol. Similarly 'Red' is the symbol which stands for the concept of 'redness'.

These symbols and signs stimulate and economize thinking. They at once tell us what to do or how to act. For example, the waving of the green flag by the guard tells us that the train is about to move and we should get in the train. Similarly, the mathematical symbol for addition (+) tells a child what he has to do. The conclusion drawn by Boring, Langfield and Weld in this connection is worth mentioning:

> *Symbols and signs are thus seen to be the pawn and pieces with which the great game of thinking is played. It could not be such a remarkable and successful game without them.* (1961, p. 199)

Therefore, it is clear that our thinking process makes use of symbols and signs as its tool.

Language

Language, besides serving as a link for inter communication, functions as a tool in thinking. It consists of words and therefore uses symbols. Sometimes instead of words we use gestures in our language. The showing of thumb, or smiling or lifting of the eye brows or shrugging of shoulders carries a lot of meaning. When one listens, reads or writes words, phrases or sentences or observes gestures in any language, one is stimulated to think. Language is the most efficient and developed vehicle used for carrying out the process of thinking. It makes us think and serves as an effective aid in the process of thinking.

TYPES OR KINDS OF THINKING

Thinking, as a mental process is usually classified into the following types:

Perceptual or Concrete Thinking

It is the simplest form of thinking. The basis of this type of thinking is perception. *Perception* is defined as the process of interpretation of sensation according to one's experience. When an apple is offered to a child, he thinks for a moment and at once refuses to take it. His thinking at this time is purely perceptual as it is based on the interpretation of sensation according to his previous experience. He remembers the taste of a green apple which was offered to him a few days ago.

This type of thinking is also named as concrete thinking as it is carried over the perception of actual or concrete objects and events. Small children are much benefited through this type of thinking.

Conceptual or Abstract Thinking

Unlike perceptual thinking, it does not require the perception of actual objects or events. It is an abstract thinking where one makes use of concepts; the generalized ideas. Language plays a big part in the development of such conceptual thinking. This type of thinking is regarded as superior type of thinking to perceptual thinking as it economizes efforts in understanding and helps much in discovery and invention.

Reflective Thinking

It is a somewhat higher form of thinking. It can be distinguished from simple thinking in the following ways:

(i) It aims at solving complex problems rather than simple problems.

(ii) It requires re-organization of all the relevant experiences and finding new ways of reacting to a situation or of removing an obstacle instead of simple association of experiences or ideas.

(iii) Mental activity in reflective thinking does not undergo any mechanical trial and error type of effort. There is an insightful cognitive approach in reflective thinking.

(iv) It takes logic into account in which all the relevant facts are arranged in a logical order, in order to find a solution to the problem in hand.

Creative Thinking

This type of thinking is chiefly aimed at creating something new. It is in search of new relationships and associations to describe and interpret the nature of things, events and situations. It is not bound by any pre-established rules. The individual himself, usually, formulates the problem and he is free to collect evidence and invent tools for its solution. The thinking of the scientists or inventors is an example of creative thinking.

DEVELOPMENT OF EFFECTIVE AND CORRECT THINKING

Thinking is one of the important aspects of the teaching-learning process. Our ability to learn and solve the problems depends upon our ability to think correctly. It helps us in adjustment and is necessary for successful living. Only those, who can think distinctly, consecutively and carefully, can contribute something worthwhile to the society. But one is not a born thinker. One has to learn to think just as one has to learn to perceive. Learning to think is not an easy road. It requires the knowledge of the techniques and practice of proper thinking. Though it is difficult to list the measures for developing effective and correct thinking, the following discussion may prove fruitful in this direction.

Adequate Knowledge and Experiences

One does not think in vacuum. Thinking, no matter how simple or complex, rests on the previous knowledge and experiences of the thinker. Adequacy of knowledge and experiences brings adequacy in thinking. Lack of knowledge and experience or defective knowledge and faulty experience is the common cause of bad thinking. Therefore care should be taken to equip the children with adequate knowledge and experiences. It may be done in the following ways:

(i) Knowledge and experiences are acquired through sensation and perception. It is very important therefore that children should receive correct sensation and be able to interpret them correctly. Thus training in correct observation and interpretation should be given to the children.

(ii) One should be provided opportunities for getting adequate experience and one should be encouraged for self study, discussion and participation in healthy, stimulating activities.

Adequate Motivation and Definiteness of Aim

Thinking is a purposeful activity. Unless there is a definite aim or purpose, thinking cannot proceed on the right track. It is a problem-solving behaviour that ends in the satisfaction of felt needs and motives. A person does not think because he thinks, but because he has a need. Therefore, there is a motive behind any valid thinking. It helps in mobilizing our energy for thinking and makes us deeply absorbed in the task of thinking. It creates genuine interest and voluntary attention in the process of thinking and thus helps a lot in increasing the adequacy and efficiency of our thinking. Therefore, one should try to think on the definite lines with a definite end or purpose. The problems we solve should have intimate connection with our immediate needs and basic motives. The aimless wandering of our thinking should be checked and our energy should be concentrated on creative and productive activities.

Adequate Freedom and Flexibility

Thinking should not be obstructed by imposing unnecessary restrictions and narrowing the field of thought process. On the other hand, it should not get unbridled freedom for tempting one to roam into a world of pure imagination. Actually one should have a flexible attitude on one's part so that one can set one's thinking according to the requirements of the situation. For example, if the past experiences or habitual methods do not help in solving the problem, we should strive for new association, relationships and possibilities for arriving at satisfactory results.

Incubation

For bringing adequacy in the process of thinking, the use of the phenomenon of incubation is very helpful. When we set ourselves to solve a problem but fail to get success in spite of our strenuous and persistent thinking, it is advisable to lay aside the problem for some time and take rest for a while or engage ourselves in some other activity. During this interval, our unconscious mind starts working on the problem and just as eggs are hatched by incubation a solution is evolved through the efforts of our unconscious mind. Thus, we can bring fresh life and avoid fatigue in thinking by incubation.

Intelligence and Wisdom

Intelligence is defined as the ability to think properly and thus proper development of intelligence is essential for bringing adequacy in thinking. Wisdom is also regarded as an effective instrument for carrying out the process of thought. It helps in the insightful solution of a problem. Therefore, proper care should be taken to use intelligence, wisdom and other similar cognitive abilities for carrying out the process of thinking.

Proper Development of Concepts and Language

As discussed earlier, concepts, symbols and signs and words and language are the vehicle as well as instruments of thought. Without their proper development one cannot proceed effectively on the path of thinking. Their development economizes, stimulates and guides the thought process. Improper development and faulty formation of concepts and likewise symbolic behaviour not only hamper one's progress in thinking but also prove fatal as they may give birth to incorrect thinking and wrong conclusions. Therefore, proper care should be taken to have proper concepts and linguistic ability (using various symbols, signs and formulae, besides words and language) for their needed use in the process of thinking.

Adequacy of Reasoning Process

Thinking is also influenced by the mode of reasoning one adopts. Illogical reasoning often leads to incorrect thinking. Logic is the science of correct reasoning which helps to think correctly. Therefore, we should cultivate the habit of logical reasoning among our children.

Besides the above considerations, we should be quite cautious in keeping ourselves well guarded against the elements that bring inadequacy in thinking. These are the factors that either arrest one's thinking or hamper its progress. One of such factors is the state of emotional excitement. Under emotional current one loses one's balance of mind. Therefore, it is essential to train ourselves in exercising control over our emotions. Prejudice, superstitions and incorrect beliefs also arrest thinking and make it biased and one-sided. Valid and correct thinking calls for elimination of all such obstructing factors and we should always attempt in this direction.

REASONING—MEANING AND DEFINITIONS

Thinking is defined as an implicit problem-solving behaviour. Reasoning is also an implicit act and involves problem-solving behaviour. Therefore, it becomes difficult to make clear-cut distinction between these processes. However, reasoning is regarded as the highest form of thinking. It is a complex mental process that needs a well organized brain. It also requires some deliberate efforts on the part of the individual who reasons.

The following definitions given by some eminent scholars can throw more light on the *meaning and nature of reasoning:*

Garrett
Reasoning is step-wise thinking with a purpose or goal in mind. (1971, p. 353)

Gates
Reasoning is the term applied to highly purposeful controlled selective thinking. (1947, p. 428)

Woodworth
In reasoning, items (facts or principles) furnished by recall, present observation or both, are combined and examined to see what conclusion can be drawn from the combination. (1945, p. 523)

Skinner
Reasoning is the word used to describe the mental recognition of cause and effect relationships. It may be the prediction of an event from an observed cause or the inference of a cause from an observed event. (1968, p. 529)

Munn
Reasoning is combining past experiences in order to solve a problem which cannot be solved by mere reproduction of earlier solutions. (1967, p. 339)

Bhatia
Reasoning consists in making a new judgement on the basis of judgement or judgements already formed and is commonly defined as 'perceiving relations among judgements' or see agreement or disagreement among judgements already made. (1968, pp. 233–34)

A close analysis of these definitions can reveal the following characteristics of reasoning:

(i) Reasoning involves a definite purpose or goal.

(ii) We resort to reasoning when the initial attempts of solving a problem by habitual behaviour fails.

(iii) One makes use of one's previous knowledge and experiences in reasoning. All our past experiences or the knowledge of the rules, principles and techniques are closely analyzed. We try to see relationship among them and judge their utility in the present context. In the light of this association and generalization, we try to infer new principles, rules or techniques to solve our problems.

(iv) In reasoning, we try to explore mentally the reason or cause of an event or happening. The attempt to find the solution of the questions like "Why is it so?" "How does it happen?" is nothing but application of our reasoning ability to find the cause and effect relationship.

Not only are we engaged in finding the causes but we are also interested to know the possible effects of actions and stimuli. In thinking, what will happen if this or that is done, one is apt to make use of one's reasoning ability. Thus reasoning has a unique advantage that it helps us to arrive at certain conclusions concerning the future finding or a solution concerning the problem without actually engaging in any motor exploration.

(v) Like thinking, reasoning is a highly symbolic function. The ability to interpret various symbols, development of concepts and linguistic ability help much in reasoning.

(vi) It is a careful, systematic and organized thinking. It follows some definite steps which are given below:

(a) Realization of the difficulty or felt awareness of the problem.
(b) Understanding of the problem and setting up of definite goals.
(c) Mental exploration of all the possible ways of realizing the set goals.
(d) Selection of the most appropriate way or theoretical solution.
(e) Testing the validity of the theoretical solution.

TYPES OR KINDS OF REASONING

Reasoning may be classified into two broad types—Inductive reasoning and Deductive reasoning. Below we try to discuss them briefly.

Inductive Reasoning

In this type of reasoning, we proceed from particular facts to a general conclusion. Experimentations and observations form the basis of this reasoning. On the basis of the facts observed and experienced under similar conditions, we try to discover universal relations or generalization. For example, the following reasoning is the inductive reasoning:

Ram is mortal;
Karim is mortal;
Mohan is mortal;
Edward is mortal;
Therefore, all men are mortal.

In this way, in inductive reasoning, from many particular truths or judgements, universal truth or judgement is inferred.

Deductive Reasoning

In Inductive reasoning, we start by completely agreeing with some already discovered or pre-established generalized fact or principle and try to apply it to particular cases.

For example the following reasoning is deductive:

All men are mortal;
I am a man;
Therefore, I am mortal.

In this way, in deductive reasoning we try to apply the universal truth or generalized principle in solving particular problems.

Training in Reasoning

Reasoning plays a significant role in one's adjustment to one's environment. Not only does it control one's cognitive activities, but also the total behaviour and personality is influenced by proper or improper development of one's reasoning ability. Therefore proper care should be taken in developing reasoning powers of children.

As pointed out earlier, reasoning is said to be a typical thinking – a productive and advanced stage in the complex process of one's thinking. Therefore what has been said earlier in the case of training in thinking equally applies to the training in reasoning. It is better not to repeat it. The cultivation of proper habits of correct thinking will surely improve one's reasoning ability. However the following points deserve mention in this connection:

(i) Intelligence and hard-working attitude coupled with strong motive and firm determination helps much in the strenuous and persistent efforts of reasoning. Therefore, we should take care of these factors in developing reasoning ability.

(ii) For proper reasoning, it is essential to have adequate insight in the problem in hand. It requires adequate knowledge and experiences. Therefore, children should be stimulated to enrich their experiences and make efforts to increase the span of their knowledge.

(iii) Initially, children should be encouraged to employ induction for their reasoning process so that they may acquire the ability to reason independently. Later on they must also be trained in making use of deduction. But in no case, they should blindly follow the deduced results. They should be acquainted with the process of deriving these results so that they may apply them intelligently.

(iv) Reasoning is said to be a systematic and organized thinking that follows some systematic steps. Children should be given proper knowledge of these steps and encouraged to proceed systematically in their reasoning.

(v) Logic is said to be the science of correct reasoning. It provides a body of rules for examining the validity of our reasoning. Therefore, adequate training in logic should be imparted to children.

PROBLEM-SOLVING—MEANING AND NATURE

Everyone of us is constantly facing one problem or the other. There are needs and motives that ought to be satisfied. For this purpose definite goals or aims are set. In an attempt to realize them, one experiences obstacles and interferences. It poses a problem for him that needs serious attention and a deliberate effort on his part to overcome the obstacle or interference in the attainment of the objectives. For this purpose, one has to set oneself to think and reason and proceed systematically in a scientific manner.

The productive work as a whole discussed above is known as problem-solving. It has been found very useful for the progress of the individual as well as society. The meaning and nature of this term can be made clearer still through the following definitions.

Woodworth and Marquis

Problem-solving behaviour occurs in novel or difficult situations in which a solution is not obtainable by the habitual methods of applying concepts and principles derived from past experience in very familiar situations. (1948, p. 623)

Skinner

Problem-solving is a process of overcoming difficulties that appear to interfere with the attainment of a goal. It is a procedure of making adjustment in spite of interferences. (1968, p. 539)

Analysis of the above definitions brings the following facts into the limelight with regard to the meaning and nature of problem-solving behaviour.

(i) In the satisfaction of one's needs and realization of the set goals, problem-solving behaviour arises only when (a) the goal is quite purposeful and essential for the individual, (b) there is serious interference in the realization of this goal, (c) this interference or obstacle cannot be overcome by simple habitual acts or mechanical trial and error methods.

(ii) The individual has to utilize his thinking and reasoning powers and engage in serious mental work (by following some well organized systematic scientific steps) for the removal of the difficulties and obstacles.

(iii) The problem-solving behaviour involves quite deliberate, conscious and serious efforts on the part of the problem-solver.

(iv) Problem-solving behaviour helps in the removal or adjustment with interferences and ultimately makes an individual reach his goal and satisfaction of his motives.

(v) Problem-solving behaviour helps an individual in the growth and development of his personality and making him happy and wiser by getting him adequately adjusted. It also contributes a lot towards the progress and development of society.

So based on the above study *problems-solving behaviour may be understood as a deliberate and purposeful act on the part of an individual to realize the set goals or objectives by inventing some novel methods or following some planned steps for the removal of the interference and obstacles on the path of the realization of these goals, when usual methods like trial and error, habit formation and conditioning, fail.*

SCIENTIFIC METHOD OF PROBLEM-SOLVING

The question arises as to which scientific procedure should be followed in a problem-solving behaviour? Let us describe its systematic steps.

1. **Problem-awareness:** The first step in the problem-solving behaviour of an individual concerns his awareness of the difficulty or problem that needs a solution. He must be confronted with some obstacle or interference in the path of the realization of his needs or motives and consequently he must be conscious of the felt difficulty or problem.
2. **Problem-understanding:** The difficulty or problem felt by the individual should be properly identified by a careful analysis. He should be clear about the problem. The problem should then be pinpointed in terms of specific goals and objectives. Thus all the difficulties and obstacles in the path of the solution must be properly named and all that would go in the problem-solving efforts should then be properly analyzed.
3. **Collection of Relevant Information:** In this step, the individual is required to collect all the relevant information about the problem through all the possible sources. He may consult experienced persons, read the available literature, revive his old experiences, think of possible solutions and put in all relevant efforts for widening the scope of his knowledge concerning the problem in hand.

4. **Formation of Hypotheses or Hunch for Possible Solutions:** In the light of the collected relevant information and nature of his problem, one may then engage in some serious cognitive activities to think of the various possibilities for the solution of one's problem. As a result, he may start with a few possible solutions of his problem.

5. **Selection of a Proper Solution:** In this important step, all the possible solutions thought of in the previous step are closely analyzed and evaluated. Gates and others (1946) have suggested the following activities in the evaluation of the assumed hypotheses or solution:
   - (i) One should determine the conclusion that completely satisfies the demands of the problem.
   - (ii) One should find out whether the solution is consistent with other facts and principles which have been well-established.
   - (iii) One should make a deliberate search for negative instances that might cast doubts on the conclusion.

   The above suggestions can help the individual think of a proper individual solution of his problem out of the many possible solutions. But for all this, he has to use his own discretion by utilizing his higher cognitive abilities for the proper identification of the appropriate hypothesis or solution by rejecting all other hypotheses.

6. **Verification of the Concluded Solution or Hypothesis:** The solution arrived at or conclusion drawn must be further verified by utilizing it in solving various other likewise problems. In case, the derived solution helps in solving these problems, then and only then is one free to agree with his findings regarding the solution. The verified solution may then become a useful product of his problem-solving behaviour that can be utilized in solving other future problems.

STRATEGIES OF PROBLEM-SOLVING

The task of problem-solving depends to a great extent upon the nature of the problem, the means and material available for its solution and the ability and competency of the problem solver. However, psychologists and educationists, as a result of extensive research in the field of problem-solving, have recommended a few special strategies and tactics that can help a lot in finding the ways of solving the problem in quite an economical and effective way. Let us have a look at the mechanism of a few such useful devices.

Algorithms

Algorithm may be defined as a strategy for generating a solution that exhausts every possible answer till it comes up with the direct solution. It is in fact a set of rules which, when followed, must lead to a solution because it is systematically applied in a specific order to all the possibilities and their outcomes. Let us illustrate the use of algorithm as a strategy for the solution of a problem.

Problem: There is an Anagram UBC. You have to build up a meaningful word using the three letters U, B and C of this given anagram.

Solution: Using algorithms, we will put the three letters U, B and C in every possible combinations like, C B U, B U C, B C U, U C B until the correct order C U B (a meaningful word) is found.

In this way, the use of algorithms may help us a lot in finding the solution of our problem. However, their use and application need a very cautious approach. It has its own shortcomings and limitations like those listed below:

- Algorithms cannot be applied to every situation as they do not exist for many problems.
- These are quite expensive in terms of the time and energy as one has to test all the available alternatives and hypotheses for arriving at the final solution. It may make the problem-solver tired, bored, or fatigued before reaching the final stage of the solution.
- Their use also may prove impracticable except for a few simple problems.

Heuristics

In comparison to algorithms, heuristics as a strategy of problem-solving are more economical in terms of time and labour. Their use and application are also simple and less demanding. As a matter of definition, *these heuristics represent such problem-solving strategies in which we make use of some mental shortcuts or rules of thumb for restructuring a problem in a certain way to arrive at its quick solution.*

The weakness of the heuristics is the fact that there is no guarantee of finding the correct solution of the desired problem. One may or may not arrive at the correct solution with such shortcuts. The application is simple, less time consuming, least tiring or boring to the individual but the correctness of the solution is not so sure as in the use of algorithms. The use of algorithms, however tiresome, lengthy and time consuming may be, always results in a hundred per cent guarantee of the correctness of the arrived solution at the end. However, as a quicker and fast means of finding the solution of the problems, the use of heuristics is quite commendable. The most commonly used heuristics as a problem-solving strategy may be named as under:

(i) Sub-Goal Analysis
(ii) Means-End Analysis
(iii) Working Backward
(iv) Using an Analogy

Let us discuss their application in problem-solving one by one.

Sub-Goal Analysis

In this strategy, the complex goal or target reached for the solution of a problem is divided into easily attainable sub-goals. In other words, a complex problem is reduced to a series (or hierarchy) of smaller, more easily solvable problems. It is similar to covering a long, tedious and difficult journey by dividing it into short easily coverable lengths instead of feeling frustrated by resorting to its coverage at a single stretch.

Means-End Analysis

While solving a problem, it is always better to have a proper analysis of the nature of the problem in perfect coordination with the means, materials and resources in our hand. Where we have to reach, what needs to be done, what type of solution does the problem need, all these issues should be carefully analyzed with respect to the means available for coping with these issues.

Hence the Means-end Analysis strategy for the solution of the problems stands for:

(a) The identification of the difference between the current state and the one that is desired in relation to the nature and solution of the problem, and then
(b) taking action to reduce this difference for arriving at the solution of the problem.

WORKING BACKWARD

While using this strategy for the solution of one's problem, one has to start with the desired result (What is to be found out or aimed at) and try to work backwards until the initial state is attained. For example, suppose we have a problem in geometry : Prove that the sum of the three angles of a triangle is equal to two right angles.

Here while making use of 'working backward strategy' we will start from the end, the concluded result and then may proceed as under:

- The three angles of a triangle are equal to two right angles.
- Which one of the angles is equal to two right angles? Surely it is called a straight angle?
- How can we demonstrate the three angles of a triangle through a straight angle?
- Which one of the three sides of the given triangle is to be extended for the construction of a straight angle?
- How can this straight angle be proved as equal to the sum of the three angles of the given triangle.

In this way, we can utilize such backward chaining for discovering the proof of a given geometrical theorem.

Similarly, we can utilize this working backward strategy in solving the problems related to other areas of knowledge. In case you have forgotten where you kept the key of a room, you can find by working backward. You are at present here but where were you prior to your arrival at the present place and thinking in retrospect about the place of your presence or working, you would certainly remember your misplaced or forgotten keys. Let us further substantiate the use of this working backward strategy by employing it in the solution of the following problem.

"Divide 100 into such four parts, that is (*i*) one part is multiplied by four, (*ii*) second is divided by four, (*iii*) in the third we add four and (*iv*) from fourth if we subtract four, the results in all the four cases remain in the form of same figure. For the solution of such problems, we always start from the end by following the sequence as under:

$$(x/4) + (4x) + (x - 4) + (x + 4) = 100$$

or

$$x + 16x + 4x + 4x = 400 - 16 + 16 = 400$$

or

$$25x = 400$$

or

$$x = 16$$

In this way, we can divide 100 into the parts.

(16/4), (16 × 4), (16 – 4), (16 + 4), *i.e.*, 4, 64, 12, 20 the sum of which is equal to the given figure 100.

USING AN ANALOGY

In this strategy one makes use of one's own experience, training and practice work carried out for the solution of the likewise problems. Here while solving a particular problem, one formulates or hypothesizes a problem similar to the problem in hand, but with a known solution; and this known solution is then used to devise a solution for the current problem. We make use of this strategy in finding the solution of any new problem faced by us by searching for its analogy in any of the problem faced and solved by us in the past. Every textbook of mathematics of any class duly emphasizes this strategy. To begin with any topic, it provides certain problems with their proper solutions, as illustrations or examples for developing understanding about the ways of solving these problems. Afterwards it provides a number of similar problems for the drill or practice work. Students then try to adopt the analogy strategy for the solution of these drill or practice work problems. They simply search for the analogy between the problems in hand. The previous experience gained through the understanding of the solved examples help them to find out the solution for the current problems.

FACTORS AFFECTING PROBLEM-SOLVING

Every one of us in life faces one or the other problems at one or the other time. We make our attempts with all the resources in our hand for finding out the solution of these problems. In doing so, many times we get success but it may not be so always. There are so many things that may be held responsible for our success or failure in finding the solution of the problems. Actually these things or factors which, one way or the other are attributed as the cause for our success or failure in the problem-solving behaviour, are generally known as the factors affecting problem-solving. There are a number of such factors which may be broadly put into two categories. In the first category we may include the factors that are directly linked with the nature and type of the problem and in the second category, we may include the factors that may have a direct relation with the nature and capacities of the problem solver and his approach to problem-solving. Let us now discuss the various things and factors affecting one's problem-solving behaviour under the heads of this two fold classification.

Factors Inherent in the Nature of the Problem

The problem-solving behaviour depends to a great extent on the nature of the problem. Some of the important factors or the attributes related with the nature of the problem may be outlined as

- The simplicity or complexity of the problem.
- The size or shape of the problem.
- Appropriate or inappropriate defining of the problem.
- The nature of the definiteness of the problem.
- Its similarity or analogy with the problems experienced or solved in the past.
- The nature of the help available from the present circumstances and resources at hand.
- The effect of the unfavourable circumstances or lack of resources in the solution of the problem.

Factors Associated with the Problem Solver

The problem solving behaviour also depends much on the factors associated with the nature, capacities and many other things inherent in the problem solver. These things or factors related with the problem solver may be outlined as under.

LEVEL OF PREVIOUS LEARNING OR TRAINING

One can solve a problem easily if it has some connection with one's past experiences or specific training received for the solution of similar problems. Hence the level of proficiency gained through some learning or training of one or the other types of problems always works as a deciding factor for the problem-solving behaviour of an individual.

INTEREST AND MOTIVATIONAL LEVEL OF THE PROBLEM SOLVER

Interest and motivation are known as the key factors and moving forces behind any activity or behaviour carried out by an individual. It equally applies to one's problem-solving behaviour. The nature of the interest and motivation thus should always be regarded as important factors affecting one's problem-solving behaviour. It is one's interest and motivation in terms of seeking the desired goals, motives, satisfaction of needs, etc. that makes one do all that one does for the solution of the problem.

ANALYSIS OF THE PROBLEM BY THE PROBLEM SOLVER

Every problem needs its careful analysis for a desired solution. One who does not care for an appropriate analysis of his problem is bound to suffer in finding the solution of his problem. It is through the analysis of the problem that one knows many things essential for solving the problem. What is the problem? What is its nature? What is given in the problem? What do we have to find out in the problem? In how many ways is it similar to other problems solved in the past? What type of help is available for finding the solution of the problem? Thus there are many issues, the solution of which can only be found through a systematic and careful analysis of the problem. Those individuals who care and know the techniques of the proper analysis of a problem thus may always get success in solving their problem in comparison to others who either do not care or do not know the proper way of the analysis of a given problem.

MENTAL SET

Our problem-solving behaviour depends much on a particular type of mental set-up woven around the ways and means of finding the solution of one or the other types of problems. It is on account of our previous learning and experiences that go deep into our nature, giving birth to a certain fixed type of problem-solving behaviour. As a result we always try to solve a given problem in the light of a mental picture of its solution already set in our mind. Thus mental set may be regarded as way of perceiving the things in the light of their *mental images already fixed in our mind on account of the past experiences or habit formation.* Consequently influenced by our mental set, we try to solve a problem in the ways and means covered through our mental set. Let us illustrate the effect of the mental set on the problem-solving behaviour through an example.

Suppose, you are asked that there were 12 oranges of which you have taken 5 oranges, tell how many oranges would then be lying with you. The correct answer is 5 but most of us would say 7. Why do people commit such a mistake? It is certainly on account of the strong impact of their mental set-up to make use of the process of mathematical addition or subtraction in finding out the solution of such problems. Their mind is already set to work in a particular direction to find the solution of such similar computational problems by adding or subtracting. When asked, "what's lying with you," they just worked according to the set direction—finding the result through subtraction which resulted in a faulty solution of the given problem.

FUNCTIONAL FIXEDNESS

Functional fixedness refers to our rigidity or fixedness in our functions or ways of behaving. As a result, we always tend to provide similar responses to the same stimuli. We have a fixed pattern of problem-solving behaviour for the solution of a particular type of problem. We can't think of any alternative or new solution other than the one habitually adopted by us for their solution. It may work in those cases when the problems faced are quite similar to those faced earlier. However, the results are not always as desirable or satisfactory as they should be. Mere repetition or reproduction of such problem-solving behaviour can't help us to devise more suitable, economical and rewarding ways of problem solving. Moreover, in many situations we may face a lot of difficulties and obstacles in finding the solution of the problems which are somewhat new or differ from the old ones in some or the other aspects (no matter how minutely it may be). Our functional fixedness does not allow us to experiment something new for the solution of these problems and as a result we are bound to waste our energy, time and resources due to our beating about the bush. We can't just see the new perspectives for the solution of the problem which are more simple, practicable and rewarding only on account of the fixedness or rigidity of our problem-solving behaviour.

One who can overcome such functional fixedness in such a situation, is sure to win the race. He may find the most appropriate solution of the given problem by adopting new ways and means by giving his rigidity or fixedness of the problem-solving behaviour. Hence we must always be careful about the obstruction mechanism of the rigidity or fixedness of our problem-solving behaviour and should always follow a dynamic and flexible approach for developing originality, creativity and inventiveness in our problem-solving behaviour.

MENTAL AND PHYSICAL STATES OF THE PROBLEM SOLVER

The mental and physical states of an individual at the time of solving a problem definitely exercise their favourable or unfavourable impact over the processes and products of his problem-solving behaviour. If one is alert, attentive, capable and active in putting in one's physical and mental abilities in the solution of the problem, one is sure to proceed properly on the path of the problem solving. In the opposite case, there will be a lot of difficulties in getting success in the task of problem-solving. Take the case of anxiety, *i.e.*, state of anxiousness. It may help the individual in his problem-solving task as an energizer of his otherwise motivated behaviour, provided it remains within his control. But in case it exceeds and goes out of control, it may prove a great obstacle in the path of problem-solving. The same is true with emotions. One can cross many hurdles in the path of one's problem-solving with the favourable wind and tides of the favoured emotions if he is able to exercise desirable control over their manifestations and reactions. On the other hand, the abruption of untimely emotions at a disproportionate or uncontrolled amount may cost dearly to the individual in his task of problem-solving.

The other important cognitive factors that affect both the processes and products of one's problem-solving behaviour, may be named as (*i*) the ability to think and reason, (*ii*) the nature of attention and concentration, and (*iii*) the power of retention and retrieval. One may get success or failure in his task of problem-solving depending upon the quality and nature of these cognitive factors. If one can think and reason well, pays proper sustained attention to his task, can utilize his past learning and experiences on the basis of his good memory, he is sure to get success in his problem-solving task. Whereas in case of lack of attention, reproduction and ability to think and reason, one may struggle with his problem without any commendable results. In this way, not only the mental state but also the physical states of one's well being effects his problem-solving behaviour favourably or adversely. When one is suffering from headache, stomach ache or any other problems in his body or feeling uncomfortable on account of the seating arrangement, light, ventilation, noise and extremes of weather and climatic conditions, then how can we expect him to be at home with his problem-solving behaviour? In such unfavourable physical state his problem-solving ability is likely to be affected adversely resulting in his under-achievement or failure in the task of problem solving.

TIME SPENT ON SOLVING THE PROBLEM

Every problem needs it own time for its solution. Hence the minimum desired time spent on solution should depend upon its nature and complexity from the viewpoint of the problem solver. However, in case one is in haste or does not care to give required time to the solution of his problem, he may not get the desired success.

The utilization of the time in problem-solving may also be considered from another angle. If we take some rest or get ourselves engaged in some recreational or other work activities, that period may also be counted as spent, although unconsciously, on the solution of the problem. This time related phenomenon is named as 'incubation' in the language of psychology. It often happens that we do not find the solution of our problem despite our constant efforts and struggling with it. What do we do then? We suspend or give up our attempts. As an alternative we may take some rest, go to sleep, engage ourselves in some recreational or work activities and thus remain physically away from our problem. However, during this time, we mentally do not go away from our problem. Our unconscious mind may continuously work towards the solution of the problem and as a result we suddenly get the way of solving the problem. The solution so found through our unconscious attempts in the absence of actual conscious efforts is said to be the consequence of the mechanism of incubation. In this way, the unconscious efforts through incubation affects one's problem solving behaviour in a big way.

As a conclusion we can say that there are many factors or things lying within the problem solver and the environment available for the solution of the problem that go in a big way for influencing and affecting the processes and products of one's problem solving behaviour. However, much depends upon the abilities and capacities of the problem solver including his interests, attitudes, level of aspiration and motivation, determination and will power for finding out the solution of his problem. If one is set for reaching one's goal, one is bound to get success in spite of heavy odds and barriers in the path of one's problem solving.

SUMMARY

Thinking refers to a pattern of behaviour in which we make use of internal representation (in the form of symbols, signs etc.) of the things and events for the solution of some specific problem. It is always directed to achieve some end or purpose and is essentially a inner cognitive process that is carried out with the help of mental manipulation of the objects, activities and experiences.

Tools employed in the process of thinking usually consists of images (mind pictures of the actual objects, experiences and activities) concepts (generalized idea about a thing, person or event), symbols and signs (like '+' or '–', railway signals, badges or flags) and language.

All genuine and purposeful thinking may be classified into certain specific types like perceptual or concrete thinking, conceptual or abstract thinking, reflective thinking and creative thinking. In the development of thinking, among children, we can start from the first and then the second form, *i.e.* concrete and abstract thinking but in its developed and higher form, we should always aim for the development of reflective and creative thinking among them.

The measures for the development of effective and correct thinking among our children may include adequacy of their knowledge and experiences, adequacy of their motivation and definiteness of aim, adequate freedom and flexibility, incubation, intelligence and wisdom proper development of concept and language and adequacy of the reasoning process.

Reasoning refers to a specialized higher type of thinking carried out through some well organized systematic steps for the mental exploration or solution of a felt problem. It is of two types

– inductive and deductive. In inductive reasoning we try to arrive at a generalized principle or conclusion on the basis of the facts observed and experienced under similar conditions. In deductive reasoning, we start by completely agreeing with some deduced result or principle and then try to apply it to particular cases.

For the development of reasoning power among our children, we must begin with the cultivation of the proper habits of correct thinking. For better results, it should then be supplemented by the inculcation of good habits and practices like hardworking attitude and firm determination, adequate insight into the felt problem, inductive approach followed by deduction, being systematic and organized in thinking and adequate training in the logical analysis etc.

Problem solving refers to a deliberate and purposeful act on the part of an individual aiming to realize some set goals or objectives by making use of some novel methods, higher thinking and systematic steps. The systematic steps followed in a scientific method of problem-solving may be identified as problem awareness, problem understanding, collection of relevant information, formulation of hypotheses, selection of a proper solution, and verification of the arrived solution.

Strategies of effective problems solving refer to those special strategies and tactics that can help a lot in finding the ways of solving the problem in quite an economic and effective way. Usually these may include algorithms, (strategy to generate a solution by exhausting every possible answer for ending up with the correct solution) and heuristics, the rule of thumb for arriving at a quick solution like sub goal analysis, means–end analysis, working backward and using an analogy etc.

Problem solving behaviour of an individual depends upon a number of factors broadly classified in two categories–factors lying in the nature of the problem (like its simplicity or complexity, its similarity or dissimilarity with the problem solved in the past etc.) and factors associated with the problem solver like his level of previous learning, interest and motivation, way of solving the problem, his mind set, functional fixedness, mental and physical status and the time spent by him on solving the problem and the situation and facilities available for him in his environment at the time of problem solving etc.

References and Suggested Readings

Boune, L.E, Dominowski, R.L., and Loftus, E.F., *Cognitive Processes*, Prentice-Hall, Englewood Cliffs, New Jersey, 1979.

Bartlett, F., *Thinking*, Basic Books, New York, 1958.

Boring, E.C., Langfield, H.S. and Weld, H.P. (Eds.), *Foundation of Psychology*, John Wiley, New York, 1961.

Bransford, J.D. and Stein, B.S., *The Ideal Problem Solver: A Guide for Improving Thinking, Learning and Creativity*, Freeman, New York, 1984.

Burner, J.S., Goodnow, J.J. and Austina, G.A., *A Study of Thinking*, John Wiley, New York, 1956.

Davis, G.A., *Psychology of Problem Solving*, Basic Books, New York, 1973.

Fantino, E. and Reynolds, G., *Introduction to Contemporary Psychology*, W.H. Freeman, San Francisco, 1975.

Levin, M.J., *Psychology: A Biographical Approach*, McGraw-Hill, New York, 1978.

Mohsin, S.M., *Elementary Psychology*, Asia Publishing House, Calcutta, 1967.

Munn, J.L., *An Introduction to Psychology*, Oxford & IBH, New Delhi, 1967.

Mangal, S.K., *Advanced Educational Psychology,* Prentice-Hall of India, New Delhi, 1993.

Roediger, H.L., Rushton, J.P. et. al., *Psychology,* 2nd ed., Little Brown, Boston, 1987.

Skinner, C.E. (Ed), *Essentials of Educational Psychology*, Prentice-Hall, Englewood Cliffs, New Jersey, 1968.

Stagner, R. and Karwoski, T.F., Quoted by L.D. Crow and A. Crow, *Educational Psychology*, Eurasia Publishing House, New Delhi, 1973.

Valentine, C.W., *Psychology and its Bearing on Education,* The English Language Book Society & Methuen, London, 1965.

Vinacke, W.E., *The Psychology of Thinking*, 2nd ed., McGraw-Hill, New York, 1974.

Wortheimer, M., *Productive Thinking*, Harper, New York, 1945.

Woodworth, R.S. and Marquis, D.G., *Psychology*, 5th ed., Henry Holt, New York, 1948.

31

The Concept and Structure of Personality

CHAPTER COMPOSITION

- The concept of Personality
- Meaning and Definitions of the Term Personality
- Structure of Personality
- Summary
- References and Suggested Readings

THE CONCEPT OF PERSONALITY

To throw some light on the concept of personality, we can consider this issue in the following steps:

1. Wrong notions and misconceptions about personality
2. Meaning and definitions of the term personality
3. Facts regarding personality
4. Structure of personality (as explained through various theories).

Let us discuss them one by one.

Certain Wrong Notions and Misconceptions

Let us first make ourselves acquainted with the wrong notions and misconceptions about the term 'personality'.

Etymologically, the word *personality* has been derived from the Latin word 'persona'. At first this word was used for the mask worn by the actors to change their appearance but later on, it began to be used for the actors themselves. Since then, the term 'personality' has been used to depict outward appearance or external behaviour etc. It is in this sense that we have developed a wrong notion about the term 'personality'. We often listen to comments like this man has a fine or magnetic personality or that man has a poor personality. We try to paste such labels as fine, good or poor on individuals on the basis of their physical make-up, their manner of walking, talking, dressing and a host of other similar characteristics.

Sometimes, we use personality as equivalent to one's character. This too is a wrong notion. Character is, by all means, a moral or ethical term which refers to the standards of right and wrong, whereas personality is purely a psychological term and hence it is not proper to use it in reference to the study of ethical values.

Moreover, we cannot take personality as an equivalent word for outward appearance or behaviour. It would be a very superficial approach. We cannot ignore the inner aspect of one's personality. Personality includes the totality of one's behaviour and hence, both inner and outer (covert as well as overt) behaviour should be taken into consideration.

MEANING AND DEFINITIONS OF THE TERM PERSONALITY

Psychologically speaking, personality is all that a person is. It is the totality of one's behaviour towards oneself as well as others. It includes everything about the person, his physical, emotional, social, mental and spiritual make-up. It is all that a person has about him.

So definitely, the term personality signifies something deeper than mere appearance or outward behaviour. How should it be given a proper meaning or definition is a difficult problem. Actually subjective nature does not allow to reach to a clear-cut, well agreed definition. That is why, it has been defined by many psychologists in so many ways according to their own points of view. Let us first begin with J.B. Watson (1930) the famous behaviourist. He defined personality in the words given below.

Personality is the sum of activities that can be discovered by actual observations over a long enough period of time to give reliable information. (1930)

Thus, Watson gives emphasis on the behaviour of an individual and considers personality as nothing but the useful effect one makes upon the person coming in his close contact.

Morton Prince, accepting the role of both heredity and environment, defines it as:

> *Personality is the sum total of all the biological innate dispositions, impulses, tendencies, appetites and instincts of the individual and the dispositions and tendencies acquired by experience.* (1929, p. 532)

After evaluating 49 definitions of personality written by many eminent persons, Allport summarizes his own concept in the following words:

Personality is a dynamic organization within the individual of those psycho-physical systems that determine his unique adjustment to his environment. (1948, p. 28)

Although Allport has tried to give a comprehensive definition of the term 'personality' by including the words organization, dynamic, psycho-physical system, unique adjustment and environment etc. yet he, like his predecessors, only describes it. By emphasizing merely on theoretical aspect and describing it in terms of behavioural or dynamic concepts, the true nature of personality cannot be understood. Contemporary psychologists like R.B. Cattell and Eysenck have so opined. They very strongly feel that if personality cannot be demonstrated, measured and quantified, it should be called philosophy or art and not personality theory in psychology.

Below we give their ideas vis-a-vis the meaning of the term 'personality'.

R.B. Cattell

Personality is that which permits a prediction of what a person will do in a given situation. (1970, p. 386)

Eysenck

Personality is the more or less stable and enduring organisation of a person's character, temperament, intellect, and physique, which determine his unique adjustment to the environment. (1971, p. 2)

Let us have a close view of the Eysenck's definition. He has tried to make certain terms clear in the following way:

Character denotes a person's more or less stable or enduring system or orgainsation of conative behaviour (*Will*).

Temperament denotes a person's more less stable or enduring organization of affective behaviour (*Emotions*).

Intellect denotes a person's more or less stable or enduring organisation of cognitive behaviour (*intelligence*).

Physique denotes a person's more or less stable or enduring organisation or bodily configuration and neuro-endocrine endowment (*glands + nervous system + bodily configuration*).

Evaluation of Eysenck's Definition

(i) The definition gives a balanced consideration to heredity and environment in building one's personality.

(ii) Eysenck stresses on the concept of structure and organisation and criticises just naming of some of the behavioural characteristics like bricks in describing a home.

(iii) This definition gives personality a physiological base.

(iv) It gives a complete picture of the human behaviour patterns by including cognitive, conative, affective and somatic (constitutional) aspects.

(v) This definition aims at making personality somewhat measurable and assessable and thus gives it a scientific base.

The above-mentioned characteristics do not suggest that Eysenck's definition has explained everything about the term 'personality' nor does it claim that it does not have any weakpoint. Like other definitions, this definition also suffers from some limitations and drawbacks, which are given below.

(i) Eysenck advocates that personality must have a physiological base, but such is not the case always. Due to the very complex nature of personality, we cannot always have a physiological base.

(ii) His definition leads us to form an opinion that personality is fixed and cannot be changed.

This is an extreme approach. It is true that personality should be evaluated on the basis of generality of the behaviour (behaviour must be consistent in a number of situations). However, on the other hand, changes cannot be denied. A person, who is an extrovert, may turn into an introvert depending upon so many intervening factors.

Thus for understanding the concept of personality, the evolution of an ideal definition still needs further research. In fact, concepts like personality are difficult to be explained as they have the identity like sound or electricity where the impact can be felt but their real nature is always undisclosed. Something about them can be known by their utility or by describing some of their characteristics and distinguishing features. Let us seek the meaning of the term 'personality' on similar lines.

SOME GLARING FACTS ABOUT PERSONALITY

Based on our discussions so far, we can conclude the following things about personality:

1. Firstly, personality is something unique and specific. Each one of us is a unique pattern in ourselves. No two individuals, not even identical twins, behave in precisely the same way over a period of time. Everyone of us has specific characteristics for making adjustments.
2. The second main characteristic of personality is self-consciousness. The man is described as a person or as having a personality when the idea of 'self' enters into his consciousness. In this connection H.R. Bhatia (1968) writes. *"We do not attribute personality to a dog and even a child cannot be described as a personality because it has only a vague sense of personal identity."*
3. Personality includes everything about a person. It is all that a person has about him. It includes all the behaviour patterns, i.e. conative, cognitive and affective, and covers not only the conscious activities but goes deeper to semi-conscious and unconscious levels also.
4. It is not just a collection of many traits or characteristics that is known as personality. For instance by only counting the bricks how can we describe the wall of a house? It needs something more and actually personality is more than this: It is an organisation of some psycho-physical systems or some behaviour characteristics and functions as a unified whole. Like when describing an elephant, we cannot say that it is like a pillar only by examining its legs. Similarly by looking at one's physique or sociability, we cannot pass judgement about one's personality. It is only when we carefully study all the aspects—biological as well as social—we can form an idea about his personality.
5. Personality is not static, it is dynamic and ever in the process of change and modification. As we have said earlier, personality is all that a person has about him. It gives him all that is needed for his unique adjustment in his environment. The process of making adjustment to environment is continuous. One has to struggle with the environmental as well as the inner forces throughout one's life. As a result, one has to bring modifications and changes in one's personality patterns and it makes the nature of personality dynamic instead of static.
6. Every personality is the product of heredity and environment. Both contribute significantly towards the development of the child's personality.

7. Learning and acquisition of experiences contribute towards growth and development of one's personality. Every personality is the end product of this process of learning and acquisition.
8. Everyone's personality has one more distinguishing feature, that is aiming to an end or some specific goal. Adler, in his book 'Individual Psychology' opined that a man's personality can be judged through a study and interpretation of the goals he has set for himself to achieve and the approaches he makes to the problems in his life. In this way, he gives a very concise meaning to the personality of an individual by calling it *'lifestyle of an individual'*.

Indeed this short and concise explanation of the term has a wide meaning. It draws a beautiful portrait of an individual's totality. It may be understood as the sum total of one's way of behaving towards oneself as well as others. It also predicts one's nature of behaviour as to how will one behave in a particular situation and one's pattern of adjustment to the everchanging forces of environment.

STRUCTURE OF PERSONALITY

The search for the nature of personality will be rather incomplete if we do not mention some important theories regarding it. This helps us in classifying the people into categories according to their personality characteristics and gives a base for the assessment of their personality. The theories of personality, in general, can be classified into four broad categories according to their modes of approach.

Theories which Adopt Type-approach

The viewpoints of Hippocrates, Kretschmer, Sheldon and Jung belong to this category. They hold that human personalities can be classified into a few clearly defined types and each person can be put in one or the other type according to his personality traits.

Theories which Adopt Trait-approach

Worth mentioning in this category is Cattell's theory of personality. This approach believes in the mathematical analysis and quantification of the personality constituents and helps in the prediction of human behaviour in a particular situation.

Theories which Adopt Type as well as Trait-approach

Eysenck's theory of personality belongs to this category. He goes a step ahead to the approach adopted by Cattell. He not only mentions the personality traits for assessing one's personality but also tries to give definite personality types.

Theories which Adopt Developmental Approach

These are the theories which try to explain the growth and development of personality. The psycho-analytical theory of Freud and theory of Individual Psychology by Adler come under this category.

Let us discuss xsome of these approaches and theories in detail.

Type Approach

the psychologists adopting Type approach advocate that human personalities can be classified into a few clearly defined types and each person can be put in one or the other type depending upon his behavioural characteristics, somatic structure, blood types, fluids in the body, or personality traits. Based on such approach, the physicians of ancient India broadly categorized all human beings into three types. This classification was based on the three basic elements of the body, i.e. *pitt* (bile), *bate* (wind) and *kuff* (mucus). Almost the same approach was followed by the Greek physicians like Hippocrates, one of the disciples of the great philosopher Aristotle. In the subsequent years, many more scholars and psychologists tried to divide persons into certain types depending upon their specific criterion. Let us describe a few of such approaches.

Hippocrates' Classification

According to Hippocrates, the human body consists of four types of humours of fluids—blood, yellow bile, phlegm (mucus) and black bile. The predominance of one of these four types of fluids in one's body gives him unique temperamental characteristics leading to a particular type of personality summarized as in Table 31.1.

Table 31.1 Hippocrates' Classification

Dominance of fluid type in the body	*Personality types*	*Temperamental Characteristics*
Blood	Sanguine	Light hearted, optimistic, happy, hopeful and accommodating.
Yellow bile	Choleric	Irritable, angry but passionate and strong with active imagination.
Phlegm	Phlegmatic	Cold, clam, slow or sluggish, indifferent.
Black bile	Melancholic	Bad tempered, dejected, sad, depressed, pessimistic, deplorable and self-involved.

Kretschmer's Classification

Kretschmer classified all human beings into certain biological types according to their physical structure and has allotted definite personality characteristics associated with each physical make-up as given in Table 31.2.

Table 31.2 Kretschmer's Personality Types

Personality types	*Personality characteristics*
I. Pyknic (having fat bodies)	Sociable, jolly, easy going and good natured.
II. Athletic (balanced body)	Energetic, optimistic and adjustable.
III. Leptosomatic (lean and thin)	Unsociable, reserved, shy, sensitive and pessimistic.

SHELDON'S CLASSIFICATION

Like Kretschmer, he also classified human beings into certain types according to their physical structures and attached certain temperamental characteristics to them as given in Table 31.3 (also Figure 31.1)

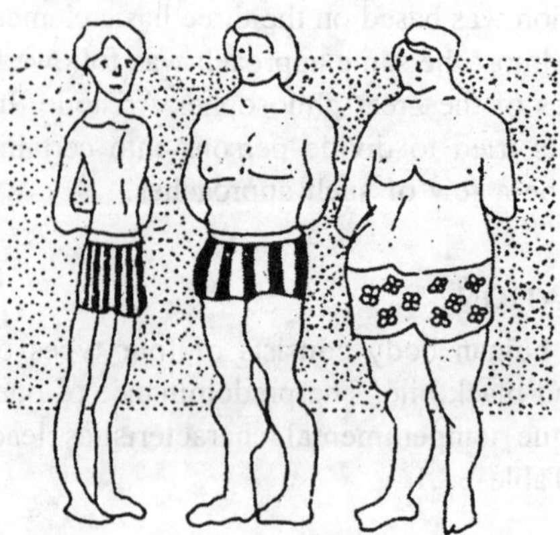

Fig. 31.1 Sheldon's personality types.

Table 31.3 Sheldon's Personality Types

Personality types	*Somatic or body structure description*	*Personality characteristics*
(i) Endomorphic	Person having highly developed viscera but weak somatic structure. (Like Kretschmer's Pyknic type).	Easy going, sociable and affectionate.
(ii) Mesomorphic	Balanced development of viscera and somatic structure. (Like Kretschmer's Athletic type).	Craving for muscular activity, self-assertive, loves risk and adventure.
(iii) Ectomorphic	Weak somatic structure as well as undeveloped viscera. (Like Kretschmer's Leptosomatic).	Pessimistic, unsociable and reserved.

The approach adopted by the above psychologists to classify on the basis of correlation between structure of the body and personality characteristics, is lopsided. It is somewhat misleading. There does not exist such perfect body-mind or body-heart correlation as the propagators of these approaches have assumed.

JUNG'S CLASSIFICATION

He divided all human beings basically into two distinct types—Introvert and Extrovert—according to their social participation and the interest they take in social activities. Later on, he further sharpened his two-fold division by giving sub-types. In this process, he took into consideration the four psychological functions—thinking, feeling, sensation and intuition—in relation to his previous extrovert and introvert types. We will describe this classification in details later in the chapter.

FRIEDMAN AND ROSENMAN'S CLASSIFICATION

This classification of personality type is given by Meyer Friedman and Ray Rosenman. It classifies the people into two personality types, type A and type B, on the basis of their personality traits and then points out which type of people are more prone to heart ailments particularly coronary heart disease.

In coronary heart disease, there is malfunctioning of the heart on account of the deficiency in supply and circulation of the blood through arteries and veins. For a long time it was thought that cholesterol deposits in the arteries and veins obstructs the free flow of blood which in turn proves a potent factor for the deficiency in supply and circulation of blood to the heart. Friedman and Rosenman with the active assistance of some medical experts tried to establish through their researches that stress is an important causative factor for the coronary heart disease. They further established that a particular type of people possessing a set of particular personality traits named as type A are more prone to the stress producing behavior in sharp contrast to the people belonging to type B. They further outlined the typical personality traits associated with these personality types 'A' and 'B' in the following way.

A Type Personality

Emotionally unstable, tense, worried, irritating, competitive, high achieving motive, moody, indifferent, active and restless, aggressive, crazy, perfectionist, idealist, rigid, much worried about punctuality and rules, hasty, jealous, dissatisfied with the self and others, suspicious, sensitive, insecure, believer in action and not in fate and fortune, etc.

B Type Personality

Emotionally stable, tension-free, happy and jolly, average achieving motive, insensitive, patient, self-satisfied, calm and quite flexible, tolerant, realist, optimist, having faith and trust in one's self and others, adjusted to one's self and others, believer in the philosophy of fate and fortune, sincere but not too serious about the execution and result of the work etc.

Trait Approach

The approach that makes use of the personality traits for identifying and describing the personality of an individual is known as Trait approach. The main propagators of this approach are the famous psychologists Gordon Allport and R.B. Cattell. Let us know about their attempts in this direction.

ALLPORT'S TRAIT APPROACH

G.B. Allport (1897-1967) was the first personality theorist who adopted trait approach in providing a theory of personality. According to Allport, personality trait are the basic units of the structure of our personality. Allport tried to search these basic units of human behaviour. The problem before him was to decide the number of personality traits representing the human behaviour in its totality. He, along with one of his colleagues listed 17,953 words in the English language with the help of available dictionaries for the description of the personality or behaviour of human beings. After analysis and rejection of the words on the basis of synonym and inappropriateness, he arrived at 4,541 words for classifying these into three main types named as cardinal traits, central traits and secondary traits.

Cardinal Traits are the most active and dominant traits of one's personality. Although present in a very small number as one or two, these are enough to colour the personality according to their characteristics. As an example we can cite sense of humour as a cardinal trait in one's personality. This trait may colour a person's personality in a specific way so much so that he may be identified or known through his behaviour almost dominated by the sense of humor at all the times and occasions.

Central Traits are those traits that are frequently employed for identifying and describing one's personality, e.g., honesty, kindness, timidity, shyness, rigidity, cruelty etc. Usually seven or eight such central traits are enough for knowing and describing the personality of an individual.

Secondary Traits are those traits of an individual's personality that play quite a secondary or insignificant role in the identification and description of one's personality. These are in fact not the essential part of one's personality. That is why these are reflected quite rarely in one's behaviour like a person named as miser, selfish, greedy.

So according to Allport, one's cardinal traits alongwith a few selected central traits may play a dominant and significant role in the proper identification of one's personality from others. Thus, they may provide speciality and separate identification to different individualities of the persons. The rest of the central traits alongwith a few secondary traits can then make a group of common traits which are generally found in most of the people. Hence, in the task of identification, naming and describing the individuals on the basis of their personality characteristics or traits, we should mainly take into account the cardinal and central traits present in their behaviour.

CATTELL'S TRAIT APPROACH

R.B. Cattell, a British-born American researcher, tried to further advance the trait approach advocated by Allport. For this he made use of the same 17,953 dictionary words pointed out by Allport (capable of describing human behaviour and personality) for arriving at some fundamental dimensions or factors for the measurement of one's personality through the following simple non-technical description.

1. He began his task in 1956 with approximately 4,000 of Allport's 17,953 terms and narrowed the list down to 171 by eliminating the repeated ones and synonyms. In this way, he arrived at the final list of 171 words (dictionary words) related with personality and called them *trait elements.*
2. The next step was to find out how they are related. He found that each trait element correlated high with some and low with others. In this way, he managed to form some specific groups and called them *Surface Traits.* These identified surface traits were 35 in number.
3. He once again went on to examine these surface traits in terms of their inter correlations. There was overlapping. The removal of such overlapping gave him the desired basic dimensions which he called *Source Traits, i.e.,* the real structure influence underlying personality.
4. He ultimately concluded that *16 Factors or Basic Dimensions* of personality given below are sufficient to describe one's personality. Each of these factors may be seen to carry a set of opposite personality traits, i.e., Relaxed V/s Tense or Practical V/s Imaginative etc. as shown in the Table 31.4.

Table 31.4 The Set of Personality Traits Existing in Cattell's Sixteen Personality Factors

Name of the factor	*Trait*	*Opposite trait*
A	Reserved	Outgoing
B	Less intelligent	More intelligent
C	Affected by feelings	Emotionally Stable
E	Submissive	Dominant
F	Serious	Happy-go-Lucky
G	Expedient	Conscientious
H	Timid	Venturesome
I	Tough-minded	Sensitive
L	Trusting	Suspicious
M	Practical	Imaginative
N	Forthright	Shrewd
O	Self-assured	Apprehensive
Q1	Conservative	Experimenting
Q2	Group-dependent	Self-sufficient
Q3	Uncontrolled	Controlled
Q4	Relaxed	Tense

5. Cattell made use of his 16 factors or basic dimensions of the personality in the construction of a personality inventory known as Cattell's Sixteen Personality Factors or Sixteen P.F. Inventory. This inventory is widely used for the measurement of the personality. In this way, efforts made by R.B. Cattell to know and measure one's personality using trait approach may be said to be appreciable.

FURTHER DEVELOPMENT IN TRAIT APPROACH

Further researches in the field of trait conception of the personality have highlighted the repetition and similarity of the terms used by Cattell for describing human behaviour in terms of 16 dimensions. For example, there stands much similarity and high correlation between the traits represented by factors 1 and 16 and also by factors 3 and 7. An individual who is calm is automatically relaxed and one who is tense can be described as emotional or easily upset. Similarly someone who is shy and timid can be described as reserved or unfriendly and an outgoing friendly personality will be also found venturesome. Therefore, the latest researchers have been able to reduce the number of traits as well as the number of dimensions (factors) for describing personality. (Piedment, Mccral and Costa, 1991) as given in Table 31.5.

Table 31.5 Five Dimensions of Personality and the Related Traits

Dimension or Factor	*Traits*
1. Extroversion	Traits like Talkative, sociable and adventurous.
2. Agreeableness	Traits like good natured, cooperative and likeable.
3. Conscientiousness	Traits like demonstrating responsibility, neatness and task motivation.
4. Emotional stability	Traits like calmness, poise and composure.
5. Culture	Traits like intelligence and interest in philosophy and art.

Type-cum-trait Approach

This approach tries to synthesize the type and trait approaches. Starting from the trait approach, it yields definite personality types. The Eysenck theory of personality reflects such an approach.

Eysenck's Theory of Personality

While Cattell tried to give dimensions to personality by giving traits, Eysenck gave it more specification by grouping traits into definite types.

How the individual behaviour is organised and gets the shape of a definite type is revealed in the Fig. 31.2.

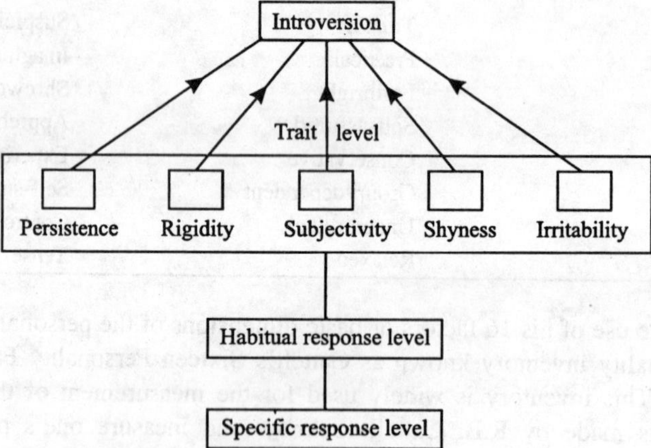

Fig. 31.2 Organisation of individual behaviour.

We have four levels of behaviour organization.

(i) At the lowest level, we have specific responses.
They grow out of particular responses to any single act. For example, 'blushing' is a specific response.

(ii) At the second level, we have habitual responses. If an individual reacts in the similar way, when the same situation reoccurs we get habitual responses. Examples of such habitual response are:
   (a) Not easily making friends.
   (b) Hesitant to talk to strangers etc. are habitual responses.

(iii) At the third level, we have organisation of habitual acts into traits. Similar behaviour acts are said to belong to one group called trait. In the above example, the habitual responses like (a) and (b) give birth to a group of trait called 'Shyness'.

(iv) At the fourth level, we have organisation of these traits into a general type. A type is defined as a group of correlated traits. The traits which are similar in nature give birth to a definite type. Just as in the Fig. 31.2 the traits like persistence, rigidity, shyness etc. have been grouped into a type which is 'Introversion'.

Now at this final stage, ultimately we obtain a definite type. A person, now can be classified as introvert if he has traits as described at level III, habits and habit systems as described at level II and responds specifically as described at level I.

Eysenck has given the following distinct types:

(1) Introversion (2) Extroversion
(3) Neuroticism (4) Psychoticism

He has also tried to link different traits and characteristics with each of these types.

PSYCHO-ANALYTIC APPROACH OF FREUD

This approach for understanding and knowing about personality belongs to the school of psycho-analysis. The famous psychologist Freud is said to be the propounder of this school of thought. Let us try to have a look at the ideas and thoughts propagated by Freud through his psycho-analytic approach.

1. Basic instincts are the basic guiding factors of human behaviour. Two of these instincts play quite an effective role in this direction. These are known as Life and Death instincts. While **life instinct** provides a burning desire and positive urge to remain alive and lead the life in a satisfactory way, the **death instinct** builds up a negative attitude towards life and guides one's behaviour towards destruction, revolt, aggression or detachment and suicidal tendencies.
2. Human behaviour is by all means centred around the sex needs. The adjustment or maladjustment in one's life mostly depends upon the degree of the gratification of one's sex needs.
3. Mind or psyche plays quite a significant role in directing one's behaviour. According to Freud, human mind or psyche can be divided into three compartments in the form of conscious, semi-conscious and unconscious. These three divisions of human mind are responsible for the three types of human behaviour, namely conscious, semi-conscious and unconscious. The unconscious behaviour being 9/10 part of the total behaviour, always dominates the total behavioural aspects and personality make-up of an individual.
4. Freud put up the idea that the anatomy of our personality is built around the three unified and interrelating systems—Id, Ego and Super Ego—occupying their positions as shown in Fig. 31.3.

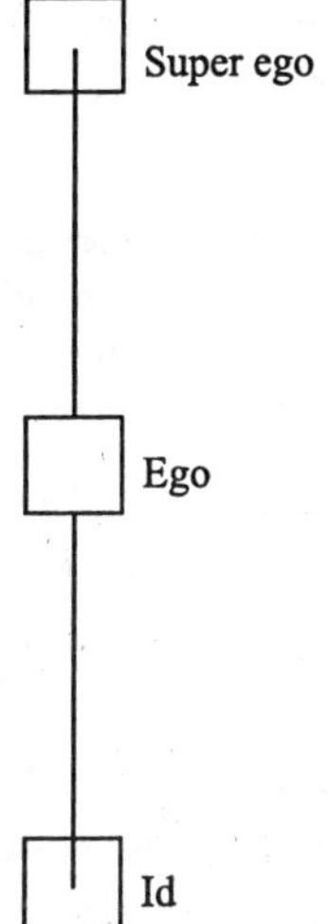

Fig 31.3 Relative position of Id, ego and super ego.

The Id is the raw, savage and immoral basic stuff of a man's personality that is hidden in the deep layers of one's unconscious mind. It consists of such ambitions, desires, tendencies and appetites of an individual as guided by pleasure seeking principle. It has no values, knows no laws, follows no rules, does not consider right from wrong and considers only the satisfaction of its needs and appetites.

Obviously, the Id cannot be allowed to discharge its energy wildly and irresponsibly and thereby a second system, the ego functions as a policeman to check the unlawful activities of the Id. It is the executive with Veto powers. It follows the principle of reality and acts with intelligence in controlling, selecting and deciding what appetites have to be satisfied and in which way these are to be satisfied.

The third system of personality is super ego. It is the ethical moral arm of the personality. It is idealistic and does not care for realities. Perfection is its goal rather than pleasure. It is a decision-making body which decides what is bad or good, virtue or vice according to the standard of society that it accepts.

The above mentioned constituents of personality play a significant role in deciding the personality of an individual. Let us see how.

1. The individuals who have a strong or powerful ego are said to have a strong or balanced personality because in their cases, ego is capable of maintaining proper balance between super ego and Id.
2. In case an individual possesses a weak ego, he is bound to have a maladjusted personality. Here two situations may arise. In one situation the super ego may be more powerful than ego. In such a case, it would not provide a desirable outlet for the repressed wishes and impulses. Consequently, it may lead to the formation of a neurotic personality. In another situation, Id may prove more powerful than ego. The person, thus may engage himself in unlawful or immoral activities leading towards the formation of a delinquent personality.

Freud tried to explain the gradual development of the human personality through his well-known concept of psycho-sexual development explained in detail as under.

According to Freud, sex is the life urge or fundamental motive in life. All physical pleasures arising from any of the organs or any of the functions are ultimately sexual in nature. Sexuality is not the characteristic of only the grown-ups. Children from the very beginning also have sexual desires. This, he termed as infantile sexuality. A child passes through the following five stages with respect to his psycho-sexual development:

The Oral Stage: According to Freud, mouth represents the first sex organ for providing pleasure to the child. The beginning is made with the pleasure received from the mother's nipple or the bottle. Thereafter, it is used to derive pleasure by putting anything like candy, stick, his own thumb, etc. in his mouth.

The Anal Stage: At this stage, the interest of the child shifts from mouth (as the erotogenic zone) to the organs of elimination, i.e., anus or the urethra. He receives pleasure by holding back or letting go of the body's waste material through the anus or urethra. This stage, generally, ranges from two to three years.

The Genital Stage: Duration of this phase, in the development of the child, ranges from 4 to 6 years. At this stage the child's interest gets shifted from the eliminating organs to the genitals. The children now come to note the biological differences between the sexes and derive pleasure from playing and manipulating the genital organs. This type of awareness about sex organs according to Freud, may give birth to a number of complexes.

The Latency Stage: This period starts from six years in the case of girls and seven to eight years in the case of boys and extends till the onset of puberty. At this stage, boys and girls prefer to be in the company of their own sex and even neglect or hate members of the opposite sex.

The Phallic Stage: Puberty is the starting point of the phallic stage. The adolescent boy and girl now feels a strange feeling of strong sensation in the genitals and attraction towards the members of the opposite sex. At this stage they derive pleasure by self-stimulation of the genitals, may fall in love with one's own self by taking interest in beautifying and adorning their own body organs and may take interest in making sexual relations with the members of opposite sex. Thus their behaviour is now centred around the satisfaction of the sexual needs either through homosexual or heterosexual relationships.

In this way, Freud adopted a somewhat different and unique approach for knowing and understanding the mechanism of personality. However, some of his views, specially related to the dominance of sex motive, proved undigestable to the followers of his school of psycho-analysis. As a result his own disciples Alfred Adler and Carl Jung broke away from him to propound their own views on personality and human behaviour.

INDIVIDUAL APPROACH OF ADLER

Adler, while opposing the Freud's sex-centred approach, argued that sex is not the life energy or the centre of all human activities. Actually, power motive is the centre urge. Human beings are motivated by the urge to be important or powerful. All of us strive towards superiority but each strives in a different way. He named it as 'style of life'. Therefore, what kind of personality one possesses can be understood by studying his style of life, i.e. the goals of life he has set for himself and the way of striving for achieving these goals.

In this way, he gave birth to individual approach in the study of personality pattern and maintained that there are no definite personality types or classes. Each individual is a unique pattern in himself because everybody has definite goals and style of life.

ANALYTICAL APPROACH OF JUNG

Carl Gustay Jung, another bright disciple of Freud, almost at the same time while opposing his Guru, put forward a different approach for understanding personality and human behaviour, known by the term Analytical approach. The major concept of this approach may be summarized briefly as below:

Structure of the Psyche: The structure of one's mind consists of one's conscious, the personal unconscious and the collective unconscious. The conscious is the seat of one's ego and conscious behaviour. Beneath it lies the personal unconscious—containing all the repressed material connected with one's private and personal life. The collective unconscious lies beneath the layer of one's personal unconscious. It is common and universal to all individuals and contains the experiences of the whole race collected over millions of years specifically in the form of universal ideas or images called archetypes. These archetypes are available in abundance in old myths and fairy tales and folklore in religious and cultural traditions in enduring literature and art. Jung has named a variety of such archetypes like the mother archetype, the father archetype, the hero and the persona, the anima and the animus and the shadow and the self. As examples of these archetypes we may consider the mother archetype, i.e. the image of the mother is always that of pious, warm, loving, protective and nourishing almost everywhere in the world.

Self-actualization Motive: In his approach to understand human behaviour and personality, Jung emphasized that human behaviour is neither directed through the sex motive (as advocated by Freud) nor through the power motive (as advocated by Adler). Rather it is guided and directed by the motive or urge of self-actualization. Each one of us tries in one's own way for expressing or actualizing one's own self. The way he is able to do so or the success or failure he gets in doing so decides his behaviour pattern and personality make-up.

Libido and Personality Development: Jung tried to give a very comprehensive meaning to the term 'libido' in contrast to the narrower meaning i.e. sex gratification, assigned by Freud. He equated it with the life urge or life energy responsible for every type of human activity including, of course, sex gratification. Its normal flow makes an individual normal while its repression, blockage or damming up may lead to abnormalities. In the case of normal flow also, the personality of the individuals may be fashioned as introvert or extrovert. The persons in whom life energy (libido) flows inward are known as 'introverts' while, persons in whom the life energy flows outward are termed as 'extroverts'.

Personality Types: Based on the notion of libidonal flow of human life energy, Jung thus tried to divide human beings basically into two distinct types—Introvert and Extrovert—according to their social participation and the interests which they take in social activities. Later on, he further sharpened his two-fold division by giving sub-types. In this process he took into consideration the four psychological functions—thinking, feeling, sensation and intuition—in relation to his previous extrovert and introvert types. Diagramatically, we can represent this division, alongwith main characteristics of each sub-types, as shown in Fig. 31.4.

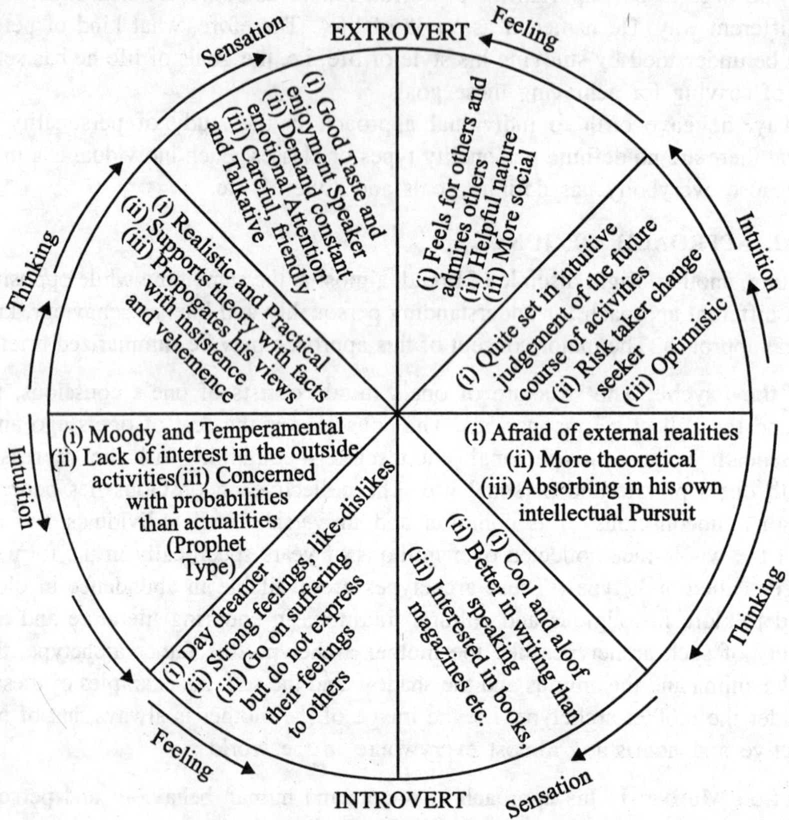

Fig. 31.4 Jung's personality types.

The classification has been criticised on the ground that in general, such different types of classes as suggested by Jung do not exist. Most of us, on the basis of typical characteristics prescribed for extrovert and introvert, may belong to both of the categories. This brings complication in the categorization of the human beings into two broad classes and their subsequent sub-classes. Reacting to such criticism, Jung later postulated that in practice both introvert and extrovert tendencies are ordinarily present in the personality of an individual. This is why an extremely extrovert person may be found to dissolve himself into typical introvert tendencies and vice versa depending upon the prevailing environmental situations and one's psychological state of mind. The presence of the both the introvert and extrovert tendencies, in somewhat equal proposition, may then lead to rename the individual as ambivert i.e. a synthesis of introvert and extrovert.

SUMMARY

In associating one's personality with his outward appearance or external behaviour etc., we have developed certain wrong notions about the term 'personality'. It has resulted in evaluating one's personality exclusively in terms of his appearance, physical manners, character and temperament etc. Although all these attributes of one's self need to be included in evaluating one's personality, yet it is wrong to equate personality with any of these attributes or even with the sum of all these attributes. Personality includes everything about a person. However it is not just a collections so many traits or characteristics that is known as personality. It may be defined as a complex blend of a relatively enduring but constantly changing pattern of a person's unique behaviour evolved as a result of his interaction with his environment.

Various theories have been propagated for explaining the structure of personality by adopting different approaches like type, trait, trait-cum-type, psychoanalytic, individual, analytical approach etc. Theories adopting type approach hold that human personalities can be classified into a few clearly defined types and each person can be put in one or the other types according to his personality traits. Accordingly Hippocrates classified peoples into four types according to the humour or fluids—blood, yellow bile, mucus and black bile. Kretschmer and Sheldon described specific biological types based on body structures and attached certain personality characteristics to them. Jung while adopting type approach tried to classify people basically into two distinct types introvert and extrovert. Friedman and Rosenman classified people into two personality types—type A and type B on the basis of their personality traits and then described which types of people are particularly more prone to heart ailments.

Theories adopting trait approach try to make use of the personality traits for underlying and describing the personality of an individual.

The personality theories put up by Gordon Allport and R.B Cattell belong to this category. Allport identifies three types of traits namely cardinal, central, and secondary, contributing towards the personality make-up of an individual. Cattell used factor analysis to identify surface traits and source traits and ultimately arrived at 16 factors or basic dimensions for describing one's personality. Latest researches have been able to reduce these traits to five namely Extraversion, Agreebleness, Consciousness, Emotional Stabilty and culture.

Theories adopting type-cum-trait approach like Eysenck's theory of personality try to synthesize the viewpoints of both the type and trait approach. They start with the description of trait initially and then end up with some distinct personality types. Eysenck in his theory has given four such distinct personality types namely introversion, extroversion, neuroticism and psychoticism by linking different personality trait with each of these types.

Psycho analytic approach of Freud holds that the anatomy of our personality is built around three unified and inter-relating systems Id, Ego and Super ego. The dominant and submissive role played by one's Id and Super ego in relation to one's ego plays a significant role in deciding the structure of one's personality, like balanced, neurotic or psychotic personality. Freud while providing much importance to sexuality, laid down five stages namely, oral, anal, genital, latency, phallic stage through which a child passes with respect to the psycho sexual development of his personality.

Adler, while opposing Freud's sex-centered approach, held that power motive plays a dominant role in structuring one's personality. In the course of one's struggle for power, one picks up a distinct style of one's life for attaining his life goals. Since everybody has an unique way of striving and has definite goals in his life, he is distinguished with his own individuality (style of his life) and unique personality. The views so expressed by Adler thus gave birth to individual approach and tendencies for the study of human personality.

Jung provided analytical approach for explaining the structure of personality. He postulated that one's mind consists of one's conscious, the personal unconscious and the collective conscious and the human behaviour in one or the other form is very much directed by the relative roles played by these elements of one's mind. He also asserted that neither the sex motive nor the power motive but the self actualization motive plays a dominant role in structuring one's personality. In addition one's libido, i.e. life urge or life energy, is also responsible for structuring one's personality. The persons in whom life energy (libido) flows inwards are known as introverts. On the other hand, persons in whom the life energy flows outward are termed as extroverts.

References and Suggested Readings

Adler, A., *Practice and Theory of Individual Psychology,* Harcourt Brace and world, New York, 1927.

Allport, G.W., *Personality—A Psychological Interpretation,* Holt, New York, 1948.

———, *Pattern and Growth in Personality,* Holt, New York, 1961.

Bhatia, H.R., *Elements of Educational Psychology,* 3rd ed., Orient Longman, Calcutta, 1968.

Cattell, R.B, quoted by C.S. Hail and G. Lindzey, *Theories of Personality,* (2nd ed.), John Wiley, New York, 1970.

Eysenck, H.J., *Dimensions of Personality,* Kegan Paul, London, 1947.

———, *The Structure of Human Personality,* 3rd ed., Methuen, New York, 1971.

Freud, S., *An Outline of Psychoanalysis,* Hogart, London, 1953.

Hall, C.S. and Nordby, V.J., *A Primer of Jungian Psychology,* New American Library, New York, 1973.

Hall, C.S. and Lindzey, *G., Theories of Personality,* 3rd ed., John Wiley, New York, 1978.

Jones, E., *The Life and Work of Sigmund,* Freud Lionell Trilling and Steven Marcus (Eds.), Anchor, New York, 1963.

Kretschmer, E., *Physique and Character,* Harcourt Brace, New York, 1925.

Mangal, S.K., *Advanced Educational Psychology,* 2nd ed., Prentice-Hall of India, New Delhi, 2002.

Piedment, Mccral and Costa, Quoted by J.G. Seamen and Douglas T. Kenrick, *Psychology,* Prentice-Hall, New Jersey, 1991.

Prince, Motion, *The Unconscious,* Macmillan, New York, 1929.

Sheldon, W.H., *The Varieties of Temperament, Psychology of Constitutional Differences,* Harper, New York, 1942.

Watson, J.B., *Behaviourism,* Kegan Paul, London, 1930.

———, *Behaviourism,* Norton, New York,-1970.

32

Determinants of Personality

CHAPTER COMPOSITION

INTRODUCTION

The personality of an individual is all about what a person is in his totality. It includes everything about a person, his internal body system and outward appearance, his covert as well as overt behaviour, his conative, cognitive and unconscious layers of behaviour. What we are today as a person are the result of a constant process of growth and development. The forces of heredity and environment play their interactive roles in pushing us up at our present personality make-up. Our lives start with the conception in the mother's womb and right then, the process of our personality formation begins covertly as well as overtly by so many forces, the key of which lies in heredity contributions, biological factors, our psychological make-up and the various social and cultural factors present in our environment. All these and other factors that try to shape our personality make-up from the conception till death are termed as determinants of our personality. These factors determine the course of our personality make-up and influence the personality's development in so many ways. A personality characterized as good or bad, poor or magnificient, weak or strong, extrovert or introvert, social or unsocial, normal or abnormal is the result and outcome of these determinants.

CLASSIFICATION OF DETERMINANTS OF PERSONALITY

The things and factors that are said to play a determining and decisive role in the development of personality can be categorized in two different ways as outlined below:

1. One way of categorizing the determinants of personality is to divide them into two broad categories—internal or personal and external or environmental.

   Internal or *personal factors* include the factors or things that lie internally within an individual and not externally in the environment. These may include factors like physical structure of the individual, (his physique, sex, nervous system and glands etc.); his intelligence, motivation, emotional reactions, attitudes, interests, temperament and sentiments, etc.

   External or *environmental factors* are associated with the forces of the environment lying outside the individual. The influence of physical environment like climate and other physical facilities available to the individual as well as the impact of culture and social forces like home, family, school and society are included in this category.

2. Another way of classifying the determinants of personality is based upon the viewpoints and angles from which personality is conceptualized. It includes biological, psychological and social and cultural perspectives. Accordingly the determinants of personality may be classified as:

   (i) Biological determinants,
   (ii) Psychological determinants and
   (iii) Social and cultural determinants.

Let us now try to discuss the determinants of personality by taking into account the later mode of classification.

Biological Determinants

The Biological determinants of personality include factors like

(i) Hereditary influences
(ii) Nervous system
(iii) Ductless glands
(iv) Physique or somatic structure, and
(v) Body chemistry

HEREDITY INFLUENCES

Heredity influences transmitted at the time of child's conception through genes and chromosomes provide the base and structure for the future development of the personality. One's growth and development is in proportion with the contribution of the hereditay forces in the course of his personality development. In case he gets less from the hereditary stock, he has to work hard for attaining desired level of personality development. The somatic structure one inherits, the nervous system he gets, the nature of intelligence and abilities he receives, all prove important in his future personality development.

NERVOUS SYSTEM

Our behaviour, to a great extent, is controlled by our nervous system. How one behaves in a particular situation depends upon the judgement of one's brain. The sense impressions, which we receive through our sense organs, are meaningless unless they are given meaning by our nervous system. Therefore, our observation and perceptions are controlled by nervous system. How intelligently we would react or make use of our mental power is again decided by our nervous system, particularly by the brain apparatus. The proper growth and development of nerve tissues and nervous system as a whole, helps in the task of proper intellectual development. Any defect in spinal cord or brain apparatus seriously affects the intellectual growth. Similarly, physical as well as emotional development is also influenced by our nervous system. Our autonomic nervous system plays a leading role in this direction. It controls the activity of involuntary processes like blood circulation, digestion, respiration and action of the glands.

These processes not only control the physical or emotional activity of an individual, but also exercise a great deal of influence over his physical and emotional development. Nerve tissues also cause the change in the secretion of hormones by some glands and consequently influence the emotional behaviour of an individual. Moreover, the nervous system acts as a coordinating agency for many operations going inside the body and harmonizes the activities and functions of the body parts—internal as well as external. Hence, nervous system should be considered as one of the important components of the human machine that plays as significant role in the growth and development of the personality of an individual.

DUCTLESS GLANDS OR ENDOCRINE GLANDS

The ductless glands, with the secretion of their specific hormones, have a great influence in shaping the behaviour and personality of an individual. Let us try to discuss the location of these glands (Fig. 32.1) and their influence on the development of our personality.

Thyroid gland: It lies at the base of the neck in front of the wind pipe. It secretes a hormone called thyroxin, the main constituent of which is iodine. The thyroid plays a leading role in controlling the process of oxidation of food. It regulates the body's oxygen consumption and the rate of metabolism. Underdevelopment of this gland results in the undergrowth of the individual. The deficiency of thyroxin causes underactivity of the thyroid gland which not only retards the growth of the body but also causes mental retardation and disorders. Over-activity of this gland is equally harmful. It leads to unusual excitement, restlessness and irritability.

Parathyroid glands: These glands are located on the posterior of the thyroids and are generally four in number. The parathyroid hormone tries to counter-balance the exciting activity of the thyroid hormone. These glands remove the toxic products from the body and restore the nervous system to relative calmness. Their under-activity produces muscular tension and overactivity produces lack of interest, fatigue and lethargic conditions.

The Pituitary Gland: This gland is situated at the base of brain. It is called the "master gland" because its hormones affect most of the other glands. This gland has two lobes—an anterior and a posterior.

The anterior lobe exercises great influence on the growth of bones. Its underactivity causes incomplete development and can lead to dwarfness, whereas an overactive anterior lobe result in gigantic growth of the human beings. The hormones produced by the lobe also supplement the activities of other glands like thyroid, adrenal and sex glands.

The posterior lobe also secretes valuable hormones. These hormones help in regulating blood pressure.

Adrenal gland: These glands, two in numbers, surround the two kidneys separately. They are believed to secrete two separate hormones—cortin and adrenaline. The function of cortin is not

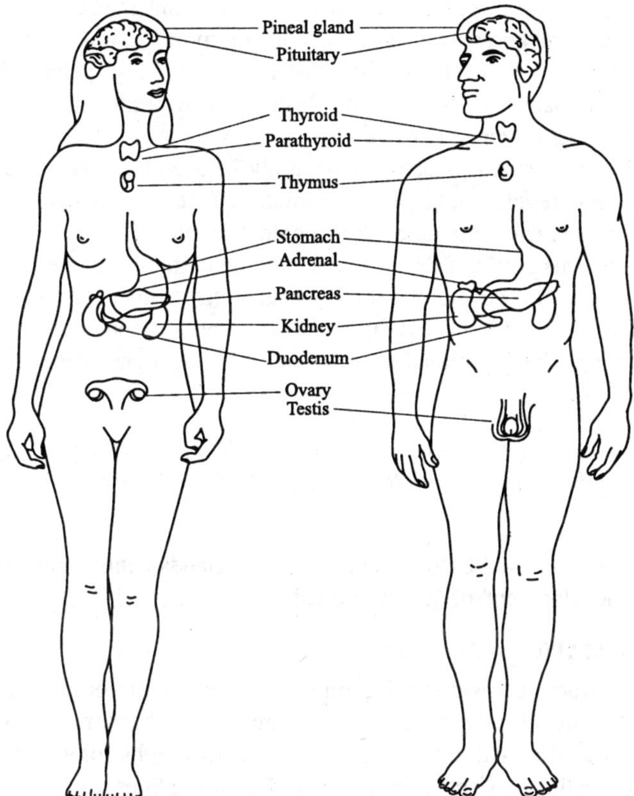

Fig. 32.1 Location of the major endocrine glands in the human body.

definitely known. But adrenaline is known to exercise great influence over nervous, muscular and sexual functions. Adrenal glands are generally known as glands of survival as their underactivity makes an individual progressively weaker day-by-day.

During emotional current, the adrenal gland is known to perform a useful function. In such a situation more adrenaline is secreted that prepares an individual's organs for the particular emotional state. Their overactivity makes an individual highly active and energetic. It may also cause sexual maturity at an early age. A little girl or a boy may acquire secondary sex characteristics of mature man or woman. In some case over-development of the adrenal glands results in increased masculine characteristics which in the case of women may produce extremely masculine characteristics like the growth of beard and moustache.

The sex glands or gonads: The sex glands or gonads are different in different sexes. Men possess male gonads and women have female gonads. The male sex glands or gonads are located in the testes. The hormones produced by the testes are known as androgens. The female sex glands are located in the ovaries. The hormones produced by the ovaries are known as estrogens.

The underactivity or overactivity of these glands caused by the deficiency or excess of the hormones secreted by them as well as by the co-acting influence of other glands like thyroid, pituitary and adrenal, not only affects the sexual growth and development of the individual but also his entire behaviour and developmental process. A slight imbalance of these glands can cause restlessness, anxiety and weakness. Our physical strength, morale, thinking and reasoning power and decision-making ability—all depend upon the functioning of these glands. In short, these glands are found to play a dominant role in one's life. Without their proper functioning, a man or woman finds difficulty in leading a happy normal life.

All the endocrine or ductless glands discussed above exercise a great influence on the various aspects of growth and development. These glands affect the behaviour of an individual by controlling his emotional behaviour and physiological activities. In this way, they have a direct bearing upon the total personality of an individual. Actually, the hormones secreted by these glands are the ones responsible for developing the typical personality characteristics in an individual. These hormones are circulated throughout the body and influence all those tissues on which functioning of body system, emotional actions and even thoughts depend. As Gardner Murphy remarks:

> *These hormones, ultimately, may be regarded as bathing the nervous system, including the brain and all the organs of the body in their own appropriate chemical juices.* (1968, p.52)

Thus, the hormones secreted by different endocrine glands control the behaviour as well as the overall personality development of an individual.

Physique or Somatic Structure

Physique or somatic structure besides being one of the important components of one's personality affect the personality development in a significant way. The somatic structure and physical characteristics of the individual concerning his height, weight, physical appearance, physical strength or general health, physical deformities and abnormalities etc. influence the development of personality of an individual. This influence is exercised in two ways.

(i) The individual's gain or loss in these physical characteristics may influence his style of life—his modes of behaviour action, tendencies, goals of life and the ways of striving towards these goals etc. Every person walks a sizable distance along a course according to his strength and stamina and so is the case with the process of personality development.

(ii) The physique itself does not directly contribute towards the development of personality but the self image formed by the individual through the reactions of his associates and other members of the society to his physical appearance play a significant role. It makes him conscious of his superiority or inferiority and develops such complexes as to affect his behaviour pattern.

Body Chemistry

The chemistry of one's body also exercises a great influence in determining one's behaviour and developing one's personality. Our body gets essential energy for its functioning on account of the chemical changes going inside our body. Sugar is converted into glucose, food is digested, oxidation takes place through the intake of oxygen and a number of similar chemical reactions take place continuously in our body. Our behaviour and functioning is largely governed by our body chemistry. In case there is some irregularity or malfunctioning in our body chemistry, it seriously affects our behaviour and personality make-up. For example a slight increase in the amount of nervous fluid in the body may cause nervousness in the individual. Similarly, the low or high level of sugar in the body may seriously affect the physical and mental state of the individual.

Psychological Determinants

Psychological factors play a big role in the functioning of the human behaviour and development of one's personality. A few important ones are discussed below.

Intelligence and Mental Functioning

One's intelligence and mental functioning play a significant role in the development of his personality. How one behaves is almost determined by his power of intellect and adjustment involving learning, acquisition of knowledge and skills, besides the way of taking decisions and dealing with the people and situation. In this way, the behaviour pattern of an individual is effectively controlled by his intellect and his personality is shaped according to the functioning of his mental powers.

Interests and Attitudes

The pattern of one's interests and attitudes try to colour one's behaviour, ways of looking towards the things and people, his learning and striving for the goals in his life. He tries to move towards the things and people in which he has interests and favourable attitudes and it determines the development of his personality.

Level of Aspiration and Achievement Motivation

One can get success in a designed direction depending upon the level of his aspiration and achievement motivation. He, who does not aspire or desire for a thing, cannot be expected to attain satisfactory progress. Those who have high achievement motivation are found to struggle for their accomplishment, demonstrating distinct life style in comparison to those who have no aspiration or, low achievement motivation.

Will Power

One's will power determines his way of behaviour and personality make-up. The persons with strong will power are found to be credited with emotional stability, decision-making ability and persistence etc., while those with weak will power are found to possess negative traits in their personality.

Emotional and Temperamental Make-up

The emotional and temperamental make-up of an individual cast a strong influence over his behaviour pattern and personality development. The presence of negative and positive emotions, the quality of emotional maturity, his temperament and the organisation of habits and sentiments etc. colour his way of behaving and dealing with the things, ideas and people. He reacts according to his emotional, potential and temperamental make-up and his personality is fashioned accordingly.

Social and Culture Determinants of Personality

Most of our behaviour is learned and learning is controlled mostly by the environmental factors lying in one's society and cultural set-up. Consequently, the development of one's personality is largely carried out by the social and cultural determinants outlined below.

Home and Family

No matter what the traits of the personality are, their development and fundamental pattern is always initiated and directed by the life at home. From the very birth of the child, the parents and the home and family atmosphere provide the foundation for the normal growth and development of his personality. If the child finds a healthy atmosphere at home, he has all the chances to develop his personality in the right direction. On the other hand, poor and uncongenial atmosphere develops him into maladjusted personality. Following are some important constituents of home and family environment that influence the development of one's personality.

(i) **Parents:** Their education, personality characteristics, their emotional and social behaviour, their mutual affection, love and quarrels, their interests and attitudes, and general character etc., all play a major role in the personality development of the child.

(ii) **Parental Attitude:** How they behave with the child and their overprotective or rejecting attitude towards him.

(iii) **Size of the family and birth order:** How many sisters or brothers does the child have, the number of male and female children in the family, his own birth order, etc.

(iv) **Economic and social status of the family:** Besides parents, the behaviour and personality traits of other members of the family also cast a desirable impact on the personality development of the children.

SCHOOL ENVIRONMENT

School atmosphere also contributes a lot in the development of the personality of a child. The personality characteristics of the teachers, headmaster, classmates, the teaching methods, curriculum, opportunities for co-curricular activities, the values and ideals maintained by the institution and the general atmosphere of the class-room and school—all influence the personality development of the child. This is why there is a great demand and rush for the admissions in good and reputed schools as they try to provide all that is desired for the balanced personality development of the children.

OTHER FACTORS IN THE SOCIAL ENVIRONMENT

Besides one's home, family and school influences, there are many other social agencies and institutions that play vital role in the growth and development of the personality of the child. These can be named as under:

Neighbourhood: Its proximity to the child and his family makes it a potent factor for casting its influence on the behaviour pattern and personality of the developing child. Whatever a child observes in his neighbourhood, he tries to imitate. The playmates chosen from his neighbourhood not only provide him company but also affect his behaviour and set the direction of his personality development.

Religious institution: Religious institutions like temple, church, gurdwara and their religious activities, fairs and ceremonies etc. make a silent and sound appeal for the shaping of the child's personality according to their ideals.

The other social groups and institutions: There are other social groups agencies and institutions like social clubs, means of entertainment and communications (Radio, television films), advertisement material, newspapers, magazines and other material and literature etc. available in the social environment of the child that are capable of casting strong impact on the personality of the developing children. A child sees crime and fight scenes on the television screen and they may prove quite enough for his bullying and aggressive behaviour in the school or with his brothers and sisters at home. Similarly, he or she may be greatly influenced by the role of a character read in the novel and may like to imitate personality traits of the character in his own behaviour. In this way, what is observed and experienced in the society by the children plays a significant role in his personality development.

The cultural environment: The cultural environment of the child possesses a vital potential for shaping and determining his personality. This environment is characterized by the mode of the living of the people of the society, caste, and social group to which the child belongs. How do these people think, eat, dress, feel, behave with each other, deal with the strangers, respect the members of other sex and observe rituals and ceremonies, their style of living and philosophy of life etc. cast a strong influence on the behaviour of the developing children and their personality is almost fashioned and tailored according to the pattern of their cultural environment. A cultural environment in which parents and elders are neglected by the younger generation and no responsibility is shared for their looking after especially in the old age will definitely shape the behaviour and personality of the concerned individuals in the same way. On the other hand, in Indian society where old cultural values of respecting the old age are present, the behaviour patterns and personality of the young and old generations will be tailored differently with a respect and a feeling of obligation towards each other in the environment of mutual love, cooperation and trust.

In this way, the development of the behaviour pattern and personality of children is influenced and determined by many a factors, things and conditions broadly categorized as biological, psychological, social and cultural determinants. However, these can never be said to act independently for exercising their influence on the development of the personality of an individual. The determinants, in one way or the other way, have affiliation with one's heredity and environment in the task of personality development of the individual. It is easy to think that all these three determinants of personality act and interact with each other for influencing and shaping one's personality.

SUMMARY

Determinants of personality refers to those things and factors that play a determining and decisive role in the development of one's personality. These can be broadly classified as internal and external factors or determinants of personality. Internal or personal factors refer to those things or factors that lie internally within the individual (like his physique, sex, interests, attitudes etc). On the other hand, external or environmental factors are linked with the forces of environment lying outside the individual like impact of physical environment, social and cultural environment etc.

All these internal and external factors or determinants of one's personality can be re-grouped or categorized in three distinct types namely Biological, Psychological and Socio-cultural determinants of one's personality.

In the category of biological determinants of personality, we can include factors or things like (i) hereditary influences transmitted at the time of child's conception through genes and chromosomes (ii) the structure and functioning of one's nervous system (iii) the nature of the secretion of specific hormones by ductless or endocrine glands (iv) one's physique or somatic structure and (v) one's body chemistry.

In the category of psychological determinants, we can include factors or things like one's intelligence and mental functioning, interests, attitudes, the level of aspiration and achievement motivation, will power and emotional as well as temperamental make-up.

In the category of socio-cultural determinants of one's personality, we may include all those factors or thing lying in one's cultural and social environment which are responsible for influencing and shaping one's personality. The area of influence of these factors may start right from one's home and family. Here the parents, their personality characteristics, behaviour and attitude towards the child, size of the family and birth order and economic as well as social status of the family prove quite a potent factors in shaping one's personality. School environment linked with the personality characteristics and behaviour of the teachers, classmates, school authorities and experiences encountered by the child in the shape of curricular and extra curricular activities all prove quite effective in shaping the personality of the children. The other factors lying in one's socio-cultural environment like impact of neighbourhood, religious institutions, social groups, clubs, means of entertainment and communication, the cultural traditions, attitudes and mores prevailing in one's society all have a great potential in exercising control over the development of one's personality.

We should always keep in mind that all these types of factors or determinants of one's personality, categorised in whichever ways, can't work independently or mutually exclusive to each other. In one way or the other, these are associated with the hereditary and environmental influences to which we human being are exposed since our conception till death. Therefore by all means we must regard the development of our personality as a coefficient of friction between ourselves and the environment.

References and Suggested Readings

Allport, G.W., *Pattern and Growth in Personality*, Holt, New York, 1961.

Janis, I.L., and Mahl, G.F. et al., *Personality Dynamics, Development and Assessment,* Harcourt Brace, New York, 1969.

Maslow, A.H., *Toward a Psychology of Being*, Van Norstrand, Princeton, New Jersey, 1962.

Murphy, Gardner, *An Introduction to Psychology*, Oxford & IBH, New Delhi, 1968.

Rogers, C.R., *A Way of Being*, Houghton Mifflin, Boston, 1980.

33

Assessment of Personality

CHAPTER COMPOSITION

INTRODUCTION

Everybody is curious to know about his own personality or that of others. We want to describe it and know what type of personality or the personality traits are possessed by us or others. It needs the knowledge and skill for the assessment or measurement of personality. There are various methods and techniques which can help us in this task. But before discussing these methods and techniques, let us first decide about using the terms assessment and measurement since it is often argued that personality can't be measured, it can only be assessed.

WHETHER PERSONALITY IS MEASURED OR ASSESSED?

The answer of this question lies in a question itself—Is the measurement of personality possible? If not then let us analyse difficulties that one faces while trying to measure it.

Difficulties in the Measurement of Personality

There are three basic elements involved in any process of measurement which are responsible for the success or failure of this process. They are-

(i) Nature of the thing we want to measure.

(ii) Nature of the instruments with the help of which we have to measure it.

(iii) Nature of the person who is going to measure.

Let us evaluate the personality measures on the above criteria.

NATURE OF THE THING (PERSONALITY)

Nature of the thing (personality) is so complex that it is hardly possible to make it an object for measurement. Firstly, because, personality is not a thing, it is an idea, an abstraction. While attempting for its measurement, we wrongly try to give it a concrete shape. Secondly, what is there in the personality, which we want to measure, is not clear. Psychologists have no agreement about the dimensions or elements of the personality. Thirdly, personality is a dynamic phenomenon. It is not static. How can we measure a thing, which is ever in a process of change and modification. The measurement will certainly differ from time to time and hence it is not proper to call it measurement.

NATURE OF THE INSTRUMENTS

The process of measurement, in addition to the subject of measurement, requires the tools and the satisfactory units of measurement. In personality measurement, we also encounter difficulties in this direction such as:

(a) There is no zero (starting point) for reference as the base of personality. After all, no child is born with zero personality.

(b) In measuring a rod, we can measure it in terms of the units of length like centimeters, inches etc. In measuring temperature, we have units in terms of degrees but in psychological measurement, we do not have any such equal or regular unit of measurement.

(c) For measurement, we require scales or measuring instruments that are exact, reliable and valid in terms of their results. In the field of personality measurement, we do not find such satisfactory instruments.

THE NATURE OF THE PERSON (EXAMINER)

To a great extent, the objectivity, reliability and validity in any process of measurement depends upon the competency and impartiality or objectivity on the part of the person who performs the task of measurement. After all he is a human being with his own beliefs, likes and dislikes, tastes and temperaments and hence we cannot check the influence of his subjectivity on any work of personality measurement.

In this way, the actual measurement (which defines itself in terms of objectivity, reliability and validity) of personality is not possible. Also it is very difficult to search for all the constituents or elements of personality, most of which are unknown. Moreover, prediction of the future status is the most essential aim of measurement. In case of a dynamic phenomenon like personality, such prediction is not possible and hence it is not justified to use the term measurement. We can only have the estimate or assessment of personality.

TECHNIQUES AND METHODS USED FOR THE ASSESSMENT OF PERSONALITY

The methods used for the assessment of personality are often classified as (i) Subjective methods (ii) Objective methods (iii) Projective methods. But this classification suffers from many drawbacks. It is difficult to draw a straight line between subjectivity and objectivity, even projective techniques cannot be saved from the subjectivity and self-projection of the examiner. Actually speaking, there is nothing like absolute objectivity in these methods. Objectivity (if at all we can have it) is nothing but subjectivity pooled together. Therefore, it is proper to seek other ways of classifying the methods of personality assessment.

We can classify these techniques in the following five categories:

Firstly, there are 'techniques, where we can see how an individual behaves in actual life situations. The main techniques in this category are: (a) Observation technique, (b) Situation tests.

Secondly, there are techniques by which we can find what an individual says about himself. The main techniques in this category are: (a) Autobiography (b) Questionnaire and Personality Inventory (c) Interview.

Thirdly, there are techniques by which we can find what others say about the individual whose personality is under assessment. The main techniques in this class are:

(a) Biographies (b) Case history method (c) Rating Scales (d) Sociometric techniques.

Fourthly, there are techniques by which we can find how an individual reacts to an imaginative situation involving fantasy. All kinds of projective techniques are included in this class.

Fifthly, there are techniques by which we can indirectly determine some personality variables in terms of physiological responses by machines and technical instruments.

Observation

Observation is a popular method to study the behaviour pattern of an individual in actual life situation. What personality traits or characteristics the observer needs to know are first decided by him and then he observes relevant activities of the subject in real life situations. The observation can be done in two ways. In one, the observer does not hide his presence. He rather becomes more or less a part of the group under observation. While in the other, he takes a position at a place where his presence is least disturbing to the group but from where he can observe in detail the behaviour of the individual under observation. To get a clear idea, the observer can make use of tape-recorder, photographic cameras, telescope etc. To ascertain whether the observer can rely on the observed results, he can repeat observations in the same situation a number of times, or the subject may be observed by a number of observers and the results may be pooled together.

Situational Tests

Here the situation is artificially created in which an individual is expected to perform acts related to the personality traits under testing. For example, to test the honesty of an individual, some situations can be created and his reaction can be evaluated in terms of honesty or dishonesty. Does he feel temptation of copying? Does he try to pick up the one rupee note in a given situation? All such instances can lead towards the assessment of the trait of honesty in the individual.

QUESTIONNAIRE

What is a questionnaire can be understood by the following description:

Goode and Hatt

In general the word questionnaire refers to a device for securing answers to questions by using a form which the respondent fills in himself. (1952, p. 33)

This definition makes it clear that in collecting information from the subject himself about his personality characteristics, a form consisting of a series of printed or written questions is used. The subject responds to these questions in the space provided in the form under the columns yes, no or cannot say (?), etc. These answers are then evaluated and used for personality assessment.

Items, like the following, are included in the questionnaires:

Do you enjoy being alone?	Yes, No, ? (not definite)
Do you enjoy seeing others successful?	Yes, No, ? (not definite)
Do you laugh at a joke on you?	Yes, No, ? (not definite)
Do you get along well with your relatives?	Yes, No, ? (not definite)

It is the most popular method and is quite useful in collecting quantitative as well as qualitative information.

Personality Inventory

It resembles questionnaires in many aspects like administration, scoring, interpretation etc. The difference can be seen in two aspects.

Firstly, the questionnaire is a general device and can be used for collecting all kinds of information (not only connected with personality traits or behaviour of an individual). Personality Inventory is specially designed to seek answers about the person and his personality.

Secondly, the questions set in the questionnaire are generally addressable to the second person like:

Do you often feel lonely? Yes, no, ?

However, in the personality inventory, they are usually addressed to the first person such as:

I often feel lonely. Yes, no, ?

The best known Personality Inventory is the Minnesota Multiphasic Personality Inventory (MMPI). The questions, included in this inventory are such that their answers are known to indicate certain specific personality traits. It consists of 550 items. Some of these items are presented below for illustration:

I sweat very easily even on cool days.
There is something wrong with my sex organs.
I have never been in love with any one.
I like to talk about sex.

Each item is printed on a separate card. The subject reads the questions and then, according to the category of his response—yes, no or doubtful—puts it down in the space provided for the purpose. With the help of these responses, evaluation in terms of the important personality traits can be obtained.

The questionnaire and Personality Inventory suffer from the following drawbacks:

(i) It is difficult to get response to all the questions.
(ii) The subject may give selected responses rather than the genuine one (hide his weaknesses etc.)
(iii) He may be ignorant of certain traits or qualities which he may possess.

Rating Scale

Rating scale is used to know from others where an individual stands in terms of certain personality traits. Usually with the help of this technique, we try to have some specific idea about some of the personality traits of an individual (whom we do not know well), from someone, who knows him very well. It reflects the impression the subject has made upon the person who rates him. The three basic things involved in this technique are.

- The specific trait or traits to be rated.
- The scale by which degree of possession or absence of the trait has to be shown.
- The appropriate persons or judges for rating.

First of all, the traits or characteristics, which have to be evaluated by the judges, are to be stated and defined clearly. Then a scale for rating work is to be constructed. How it is done can be understood through the following example.

Suppose we wish to have rating on the 'Quality of Leadership' of the students of a class. We can have divisions of this quality into degrees such as very good, good, average, poor, very poor etc. Now the arrangement of these divisions along a line at equal intervals, from high to low or otherwise will be named as Rating Scale for assessing the quality of leadership. Usually the degrees are indicated by numbers, 1 to 3, 1 to 5 or 1 to 7, comprising three points, five points or seven points scale. The seven-point scale is of the following type.

7	*6*	*5*	*4*	*3*	*2*	*1*
Excellent	Very good	Good	Average	Below average	Poor	Very poor

Now the raters, who are in a position to rate the individuals properly, can be asked to rate them and give them scores, ranging from 1 to 7, according to the degree of leadership they possess.

Rating techniques suffer from some drawbacks like subjective bias and halo effect. In the former, the rater may have his own likes and dislikes and this may colour his estimates about the individuals under rating, whereas under the halo effect, he may rate an individual (on the basis of general impression) to be more honest or likeable than his actual potentialities.

To bring some reliability it has been suggested that instead of having rating by only one judge, we can assign the rating work to a number of judges, for example to different teachers, classmates, parents etc., who can pool in their judgements or ratings.

Interview

Interview is a technique of getting information directly from the subject about his personality in face-to-face contacts. It gives an opportunity for mutual exchange of ideas and information between the subject and the psychologists. For this purpose, the psychologist tries to fix a face-to-face appointment with the person or persons under assessment. He makes sure of the personality traits or behaviour he has to assess and then he plans accordingly. Usually, a list of questions to be put is prepared and after taking the subject into confidence, the psychologist tries to seek answers to his pre-planned questions. He not only takes care of the content of the responses but the tone, behaviour and other similar factors, are also kept in mind for the proper evaluation of the desired personality pattern of the individuals.

The limitation of this technique is that it needs a well-trained competent interviewer. It is costly in terms of labour, time and money. It also suffers from the subjective bias of the interviewer. Here again, like questionnaire and personality inventory, we cannot have any safeguard to stop the subject to hide his feelings or to respond in terms of selective answers. On the credit side, cent per cent answers to the questions put to the subject, are obtained through interview. There is very little danger of not getting answers to the questions and moreover we can get the most confidential informations from the subject which he would have otherwise hesitated to reveal through writing.

In fact, interview is a relatively more flexible tool. It permits explanation, adjustment and variations according to the situation and thus proves one of the essential and important tools for personality assessment.

Projective Techniques

So far we have discussed only those techniques which usually evaluate the overt or conscious behaviour of an individual. The covert or unconscious behaviour is not so insignificant; rather it is more significant than the former, as Freud believes that our conscious behaviour is only one-tenth of the total behaviour. Therefore, there should be some other techniques which not only emphasizes the observable part of the human personality but can reveal the inner or private world and go deeper in the unconscious behaviour of an individual to unearth the repressed feelings, wishes, desires, fear, hopes and ambitions.

Projective techniques are devised to accept the challenge. They try to assess the total personality of an individual and not in fragments. Let us see what these techniques are.

WHAT ARE THE PROJECTIVE TECHNIQUES?

These techniques are based on the phenomenon of projection. In these techniques relatively indefinite and unstructured stimuli (like vague pictures, ink-blots, incomplete sentences, etc.) are provided to the subject and he is asked to structure them in any way he likes. In doing so he unconsciously projects his own desires, hopes, fears, repressed wishes etc. and thus not only reveals his inner or private world but gives a proper clue to estimate his total personality.

The common Projective Techniques are:

THE RORSCHACH INK-BLOT TEST

This technique has been developed by Swiss psychologist, who was the son of an art teacher

Mr. Harmans Rorschach. Material of the test consists of 10 cards with ink blots. Five of them are in black and white and five are multicoloured. These ink-blots are completely unstructured, that is the shapes of the blots do not have any specific meaning as shown in Fig. 33.1.

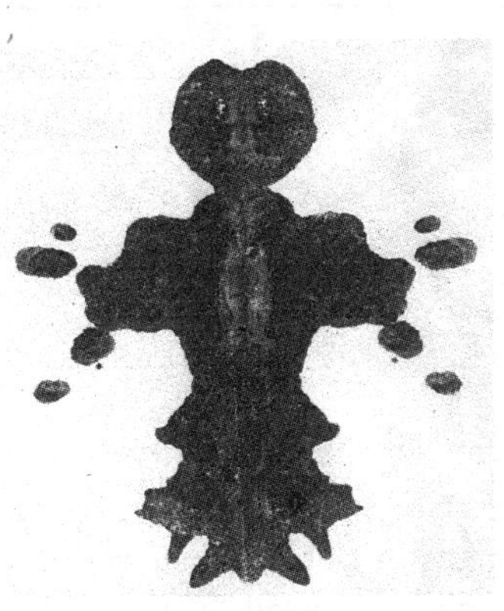

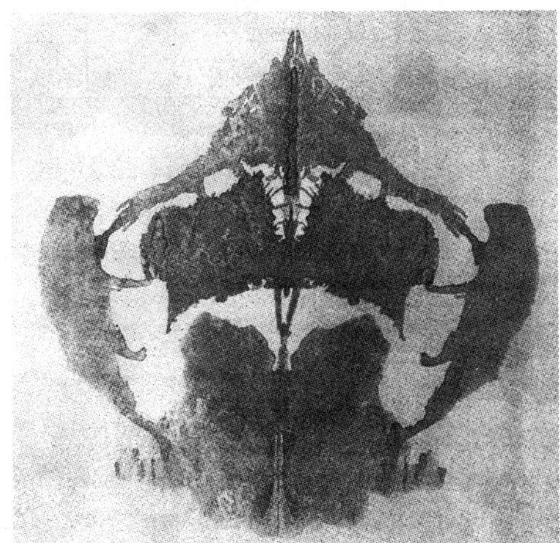

Fig. 33.1 Two inkblots of the type used in Rorschach inkblot test.

Administration of the Test

(i) The cards are presented one at a time in a specified order. When the subject takes his seat, the examiner gives him the first card with necessary instructions. He is asked to say what he sees in the card, what does it look like etc.

(ii) The subject is allowed as much time as he wants for a given card and is permitted to give as many responses to it as he wishes. He is also allowed to turn the card around and look at it from any angle to find things in it.

(iii) Besides keeping a record of the responses of the subject concerning these ink-blots on different pieces of paper, the examiner notes the time taken for each response, position in which cards are being held, emotional expression and other incidental behaviour of the subject during the test period etc.

(iv) After all the cards have been presented, the second phase of inquiry follows. It is intended to seek clarification or addition to original responses.

Scoring, analysis and interpretation of the test

For the purpose of scoring, the responses are given specific symbols which are entered in four columns.

These scoring categories are named as:

(i) Location, (ii) Contents, (iii) Originality, and (iv) Determinants.

Location (the first column). Location refers to the part of the blot with which the subject associates each response. The symbol W, D, d and s are used for scoring the location responses. The symbols stand for the things given ahead:

W for that response which shows that the subject is seeing the card as a whole.

D indicates large details.

d indicates small details.

s indicates the subject's response to the white spaces within the main outlines.

Contents (second column). This column concerns itself with the contents of the responses. It simply takes note of what is seen by the subject and not the manner of its perception.

Some of the symbols used for scoring the content of the responses have been explained in the list below:

Scoring symbol	*Content of the response*
H	Subject sees human forms
A	Subject sees animal forms
Ad or Hd	Subject sees animal detail or human detail
N	Subject sees natural objects like rivers, mountains, green fields etc.
Ob	Subject sees inanimate objects like lamp shade, pot etc.

In this way, for details of the contents the symbols are used and entered into the second column.

Originality (third column). For each of the 10 cards, certain responses are scored as popular by symbol P, because of their common occurrence while some others in which something new is given, and thus indicate some type of originality, are scored as original depicted by the symbol O.

Determinants (fourth column). This column measures the manner of perception, i.e. the particular characteristics which have helped the subject in determining the blot or deciding his manner of perception. The main determinants are:

(i) the form (F) of the blot, (ii) its colour (C), (iii) movement (M), and (iv) shading (K).

For example, if the subject responds to a blot as butterfly, then, we can say that it is the "form" which led to this way of seeing it and then we score the response as F. On the other hand, if the subject sees something like fire, blood etc. then the determinant is certainly the "colour" and we enter C in the fourth column.

Subject's responses on account of "shading", e.g. perception of rough or smooth surfaces, smoke, cloud etc., are scored as K, whereas if the subject responds in terms of "movements"—movement of human beings (like boy running, dancing etc.), animal being (*like* dog barking) or inanimate objects (water flowing, cloth moving etc.), the symbols, M, f_m or m are entered in the 4th column of determinants. We can have cases where we note them by mixed symbols as (CF), (FK) etc.

Interpretation

Now in all the four columns different symbols are counted. It gives an idea of the relative frequencies of the different kinds of responses. The entry of scores (in symbols) in different columns can be roughly made in the following way:

	I Column					*II Column*					*III Column*		*IV Column*				*V Column*
Symbols	W	D	d	s	H	A	Ad	Hd	N	O_b	P	O	F	C	K	M	Mixed Category
Frequency																	

The relative frequencies of the different symbols within the scoring categories and among the several categories help the interpreter to decide the personality characteristics of the subject. For example, if

(i) the number of Ws are greater than d or D; then the person is said to be mature, intelligent and is expected to possess the ability to synthesize,

(ii) More frequency on the side of the colour at the expense of human movement indicates an extrovert nature while domination of M over colour, an introvert,

(iii) Dominance of shading responses expresses anxiety, depressed attitudes and feeling of inferiority, and

(iv) Relatively more emphasis on movement indicates richness of one's imaginative life.

It is not only the relative importance or occurrence of certain kinds of responses which help in interpretation, the various other factors like time factor, the behaviour of the subject at the time of reactions etc. also have their meanings.

Therefore, it is only through various kinds of relationships, observations, records and integration of results from various parts that a final global picture about a subject's personality can be drawn. The test demands a lot of training and skill in scoring and interpretation on the part of the examiner and therefore, the work should be considered as a serious one and should only be done by an experienced and trained psychologist.

TAT OR THEMATIC APPERCEPTION TEST

The test consisting of perception of a certain picture in a thematic manner (revealing imaginative themes) is called TAT or Thematic Apperception Test. This test was developed by Murray and Morgan (Fig. 33.2).

Fig 33.2 A sample picture from TAT.

Test material and administration: It consists of 30 pictures which portray human beings in a variety of actual life situations. Ten of the cards are meant for males, 10 for females and 10 for both. In this way, the maximum number of pictures used with any subject is 20. The test is usually administered in two sessions, using 10 pictures in each session. The pictures are presented one at a time. They are vague and indefinite. The subject is told clearly that this is a test of creative imagination and that there is no right and wrong response. He has to make up a story for each of the pictures presented to him, within a fixed time. He has to take care of the following aspects while knitting the story:

(i) What is going on the picture?
(ii) What has led to this scene?
(iii) What would happen in such a situation?

In making up the stories the subject unconsciously projects so many characteristics of his personality. There is no time to think. Therefore, the stories express his own life-natural desires, likes and dislikes, ambitions, emotions, sentiments etc. Its special value resides in its power of exploring the underlying hidden drives, complexes and conflicts of the personality. An expert examiner can know much about the personality of his subject by carefully interpreting the given responses.

Scoring and interpretation: Originally Murray analyzed the contents of the stories according to the need and presses (the need of the hero and the environmental forces to which he is exposed). Today this way of interpretation is not generally followed. Nowadays, the system of scoring and interpretation takes into account the following:

(i) **Hero of the story–** What type of personality does he have?
(ii) **Theme of the story–** What is the nature of the theme or plot used in making the story?
(iii) **Style of the story–** Length of the story, language used, direct or indirect expression, forced or poor expression, organisation of the contents, originality and creativity etc.
(iv) **The content of the story–** What interests, sentiments, attitudes do they depict. In which manner (reality or fantasy) has the behaviour been expressed? What inner state of the mind does the story reveal?
(v) **Test situation as a whole–** The subject's reaction to be listed as whole.
(vi) **Particular emphasis or omissions–** The omission, addition, distortion and attention to particular details.
(vii) **Subject's attitude towards authority and sex.**
(viii) **Outcome.** Conclusion of the story—happy, unhappy, comedy etc.

As a whole, the recurring themes and features contribute more than a single response towards interpretation. Moreover, the global view of one's personality should be based on the responses of all the 20 pictures shown to the subject. There are so many chances of misinterpreting the stories contents by an immature examiner. Therefore, the future of TAT hangs on the possibility of perfecting the interpreter more than in perfecting the material. He should be given full opportunity for acquiring essential knowledge and training for this purpose.

CAT (Children Apperception Test)

TAT test works well with adults and adolescents but for children it is not suitable. For children between 3 to 10 years, the CAT was developed by D. Leopold Bellak.

Description of the Test: It consists of 10 cards. The cards have pictures of animals instead of human characters since it was thought that children could identify with animal figures more readily than with persons. These animals are shown in various life situations. For both sexes, all the 10 cards are needed. The pictures are designed to evoke fantasies relating to a child's own experiences, reactions and feelings. Whatever story the child makes, he projects himself. It is a colour-free test but it demands some alterations according to the child's local conditions.

Administering the test: All the 10 cards are presented one by one and the subject is asked to make up stories on them. The child should have confidence and he should consider story-making a pleasant game.

Interpretation: Interpretation of the stories is centred around the following eleven variables:

(i) **Hero:** The personality traits of the hero as revealed in the story.
(ii) **Theme of the story:** What particular theme has he selected for the story building?
(iii) **The end of the story:** Happy ending or unhappy, wishful, realistic or unrealistic.
(iv) **Attitude towards parental figures:** Hatred, respect, devotion, grateful, dependent, aggressive or fearful.
(v) **Family role:** With whom does the child identify himself with in the family.
(vi) **Other outside figures introduced:** Objects or elements introduced in the story but not shown in the picture.
(vii) **Omitted or ignored figures:** Which figures are omitted or ignored should be noted as they may depict the wish of the subject that the figures were not there.
(viii) **Nature of the anxieties:** Harassment, loss of love, afraid of being left alone etc., should also be noted.
(ix) **Punishment for crime:** The relationship between a crime committed in the story and severity of punishment given for it.
(x) **Defence and confidence:** The type of defences, flight, aggression, passivity, *ted* regression etc. the child takes, nature of compliance or dependence, involvement in pleasure and achievement, sex desire etc.
(xi) **Other supplementary knowledge:** The language, the overall structure of the stories, time taken for completing them and the reactions of the subject at the time of making the story etc.

With all this knowledge an expert interpreter can pronounce judgement on the various aspects of the child's personality.

WORD ASSOCIATION TEST

In this technique there are a number of selected words. The subject is told that:

(i) the examiner will utter a series of words, one at a time,
(ii) after each word the subject is to reply as quickly as possible with the first word that comes to his mind, and
(iii) there is no right or wrong response.

The examiner then records the reply to each word spoken by him; the reaction time and any unusual speech or behaviour manifestations accompanying a given response. The contents of the responses along with the other recorded things give clues for evaluating the human personality and thus help a psychologist in his work.

SENTENCE-COMPLETION TESTS

These tests include a list of incomplete open-ended sentences, which require completion by the subject in one or more words. The subject is asked to go through the list and answer as quickly as possible (without giving a second thought to his answers). For example, we can have the following sentences:

I am worried over....................................

My hope is ....

I feel proud when ....

My hero is ....

The sentence completion tests are regarded as superior to word association because the subject may respond with more than one word. Also there it is possible to have a greater flexibility and variety of responses and more area of personality and experiences may be tapped.

In addition to the projective techniques mentioned above, there are some others which may prove useful in many situations. These are play technique, drawing and painting tests etc. Both these techniques are very useful in the case of small children. In the former, the examiner observes the spontaneous behaviour of the children while playing or constructing something with the help of given material and in the latter, the natural free hand drawing and paintings of the children are the matter of the study. Both these techniques provide a good opportunity for the careful analysis of a child's personality.

EVALUATION OF PROJECTIVE TECHNIQUES

Merits

Projective techniques have some outstanding features which give them some sort of superiority over the other techniques of assessing the personality. They are given below.

1. The nature of appraisals being made by these techniques is usually well-disguised. The subject is ordinarily not aware of the true purpose of the test and even if he has knowledge, he cannot know what aspects of his responses are significant or what significance do they have. Therefore, there is no danger of distortion of the response or to give selective responses by the subject.
2. In these projective techniques, the tasks presented to the individual are usually both novel and unstructured. The subject cannot depend upon an established, conventional and stereotyped pattern of responses. He is to respond quite independently. Therefore, by these techniques, we can be saved from the danger of practice and coaching effects from which most tests suffer.
3. Scope and area of their application is very wide. They make little or no demand on literacy or academic skills and are equally useful for children as well as adults.
4. Most of the essential aspects of the unconscious behaviour, of which the subject himself has no knowledge, can be revealed through these techniques. In this way, these techniques play a great role in disclosing the private world of the subject and hence have a unique advantage of evaluating the total personality of an individual.

Limitations

Despite all these good points at their credit, the projective techniques also suffer from some weaknesses. They are:

(i) Standardised projective tests are costly. Also there is a shortage of such tests.

(ii) The standardised work suffers from many weaknesses. Proper norms and objective interpretation are hardly available for these tests. Also they are not highly reliable and valid.
(iii) They are time-consuming both in administration and scoring.
(iv) The interpretation task is subjective and needs well-trained and experienced persons, who are generally not available.

But these above mentioned limitations on the part of projective techniques do not make them less significant. In fact, with the essential training and knowledge at his command, an expert psychologist is sure to gain important information about the subject, which is otherwise not available. On the other hand, it is also true that the projective techniques alone are not the answer to all the questions regarding human personality and adjustment. They should always be supplemented with other techniques of the personality so that comprehensive and detailed picture of the personality make-up of an individual is obtained.

SUMMARY

The task of actual measurement in the case of personality is not possible. We can only estimate and assess it by a variety of techniques like observation, situational tests, questionnaire, personality inventory, rating scale, interview and projective techniques.

In adopting observation technique, observer tries to observe the relevant activities concerning one or the other personality traits of the subject in real life situations. In the situational tests, situation are artificially created for the observation of one's behavior related to the personality traits under testing. Questionnaires as a technique of personality assessment refers to a form consisting of some questions related to the personality characteristics requiring responses on the part of the subject for the assessment of his personality.

Personality inventory resembles questionnaire in many aspects like administration, scoring, interpretations etc. However, it differs from questionnaires in the sense that it is specially designed for seeking information about the personality traits or behaviour of an individual rather than collecting all kinds of information like questionnaire. Rating scale refers to a technique of rating (telling where an individual stands in terms of some personality traits) on three, five or seven point scale for getting idea about some of the personality traits of an individual whom we don't know well from someone who knows him very well. Interview refers to a technique of getting information directly from the subject about his personality in face-to-face interactions.

Projective technique are based on the phenomenon of projection. In these techniques relatively indefinites and unstructured stimuli like vague pictures, ink blots, incompletes sentences etc. are provided to the subject and he is asked to structure them in anyway he likes. In doing so, he unconsciously projects his own desires, hopes, fears, repressed wishes etc. and then not only reveals his inner or private world but gives a proper clue for the assessment of his total personality. The various techniques involved in this category may be named as Rorschach Ink Blot Test, Thematic Apperception Test (TAT), Children Apperception Test (CAT), Word Association Test and Sentence Completion Test etc.

References and Suggested Readings

Anastasi, A, *Psychological Testing*, 2nd ed., Macmillan, New York, 1961.

Butcher, James, N., *Objective Personality Assessment*, Acamedic Press, New York, 1972.

Chronbach, L.J., *Essentials of Psychological Testing,* 3rd ed., Harper & Row, New York, 1970.

Goode and Hatt, *Methods of Social Research,* McGraw-Hill, New York, 1952.

Klopfer, Band and Kelly, D., *The Rorschach Technique*, World Book, Yonkers, 1946.

Mangal, S.K., *Advanced Educational Psychology*, 2nd ed., Prentice-Hall of India, New Delhi, 2002.

Mischel, Walter, *Personality and Assessment*, John Wiley, New York, 1968.

Murray, H.A., *The Thematic Apperception Test*, Harvard University Press, Cambridge (Mass.), 1943.

Vernon, P.E., *Personality Test and Assessment,* Rev ed., Methuen, London, 1965.

34

Exceptional Children

CHAPTER COMPOSITION

MEANING OF THE TERM 'EXCEPTIONAL CHILDREN'

Exceptional children are those children who deviate significantly from the normal ones. In other words, children who show a considerable deviation from what is supposed to be the normal or average to their group are labelled as exceptional children. The deviation may fall on either side and therefore, exceptional may be significantly below or significantly above average in the various aspects of human growth and development. Such children are so exceptionally inferior or superior to the normal children in terms of physical development, mental ability, social behaviour and emotional reactions that they experience a sort of maladjustment in life. They need special care and education for their proper adjustment and maximum utilisation of their abilities.

Crow and Crow have tried to explain the term exceptional in the following words:

> *"The term 'atypical' or 'exceptional' is applied to a trait or to a person possessing the trait if the extent of deviation from normal, possession of the trait is so great that because of it the individual warrants or receives special attention from his fellows and his behaviour responses and activities are thereby affected."* (1973, p. 508)

Telford and Sawrey have also expressed similar views about the term exceptional children. They write *"The term exceptional children refers to those children who deviate from the normal in physical, mental, emotional or social characteristics to such a degree that they require special social and educational services to develop their maximum capacity"* (1977, pp. 10–11)

The above cited definitions may help us to draw the following conclusion about the nature and characteristics of exceptional children.

- Exceptional children are quite deviant, distinct and different from the average or normal children.
- Their deviation from the normal or average may fall on either side—positive or negative—in any dimension or aspect of their personality like physical, mental, social, emotional and moral etc.
- However, the differentiation and deviation from the normal or average children with respect to possession of a particular trait (making one exceptional) must be so great that on account of it (i) he may experience unusual or peculiar problems regarding his adjustment to the self and the environment and (ii) may also require special type of bringing, care and education for his adjustment, proper growth and development as well as for nurturing of capabilities.

TYPES OF EXCEPTIONAL CHILDREN

Judging on the basis of the characteristics laid down above, we may have a variety of children labeled as exceptional with respect to their possession of the exceptional traits related to the various dimensions of their personality. In physical dimension, we may come across children having unusual or exceptional physical abilities and capacities in terms of height, weight, physical strength and stamina on the positive side and disabilities and handicapness on the negative side. Similarly, in the mental dimension where we may have intellectually geniuses on the positive side while the educationally low, slow learners, backward and mentally disabled may be on the negatively extreme side. Similar is the case with the other aspect of human personality where we may have extremes or exceptionality on both the positive and negative sides.

Now the question arises as to in how many categories, classes or broad nomenclature should the exceptional children be divided? Should we include all types of seriously deviates in all dimensions of the personality in the term exceptional or restrict its use to some or the other type of children in some or the other ways?

To term one as 'exceptional' we may take the help of characteristics mentioned abovd. Here one of the essential conditions is that one should face a lot of difficulty and problems in his adjustment on account of his exceptional traits to the extent that he requires special care, provisions and education for the adjustment and adequate development of his abilities. Based on this, we usually exclude the children whose traits are on the extreme positive side of the personality dimensions like physical, emotional, social, moral etc., since they ordinarily do not demand any special provision and care for their adjustment and development.

Thus considering general welfare and educational angel for the proper adjustment and development of the children, the following types of children are usually included in the term 'exceptional children'.

(1) Physically disabled or handicapped children
(2) Mentally disabled or mentally handicapped children
(3) Gifted children
(4) Creative children
(5) Delinquent or socially handicapped
(6) Emotionally disturbed children
(7) Learning disabled children
(8) Backward children or slow learners

Let us discuss all these types of children in this chapter except the creative children which we have already covered in the earlier chapter of this text.

THE GIFTED CHILD

Meaning and Defintion of the Term 'Gifted Child'

The term 'gifted child' has been defined by various authors in the ways given ahead:

Havighurst

The talented or gifted child is one who shows consistently remarkable performance in any worthwhile line of endeavour. (1958, p. 19)

Prem Pasricha

The gifted child is one who exhibits superiority in general intelligence or the one who is in possession of special abilities of high order in the field which are not necessarily associated with high intelligence quotient. (1964, p. 301)

The above definitions bring into focus the following characteristics of the gifted children:

(i) The gifted child is essentially an exceptional child,
(ii) In comparison to his peers he is superior in some ability or a group of abilities,
(iii) In most of the cases, gifted children always exhibit superior performance in the area or areas of their giftedness only.
(iv) The 'gifted children' category includes not only the academically talented children but also those who show promise in:
  (a) Music, dance, drama, painting, sculpture, writing and other creative arts.
  (b) Mechanical work.
  (c) Social leadership and human relationships.
  (d) Creative scientific experimentation and exploration.
  (e) Physical activities like games, sports and gymnastics.
(v) It is not essential that a gifted child should possess a very high I.Q. showing his superiority in general intelligence over his peers.
(vi) On receiving proper attention and opportunity for self-expression and development, he can contribute something remarkable to the welfare of his society, nation and humanity at large.

Needs and Problems of the Gifted Children

Like other children, the gifted children also have certain basic needs like the need for security, for love, for belongingness and the need to be accepted as an individual. In addition to these basic needs, the gifted children may have the following special needs like,

(i) the need for knowledge and understanding.
(ii) the need for creativity and ingenuity.
(iii) the need for the development of his exceptional ability or abilities.
(iv) the need for self-actualization or self-expression.

In this way, the gifted child does not only strive for the satisfaction of his basic needs but also needs the opportunity as well as the facilities for the realization of his specific needs. In case he finds it difficult to accomplish these needs, he becomes mentally as well as emotionally disturbed. This brings a sort of maladjustment and he turns into a problem child.

Gifted child needs proper environment for his development. He wants to be understood carefully in response to his different needs and problems. The gifted child is exceptionally curious and has a thirst for knowledge. Thereby, he is in the habit of asking the truth-searching questions. The parents as well as the teachers who do not understand the necessity of his urges, usually snub him. Sometimes, he wants appreciation for his ingenuity in scientific field or creativity in arts, but he does not get it. Consequently, he feels insecure and rejected. A sort of mishandling or carelessness on the part of teachers or parents further aggravates the situation and he is turned into a nuisance. Below we cite some reasons of his such maladjustment.

In case the gifted child gets undue attention and appreciation, he becomes too much conscious of his superiority and develops a boastful and aristocratic attitude. He cannot make himself adjusted along with the other fellow students. He thinks them inferior as well as a foolish and even hates them; on the other hand, the other children become jealous of such a child. They do not accept his superiority and begin to reject him. The gifted child, in this way, does not get recognition from his companions and faces a sort of social rejection. This makes him quite perturbed. As a result, he either becomes withdrawn or aggressive and hostile.

From another angle also, in our usual system of classroom education, the gifted children are faced with the problems of adjustment. We in the classrooms plan work for an average child. The same task is assigned to the entire class. For the gifted child, it has no challenge and he finishes it in no time or takes no genuine interest in it. As a result, he becomes restless, careless, inattentive and idle. He often utilizes his extra time and surplus energy in getting into mischiefs and creating problems of discipline both in the classroom and outside the school.

In this way, due to lack of adequate facilities, suitable environment and ignorance about their specific needs and problems, the gifted children have the possibility of being turned into maladjusted or abnormal personalities. Under these circumstances, the superior talents go wasted. Therefore, there is a need for special care and proper education to the gifted children.

Identification of the Gifted Children

The first step in the direction of planning special education for the gifted children is to identify or separate them from the average children. In the absence of identification and adequate provision, many of the gifted children, like the flowers in a desert or diamonds in a coalmine, go unnoticed.

For the adequate identification of the gifted children, we must make a proper distinction between the intellectually gifted children and children with special talents who show superior performance in some or the other areas.

In the identification of intellectually gifted or academically talented children, intelligence tests are more often used as a screening instrument. Psychologists have difference of opinion regarding demarcation drawn by I.Q. between the average and the gifted children. Some consider children with 125 I.Q. and above as the gifted children while there are others who have raised this limit to 135 or 140. The criterion is quite arbitrary and not universal. However I.Q. of 130 or above (as measured by an individual intelligence test) is usually accepted as the most agreed criterion for separating the gifted children from the average population.

In addition to the intelligence, the following list of identifying characteristics prepared by De Haan and Kough (Dutt, 1974, p.201) can be of great help in the identification of intellectually gifted or academically talented students:

1. Learns rapidly and easily.
2. Uses a great deal of common sense and practical knowledge.
3. Reasons things out. Thinks clearly, recognizes relationships, comprehends meanings.
4. Retains what he has heard or read without much rote drill.
5. Knows about many things of which most students are unaware.
6. Has a large vocabulary which he uses easily and accurately.
7. Can read books that are one or two years in advance of the rest of the class.
8. Performs difficult mental tasks.
9. Asks many questions and has a wide range of interests.
10. Does some academic work one or two years in advance of the rest of the class.
11. Is original in his thinking, uses good but unusual methods.
12. Is alert, keenly observant and responds quickly.

As mentioned earlier, there are some gifted children who, although do not possess superior general intelligence, exhibit special abilities or talents in one or the other fields. Such children are not able to be identified by intelligence tests. Such type of children need careful observation and study so that the specific areas of their giftedness can be spotted out. Aptitude tests can render valuable help in this direction. Interest inventory, anecdotal records, opinions and reports of friends and teachers often help in exploring the latent gift. Sometimes self-analysis also helps in acquainting oneself with the kind of gift one possesses. In addition to this, the overall behavioural assessment through personality tests and sociometric techniques also reveal the special abilities of a child. Some children show their talents when they are provided opportunities for self-expression and self-actualization. Some need a little more stimulation and encouragement. A wise and expert teacher, therefore, should try to put an all-round effort for detecting and recognizing the specific abilities and talents of these children so that they may be helped properly in achieving success in the specific fields.

Education of the Gifted Children

At the present juncture, students all over the world appear to be in revolt. There is a general feeling among them that their lives is without any ideal or objectives to strive for. It is also an alarming fact that the leaders of these angry youths are found to be the most brilliant and the gifted ones. It makes us think what is wrong with the present system of education. Why is the stream of valuable human energy and the talents of such gifted individuals drifting in a negative direction?

Surely, there is an urgent need of a well-thought programme or scheme of special education for the gifted children. Following plans have been put forward by different thinkers for this purpose:

1. Separate Schools.
2. Ability grouping or separate classes.

3. Acceleration or double promotion.
4. Enrichment programmes.

It is often suggested that we should have separate schools for gifted children and adequate facilities should be provided in these schools so that gifted children may be helped in developing their specific abilities and potentialities. Such segregation is often criticised and labelled as undemocratic. The products of public schools, where we have the provision for selected special education, also justify our fears and doubts. The students from these schools develop an aristocratic and conceited attitude which may widen the gap between educated and uneducated or privileged and unprivileged.

Similarly, the segregation of the gifted children into a separate section within the same school also spells similar danger. This plan is known as ability grouping. Here a given grade is divided into different sections on the basis of ability, the range of ability within each section being relatively narrow. The non-feasibility of both these plans, involving segregation, is obvious in the Indian context. Neither can we afford such segregation as it involves huge expenditure nor can it bring much fruitful results. A gifted child is gifted or talented in his area of giftedness only. He may or may not possess a superior general intelligence. The children who possess talents in a particular area may be one or two per cent of the total population of their class. Therefore, it is unwise to think of having a separate section comprising these few children only. In case we have segregation on the basis of I.Q., there is no guarantee that homogeneity would be maintained in grouping.

Another concept in the education of the gifted children is 'acceleration', commonly referred to as double promotion. According to this plan, the gifted child is allowed accelerated progress. He is either promoted to advanced grade in the mid of the session without completing prescribed full-term or is permitted to skip a grade or class at the end of the term. The plan, although quite feasible, suffers from a serious defect that it creates a wide gap between educational ability and experience. Those children who get early promotion in the advanced grade are usually not able to adjust with the children who are senior to them in age. Though intellectually at par with them, they lag behind in emotional, social and physical dimensions and thus become the victim of adjustment problems.

Another proposal for the education of the gifted children is what is technically known as 'enrichment'. Basically, it involves selection and organisation of learning experiences and activities appropriate for the child's adequate development. Thus, the enrichment of education should be considered a need of all students. However, in the case of gifted children, it will definitely imply an urgent need to impart a greater variety of experience or task at a more advanced level to them. Thus, enrichment programmes proposal aims to bring additional educational opportunities for the gifted children. For example, it may include the following:

(i) Special assignments (within or outside the syllabus).
(ii) Work on independent projects.
(iii) Preparing reports and participation in panel discussion.
(iv) Independent library reading.
(v) Visits to various places for getting first hand information.
(vi) Construction of models, aid-material and improvised apparatus etc.
(vii) Participation in the organisation of cocurricular activities.
(viii) Experimentation and independent research.

Hence learning experiences should be so enriched that gifted children find something new and challenging for themselves. In this situation, they can get adequate opportunities for their proper development. Enrichment of the learning experiences or programmes provided in the school, in my opinion, is the most suitable way of the education of the gifted children in our country, wedded to democracy and socialism. It not only provides facilities for the full development of the special abilities and potentialities of the child but also cares for the development of his total personality. It tries to satisfy the basic needs of the gifted children and helps them in their proper adjustment. Moreover, it helps in involving a school programme that is beneficial to both the average and gifted. Both of them can develop according to their own abilities and capacities without interfering in the development of others. In this way, 'enrichment' provides all the essential facilities for a gifted child within the same structure of our educational system and does not bring any extra hardship or financial burden on the shoulders of our educational institutions. Therefore, in any scheme of education for the gifted children in our country, adequate provision should be made in the school curriculum for the enrichment of the learning experiences according to their needs and requirements.

THE BACKWARD CHILD

Definition and Meaning of the Term 'Backward Child'

The terms 'backward child' and 'backwardness' have been defined in many ways. Below we give some of the well-known definitions:

Barton Hall
Backwardness, in general, is applied to cases where their educational attainment falls below the level of their natural abilities. (1947, p. 02)

Schonell
Backward pupil is one who compared with other pupils of the same chronological age shows marked educational deficiency. (1948, p. 54)

Burt
Backward child is the one who in mid-school career is unable to do the work of if the class next below that which is normal for his age. (1950, p. 77)

All the above definitions lead us to conclude the following facts about a backward child,

- He is a slow learner and finds difficulty in keeping pace with the normal school work.
- Educationally, he is not able to attain what he should. In other words, his educational attainment falls below his natural abilities.
- He falls far behind other children of his age in matters of study. Usually such children remain in the same class for a number of years.
- Not only is he unable to learn in his class with the children of his own age but also he finds it difficult to learn with the children of lower classes, who are younger to him in age.
- He is necessarily a failure in the academic field and shows educational impoverishment.
- Like mentally retarded and mentally handicapped children, we cannot call a child backward merely on the basis of his I.Q. Therefore, no definition suggests an I.Q. level below which a child can definitely be called backward.

Infact intelligence is no guarantee against backwardness. On the other hand, a lower I.Q. also does not necessarily make a child backward. Consequently, the backward child should not be misunderstood and labelled as mentally retarded or dull. Barton Hall (1947) has emphasized this fact in the following words:

> *A child may be both dull and backward but he is not necessarily backward because he is dull.* (p. 102)

In actual sense, we can call a child backward only if his attainment falls below his natural ability. In order to decide whether a child having lower I.Q. is backward or not, he should be compared wth the children possessing the same I.Q.

Another striking fact about backward children is that they may be the individuals possessing very superior intelligence or special ability and talents. These gifted students are found to be indifferent towards the school work due to so many environmental and psychological reasons and thus lag behind in achievement. Therefore, backwardness is not supposed to be the characteristic confined to dull, mentally deficient or retarded children. An average, superior or even genuis child may also show backwardness. In true sense, any child who does not progress at the rate at which his abilities permit him can be termed as backward. Superior child possesses superior abilities and potentialities and should, therefore, be supposed to show his intellectual superiority and if he does not show such superiority, he should be termed as backward. But on the other hand, if a dull child does not achieve as much as an average or superior child achieves, he cannot be called backward unless he lags behind in achieving what he is supposed to achieve according to his abilities.

Kinds of Backwardness

Backwardness is supposed to be of two kinds. One is general backwardness which is, in fact, an all-round backwardness. A child suffering from such backwardness is found to be weak in all the subjects of the school curriculum. The other is specific backwardness. A child suffering from such backwardness lags behind in one or two specific subjects only, when in others he shows satisfactory or even extraordinary progress.

Causes of Backwardness

It is difficult to list the general causes of backwardness as it is an individual problem and every individual problem is unique. But it is certain that the roots of backwardness of a child must lie within or outside him in the environment. Moreover, it is also found that usually there are so many factors or causes that operate together in a particular case of backwardness. Below we try to have a look at some possible causes or factors leading to backwardness.

FACTORS LYING WITHIN THE CHILD

1. *Physiological or Physical factors:* Physiological or physical condition of the child at every stage affects his educational attainment. Studies of Burt, Schonell and others have shown that majority of the educationally backward children suffer from some kind of development or physical retardation. Either they are born with poor health, inherited lack of vitality and physical deformities or become the victims of the poor environment and thus suffer from physical ailment, chronic diseases and bodily defects. Their bodily defects like defective vision, faulty hearing, speech defects, left handedness etc. make them handicapped and they are necessarily developed as backward. On the other hand, the physical ailments due to some or the other disease seriously interfere with the attendance in school and study at home. Also it brings down their health to such an extent that they cannot devote proper time and energy to their studies. Consequently, such children are developed into educationally subnormal and termed as backward.
2. *Intellectual factors:* Intellectual inferiority is also found to be an important contributory factor. Some children are born with some defects in their brain system or intellectual subnormality. These mentally handicapped or intellectually inferior children cannot keep

pace with the normal school activities and prove to be very slow in learning. Burt (1953) on the basis of his studies, asserts that "*in majority of the causes defective intelligence or lower I.Q. has been found to be the sole causes of the backwardness.*" (p.42) In our common observation also, we can find that the students, whose intellectual powers like thinking and reasoning, concentration, observation and imagination powers are not properly developed for one reason or the other, are generally drifted towards educational subnormality. Such children are not only affected in terms of quick understanding and grasping the meaning or remembering but also suffer from emotional imbalance and social maladjustment which impedes progress in school subjects.

ENVIRONMENTAL FACTORS

Apart from the above factors present within the child himself, environmental forces, specially home, neighbourhood and school atmosphere, exercise a good amount of influence upon the educational attainment of an individual. We are describing these environmental factors ahead:

1. *Home influences*: Parents, the family relationships and the home atmosphere have a direct relationship with the educational attainment of the child. We can summarise this influence as follows:
   (a) The privileged homes and well-to-do families are able to provide best amenities of living and proper facilities for getting education. In poor families, not only the educational facilities but the most essential necessities of life are denied to the children. Due to unhygienic conditions and malnutrition, the health of these poor children is adversely affected. It reduces their learning capacity and thus makes them backward. In such atmosphere the child is also deprived of the elementary fund of general knowledge and experiences. He does not get opportunities for gaining richer experience in the form of varied social contacts, trips and excursion etc. Consequently, he faces difficulty in grasping the ideas related to these experiences and becomes educationally subnormal. Usually in poor homes, children are required to perform many household activities or to help in family occupation. As a result, they devote lesser time in their studies. They also become tired with the hard work and thus are not able to pay proper attention to their studies at home as well as in school.
   (b) Besides poverty, the intellectual inferiority and illiteracy of the parents also contribute towards the subnormal educational attainment of children. Such parents neither possess a positive attitude towards education nor do they have sufficient ability to guide and help in studies.
   (c) The family relationships and the behaviour of the family members also contribute much in the direction. Strained relationships and improper behaviour not only disturbs the harmony of the home but also creates many emotional and social problems. A child whose parents have divorced or who has stepfather or mother or if their attitudes are either too harsh or too indulgent or of slackness and carelessness or where there are unusual conflicts and quarrels, the child's psychological and social needs are not satisfied. In such environment, the child neither feels secure nor gets proper love, affection and guidance from his parents and hence becomes educationally subnormal.
2. *School influence:* Improper school atmosphere and unfavourable conditions also contribute to the problem of backwardness. More often irregular attendance or prolonged absence from

school contributes much towards the scholastic subnormality of a child. Besides this, there may be the following factors operative in school which affect the educational attainment of child:

(i) The defective, uninteresting and ineffective teaching.
(ii) Lack of equipment, facilities and provision for revision, experimental and creative work, cocurricular activities and varied experience etc.
(iii) Defective curriculum and examination system.
(iv) Lack of guidance and wrong choices made in the selection of subjects by children.
(v) Poor administration and indiscipline.
(vi) No regular checking of home assignment and lack of proper incentives and stimulation.
(vii) Improper attitude of the teacher and interpersonal relationships among the staff members and students.

3. *Neighbourhood and other social agencies:* The social environment of the child does not confine itself within the boundary walls of his home or the school. The neighbourhood where the child has his home, the companions with whom he plays and the gang with whom he associates himself, the members of the society who come into his contact, the press, radio, cinema, clubs, religious and social places that he visits, all contribute to the problem of educational subnormality. It may colour his attitude towards life, work or studies and also divert his attention to other socially undesirable activities instead of school studies and consequently cause scholastic backwardness.

In this way, environmental forces, to a great extent, control and direct the scholastic progress of a child. His interests, attitudes, habits of work and study, thinking and reasoning process, understanding and observational powers—all get affected by the kind and nature of environment in which he lives and consequently he attains what his environment allows him to attain.

Education of the Backward Children

Backward child as we have seen above suffers from mental, emotional and social problems. Besides defective intelligence and inherited-physical characteristics, to a great extent he is a product of maladjustment and maltreatment. Like other children, he needs security, love, affection and satisfaction of his urges of construction, self-assertion etc. In case he is denied the satisfaction of his social and emotional needs due to some or the other reason, he becomes mentally and emotionally disturbed and suffers from serious adjustment problems. As a result, he fails to pay required attention to his studies and thus becomes educationally subnormal or backward. After being named as backward, he again becomes victim of serious maladjustment and behavioural problems. He becomes conscious of the backwardness and develops inferiority complex. Socially he becomes isolated or is turned into a delinquent child. Thus, his backwardness not only becomes a problem for him but it affects adjustment and progress of other children in his class or group as well. Therefore, the backwardness needs careful attention. There is an urgent need of special education for the backward. It will help us in saving huge wastage and stagnation and check the growth of problem children. Let us think what can be done in this direction.

Diagnosis of the Cause or Causes

The primary task in planning for the education of a backward child is to ascertain the possible and more probable causes of backwardness. This can be done in the following ways:

1. Attainment tests as well as the diagnostic tests should be used to assess the extent and nature of backwardness in specific subjects.
2. Intellectual level of the backward child can be assessed by any standard test of intelligence. As far as possible, both verbal and performance type of tests should be used for this purpose.
3. The child's special abilities should also be ascertained by means of other psychological tests.
4. The child's behaviour as a whole and his specific behaviour in particular in a situation should be judged through situational tests and observation method. His emotional characteristics, social relationship and temperamental traits should also be carefully assessed.
5. A thorough physical and medical examination is also essential for knowing the physical or physiological condition of the backward child. The child's developmental history from early childhood with regard to physical ailments, any disabilities and defects etc. should also be studied.
6. The socio-economic status of the child's family, the living conditions, education of the parents, size of the family, birth order, relationship within the family, the nature of the gang influence and the social environment in which the child is living should also be carefully studied.
7. The school environment, including methods of teaching, courses of instruction, the facilities available for co-curricular activities, student-teacher interaction, etc., should be carefully assessed.
8. The scholastic history of the child should be properly studied and his day-to-day individual and group behaviour should be carefully evaluated.

EDUCATIONAL GUIDANCE OR TREATMENT OF BACKWARDNESS

After diagnosing the probable cause or causes of backwardness, we should make conscious efforts in helping the child to get rid of his backwardness. The remedy of backwardness lies solely in its nature and extent as well as in the causes that produce it. Moreover, there is no single or simple remedy applicable alike to every case of backwardness. Each case is unique and therefore needs individual attention and planned treatment depending upon the kind of the backwardness. However, the following points may prove helpful in planning educational programme or suggesting possible remedial steps for the backward children:

1. *Regular medical check-up and necessary treatment:* In cases of backwardness where physical defects and ill health are found a contributing factor, there is a need of essential arrangement for regular medical check-up. School authorities with the cooperation of the parents and government should take steps for the treatment of such children.
2. *Readjustment in the home and school:* Most of the backward children due to many environmental factors have temperamental and emotional difficulties and suffer from mental conflicts. Such children should be helped in their readjustment in homes as well as in the school. Such emotionally starved and mentally perturbed children need proper love, affection and security. They should be properly understood and encouraged. There is a need of close contact with parents so that the root cause of the emotional and mental disturbances is discovered. Parents also need to be educated about the proper handling of these students. Social agencies and government should come forward not only for educating the parents but also for giving proper attention to remove the miserable handicap caused to the children due to their poverty and other social maladies.

3. *Provision of special schools or special classes*: The provision of special education for the backward child is also a right remedial step. Under this provision, backward children are segregated from other children and kept in small groups either in special classes or in special schools. Emphasizing the need of such segregation, Professor Udai Shanker (1958) writes. *"If they are kept with normals, they will be pushed back and the backward will become more backward with children of their own level. But they will be less conscious of their drawbacks and they will feel more secure in a group of their own type where there will be more encouragement and appreciation and less competitions."*
4. *Provision of special curriculum, special methods of teaching and special teachers*: The group of those children suffering miserably with acute backwardness rightly deserves special care. Such children should have special curriculum, special methods of teaching and also suitable special teachers. Their curriculum should not be as wide as the curriculum meant for the normal children. It should include more practical and concrete aspects so that they may be made competent workers and intelligent citizens rather than scholars. Methods of teaching for such children should be accordingly modified. They require short and simple methods of instruction based on concrete living experiences with concrete materials. There is a need of using appropriate aids and providing rich direct experiences to such children. Also the backward children should be taught by competent and specially trained teachers so that they may be properly understood and their difficulties be removed.
5. *Special coaching and proper individual attention*: Once the area and nature of the weakness has been spotted by proper diagnostic tests in various subjects, arrangement for special coaching should be made for backward children individually or collectively as the situation demands. It can be given in terms of more practice, drill, repetition, review or explanation. By providing such special coaching, their deficiencies and gaps can be removed.
6. *Checking Truancy and Non-attendance:* Backwardness in some cases may be the result of irregular attendance, truancy or long absence from the schools. Such cases should be discovered and desirable steps should be taken to remove them.
7. *Provision of co-curricular activities, rich experiences and diversified courses:* In some cases, the backwardness is caused due to lack of interest in the school studies or a particular subject. The child sometimes does not find anything challenging or stimulating in the routine class instruction or does not get opportunity of studying the subject or performing activities of his choice. Therefore, adequate provision should be made for diversified courses and varied rich experiences in the form of various co-curricular activities and instructional programmes.
8. *Maintenance of proper progress record:* Examination and testing programme of schools need essential modifications. There should be a well-planned regular evaluation of the progress of the children in all curricular or co-curricular aspects. The record of this regular evaluation should be maintained properly. For this purpose, progress charts and cumulative record card can be kept. It helps in knowing the child's attainment level and his speed of progress.
9. *Rendering guidance services:* Lack of guidance in making proper choices for the selection of courses of instruction and field of work is also considered one of the factors contributing towards backwardness. Therefore, in every school, guidance services should be organised properly. State authorities should also pay due attention in making the parents aware of their children's ability, interest and aptitudes and accordingly aspiring for the careers of their children.

10. *Controlling negative environmental factors:* The social surroundings and gang or peer group influences play a dominant role in colouring one's interests, attitudes and vision of life. Therefore, due care should be taken to remove or at least reduce the influence of any negative environmental factors that is responsible for the backwardness of the child.
11. *Taking help of experienced educational psychologists:* Services of some experienced educational psychologists can also prove valuable in planning the education of backward children. He may give valuable guidance to the teachers as well as the parents for taking remedial steps in removing the causes of backwardness of their children.

Above, we have tried to think about the possible remedial task by suggesting some of the guidelines for the teachers. But the problem is so complicated and interwoven that it needs a multi-dimensional strategy. Not only the teachers or school authorities but parents, psychologists, social workers and state authorities should join them in discovering and rectifying the causes of backwardness. Then only can the disease be properly uprooted and the millions of our future citizens can be given proper opportunities for their self-development and self-realization.

JUVENILE DELINQUENT

Meaning and Definition of the Juvenile Delinquent

Every society establishes some social and moral norms to maintain harmony and order in its structure. It persuades its members to follow them strictly by framing legal laws and codes. The behaviour, which is contrary to these established norms, is referred to as antisocial behaviour or crime. It involves injury to either to the property or the people in the society. Society for its protection from such antisocial elements or criminals has due provision of punishment and often such people are kept behind the bars. Such antisocial behaviour or criminal tendency is not only found among the adults or grown-ups, but even minors suffer from such social diseases. Such children and adolescents are known as 'Juvenile Delinquents' or 'Young Delinquents'. Therefore, juvenile delinquents are essentially the criminals, minor in age and are usually referred to as minors with major problem. They violate the law of the land and commit offences like theft, gambling, cheating, pick-pocketing, murder, robbery, dacoity, destruction of property, violence and assault, intoxicating, vagrancy, kidnapping, abduction and sexual offences.

Therefore, the term 'juvenile delinquent' or 'young delinquent' in my opinion, can be defined as: *Juvenile delinquent or young delinquent is a child or young (minor in age) who deviates seriously from the norms of his culture or society and commits such acts, that, if committed by an adult would be punishable as crimes.*

Juvenile delinquency should, therefore, be taken as a red signal and serious challenge to the well-being of the society. The young delinquents, if not handled properly, can become a permanent nuisance to the society. Therefore efforts should be made to root out the diseases before it gets out of hand. For this, one should have a clear understanding and genuine insight into the nature of this disease. How does it originate and grow? What are the factors responsible for turning an innocent into an undesirable criminal personality. Let us try to seek answer to such questions.

Causes of Delinquency

From time immemorial, psychologists and other social scientists have been engaged in discovering the possible causes of delinquency. As a result, various factors, from time to time, have been blamed for juvenile delinquency. Let us try to evaluate them one by one:

HEREDITARY FACTOR

Earlier period of these researches was dominated by the hereditarians who blamed heredity for delinquency. The claim of hereditarians (like Henry, Maudsley, Tredgold and Dugdale etc.) that delinquency is inherited was tested through various studies conducted by personalities like William Healey, Cyril, Burt, Conrad and Jones, Wingfield and Sandiford. All of them concluded that delinquency is not inherited and therefore, it is unjustified to blame heredity for delinquent behaviour.

CONSTITUTIONAL OR PHYSIOLOGICAL FACTORS

Later on constitutional factors like defective constitution or glandular system were offered to explain the causes of delinquent behaviour. Professor Udai Shanker (1958) in his studies also observed that "*Poor health, short or too big stature or some deformity which give rise to feeling of inferiority, dispose one to more aggression, as a compensatory reaction for his inadequacies*" (p. 30), and consequently one develops delinquent behaviour. Apparently this allegation seems to be well founded but it is not so. For its support, not much scientific evidence has been reported so far. However, in some cases, it may be taken as one of the causes of delinquent behaviour.

INTELLIGENCE FACTOR

Intellectual deficiency as the cause of delinquent behaviour has also been one of the old controversial notions. While earlier writers like Lombroso, Goddard etc. emphasized that the greatest single cause of delinquency and crime is mental retardation, Burt, Healey, Bronner, Merrill and others have strongly rejected the chain. In fact, a direct causal relationship between defective intelligence and delinquency is almost doubtful. High intelligence is no guarantee for good behaviour. In many cases, persons with superior intelligence have been found to be the leaders of notorious gangs, and antisocial organisations.

Sometimes on the basis of the statistics, it is argued that the majority among the delinquents possess low intelligence, therefore, defective intelligence causes delinquency. But this concept is not well-founded. The collected statistics in such cases may present an unreal picture. Intelligent individuals may not be caught red-handed whereas those with low intelligence may always be caught and taken in custody. Moreover, defective intelligence may lead to delinquency in one situation and may be a barrier to it in another situation. Therefore, it is not proper to blame low intelligence for the delinquent behaviour.

ENVIRONMENT AND SOCIAL FACTORS

It has been proved by different researches in the field of delinquency that delinquent behaviour is a learned reaction. Delinquents do not inherit delinquent character from their parents or ancestors but are made so by the uncongenial environmental and social conditions. In this connection, the conclusion drawn by Prof. Udai Shanker (1958) is mentionable. He writes:

> *Delinquency is, therefore, not inherited, it is the product of social and economic conditions and is essentially a co-efficient of the friction between the individual and the community. The most important causes of antisocial behaviour are environmental and sociological in character.* (p. 30)

Therefore, it is proper to blame uncongenial atmosphere of the family, school, neighbourhood and society for the antisocial behaviour of the child as he picks up delinquent traits from such situations. Let us see how far such atmosphere is responsible for the delinquent character formation among the children.

Home environment and delinquency: Defective and deficient family environment is a fertile ground to germinate the seeds of delinquency and in many cases seeds are also available within the family environment. Various researches on delinquency have revealed that family life and delinquency are closely correlated. If we try to summarize the findings of such studies we would find that family environment, where the following types of relationship or conditions prevail, is most susceptible to delinquency.

(i) Broken home, where the family is incomplete due to death, desertion, separation, divorce.
(ii) Improper parental control.
(iii) Delinquent and criminal behaviour of the parents or other family members.
(iv) Domestic conflicts.
(v) Economic difficulties and poverty in the family.
(vi) Dull, monotonous and uninteresting home environment.
(vii) Denial of reasonable freedom and independence to the youngsters.
(viii) Maltreatment and injustice done to the youngsters.

In the above mentioned situations and environment, the child does not get opportunities for the satisfaction of his basic needs. He becomes a victim of emotional problems like inferiority, insecurity, jealousy and being thwarted etc. It makes him a maladjusted individual and consequently turns him into a hostile rebellious and antisocial personality. In this way, uncongenial home conditions deserve to be blamed for juvenile delinquency and in all cases of delinquent behaviour, one must investigate deeply the family background and home environment.

Uncongenial social environment outside the home: While home provides the roots for delinquent behaviour, the social environment outside the home nourishes it by supplying some substitute for the satisfaction of unsatisfied basic needs and urges. For example, the peer group or gang presents itself as a substitute for family love and belongingness. It also satisfies the need of recognition and gives him opportunity for self-dependence and adventurism. Antisocial activities of his peer group drag him into antisocial behaviour and companionship, persuades him to engage in delinquent acts. Neighbourhood and the places of social contacts and social situations where the elder members of the society are found engaged in antisocial activities or massmedia like newspapers, books, magazines and cinema that acquaint the children with normal and antisocial acts, provide serious temptation for the youngsters to become delinquents in order to satisfy their unfulfilled desires and needs.

Maladjustment in School: In many cases of delinquency, uncongenial social environment can be labeled as a significant stimulating factor. It brings serious maladjustment and consequently increases the probability of delinquent character formation. Such uncongenial environment may involve the following elements,

(i) Defective curriculum.
(ii) Improper teaching methods.
(iii) Lack of curricular activities.
(iv) Lack of proper discipline and control.
(v) Slackness in administration and organisation.
(vi) Antisocial or undesirable behaviour of the teachers.
(vii) Maltreatment and injustice done to the child.
(viii) Failure or backwardness.

The foregoing discussion can lead us to conclude that delinquency is an environmental and social disease. Delinquent acts are learned and acquired acts. No child is born as delinquent and delinquent behaviour is not the product of genes. The delinquents are not born with some specific innate physical, mental or emotional characteristics. They are normal individuals with normal needs and desires. Like other normal children, they also want to love, to be loved and to satisfy the need of security and recognition etc. Denial of the satisfaction of these basic needs bring maladjustment and makes them hostile and rebellious.

In this way, the delinquent behaviour should be considered a sort of reaction or resentment against the prevailing social and environmental conditions. It is an open revolt against parents, teachers or other social organisations which do not provide them the essential environment for the satisfaction of their basic needs and urges. Therefore, the delinquent child needs a very careful handling. Delinquency is a serious behavioural disease that needs planned attempts for its prevention and treatment. In the following pages we will like to discuss the remedial measures for delinquency.

REMEDY-PREVENTION AND TREATMENT OF DELINQUENCY

In controlling delinquency, the principle of an eye for eye and a tooth for tooth does not work. Delinquency, besides being a legal problem, is basically a psycho-social problem. All types of delinquents, in all their shades, are essentially maladjusted personalities and the product of faulty upbringing and maltreatment. The solution of this problem essentially requires two-dimensional attack:

1. **Preventive Measures:** Initially it will involve improvement of the social or environmental conditions which thwart the satisfaction of the basic needs of the individual and thus will help in the prevention of delinquency.
2. **Curative Measures:** It is the rehabilitation and reformatory front which involves special arrangement for the rehabilitation and education of the delinquents by the government or voluntary organisations.

Preventive measures (Improvement of social and environmental conditions):
Following suggestions can work well in this direction:

(i) *Parental education:* Parents should know something about the psychology of delinquency so that they can treat and handle their children properly and provide them proper environment for the satisfaction of their basic needs and urges. It requires parental education. Help from the guidance services, clinics and other voluntary social services can be taken for this purpose.

(ii) *To save the child from the bad company and antisocial environment:* Parents, family members and the school authorities should have a close watch on the activities and social environment of the children and take care that he does not fall in bad company. Some antisocial elements and criminals try to hire youngsters for their own purpose. Attempts should be made to save children from their clutches and children should get proper education for keeping themselves away from such elements.

(iii) *Providing substitutes for the defective environment*: Sometimes it is difficult to bring change in the defective family environment or bad influences of the neighbourhood and peer group are uncontrollable. In such cases, children should be removed from their original environment and placed either in foster homes or well-managed reformatories and special schools so that they may be provided with healthy environment for their proper emotional and social adjustment.

(iv) *To rectify the school education and school environment:* School environment should be made healthy and congenial. The curriculum, methods of teaching, discipline, classroom behaviour of the teacher and the social atmosphere of the school should be rectified in such a manner that children do not involve themselves in emotional and social maladjustment problems. There is a need of great change in the attitude of teachers who impose their authority on children and do not try to understand their basic needs. The headmaster as well as the teachers should have proper knowledge of the psychology of individual difference and delinquency.

Curative measures: The problem of juvenile delinquency in any circumstance should not be regarded as a penal problem. It is an educational and welfare problem. Therefore, juvenile delinquents should not be put behind the bars and treated through the normal channel of the penal system. Delinquency requires reforms in the shape of rehabilitation and re-education and therefore, special legal provision should be made to deal with the juvenile delinquents. In the progressive communities of the world, the legal dealings with the juvenile delinquents have been changed. The system of U.K. maintained under "Children's and Young Person's Act" is worth appreciating. We can adopt it with some essential changes in our country. Essential features of this system are as follows:

(i) Establishment of Special Juvenile Court with specially trained magistrate to deal with Juvenile delinquents.
(ii) Appointment of trained social workers, probation officers for taking charge of delinquent cases.
(iii) Taking help from clinical psychologists and psychiatrists for understanding the delinquent behaviour of the child.
(iv) Establishment of special schools where the essential provision for the eduction, correction and rehabilitation is possible.
(v) Provision of giving the children in the custody of fit persons or social agencies,
(vi) Establishment of remand homes where the juvenile delinquents are placed when they wait for their trial or for approved school placement or for being given to the custody of fit persons or as asked by probation officer before employment and after discharge from the approved schools.

Provision of special school or '*approved school*' needs special mention in this programme. These schools have specially trained staff. The curriculum of these schools is flexible and provides opportunities for self-expression, recreation, manual work and learning of useful crafts. Here, provisions are made to satisfy the basic needs and urges of the children and thus he is helped in his social and emotional readjustment. In this way, the child is helped to get rid of his delinquent behaviour and learn the proper way of responding to social situations and conditions.

In our country also, the attitude towards delinquency is changing. In most of the states the State Children Act has been enforced and some of them have gone much ahead in the work of rehabilitation and re-education of the young offenders. Separate Child Welfare Boards for dealing with the problem of delinquency has been established and 'approved schools' have come into existence. Some states have encouraged the voluntary organisation to take custody of the delinquent children. Provisions for the look after of the neglected and destitute children are also made so that they may not develop into delinquents. Some states have started foster care programme on the British pattern. Under this programme, the court gives custody of a child to a fit person. Under certain conditions, Remand homes and appointment of probation officers, etc. are also prevalent in many states.

In this way, some efforts are already in the way to deal sympathetically with the problem of delinquency, but still a good deal remains to be done. States need to take genuine steps in this direction. The greater need, however, is to arouse public consciousness regarding this problem. No government can solve any problem without public co-operation. Therefore, there is a need to change our attitude towards delinquents so that they may be helped in their readjustment and rehabilitation.

PHYSICALLY DISABLED CHILDREN

Who are Physically Disabled or Handicapped Children?

The children who suffer adversely in terms of

(i) *performing their daily business,*
(ii) *seeking their social and emotional adjustment, and*
(iii) *realizing their educational and developmental needs on account of the deficiencies, defects and impairments in their physical organs and as a result need special care attention and educational efforts from their parents, family, school and society are termed as physically disabled, handicapped or crippled children.*

These children deviate seriously from the otherwise normal children because of their physical impairment and disabilities. Their impairment and disability proves too costly to them in terms of their normal adjustment and development. They can neither attempt for the normal achievements and progress like the normal children in their lives nor do they have the necessary abilities and capacities for doing so in case they attempt to do so.

A physically handicapped child on account of his physical impairment and defect in one or the other physical organs feels and exhibits his limitation or inhibition for the required participation in normal activities and social as well as emotional adjustment. This fact is very well noticed by the peers and colleagues and as a result they may begin to shower sympathy or ignore, ridicule and even use derogatory and abusive language for him. This makes him more conscious of his physical deficiency and impairment and thus aggravates as well as precipitates the already existing problem of impairment, deficiency and physio-psychological maladjustment. In such circumstances, he is bound to become victim of the inferiority complexes, and maladaptive behaviour and may thus require special provisions for his adequate adjustment and education.

TYPES OF PHYSICALLY HANDICAPPED CHILDREN

Generally we may classify the physically disabled or handicapped children into some of the following main types:

1. Visually impaired or handicapped children.
2. Orally handicapped or hearing impaired children.
3. Orthopaedically impaired or crippled children.
4. Speech handicapped or impaired children.
5. Perceptually impaired children.

Let us try to discuss herein this chapter the children belonging to the above first three categories i.e. visually, hearing and Orthopaedically impaired children.

Visually Impaired or Handicapped Children

MEANING AND TYPES

Visually impaired or handicapped children are those children who suffer from the impairment and defects of their eyes to such a degree that it makes them disabled or handicapped in terms of their visual ability and perception. This handicap or disability may represent a continuum, ranging from poor and defective vision to no perception of light at all. As a result of such variance the visually impaired or handicapped children are often given different names and classifications like partially sighted, children having low vision, legally blind, totally blind and so on. Let us try to understand these terms.

The term **partially sighted** stands for those visually handicapped who have some visual problems due to which they have partial perception of the objects seen. The term **low vision** generally refers to a severe visual impairment, not necessarily limited to distance vision. Low vision applies to all individuals with sight who are unable to read something from a normal viewing distance, even with the aid of eye glasses or contact lenses. The term **legally blind** stands for the persons having less than 20/200 vision in the better eye or a very limited field of vision (20 degrees at its widest point).

The term **totally blind** refers to the persons who have no vision, i.e. no perception at all, of the objects seen and can learn via braille or other non-visual media only.

However, in this chapter for the useful educational discussion we would like to merge the above four categories into two broad categories:

1. Totally and nearly totally blind children.
2. Low vision and partially blind children.

The first category includes those children who are learning with the aid of braille or other non-visual media in schools meant for blind.

In the latter category of low vision and partially blind, we would include the children suffering from problems (after correction) such as dimness of vision, haziness, film over the eye, foggy vision, extreme near or far-sightedness, distortion of vision, spots before the eyes, colour distortions, visual field defects, tunnel vision, no peripheral vision, abnormal sensitivity to light or glare, and night blindness.

Causes of Visual Impairment or Disability

The causes of visual impairment and disability of the children lie well within one's heredity endowment as well as socio-psychological and physical environment. The main underlying causes in this respect may be outlined as below:

1. The transfer of genes and chromosomes associated with visual impairments to the children from their parents at the time of conception.
2. Carelessness on the pregnant mothers' part in their diet, malnutrition, use of strong drugs, being affected from chronic diseases and by serious accidents and incidents, abnormal and stressful psyche states, unhealthy living and socio-psychological environmental conditions faced by the mothers during their pregnancy.
3. The mishaps and incidents at the time of the birth of the child, pre-mature delivery, effects of anesthetic agents and instruments used in delivery, infections caused to the children during delivery etc.
4. Starvation, malnutrition, unhygienic, uncongenial and unfavorable conditions faced by the children in their early years.
5. The ill effects of infectious diseases like small pox, chickenpox and measles etc.
6. Diseases of the eye and infection.
7. Deficiency of vitamins and other nutrition components essential for health and well-being of the eyes.

8. Evil effects of fatal diseases like cancer, growth of tumours, skin diseases, typhoid, malaria etc.
9. Improper postures adopted at the work place and specially at the time of reading and writing.
10. Ill effects of reading, writing and working in defective and improper light conditions such as dim lights, moving lights, intensive lights, scorching or fast coloured artificial lights. The exposure to electronic devices, radioactive substances and rays. Excessive viewing of programmes on the television screen and working with computers have added to many problems and defects of the eyes in the children nowadays.
11. Injury and ill effects caused to the eyes due the carelessness adopted in the day-to-day functioning as well as in professional activities.
12. Damage of the eye organs and other organs of the body responsible for proper sensational and perceptual activities due to fatal accidents.
13. The ill effects of poisoning and intoxicating substances, alcoholism and drugs addiction.
14. Ill effects of external objects like dust, smokes, and pollution etc.

EDUCATION AND ADJUSTMENT OF THE VISUALLY IMPAIRED

The visually impaired, on account of their impairments and deficiencies, have certain limitations, needs and problems with regard to their adjustments and education. They are so handicapped in their movements that they can't even travel independently. The deficiency with regard to the most important sense organ makes them disabled to learn from nature and similar other visual objects and activities unlike their 'normal' peers. The problem becomes more acute and severe depending upon the degree of their blindness. Therefore measures for the adjustment and education for the totally visually impaired differs from the partially impaired. Let us discuss these measures under separate heads.

Education and adjustment of the totally blind or nearly blind children: Those children who are completely or nearly blind can't be educated with the normal children in normal schools. They have to be sent to the special boarding schools meant for the blinds. There are special teachers and staff employed in these schools specially trained and equipped with the special technique of teaching and dealing with the blind children. The methodology here usually requires the use of senses other than the sight. Touch, smell and hearing become important instruments for the communication of learning experiences and adaptation to physical and social environment. Teaching-learning process of the classroom is carried out through braille scripts. By this script, they are taught to read and grasp the written communicated ideas through their sense of touch. Later, the writing skill is developed with the help of other special devices.

In the beginning of their education, much emphasis is laid on the attempts to make them adjusted to the physical and social world and arouse their interest towards learning. Their earlier curricular experiences are directed towards making them learn the simple facts of reading, writing, arithmetic and knowing the local environment. Gradually, they may be given more knowledge and understanding through braille books and classes. The specially organised curricular experiences and communication process for the blind children in blind schools is thus primarily aimed for the following provisions:

1. Blind children are trained to become independent in terms of carrying out their day-to-day activities and have necessary movements related to their social environment and work situations. With the use of sticks and their sense of hearing and touch, they are specially

trained in their physical movements so much so that they are able to cross the busy roads as independently as possible.

2. They are trained to carry out the different types of co-curricular activities with the help of special programmes and equipment used in these schools. As a result, they can learn many things regarding physical education activities like sports and games, debates and declamation contests, literary activities like poem, recitation, dramatisation and acting, music and dancing, working with clay and plasticine, and so on.
3. Blind children have special aptitude for music and other activities involving hearing and listening, touching and smell sensations. Therefore, much attention should be paid to train and provide curricular and co-curricular experiences to them in the activities related to these sensory experiences.
4. Blind children can be properly trained in craft activities and vocational works of varying nature so that they become economically independent and are usefully employed in the government and privately managed establishments or even opt for self-employment to earn their livelihood. As a result, they may be seen carrying out simple organisational activities like running a telephone booth and operating delicate machines and computers.

There are many blind institutions running in almost all the states and union territories of India by government and non-government organisations for the welfare, adjustment and education of the blind and partially blind children. There have been quite pleasant and praiseworthy outcomes of these attempts in making the blind children not only economically independent but also a boon and helping hand for the society in many of the social, cultural, vocational and professional areas. The research work is also being encouraged for making the adjustment and education of the blind children as effective as possible. One such institution, National Institute for the visually handicapped, has been functioning since 1971 at Dehradun. Similarly, another national level institution known as National Association for the Blind has also been functioning well for the education, adjustment and rehabilitation of the blind children. It has its branches throughout the country which are functioning successfully for the welfare, adjustment and education of the blind children, especially the totally and nearly total blind children.

Education and adjustment of low vision and partially blind children: The children who have low vision and are partially blind are generally not cared and educated in the residential boarding schools like totally blind children. With some extra efforts and means, these children can utilise vision as an important channel of learning contrary to the totally blind who have to rely on senses other than vision. Therefore, there is a larger scope of educating the low vision and partially blind children along with the normal children in the normal schools with a little extra efforts, care and provisions like below.

1. The first and the most important thing to do with these children is to attempt for the corrective measures of their eye impairments. For this, there is a need of proper medical check-up of the eyes of these children with the active cooperation of their parents. Proper follow-up in the form of suitable corrective measures like spectacles with numbered glasses etc. then must be taken for helping these children to make use of their vision in every possible way. They should be made to learn the use of corrective measures, spectacles etc. in a proper way and also become habitual in their use with ease and convenience.
2. Since by definition, low vision or partially sighted children are those children who have defective vision or impairment even after adopting corrective measures, their sense of sight must be utilized in their education as minimum as possible. Consequently, they should

never be loaded with unnecessary reading and writing task. Similarly delicate artistic work, geometrical construction, drawing and painting, minute observation work etc. should be altogether avoided with such students.

3. A little extra care in terms of the usual set up of the classroom and work places may also be taken for these children. They must be made front liners in the teaching-learning situations and adequate arrangement for proper lighting must also always be made so that these children may be helped to make maximum use of their low vision.
4. Besides these, a number of other measures may also be undertaken for making the things helpful to them. A few mentionable are:
   (i) Paying individual attention for removing their difficulties with regard to their perception of the instructional material written on the blackboard, charts, maps etc.
   (ii) Taking extra care in speaking out the things written on the blackboard and other visual aids.
   (iii) Making much use of the aid material and devices requiring senses other than the vision, e.g. making use of audio cassettes, radio broadcasting, tape recorder etc.
   (iv) Equipping them with the extra vision equipment like hand lens, magnifying glass etc.
   (v) Provision of having bold lettered books in the library for these children.
   (vi) Taking other helpful measures for making the things perceived depending upon their disability, e.g. a colour blind or any such perception impaired child may be told about the facts in some other ways.

Hearing Impaired Children

MEANING AND TYPES

Hearing impaired children are those children who suffer from a wide range of hearing losses (including deafness) making them wholly or partially disabled in utilizing their hearing organs for getting and exchanging information with others.

The hearing losses as such thus affect the ability of the children to communicate with others. Since communication, i.e. exchange of information, is the key component of any knowledge acquiring process and the subsequent adjustment to one's environment, the children suffering from hearing impairment are bound to suffer adversely in terms of their adjustment and educational development. The situation gets worsened depending upon the intensity and severity of the hearing loss.

In terms of physiological and medical language, the hearing losses are usually classified into the following four types-

Conductive hearing losses are caused by diseases or obstructions in the outer or middle ear (The conduction pathways for sound to reach the inner ear). Conductive hearing losses usually affect all frequencies of hearing evenly and do not result in severe losses. A person with a conductive hearing loss is usually able to use a hearing aid well or can be helped medically or surgically.

Sensorineural hearing losses result from damage to the delicate sensory hair cells of the inner ear or the nerves that supply it. These hearing losses can range from mild to profound. They often affect the person's ability to hear certain frequencies more than others. Thus even with amplification to increase the sound level, a person with a sensorineural hearing loss may perceive distorted sounds, sometimes making the successful use of a hearing aid impossible.

A mix hearing loss refers to a combination of conductive and sensorineural loss and means that a problem occurs in both the outer or middle and the inner ear.

A central hearing loss results from damage or impairment to the nerves of nuclei of the central nervous systems, either in the pathway to the brain or in the brain itself.

Such type of classification of hearing losses and the subsequent distinction among hearing impaired is neither needed nor seems practicable in the field of education for devising ways and means of their adjustment and educational development. Therefore it is more useful and feasible to classify the learning losses as slight, mild, moderate, severe or profound, depending upon how well a person can hear the intensities (loudness) of the sound measured in units called decibels-dB, or frequencies (pitch) of the sound measured in units called hertz-Hz. Generally, only children whose hearing loss is severe or profound, i.e. greater than 90 decibels (dB) are considered deaf, while the remaining ones suffering from slight, mild or moderate hearing losses are termed as 'hard of hearing'.

In this way, we can attempt to classify the hearing impaired children into two broad types (i) deaf, and (ii) hard of hearing for the clear purpose of helping them according to the degree of their disability.

Here we must be again clear in our conception that the term 'deafness' stands for the state or condition that prevents a child from receiving sound in all or most of its forms. In addition, he may also be dumb in case his deafness is by birth.

Consequently, he will hardly be profitted from the sensory experiences associated with hearing even speech.

Contrarily, a child termed as 'hard of hearing' can generally respond to auditory stimuli, including speech, and therefore he has the probabilities of making profits from the experiences associated with the sense of hearing. Such distinction between these two types of hearing impaired can thus probe a solid base for planning and structuring any educational and adjustment scheme for them.

Causes of Hearing Impairment

Hearing impairment is usually linked with the defects and deficiencies associated with our organs helpful in hearing sensation and its perception. Both hereditary as well as environmental factors may be responsible for making one hearing impaired and thereby the main causes underlying this impairment may be cited as below.

1. The child may inherit the genes and chromosomes related with hearing impairment from his parents at the time of conception.
2. He may fall victim to the uncongenial environment available to him in the womb of his mother. The physical and mental health of the mother, her food habits, malnutrition and starvation, fatal accidents and chronic diseases, addiction to drugs and intoxicating substances, poisoning and exposure to radioactive elements etc., may cast harmful effects in the form of damaging the vital hearing organs of the child.
3. The unhygienic and defective environment as well as the physical and mental health of the mother, along with the careless attitude adopted by the persons associated with the delivery of the child, may affect the child's health in terms of the damage of the vital hearing organs of the child at the time of the delivery. Premature delivery, using of the forceps, operational hazards, infections caught and many other things can result in such hearing losses.
4. The early few years of the child known as formative years are said to be very important from the children's health point of view. Any type of deficiency of vitamins and other

nutritional elements essential for hearing abilities suffered during these years cost heavily to the growing children in terms of hearing impairments.

5. In some cases, the causes of hearing impairments are purely psychological. The child may unconsciously learn hearing loss as an escape from the unpleasant and untolerable situations of his life.
6. In some cases the sound pollution and its adverse effects may become the germinating as well as precipitating cause of the impairment.
7. There is never an end to the incidents and accidents in one's life causing physical injury to the sensory and perceptual organs of the hearing system resulting into hearing impairment.
8. The ignorance regarding proper care and maintenance of the hearing organ, particularly the ears, may cause dearly to the children resulting into some or the other types of hearing loss. Penetration of pointed and sharp objects in ears for removing dirt and other external objects or as a measure of relief from irritation may damage some or the other vital part of the ear.
9. The hearing impairment may be caused at any time in the life of an individual on account of the bodily diseases, their consequences and side effects and reactions of the medicines and drugs used for their cure. These diseases may be directly related to the auditory organs or may affect them on account of the general weaknesses and deficiencies suffered by the body. It usually happens with the patients suffering from cancer, brain-fever, brain tumour, typhoid, wooping cough, malaria, encephalitis and mumps etc. Overdose of strong drugs like streptomycine, quinine and L.S.D. in some cases have been found to be the major or sole cause of hearing impairment. In many other cases, aftereffects and side effects of skin diseases, disease of throat and nose and infectious diseases like small pox, chicken pox, etc. have been found to be the potent causes for such impairment.
10. Many a time there is an abnormal growth or pathological changes in the hearing organs located in the ears, auditory nerves and parts of the brain responsible for auditory perception. Such abnormalities essentially result in hearing impairment.

EDUCATION AND ADJUSTMENT OF HEARING IMPAIRED CHILDREN

Any scheme or planning for the education and adjustment of the hearing impaired children essentially depends upon the degree of the severity of their hearing impairment In fact, in this respect, it should be an individual phenomenon. However, considering the practical side of the problem it is usually carried out at two fronts.

(a) Education and adjustment of the deaf children, and
(b) Education and adjustment of the hard of hearing.

Education and adjustment of the deaf children: On account of their severe or profound hearing losses, deaf children need much more special attention and care for their adjustment and education. In fact, the nature of their hearing loss makes them quite different from the normals in terms of their needs and adjustment problems like below:

- Deaf children cannot communicate orally. Therefore, the use of oral means, i.e. the use of sense of hearing, in their education needs to be totally avoided.
- The hearing disability puts many hurdles in their paths to lead even the normal day-to-day life. As a result, they may face many physical, social and psychological maladjustment and security problems.

- Their problems become more acute in the cases when they are also dumb besides being deaf, as they can't even call others for help in case of any danger and difficulty faced by them on account of their hearing disability.

The needs and problems like above make a strong case for some very special provisions for the adjustment and education of the deaf children. In any case, they can't be taught along with the normal children in normal schools. That is why, it is always advisable to send them right from an early age to the residential boarding schools or special schools known as the schools for deaf and dumb.

In these special schools, special provisions can be made for their adequate adjustment and educational progress by professionally trained special teachers with the help of special methods, aids and techniques. Some of the special provisions of these schools are mentioned below:

1. Hearing impaired children are here specifically trained in learning special means and methods of visual communication modes such as sign language, finger spelling and cued speech, (as you must have seen in the news broadcast for hearing impaired on the television).
2. Great pain is taken for the language development of these children with the help of training received in visual communication as well as utilisation of other senses (senses of sight, smell, touch and taste). Special provision is, therefore, made in their curriculum for making them learn vocabulary, grammar, word order, idiomatic expressions and other aspects of verbal communication.
3. Their curricular and co-curricular experiences are organised so as to impart them all the necessary education for their adjustment and education with the help of the utilisation of all other senses, besides hearing. They may thus be allowed and encouraged to see, touch, taste, smell and work out the things and experiences by themselves for getting the desired learning experiences.
4. Deaf children are seen to be specifically endowed with the increased abilities and capacities in terms of their power of sight, smell, touch, taste and physically as well as mentally working capacity etc. as a matter of compensation for their hearing disability. Therefore, special provisions in the form of curricular and co-curricular experiences are always made for deaf children so as to develop their inner abilities to make them good artists, cartoonists, writers, fashion designers, architects, scientists, and craftsmen etc.
5. Vocational training and education is also made a compulsory part of their curricular programmes in these schools to enable them to learn the means of their livelihood and become self reliant in future.
6. With the change of time and subsequent progress in educational and communicated technology, many of the progressive deaf and dumb schools have started to make use of computer education and developed technology for the education and adjustment of the deaf and dumb children. Now communication and as a result teaching-learning work is facilitated by the use of developed electronics media, computer and communication technology. As a result, deaf children may now have many useful devices available to them. The facilities regarding text telephone (enabling persons to type phone messages over the telephone), having e-mail messages and web text material can make the task of such children's adjustment and educational development easy and interesting.

EDUCATION AND ADJUSTMENT OF THE HARD OF HEARING

The task of educating and adjusting those hard of hearing is relatively simple than those of the deaf children. With a little more effort, they can be made to learn the art of better adjustment and educational development alongwith the normal children in a normal school set-up. The important aspects regarding their education and adjustment are outlined below.

1. The first and foremost task in the education and adjustment of the hard of hearing is to help them acquire specific bearable hearing aids (selected according to the degree of hearing loss) and make them habitual in their proper use and handling. The early bearing of such hearing aid may prove quite advantageous to some of the hearing impaired as it may bring desirable improvement in their hearing functioning.
2. Care should be taken in their upbringing and schooling so that they do not feel inferior on account of their hearing impairment. They should never be ridiculed, made a matter of amusement or sympathy or ignored and hated. Contrarily, they should always be treated in a normal way like other normal children so that they are not unnecessarily conscious of their disability.
3. Teachers and audiologists both should try to work together to teach the child to use his or her residual hearing to the maximum extent possible for the task of adjustment and educational progress.
4. These children as well as the parents and teachers should be trained in the utilization of proper means of communication in the task of adjustment and education of these children. The oral or manual means of communication or a combination of the two can be utilised with these children. Oral communication includes speech, speech reading and the use of residual hearing. Manual communication involves signs and finger spelling. Total communication as a method of instruction may thus be a combination of the oral method plus signs and finger spelling.
5. The hard of hearing may be trained and made habitual to listen to the sound of low intensity and frequency (by keeping the hearing aids at the time of training) with the help of the services of audio-aids like radio, tape recorder, VCR, television and computer-assisted multimedia presentation etc.
6. The use of television, video recording and computer-assisted multimedia presentation as well as the living efforts of the teachers, parents and instructors may help the hard of hearing not only to get the desired learning experiences and instructional material like the normal children but also to make them trained in making maximum use of their residual hearing in close combination with learning the art of lip-reading and language of the body movements, gestures and postures.
7. The hard of hearing usually remains backward in terms of proper language development specifically in the areas related to communication of speech. The specific efforts should be made for the proper development. For example, some of them are unable to maintain a proper language, level of the loudness or pitch of their voice in their communication. It happens since they have no idea about the proper level of the loudness or pitch in a communication at a given situation or time. Here they should be helped and trained for communicating properly with the proper intonation, intensity and frequency, pronunciation etc. specifically with the use of modern aids and equipment.
8. In the case of hearing impairments of psychogenic origin, the services of qualified therapists, counsellors and psychologists may be utilised for providing necessary assistance to the affected children for getting rid of the maladpative behaviour and symptoms of hearing impairment.

9. Help of the one or the other suitable special educational services and measures like the ones listed below may also be taken for helping the hearing impaired in their proper adjustment and educational development.
   - Favourable seating in the class and other learning situations (front bench and closer to the teacher).
   - Taking regular help of blackboard writing, sketching, charts, maps and other visual presentation alongwith the oral communication.
   - Using captioned films/videos etc. in the instructional process.
   - Regular speech, language and auditory training from a specialist.
   - Services of an interpreter for those students who use manual communication.
   - Use of amplification systems.
   - Assistance of a note-maker, who takes note for the hearing impaired, so that the impaired child can be fully benefitted from the instructions.
   - Training facilities for the parents, teachers and peers in alternative communication methods such as sign language, speech reading, body language etc.
   - Appropriate counselling and therapeutic measures for the proper adjustment of the hearing impaired to the socio-psychological environment.
   - Use of the modern helpful devices available to hearing impaired like text telephones, computer assisted or managed instructions and multimedia presentation etc.

Orthopaedically Impaired or Crippled Children

Meaning

Orthopaedically impaired or *crippled children* are those children who suffer from such defects and deformity of their bones, muscles or joints that may interfere with their normal functioning and adjustment to the general and specific demands of their environment to the extent of requiring special measures for their well-being, adjustment and educational progress.

Functional limitations caused by orthopaedical impairment

The physiological and functional problems suffered by crippled children are complex and diverse and their disabilities may be temporary, intermittent, chronic, progressive or terminal and may thus differ from individual to individual. However, generally the following types of functional limitations may be observed in the population of the crippled children,

(i) Poor muscle control.
(ii) Weakness and fatigue.
(iii) Difficulty in walking, talking, seeing, speaking, grasping (due to pain or weakness).
(iv) Difficulty in reading.
(v) Difficulty in doing complex or compound manipulations (push or turn).
(v) Inability to use the limbs.
(vi) Difficulty or total inability with regard to twisting motion.
(viii) Inability in operating even well-designed products directly without assistive devices (including mobility aids like crutches, wheelchairs, communication aids like single switch based artificial voice etc.).
(ix) Paralysis (total lack of muscular control in part or most of the body).
(x) Interference with control like problems in accuracy of motor programming and coordination, uncontrolled and purposeless motion, tense and contracted muscles, etc.

(xi) Joint movement limitation (either mechanical or due to pain).

(xii) Difficulties and inabilities faced in motor functioning due to smallness of limbs, missing limbs or abnormal trunk size.

CAUSES OF ORTHOPAEDICAL IMPAIRMENT

Heredity, in any way, can't be said to be a direct contributing factor for transmitting the orthopaedical impairment as the impairment as such cannot be carried through genes and chromosomes at the time of conception of the child. However, there is some possibility of inheriting defective body and psyche-structure or diseases responsible for the development of the orthopaedical impairment at the later stage. As an example, we may cite muscular dystrophy—a group of hearing hereditary diseases causing progressive muscular weakness, loss of muscular control contractions and difficulty in walking, breathing, reaching and use of hands involving strength. After conception, the impact of various environmental factors causing orthopaedical impairment may be outlined as below:

1. **Causes operative in the womb of the mother:** You may have seen that many children are born with some or the other types of orthopaedical impairment. It justifies the impact of negative and unfavourable influences experienced by the children in their proper growth in the womb of their mothers. Such factors may be named as the poor and defective physical and mental health of the pregnant mothers, maternal malnourishment and subsequent nutritional deficiencies suffered by the children, effect of chronic diseases, accidents and injuries caused to mothers and the children in the womb, ill effect of hard drugs, intoxicating objects, poisoning, radioactive rays exposure, etc. transmitted from the mother to the child.
2. **Causes operative at the time of birth:** There are premature deliveries and as a result, there may be many deficiencies in the growth and development of the children leading to orthopaedical impairment. In many cases, children are delivered after being operated. There may be many hazards in such operations. Sometimes newborn children get infected with chronic diseases, or get injured causing orthopaedical impairment on account of prevalent unhygienic conditions prevalent and carelessness attitude adopted by the persons associated with delivery.
3. **Accidental and incidental factors:** Mishappenings, bad incidents and accidents know no limits, age and time in one's life. From the time of conception till death, one is always exposed to such hazards in his life. Their consequences are also limitless. A simple accident like slipping in the bathroom, stumbling on the road or being hit by a light object may cause a big injury leading to serious orthopaedical impairment. You may be witnessing such scenes and reading in the newspapers, the consequences of the fatal accidents, mishappenings, nature and manmade catastrophies and calamities. People may get burnt, badly injured losing one or other limbs and important body organs including head, spinal cord, brain and other sensitive part injuries. These accidents and mishappiness may thus be considered as one of the major contributing factors of the orthopaedical impairment.
4. **Nutritional deficiency:** Many of the orthopaedical impairments in children may be caused on account of acute deficiencies of one or the other nuitritional elements or components that are essential for the growth and development as well as proper activation and functioning of the bones, muscles and their joints, the sensory and motor nerves and important parts of the brain responsible for proper cognitive and motor functioning.

Such deficiency proves too costly to the children in their early formative years of life so much so that it can make them impaired for the life time.

The effect of infection and diseases: In many cases, the orthopaedical impairment is the result of the infections received and diseases suffered by the children during the period of their growth and development. Polio, the major contributor of the orthopaedical impairment in the children, is an infectious disease. A slight carelessness or ignorance on the parts of parents and concerning health authorities leading to the non-introduction of polio drops to the child at the proper age and time may turn an otherwise normal child into an orthopaedically impaired one.

Similarly there are many other diseases, infectious or otherwise, that may cause orthopaedical impairments among the children. A few of such diseases are mentioned below:

(i) **Arthritis:** It is defined as pain in joints, usually reducing range of motion and causing weakness. Rheumatoid arthritis is a chronic syndrom. Osteoarthritis is a degenerative joint disease. All such forms of arthritis prove a potent cause for the development of orthopaedical impairments.

(ii) **Multiple Sclerosis (MS):** It is a disease of the central nervous system characterized by the destruction of the insulating material covering nerve fibres. It usually occurs between the ages of 10 and 40. This neurological disease may result into serious orthopaedical impairments characterized by poor muscle control, weakness and fatigue, difficulty in walking, talking, seeing, sensing or grasping objects, and intolerance to heat.

(iii) **Amyotropic Lateral Sclerosis (ALS):** It is a fatal disease of the central nervous system characterized by slow progressive paralysis of the voluntary muscles. It may result into progressive muscle weakness involving the limbs, trunk, breathing muscles, throat and tongue leading to partial paralysis and speech difficulties.

EDUCATION AND ADJUSTMENT OF ORTHOPAEDICALLY IMPAIRED

Where should the orthopaedically impaired children be cared and educated is an important question that can be raised at this stage. This question can be answered on the basis of the degree of impairment suffered by the indiviudal child. In case of a severe and profound impairment, the placement is necessarily to be made in the hospitals followed by the home or any other suitable boarding place. The educational and adjustments efforts should be linked and collaborated with medical and home/family attention. However, fortunately, thc number of such severally crippled and seriously impaired children is not so large. The majority belongs to the mild and moderately impaired children. Many of these orthopaedically impaired have no restrictions on what they can do and learn, unlike others who are limited to certain extent in their activities. Therefore, as far as majority is concerned their adjustment and education with a little extra effort is very much possible along with the normal children in the normal educational set up. This idea of integration with the normal children in the normal schools also suits the conditions and infrastructure of the developing countries like ours.

Now the question arises as to what should be done for these children in their adjustment and education in the normal school set-up. It is also an undeniable fact that the orthopaedically impaired children have their own needs and problems other than those of the normal children. Therefore their adjustment and education needs a little more planning and extra efforts.

The environmental as well as the educational efforts need desired enrichment in terms of curricular and co-curricular planning and experiences, methodology of providing experiences, modification and adaptation to the school environment according to their needs and adjustment, guidance and counselling etc.

Keeping all the above discussion in mind, it is advisable to proceed with the education and adjustment of the orthopaedically impaired on the lines given below:

Adopting Team Approach: The education and adjustment attempts regarding orthopaedically impaired needs coordinated efforts. The parents, teachers, school authorities, medical professionals and guidance and counselling workers all should join hands for a team work in the best interests of the impaired children. While the help from the medical professionals is required for regular medical and physical check-up of the impaired, the counsellors, therapists or psychiatrists are needed for their proper psycho-social adjustment and adaptation to environmental needs.

Development of Enriched Programmes: In the integrated educational set-up alongwith the normal children, there is a need of well-thought enriched programmes for those orthopaedically impaired. For the purpose of developing such educational programmes we must take care of the following five basic goal areas:

(a) Physical independence including mastery of daily living skills
(b) Self-awareness and social maturation
(c) Communication
(d) Academic growth including balanced personality development
(e) Life skills training including economic independence and employment abilities

Proper Implementation of the Enriched Programmes: What is thought essential for the proper education and adjustment of the impaired children should be translated into action as effectively and honestly as possible by adopting the following measures:

(i) The prime need of the orthopaedically handicapped is to make themselves self reliant in terms of the disability and handicap faced by them in managing their day-to-day affairs. The essential training for this purpose must be made an integral component of their education. In cases when the help of additional aids and equipment for their proper movements and activities are needed, they should be helped in acquiring and adapting to their use.
(ii) They must be given all possible opportunities through curricular and co-curricular experiences for their proper academic growth and balanced personality development, as provided to their normal peers. At no time should we make them feel that they are different or in any way inferior to the normal children in the matter of learning and acquiring curricular facts.
(iii) The awareness of the self, the acquaintance with the abilities and disabilities is very essential for any individual for his proper progress. Therefore, there is no harm if the impaired knows the hard facts of his disability and handicap. However, the main thing is that they should not be allowed to develop any complexes, anxiety and frustrations on account of their disability. On the contrary, they should be made to learn to make their lives more adaptable, enjoyable and optimistic by using suitable adaptive modes including social maturation, interactive and communication skills.
(iv) The vocational training and learning of such experiences so as to make them economically self-reliant, self-employed or in getting suitable employment must be made an integral part of their educational programme.
(v) They must be given such concrete experience, knowledge and skills that may successfully equip them for their better adjustment in their future life activities and socio-psycho-physical environment. These experiences may be given through various co-curricular activities and other community and social participation processes.

(vi) Nature has compensated for the disabilities and handicap and limitations felt by the impaired children in one area by rewarding them with necessary abilities, interests and aptitudes for excelling in another areas and avenues of life. As a teacher and parents, we must consciously and deliberately find out the areas and avenues where an individual impaired child may excel with a little motivation, training and educational efforts.

Proper modification and adaptation of the school environment: In the normal schools, we have an educational set-up and facilities suited to the needs and requirements of normal children. In case we plan an integrated education, we have to take care of the needed modification and adaptation of the school's facilities and environment according to the adjustment and educational needs of the impaired. Such modification and adaptation may require some provisions like below:

- The children who face difficulties in writing must be assigned little or no written assignments. The provision of oral tests instead of written should also be made for them. In some cases where the need arises they should be given more time for completing their assignments or answering the questions.
- They must be provided seating arrangement, i.e. table, chair and other working seats, according to the needs and requirements of their deformities.
- The classroom and work places should have a large area as to allow the orthopaedically handicapped move and work easily. The laboratory, reading room and library facilities, workshop areas and facilities, toilet and drinking facilities etc. must have adequate provisions and amendments according to the needs and requirements of the handicapped.
- There must be specific guidelines available to the orthopaedically impaired for being followed so that they can manage and adjust to the available environment and facilities provided in the school as easily as possible.
- Essential support services should be arranged for the adjustment and welfare of the orthopaedically impaired. These services may include the services like transportation, diagnostic services, school health services, physical therapy, occupational therapy, counseling, school social work services and medical emergency services etc.

However, in arranging support services and modifying the school environment, it should be properly taken care of that all these attempts are not more restrictive than absolutely necessary so that the student's school experiences can be as normal as possible. Over protection of any sort should always be avoided and whenever possible, handicapped children should be allowed to take risks just as their able bodied peers do.

Provision for Treatment and Welfare Measures: The school authorities with active corporation of the parents, members of the society and government and non-government agencies should work towards the welfare and treatment measures for those orthopaedically impaired. The impaired children thus should be helped in getting rid of their impairment with the help of suitable medical facilities therapies, operation, medicines etc. to the maximum extent possible. In case of incurable impairment, they must be made to adjust and live comfortably with their impairment with the help of proper medical facilities, therapies and guidance. Wherever the need arises, they must be helped in adopting artificial limbs for reducing the discomfort of their disabilities. The help of the recent advances in technology may also be taken to make their lives as close to normal as possible. For example, children with cerebral palsy (damage to the motor areas of brain prior to brain maturity) caused impairments may be helped to use computer terminal for communication. By adopting suitable technological means, even children suffering from most severe handicap can have greater control over communication and daily living skills.

In fact the task of helping the orthopaedical impaired in their adequately adjustment and educational development is quite challenging. It needs a lot of patience, hard work, sincerity and humanistic touch from all those who are concerned with such responsibilities. As emphasized earlier, it is a team work that needs joint efforts and cooperation of the teachers, parents, educational authorities and voluntary as well as governmental, social and medical agencies working in the field of education, health and rehabilitation of the handicapped. Fortunately, we have such non-government agencies as well as state and central government controlled departments and institutions that are serving the cause of the orthopaedically handicapped in many ways. We must take their services for the adjustment and educational progress of the impaired children. We can have economic assistance for their education, purchasing of aids, equipment, adoption of artificial limbs, vocational training, rehabilitation and employment etc. from these agencies. The availablity of artificial limbs and aids etc. is no longer a problem in our country. These are being manufactured at many places. The mentionable and praiseworthy work is being done by the artificial limb manufacturing establishment located at Jaipur. The work done by social welfare of the central and state governments is also praiseworthy. Rehabilitation council of India with its functionaries is also doing commendable job in this direction. Similarly a number of institutions and agencies are also taking up the challenging task of doing research in the areas of education and adjustment of the orthopaedically impaired. National Institute of orthopaedically Handicapped, a national level institute working at Calcutta, has been contributing a lot since 1981 by serving the various purposes of orthopaedically handicapped in terms of their adjustment, rehabilitation and educational progress.

Mentally Disabled or Retarded Children

Meaning and Definition

In the mental or intellectual dimensions of one's personality, while the gifted lies on the top of the scale, the mentally disabled occupy the lowest end. These are the children who are handicapped or disabled in terms of the functioning of their mental abilities or capacities in the same sense as the physically handicapped demonstrate their inabilities or incapacities in performing some or the other physical functions. As a matter of terminology, such children are known by so many names other than mentally disabled such as "mentally retarded", "feeble-minded", "mentally handicapped", "mentally deficient", "mentally subnormal" or "mentally sub average" etc. By whatever name we may call them, these are the children who possess sub-average intellectual functioning or suffer from mental retardation on one account or the other. It will be, therefore, appropriate to understand the meaning of the term 'mental retardation', before attempting and defining the term 'mentally retarded' or 'mentally disabled'.

Mental retardation as a term stands for a special type of psychological disorder associated with the arrest or incomplete development of one's brain, beginning usually at birth and leading to a diminution of intellectual powers relative to his chronological age. Actually *retardation* as a term is frequently used in the subjects physics and engineering as antonym to the term 'acceleration'. Here acceleration stands for uniform increase in the velocity of a moving object and retardation for a gradual decrease.

The same sense is conveyed here in the subject psychology through the term mental retardation. The rate of growth and development of one's intellectual powers gets diminished or arrested. It does not pick the normal speed expected from the children of that very chronological age. Certainly such affected children lag behind and become handicapped in performing expected normal intellectual behaviour. That is why they are also named as 'mentally handicapped' children. The other common term used for these children is 'mentally deficient' children indicating that these children certainly suffer from a certain type of deficiency or incompleteness in terms of the expected normal intellectual development.

Let us further know about the meaning and nature of the term 'mental retardation' or 'mental deficiency' through some well-known definitions:

J.D. Page
Mental Deficiency or Retardation is a condition of subnormal mental development present at birth or early childhood and characterized mainly by limited intelligence and social inadequacy. (1976, p. 354)

American Association on Mental Deficiency
Mental retardation refers to significantly sub-average intellectual functioning existing concurrently with deficits in adaptive behaviour and manifested during the developmental period. (1973, p. 326)

British Mental Deficiency Act
Mental retardation is a condition of arrested or incomplete development of mind existing before the age of 18 years whether arising from inherent causes or induced by disease or injury. (1981, pp. 197–198)

A close analysis of the above definitions may reveal the following things about the meaning and characteristics of mental retardation or mental deficiency.

- Mental retardation is a condition or state of mind.
- It is not a disease or illness of the mind.
- It is related to the subnormal development of the mind or brain.
- It is also related to one's inadequate adjustment with the environment.
- The deficiency may be observed at birth or in early childhood.
- Both the inherent and external factors may cause mental retardation.

Equipped with the above meaning and characteristics of mental retardation, we may now be able to evolve a definition of the term 'mentally retarded' or 'mentally disabled' children in the following way:

Mentally retarded or disabled children are those children who suffer from the retarded, subnormal or deficient growth and development of their brain affecting their intellectual capacities to the extent that they feel handicapped in their adaptation to the environment and thus require special care and provision for their welfare and development of their capacities.

TYPES OF MENTALLY RETARDED OR DISABLED CHILDREN

There have been many attempts to devise certain ways and means for classifying the mentally retarded into some definite types according to the degree of the seriousness of their mental deficiency or retardation. Two of such attempts based on I.Q. and adaptive behaviour are quite popular. Let us try to discuss these attempts now.

Classification Based on Intelligence Tests: The concept of I.Q. and scores on intelligence tests have been found useful in labeling the individual as gifted, average (normal) or subnormal (retarded). Terman, using Standford Binet Scale, tried to label the individual with I.Q. between 90 and 100 as normal or average and persons with I.Q. below 90 as below average or subnormal. The subnormals were further categorized as under:

Table 34.1 Categories of Mental Retardation

Category	*Range of I.Q.*
Idiots	below 25
Imbeciles	from 25 to 50
Morons	from 51 to 75
Border line and the dull	from 76 to 90

The individuals falling into the above categories (except a few border line cases as they have the equal chances of drifting towards subnormal and normal categories) are labeled as idiot, imbecile, moron and dull are known as mentally retarded or mentally handicapped.

But this classification based on I.Q. is quite arbitrary and we can find differences of opinion regarding the range of I.Q. and its corresponding category. But one thing is certain that all mentally retarded or mentally handicapped children possess sub-normal intellectual capacities i.e. they are basically less capable of intelligent behaviour than normal children of their age. Diagnosis of such sub-normal intellectual capacities is not a simple task. Intelligence tests alone do not suffice. Also latest researches in the field of sub-normality have raised doubts about the creditability of I.Q. scores. It was felt that a certain level of I.Q. score does not by itself designate an individual a mental retarded. He must also be unable to adapt to the natural and social demands of the environment. Consequently, the importance of assessment of adaptive behaviour in the identification and demarcation of the level of mental subnormality has been realised.

Adaptive Behaviour as a Means of Classification

This criterion describes one's adaptive behaviour expected of his age and cultural group in two ways for the required assessment.

- The degree to which the individual is able to function and maintain himself independently, and
- The degree to which he meets satisfactorily the culturally imposed demands of personal and social responsibility.

Attempts have been made to devise measures for the assessment of deficiency in adaptive behaviour through Vineland Social Maturity Scale, Adaptive Behaviour Scale (AAMD) and Maxfield Buck Holz Social Maturity Scale.

The consideration of deficiency in adaptive behaviour alongwith the very low scores on an intelligence test resulted in the development of an altogether new classification of sub-normality. The terms moron, imbecile, or idiot are now completely avoided for determining the level of retardation. The new terminology in terms of obtained I.Q. on different tests scale is represented in Table 34.2.

Table 34.2 Levels of Mental Retardation

Level of retardation	*Intelligence Quotient*	
	Stanford Binet	*Wechsler scales*
Profound	Under 20	Under 25
Severe	20-35	25-39
Moderate	36-51	40-54
Mild	52-67	55-69

In view of their typical sub-normal intelligence and deficient adaptive behaviour, these categories are described below:

Mild retardation

A majority of approximately 85 per cent of the retarded belongs to this category. They are found to possess the following main characteristics:

- In adult life, these individuals attain intellectual levels comparable to that of the average ten years old child. Their social adjustment may be compared with that of the adolescent. Here too they lack the innovative and vigorous nature of normal adolescents.
- They show signs of delayed development early in life and learn to walk, talk, feed and toilet themselves an year later than the average. They may be identified in schools as slow learners and are frequently required to repeat early grades. Speech disturbances are common among them.
- In comparison with normal individuals, the mildly retarded exhibit immature behaviour, have poor control over their impulses, lack judgment and fail to anticipate the consequence of their actions. Their sexual behaviour and adjustment, in spite of the normal sexual development and fertility, is unpredictable and leads to a variety of problems and difficulties.
- The mildly retarded individuals generally do not show any organic pathology and require little supervision.
- They are considered to be educable. With early diagnosis, parental assistance, and aid of special classes, they can be expected to reach a reasonable degree of educational achievement and to make an adequate social and economic adjustment in the community.

Moderate mental retardation

About 10 per cent of the total mentally retarded belong to this category. Their main characteristics may be summarized as below:

- In adult life they attain intellectual level similar to that of the average six-year-old.
- Physically they appear clumsy, suffer from lack of motor co-ordination and present an affable, dull and somewhat vacuous personality.
- As a result of their inadequate development and deficient capacities and abilities they are regarded as 'trainable' instead of being 'educable' like the mildly retarded.
- From early infancy or childhood they show signs of retardation in almost all areas of development, and though they manage to speak, their rate of learning is too slow. They are unable to do any work that requires initiative, originality, abstract thinking, memory or consistent attention, and cannot be expected to acquire the basic skills of reading and writing.

However, with early diagnosis, parental help and adequate training and support, most of the moderately retarded can achieve considerable independence in all spheres of life. Nevertheless, they require constant supervision and support and need institutionalization depending on their general level of adaptive behaviour.

Severe mental retardation

Nearly 3.5 per cent of the total retarded individuals—mostly children and adolescents—belong to this category. Their main characteristics may be summarised as below:

- They never attain an intellectual level greater than that of the average four-year-old child.
- The mortality rate due to high susceptibility to disease is quite high among these individuals.
- They are grossly retarded in development from birth or infancy onward and show severe motor and speech retardation. Sensory defects and motor handicaps are common.
- The majority of them display relatively little interest in their surroundings and many of them never master even the necessary skills and functions like feeding and dressing themselves, or bladder and bowel control.
- The severe mental retardates are neither 'educable' nor 'trainable' and the majority of them remain dependent on others throughout their lives. They need care and supervision of others with a great need for institutionalization.
- They may profit with proper care, timely treatment and specialized training for managing their own physical well-being and doing manual labour,

Profound mental retardation

This group makes 1.5 per cent of the total mentally retarded population. It is characterized by the most severe symptoms of mental retardation as given below:

- The individuals belonging to this category never attain in adult life an intellectual level greater than that of the average two-year-old child.
- They are severely deficient both in their intellectual capacities and adaptive behaviour. The symptoms associated with them are retarded growth, physical deformities, pathology of the central nervous system, autism, severe speech disturbances, motor incoordination, deafness and convulsive seizures.
- They are unable to protect themselves from common dangers and are unable to manage their own affairs and satisfy their physical needs.
- Their life span, as a result of their low resistance, is too short.
- Such individuals are completely dependent on others and need the care and supervision given to an infant.
- Essentially, they need to be institutionalized as their condition deteriorates on account of the biased attitude of the parents and stressfull demands of their environment.

Causes of Mental Retardation

It is difficult to postulate some standard causes for mental retardation that can be applicable to every case of mental retardation. Mental deficiency or retardation is an individual problem and should be treated as a unique case in itself. However, for the general diagnosis of such cases, the characteristics of mentally retarded or handicapped individuals besides his I.Q., can serve a useful purpose. The knowledge of the probable causes may also help in this direction. These causes can be listed as under:

Factors operative at the time of conception

Mental retardation may be caused by some defective genes in the chromosomes of one or both parents at the time of fertilization.

Factors operative inside the womb of the mother

When the child is in the womb of the mother, which is approximately for the period of 9 months, improper and deficient intra-uterine environment may cause mental retardation. Abnormal emotional and mental conditions of the mother during pregnancy, her severe illness and chronic infections; and the deficiencies with respect to food which a human embryo receives from the blood stream of the mother are some of the factors that may lead to mental deficiency.

Factors operative at the time of delivery

It is possible that at the time of delivery, too short or too long labour or use of mechanical instruments may cause head injuries to the child. Such head injuries often cause mental retardation.

Post natal factors (Factors operative from birth to death)

In addition to the causes mentioned above, mental deficiency may be caused by the following post natal factors:

(i) Head injuries due to accidents.
(ii) Infections and chronic diseases in early childhood.
(iii) Food deficiency and malnutrition.
(iv) Socio-cultural and educational deprivation.
(v) Emotional maladjustment and mental conflicts.

PREVENTIVE AND REMEDIAL MEASURES

If we review all the possible causes of mental retardation given above, we can find that mental retardation is the product of both heredity and the environment. Therefore, it is not proper to blame heredity alone for the child's mental deficiency. The realization of such environmental effects increases the responsibility of parents, teachers, responsible members of the society and state authorities. They may join their hands in the task of providing proper atmosphere for the growth and development of the children so that the environmental forces may not get free hand in causing mental deficiency among the children. Definitely something can be done regarding the improvement and controlling of environmental situation but we are helpless in controlling heredity and accidental factors. Therefore, the cases of mental retardation are sure to exist and consequently, we have to think about the measures for the treatment and cure of mental retardation.

Regarding the cure of mental retardation, it has been already said that by virtue of its definition it is incurable, in the sense that mentally retarded child cannot be given more intelligence and made normal. But attempts can be made to educate and train him so that he may become useful for himself as well as for the society. The first step in the education of such children is to make their parents realize the truth about their children. They should be persuaded to send their children to special boarding schools meant for mentally handicapped children. It is the best place for their education and training. In homes, the involved attitudes of the parents interfere with the proper development of the retarded child. These schools should be managed properly so that they may provide essential environment for maximum development of the personality of the child. Curriculum, method of teaching and tools for the evaluation should be adjusted according to the individual needs. More emphasis should be given on co-curricular experiences and they should be given training for manual work and crafts. Care should also be taken for their social and emotional development and they should be enabled to manage their affairs independently.

Learning Disabled Children

Meaning and Definitions

Children suffering from serious learning disabilities are labelled as learning disabled children. Now question may arise as to what are these learning disabilities.

In fact learning disability is nothing but a sort of handicap or helplessness that can be felt by the sufferer in terms of his or her academic performance (learning or understanding something) in the same way as experienced by a mentally disabled in terms of his mental functioning or by a physically handicapped or disabled in terms of his physical functioning.

Interpreting in this way, a learning disabled child suffers with the inconveniences and problems in the learning areas in the same way as experienced by a mentally handicapped in mental or cognitive areas, or by a physically handicapped in the physical and motor areas or even by a socially or emotionally handicapped in the social and emotional areas.

Let us try to know more about the terms 'learning disabled' and 'learning disabilities' with the help of a few well known definitions given below:

S.A. Kirk

The term learning disability is not meant to be used for children with minor or temporary difficulties in learning but with a severe discrepancy between ability and achievement in educational performance and such severed discrepancy described as learning disabilities with significant learning problems that cannot be explained by mental retardation, sensory, impairment, emotional disturbance or lack of opportunity to learn. (1971)

National Joint Committee on Learning Disabilities, USA

Learning disabilities as a generic term refers to a heterogeneous group of disorders manifested by significant difficulties in the acquisition and use of listening, speaking, reading, writing, reasoning or mathematical abilities. These disorders are intrinsic to the individual presumed to be due to central nervous system dysfunction and may occur across the life span. Problem in self-regulatory behaviours, social perception and social interaction may exist with learning disabilities but do not by themselves constitute a learning disability. Although learning disabilities may occur concomitantly with other handicapping conditions (for example, sensory impairment, mental retardation, serious emotional disturbance or social maladjustment) or with extrinsic influences (such as cultural differences or lack of opportunity to learn), they are not the result of those conditions or influences. (McLoughlin and Netick, 1983, pp. 21–23)

Kavale & Forness

People with learning disabilities belong to a group of very diverse individuals but they do share one common problem. They do not learn in the same way or as efficiently as their non-disabled peers. Although most possess normal intelligence, their academic performance is significantly behind their classmates. Some have great difficulty in learning mathematics, but most find the mastery of reading and writing to be their most difficult challenge. (1966)

A close analysis of all these definitions may reveal the following things concerning meaning and concept of the terms *learning disabilities* and *learning disabled.*

1. Learning disabilities refer to certain kinds of disorders in the basic psychological processes of an individual.
2. These disorders are mainly caused by intrinsic factors (lying within the individual) like central nervous system dysfunction (some brain or neurological damage impending one's motor or learning abilities), specific deficits in information processing or the ability to learn.

3. Although one or the other learning problem may be caused by extrinsic factors like mental retardation, sensory impairment, emotional disturbance, cultural differences, lack of educational opportunities, poverty etc. Learning disability is not the direct result of such external factors or conditions.
4. Disorders associated with learning disabilities are usually manifested into some specific severe learning problems confined to one or two cognitive areas like inability to grasp or understand the things, difficulty in language related areas such as communication, written language or reading, or handicap in terms of acquiring mathematical or social skills.
5. Individuals with minor or temporary difficulties in learning are not termed as learning disabled. Only those who have severely impaired learning inefficiency and serious learning problems are included in this category.
6. The learning disability may allow an individual to have intelligence scores within the normal range but it essentially makes them substantially delayed in academic achievement. He always lags behind in terms of his educational progress in comparison to the peers of his age and class.
7. The impaired learning inefficiency coupled with serious learning problems in one or the other cognitive areas leads to a distinctive gap between an individual's potential and actual education achievement and as a result he becomes disabled or handicapped in one or the other learning areas so much so that he needs special care, attention and educational services for his adjustment and welfare.

In this way learning disability provides a lot of obstacles and difficulties in the path of learning. Gradually the learning problems become so acute as to cause severely impaired learning inefficiency in one or the other cognitive areas. It leads to a distinctive gap between one's potential and actual educational achievement which require special care, attention and remedial measures and when it happens the learner is labelled as learning disabled.

NATURE AND CHARACTERISTICS OF LEARNING DISABLED

Researches in the fields of education and psychology have brought into notice a number of significant behavioural and personality characteristics as well as general outcomes of the nature and characteristics of the learning disabled children. Let us mention a few important ones.

1. Learning disabled children essentially suffer from serious learning problems or disorders for a number of reasons.
2. Their problems and disorders are usually manifested by significant difficulties in the acquisition and use of language (listening, speaking, reading, writing etc.), reasoning or mathematical ability or of social skills.
3. They may exhibit symptoms of hyperactivity and impulsiveness.
4. Most of them may suffer from emotional problems and demonstrate signs of anxiety, moodiness or ups and downs in their behaviour.
5. Their learning disability is neither apparent in the physical appearance, nor demonstrable through their I.Q. scores. They may have robust body, good vision, sound ears, and normal intelligence.
6. They essentially suffer from severely impaired learning efficiency or a handicap, which is just as real as a crippled leg.
7. All of them essentially exhibit a significant educational discrepancy, *i.e.* a wide gap between their learning potential and actual educational achievement.
8. Some of them may demonstrate equivocal neurological signs and EFG irregularities.

9. They may exhibit disorders of memory, thinking, attention general coordination perception and motor functioning etc.
10. Main problem for all these children lies in their observable deficiency in learning and mastering academic tasks. They are handicapped in learning and acquisition in the same way as physically and mentally handicapped are in physical and mental performances.
11. They usually exhibit the following learning characteristics responsible for their learning impairment (i) lack of motivation, (ii) inattention, (iii) inability to generalize, and (iv) lack of adequate ability in problem solving, information processing and thinking skills, etc.
12. Their learning impairment is so severe that they essentially require special attention, care and remedial programmes for the rectification of their learning problems and disabilities.

CAUSES OF LEARNING DISABILITIES

Depending on the types of learning disabilities found in the children, a number of researches have been conducted to find out the possible factors or causes of learning disabilities. Generally the factors causing learning disabilities may be found to fall in the following three categories:

Genetic or heredity factors

In some cases, the genetic or heredity factor is found to be the major cause for generating learning disabilities among children. On the pattern "Like begets like," it has been found that many characteristics commonly found in the learning disabled are transmitted from generation to generation. This relationship between inheritance and disabilities has been established on the basis of the following results:

(a) Nearly 20 to 25 per cent of the hyperactive or impulsive children have been found to have at least one parent of this nature.

(b) Emotional imbalances, disorders of memory and thinking, speech and learning have been found to run in families.

(c) Going deep into the genetic research, US scientists and psychologists have attained success in identifying particular genes that may be held responsible for reading and other learning problems.

Organic or physiological factors

Study of most learning disabled cases reveals that they suffer from malfunctioning or dysfunction of their central nervous system consisting of brain, spinal cord and message carrying nerves etc. This dysfunction, however minimal, is caused by the factors like:

(a) Brain damage caused by an accident or by lack of oxygen before, during or after birth resulting in neurological difficulties that may affect their ability to learn.

(b) Damage or injury caused to the spinal cord and message carrying nerves etc. leading to their malfunctioning and subsequent learning difficulties.

(c) Dysfunction of the central nervous system may be caused by biochemical imbalances generated by the factors like:

  (i) Colouring and flavourings in many of the food items consumed by the children may cause hyperactivity, impulsivity, emotional imbalance etc. leading to the malfunctioning of the central nervous system.

  (ii) Vitamin deficiency may cause inability of a child's bloodstream to synthesize normal amount of vitamins essential for normal functioning of the central nervous system.

In short, it can be concluded that one's learning capacities and abilities are very much dependent on proper functioning of one's central nervous system. Dysfunction of the central nervous system in any form may thus affect and cause serious learning difficulties and hence any factor that can cause neurological damage to our central nervous system may lead to its malfunctioning and subsequent learning difficulties.

Environmental factors

In many cases, learning disabilities may be caused by the improper and uncongenial conditions and factors present in an individual's physical, social, cultural and educational environment. Some of these factors have been cited as under:

(a) The poor nourishment and defective environment received by the foetus in the mother's womb.
(b) Pre-mature delivery, uncongenial and improper environmental setting at the time of birth or a defect in the central nervous system.
(c) Diet deficiency in the early age, severe diseases, accidents and injuries that may cause central nervous system dysfunction.
(d) Children who do not receive proper medical care and attention and as a result suffer from any impairment in their senses of hearing, sight, taste, touch, smell and other neurological functioning become handicapped in terms of learning.
(e) Insufficient early experiences and stimulation in terms of learning and acquisition received on account of defective educational set-up.
(f) Poor or inadequate instructions received on account of their own family set-up or lack of motivation, skill and ability on the part of teachers.
(g) Emotional disturbance and lack of motivation on account of many factors present in a person's environment and even on account of malfunctioning of his physiological processes.
(h) Inadequate and improper development of langauge skills, lack of concentration and adequate attention.
(i) Use of drugs and intoxicating substances like alcohol.
(j) Imitation and the company of defective learning models present in one's cultural social and educational environment.
(k) Social and cultural deprivation.

Identification of Learning Disabled Children

Identification of learning disabled children may be done mainly in two ways—the employment of non-testing and testing devices.

Non-testing Devices

In this category, we may include techniques like observation, rating scale, check list, interview etc. By employing these devices, we can identify the learning disabled in relation to their general personality and characteristics. We may find a list of these characteristics common with the learning disabled and then weigh the observed child in relation to these for the identification of the degree of disability. We may also seek the opinion of teachers and other persons regarding the learning abilities, mental level, scholastic potential etc. through such devices for the diagnosis and identification of learning disabilities of the children.

Testing devices

Testing devices include different types of tests that can be used as diagnostic measures for the identification and assessment of children with different kinds of learning disabilities. Generally, the following types of tests fall into this category

(a) **Standardized diagnostic tests** Many such tests available in our country as well as abroad. With the help of norms given in these tests, we can assess the relative educational standard of the children of same age or grade and thus may be acquainted with the educational deficits and deficiencies of a particular child. As a result we can have a reliable and valid diagnosis of the learning difficulties in various areas of scholastic performance especially in language, mathematics, social and experimental skills etc. Example of such available standardized diagonostic tests are:

   (i) *Diagnostic test in Decimal Systems and Percentage* by V.P. Sharma and Shukla.
   (ii) *Durrell Analysis of Reading Difficulty* by Durrell.
   (iii) *The Stanford Diagnostic Arithmetic Test* by Betty, Madden and Gardner.
   (iv) *The Spache Diagnostic Reading Scales* by Spache.
   (v) *The Gates Mckillop Reading, Diagnostic Test* by Gates and Mckillop.

(b) **Ability tests or process tests** Learning disabled suffer from the inability or incapacity in their process of learning and understanding. The ability tests or process tests are so designed as to assess the degree of their inability or poor ability to understand and learn. Since the learning of a child is processed through his abilities of visual perception, auditory perception, eye motor coordination, psycho-linguistic understanding etc., the ability tests or the process tests are designed to test the abilities of the children related to these areas. Examples of such tests are:

   (i) *The Marianne Frosting Development Test of Visual Perception* by Frosting Lefever and Whittlesey.
   (ii) *Illinois Test of psycholinguistic Abilities* by Kirk, McCarthy and Kirk.

(c) **Achievement tests** These tests are designed to assess the degree of achievement of children in various knowledge, skills and performance process areas. These may be of two types, namely *Standardized achievement tests and Teacher made tests.* While the former are structured by an outside agency and are readily available for administration, the latter are constructed by individual teachers in their respective subjects or areas for assessing the degree of the children's achievement or diagnosing their learning difficulties and diasbilites. The performance of the individual students in these tests may reveal many things about the nature and extent of the learning deficiencies and deficits vis-a-vis various learning areas.

(d) **Daily assessment system** There can be a systematie, well-planned regular assessment system on a daily basis in schools for recording the children's achievement on various specific knowledge, skill and performance areas. This process of continued information may bring into limelight many important things related with the nature and extent of learning deficiencies and deficits of individual learners, particularly in relation to the processes of their learning and understanding.

Educational Provisions for the Learning Disabled

Let us think what can be done to the learning disabled children once they have been identified. Their identification clearly reveals that they suffer from somewhat a severe learning inefficiency, deficiency or deficit resulting into a serious gap between their potential and actual educational achievement. One or the other factors lying within them or their environment may be the reason for it. We can find diversity in terms of their learning disabilities, their nature, types, degree of handicapness and etiology. As a result it is not proper to treat them as a group for their learning deficiencies and disabilities. Each one of them is unique. Therefore no uniform treatment or remedial measure can be prescribed to all the learning disabled. Each one of them is to be cared and treated as a separate and individual case. This is why great care should be taken for the proper identification of the nature and amount of learning disability or disabilities of a particular child. The treatment then should be given on the basis of proper analysis and evaluation of the identification data. The researches in this field have devised many ways. Let us discuss a few of such measures.

Provision of specialized schools or classes

This provision is based on the assumption that learning disabled children are quite distinct from other children of their schools or classes. They cannot be taught along with others as they suffer from severe learning deficiencies and deficits. Hence there should be special schools or at least separate classes for them where they can be taught by specialized teachers through special methods and techniques essentially on the same curriculum with greater care and attention.

In the specialized schools, learning disabled children thus find a complete specialized segregated setting. However, in the specialized classes in a regular school there is somewhat less segregation in comparison to the specialized schools. Here there is a provision for special instruction by special teachers for overcoming the learning deficiencies of the sufferers. In this task the help of the regular classteachers may also be counted for providing assistance in teaching subject matter. Alongwith the instructions related to academic subjects, experiences related to social and co-curricular activities are also provided alongwith the other normal students.

However, the segregated setting, whether in the form of separate schools or classes, suffers from serious defects and limitations. In fact, such segregation is neither feasible nor practicable. It is far from ground realities and may prove futile as we cannot arrange segregation or separation based on the individualized learning inefficiencies and deficits. Each of the learning disabled is a unique case in himself. He or she needs individualized attention, care or even different methods, techniques and treatment for the rectification of his or her deficiency and overall adjustment. Therefore, the provision of putting the learning disabled in separate schools or classes cannot work well and hence we should now try to evaluate the other two provisions.

Provision of special remedial and educational programmes

This provision can work well in the existing school and educational set-up. Here the beginning can be made with the proper identification of the nature, type and amount of learning difficulties, deficiencies or deficits. Then proper special remedial and educational programmes may be made out of the readymade programmes available in the market or at other places having provision for such educational services. The Resource Centre of the Colleges of Education, DIETS, SCERT, NCERT, Extension Department of Universities and many other social and community organisations usually provide such educational services and necessary help from these centres simply on the institution to institution transaction basis can be obtained for the required pupose. The remedial programmes, material and guidance available through such sources may definitely help the cause of learning disabled. For example, if the deficiency and deficits of the suffering children are related to the neural impairments in sensory motor system, we can follow remedial programmes like (i) The Strauss Lehtinen-Cruickshank Perceptual Motor Programme, (ii) Getman's Visuo-Motor Programme etc.

Similarly if their deficiencies and deficits are related to their psycho-linguistic ability, these can be rectified through standardized remedial programmes like (i) Witmer's Psycho-Educational, (ii) The Fernald Kinesthetic Remedial Reading Method, (iii) The Pragmatic General Diagnostic Remedial Approaches by Blanco or Morgan etc.

Structuring and improving the existing environmental set-up

Many of the learning difficulties and deficiencies of children are caused by uncongenial, improper and negative factors present in their physical, social, cultural and educational environment. Therefore, attempts should be properly and honestly made for the adequate structuring and improving of the existing environmental set-up. It will definitely help in reducing the case of learning disabled by providing them due assistance, care and guidance for the rectification of their learning disabilities. The task requires the joint efforts of all those who are concerned with the upbringing, education and welfare of the children. The parents, members of the family, teachers, guidance and counselling workers, educational authorities, social and community agencies etc. all should join hands for providing due care, attention and remedial and educational programmes to the learning disabled. They should help them in acquiring desirable personality traits by overcoming their deficiencies with regard to their educational progress and behavioural drawbacks. What can be expected from them can be summarized in the following way:—

(a) Great care should be taken by the parents and teachers, in picking up proper methods of learning, communication, perceptual motor movements and general coordination etc.

(b) Efforts should be made to restructure and improve the man-material facilities provided in the schools so as to suit individual learners as per their needs, interests and abilities. There must be proper integration of theory with practice as well as of curricular with co-curricular activities. Methods of teaching as well as the handling the students should be structured so as to cater to the needs and difficulties of the learning disabled present in a particular group, section or class.

(c) If the learning disabilities are so severe that it demands very special care and attention, then learning disabled should be placed in full time special learning set-up under the guidance of a specially trained teacher. Here they must be given full opportunity and training for improving their poor study habits, methods of improper learning and for modifying their undesirable and inappropriate socio-emotional and psycho-educational behaviour. After putting the learning disabled into a highly structured environment and getting satisfactory results, he should be moved back into a less isolated setting and subsequently into a normal classroom setting.

(d) Whether we employ specialized trained teachers or the usual classroom or subject teachers with some extra knowledge and training to deal with learning disabled, the one most important thing is their behaviour and attitude towards these children. One should not lose patience as these children are essentially slow learners, underachievers and far from satisfactory in their socio-psychological behaviour. They should be accepted with all their weaknesses and deficiencies. Snubbing, ridiculing, or punishing these children in any form leads to negative and harmful results. The parents, elders and teachers all should exhibit love and care while dealing with them. Our approach towards them, as far as possible, should be very constructive, pleasant as well as encouraging so that these disabled children may learn the proper method of learning and behaving and develop required self-confidence and positive attitude of their educational progress by getting rid of at least some learning difficulties and deficiencies from their behaviour.

(e) In schools as well as in community setting, there should be proper arrangement with regard to a well-structured educational setting or resources centre with adequate learning material, equipment and some trained specialized teachers, experts in guiding and helping the learning disabled. With the help of available men and material resources, the learning disabled should be helped in overcoming their deficits and deficiencies in skills like spelling, handwriting, memory, verbal expression, comprehension, mathematical skills, experimentation and observation, thinking and reasoning skills, visual and auditory perception, sensory motor development, social skills, and so on.

EMOTIONALLY DISTURBED CHILDREN

Meaning and Concept

In a generalized way, children who suffer from emotional maladjustment or deviant and defective expression of their emotional behaviour, causing problems to their self and others are referred to as *emotionally disturbed children*. However, in practical sense the term 'emotionally handicapped' is conceptualized by different individuals in the different ways. From the viewpoint of teachers it may be used for those children who are too agressive, shy or withdrawn, or those who disrupt the general atmosphere of the class and school and thus put undue pressure on the teachers.

From the viewpoint of the parents, children who do not obey their commands, demonstrate extremely aggressive or withdrawn behaviour, create problem situations for members of the family or become scape goat on account of the emotional disturbances of parents are termed as 'emotionally disturbed children'.

From the angle of psychiatrists and guidance personnel, those children who are the victims of uncongenial especially the frustrating environment at their homes, in schools or in other socio-cultural situations fall prey to emotional disturbance. They opine that children whose basic needs are not gratified to the extent of causing serious adjustment problems to their self and the environment become emotionally maladjusted and disturbed.

So people are found to possess their own conception of emotionally disturbed children. Let us try to form a somewhat proper and more agreeable concept of the term 'emotionally handicapped' children by taking into consideration the definitions put forward by some eminent scholars and authorities.

Phillips, E.I. (1967) in his article "Problems in education of emotionally disturbed children" has tried to define this term as under.

"Emotional disorder or disturbance in children can be defined in terms of certain observable characteristics such as hyperactivity, withdrawn behaviour, failure to achieve a level reasonably commensurate with ability or tendency towards fighting and other aggressive behaviour, resentment and antagonism towards authority and rules and regulations, and general problem in learning and concentrating not associated with known organic or sensory defects."

American Psychiatric Association (1980) in its Diagnostic and Statistical manual of mental disorders (DSM III) has defined the term emotional disturbance as under.

"It is a type of psychiatric disturbance without clearly defined physical cause or without structural damage to the brain".

Bower, E.M. (1981) in his book "Early identification of emotionally handicapped children in school" has defined the term emotionally disturbed children as under.

Emotionally disturbed children are those children who are characterised with any one or more of the five characteristics namely, (i) learning problems not explained by intellectual, sensory, or health factors, (ii) difficulties in initiating and maintaining interpersonal relationship, (iii) behavioural or emotional reactions are not appropriate to circumstances, (iv) pervasive unhappiness or depression, and (v) development of physical symptoms or fears related to school or personal problems.

From the above definitions, we may know that the state of emotional disturbance of a child comprise some observable characteristics of the abnormality of the behaviour, the problems felt and the consequences arrived as a result of such problems. Emotional disturbed children are usually found to suffer with the psychiatric or behavioural problems so much so that it may make them handicapped in terms of their adequate adjustment and needed progress.

We may thus conclude that *emotionally disturbed children are those children who suffer from one or the other psychiatric or behavioural disturbances or disorders (not caused due to organic or physical factors) to the extent of making them handicapped in terms of their adequate adjustment to their self and environment and obstructing their needed progress in all walks of life.*

Classification of Emotionally Disturbed Children

Typically, all the children suffering from emotional disturbances exhibit remarkable symptoms of childhood psychiatric or behavioural disorders. Depending upon the nature of their disturbances, these children may be classified into seven types described as under:

Children Suffering from Depression

These children suffer from pervasive unhappiness or depression. Such children are found to harbour intense feelings of dejection, discouragement and sadness. There is a high level of anxiety and apprehensiveness and extreme feelings of self condemnation. The child suffering from depression is unable to concentrate and his level of activity and initiative is lowered. In its most severe form, the anxiety and desperation are heightened to such an extent that the child is unable to study or do related work and sits alone in despair viewing the dark side of life and sometimes have suicidal thoughts. Depression of these children may be viewed as the type of such emotional disturbance where the suffering child tries to direct his hostility or anger towards the self instead of being turned outward. Instead of blaming others, the individual blames himself for the loss and the distressing situation.

Children Suffering from Anxiety Disorders

A number of emotionally disturbed children suffer from anxiety disorders. Such children exhibit a maladaptive behaviour pattern dominated by chronic apprehensiveness with recurring episodes of acute anxiety, helplessness and resentment so much so that it seriously interferes with their adjustment and well being. Their intense feelings of anxiety may lead them to an intense state of tension, panic, stress and discomfort visible through symptoms like difficulty in breathing, disturbances of sleep and appetite, heart palpitation and faintness, tremors of the hands and limbs etc.

Children Suffering from Phobias

Phobias occur when anxiety and its somatic or behavioural concomitants are displayed in the presence of a feared object or situation. Children suffering from such emotional disturbance are seen to experience persistent, intense and irrational fear of a specific situation or object. They may have a fear of height of open places, of darkness, of crowds, of water and so on. They may also exhibit a specific kind of phobia named as school phobia. It is a specific phobic reaction resulting from fears about school experiences, separation from parents or a combination of both.

CHILDREN SUFFERING FROM PSYCHOSOMATIC OR PSYCHOPHYSIOLOGICAL DISORDERS

In such disorders, children are known to exhibit changes in their physiological functioning due to stress and emotional factors. A few mentionable disorders of this type are migraine (extremely painful headache), anorexia nervosa (loss of appetite leading to weight loss to the point of emaciation), peptic ulcer, hypertension, asthma, diarrhoea, vomiting, abdominal pain, hysteria etc. Indeed such type of psychosomatic dysfunction (caused by the interaction of biological, social and psychological factors) constitutes one of the major causes of school absence.

CHILDREN SUFFERING FROM PERSONALITY DISORDERS

Personality disorders are also often named as conduct or character disorders. These are characterized by the impairment of one's ability to maintain normal social relationships and repeated conflicts with the norms and values of the society one lives in. Children and adolescents suffering from these disorders are those who suffer by a general failure to acquire effective habits of adjustment and adequate social relationships and as a result are found to display a pattern of disturbed or antisocial behaviour. Children suffering from delinquents, alcoholism and drug addiction, sexual deviations, etc. may be included in this category. However, based on symptom clusters, we may try to group the children's personality disorders into the following three categories:

(i) Emotional constriction, rigidity, aloofness and the inability to maintain interpersonal relationships, (e.g. Schizoid, Paranoid and Schizotypal personality disorders).

(ii) Dramatic, emotional, self-centered and unstable behaviours (e.g. identity disorders, conduct disorders, histrionic, narcissistic and antisocial personality disorders).

(iii) Intra psychic struggles between anxiety and defenses against anxiety (e.g. avoidant disorder, dependent disorder, compulsive disorder and passive-aggressive disorder).

CHILDREN SUFFERING FROM PSYCHOTIC DISORDERS

Psychotic disorders represent the most serious psychiatric disorders (disorders of the mind). The most striking example of the type of disorder is childhood schizophrenia. The children suffering from such disorders exhibit serious forms of emotional and personality disturbances like:

(i) Periodic or prolonged loss of contact with the real world.

(ii) Manifesting symptoms of the nature like delusions (beliefs contrary to reality), hallucinations (perception contrary to reality like hearing voices in a completely silent room), stupor (state of immobility with partial or complete unconsciousness), incoherence (disconnected and unrelated thoughts) or violent reactions.

CHILDREN SUFFERING FROM BEHAVIOUR DISORDERS

Such type of children exibit one or the other type of behavioural problems in their behaviour pattern. In the school setting, they may be found to experience enormous frustration, intrapsychic conflicts, poor self esteem, feelings of failure and high anxiety levels. They may exhibit their frustrations in an aggressive way or through withdrawal symptoms like extreme shyness, aloofness, etc. They may also exhibit a variety of immature behaviour like thumb sucking, crying, whining, negativism and baby talk indicative of some underlying, perhaps transient, problems at home or elsewhere in the child's environment. Sometimes very bright and the otherwise good students of the class may also exhibit quite immature or disturbed emotional behaviour (in the form of too much deficient in social behaviour) especially those who are overprotected by their parents and other members of the family.

ETIOLOGY (CAUSES LYING BEHIND THE EMOTIONALLY DISTURBED BEHAVIOUR)

Why do the children become emotionally disturbed? What are the causative factors responsible for the incidence of emotional disturbances among children? Let us find the answers to these questions.

The common causative factors responsible for the eruption of emotional disturbances among the children may be divided into the following categories.

1. Hereditary or Genetic factors
2. Biological or physiological factors
3. Socio-environmental factors

Let us try to know about them in detail.

HEREDITARY OR GENTIC FACTORS

Defective genes transferred to the offspring at the time of conception are in some ways responsible for the transmission of a certain genetic predisposition related with the emotionally disturbed behaviour. For example Huntington's chorea, a degeneration marked by speech impairment, intellectual impairment and emotional disturbance is caused by the transmission of genes. Similarly in more severe forms of psychopathology like child schizophrenia, heredity is a strong predisposing factor.

BIOLOGICAL OR PHYSIOLOGICAL FACTORS

While hereditary factors are more or less predisposing factors (the starting base and fertile ground for the germination of the seeds of emotional disturbances), the biological ones constitute both predisposing and precipating factors (immediate causes for igniting the disturbances).

In biological or physiological factors, the somatic structure and physiological factors within the individual plays a significant role as a predisposing and precipitating factors responsible for the child's emotional disturbance. For example disatisfaction with one's somatic structure, coupled with unusual remarks or reactions of other people, may give birth to many complexes, guilt feelings and frustrating encounters which in turn, may lead to mild or severe emotional disturbances. Similarly physiological factors like overactivity or underactivity of the endocrines or ductless glands may lead to significant physiological anomalies which in turn may provide fertile ground for the growth of the emotionally disturbed behaviour. Similarly children suffering from the problems of chronic health or other physical disorders may create added anxiety and stress to themselves and the members of their family, and this in turn may give birth to many problems related to emotional disturbances.

SOCIO-ENVIRONMENTAL FACTORS

The most striking reasons for the germination as well as perpetuation of the emotionally disturbed behaviour of the children lie in their socio-cultural environment. There are many things, situations and incidents from the past and present of one's socio-cultural environment that may cause a variety of frustrations, conflicts, stresses and pressures in the minds of the growing children and result in disorganized personality and emotionally disturbed behaviour. A few of such uncongenial factors or situations present in children's socio-cultural environment may be named as below.

1. Broken homes on account of separation, divorce or death of one or both the parents.
2. Seriously neglected and/or emotionally, physically and even sexually abused by a parent or surrogate parent.
3. The emotional malfunctioning and maladaptive behaviour of the parents and members or the family learned as a model behaviour by the child.
4. Maltreatment and improper behaviour of the parents and/or members of the family towards the child.
5. Frequent quarrelling, fighting and other types of uncongenial environmental conditions prevalent in the home and family environment.
6. Uncongenial environmental conditions and improper teaching-learning facilities available in the school.
7. Improper behaviour of the teachers or senior students towards the child.
8. Inappropriate models present in the school environment for the learning of emotionally disturbed behaviour.
9. Reinforcement of inappropriate behaviour by the teachers, peers or other factors available in the school.
10. Inappropriate high expectations of the teachers and parents from the child.
11. Disadvantages suffered by the child on account of extreme poverty, social and cultural deprivation, low social status of the family.
12. Discrimination suffered on account of cast, colour, sex, religion, language or regionalism, etc.
13. Mismatch between the child's temperament and the parental and other environmental expectations.
14 Defective and uncongenial environment and improper role models available to the child in his neighbourhood, community, on television, movies, etc.

Thus, the children may acquire or develop emotional disturbance in their behaviour as a result of the presence of one or the other types of causative factors explained above. However, in most of the cases the emotionally disturbed behaviour may be taken as a coefficient of friction between the individuality or personality of the child with the forces of his socio-cultural environment. While the genetic or biological factors may provide fertile ground and seed for the germination of the emotionally disturbed behaviour, the environmental factors ignite the fire through the available immediate causes. In some cases, even the seed as well as the ground is supplied by the environmental forces for their growth and perpetuation. Therefore, in most cases, the environmental forces are to be largely blamed for the birth and growth of the emotional disturbances among the children.

Identification of Emotionally Disturbed Children

How can emotionally disturbed children be identified in a classroom set-up or from among the general population? This question may be answered by pointing out two types of measures, namely, testing and non-testing devices. In testing devices, one makes use of certain standardized personality tests and adjustment inventories for the diagnosis of the emotional disturbance and behavioural problems of the children. Some of these tests are:

California Psychological Inventory, Children Apperception test, Thematic Apperception test, Rorschach Ink blot test, Money's Problem Checklist, Bell's Adjustment Inventory, Walker Problem Behaviour Identification checklist, Burk's Behaviour Rating Scales.

Through the administration and interpretation of such testing devices, we may be able to screen or separate the emotionally maladjusted or disturbed children from the emotionally adjusted.

Besides the use of testing devices, non testing devices in the form of observation and interview may also help in the diagnosis and identification of emotionally disturbed behaviour among the children observed or interviewed by one or a group of examiners. In such observation and face-to-face interview techniques, the typical characteristics and behaviours associated with emotional disturbance may prove quite advantageous. We have already given useful hints for such observable behavioural characteristics in the definition and concept of the term 'emotional disturbance'. However, we may again summarize and pinpoint some of the significant characteristics and behaviours displayed by the emotionally disturbed children over a long period of time (signaling that they are not coping with their environment or peers).

(i) Hyperactivity (Short attention span, impulsiveness)
(ii) Aggression/self injurious behaviour (acting out, fighting)
(iii) Withdrawal (failure to initiate interaction with others, retreat from exchanges of social interaction, excessive fear or anxiety)
(iv) Immaturity (inappropriate crying, temper tantrums, poor coping skills)
(v) Learning difficulties (academically performing below grade level)

In addition to this, children suffering from severe emotional disturbances may exhibit serious psychiatric problems like distorted thinking, excessive anxiety, bizarre motor acts, and abnormal mood swings and are sometimes identified as children suffering from severe psychosis or schizophrenia.

Remedial measures and Educational Provisions

Those children suffering from significant emotional disturbances need timely remedial measures and treatment for the rectification of their emotional problems before considering any educational provision for their proper educational progress. Let us therefore discuss the various treatment measures applicable in the cases of emotionally disturbed.

Remedial Measures or Treatment

In treating emotionally disturbed children, one thing that must be properly accepted is that there in no universal formula or cookbook method of treating all types of emotionally disturbed children. The remedy or treatment measures therefore should always be taken in view of the type of emotional disturbance shown by the child alongwith his unique personality, temperamental characteristics and the prevalent environmental situations. However, we may discuss the various general therapeutic measures taken for emotionally disturbed children as below.

1. **Psychodynamic Therapy.** In such type of therapy, the child suffering from emotional disturbance is treated for the underlying psychological causes creating tensions, frustration, complexes, fears, fantasies, daydreaming etc. in the mind of the child instead of the overt symptoms of his emotionally disturbed behaviour. These days we make use of modern psychodynamic therapies like play therapy, art therapy, music therapy and hypnosis instead of solely depending upon free association and dream analysis. In these therapies, feelings, fantasies and fears are played out by the child to get rid of the underlying causes giving birth to disturbing emotional behaviour.
2. **Behaviour Therapy.** The basic assumption underlying behaviour therapy is the belief that all behaviour is learned. The emotionally disturbed behaviour thus grows out of

maladaptive or defective learning. Consequently in behaviour therapy, attempts are made to provide corrective learning experiences for the removal of overt symptoms of disturbed behaviour by adopting behaviour correction/modification techniques like counter conditioning (de-conditioning), desensitization methods like relaxation, and flooding or aversive conditioning or modeling, etc.

3. **Group psychotherapy.** In this therapy, two or more children are analysed by a therapist or a technique of group dynamics/group situation is adopted for treating a child. It is especially helpful for children experiencing peer or social interaction problems. The orientation of the child or group under treatment may be behavioural, psychodynamic, or supportive, but it is always designed so as to increase the child's awareness and control of his or her emotions.
4. **Family therapy.** Such type of therapy is needed when it is perceived that unhealthy intra-familial relationships are responsible for the emotional disturbance of a child. In such cases, attempts are made to identify and modify maladaptive family patterns that are responsible for the germination and perpetuation of the problems. Quite often parents are approached for teaching means of modifying behaviour at home, to offer advice on child rearing, to explain a child's behaviour and to arrange their essential support for helping the child in getting rid of his or her emotional disturbance.

EDUCATIONAL PROVISIONS

Another priority, besides helping the emotionally disturbed children, in facing the problems of emotional disturbance lies in simultaneous planning for their proper educational progress. This again depends upon the type of emotional disturbance experienced by the child and the resources as well as facilities available for planning about his education. However, in general the following three types of provisions can be made for the education of the emotionally disturbed children.

Provision of Special classes in regular schools

This provision is based on the assumption that it is not appropriate to keep emotionally disturbed children in the same class along with the otherwise normal children as it may serve no useful purpose vis-a-vis their educational progress. Besides it can also create disturbances and adjustment problems in the normal setting and working of the class. Therefore it is suggested that emotionally disturbed students be placed in a separate class or section so that proper provision for their education and adjustment may be made within the regular schools. Here we may follow separate curriculum, methods of teaching, behavioural treatments, innovative special techniques for the adjustment and educational progress of these children with the help of special attention paid by specially trained teachers, resource personnel, guidance workers and other personnel's especially helpful in the task.

Provision of Special Schools

We may have separate residential schools or day schools especially meant for the adjustment and education of the emotionally disturbed. It is needed in more severe cases of emotional disturbance. Here we can have special care, treatment as well as educational measures for them under the supervision of the specifically trained staff and guidance personnel. Special curriculum, methods of teaching, ways of doing assignments, project works or even the method of evaluation are so planned that it caters the specific needs of the emotionally disturbed in such special schools. These schools thus have their own programmes and provisions especially suited to the adjustment and educational progress of the emotionally disturbed.

Provision of Integration and Mainstreaming

Both the above-mentioned provisions related with the placing of emotionally disturbed students into special classes or schools rest on the principle of segregation or separating them from the rest of the students' population. Such provisions are neither practicable nor feasible in the circumstances prevalent in our country. We cannot afford such exclusive resources for meeting the needs of the few. Moreover, emotionally disturbed children differ significantly with respect to the types of disturbances suffered and the degree of the severity of such disturbances. Therefore, it is quite impossible to provide such wide segregation to such wide variety of heterogeneous groups. In fact each case is unique in itself and hence needs specific provision for its adequate adjustment, education and welfare. So in such a situation what is most needed is the specific individual attention and if it can be arranged in the mainstream itself, then there is absolutely no needs of their segregation. Hence, these days more emphasis is laid on the provision of integration and mainstreaming for the adjustment and education of the emotionally disturbed.

In this provision, attempts are made to integrate emotionally disturbed children and the otherwise normal children in a school setting where all the children share same resources and opportunities for their adjustment and learning on a full time basis. In the regular classroom setting, attempts are made to provide needed individual attention, care, suitably designed educational programs and behaviour modification techniques for the emotionally disturbed as per their needs of adjustment and educational progress. The idea is to help the emotionally disturbed children in their proper adjustment and education through proper individualized educational programme, care and attention by placing them in the least restrictive environment. The results of such placement and provision for the emotionally disturbed have been quite successful. Leaving aside the more severe cases, integration of the emotionally disturbed with the regular students, has resulted in a better educational performance with a little more individual attention, assistance of a resource person, aids and care.

Therefore, the provision of integration and mainstreaming coupled with specialized individual attention is now considered a better approach for the needed adjustment and educational progress of the emotionally disturbed.

SUMMARY

Exceptional children are those children who deviate seriously from the normal in terms of the possession of one or the other trait often related to the various dimensions of their personality to the extent of requiring special attention and education for their upbringing, welfare and adjustment.

Gifted children are those exceptional children whose performances are significantly above average, praiseworthy and remarkable in any worthwhile field of human endeavourer. The truly gifted children not only includes the intellectually gifted or academically talented children but also the children who show promises in other works of life, e.g. music, dance, sports, social leadership, arts, etc. While for the identification of the former, intelligence tests can be safely employed as a screening instrument, the latter need careful observation and study for spotting the specific areas of their giftedness. Aptitude test, interest inventory, anecdotal records, opinions and reports of the parents, teachers and friends can also help in exploring their latent gift. Several schemes like establishments of separate schools, placing them in separate groups or classes, acceleration or multiple promotion and enrichment programmers are suggested for the education of these children. However, "enrichment"(enriching the already existing programmes of education in view of the developmental needs of the gifted) may be considered the best for the countries like ours wedded to democratic socialism.

Backward children are those exceptional children whose attainment in one or the other field falls below the level of their natural potentialities. They are also termed as 'slow learners' on account of their below-average progress in the acquisition of new behaviours. However, intelligence is no guarantee against backwardness. The child showing above average intelligence may also lag behind and be declared as backward for not performing at the level which can be expected from him on account of his natural abilities. The causes of backwardness lie in the children themselves (such as their physiological and intellectual sub normality) and also in the environmental influences (cast by home, neighbourhood, school and other social agencies). In planning remedial work for the backward, we must try first to diagnose the extent, nature and causes of their backwardness and then suitably plan for the needed remedy in view of the findings of such diagnosis.

Juvenile delinquents are those exceptional children (essentially minor in age) who deviate seriously from the norms of their culture or society and commit such acts that, if committed by an adult would be punishable as crimes. The causes of delinquent behaviour lie in faulty upbringing, improper environmental influences and maltreatment. Its remedy needs both preventive as well as curative measures. In taking preventive measures we have to take care of the things in such a way as not to allow the children to feel maladjusted, get wrong influence from the antisocial elements or turn into rebels against society. In taking curative measures for an offender, we should not resort to punitive measures and put him in the prison along with the hardened criminals but should take psychological measures through the educational correction and rehabilitation programmes.

Visually impaired or **handicapped children** are those children who suffer from the impairment and defects of their vision to such an extent that make them disabled or handicapped in terms of their visual ability and perception. The causes regarding the visual impairment and disability of the children lie well within one's hereditary endowments as well as socio-psychological and physical environment. For taking appropriate measures for the education and adjustments of the visually impaired children, we must first distinguish and divide them into two categories (1) Totally and nearly totally blind children and (2) Low vision and partially blind children. It is better to send the former ones in special boarding schools meant for the blinds but the latter ones can be educated with the normal children in normal schools with a little extra efforts, care and needed special provisions.

Hearing impaired children are those children who suffer from a wide range of hearing loss (including deafness) making them disabled wholly or partially in utilizing their hearing organs for getting and exchanging information with others. Both hereditary as well as environmental factors may be termed responsible for making one hearing impaired. For taking appropriate measures for the education and adjustment of the hearing impaired, we can classify them into two broad categories, namely deaf and hard of hearing, for the clear purpose of helping them according to the degree of their disability. It is advisable to send the former ones right from the earlier age to the residential boarding schools or special schools known as the schools for the deaf and dumb. The latter ones, however, can be safely educated along with the normal children in the normal schools set-up with a little more effort and special provisions.

Orthopaedically impaired or **crippled children** are those children who suffer from such defects and deformity of their bones, muscles or joints that may interfere with their normal functioning and adjustment to the general and specific demands of their environment to the extent of requiring special measures for their well being, adjustment and educational progress. Defects and deformities to the offspring cannot be carried out as such through geans and chromosomes. After conception, these are acquired through the negative and unfavorable influences received in the womb of the mother, causes operative at the time of birth, accidental and incidental factors, nuitrional deficiency and the effect of infection and diseases. The adjustment and education of most of those orthopaedically impaired is quite possible along with the normal children in normal educational set-up with a little extra effort by making the school environment properly friendly to them.

Mentally disabled or **retarded children** are those exceptional children who besides possessing a low IQ suffer from the impairment or deficiency in adaptive behavior to the extent of requiring special care and provision for their welfare and development of their capacities. Mental retardation can be classified into four levels, namely mild, moderate, severe and profound, according to the degree of the severity of the mental retardation. From the educational as well as their adjustment angle, while the mildly retarded are considered educable and the moderately retardates trainable, the severe and profoundly retardates are considered neither educable nor trainable. Both of these are in need of custodial care and supervision by others on account of their inability to cop with their environmental needs.

Learning disabled children are those children who suffer seriously from the impaired learning inefficiency to the extent that they essentially require special attention, care and remedial programmes for the rectification of their learning problems and disabilities. Cause of the learning disabilities may be located in one's (1) heredity endowments (2) organic or physiological factors causing dysfunction of their central nervous system (3) improper and uncongenial conditions present in one's environment. The identification of learning disabilities among children may be carried out by means of (1) Testing devices like standardize diagnostic, ability or achievement test etc. and (2) Non testing devices like observation, rating scale, check list, interview etc. For taking educational measures for the learning disabled, we should not lay emphasis on the segregated setting, whether in the form of separate schools or classes, but try to provide due care and attention within the existing educational set-up by adopting suitable remedial and educational programmes as well as for improving the existing environmental set-up in accordance with special requirements of these children.

Emotionally disturbed children are those children who suffer from one or the other psychiatric or behaviour disturbances or disorders (not caused due to organic or physical factors) to the extent of making them handicapped in terms of their adjustment and progress in life. Depending upon the nature of their disturbances, these children may be classified as children suffering from depression, anxiety disorders, phobias, psycho-physiological disorders, personality disorders, psychotic disorders and behavior disorders etc. The causes of their emotional disturbances may lie well in their heredity influences, biological or physiological factors and socio environmental factors. Their identification may be carried out through testing measures (like standardized personality and adjustment inventories, problem check lists, projective techniques etc.) as well as non testing devices like observation, rating scale, interview etc. The treatment measures for the rectification of their behavioural problems may involve psychodynamic therapy, behavior therapy, group psychotherapy and family therapy. While making educational provisions for these children, it is better to prefer their integration and mainstreaming with the normal children in normal school settings instead of getting them segregated through separate schools and separate classes. In such settings, however, we must try to make provision for the specialized individual attention and services of the psychologists, resource persons etc. for meeting the special needs and requirements of these children in the path of their proper adjustment and educational progress.

References and Suggested Readings

American Association on Mental Deficiency (1973) as cited by Kisker, George W, *The Disorganized Personality*, McGraw-Hill (International student Edition III), 1964.

American Psychiatric Association, *Diagnostic and Statistical Manual of Mental Deficiency*, 2nd ed., DSM-II, Wasington, D.C., 1968.

American Psychiatric Association, *Diagnostic and Statistical Manual of Mental Disorders*, DSM-III, Wasington, D.C., 1980.

Barton, Hall, *Psychiatric Examination of the School Child,* Edward Arnold, London, 1947.

Bower, E.M., *Early Identification of Emotionally Handicapped Children in Schools*, 3rd ed., Spring Field, II, Thomas, 1981.

British Mental Deficiency Act (1929) as cited by Shanmugam, T.E., *Abnormal Psychology*, Tata McGraw-Hill, New Delhi, 1981.

Brown, J.F., *The Psychodynamics of Abnormal Behaviour*, Asia Publishing House, New Delhi, Indian reprint, 1969.

Burt, C., *The Young Delinquent,* 3rd ed., University of London Press, London, 1938.

———, *The Subnormal Mind,* 3rd ed., Oxford University Press, London, 1955.

Coleman, James C., *Abnormal Psychology and Modern Life*, 3rd ed., D.B. Taraporewala & Sons, Mumbai, 1970.

Crow, L.D. and Crow, Alice, *Educational Psychology*, Eurasia Publishing house, New Delhi, 1973.

Davison, G.C. and Neale, J.M., *Abnormal Psychology*, 2nd ed., John Wiley, New York, 1978.

De Haan and Kough, quoted by Dutt, N.K., *Psychological Foundation of Education,* Doaba House, New Delhi, 1979.

Grossman, H.G. (Ed.), *Classification in Mental Retardation*, American Association on Mental deficiency, Washington, D.C., 1983.

Havighurst, R.J., Quoted in N.B. Henry (Ed.) *Education for the Gifted,* Fifty-sevnth yearbook of National Society for the Study of Education, Part II, Chicago.

Kavale, K.A. and Forness, S.R., *The Science of Learning Disabilities*, College Hill, San Diego, CA, 1985.

Kirk, S.A. and Kirk, W.D., *Psycholinguistic Learning Disabilities: Diagnosis and Remediation,* University of Illinois Press, Urbana, IL, 1971.

Lerner, J., *Children with Learning Disabilities,* Houghton Miffilin, Boston, 1976.

Mangal, S.K., *Advanced Educational Psychology*, 2nd ed., Prentice-Hall of India, New Delhi, 2002.

McLoughlin, J.H. and Netic, A., "Defining Learning Disabilities: A New and Coperative Direction", *Journal of Learning Disabilities*, **16,** pp. 21–23, 1983.

Page, James D., *Abnormal Psychology*, Tata McGraw-Hill, New Delhi, 1976.

Pasricha, Prem, *Educational Psychology*, Delhi University Publishers, New Delhi, 1963.

Phillips, E.I., "Problems in Education of the Emotionally Disturbed Children," in N.G. Harringand R.L. Schienfelbas (Eds), *Methods in Special Education*, McGraw-Hill, New York, 1967.

Schonell, F.J. (Ed.), *Backwardness with Basic Subjects,* Oliver & Boyd, Edinburg, 1948.

Shanker, Udai, *Problem Children*, Atma Ram & Sons, New Delhi, 1958.

———, *Exceptioal Children*, Sterling Publishers, New Delhi, 1976.

Tannenbaum, A.J., *Gifed Children Psychological and Educational Perspectives*, Macmillan, New York, 1983.

Telford, C.W. and Sawrey, J.M., *The Exceptional Individual*, 3rd ed., Prentice-Hall, New Jersey, Englewood Cliffs, 1977.

Verma, S.C., *The Young Delinquents,* Lucknow Pustak Kendra, Lucknow, 1970.

35

Behavioural Problems—Meaning, Concept and Treatment

CHAPTER COMPOSITION

BEHAVIOURAL PROBLEMS—MEANING AND CONCEPT

Under our normal behaviour what we do or perform has some definite purpose, aim or motive. Thus all our activities are always directed towards the satisfaction of our basic needs, desires, ambitions, instincts and emotions. Our such goal-directed and purposeful behavioural activities help us in seeking adjustment to our self and the environment. As a social being, we try to maintain proper give and take relationship in the society, where society provides us means and materials for our maintenance and proper development and we, in turn, contribute towards its progress and advancement according to our capacities. The way in which this give and take relationship is maintained decides the course of our adjustment with the society. Satisfactory adjustment gives satisfaction to us and the society. Consequently our actions and behaviour are adjudged proper and get rewarded or praised. Contrarily when our equilibration, the balance between our self and the social environment, is disturbed, we begin to suffer from social maladjustment. Then it becomes difficult to maintain harmony in our relationship with the society. We are forced to drift away from the norms, rules and regulations and expectations of the society and there begins a war like situation between our 'self' and the social environment. We are confronted with the feelings of insecurity, anxiety, frustration and other similar emotions resulting in various abnormalities in our behaviour. As a consequence, our behaviour no longer remains a social behaviour but becomes anti-social or abnormal leading to many behaviour problems to our self and the society.

Such type of behavioural problems are quite common and universal, existing at all the stages of our life from infancy to old age. However, these are most common and usual with children and adolescents. The reason for this can be their lack of required maturity and understanding for coping with the needs of the environment. Due to this, they fall easy victims to many behavioural problems like:

(i) Bed wetting, (ii) Nail biting, (iii) Autism (inability to relate socially), (iv) Thumb sucking, (v) Temper tantrums, (vi) Lying, (vii) Truancy, (viii) Stealing, pickpocketing and other types of juvenile delinquency, (ix) Bullying or fighting, (x) Hair plucking, (xi) Phobia about insects like cockroach, spiders, lizards etc., (xii) Speech disorders like stammering, (xiii) Extreme fearfulness and anxiety (xiv) Copying (xv) Negativism, (xvi) Sexually deviant behaviour, and (xvii) Drug addiction etc.

The above examples of the children and adolescents behavioural problems may clearly reveal that their behaviour related with such problems is essentially away from the otherwise normal behaviour expected from them at their age level. It is noticed and takes into account other cognition only because it is somewhat different from the expected or otherwise normal behaviour. It becomes a subject of serious consideration only when it is grown and committed in such a way that it becomes a problem for the parents, classmates, neighbours, elders or the society as a whole. In this way, a behaviour which is somewhat away from the normal is entitled to be included in the category of problematic behaviour, provided it relates to the point of causing problems to the individual himself as well as to the members and resources of the society.

However, such problem child or adult has abnormality only in terms of the problems related with behaviour, otherwise he is as normal as others. It is not essential for him to demonstrate signs of other abnormalities or maladaptations like mental retardation, physical or mental handicap, immorality or criminal record, neurotic or psychotic disorders etc. In this way children or individuals affected with behavioural problems should never be confused with the individuals suffering from developmental disorders and mental illness.

On the basis of what has been discussed about the meaning and nature of the term behavioural problem so for, we are now in a position to define it as:

The term behavioural problem or problematic behaviour stands for that type of serious abnormality in the behaviour of an individual (child or adult) which, while causing a problem for his proper adjustment to self and the environment, proves quite detrimental to his own welfare along with that of the society.

In reference to the above cited definition, we would like to illustrate it further by discussing in detail the following types of the common behavioural problems of the children and adolescents in this chapter.

1.Truancy, 2. Lying, 3. Stealing, 4. Temper Tantrums, 5. Drug Addiction.

Juvenile Delinquency related with serious behavioural and social problems of children and juvenile youth have already been discussed in Chapter 34 of this book.

Truancy

Meaning

Truancy as a behaviour problem is related with the school life of a child. *Those children who willingly make themselves absent from the classroom or outside classroom activities of the school without the prior permission of their parents, teachers or school authorities are termed as truants and their such absenteeism related behaviour is termed as truancy.*

Defined in this way, we can say that truants try to challenge and defy the rules and regulations of the school and the authority of their parents and teachers. They are used to deceiving their parents, elders and teachers by making various excuses for their behaviour. The parents are assured that their child is attending the school, but he behaves otherwise by playing truant and wasting his time elsewhere. Similarly at the initial state of truancy, he offers a number of explanations and excuses for his absenteeism. He might say that his mother is ill or that he has to manage one or the other household affair or he is to visit some relative or place along with his family members, and so on. By such pretence, he makes a fool of the teachers and school authorities for playing truancy. The initial truant behaviour is then reinforced on account of many factors. Once he is habituated, it becomes quite difficult for him to get adjusted with the school activities. He is unable to do the class or homework, fails in the monthly, terminal and other examinations and ultimately forces himself away from what is happening in the class and the school. Now he becomes careless and seldom thinks of any type of permission, excuses, or repent for his truant behaviour. Gradually it leads him to different types of abnormalities resulting into serious problematic, antisocial and delinquent behaviour.

Causes of truancy

Truancy, in all its kinds and shapes, is a behavioural problem and is thus the outcome of one's maladjustment and maladaptation with his self and the environment. The causes of his maladaptive behaviour resulting into truancy, thus lie well within the factors and circumstances related to one's physical, social and educational surroundings discussed as below:

1. **Physical health of the child:** Some children have very poor health and physique. They are frequently subjected to physical ailments and diseases. Some suffer from severe headache, backache, stomach or intestine troubles etc. With such physical and physiological troubles, they are compelled to remain absent from the regular classroom as well as other practical and cocurricular activities. It results into their lagging behind in comparison to their fellow students. As a result, they feel distracted and show distaste in continuing the school. However, the fear of their parents compels them to attend the school. They can't come up with new excuses for being away from the class and the school and in such circumstances, they are persuaded to play truancy and once named for such behaviour, they feel satisfied in remaining so.

2. **Mental health of the child:** Some children are found to have poor mental health. They remain quite tense, anxious, perturbed and stressed. A sense of insecurity and fearfulness is always prevalent in them. It may happen on account of their defective family environment or some other socio-psychological reasons. Such children do not fit well in the normal school environment and feel a lot of difficulty in getting adjusted according to the needs and requirements of their school. They continue to search other adjustment alternatives well outside the boundaries of the classroom and the school and as a result learn to play truancy.

3. **Level of physical and mental abilities:** The curricular and cocurricular activities of the school expect a reasonable minimum level of physical and mental abilities from a student of a particular course and class. Naturally, children with inferior abilities and capacities will find themselves in trouble when exposed to normal classroom or other practical activities.

In such a situation, they feel embarrassed and specially so when they are rebuked and punished for their inferior performances either in the curricular or cocurricular activities. The alternative they now try is truancy. It helps them to provide safeguard from the otherwise unhappy situation in the school and defying the school authorities temporarily boosts their ego.

Thus where the deficiency in terms of the physical and mental abilities makes one a truant, the over-presence of such abilities may also work in the same direction. Those children who have quite high superior abilities and capacities may also find themselves maladjusted with the normal work and activities of the school. Nothing is challenging to them and out of boredom, they may try for alternatives outside the classroom or the school and thus may learn to play truancy.

4. **Behaviour of the teachers:** A teacher's behaviour and personality traits play a significant role in forcing the students to play truancy. A school is said to be an extension of one's home. Children expect the affectionate parental behaviour from their teachers. However, when they are confronted with an almost opposite behaviour characterized with favouritism, partiality, negative attitude, damaging criticism, egoism, abuse and physical assault etc., they feel suffocated and as a result try to run away from the classroom or school activities conducted in the supervision of those teachers. Sometimes teachers resort to very hard punitive measures for a minor incident of noise and disorder, non-doing or incorrect home or drill work, non-compliance with their instructions etc., without caring to know the rootcause of such behaviour of their students.

   Apart from this, there are a few teachers who cross all the limits of negative behaviour. They tease, abuse and beat an otherwise good child for simple reasons like he is not taking tuition from them or he belongs to a particular caste or religion or he does not oblige him by meeting his appropriate or inappropriate demands. A child very well understands the evil intentions and unjust behaviour of his teacher. But since he has limitations on inducing any positive changes in the behaviour of his teacher, he resorts to escapism and is forced to play truancy.

5. **Study and teaching methods in schools:** Sometimes what is taught in the school or the methods employed for providing learning experiences to the children do not suit the children or an individual child. He is unable to grasp and understand the classroom teaching or learn necessary skills for practical work. In such a situation, he lags behind in his studies and finds it difficult to complete his home and classroom assignments. His such failure may agitate the teacher who may give him negative score or take other punitive measures. Finding no other suitable ways, the child may then react by resorting to truant behaviour. In this way, a defective curriculum or improper methods of teaching may prove a potent cause for the children's apathy towards the subjects and activities of the school to such an extent that he may be forced to resort to truancy.

6. **Lack of cocurricular activities and hobbies:** Children differ in terms of the possession of interests, attitudes, aptitudes, abilities and capacities. Such diversification of their nature demands diversification of learning facilities in terms of curricular and cocurricular experiences so well. However, this need can be properly realized through the proper organization of various cocurricular activities and suitable provision for diversified hobbies. It is a sad commentary on the part of our existing school system that such provision is hardly made in our schools. As a result children find school work dull, boring

and unchallenging. Contrarily, they find activities of their choice and likings just outside the boundary walls of the school in the form of movies, computer cafés, entertainment clubs, games and other gang activities along with their peers. Such attractions, then automatically persuade them to learn and develop the truant behaviour.

7. **Indiscipline in schools:** School administration plays quite an effective role in providing proper teaching-learning facilities to the students. It also sets the tone of the discipline prevalent in the school. Some schools follow very strict norms in the name of discipline, and students are subjected to hard punishment on even minor things and petty matters. In such autocratic administration, sensitive children feel quite insecure and fearful in attending the class and school activities and as an alternative, adopt the mechanism of escapism, *i.e.* playing truancy. On the other hand, in schools where administration is poor and lenient, there remains no discipline. In such free for all situation there remains no systematic record of the student's attendance or in case some record is maintained, children do not fear of any action. Besides, there lies no proper arrangement and care for the regular and methodological holding of the classes and other activities. Such type of loose administration provides ample opportunities for the germination and perpetuation of truancy among the children.

8. **Ill effects of bad company:** In some cases, children adopt truancy in the company of their fellow truants or are forced to do so by the anti-social elements. A child who keeps the company of such friends or colleagues, who have no taste left for study and who have fallen in the company or trap of some anti-social elements, is bound to pick-up their habits, play truancy and learn their style of living.

9. **Home environment:** The behaviour and conduct of the parents or other members of the family, alongwith the non-congenial environment prevalent at one's home, may lead a child to truancy. He may take undue advantages of the ignorance and illiteracy of his parents. Their mutual conflicts, tensions, suspicions, distrust and fights may persuade and force him to play truancy for one or the other reason. In such an environment, he may get less time and opportunities for doing the assigned homework and revising or practicing the lessons or activities learned in the school. It may also happen in the situations where the parents or other members of the family tend to engage the child in day-to day household or professional activities without caring for his studies. Whatever the reason or situations may be, it is the child who suffers miserably on account of the availability of less or no time as well as facilities for carrying out his studies at home. In case the home assignments are not completed and he lags behind in his studies, he will have little or no interest in facing his teachers and attending the classes.

   However, in case he attends the classes with the mind loaded with home conflicts, tensions and stresses, it would be rather impossible for him to take his work and studies seriously in the school. Due to his absent mindedness, he will face wrath and insulting behaviour of his teacher and in such a situation he may feel safer in playing truancy. In another situation when he gets quite aggrieved, tensed or agitated on account of the harsh, partial and undesirable behaviour of his parents or members of the family, he may decide or be forced to play truancy as a result of over reactions and frustrations.

10. **Difficulty in the satisfaction of basic needs:** In case the basic physical, and socio-psychological needs of a child are not gratified or there comes hurdles in their proper gratification it may lead to behavioural problems. Such type of maladjustment of the child,

in the real sense, is the root cause of his all types of problematic behaviour including truancy. Home and family, school and its environment, time and opportunities in the social situations may somewhat or somewhere create a number of hurdles and obstruction in the proper gratification of one's important needs, desires and motives. In such a situation of non-gratification, one may be tempted, persuaded or forced to satisfy it through the otherwise abnormal, illegal and unsocial means. A child who belongs to a very poor family may automatically try one or the other means for getting the things used by his friends and colleagues. It would not be surprising if it drifts him towards the extremely unfair means available in the company of anti-social elements possible through playing truancy.

11. **Desire to escape from work:** Some of the children lack the tendency for work. They are extremely careless and insincere towards their studies and responsibilities. They are always in search of excuses for spending time and energy towards things and events other than their studies and school activities. Such tendencies and habits may be the outcome of their previous experiences or learned behaviour including work culture available to them at their home and the society. Such tendency and hobbies lead to their disinterest and negligence in the classroom and school activities. As a result, they may be seen to suffer in terms of their progress. It may then became a source of conflict between them and their teachers. Since they are not in the habit of doing any extra hard work for overcoming their deficiencies, they are forced to seek its alternative by playing truancy.
12. **Social and emotional maladjustment:** Some children do not have their social and emotional development well in tune with their chronological age. Thereby, they may feel difficulty in getting along with their peers in the classroom and other school activities. Some children who are gifted and genius may acquire the higher grades despite their lower chronological ages. Such children prove misfit and maladjusted with other fellow children, due to their superiority not only in terms of their chronological age but also in terms of physical, social and emotional maturity.

    Similarly, those children, who on account of their repeated failures or some other reasons reach higher chronological age and level of physical, social and emotional maturity, may find themselves quite misfit and maladjusted with the other younger children of their class.

    In another situation, a child may feel maladjusted on the grounds that he is quite different from others in terms of his socio-economic status, caste, colour, creed, religion, language, region or nationality, etc. Sometimes his own temperament, timidity and fearfulness, shyness and frigidity, aggressiveness and over dominance, jealousy and envy may cause serious adjustment problems with the fellow children and school environment. As a result he resorts to escapism and learns to play truancy in order to save himself from the unhappy maladjustment outcomes.
13. **Desire to prove superiority and courage :** It is set in the minds of some children that their deviant behaviour and negativism, like not listening to the teachers, not doing home work and drill work, not attending to the classroom and school activities and playing truancy, may make them a hero in the eyes of their peers. They may dream of such outcome of their otherwise negative and undesirable behaviour but things usually happen in the opposite direction. They fall in the eyes of the teachers and school authorities to the extent that there remains no way for them other than remaining absent or playing truancy.

Remedial measures for truancy

The remedy of truant behaviour needs two-sided attack involving both preventive and curative measures. The first important task is to save the children from becoming truants and in case they somehow become truants then attempts should be made to bring them back to the mainstream.

Preventive Measures

We can consider the following measures for the desired prevention:

- Parents and guardians must be provided adequate guidance and counseling so that they may properly fulfill their obligations like—(i) proper dealing with their children, (ii) making the home and family environment congenial, (iii) providing adequate care and attention in the upbringing of their children, (iv) remaining careful for the proper satisfaction of the basic needs of their children, and (v) cooperating with teachers and school authorities in the proper progress and development of their children.
- Parents, teachers and elders should have proper vigilance over the activities particularly the company of the children. It should be fully taken care of that they do not fall victims to the evil designs of the anti-social elements.
- It should be made sure by the parents, teachers and all the well-wishers of the children that their essential physical and socio-psychological needs remain gratified to a certain appropriate level. It should be properly observed that the children do not suffer from a sense of insecurity, neglect and lack of love and affection in any way on account of their deficient environment.
- The physical and mental health of the children should be properly taken care of. The children can be saved from the evil effects of tensions, anxieties, and stresses by showering on them adequate affection and love, giving patient hearing to their problems and outbursts, showing sympathy and providing adequate emotional and physical security to them. For their physical health, they should be helped in developing proper habits for keeping them healthy, disease-free and physically strong. They should be provided with balanced diet and arrangement for their physical and medical check-ups. The follow-up work in terms of the correction of any type of deficiency and ailment should be properly taken with proper consultation and cooperation of parents.
- There should be serious attempts for restructuring and modifying the school environment so as to make it more congenial and suitable for the proper care and education of the children as per their needs, interests and abilities. It may include measures like appropriate behaviour of the teachers with the children, reforms in the curriculum and teaching methods, working towards constructive and self imposed discipline, desired modification in the means and ways of school administration and organization, proper arrangement of hobbies and cocurricular means, adequate arrangement for healthy competitions and cooperative activities and adequate arrangement for proper guidance and counseling etc.
- Proper attention should be paid to adequate social and emotional development as well as adjustment of the children. All the obstructions in this direction should be timely removed and by all ways and means, children should be made to realize that their progress and welfare rest in studying and working together in a proper harmony.

Curative Measures

The most important thing in the treatment of a truant lies in the fact that such behaviour should not get any type of reinforcement through one or the other means. This is why punitive measures like imposing fines, caning, physically assaulting, reproofing and rebuking, stricking off the name from the school roll etc. prove quite counterproductive. Such children need sympathy. It is futile to waste our energy by losing temper and showing our hatredness towards these children. As far as possible the truant behaviour at its initial stage should be completely ignored and should not be subjected to any reinforcement. In such a way it may have its natural extinction. However, if repeated considerably, it should be attended for knowing about its rootcauses. Every truant behaviour has its own reasons and causes, and so its treatment lies well in our attempts, first to find out such causes and then try for the eradication, removal and modifications. Quite often not only one or two but many factors are found to be operating jointly to develop truant behaviour in the children. Therefore, attempts should be made to proceed systematically in view of modifying and restructuring the defective environment and conditions as summarized below:

- Attempts should be made for adequate adjustment of the child with his family environment. The parents and elders must be made to realize the need of proper love and affection as well as physical and emotional security and safety to their children.
- Attempts should be made for the removal of the deficiencies and deficits with regard to the physical and mental health of the children.
- Attempts should be made to break their relationships with their bad company. However, it needs quite a cautious approach. No coercion should be applied for this purpose. Instead, one must try to win over the child through love and affection and slowly convince him about the consequences of his bad company.
- If what he gets outside the class or school through truancy is also available to him in the school, then the attraction or compulsion of playing truancy will naturally diminish. Consequently, attempts should be made to make provision for the fulfillment of his attraction through cocurricular and curricular experiences in such a way that on one hand it helps in his all-round development and on the other it puts an end to the development of undesirable habits and objectionable behaviour.
- There is need for lot of patience, sincerity, hard work and repeated attempts on the part of teachers, parents and other elders for bringing back the truants on the right path. A child who has developed complete distaste for studies and other school activities or who hates his teachers and the school environment can't be expected to give up his truant behaviour and return to the mainstream easily. It is easy to get spoiled but reform takes its own time. We will have to win over the child, get him into confidence, provide him with the work and activities of his choice and get along with him so as to remove his fears, doubts, suspicions and misgivings for making him adjusted to the classroom and school environment. The task is not so simple. It needs the cooperative efforts of everyone from the parents and members of the family, teacher and other school authorities to all those who in one way or the other are interested in the welfare and progress of the child.

Lying

Meaning

Lying and speaking the truth represent the two opposite and contradictory dimensions of one's personality. While truth is associated with the virtues like honesty, integrity, and transparency in one's behaviour, lying is said to be in close relationship with the vices like dishonesty, fraud, deceit and indecency. So while speaking of truth is always appreciated and encouraged in our society, the telling of lie is considered bad, undignified and immoral. In our books and literature, we are always told and preached that we should not tell lies. However, despite such widespread opposition to lying, we all, including small children, tell lies. The question arises as to what makes such innocent children pick up the evil habit of lying in its many ways and styles. Let us study this problem in detail.

TYPES OF LIES

Lies can be classified mainly into two following broad types and styles.

A. *The lies that are told knowingly in the state of full consciousness with some definite purposes.* The examples of such lies are:

- Lies told on account of fear or for saving the self from punishment or some other personal losses.
- Lies told for the safety of others
- Lies told for taking revenge
- Lies told for a good laugh by making fool of others
- Lies told in the form of gossips or exaggeration of events for proving one as a super hero.
- Lies told for acquiring a thing somehow for the satisfaction of one's own interests.
- Lies told as an imitative act or group behaviour along with the other group members.
- Lies told for winning a game or competition.
- Lies told on the advice and instruction of one's parents, teachers and other elders.

B. *The lies that are told unknowingly in the absence of essential consciousness* are included in this category. These are mainly generated through one's unconscious mind. Examples of such lies have been cited as follows:

- Lies related to an incomplete, improper or wrong reporting of the facts on account of inadequate rememberance of the things or events.
- Lies for the expression of one's unconscious motives and desires.
- Lies based on things and events related purely to one's world of imagination.
- Lies told simply on account of the children's ignorance or innocence.

CAUSES OF LYING

The types of lies we have mentioned above may be found to have some of the following reasons for their presence in a child's behaviour.

1. A child does not notice any evil in telling lies, simply because he observes the behaviour of his elders, including his parents and teachers, doing the same. "Papa is saying that at present he is not at home," such lies beautifully portray child's innocence and the purity of his heart and mind. However, with repeated emphasis, inspiration, instruction and order from the elders, a child may be persuaded or compelled to tell lies. The repetition of such behaviour may gradually make him a habitual lier with no traces of retrogressive thinking or introspection.
2. We find that most of the child's behaviour is learned through imitation. In the society where there is a widespread practice of lying, how can we expect that a child will not follow or imitate the practices of his elders or companions.
3. A child is quite sensitive by nature. He needs lot of love, affection, surety, safety and security for his well being and development. In adverse situations, he may soon get afraid, tense and stressed and then as a means of protection may resort to lying. For example, to save himself from the expected rebuking or beating by the teachers for not doing home

work or not coming to the school, he may resort to lying about the illness of his mother or some urgency and distress at home. Gradually such lies in terms of false excuses may turn into a habit that may accompany them throughout their lives as may be evident by the nature of excuses put up by such persons to their employers or wives for their late arrival.

4. When a child learns that he can achieve his goal easily by lying, he is naturally persuaded to repeat his behaviour. When children are able to get money from their parents or family members by telling lies and use it for fun and enjoyment or for purchasing things of their choice, their lying behaviour remains in the process of gradual reinforcement. As a consequence, they remain in search of new excuses and methods of lying for bluffing their elders and thus become a habitual liar.
5. Many a time, children resort to lying to take revenge or for expressing their hatred, envy and jealousy towards other children. In some situations they may feel that they are insulted, rebuked and punished on account of the complaint or good behaviour of a particular child or group of children. As a matter of reaction, they may then resort to lying for taking proper revenge by getting them down in the eyes of the elders.
6. Sometimes, group loyalty and friendship may also persuade them to tell lies. They may resort to any type of lying for saving their friends from the expected punishment or getting them benefited in some other ways. It also happens to a child when he behaves under the influence of the group behaviour. The child necessarily does what the other members of the group do. He tells lies if the group expects him to do so. Later on as a grown-up individual he becomes habitual of repeating this group loyalty based lying behaviour.
7. In many situations children pick up the habit of lying simply for the sake of entertainment and amusement. This behaviour is also learned by observing and imitating the lying behaviour of their elders. On 1st April, the fool's day, he observes his elders making fool of others by lying in so many ways. Similarly in other situations it is repeated by them for cracking jokes and entertaining themselves at the cost of others. Such behaviour is then learned by the children by way of imitation. They begin to entertain themselves through their lying behaviour of befooling others. Such habit may cost them heavily in their life like the legendary shepherd boy who had to pay heavy price in terms of his life for befooling others by telling lie of being attacked by the wolf.
8. Children are ego-centric by nature. They want to show that they are superior to their peers in terms of many things like the status of their family, the qualities and characteristics of their family members, their own future plans etc. They may even resort to lying for realizing such objectives. They may boast about their foreign-based uncles or cousins, the brave acts of their relatives serving in forces, luxuries and riches of their family etc. to influence their friends. Gradually such type of behaviour makes them quite efficient in baseless gossiping and lying.
9. Children are never willing to accept their defeat. They always like to be victorious in words or deeds by one way or the other. This spirit works against the established norms of sportsmanship and they indulge in baseless lies and foul play for avoiding their defeats in any competition or show. Once they get success through lying or foul play, they pick it up as a habit through their sufficiently reinforced behaviour.
10. Children have short memory about the things and events they have heard or seen. As a consequence, when they try to describe a thing or event on the basis of their memory, they can give an incomplete or distorted picture of what was seen or heard by them in reality.

In doing so, they may often commit serious mistakes like telling incorrect names of the persons and places, incorrect dates and timings or incomplete wrong reporting of the incidents and events. Although all this happens quite unknowingly, they may be labeled as gossipers or liars on account of the significant observable differences between the reality and the picture portrait by them through their distorted description. Once declared a liar or a gossipy, they accept it as an honourable distinction and begin to behave as one in real sense.

11. Children are quite imaginative. They always wander in the world of their dreams and strange imaginations full of princes and princesses, angels and fairies, evil spirits and ghosts, magicians and supermen, heroes and heroines, and so on. While living in their dreams, they begin to imagine them happening in their day-to-day life. Their unconscious mind begins to provide false portrait and description of their ungrounded imagination. They may then claim, "Listen I have actually seen with my own eyes—a beautiful, well dressed angel descending here on this ground," or "Suddenly before me that bush turned into an evil spirit and began to grow in size," and so on and so forth. So all that they narrate is nothing but the product of their imaginative world. To others who are familiar with the realities of life, it is bound to appear as a bundle of pure lies. The children's imaginative expressions are thus labeled as lies by the elders. Children themselves initially feel quite elevated and satisfied with such labeling and may gradually be habituated to tell such lies in the later life.
12. Some children by some way or the other get quite maladjustment with their self and the environment. To protect themselves from the ill effects of the feelings of insecurity, anxieties, stresses and frustrations, they may take the shelter of lying behaviour as a defence mechanism.

Remedial measures for lying behaviour

The prevention and treatment of any problematic or maladaptive behaviour lies in the removal or eradication of the inherent cause of that behaviour. The same applies to the prevention and treatment of lying behaviour also. By following the maxim "prevention is better than cure", first the efforts for the prevention of this behaviour should be made in all the possible ways. However, in case the child gets habituated to telling lies then attempts should be made to bring desirable modification in his behaviour. In all such attempts the following measures may prove quite fruitful.

1. Children should be educated to differentiate between virtues and vices, good and evil, and truth and lies. The evil effect of telling lies and an all-round pleasing effect of speaking truth must be made noticeable to the children. Various suitable measures like showing of relevant films and picture stories, narrating ideal stories and life events, emphasizing on such related study material already included in the school curriculum etc. must be taken for generating attraction towards the truth and distraction and hatredness towards the lying behaviour.
2. The environmental situations inside and outside the family should be so attended and taken care of that children are not able to pick up the habit of lying as an ideal behaviour imitated by their parents, teachers and elders. These elders should always set their own example for the fruitful behaviour. In no way should the children be asked, persuaded or forced to tell any kind of lie by the elders for the sake of their petty individual interests.
3. The children should not be encouraged for telling lies in order to take revenge and hitting others. They should be made to realize with proper patience, love and affection that there

is no use of increasing bitterness and enmity. Hatredness always breeds hatredness. Therefore, one must always try for reducing the gap of misunderstandings and spoiled relationships by not resorting to revengeful means. Hence one should never take the help of lies for settling one's scores with others. As a next step, elders should also take the necessary initiatives for the removal of enmity between the children.

4. The children should also be made to realize that it is not good to make use of lies for the sake of entertainment and amusement. Many a time it leads to troubles and brings disasters, just as if one tells a lie about the death or injury of a child, it may cause a heart attack to the emotionally attached parents or cause any other type of damage to the family. The narration or experiences about such outcomes of the lying behaviour may thus persuade the children to refrain from telling lies for amusing themselves at the cost of others.
5. The children should be provided with adequate opportunities for sports, games, recreation and other constructive cocurricular activities in the school. It provides a better outlet and catharsis for their inner feelings, specially those connected with their unconscious. They can now better actualize their world of dreams by getting proper wings of imaginative thinking and creativity through a number of diversified constructive activities. Now since there remains no need of taking the help of imaginative lies, they may be saved from being termed as a liar.
6. The children who tell lies for establishing their superiority or boasting about them and their families should be made to realize that it is of no use to build castles in the air. The truth is bound to be known someday and when it happens, they will stand nowhere. Hence it is always better to concentrate on the development of our present abilities and capacities instead of living in fool's paradise and unnecessarily boasting about the things that are not with us.
7. Attempts should be made to develop the play and sportsmanship spirit among the children. They must be made to realize that one has to lose for enabling others to win. By all means they must improve themselves for winning a game or competition but in no way should they resort to foul play or lies.
8. We must try to arrange certain inspiring slogans like "Truth is always victorious", and "Truth is virtue and lying is sin" on the classroom walls or the school verandah, for developing positive attitude towards truth and negative towards lying.
9. Sometimes children resort to lying for the satisfaction of their day-to-day petty needs. The teachers should try to investigate about these petty needs of the children and get them satisfied with the active cooperation of the parents, other family members and school authorities. It may save the children from telling lies or becoming a tool of the anti-social elements.
10. Company plays a leading role in making and marring the future of the children. Hence it should be properly ensured that children do not fall in the company of the established liers and anti-social elements. In case one falls in their trap, we must adopt a very cautious approach for bringing the child into the mainstream. On one hand we have to remain alert about the reaction of the bad elements and on the other, the child should be made to realize that it is in his best interest to leave their company.
11. It is no use of resorting to punitive measures for correcting the lying behaviour of the child. It may instead strengthen his habit of lying through its reinforcing consequences. In such a situation, instead of bringing any positive results, the lying behaviour may be intensified by leaving an impression on the minds of the child that in doing so—(i) he becomes the

center of undue attraction, (ii) he may get opportunity for taking revenge with his parents and family members as they are hurt or their prestige is at stake, and (iii) he may save himself by entrapping others.

12. The best way of breaking the lying habit is in completely ignoring it. In any way, it should not get any undue attention or reinforcement. Initially when a small child tells a lie, his lying behaviour should not be reinforced by comments like "Look, how the naughty chap is telling a white lie." He should neither be rebuked nor slapped but simply his behaviour should be completely ignored and he should be made to realize that nobody is taking any notice of his lying behaviour and everybody present feels that his behaviour is not proper or worthwhile for future repetition.
13. The children who speak the truth must be rewarded and appreciated for their truthful behaviour. In the process of behaviour modification, a lying child should get an immediate proper reinforcement at the first sign of his truthfulness. He may be appreciated and rewarded in the presence of other children and teachers. Such reinforcement will certainly boost his morale and he will feel attracted and motivated towards truthfulness. As a result, his steps will automatically lead him on the path of the truth instead of lies.

Stealing

Meaning

Stealing refers to that behaviour of an individual or child in which he (i) engages himself in picking up or taking away some thing (money or material object) belonging to others without their consent or knowledge; (ii) pleads or exhibits his ignorance about the whereabouts of the object and (iii) keep an unauthorized possession of the picked up object with him or derives benefits by selling or giving it to somebody else of his choice.

This behaviour of both the children and the adults is considered quite undesirable, unsocial, immoral or even unlawful. Its seriousness is linked with the age of the involved individual. Generally if such act is committed by an infant or a child below the age of five (In true sense till the development of the concept of stealing and non-stealing, mine and yours and law of property etc.), it is not termed as stealing. After that, the behaviour is definitely named as 'stealing'. It is considered an offence that is to be dealt with the law of the land. However, if committed by a minor (below 18 years of age), the child or youth is named as delinquent but in the case of a major (individuals more than 18 years), it is considered a serious offence and the individual who commits such an act is called a criminal. Such criminals (usually named as thieves) are often put behind the bars and dealt with seriously as per the laws of the land. In this way, an ordinary way of picking up things by innocent children may turn into an immoral, unsocial and unlawful stealing habit of the future capable of damaging the very social fabric and lawful system of the society.

The ultimate consequences of the habit of stealing may thus compel us to think about the ways and means of saving the children from the clutches of this bad habit. In case someone falls victim to this habit, we must have some remedial measures and rectification programmes ready so that he may not enlisted as hardened criminal. Let us have some necessary thinking on these issues, but first of all let us try to know what makes an innocent child steal something.

Causes of Stealing

While searching for the probable causes of stealing behaviour among a wide variety of children, one comes across the following list of reasons:

Ignorance and Mental Retardation: Children who have not yet learned the concept of mine and yours, stealing and non-stealing, etc. may pick up the object belonging to others on account of their sheer ignorance. They do not see any evil in such an act. They just pick up or take possession of other's object because they like it or because it is of some immediate use to them. Generally, it happens with small children and children with intellectual deficiency.

Imitation: When a child observes that the elder children and members of his family pick up the objects belonging to him or others without telling anything or taking consent of the owner, he begins to imitate the behaviour of his elders. He also picks up money or material objects of others without informing or taking their consent. This behaviour is then carried out outside the home and family environment to neighbourhood, school and other social places. When this happens, the child is charged with committing the offence of stealing. Once termed a thief, he drifts towards the forced evil of stealing.

Defective Family Environment: Family is the first premier institution that makes a child learn good or bad habits through its strong impact and desirable or undesirable influence on the tender minds of the youngsters. Parents and other members of the family work as ideal figures or models for the children. Their behaviour patterns are easily imitated by the children. This is why the stealing behaviour of the elders may be learned easily by the youngsters of the family. In addition to this, there are many other things that may lead the child towards stealing behaviour. A few significant ones may be mentioned as below:

- On account of poverty and some other reasons, the child may feel deprived of the objects of his tastes and likings like certain food or drink items, toys and other play material, books and other reading and writing material etc. To get these object, he may then resort to stealing either in the form of cash or kind.
- There is lot of negligence on the part of the family members. They are used to putting cash or valuables in unsafe or unaccountable way so much so that these are at risk of being picked up by their children or servants. The children in such a loose environment may take undue advantage and pick up money or valuables for their fun and other unessential expenditures. Sometimes, parents take such stealing behaviour of their children in light and insignificant way. Such relaxed and loose environment may encourage the child to later develop stealing as a trait of his personality.
- Sometimes there prevails an extremely harsh, dominating and fearful autocratic environment at home. Why have you broken this toy, how did this object get damaged or spoiled, why have you forgotten or lost your book or pen? Such hitting questions or enquiry approach accompanied with the fear of getting reproof and corporal punishment by the elders, may make the child replace the broken or lost object by way of stealing.
- In some situations, children are found to resort to stealing behaviour simply to take revenge for the aggressive, unjust and harsh behaviour of their elders and parents. They deliberately and knowingly steal the cash or articles to hurt the feelings and sentiments of their elders.

Effect of Bad Company: Most children's habits are the product of good or bad company they enjoy in the neighbourhood, school or other social set ups. In case there are neighbours, playing mates, class or school mates habitual of stealing, then there are high chances that the child would imbibe the habit of stealing in his own conduct. He may be easily attracted to their acts of stealing as it gets them cash or valuable with a little effort and once impressed, necessary training in stealing may then be easily available from his thief companions.

Showing Courage and Fearlessness: In some cases, false egoism and display of unnecessary courage and fearlessness before his companions may make a child steal some or the other objects. He may pick up mangoes or guavas from the neighbour's garden or steal some or the other articles from a shop only to show that he has enough guts and courage to do so. These children resort to such stealing behaviour on the assumption that by doing so they will earn the heroic and leadership position in their group.

Psychological Causes: In some cases, stealing behaviour of the children is the direct result of their emotional and social maladjustment. The children who remain tense or are grippled with the feelings of vengeance, may be forced to feel relaxed and satisfied by way of stealing one or the other object irrespective of its utility to them.

Abnormality in behaviour: In some cases, stealing is a visible sign of abnormality in one's behaviour. In the terminology of abnormal psychology, such compulsive abnormal behaviour is named as 'kleptomania'. Under the influence of such compulsive behaviour one is forced to steal a particular type of objects like the undergarments of the opposite sex, spoons, etc.

Encouragement and Reinforcement: Any improper or undesirable behavioural act performed consciously or unconsciously by a child may turn into a habit only when it is reinforced properly in one way or the other by the factors and conditions prevalent in his environment. When a child picks up mangoes or guavas from the neighbour's garden or steals tablespoon from a social gathering and gets appreciated by his mother, elder family members or friends for his act, he is bound to pick up this behaviour as a fixed pattern or trait.

REMEDIAL MEASURES FOR STEALING BEHAVIOUR

Stealing in all its shapes and forms is definitely a bad habit and undesirable as well as unsocial behaviour. Children should be saved from the clutches of this bad habit. The first and foremost thing is to attempt for the preventive measures but in case the children fall victim to this evil, we have to seek the remedial measures. In general, however, the following things may prove quite helpful in dealing with the stealing behaviour of the children.

1. The children should be clearly told about the desirability or undesirability of their behaviour. They must be made to distinguish between the stealing and non-stealing behaviour. The concept of property, in terms of mine and their, should also be developed among the children. It should also be emphasized that it is not proper to take the money or objects belonging to others without taking their consent. The children behaving accordingly should be duly appreciated before other children for being projected as a model of proper behaviour.
2. There is no point in lecturing about stealing as a bad habit. The children need live solid examples for the learning of good ways, manners and habits. For this purpose, the parents and elders need to attempt in the following ways:
   - They should not pick up anything belonging to their children or others without their consent or knowledge.
   - They should not tell or narrate any incident involving theft or stealing in such a way that it portrays stealing as a heroic deed or desirable behaviour.
   - He must be told and convinced about the ill effects and damaging consequences of the habit of stealing through well narrated incidents and stories, displayed pictures and illustrations, literature and movies etc.

3. The family environment should be so controlled and regulated that children do not get anything helpful in drawing their behaviour towards stealing. Any incidence or behaviour of any member of the family should in no circumstance be allowed to become a subject of modeling or base for the stealing behaviour of the children. Necessary attention should always be paid to the satisfaction of their essential material needs. They should be made to learn to live their life honourably and satisfactorily within their family means. They must be made to realize that there is no end to one's requirement or needs and therefore it is not proper to steal other's things for satisfaction of one's unlimited or even essential desires.

   In fact poverty alone can't turn a child into a thief. It is the lack of satisfaction of one's emotional affection and security needs that proves a major cause for drawing a child towards stealing behaviour. Hence if the parents and family provide him the necessary attention for the satisfaction of his physical and psychological needs, then he will not be compelled to pick up stealing as a substitute or means for the satisfaction of his otherwise unsatisfied social, economical and material needs.
4. Attempts should be made to bring those children on the right track who resort to stealing for projecting themselves as hero, brave or courageous figures in the eyes of their colleagues. They should be made to realize that stealing is a cowardice act rather than a heroic or brave adventure. Apart from this, these children should be provided with ample opportunities in the form of co-curricular activities and social openings for exhibiting their courage and adventurism through mountaineering, scouting or N.C.C., competing in sports and games or doing social service at the hours of crises and calamities.
5. The mentally disturbed, emotionally upset and tense children should be properly attended by the parents, elders and teachers through proper care, love and affection. They should not feel so insecure that they resort to stealing so as to do away with any anticipated ill-treatment by their elders.
6. We should not come to any hasty conclusion regarding the stealing behaviour based on any single incidence reported about a child. It should be properly investigated by going to the rootcause or bases for the eruption of such a behaviour. A child may indulge in stealing merely on account of his sheer ignorance, misguidance or willful manipulation of some vested interests.
7. Punitive and hard measures do not bring desired positive results in breaking the habit of stealing. The real remedy lies in bringing desired modification in the otherwise undesirable behaviour of the child. We must win over his heart and make him realize the undesirability and nonfunctionability of his stealing behaviour. He must feel that his stealing behaviour is quite detrimental to the welfare of his self and the society. It does not mean that the child should not be punished in any way for his stealing act. Punishment, if any, may be given to the child for the correction of his undesirable behaviour, but it should be given in such a way that child realizes that his behaviour has given a serious setback to the feelings and sentiments of his parents, elders or teachers and they have been forced to take such disciplinary measure only for the correction of his undesirable and unsocial behaviour.
8. Any behavioural act of stealing performed by the child consciously or unconsciously should in no way be given any type of reinforcement, either positive or negative. As far as possible, it should not be given any undue attention or importance. By no means and in no way should it be appreciated or made a subject of mockery. It should be dealt with desired patience and tolerance on the part of the parents, elders and teaches. Angry outbursts and reaction on their part may provide unnecessary reinforcement to the stealing

behaviour of the child. However, in any case the stealing behaviour or any first such step should never be taken as non-existent or non-significant. It should be properly investigated with necessary tolerance and patience on the part of elders and necessary remedial step should essentially be taken for weeding out the disease from its roots. In any case, the child should not feel that his undesirable behaviour has an approval of his elders or it may prove a weapon in his hand for taking revenge on one account or the other.

9. The children who resort to some special type of stealing behaviour like kleptomania on account of the abnormality in their behaviour should be provided adequate treatments by the psychologists and psychiatrists.
10. The behaviour therapy and behaviour modification techniques should be properly adapted for correcting the stealing behaviour of the children. As soon as the child steps in for the correction of his behaviour, he should be properly appreciated and his efforts for modifying his behaviour should be immediately reinforced through suitable reinforcement schedules. His changed good behaviour should be appreciated and acknowledged in public for boosting his changed self image and he should be given all help and assistance for getting rid of his undesirable stealing behaviour.

Temper Tantrum

Meaning

Temper tantrum or temper outburst is a common sight for any professional who deals with the problems of the children. It occurs more frequently among younger children who exhibit a variety of learning, physical or emotional problems. *As a matter of definition, temper tantrum may be termed as an intense uncontrollable outburst of anger expressed through cursing, kicking, hitting, biting, screaming, rolling on the ground, destruction of property and related behaviour that may be dangerous to those around as well as to furnishings.*

In general, temper tantrum seem to occur only when the child is in the presence of an adult particularly the one quite familiar and near to him like his parents, grandparents, teachers or in an institutional setting, the childcare workers. In this way, by its own typical demonstration, the temper tantrum seems to be a pure attention-seeking behaviour. It often appears when the child fails to realize his objectives by some other ways or becomes conditioned to realize them through the intense uncontrollable rage.

Causes of Temper Tantrum

Much to our dismay, young children often display temper tantrums. The following list may help us to understand why children act in this way.

1. Temper tantrum is more likely to arise when a child is feeling hungry, thirsty, tired or sick. Children who want or need attention may also act aggressively to get it.
2. Children occasionally resort to temper tantrum as a means of asserting themselves. You may notice a three-year-old toppling over a playmate's block tower. While this act may appear to an adult to be a sort of hostile takeover, it's more likely to be a declaration of independence, assertiveness or an attempt to initiate play. Nonetheless, children need to learn more appropriate vehicles of expression.
3. Children who witness violent behaviour—either on television, in movies or firsthand—are likely to imitate aggressive actions in their interactions with peers, teachers and family members. Likewise, children who are witnesses to or victims of abuse or violence at home or in school are likely to respond with temper tantrum in their play or any social situation.

4. Children who have not learned self-control often act aggressively. When the adults in their lives set clear and consistent limits, young children will eventually learn to set limits on their own behaviour. However, when children have limited or inconsistent guidance from parents and caretakers, they have difficulty in recognizing and monitoring their aggressive behaviours.
5. Children who have not learned more appropriate problem-solving techniques often resort to violence as a means to resolve conflict. When children become frustrated because their playmate don't share a favourite toy, a parent is busy talking on the phone or a sibling has got favour and recognition, they often respond with aggressive behaviour. Children need guidance in finding other strategies for solving these types of problems and venting their frustration.
6. Angry defiance may be associated with the feelings of dependency and angry outburst may be associated with sadness and depression. In childhood, anger and sadness are very close to one another, and it is important to remember that much of an adult experiences as sadness is expressed by a child as temper tantrum.
7. The uncongenial home and family environment may prove a germinating soil as well as nourishing agent for the aggressive behaviour of the child. When a child is unable to satisfy his basic physiological and socio-psychological needs, he begins to drift towards maladaptive styles of behaviour including temper tantrum. In the environment, where child feels that he is unnecessarily ridiculed, rebuffed and punished and is subjected to partial, prejudiced, cruel and unjust behaviour at the hands of the elders, he resorts to angry and aggressive behaviour for his self defence to cover the feelings of insecurity or to take revenge.
8. Many a time the aggressive mode of the child's behaviour in the form of temper tantrums get linked with the reinforcement received by him through the satisfaction of his desires or needs through his temper outbursts. Once he realizes his objectives through such means, he is habituated to repeat it whenever he needs so in future.
9. According to Alder, the famous psychologist belonging to analytical School of Psychology, the need to dominate or self assertion is the prime motive or spring board of human behaviour. In some of the children, it is found in excess which may compel them for resorting to temper outbursts or uncontrolled rage in order to make others fearful and accept their dominance.
10. In some cases, biological factors may also play a decisive or side role for inciting or paving the way for sudden emotional outbursts and aggressive behaviour. The malfunctioning of the glands and nervous system may well trigger off such situations in some or the other cases.

Remedial Measures for the Temper Tantrum Problem of the Children

Handling children's temper tantrums can be puzzling, draining, and distressing for adults. In fact, one of the major problems in dealing with anger in children is the angry feelings that are often stirred up in us. It has been said that we as parents, teachers, counselors, and administrators need to remind ourselves that we were not always taught how to deal with anger as a fact of life during our own childhood. We were led to believe that to be angry was to be bad, and we were often made to feel guilty for expressing anger.

It will be easier to deal with children's temper tantrums if we get rid of this notion. Our goal is not to repress or destroy angry feelings in children—or in ourselves—but rather to accept the feelings and to help channel and direct them to constructive ends. Parents and teachers must allow children to feel all their feelings. Adult skills can then be directed toward showing children acceptable ways of expression. Outbursts should not always be viewed as a sign of serious problems; they should be recognized and treated with respect.

Although like other behavioural problems, the temper tantrum is to be handled as an individual case in itself. In general, the following points may prove quite helpful to parents, teachers and elders in dealing with the temper tantrum problem of their children.

1. Try to anticipate a melt-down. Being aware of when your child is feeling hungry, tired, sick or frustrated is your first line of defense against aggressive behaviour. If you know when aggressive behaviour is likely to strike, you can head it off with a diversion like food, a new activity or a break in the action.
2. Encourage your child to use words for describing his feelings. When your child seems out of control, help him talk about how he is feeling and let him know that you understand his feelings. 'I can see that you're feeling really angry right now because you want to stay at the playground. But it's time to go home now.' Let your child know that it's okay to express the feelings in words. Help him generate a list of words—angry, mad, sad, upset, grumpy, etc.—for describing his feelings.
3. Introduce acceptable strategies for dealing with temper tantrums. With younger children, it is sometimes helpful to offer an invigorating physical activity such as bouncing on a trampoline, running around the outside of the house three times or stamping their feet on the driveway to help them blow off steam.

   With older children (six and above), discuss appropriate times and places for handling anger. Teach children to count backward from 10 before acting out. If your child is on the verge of a breakdown in the middle of the shopping mall, remind her that a public place is not the appropriate spot, acknowledge her feelings and let her know that you'll discuss the situation with her as soon as you get home.

   Follow through with your commitment and be sure to give her plenty of time to vent her frustration. Children of all ages often find drawing a picture about a difficult moment or writing an apology letter to be helpful cooling off techniques.
4. Set clear limits about aggressive behaviour. Make sure your children understand the consequence for incorporate actions and be consistent in following up on them. When your child initiates a loud tantrum during a play date, remove her from the situation immediately. Tell her, "It's not okay for you to behave that way. When you kick and scream, then we have to go home." Once you've established a rule, don't open it up for negotiation.
5. Help your child develop appropriate problem-solving strategies. With every young child, you'll have to initiate the technique. For example, with a two-year-old who's having difficulty sharing a favourite play thing, set a timer so that each child has equal time.

   Encourage older children to work independently to develop solutions. Intervene only when necessary and limit your involvement. When siblings are arguing over the last cookie, state the problem and ask for solutions—"So, there's only one cookie left. What could you do so that all three of you could have a snack?" Then step back and let them negotiate among themselves.
6. Pay close attention to television viewing, video game playing and online surfing. Set limits on the amount and type of television programming your children watch. Watch television along with your children and encourage discussion about program content. Don't be afraid

to shut off an inappropriate program. Prohibit violent computer games and closely monitor time spent online.

7. Choose books and movies that promote themes of kindness and responsibility. Ask the children's librarian at your local library for assistance in finding appropriate books for children of all age-groups. Reading aloud to children of all ages is a great way to promote conversations about values and appropriate behaviour. A family movie might provide an opportunity for similar conversations.
8. Make a consistent effort to recognize kind behaviour. Let children know that you value their kindness by pointing it out as often as possible. For example: 'I noticed that you shared the last bit of Cheerios with your sister this morning. That was very thoughtful.' Making it clear that you expect good things and acknowledging positive acts will send a clear, motivational message to children.
9. Hold male and female children to the same standards. Many parents are tempted to follow the old 'Boys will be boys' adage when it comes to managing aggressive behaviour. It's essential that both boys and girls learn to express their aggression appropriately. Make it clear that physical aggression will not be tolerated. At the same time, make sure that children of both genders are given ample opportunity to express their feelings.
10. Be a supportive role model. Above all, act kindly and compassionately toward your children and other family members as well as friends and strangers. Always use polite language towards your children and be sure to apologize for any unkind action. Avoid using sarcasm with children. Never respond to inappropriate behaviour with violent language or actions.
11. Manipulate the surroundings. Aggressive behaviour is more likely to happen or reinforced by placing children in tough, tempting situations. We should try to plan the surroundings so that certain things are less apt to happen. Stop a problem activity and substitute, temporarily with a more desirable one. Sometimes rules and regulations, as well as physical space, may be too confining. Hence if you know what situations trigger temper tantrums in your child, try to avoid them.
12. Use closeness and touching. Move physically closer to the child to curb his or her angry impulse. Young children are often calmed by having an adult come close by and express interest in the child's activities. Children naturally try to involve adults in what they are doing, and the adult is often annoyed at being bothered. Very young children (and children who are emotionally deprived) seem to need much more adult involvement in their interests. A child about to use a toy or tool in a destructive way is sometimes easily stopped by an adult who expresses interest in having it shown to him. An outburst from an older child struggling with a difficult reading selection can be prevented by a caring adult who moves near the child to say, "Show me which words are giving you trouble."
13. Use a time-out—briefly isolating the child immediately after the aggressive behaviour occurs. Rather than scolding or physically punishing the child, place him in a quiet room or on a chair in the corner for a short period of time (many experts recommend one minute per year in age) in order to cool down.
14. Try not to resort to physical punishment. It may stop aggression temporarily, but there is evidence that in the long run such punishment may actually increase aggressive behaviour, probably because it conveys the idea that hitting is okay.
15. Reinforce the non-aggressive and good behaviour of your problem child immediately as and when it happens.
16. Reduce the time your child spends with playmates who engage in aggressive behaviour.

A FIVE-STEP PROGRAM TO REDUCE AGGRESSION

1. Make a colourful chart with a space for each day of the week. If the child is quite young, divide each day into smaller intervals to accommodate a shorter attention span. Hang the chart on the wall.
2. For each time the child does not display aggression, give the child a sticker and help him place it on the chart. Say, "Good, you didn't hit" (or bite or kick, etc.).
3. Supplement the sticker with a snack or treat or a few minutes of special attention.
4. After the child has gone a whole week without aggression (or a shorter time for a younger child), show him the stickers on the chart, and say, "You haven't hit (or kicked, bitten, fought, etc.) for a whole week. Now, you've earned a special reward." This reward can be an outing with a parent, an extra period of time alone with the mother, or anything you know your child would like. It should be unusual enough to motivate the child strongly.
5. When the child is aggressive, say, "No hitting." At the end of the day or interval, show the child the chart and say, "You didn't get a sticker this time because you had hit."

Drug Addiction

MEANING AND DEFINITION

The term 'Drug addiction' carries with it the concept of drug and addiction. Let us have a clear understanding of these concepts.

Drugs: We generally make use of one or the other drugs for preserving our health and protecting as well as curing ourselves from illnesses or diseases. In this sense, drugs are our best friends. However, this is one side of the story. All drugs are not always so helpful to us. If taken in excess or in contradiction to the need of the body, they may prove fatal. It is more true with those drugs that are associated with intoxication. Here while trying to know the meaning of the term 'drug addiction', we must be quite specific that by the word 'drug' we clearly mean the drugs associated with intoxication. What are these intoxicated drugs, how do these affect one's body and mind? We will discuss these issues again later in this chapter.

Addiction: Physiological and psychological dependence on something may be referred to as our addiction to that thing. In this sense, we may have addiction to our breakfast, lunch or dinner. We may feel craving for morning or evening tea or milk before sleeping etc. However, addiction does not have such a simple meaning when we try to integrate it with the habit of taking intoxicating drugs. Here we refer to it in the category of those harmful and relatively permanent bad habits and evils (like gambling, prostitution, alcoholism, stealing, pick-pocketing etc.) which are considered extremely fatal and detrimental to the individual and the society. Once adopted in one's behaviour, it becomes quite difficult to get rid of them irrespective of their damaging physical and social consequences. In the beginning, one may make use of such intoxicating drugs quite casually for one or the other reason. However, its excessive and prolonged use can make him quite dependent on it both physiologically and psychologically. Gradually, it becomes difficult for an individual to give up its use. The more he takes the drug, more he becomes dependent on it thus resulting in such craving that one is compelled to take it at any cost irrespective of the consequences. Hence starting from a casual intake and ordinary habit, drug addiction may take the shape of quite a dangerous personality disorder. In its developing stages this disorder may be seen to gradually affect the individual in the following ways.

1. **Initial effects of drugs:** Intoxicating drugs are very powerful and exercise instant affect on the mind and the body of the individual. These drugs provide stimulating, sedative or mind-blowing effects according to their own tendencies. One is attracted and begins to use them due to one or the other reason. He uses them again and argues that these help him in providing relief from the tension, stress, pains etc. or provides him opportunity to wander into his world of joy, happiness and wish fulfillment.
2. **Conversion into a habit:** Whatever the reasons or circumstances may be for taking the first dose of an intoxicating drug, its initial instant effect is quite powerful in persuading or compelling the individual to take the second or more subsequent doses in a chained reaction. Gradually, its use turns into an essential routine and habit of one's day-to-day life so much so that one can't live without it.
3. **Tolerance for the heavy doses of the drugs:** You have seen that people who are not used to drinking tea or coffee, employ it as a sort of medicine to get relief from cold or headache. It works for them on account of the stimulation provided by caffeine and cocaine—the main intoxicating elements present in tea and coffee. However, same is not true for the people who take tea and coffee regularly. The prolonged and excessive use of tea and coffee makes one's body so accustomed and habitual that no such stimulation is felt by the intoxicating caffeine and cocaine in the latter case.

   For generating same stimulation, one either needs heavy doses or may require some other more powerful drug for relief from cold and headache.

   The same is true for all types of intoxicating drugs. Once used on any account or reason, a drug provides them such temptation and persuasion that they continue their excessive and prolonged use. The more they use a drug, more accustomed and habitual their mind and body become to bear its effect. As a consequence of such chained reactions, one has to frequently take more and more heavy doses of the drug for obtaining the results and experiences similar to the initial ones when one had relatively less frequency and amount of the doses of the drug.
4. **Physiological and Psychological Dependence:** As said earlier, the prolonged and excessive use of an intoxicating drug leads to increased tolerance. One now has to take increased doses of this drug with the increased frequency and amount for getting the similar relief and other intoxicating effects. Consequently the individual develops an increasing physiological and psychological dependence on them to the extent that he feels agitated, disturbed and miserable whenever the particular drug is not administered. By physiological dependence here, we mean that his physical and physiological systems become so habituated to the use of the drug that his physical or physiological activities cannot be properly maintained, nor can he get relief from the pains and other troubles of his body systems without the use of that drug. Similarly by psychological dependence on a drug, we mean that one is persuaded and compelled to think that his interest and welfare lie in the use of the drug. His mind is totally set for devising the means and ways of getting that drug somehow without caring for any physical, physiological or social consequences. In this way his whole behaviour is now centered around the use and craving for that drug. Thus his mind and body both become slaves in the hands of his drug addiction.
5. **Presence of withdrawal symptoms:** The increasingly physiological and psychological dependence of the individual on the intoxicating drugs is clearly reflected through some or the other withdrawal symptoms (appearing in the case when some one is deprived of his

intake of doses) like lack of appetite, loss of weight, constipation, restlessness, nervousness, nausea, vomiting, diarrhea, disinterest in sexual and social relationships and even epileptic seizures or acute brain syndrome in some cases. Besides, there is an intense craving for that particular drug. All his actions and behaviour are directed towards gratification of the craving for the drug. He becomes restless, perturbed, uneasy, sad and tense. His pains and agonies get intensified with the denial of the drug and passage of the time.

In this way withdrawal symptoms may quite effectively reveal the intensity of one's physiological and psychological dependence on the intoxicating drugs.

6. **Developing into a behavioural problem:** Excessive physiological and psychological dependence on drugs makes an individual handicapped in terms of his proper physical, physiological and psychological functioning. All his actions and behaviour are centered around the satisfaction of his craving for the drugs. In case his carving for more and more doses of the drugs are not satisfied, he demonstrates serious withdrawal symptoms. He tries his best to get the required dose of the drugs by fair or foul means regardless of the consequences. All such developments in his behaviour consequently lead him towards the total maladjustment to his behaviour and he ultimately gets affected with a specific type of behavioural problem associated with drug addiction.

After understanding the meaning of the terms 'drug' and 'addiction', we may now define the term 'drug addiction' in the following way;

The behavioural problem associated with the drug addiction stands for that physiological and psychological state of an individual which is resulted through the prolonged and excessive use of an intoxicating drug and which may be characterized by (a) *an intense craving or compulsion to obtain or consume it regardless of consequences;* (b) *a tendency to increase the dosage with time;* (c) *physiological and psychological dependence on the effects of the drug;* (d) *manifestation of particular withdrawal symptoms on abrupt discontinuation of the drug, and* (e) *to live and work only for consuming the drug.*

DRUGS—TYPES AND EFFECTS

Depending upon the nature of their effects, drugs may be classified at stimulant, sedative and deliriant (mind-blowing).

Stimulant drugs: These drugs stimulate the brain and sympathetic nervous system resulting in alertness and increase in response and motor activity. The major drugs of this category are nicotine, cocaine, caffeine, and amphetamines like benzidine, dexedrine and methedrine.

The addiction to stimulant drugs makes an individual dependent, physiologically and psychologically, on its ever increasing doses for the continuous stimulation of sense organs. In the long run, it results in severe loss of appetite and weight, constipation, increased anxiety and irritability, sleep deprivation, gradual impairment of intellectual functioning and periodic episodes of delirium.

Sedative drugs: These drugs slow down the activities of an organism and diminish the response of the brain and nervous system. As a result they are used as pain relievers and sleep inducers and may be classified as narcotics and hypnotics. The major narcotic drugs are opium, morphine, heroin, codeine, demerol and methadrone. Hypnotic drugs include barbiturates like amytal, nembutal, seconal, and non-barbiturates like bromides and paraldehyde chloral hydrate.

The prolonged use of sedative drugs leads to increased tolerance and physiological as well as psychological craving for them. The immediate effects are pleasant and there is relief from pain and lessening of voluntary movements followed by euphoria. But these effects are short-lived and are followed by a negative phase or craving for more drug and the consequent ill effects.

The addiction to narcotics results in loss of appetite and weight, constipation, lack of sexual desire and social interests. Unlike narcotics, the addiction to hypnotic drugs lead to intellectual impairment and disturbance of the motor functions dependent on the cerebellum.

The sudden withdrawal of sedative drugs results in dangerous withdrawal symptoms like restlessness, nervousness, excessive perspiration, nausea, vomiting, diarrhoea, severe headache, marked tremors, cardio-vascular collapse and painful muscular cramps. In the case of hypnotics, the withdrawal reactions may lead to epileptic seizures and delirium. If not treated in time, the seizures can cause death. Tranquillizers like meprobamate also result in addiction and have the same results as most of the sedatives.

Deliriant or mind-blowing drugs: These drugs produce transient states resembling psychoses resulting in marked confusion, distortion in thought processes, delirium, illusions and hallucinations. Marijuana produces an euphoric state involving increased self confidence and a pleasant feeling of relaxation characterized by a feeling of floating. There is a considerable distortion of the sense of time and space. In some cases, the individual becomes irritable. There is a marked impairment in the motor and intellectual functioning but the users usually think that their efficiency has increased. This false sense of adequacy gives rise to incidents of reckless driving and other antisocial episodes. In many individuals, the intoxication of marijuana may produce acute psychotic reactions as found with hallucinogenic drugs.

The most popular mind-blowing or hallucinogenic drug is LSD-25 or lysergic acid diethylamide. Other hard drugs of this category are mescaline (an alkaloid and the active ingredient of peyote), psilocybin (a crystalline powder derived from mushroom) and bufotenine. The outward symptoms of LSD and other hallucinogenic drugs addiction bear a strong resemblance to the behaviour of schizophrenic patients. There is marked confusion, muddling in one's thinking and development of visual and auditory hallucinations. There is a false sense of well-being and the patient gradually develops a high level of tolerance and dependence.

Another drug of this category that is most abused is methamphetamine (speed) taken in the form of intravenous injection. Prolonged use of this drug results in malnutrition, brain damage, disturbance of the heart rhythm, and a dangerously impulsive, paranoid unpredictable behaviour.

How do people become drug addicts?

Nobody is born as drug addict. He acquires this behaviour from his environment gradually by passing through the following three main stages.

Initial stages: One may be initiated or persuaded to take the first few doses of an intoxicated drug under the circumstances given below:

- One may take a particular intoxicating drug as a medicine prescribed by a medical practitioner or doctor or he may have been advised by some friend or elderly person to do so for the cure and treatment of his illness.
- One may be tempted to use a drug by imitating the behaviour of his parents, friends and other members of the society.
- One may take it simply on account of his curiousity about the use of a new thing or for the sake of fun and pleasure of looking for new thrills, new kicks and possibility of mystic experience.

- One may use it for showing that he is not a child now and has enough guts and courage to consume such a drug.
- One may resort to drugs simply for giving company to friends and developing new relationships.
- One may use it on the plea of getting relief from anxiety, pressure and tensions.
- One may think of its use for seeking escape from boredom.
- One may use the drugs on the plea of generating necessary confidence, energy and initiative for committing a crime or an anti-social act.
- One may be tempted, persuaded or forced to make use of drugs under the evil influences and underhand methods used by the anti-social or criminal personalities engaged in the drug trafficking business.

Developing stage: As this stage, the behaviour learned at the initial stage is reinforced and rewarded on account of—(i) assumption and false impression of adequacy and well-being, (ii) temporary relief from anxiety, pain or stress, (iii) pleasant reverie and short-lived pleasing effects or state or euphoria created by the use of drug. Reinforced by such instant effects of the first few doses, one is tempted and persuaded to repeat the intake of the similar drug and thus falls into the trap of using it again and again (with the increased frequency and amount) and thus developing it as a habit or characteristic of his personality.

Final stage: By the time one reaches this stage, he becomes quite addicted to the drug. The excessive use of the drug leads to increased tolerance resulting into complete physiological and psychological dependence on them to the extent that he feels quite miserable, perturbed or tense whenever this drug is not administered. So what began as an innocuous experiment at the initial stage ends in disaster at the final stage. The individual now turns into a drug addict who has a strong compulsion and craving for the drug. Neither does he follow any norms nor does he listen to any advice but only cares and attempts for the required doses of his drug at any cost irrespective of the consequences. He now lives only for the sake of the drug intake and such intake becomes the only reason for running and taking away his life. His behaviour now becomes abnormal and maladaptive to the extent of being included in the category of personality disorders. He now reaches the point of no return. All the doors for his reforms are now closed. He realizes that he himself cannot give up the drug but hopes for some miracle or somebody to come for his help in getting rid of the menace of drug addiction. In such an advance stage, though it is quite difficult to save him, there is still some hope for the correction of his behaviour through systematically planned and organized attempts which we will discuss in the causative measures mentioned later in the text.

PREVENTION AND TREATMENT OF DRUG ADDICTION

Prevention: Prevention is said to be better than cure. Consequently it is always proper to think of the ways and means that may help the future generations save themselves from the clutches of this dreaded evil. The following measures may prove quite effective and fruitful in this direction.

- The beginning in this direction must be made by educating the public about the causes and consequences of drug addiction.
- There should be substantial provision in schools for educating the children through various curricular and cocurricular activities about the menace of drug addiction.
- There is a need of restructurization of unhealthy environment and reduction in the problems leading to frustration, tensions and anxieties among the youth. Job opportunities

need to be increased and the education system should be so reshaped that it includes job-oriented and employment based courses.

- The energies of the children and youth should be channelized into constructive and creative projects like rural reconstruction, welfare of the society and the nation and for helping the needy and poor. This will give them a sense of purpose and opportunity for adventure and new experiences, the things they try to seek through drugs.
- The intoxicating drugs that have limited medical application should be banned. Parents and elders should not take such medicines that carry strong intoxicating effects. As far as possible, these should not be taken in the presence of children nor administered to them as medicine.
- Drug trafficking should be checked through strict social and legal means. The individuals who try to trap the children and youth, through temptation or coercion, into drug addiction should be carefully watched and strictly dealt with through social and legal provisions.
- Parents and teachers should be quite vigilant about the company and living style of the children, especially during adolescence. They must try to meet their basic needs and remain on track with themselves and the environment. Any abnormality in their behaviour and day-to-day activities should be wisely attended and proper corrective measures should be taken for saving them from the dangers of drug addiction.

TREATMENT OF DRUG ADDICTION

In case one becomes drug addict, due to one or the other reason, he needs proper attention, care and treatment so that he can get rid of this addiction. Truly speaking, drug addiction is not a law and order problem as imagined in certain circles. It is predominantly a social and psychological problem. Addicts should be distinguished from criminals who supply them with drugs and live off their misery. The irony of addicts is that they depend on drugs to the extent of pathological craving so powerful that they try and manage to get the drug regardless of legal or other obstacles. Keeping all these things in view, the following five measures prove fruitful in the treatment of drug addicts.

Compulsory hospitalization: Compulsory institutionalization and hospitalization is a major step in the treatment of drug addicts. If the doctor waits until the patient voluntarily seeks effective treatment, he may well wait until the patient dies. Drug addicts do not want treatment, they want drugs and in their surroundings and environment they can't be deprived of drugs. The admission in hospitals may be able to cover the following major risks:

(i) Rejection by family and society, (they can neither understand nor manage the patient) makes the patient depressed. This situation worsens when drugs are not available during the withdrawal phase.

(ii) The tendency to go on to harder drugs or mixed drugs to get the desired effect may lead to disaster.

(iii) There is a risk of the patient killing himself on account of an accidental overdose or committing suicide when profoundly depressed or a mishap under the intoxicating effects of drug.

(iv) There is danger of infection or other complications when the drug is injected in the body by the individual.

Deintoxicating or drying-out the patient: Attempts should be made to deintoxicate or dry-out the patient. It may be achieved through (i) the 'cold turkey' procedure, i.e. sudden total discontinuation of drugs; (ii) giving the patient progressively diminishing doses of drug leading to complete cessation; and (iii) substituting a less addictive drug and later seeking gradual reduction in intake.

Medical measures: With some patients, specially psychotic addicts, ECT or tranquilizing drugs may prove quite helpful. Adequate care is to be taken for the provision of antibiotics as there is an inherent danger of possible infection. The withdrawal reactions should also be controlled as they lead to physical or mental disaster. Adequate dietary measures in the form of glucose and vitamins are to be ascertained for compensating the drug deficiency and also adequate feeding and fluids should be ensured.

Psychological treatment: Psychological treatment of drug addicts calls for patience and time. Long range psychotherapy and socio therapy are essential if the patient is to learn to face his problems and seek adjustment in the society without the use of the drug.

Long-term therapy and rehabilitation: The long-term therapy is also essential and it may be achieved as follows:

(i) **Re-personalization:** The drug addicts should be helped to form proper relationship with therapists, doctors and nurses before they can re-establish any personal identity.

(ii) **Specific therapy:** Withdrawal reactions and complications should be well guarded against with the help of specific drugs. For example, epileptics may need anti-convulsants or schizopherenies may need phenothiazines.

(iii) **Re-socialization:** The drug addicts must learn to socialize and adjust without the aid of drugs.

(iv) **Re-occupation:** Once cured, the drug addicts should be helped in seeking employment and occupational adjustment. They need to be trained the job skill and persistence so that they may be accepted by their employers.

(v) **Re-housing:** They should be helped in getting adequate family adjustment and re-establish themselves by learning to accommodate and fend for themselves.

The duration and extent of long-term therapy depends upon the patient's potential, and the original level of maturity which the patient has reached. If adequately cared through therapy and rehabilitation, the patient should be able to lead a full life and develop his potential abilities.

SUMMARY

The term 'behavioural problem' refers to a type of serious abnormality in the behaviour of an individual resulting into his maladjustment with the self and the environment and proving detrimental to the welfare of his self and the society. Examples of such behaviour are truancy, lying, stealing, temper tantrums, drug addiction and juvenile delinquency.

Truancy as a behavioural problem relates with the school life of a child. A child demonstrates such behavioural problem when he willingly remains absent from the classroom or other activities of the school without bringing it to notice of his teachers, parents or school authorities. Causes of truancy lie in the factors and circumstances related to one's self and the environmental surroundings like one's physical and mental health, level of the physical and mental abilities, improper behaviour and maltreatment received from the peers, elder students, teachers and school authorities, improper methods of teaching, lack of cocurricular activities and hobbies, indiscipline prevalent in the school, ill affects of bad company; defective home environment, difficulty in the satisfaction of the basic needs, desire and tendency to escape from work, social and emotional maladjustment, to prove superiority and courage by indulging in such negative behaviour etc. Remedial measures for the truant behaviour involve both the preventive as well as curative measures. We must first try our best to save the children from becoming truant and in case they somehow become so, attempts should be made to bring them back in the mainstream.

Lying as a behavioural problem is associated with a bad habit and serious compulsion of not speaking truth on the part of an individual in his communication with other people. According to their nature, causes and effect, lies can be broadly classified into two types namely (i) those told knowingly with full consciousness and definite purposes, and (ii) the lies told unknowingly in the absence of essential consciousness or purposes. As remedial measures for the lying behaviour of the children, initially efforts for the prevention of this behaviour should be made in all the possible ways. But in case the child gets habituated to telling lies, then attempts should be made to bring desirable modifications in his behaviour.

Stealing refers to that abnormality in the behaviour of an individual in which he is engaged in picking up or taking away something (i.e. money or material object) belonging to others without their consent or knowledge. The behaviour, when developed as a habit, may lead a child to be labeled as delinquent and hardened criminal as he grows older. The causes of stealing behaviour in the children may be well linked with factors like their ignorance and mental retardation, imitation of the stealing behaviour of others, defective family environment, effect of bad company, display of unnecessary courage and fearlessness, psychological factors associated with their personal emotional and social maladjustment, abnormality like the presence of compulsive behaviour for stealing behaviour etc. In attempting remedial measures for the stealing behaviour of the children, the first and foremost thing is to try the preventive measures but in case child falls victim to the evil, we have to seek the remedial measures by making him realize the undesirability of his behaviour and seeking possible ways for bringing desirable modification in his otherwise undesirable behaviour with the help of behaviour therapy and behaviour modification techniques.

Temper Tantrum refers to an intense uncontrollable outburst and expression of anger demonstrated through a number of undesirable physical acts like hitting, biting, destruction of property etc. It may prove dangerous to those around as well as to furnishings. In all its way temper tantrum by its typical demonstration seems to be a pure attention-seeking and goal realizing behaviour. A child may resort to such behaviour only to seek attention of others for making them agree or available for the satisfaction of his desirable as well as undesirable needs. This behaviour is totally acquired and not innate or inborn in any form. One learns this behaviour in order to realize his needs and objectives through the models and feedback available in one's environment. In seeking remedy for the temper tantrum behaviour of the children, we must not resort to repressing or killing angry feelings or to punishing the child, but rather to accept his feelings as well as the child in a quite natural way. Paying no attention and reinforcement of any kind (punishment is also a kind of reinforcement) may help the child in making no repetition of his temper tantrum. By making the child realize the undesirability and ill consequences of his temper tantrum, employment of proper behaviour therapy and behaviour modification technique may help much in getting rid of such undesirable social behaviour of the children.

Drug addiction refers to the behavioural problem of our adolescents and youths in which they are found to be getting addicted to the harmful drugs associated with intoxication like LSD-25, methamphetamine or speed, marijuana, morphine, heroin, methadrene, benzidine, and cocaine, etc. Drug addiction has no hereditary roots and is therefore a purely learned behaviour. At the initial stage, the first few doses of an intoxicated drug may be taken out of curiously, for getting fun, relief from pressure etc. under the influence of evil influences or by way of modeling of the behaviour of the elders. The initiated behaviour then may get reinforced and rewarded on account of a false impression of adequacy and well being — short-lived pleasure effects created by the consumption of the drug and then it may result into total dependence (physiological as well as psychological) on the use of the drug. To save youngsters from the clutches of this behavioural problem, we must first think about the preventive measures. However, in case one becomes drug addictive, then due attention should be paid for helping him to get rid of this bad habit. Compulsory hospitalization, de-intoxicating or drying out of the addict, accompanied with special medical measures, psychological treatment including long-term therapy and rehabilitation, are some of the measures that can prove helpful in the care and treatment of the children suffering from drug addiction.

References and Suggested Readings

Boston, Hall, *Psychiatric Examination of the School Child*, Edward Arnold, London, 1947.

Burt, C., *The young Delinquent*, (3rd ed.), University of London Press, London, 1938.

Carmichael, L. (Ed.), *Manual of Child Psychology*, John Wiley, New York, 1946.

Crow, L.D. and Crow, A., *Child Psychology*, Barney and Noble, New York, 1969 (reprint).

Hurlock, E.B., *Child Psychology*, MacGraw-Hill, Tokyo, 1959, (Asian Students 3rd ed.)

Shanker, Uday, *Problem Children*, Atma Ram & Sons, New Delhi, 1958.

Verma, S.C., *The Youug Delinquents*, Lucknow Pustak Kendra, Lucknow, 1970.

36

Adjustment, Frustration and Conflicts

CHAPTER COMPOSITION

MEANING AND DEFINITION OF ADJUSTMENT

"Life presents a continuous chain of struggle for existence and survivals," says **Darwin**. The observation is very correct as we find in our day-to-day life. Every one of us strives hard for the satisfaction of our needs. While struggling to achieve something if one finds that results are not satisfactory, one either changes one's goal or the procedure. For example, if one aspires to join M.B.B.S. course, one works hard to get good marks in the Pre-Medical class. In case one is not able to get admission due to one's low percentage, one may change one's goal and feel inclined or aspire to join a B.Sc. course for medical representative job.

By restoring to such means, one protects one's self from the possible injury to one's ego, failure or frustration. It is a sort of shifting to a more defensive position in order to face the challenge of circumstances after failing in earlier attempt or attempts. This special feature of the living beings is termed as adjustment. Let us now analyse this term by studying some important definitions.

L.S. Shaffer

Adjustment is the process by which living organism maintains a balance between its need and the circumstances that influence the satisfaction of these needs. (1961, p. 511)

Gates, Jerslid and others

Adjustment is a continual process by which a person varies his behaviour to produce a more harmonious relationship between himself and environment. (1970, pp. 614-15)

Vonhaller

We can think of adjustment as psychological survival in much the same way as biologist uses the term adaptation to describe physiological survival. (1970, p. 426)

Let us try to analyze these definitions.

- **Shaffer's definition** lays stress on needs and their satisfaction. One feels adjusted to the extent one's needs are gratified or in the way of being gratified. An individual tries to bring changes in his circumstances in order to overcome the difficulties in the realization of his needs. Sometimes he reduces the quantum of his need so that he may feel satisfied within the limited resources of needs and in this way, he tries to keep a balance between his needs and the capacity of realizing these needs. As long as the balance is maintained he remains adjusted. The moment it is disturbed, he drifts towards maladjustment.
- **The second definition** by Gates and Jerslid takes adjustment as a signal of harmonious relationship between a man and his environment. One has to fit oneself in the prevailing circumstances. When we adjust ourselves by this means we are changing in some way to adapt or accommodate ourselves in order to fit as per certain demands of our environment. The conditions in the environment are in a continuous chain of changes. We change our nature in order to fit ourselves in the realm of nature. Thus the process of adjustment is continuous. We try to change or modify our behaviour for bringing a perfect understanding between ourselves and our environment. For example if an urban girl is married to a rural boy and made to live a village life, she has to change her behaviour, her habits and her way of life for accommodating herself in the changed circumstances.
- The last definition by Vonhaller takes clue from the Darwin's theory of evolution. Darwin maintained that only those organisms most fitted to adapt to the changed circumstances survive. Hence the individuals who are able to adjust themselves in changed situations in their environment can live in perfect harmony and lead a happy life. In this way, adjustment as a psychological term is a new name for the term *adaptation* used in biological world. In all sense, adjustment implies a satisfactory adaptation to the demands of day-to-day life.

The above discussion can lead us to summarize in the following way:

— Adjustment is a process that takes us to lead a happy and well-contented life.

— Adjustment helps us in keeping balance between our needs and the capacity to meet these needs.

— Adjustment persuades us to change our way of life according to the demands of the situation.

— Adjustment gives us strength and ability to bring desirable changes in the conditions of our environment.

Besides the demands of one's basic need, society also demands a particular mode of behaviour from its members. In case one thinks only to fulfill one's needs by setting aside the norms, ethics and cultural traditions of one's society, one is not going to be adjusted in one's environment. Here adjustment also needs one's conformity to the requirement of one's culture and the society. In this way, adjustment does not only cater to one's own needs but also to the demands of the society. Therefore, in defining adjustment in its comprehensive way, *we can conclude that adjustment is a condition or state in which one feels that one's needs have been (or will be) fulfilled and one's behaviour conforms to the requirements of the society and culture.*

CHARACTERISTICS OF A WELL ADJUSTED PERSON

A well-adjusted person is supposed to possess the following characteristics:

- **Physically adjusted:** A well-adjusted individual enjoys wholesome adjustment in terms of his physical health, and physiological well-being. He is physically mature and sound in relation to his age-linked physical and physiological growth and development. What he has in terms of his somatic structure, physical development, strength and abilities make him feel secure and satisfied.
- **Emotionally adjusted:** A well-adjusted individual demonstrates a well-balanced emotional behaviour. He is able to express desirable emotions in a proper amount as per the needs of the situation and his own well-being.
- **Socially adjusted:** A well-adjusted individual is a socially mature individual. He has the necessary development in terms of social competency and social obligations. He knows his social environment and has a desire and capability to adjust his self to the demands of the social life.
- **Awareness of one's own strengths and limitations:** A well-adjusted person knows his strengths and weaknesses. He tries to gain from his assets in some areas while accepting limitations in the other.
- **Respecting one's self and the others:** Disliking one's self is a typical symptom of maladjustment. An adjusted individual has respect for one's self as well as of others.
- **Adequate level of aspiration:** His level of aspiration is neither too low nor too high in comparison to his own strengths and abilities. He does not try to reach for stars and also not repent by selecting an easier course for advancement.
- **Satisfaction of the basic needs:** His basic needs like organic, emotional and social needs are fully satisfied or in the process of being satisfied. He does not suffer from emotional craving and social isolation. He feels reasonably secure and maintains his self-esteem.
- **Does not possess critical or fault-finding attitude:** He knows how to appreciate the goodness in objects, persons or activities. He does not try to search for weaknesses and faults. His observation is a scientific one rather than being critical or punitive. He likes people, admires their qualities and wins their affection.
- **Flexibility of his behaviour:** He is not rigid in his attitude or way of living. He can easily accommodate or adapt himself in the changed circumstances by making necessary changes in his behaviour.
- **Capable of struggling with odd circumstances:** He is not easily overwhelmed by the odd circumstances. He has sufficient will and courage to resist and fight against odds. He has an inherent drive to master his environment rather than to passively accept it.
- **Realistic perception of the world:** He holds a realistic vision and does not wander unnecessarily in the world of ideas and imagination. He always plans, thinks and acts on the real footing.

- **Feeling at home with his surroundings:** A well-adjusted individual feels satisfied with his surroundings. He fits well at his home, family, neighbourhood and other social places. As a student he likes his school, school-mates, teachers and feels satisfied with his daily routine. When he enters a profession, he has a love for it and he maintains his zeal and enthusiasm in his profession despite heavy odds.
- **An adequate philosophy of life:** A well-adjusted person has his own philosophy of life which he tries to observe while keeping in view the demand of the changed situation and circumstances. He weaves his philosophy around the demand of his society, culture and his own self so that it does not clash with his environment on it one hand and his self on the other.

SPHERES OF ADJUSTMENT

For an adequate adjustment one has to make oneself adjusted firstly to one's self and then to one's environment. Thus the spheres, dimensions or aspects of adjustment may be divided mainly in two categories, personal and environmental. For any individual while the adequacy of his own physical and mental health, emotional adjustment and satisfaction of personal needs are vital for the overall adjustment, the need for making adjustment with the social and occupational world can also not be overlooked. Based on this, we can categorize the overall adjustment of an individual into three spheres, namely personal, social and occupational. Let us try to know more about these three spheres of one's adjustment.

Personal Adjustment

Personal adjustment is concerned with an individual's adjustment to his self. Now question arises as to what does the term 'self' mean with regard to personal adjustment. The total individuality incorporating various aspects of his growth and development, personality traits and characteristics and satisfaction of his basic needs may essentially be included in the body of the term 'self'. In this sense, the extent to which one remains satisfied with what he owns in terms of his physical and mental development and other personality characteristics and his basic needs remain gratified, he may be called adjusted within the sphere of personal adjustment. Let us now elaborate these components of one's personal adjustment.

ADJUSTMENT TO PHYSICAL DEVELOPMENT AND HEALTH

Physical growth and development follow a somewhat definite pattern. A child of a particular age is normally expected to have a certain increase in weight and height, acquire definite somatic structure and physical characteristics and have growth and development with regards to internal organs, body systems and their functioning. In case this growth and development takes place in a normal way and the individual remain satisfied, he remains adjusted otherwise it may lead to frustration and other complexes paving the way for his maladjustment. Similarly, one should keep better physical health free from stressful ailments and diseases so as to enjoy better personal adjustment. In this way if an individual's physical growth and development as well as his physical strength, abilities and capacities are in conformity with what is expected at his age and he does not feel any difficulty in his physical functioning and general progress due to any kind of defect or inability of his physical organs, he may get along well with his adjustment to his self.

ADJUSTMENT WITH REGARD TO MENTAL DEVELOPMENT AND HEALTH

The other major aspect of one's personal adjustment is related with his mental development and mental health. Like physical development, an individual of a particular age is expected to function at a certain level of intellectual growth and development. In case one does not acquire even the normal mental capacities and abilities expected at his age, he may feel handicapped in terms of intellectual behaviour and this deficiency (while compared to others) may lead to frustration and complexes. Similarly, one who is not keeping good mental health may turn into a maladjustment personality. Anxiety, distress, stressful situation, pressures, complexes, frustrations all are bitter enemies of one's mental health and these may lead a person to total maladjustment with his self.

Emotional Adjustment

Emotions play a leading role in controlling and directing one's behaviour and providing a definite shape to his personality make-up. An individual who is capable of expressing his emotions in a proper way at a proper time may be termed as emotionally adjusted. The acquisition of such emotional adjustment may automatically help an individual to act and behave in a desired way, face the life situations properly and feel adjusted in his personal and social life.

Sexual Adjustment

Sex is also a personal matter like one's physical, mental and emotional adjustments. Moreover, the gratification of sex needs is the most important aspect of our life. As long as this need remains in the state of satisfaction, the individual feels comfortable, satisfied and adjusted but as soon as the balance is disturbed, there crops up obstacles in the path of gratification of sex needs and the individual may be drifted towards maladjustment. Studies and researches in this area have established that one's proper sexual development, his proper attitude towards sex and the satisfaction of his sex needs in a desirable and proper way are the essential factors responsible for his adjustment to his self and the environment.

Adjustment with Respect to the Individual Needs

This sphere of our personal adjustment may also include all such types of adjustments that are concerned with the satisfaction of our personal needs. Among these, we may include the needs like (i) physiological or organic needs such as hunger, thrust, sleep and rest etc. (ii) material needs such as need for clothes; shelter and various other material facilities and comforts, (iii) our socio-psychological needs such as need to love and to be loved, need for expression and actualization, need to dominate, get respect and regard etc. We all, from the very beginning of our life till the end, remain busy in working and struggling for the satisfaction of these needs. In case we get success and feel satisfied, we remain adjusted or else we are compelled to drift towards maladjustment.

Social Adjustment

This sphere of adjustment is concerned with one's adjustment to his social surroundings. Such adjustment is as much essential as one's adjustment with his self. In all circumstances, one should feel reasonably satisfied with what he gets in term of his social environment. By doing so, he may get along well with others and keep himself in the category of a socially adjusted person, but if it does not happen he may become a socially maladjusted person. In such circumstances, either he may cut himself off from the society or may turn into an anti-social and criminal personality. In this sense, one's adjustment with his social set up, started from his parents, home and family and extended to the neighbourhood, state, country and encircling whole world, is quite essential for the welfare of his own and the society. Let us try to know in detail about the components of one's social adjustment.

Home and Family Adjustment

One should feel the comfort and satisfaction in one's home in the spirit of 'Sweet Home'. He must have proper cordial relationships and behavioural adjustment with the members of his family. One who is fed up with his family environment and likes to spend most of the time outside the home so as to avoid the company of the family members is surely a person who is seriously lacking in terms of his home and family adjustment. Contrary to this, when the home and family environment are quite cooperative and congenial, the members of the family get proper opportunity for the satisfaction of their mutual personal needs and social obligations. In such encouraging, mutually sharing, loving and peaceful environment each member works for the progress and welfare of the others besides the development of his own. Such family environment provides a reasonable insurance for the total adjustment and well-being of all the members of the family.

Adjustment with Friends and Relatives

The social circle of one's friends and relatives is closely linked with the social environment of his home and family. One's behaviour and personality development is very much influenced, guided and patronized by one's relatives and friends. These are the persons who come to our help in the hour of our need. One may feel secure and satisfied if he has cordial, congenial and harmonious relations with (may be few) his relatives and friends. In the contrary and opposite situations, one is bound to feel lonely, insecure and perturbed at the time of distress and casualties. In this way, the key of one's adjustment lies in getting along well with his friends and relatives.

Adjustment with Neighbours and Other Members of the Community

Next to our home is the neighbourhood and the community. Most of our physical, psychological and social needs are fulfilled through proper communication, exchange, goodwill and spirit of cooperation maintained with our neighbours and other members of the community. We can't live in harmony and peace with indifferent and spoiled relationships with our immediate neighbours and members of the community. The essential thing is to learn the lesson of togetherness and co-existence with the members of the community inspite of differences of opinions, living standards, language, caste, religion etc.

It is futile to waste our energy and resources in endless conflicts and tensions created through mutual mistrust, fear, disliking and disrespect, jealousy and envy, false pride and inflated ego. It creates a chain of reaction and ends with the state of dissatisfaction resulting in our maladjustment with our own neighbours and members of the community. Hence, it is always better to try our best to get along well with our neighbours and members of the community. Slowly this spirit of togetherness, bond of friendship, cooperation, co-existence and peaceful living should be extended to the boundaries of one's nation and even to the world as a close-knit family.

Here the question arises as to what should one do for maintaining proper relationship with the members of his family, friends, relatives, neighbours and members of the community so that he may be well-adjusted in his social set up? The answer lies in one's proper social development and adaptability to the social environment. One should essentially learn the lesson of mutual love and respect, goodwill and trust, cooperation and sharing and other similar qualities and virtues of a social being. One should try to know the norms, modes of living and expectations of the society for adapting himself in the existing pattern of one's community and society. It does not mean that he should blindly lead to conformity, but in all his efforts he must first try to get along with the social set up and then work honestly for the desired changes and needed social progress.

Occupational Adjustment

How far are we satisfied with our world of work and means of livelihood decides, to a great extent, our state or adjustment or maladjustment to our self and the environment. From the very beginning, parents aspire for a good occupation or profession for their children. They plan their education accordingly. However, entering into the profession or occupation of one's choice or being in tune with their abilities and capacities depend on a lot of factors. Whatsoever it may be, once chosen one should learn to adjust and adapt to the needs and requirement of one's profession or occupation. His success in his field of work will depend to a large extent on the sense of satisfaction he feels in performing various duties in his job. He must be reasonably satisfied and should get along well with the men and material resources available in his world of work. Such satisfaction, adaptation and adjustment to one's occupation automatically help in attaining the desired objectives in his personal and social life leading to the overall adjustment to one's self and the environment. Now at this stage, the question may arise as to who should be termed as an adjusted individual in his field of work or occupation. For this, let us think about the possible traits and characteristics generally found in such vocationally or occupationally adjusted persons.

(i) Once entered, they feel no regret about the choice of work or occupation.

(ii) They demonstrate a sense of job satisfaction through the performance of various duties regarding their job or occupation.

(iii) They feel reasonably satisfied with the working conditions and facilities available for carrying out their job duties. They are not in the habit of unnecessarily complaining about limitations and non-availability of resources.

(iv) They get along well with their colleagues and the officials of their world of work. They try to maintain cordial relationship and harmony with them for attaining desired proficiency in their work.

(v) They are committed and have a very positive attitude towards the working and value of their occupation. They do not unnecessarily dream or plan of entering into other occupations. While respecting their own profession, they always strive to achieve a sense of satisfaction by performing their duties honestly and sincerely.

(vi) They are reasonably satisfied with the opportunities provided in their personal occupation for promotion and other achievements. They do not get much perturbed despite not getting early opportunities of promotions and other incentives and believe that their work will be rewarded in one way or the other.

(vii) They are usually engaged in bringing necessary improvement and modification in the methods and processes related to their occupation for qualitative improvement. They have creative sparks in them which is often reflected through their styles of functioning.

(viii) They are reasonably satisfied with their occupations in terms of economic returns. They are not found comparing their salaries and financial returns with others and complaining about their chosen occupation.

(ix) They maintain a sense of accountability for the assigned duties and try to maintain the image and respect of their profession by extending desired cooperation to colleagues and administrators.

MEANING OF THE TERM 'MALADJUSTMENT'

Contrary to adjustment, *maladjustment* represents a condition or state in which one feels that one's needs are not (or will not be) fulfilled and he has been a failure in establishing harmony with his self and the environment.

Defined in this way a person suffering from maladjustment may exhibit serious behavioural and adjustment problems causing harm to the well-being of his self and others.

CAUSES OF MALADJUSTMENT

There is much truth in the saying that one remains adjusted as long as his basic (physiological and socio-psychological) needs get satisfied or he has some hope for their satisfaction in future. The moment he is denied the satisfaction of his needs or gets despaired, he falls victim to the forces of maladjustment. So the causes of one's maladjustment to his self and the environment may be both of personal as well as environmental nature. Let us discuss them in brief.

Personal Causes

In these types of causes, we may include the following:

HEREDITY FACTORS

The individual may inherit defective mental make up, physiological structure, colour of the skin, constitutional defects, incapacities and incapabilities making him feel depressed, inferior or causing one hurdle or the other in the way of proper satisfaction of his basic needs.

PHYSIOLOGICAL OR PHYSICAL FACTORS

In many cases, physiological or physical factors like poor health, lack of vitality, physical deformities, physical ailments, chronic diseases and bodily defects, etc. may drift one towards maladjustment. He may feel handicapped in meeting his basic needs or may develop feelings of inferiority on account of his physical deformities, sub-normalities and incompetencies etc. which may lead to the dissatisfaction to his self and the environment.

THE CAUSES INHERENT IN THE NATURE OF THE INDIVIDUAL

These causes are quite inherent in the nature and temperament of an individual. The mentionable ones may be as below:

— Unrealistic aims, goals and ideals of life.

— Lack of social maturity and adjustment.

— Lack of emotional maturity and control over the emotions.

— Improper setting of the level of aspiration.

— Unresolved conflicts and contradictory desires.

— Frustrations and desperations.

Environmental Causes

In most of the cases, environmental forces are said to be the greatest or sole contributor in the germination as well as perpetuation of the cases of maladjustment prevailing in our society. The forces of environment begin to play their role right from the conception of the child in the womb of the mother in the form of defective nourishment available to him. From his birth onwards the following types of defective environmental conditions may drift him towards maladjustment.

— Improper behaviour of the parents and elders towards child.

— Uncongenial and defective home environment on account of the factors like frequent quarreling between the parents, their separation or divorce, loss of one or both the parental figures, unsocial or anti-social behaviour of the members of the family.
— The defective environmental conditions available in one's neighbourhood, community and society which may put hurdles in the proper satisfaction of one's basic needs or may force him to pick bad habits for paving the way of his maladjustment to his self and others.
— The defective and uncongenial environment available in the school in terms of the behaviour of teachers, peers, defective curriculum and methods of teaching, lack of co-curricular activities, too much rigidity or rules, punitive measures, etc.

Detection of Maladjustment

Maladjustment must always be taken as a red signal as it may lead the child towards serious behaviour problems, mental illness and diseases. It is always better to have its early detection and find ways and means for its rectification.

The cases of maladjustment among the children in a class may be detected by the teachers by following two types of measures mentioned below:

1. Use of Testing devices like Adjustment Inventory, mental health tests, youth/child problem inventory etc.
2. Use of Non-testing devices like observation, Interview, rating scale, checklist, etc.

Let us discuss these approaches one by one.

Use of Testing Devices

The cases of maladjustment can be better diagnosed with the help of suitable Adjustment inventories. Such inventories are available for different age groups and areas of adjustment covering a wide range of people. With the help of their administration to the individual as well as to the group, we can get the scores for being classified as adjusted or maladjusted on one or the other areas of their adjustment. Examples of these adjustment inventory are:

1. H.S. Asthana's Adjustment Inventory. (Available in two forms—Students and Adults)
2. Bell's Adjustment Inventory. (Available in two forms—Students and Adults)
3. Adjustment Inventory developed by A.K.P. Sinha and R.P. Singh.
4. Mangal Teacher Adjustment Inventory (Available in long as well as short forms)

Use of Non-testing Devices

The use of non-testing devices for the detection of the cases of maladjustment rests on the principle that the cases of maladjustment may be better detected through the observation of the behaviour of the students in real life situations. For this purpose, one may resort to the techniques of observation, rating scale, interview and check list being used to note down or take care of those behavioural characteristics of the students that may help in labelling them as adjusted or maladjusted. For illustration, we may name the following qualities and characteristics observable in one's behaviour for typically identifying him as a maladjusted personality.

- Lack of self control
- Sense of inferiority
- Lack of personal security
- Nervousness and anxiety
- Aloofness and withdrawal tendencies
- Cruelty and aggressiveness
- Sarcasm and incessant scolding
- Lack of patience and tolerance
- Lack of the feelings of love, respect and affection
- Use of bizarre methods of striving to be important
- Attention-seeking behaviour
- Demonstrating problematic and anti-social behaviour
- Suffering from mental illness or diseases.

FRUSTRATIONS

Man is ambitious by nature. He has so many aspirations and desires to be fulfilled. He plans and strives hard for their realization but it is possible that despite his best planning and efforts, he may not get the desired success. At times he may find himself in the state of utter confusion and bewilderment. All the paths for going ahead seem to be blocked. Such state of affairs, along with the repeated failure in the attempts, puts one into a state or condition that can be termed as frustration. For making the term more clear, let us take some definitions coined by eminent writers.

Carroll
A frustration is the condition of being thwarted in the satisfaction of motive. (1962, p. 23)

Good
Frustration means emotional tension resulting from the blocking of a desire or need. (1959)

Kolesnic
Frustration is the feeling of being blocked or thwarted in satisfying a need of attaining a goal that individual perceives as significant.

Barney and Lehner
Frustration refers to failure to satisfy a basic need because of either conditions in the individual or external obstacles. (1953, p. 28)

These definitions reveal the following facts about the nature and meaning of the term frustration:

- Frustration is that stage or condition in which failure dominates the attempts.
- In this state one feels a major obstacle in the satisfaction of one's basic needs or in the attainment of one's cherished goal.
- The significance of the goal and strength of the "blockade" increases the degree of frustration.
- The cause of frustration lies both in the individual himself and his environment.

Causes of Frustrations

The cause of frustration may be divided into two major heads:
A. External factors. B. Internal factors.

External Factors

External factors are also called *Environmental factors*. These are the situations or conditions which are present in one's own environment. They affect the individual from outside. The main external factors are as follows:

1. **Physical factors.** Natural calamities, obstacles or events in the environment may try to block the path of an individual in the attainment of some important goal or in the satisfaction of one's basic needs and desires. In this way, they become the potential source for frustrating motivated individuals. For example, particular society and community may impose bar on the marriages of school mistresses and this may cause frustration to a young school mistress who is in deep love with a handsome boy and wants to marry him. Similarly a young man with bright prospects may feel frustrated when he is denied admission to a course simply because he does not fulfil the condition of a bonafide resident.
2. **Social factors.** Social factors also include the part played by other persons in blocking the path of the motivated individuals. A child may feel frustrated when he is denied to go to a movie with his friend or to a dance party or picnic. Similarly an employee may feel frustrated when he is thrown out instead of meeting his demands for salary hike.
3. **Economic factors.** Economic and financial factors contribute much in frustrating many of the individuals particularly in developing countries like India. Often there are news items that a young man killed himself because he was suffering from depression due to a long spell of unemployment or a mother has killed herself along with her children by jumping into a well due to the utter frustration caused by the continuous denial of the basic need—food. Similarly men who revolt against the social, political set-up witness the results of frustration suffered due to severe economic deprivation.

Internal Factors

Internal factors are the factors that frustrate an individual from within. These are also called personal factors as the person himself is the cause of such frustration. The main factors in this category are as follows:

1. **Physical abnormality or defects:** Too small or big stature, very heavy or lean and thin body, an ugly face or dark complexion, some glandular or bodily defects (such as being one-eyed, blind, lame, deaf or dumb) may constitute a source of thwarting and thereby cause frustration. Deficiency in one's intelligence or backwardness in a particular subject may also frustrate an individual who is motivated to learn a particular course or choose a particular vocation.
2. **Conflicting desires or aims:** Frustration is also caused by mutually conflicting desires or aims. Suppose a man wishes to marry a girl to whom he is in love with but also wishes to avoid it as it interferes with his ambition of going to U.K. for higher studies. Now he has to make a choice and a choice of one at the cost of the other may become a cause of frustration to him. A similar frustration may be felt by a young woman who aspires to become a mother but avoids it due to the fear of losing her job or spoiling her career.
3. **Individual's morality and high ideals:** Individual's moral standards, code of ethics and high ideals may become a source of frustration to him. He is always caught between his super-ego and Id. At the time when his ego fails to maintain a balance between the two, he becomes frustrated. Due to the weight of the moral standards of his conscience, he

possesses the unnecessary feeling of guilt or an unusual fear of punishment. For example, he may like to have friendship with some girl but his moral standard does not allow him to do so. Similarly one may be denied to smoke, to wear broad-based trousers or to see a sex movie only because of his code of ethics or high ideals. The inhibitions and possible conflicts may give birth to emotional tension within him and consequently he may feel frustrated.

4. **Level of aspiration too high:** One may let one's aspiration fly to a very high level in spite of one's incapabilities or human limitations. For example, a young man may aspire to become the captain of the Indian cricket team in the next year despite the fact that he does not even know how to play cricket. Such aspirations are bound to lead to frustration.
5. **Lack of persistence and sincerity in efforts:** Frustration may be caused by one's own weakness in putting continuous and persistent efforts with all his courage, enthusiasm and will power. For example, suppose one reads a book with no sincere willingness to understand it. After some time he takes another book and does the same thing with it. He complains that he is not able to grasp anything even after reading so much. This thus gives birth to the feeling of inadequacy that ultimately leads to frustration.

Reactions to Frustration

Frustration results in various types of reactions according to its intensity and nature of the individual experiencing frustration. Some have frustration tolerance to the extent that they bear the consequences with a little injury to the self or the society; while others (or the former in the special situations) become too violent and aggressive. In this way the reactions to frustration may be classified into two major categories.

SIMPLE REACTIONS

Under these, we may include the following four types of reactions:

Increasing trials or improving efforts. During the period of frustration, some individuals undergo introspection and to overcome the obstacles they either increase their efforts or bring improvement in their behaviour or procedure.

Adopt Compromising Means. Repeated failure in one direction may lead organisms to change the direction of their efforts. For example an I.A.S. aspirant in case of failure may direct his energy to the Provincial Civil Service examination. A girl's mother failing to marry her daughter to a fair and handsome boy may be contented with a boy of dark complexion.

Withdrawal. An individual learns to be away from the situations that cause him frustration. A child withdraws himself from the game he does not know. A young man refuses to marry because of his sexual incompetency due to some physiological deformities.

Submissiveness. Here the individual surrenders himself and accepts his defeat before the frustration causing conditions. A child may become extremely submissive after failing in his attempts in certain direction.

VIOLENT REACTIONS

In addition to the above mentioned simple reactions, an individual may become very tense emotionally and resort to aggressive activities. This aggression is of two types—External and Internal.

External aggression. "The aggression," as Carroll observes "may be directed towards either the person or persons who caused the frustration or towards a substitute or substitutes." (1967, p. 34). A clerk in his frustration of not getting promotion may quarrel with his officer or resort to rebuking his wife or beating his children. A boy experiencing frustration in the playground may try to knock the boy down who is not giving him a chance to try the ball or may use his younger brother or parents as substitutes for relieving his tension.

Internal aggression. It is an aggression that is turned inward towards the self. Instead of releasing one's emotional tensions by attacking others, one resorts to attacking one's self. Instead of blaming others, the individual blames himself. No doubt certain amount of self criticism does not do any harm but excessive aggression towards the self is sure to destroy the self. Eventually the person becomes a mental patient or tries to escape by committing suicide. Thus as far as the well-being of the individual is concerned, inward aggression is more dangerous than outward aggression.

CONFLICTS

Meaning and Definitions

The term 'conflict' is used in so many ways in our day-to-day setup. There may be conflicts between the two sets of ideologies, cultures, religions and organizations. Conflicts may arise between husband and wife, father and son and teacher and the taught. It may also show its presence among brothers and sisters, members of an organization or community, states of a country and countries of the world at large. Apart from these external or outer conflicts, there are inner or internal conflicts which are called 'psychological conflicts'. In the following text we will discuss such types of conflicts. Let us begin by giving some important definitions.

Douglas and Holland

Conflict means a painful emotional state which results from a tension between opposed and contradictory wishes. (1946, p. 216)

Barney and Lehner

Psychological conflict is a stage of tension brought by the presence in the individual of two or more opposing desires. (1953, p. 30)

L.F. Shaffer

Conflict may be defined as a state of affairs in which two or more incompatible behaviour trends are evoked that cannot be satisfied fully at the same time. (Boring, Langfield and Weld, 1961, p. 523).

These definitions help us to conclude that:

- Conflict is a painful state or condition of an individual.
- One feels intense emotional tension during this state.
- Tension is the result of the presence of two or more desires or wishes in the individual. These desires are contradictory in nature and therefore cannot be satisfied fully at the same time.
- The individual, being at the crossroads and not able to choose between the two opposing desires, becomes tense and restless.
- Thus becoming a victim of the two opposing desires, he suffers from an inner conflict to do or not to satisfy one or the other desire.

Types of Conflicts

Approach-Approach Conflicts. In such conflicts, an individual is faced with the problem of making a choice between two or more positive goals almost equally motivating and important. For example a child may have to choose between reading an interesting comic book or going out to play cricket. A young man may experience such a conflict when he has to make choice for his marriage out of the two equally qualified, beautiful and respectable offers. The conflicts of this type are of little danger and temporary in character. After all when a step is taken towards the realization of one goal, the attraction for the other automatically fades. However, there are occasions when one finds great difficulty in making a choice between two positive desires. For example, a young girl may be devoted to her family and all the same desire to have love marriage with a boy of another caste that is not acceptable to her parents.

Avoidance-Avoidance Conflicts. In conflicts of this type, an individual is caught in a situation where he must choose between two or more possible negative courses of action. For example a child who does not want to study and at the time does not wish to displease parents by failing in the final examination may experience such conflict. Similarly a boxer may have to choose between his fear of death or defeat at the hands of his rival or if he does not fight, the loss of respect from his admirers. It is just like being caught between the devil and deep sea. Because of the threat involved in such a situation, both choices are equally unattractive and hence the natural tendency is to escape from them or to do nothing. In case one is compelled to take a decision, one is likely to suffer the conflict of Avoidance-Avoidance type. Usually conflicts of this type are more serious than the Approach-Approach type conflicts.

Approach-Avoidance Conflicts. In such conflicts, one is faced with the problem of choosing between approaching and avoiding tendencies at the same time. An individual may be motivated towards a kind of behaviour activity which he perceives to be wrong, evil and degrading but at the same time the attraction of behaviour is so strong that he becomes restless without doing it. To masturbate or not to masturbate, to marry or not to marry, to tease the girls or not to are some of the situations that may repel and attract an individual simultaneously. Conflicts of this type are distinctly the most severe emotional tension and give birth to so many anxieties and complexes.

Reasons behind Conflicts

We have seen that conflicts are the creation of the dissatisfaction felt by an individual due to the non-fulfillment of his two contradictory desires. The forces of the environment are in fact responsible for these conflicts as they provide necessary ground for their occurrence but at the same time we teachers, parents and society are also responsible for giving birth to so many conflicts in our youngsters. Let us try to discuss this situation.

HOME ENVIRONMENT

Faulty upbringing at home, unhealthy or unpleasant relationship among the family members are the potential sources of conflicts in children. A child, due to over protection, dominance, submissiveness or negligence on the part of parents, does not cope with the experiences during social contacts with other children at school and thus he may become a victim of the opposing desires in future.

School environment

Uncongenial school environment, dominant or submissive role of the teachers, faulty methods of teaching, denial of opportunities for self expression, contradictory demands of the teachers and classmates are some of the bases which may give birth to conflicts.

Social and cultural environment

The social environment and cultural value may also prove a potential source of conflicts. Chief among them are the sex conflicts as the demands of our culture have not been well adjusted to the sexual need of the individual. The taboos, inhibitions and the negative attitude towards sex are the cause of so many sex conflicts in the minds of our youths. The pattern of conflicting values existing in our society and culture is responsible for a number of other conflicts. For example, on one hand we give incentive to competitive gains and on the other advocate co-operation and submission. Frustration suffered due to lack of opportunities in developing countries like India also give birth to many a conflicts. Similarly, non-fulfillment of the need for status, many financial worries and dissatisfaction with the working conditions and career fulfillment also prove to be the source of many conflicts.

Role of Teachers in the Process of Adjustment

A well-adjusted individual is an asset to himself and a boon to the society whereas a maladjusted personality brings misfortune to one's self and discomfort to others. Therefore there is an urgent need to devise some means and take precautionary measures so that we may have well adjusted personalities from our younger generation. The following measures may prove fruitful in this regard on our part as teachers.

Balanced growth and development

We must be careful in bringing balanced growth and development of a child's personality. His physical and mental health as well as his social, emotional and aesthetic development should be properly attended to. One aspect or direction of growth should not be developed at the cost of the others. There should be perfect harmony and balance between the different aspects of growth and development.

Satisfaction of the basic needs

We must provide opportunities and give necessary assistance to the child for the solution of his basic needs. The degree of one's adjustment is directly proportional to one's feelings of satisfaction with regard to one's varying needs. Therefore, the child should not suffer from physical, mental, emotional or social starvation.

Awareness of strength and weakness

The child should be helped in realizing his strengths as well as weaknesses. We should not be extremely critical of him. He should be accepted with all his limitations and shortcomings.

Setting a proper level of inspiration

The child should be helped in setting a proper level of aspiration, ideals and ambitions for going ahead in life.

DEVELOPING TENSION-TOLERANCE

We should help children in developing tension-tolerance in them so that they may not succumb under stresses and strain while facing the odds of life.

HARMONY WITH THE DEMANDS OF SOCIETY AND CULTURE

In order to help children in adjusting with the demands of the society and culture, teachers and parents should themselves try to practice the right ways and good habits. Preaching is of no benefit. The children should be made to realize the importance of the cultural and social milieu etc.

PROVIDING HEALTHY ENVIRONMENT

Maladjustment is the product of faulty upbringing and uncongenial environment at home, school and other places of social contact. Therefore, proper care should be taken by the teachers, parents and other responsible members of the society to provide healthy environment to the children. They should provide adequate care and love to the children and arrange for the satisfaction of their needs as well as actualization of their potentialities.

PROVISION OF GUIDANCE AND COUNSELING

Life is full of problems. Children should be made to face them independently. But in many cases they need proper guidance in making right choices and proper selection with respect to their education, vocation and personal world. Therefore, we should arrange for the guidance and counseling services in schools for helping children in making adjustments with their problems.

SUMMARY

'Adjustment' refers to a condition or state in which one feels that one's needs have been (or will be) fulfilled and one's behaviour conforms to the requirements of his society and culture. In fact what we understand by adaptation in the biological word is known as adjustment in the language of psychology.

A well adjusted person is supposed to be physically, emotionally and socially adjusted, aware of his own strength and limitations, respecting one' self and the others, keeping an adequate level of aspiration, feeling satisfied in terms of meeting his basic needs, not possessing critical or fault finding attitude, demonstrating flexibility of behaviour, capable of struggling in odd circumstances, realistic perception of the world, feeling at home with his surroundings and possessing adequate philosophy of life.

The overall adjustment of an individual with his self and environment can be broadly divided into three categories or spheres namely, personal, social and occupational adjustment. Personal adjustment is concerned with an individual's adjustment to his self. Social adjustment is concerned with one's adjustment to his social surroundings and occupational adjustment is concerned with one's adjustment to his world of work and means of livelihood.

Contrary to adjustment, **maladjustment** refers to a condition or state in which one feels that one's needs are not (or will not be) fulfilled and he has been a failure in establishing harmony with his self and the environment. Causes of maladjustment may lie both in the person himself (in the form of heredity, physiological factors and natures of the individuals) and his defective and uncongenial environment found in one's home, family, neighbourhood, school, society and his world of work. Since maladjustment pushes a person to a problematic behaviour, its early detection and rectification must be carried out as properly as possible. We can make use of testing devices (such as standardized adjustment inventories) and non-testing devices (like observation, rating scale, interview and check list etc.) for the detection of maladjustment among our children and can then accordingly plan for the adequate adjustment of the sufferers.

Frustration refers to a condition or stage reached on account of repeated failure or blockage experienced by an individual in the attainment of his basic needs or realization of an important goal. The causes of frustration may be external (like physical, social or economic factors) or internal (like one's physical abnormality or defects, conflicting desires, his morality and high ideals, unrealistic level of aspiration or lack of persistence and sincerity in efforts etc.).

Under frustration people may react differently depending upon their own nature as well as the intensity of the frustrating experiences. They may react violently with varying intensity by resorting to aggression towards their self or the things and persons, whom they consider responsible for their frustration. Instead of it, they may also demonstrate adjustable reactions like increasing trials or improving their efforts, adopting compromising means, surrendering and accepting their defeat or withdrawing themselves from the frustration giving situations.

Conflict refers to a painful condition or emotionally tense state of an individual reached on account of the presence of the two equally opposed and contradictory wishes at the same time. Generally the conflicts faced by us in our life may be of the types like Approach-approach conflicts (making choice between two or more equally attractive goals), Avoidance-avoidance conflicts (choosing between two or more possible negative course of action) and Approach-avoidance conflicts (choosing between approaching and avoiding tendencies at the same time). As a causative factor of the arousal of conflicts one's defective environment loaded with its contradictory demands may prove a potent source for the germination as well as perpetuating such conflicting situations.

Teachers may play a big role in making their students develop into a well-adjusted individual. For this purpose they may help their students in attaining balanced growth and development of their personality, satisfaction of their basic needs, awareness of their strengths and weaknesses, setting a proper level of aspiration, developing tension tolerance, seeking harmony with the demands of society and culture by providing healthy and congenial environment, teaching-learning situations and adequate guidance and counseling according to the individual and social requirements of their students.

References and Suggested Readings

Arkoff, Abe, *Adjustment and Mental Health*, McGraw-Hill, New York, 1968.

Adms, Henry E., *Psychology of Adjustment*, Ronald Press, New York, 1972.

Carrol, H.A., *Mental Hygiene—The Dynamics of Adjustment*, Prentice-Hall, New Jersey, 1967.

Crow, L.D. and Crow, Alice, *Mental Hygiene,* McGraw-Hill, New York, 1951.

Cutts, N.F. and Mosley, P., *Practical School Discipline and Mental Hygiene*, Houghton Miffilin, Boston, 1941.

Davision, Gerald C. and Naele, John, M., *Abnormal Psychology*, 2nd ed., John Wiley, New York, 1978.

Gates, A.S. and Jersild, A.T., *Educational Psychology*, Macmillan, New York, 1970.

Good, Carter, V., *Dictionary of Education*, McGraw-Hill, New York, 1959.

Hadfield, J.A., *Mental Health and the Psychoneurosis*, George Allen & Unwin, London, 1952.

Kartz, Barney and Lehner, G.F., *Mental Hygiene in Modern Living*, The Ronald Press Company, New York, 1953.

Leher, George and Ela Kubo, *The Dynamics of Personal Adjustment*, Prentice-Hall, New York, 1964.

Lewkan, P.B., *Mental Hygiene in Public Health*, McGraw-Hill, New York, 1949.

Menninger, K.A., *Human Mind* Quoted by R.N. Sharma in Shiksha Manovigyan, Rastogi Publications, Meerut, 1967.

Morgan, C.T., *Introduction to Psychology*, 2nd ed., McGraw-Hill, New York, 1961.

Mun, N.L., *The Fundamentals of Human Adjustment*, George G. Harrap, London, 1968.

Page, James, D., *Abnormal Psychology*, Tata McGraw-Hill, New Delhi, 1976.

Shaffer, L.F., *L.S. Shaffer's Article in Foundations of Psychology* (Ed.), Boring, Langfield and Weld, John Wiley, New York, 1961.

Shaffer, L.F., *The Psychology of Adjustment*, Houghton Miffilin, New York, 1936.

Vonhaller, Geuner, B., *Psychology*, Houghton International, New York, 1970.

Waltin, J.E.W., *Personality Maladjustment and Mental Hygiene*, 1951.

37

Mental Health and Hygiene

CHAPTER COMPOSITION

MEANING OF THE TERM MENTAL HYGIENE

Mental Hygiene, as the name suggests, is that branch of hygiene which deals with mental health of the individuals in the same way as physical hygiene is concerned with their physical health. In physical hygiene, we study the causes of physical ailments or diseases. Their prevention and curative measures are also discussed in order to save the individuals from the hazards of any physical illness or ailments. In addition to this, the principles and techniques for maintaining proper physical health, with a healthy body and desirable working habits, are also suggested. Similarly, mental hygiene takes care of the prevention as well as treatment of mental illness, disorder and maladjustment. It also suggests ways and means of maintaining proper mental health and efficiency and therefore, helps in the proper mental or intellectual growth and development of an individual.

The meaning of the term 'Mental Hygiene' can be made more clear by having the following definitions:

American Psychiatric Association
Mental Hygiene consists of measures to reduce the incidence of mental illness through prevention and early treatment and to promote mental health. (Singh & Tiwari 1971, p. 434)

D.B. Klein
Mental Hygiene, as its name suggests, is concerned with the realization and the maintenance of the mind's health and efficiency. (1965, p.2)

Drever
Mental Hygiene means investigation of the laws of the mental health, and the taking or advocacy of measures for its preservation. (1952, p. 167)

Crow and Crow
Mental Hygiene is a science that deals with human welfare and pervades all fields of human relationship. (1951, p. 4)

Crow and Crow
As conceived today, mental hygiene may be defined as the prevention of mental illness, the preservation of mental health, and the cure of mental illness. (1969, p. 199)

From these definitions, we can conclude that *Mental Hygiene is a science that attempts to develop and apply principles and techniques for the preservation and promotion of mental health as well as for the prevention and treatment of mental disorders, diseases and other abnormalities, ultimately leading to an adequate adjustment and balanced development of one's personality.*

AIMS AND PURPOSES OF MENTAL HYGIENE

Mental Hygiene, as we have seen above, does not merely limit itself to the prevention and treatment of mental disorders or illnesses. It also takes into account the preservation and promotion of mental health of the organism. In this way, we can identify the three important aspects or approaches in mental hygiene, namely the preventive, preservative and the curative approaches. These different aspects can be utilized for studying the aims and purposes of mental hygiene. Crow and Crow, (1951, p. 4), on the basis of these aspects of mental hygiene have emphasized three major purposes of mental hygiene.

1. Prevention of mental disorders through an understanding of the relationship that exists between wholesome personality development and life experiences;
2. Preservation of the mental health of both the individual and the group; and
3. Discovery and utilization of therapeutic measures to cure mental illnesses.

In the first phase, mental hygiene aims at suggesting preventive measures to save us from the dreadful clutches of conditions and situations that lead to mental illness, maladjustment and disorders. In this direction it aims:-

- to list various causes of maladjustment—personal as well as social.
- to furnish the knowledge of drives, needs, motives, conflicts of motives, frustrations and tensions etc.
- to suggest ways and means of achieving emotional and social adjustment.
- to suggest solution for inner conflicts and frustrations and thus relieving ourselves from tensions, anxieties and emotional disturbances.

The second broader aim of mental hygiene relates itself with all the possible measures of preserving and promoting mental health. Here mental hygiene may aim at finding the ways and means for—

- developing total potentialities of an individual;
- attaining emotional maturity and stability;
- achieving personal and social security as well as adequacy;
- developing healthy human relationships and group-interaction, and
- helping the individual in acquiring sound body and normal mental health.

The third end of mental hygiene is related with the treatment and curative measures. In this direction, mental hygiene may aim—

- to furnish necessary knowledge regarding types of mental illnesses, disorders and diseases;
- to suggest various forms of therapy for the treatment and cure of specific mental illness and disorders, and
- to suggest means for the rehabilitation and readjustment of the maladjusted, mentally disturbed and mentally ill persons.

In this way, mental hygiene aims at achieving proper mental health and efficiency in all the aspects. But this aim of the development of sound mental health is not an end in itself. It is rather a platform to achieve some greater ends. Mentally healthy persons acquire certain essential abilities and capacities that are helpful in their development as socially adequate and emotionally stable, well balanced personalities. They can get along well with themselves and thus lead a well contented, happy life free from unnecessary anxieties, conflicts and frustrations. In this way ultimate aim of mental hygiene, as Shaffer and Shoben put it, "*is to assist every individual in the attainment of fuller, happier, more harmonious and more effective existence.*" (1936, p. 435)

MEANING OF THE TERM MENTAL HEALTH

Mental health stands for the health of the mind as Carter V. Good in The Dictionary of Education (1959, p. 263) has termed it as "*The wholesomeness of the mind*" analogous of the wholesomeness of the body implicit in physical health. Accordingly, mental health is concerned with the health of one's mind and its functioning in the same way as the physical health is concerned with the heath of one's physical organs and their functioning. To know more about its nature and meaning, let us try to look at some of the well-known definitions.

Waltin, J.E.W.

Mental health concerns with the development of 'wholesome' balanced personality, one who does not comfort himself like a series of compartmentalized selves, - honest on Sunday, dishonest on Monday, generous today, crebbed tomorrow, reasonable and logical at times, at other times confused and inconsistent. (1951, p. 41)

J.A. Hadfield
Mental health is the full and harmonious functioning of the whole personality. (1952, pp. 1-2)

P.B. Lewkan
Mentally healthy person is one who is happy, lives peacefully with his neighbours, makes his children healthy citizens and after fulfilling such basic responsibilities is still empowered with sufficient strength to serve the cause of the society in any way. (1949, p. 68)

K.A. Menninger
Let us define mental health as the adjustment of human beings to the world and each other with a maximum of effectiveness and happiness. It is the ability to maintain even temper, an alert intelligence, socially considerate behaviour and a happy disposition. (1967, p. 46)

Cutts and Moslay
Mental health is the ability which helps us to seek adjustment in the difficult situations of our life. (1941, p. 4)

Let us try to analyse these definitions one by one.

- The first two definitions given by Waltin and Hadfield consider mental health as the means and measure for the development as well as functioning of a wholesome well-balanced and integrated personality. Considering this way, mental health has a wider scope than physical health. It concerns with the all-round development of the personality of the child and not merely with the development of one's physical or bodily aspects. Moreover, it aims at the balanced personality, a personality like the balanced physical system who is able to stand firmly in the midst of stress and strain and who can exhibit adequate emotional maturity and balance between his needs and circumstances. For this he should behave as an integrated personality and not a split personality or a mind torn between various courses of action or inconsistent behaviour patterns. Truly speaking, for passing judgement about one's mental health, we may safely take consistency of his behaviour as one of the sound criteria. The individuals who are able to take proper judgement and are consistent in their behaviour can be said to enjoy good mental health in comparison to those who are in conflicts and practice double standards in behaviour.
- The remaining three definitions suggested by Lewkan, Menninger and Cutts & Moslay consider mental health as the state of one's peace of mind, happiness and harmony brought out by one's level of adjustment with his self and his environment. Such a person is capable of successfully steering himself away from difficult situations involving stresses without losing his balance or breaking and exhausting himself. Judging in this way, we can conclude, *mental health as the health of one's mind which can prove a potent determinant of one's integrated personality and balanced behaviour identified on the basis of the level of his adjustment to his self, others and environment.*

UNDERSTANDING THE CONCEPT OF MENTAL HEALTH

There are certain well-known characteristics and findings for understanding the true concept of mental health. They have been mentioned briefly as follows:

1. **Nothing called perfect mental health:** It is difficult to see a person who is mentally healthy in all the aspects. Truly speaking, perfect mental health is a fiction and not reality. Hence, it is always better to talk of optimum mental health in place of perfect mental health.

2. **Mental health is a dynamic concept:** Mental health denotes a state of balance or equilibrium of our mind. This balance is not static, it is quite dynamic. The circumstances in our life are never static and since they are changeable, so is our adjustment. The adjustments we have achieved at any point with ourself and the environmental forces may not be helpful in future and so one's mental health is always in a state of dynamics. For example, suggestibility at the age of two may be a normal trait of personality but not so after attaining maturity.
3. **Mental health can't be achieved without physical health:** The saying that "a sound mind lives in a sound body" is quite true. For achieving an optimal level of mental health, one has to first acquire adequate physical health.
4. **Mental health and efficiency are not the same thing:** It is not essential for the successful and efficient men to be mentally healthy as well. One may be quite efficient and successful at his work or profession but he could be most unhappy, full of anxiety, etc. otherwise.
5. **Mental health and Social ability are not the same thing:** While a mentally healthy person is sociable, it is not necessary for a sociable or socially adaptable person to be healthy minded. One may be sociable but extremely anxious to please everybody. Similarly he may be amenable because of an inherent feeling of insecurity or inferiority.
6. **Mental health differs form ethical standards:** Mental health differs from ethical standards. Morality does not guarantee mental health. There exist many individuals who are very moral but suffer from serious abnormalities like phobias or sex perversions.

CHARACTERISTICS OF A MENTALLY HEALTHY INDIVIDUAL (SYMPTOMS OF GOOD MENTAL HEALTH)

A mentally healthy individual can be easily distinguished from others by his mode of living, behaviour and personality characteristics. In general, these features and characteristics can be summarized as follows:

1. He knows himself well and is in a position to evaluate his strengths and weaknesses. Therefore, he always chooses a task that is of intermediate difficulty—neither too difficult nor too easy.
2. He has adequate ability to make adjustments in the changed circumstances and situations.
3. He is emotionally mature and stable as he is able to express his emotions in a desirable way and exercise proper control over them.
4. He is socially adjustable as he possesses an adequate ability to get along well with himself and others.
5. His intellectual powers are adequately developed. He is able to think independently and take proper decision at the proper time.
6. He always lives in the world of reality rather than that of imagination and fantasy.
7. He possesses enough courage and power of tolerance for facing failures in his life. He never repents and worries over his failures and mistakes.
8. He feels quite safe and secure in his respective groups and environment. He likes others and is liked by them. He possesses an adequate sense of belonging and loyalty towards the group he belongs.
9. Although he tries to accomplish his work as nicely as possible yet he does not prove to be an extremist by becoming a perfectionist.

10. He is free from undesirable mental disturbances, disorders, conflicts, anxieties, frustrations, ailments and diseases.
11. He possesses desirable social and health habits. He is regular and punctual in performing his duties and does not suffer from forgetfulness.
12. He is self-confident and optimist. He does not exhibit undue fear and anxiety for any new assigned task.
13. He has an adequate sex adjustment and does not suffer from sex abnormalities or dissatisfaction.
14. He possesses an adequate philosophy of life that governs his conduct and activities.
15. He possesses socially desirable healthy interests and aptitudes.
16. He leads a well-balanced life of work, rest and recreation.
17. He is satisfied with his profession or occupation.

The above listed characteristics should not be taken as essential and necessary conditions for the maintenance of proper mental health and thus absence of one or the other characteristics does not necessarily mean negation of mental health. Acquisition of complete mental health, as reflected by the above characteristics, is an ideal state and therefore, although we should aim to reach close to this, we should not be unduly worried over achieving perfection with regard to these traits and characteristics.

Symptoms of Poor Mental Health

With regard to the symptoms of poor mental health, we can make a list of all the opposite negative features and characteristics of one's behaviour and personality characteristics just in contradiction to what has been said above about the symptoms of good mental health. However, in brief, these symptoms may be outlined as:

- Emotionally unstable and easily upset
- Apprehensive, suspicious and insecure
- Self-critical, empowered with a feeling of guilt
- Lacks self-confidence and will power
- No adequate adjustment with the self and the environment — physical, social and professional
- Failure in setting a proper level of aspiration
- Suffers from frustrations, unresolved conflicts, strains and stresses
- Lacks enduring power and tolerance
- Lacks decision-making ability
- Poor self-concept and achievement motivation
- Unrealistic attitude towards life and people
- Suffers from mental disturbances, disorders, ailments and diseases
- Always dissatisfied with his achievements and tries to seek perfection in his or other's work
- Lives in his own world of imagination and fantasy.

IMPORTANCE OF MENTAL HEALTH

Health is rightly called wealth. It involves one's physical as well as mental health. As said earlier, mental health has much wider scope than physical health as it aims for the development of wholesome balanced and integrated personality. The acquisition of such personality is indeed a great asset and privilege for a normal individual. He can be able to actualize his self, live his life to his satisfaction and happiness and strive as well as attain the goals of his life to his satisfaction in the perfect tune of taking and giving something to the society. It is possible only when one enjoys good mental health and one can enjoy good mental health only when one is cautious about his mental health and knows its value and importance along with the knowledge of means and ways for achieving and maintaining it. For this, let us first discuss the importance or value of mental health.

1. **Helps in the development of desirable personality:** Mental health helps in the development of a wholesome, well-balanced and integrated personality. Such individual maintains a proper balance between his self and the environmental situation, his needs and the needs of the society and provides an example of an integrated personality instead of the splitted one.
2. **Helps in proper emotional development:** There is a close relationship between one's mental health and emotional behaviour. The individuals who enjoy good mental health are supposed to demonstrate proper emotional maturity in their behaviour. On the other side, those who are tense, disintegrated and mentally unhealthy demonstrate sudden emotional outburst and emotional immaturity.
3. **Helps in proper social development:** One's mental health helps one in becoming sociable and establishing proper social relationships in the society. One who is not in conflict with oneself has sufficient time and energy available for attending others and it helps one in one's proper social behaviour and adequate social adjustment.
4. **Help in proper moral development:** The individuals who enjoy sound mental health are usually found to behave as a man of integrity and character by following the ethical standards of the society. The proper functioning of their intellect guards them against the immoral and unsocial behaviour. They are able to exercise reasonable control over their emotions and channelise their energy to the noble tasks.
5. **Helps in proper aesthetic development:** Proper mental health helps the individual in the development of appropriate aesthetic sense, artistic taste and refined temperament. A mind free of any tension, conflict, frustration, inferiority, guilt or hostile feelings, may have better chance of drifting towards aesthetic, artistic and creative channel than the mind torn between complexities and conflicts.
6. **Helps in actualizing one's potentialities:** Every one of us has a fund of natural abilities and potentialities that can be actualized through proper efforts. Exercising such efforts and striving towards the actualization of one's potentialities depend, to a great extent, on the state of one's mental health. While the children having good mental health can strive well for the actualization of their potentialities, the mentally unhealthy children fail to do so on account of the malfunctioning of their intellectual powers, disintegrated personality and maladapted behaviour.
7. **Helps in seeking proper adjustment:** A mentally healthy individual is an adjusted person. He is able to seek adequate adjustment with his self and his environment. He is able to adjust his needs as per the demands of the situations and well being of the society. Hence mental health helps the individual to seek a harmonious relationship with his self and his environment.

8. **Helps in seeking goals of life:** Mental health helps the individual to strive properly for the realization of the goals of his life. These goals may differ from person to person depending upon their lifestyles and philosophy of life. But an optimum mental health always helps the individuals to divert his energies in full capacity for the realization of these goals and live a life to his satisfaction aiming towards happiness to his self and others.
9. **Helps in the progress of the society:** Mental health helps the individuals to develop as well-balanced useful citizens who are conscious not only of their rights but also of their responsibilities. They take essentials from the society for their proper development and living but are also ready to give something to the society for its progress and development. Actually the prosperity and progress of the society is linked with the health, particularly the mental health, of its members. The desired peace, progress and happiness in the society can only be possible when its members enjoy the same in terms of their sound mental health.
10. **Helps in the prevention of mental illness:** Mental health helps an individual in protecting him against abnormalities of behaviour, maladjustment, illness and mental diseases in the same way as physical health is helpful in saving him from the physical illness, ailments and diseases. A sound mind and balanced personality has enough resistance to fight against the odds of life and bear the accidental stresses and strains of life in comparison to those with impaired mental health. Therefore, adequate preservation of mental health by the individual and proper education about it may help in a big way in reducing the cases of mental illness and diseases in the society.

PRINCIPLES OF MENTAL HEALTH

Achievements of proper physical health rests on the observation of the principles of physical health. Similarly we can help children achieve good mental health by acquainting them with some specific principles of mental health. What should be these principles is an issue that needs to be considered wisely.

It is an established fact that one enjoys mental health to the extent to which one is reasonably satisfied with one's self as well as the environment. Consequently, we can roughly divide these principles into two categories as below:

A. Principles seeking adjustment with one's self.
B. Principles seeking adjustment with one's environment.

Principles Seeking Adjustment with One's Self

One can ensure good mental health if one remains adjusted with oneself. The following seven principles may work well in seeking such adjustment.

THE PRINCIPLE OF KNOWING THE SELF

One must be quite aware with his self specifically in terms of one's strengths and limitations so that one can accordingly shape one's behaviour and direct one's attempts for the realization of the goals in life.

THE PRINCIPLE OF ACCEPTING ONE'S SELF

One who accepts and respects oneself in its very shape and existence is likely to enjoy good mental health while someone who always complains about his inadequacy or the circumstances of his life or blames others and his misfortunes, cannot be expected to lead a healthy mental life.

THE PRINCIPLE OF BALANCING THE LEVEL OF ASPIRATION

One should not set one's level of aspiration and achievement motivation either too high or too low but should try to set it at a proper level by keeping in view one's own capabilities and opportunities on one hand and the goals and objectives on the other. This can help one avoid unnecessary frustrations and failures.

THE PRINCIPLE OF BALANCING ONE'S DEVELOPMENT

Mental health aims for the development of a wholesome well-balanced personality. Accordingly one should seek and strive for the balanced harmonious development of his personality in all the dimensions—physical, mental, emotional, social, moral and aesthetic.

THE PRINCIPLE OF INTEGRATING THE SELF

The self of the person should portray itself as an integrated one and not as split personality. One should not make one's self torn between the opposing and conflicting desires and ambitions and should not fall prey to unnecessary tensions and indecisiveness.

THE PRINCIPLE OF SELF-DRIVE AND SHAPING

It is quite wrong and contrary to the principles of mental health that the child is forced into a shape that is wished by others while completely ignoring the wishes of his self. Similarly it is wrong to allow others to drive his self—contrary to his own ideals and aspirations. The individual himself must be his own driver and be allowed to freely attempt to shape his own destiny, then and only then can he be moved in the direction of satisfactory mental health.

THE PRINCIPLE OF SELF CONTROL

There is no need to exercise external control for disciplining an individual. A forced discipline may lead to aggression or regression of his behaviour. The better way to help him in gaining good mental health is to guide him for exercising control over his self.

The Principles Seeking Adjustment with Environment

Besides, seeking harmony with his self, the person must have a reasonable harmony and adjustment with the men, material and situations present in his environment. Ten principles helping in this task have been discussed below:

THE PRINCIPLE OF UNDERSTANDING OTHERS

One must not only understand his self but also try to understand others properly so that he can behave well with them according to their limitations and strengths, needs and desires, interests and attitudes, and taste and temperaments etc.

THE PRINCIPLE OF ACCEPTING AND RESPECTING OTHER'S INDIVIDUALITIES

Every person has his or her individuality, style of life and traits of one's own personality. While seeking respect for our 'self' we must not forget to pay due respect to others' selves and individualities. We might invite unnecessary quarrels, tensions and conflicts by attacking their self and showing disrespect to their individualities and personality. We must also try to accept others as they are in terms of their existing strength and limitations, good or bad habits for seeking proper adjustment with them.

THE PRINCIPLE OF SOCIALIZING ONE'S SELF

The individuals, who are better in terms of social relationship, adjustments and adaptation, are able to achieve good mental health in comparison to those who are unsocial, ego-centric, selfish and lonely. Therefore the better way of achieving good mental health of children is to seek proper socialization for them. They must be taught to harmonize their self with the self of others. They must realize that the true fulfillment of life lies in service, i.e. giving oneself to some extent to the need of others.

THE PRINCIPLE OF ADEQUATE SATISFACTION OF NEEDS

We as human beings have many needs categorized as organic and socio-psychological needs. These needs are as basic and fundamental as the need for oxygen, water and food etc. which are essential for our survival. Sex gratification and satisfaction of socio-psychological needs like the need for security, love and affection, freedom, companionship, recognition, self-actualization, etc. are also essential for the proper growth and development and happiness of the human beings. Truly speaking, the level of one's mental health depends upon the level of the satisfaction of one's needs. One remains normal and enjoys satisfactory mental health as long as his needs are gratified or are in the way of gratification. In case one is deprived of the satisfaction of his needs or these are thwarted and threatened, one gets maladjusted and drifted towards the impairment of his mental health.

Therefore, due care should be taken in the satisfaction and gratification of the needs of the individuals for making them mentally healthy.

THE PRINCIPLE OF TRAINING THE EMOTIONS

Emotional energy, if utilized properly, is a big asset for the progress and development of an individual. However, if it is drifted away from its normal expression and gets out of control, it may spell disaster. The repression of this energy is also equally dangerous as it may give birth to various problems of mental health. The best way is to have one's emotions trained so that the flow of emotional energy may be directed into constructive channels. Such training may be properly imparted by adopting the techniques of sublimation and catharsis.

THE PRINCIPLE OF ADJUSTMENT TO THE WORLD OF WORK

For enjoying normal mental health, one must be reasonably satisfied and adjusted with his world of work. Those who remain maladjusted with their work and profession can't remain adjusted in their lives and consequently suffer from mental worries and problems. The right thing is to develop a very positive attitude towards one's world of work by remembering the maxim "work is worship". A work that is done half heartedly or with a negative outlook and rebellion attitude is likely to affect not only the quality of the work but also the mental health of the workers quite adversely. Therefore, one must try to seek proper adjustment to his work and profession for the proper safeguard of his mental health.

THE PRINCIPLE OF POSITIVE ATTITUDE TOWARDS LIFE

The state of one's mental health is greatly determined by one's attitude towards life. While the positive and optimistic outlook may keep one smiling by providing sufficient strength and patience in facing the realities of life, the negative and pessimistic attitude may drift him towards the feeling of inferiority, hostility towards one's environment, frustration and agonies of life. Therefore, it is better to learn the lessons of developing positive attitude towards the activities of life by looking at each morning as a new day and not carrying the troubles of yesterday. It is in the learning of such lessons that can help the individuals gain control in terms of better mental health.

The Principle of Bearing the Stresses and Strains of Life

Life is not always the bed of roses. It often offers challenges, struggles and problems that are to be faced with patience and courage. In addition to this, there are many incidents and accidents involving stresses and strains, the pressures of which have to be borne by the individuals concerned. It is the duty of the parents to teach their children to remain strong at the time of stress and strain. They must also practice this lesson at the time of rearing their children and also set their examples of own sustaining the odds and eventualities of life. Those who make themselves trained and wise for the stresses and strains of life are able to preserve their mental health in a proper way in comparison to those who can easily break in the storms of life.

The Principle of Good Physical Health

Healthy mind lives in a healthy body. Keeping one's body and physical health in a satisfactory, normal condition is the prime and the most basic requirement for achieving and maintaining good mental health. How can we expect a physically, somatically weak man to keep his mind free from tension, worries and other negative and depressive feeling? The health of one's nervous system, ductless glands, body systems and organs are sure to affect one's mental functioning, personal and social adjustment leading to his good or poor mental health.

The Principle of Having Faith in God and Nature

In this age of extreme materialism and degradation of human values, there has been a tremendous rise in the rate of cases of mental illness and mental diseases. Everywhere in the world there is cut throat competition to outperform each other and snatch other's share for enhancing the self. 'Self is great' is the slogan of the present age and this extreme selfishness has resulted in the miseries and agonies of human beings. The results are obvious. Nobody cares for others. There is nothing like mutual trust, harmony, love and affection left among the human beings. Everybody is suspicious and jealous of others. Consequently everybody is tense and facing mental worries and problems. The loss of faith needs the imposition of faith. There must be something to provide a sense of security. The only one who can be trusted to show due affection is none than the Almighty. The wounded human psyche needs a healing touch and it can be provided by one's faith in God. The ultimate cure and measure for keeping oneself free from mental worries and tension thus lies in having faith in God and Nature. One should aim at doing one's duties and sharing one's responsibilities as sincerely as one can without caring for the fruits of one's action and leaving it to God and Nature. Such attitude and actions can certainly prove a very helping factor in achieving and maintaining proper mental health.

DEFENCE OR MENTAL MECHANISMS

Meaning of Defence or Mental Mechanisms

In our life, we have so many aspirations and ambitions but it is not possible to achieve all that we desire. There are many situations when we fail in our attempts and get frustrated. Our failures and frustrations may bring injury to our ego and give birth to the feelings of inferiority and anxiety.

Most of us do not like to face the reality by accepting our shortcomings and failures but tend to resort to certain mechanisms for defending our inadequacies or anxieties. These mechanisms or devices are called defence mechanisms or mental mechanisms.

To understand this term more clearly, let us have a look at some of the popular definitions:

Page
When psychological equilibrium is threatened by severe emotional traumat, frustrations, or conflicts, the mind resorts to a variety of protective subterfuges and debtors called mental mechanisms or dynamisms. (1976, p. 39)

Carroll
An adjustment mechanism is a device resorted to in order to achieve an indirect satisfaction of a need so that tension will be reduced and self-respect maintained. (1967, p. 53)

Arkoff
Certain patterns of behaviour that are employed for protection against threat or anxiety are called defence mechanisms or adjustment mechanisms. Sometimes they are referred to as 'ego defence mechanisms' since they serve to defend the ego or the self from threat. (1968, p. 138)

Davison and Neale
A defence mechanism is a strategy, unconsciously utilised, that serves to protect the ego from anxiety. (1978)

On the basis of these definitions, we can draw the following conclusions about the nature and characteristics of defence mechanisms:

1. Defence mechanisms are devices in the form of a certain pattern of behaviour.
2. These mechanisms provide protection against whatever threatens our ego or self-esteem.
3. There are many situations in our environment and also within ourselves that threaten our psychological equilibrium. As a result, we fall victim to anxiety, frustration, conflicts or other psychological upsets. Defence mechanisms help us defend ourselves from possible injury in such delicate moments.
4. Unfulfilled desire, need or motive may bring a state of tension leading to possible injury to one's self respect. The way out is provided by the defence mechanism in the form of indirect satisfaction of that need.
5. Defence mechanisms may be evolved by anything in conflict with our minimum ideal of what the self must be.
6. Defence mechanisms are quite temporary defence against anxiety and inadequacies. By resorting to them, one tries to deceive himself more than anybody else.
7. Since frustrations or conflicts are experienced by everyone and since everyone is compelled to maintain ego or self-respect, it follows that the defence mechanisms are used by all of us whether normal or abnormal at one time or the other.
8. Defence mechanisms are largely unconscious. They tend to operate in a machine-like or automatic way. In fact, they are always in corresponding degree, self-deceptive and thus aim at softening or disguising what is unacceptable to us in terms of our failure or inadequacies.
9. Defence mechanisms should not be confused with symptoms of neuroses or other abnormal conditions. These mechanisms are purely psychic or mental devices or ways of perceiving and desiring. Here, the individual is helped to perceive or have a matching wish to make him free of threats to his self-regard.

10. The persons employing defence mechanisms can't be labeled as abnormal or mentally deficient. Infact a person usually resorts to such mechanisms simply for saving himself (may be temporarily) from the danger of falling in the clutches of mental illness or maladjustment with one's self or the environment.
11. The excessive use or dependence upon the mental mechanisms may lead to one or the other type of abnormalities in one's behaviour causing serious disturbances in his physiological as well as psychological functioning.

Important Defence Mechanisms

Rationalization

It is a defence mechanism in which a person tries to justify his otherwise unacceptable social behaviour or act by giving socially acceptable reasons for it and thus attempts to deceive others and himself by inventing good reasons to justify his conduct. Thinking on these lines a rationalizer will view and explain his idleness as "needed relaxation", his cowardice as "caution", his severe and arbitrary discipline policies "for child's own good". A child makes use of rationalization when he tries to offer lame excuses for his failure. He may blame unfairness or ambiguity of the questions, teacher or parents or his poor health and ailments and thus try to disguise his own weakness and deficiency.

The use of rationalization is almost universal. We all, at one time or the other, interpret our behaviour in an acceptable or reasonable way in order to prevent a threat to our sense of well-being and thus try to maintain or even enhance our image. We often offer the noblest of reasons for behaviour that is actually motivated by selfish desires. The game of rationalization is well played by statesmen or nations. In announcing a specific programme a government may assert that it is for the social good of all, when actually its objective stands for bringing more power to it.

The mechanism or rationalization may be well-illustrated by considering two special types of attitudes known as sour-grapes and sweet-lemon attitudes.

In sour-grapes mechanism, based on the fable of the fox and the grapes, an individual, unable to obtain what he wants, tries to avoid the bitterness of disappointment by maintaining that he did not want it any way. The young man who fails to get the job saves face and self-respect by declaring that he did not really want the job. A boy failing to win a place in his school cricket team maintains that he actually did not want to waste his time in playing cricket. Similarly, a young man rejected by his fiancee may maintain that he did not actually want to marry her as she did not meet his standards. All such justifications, explanations and excuses help the individuals in getting relief from the tension or frustration by playing down the good points and stressing on the unpalatable ones.

In sweet-lemon type reaction, the individual maintains that whatever happens is for the best or whatever he has obtained is the best he could obtain. A senior lecturer is denied promotion to the post of principal which infact is a severe blow to him, but he adjusts to this frustration by saying that he is more happy in his present post where he enjoys comparatively more security of services and also gets to devote more time for the welfare of his family and writing. Similarly, a handicapped boy may rationalize by thinking of his broken leg as a blessing in disguise as it provides him an opportunity to catch up on his studies.

Projection

A person may have inferior impulses, traits or motives that can involve him in a threatening situation. For his defence, he may now resort to the mechanism of projection by attributing to or observing the unacceptable motives in other persons. Arkoff points out *"Used as defence, projection implies that a person has certain thoughts or feelings or actions which are threatening to him which he then denies are his and instead attributes to others."* (1968, p. 156)

When a person with some shortcomings observes and criticizes the failings of others, he may be said to make use of projection as defence. Similarly, a student who has been caught cheating in the examination may defend himself by saying that others have also cheated. A person with an unacceptable sexual urge may try to accuse his wife for her 'flirtations' and the wife may be considerably worried about the adultery of her husband. A boy who is tempted to be homosexual may accuse others of making indecent advances.

It is not necessary that the objects of one's projection must always be persons. Animals, natural and supernatural forces or even inanimate objects may serve as well. A student may blame his fortune for his failure. A badminton player may attribute his failure to his racket. The boy after falling from a chair may kick the chair for being responsible for his fall.

Thus, in projection what is desirable or unacceptable is neither explained (as in rationalization) nor counter-acted (as in reaction formation) or made up for (as in compensation), but one gets rid of it by projecting it (attributing or observing in) on others.

One gets satisfaction by projecting the undesirable or unacceptable on others and it may be explained through the following benefits derived:

One can get rid of the undesirable or unacceptable by denying ("I don't have such undesirable dirty thoughts.")

REACTION-FORMATION

While rationalization is a kind of "refutation by argument or explanation" of implied inadequacy or unworthiness, reaction-formation is a "refutation by action". Here one strives to behave in ways that are sharply in contrast with the ways that he tends to behave for protecting his self-esteem. By utilizing reaction-formation as defence, one tries to inhibit, mark or overcome certain impulses that threaten one's self or general welfare by emphasizing the opposite or contradictory ones. A mother may hate her child, but by using reaction formation as defence she may be able to inhibit, mark or overcome unworthy impulses and thus turn into an attentive, solicitous and over protective in her behaviour towards him. A person who is strongly motivated by undesirable sex needs may react by being extremely puritanical, avoiding almost all association with the opposite sex and even criticizing others for their sexual activities. In this way, he may strive to feel, think and act in ways contradictory to his own real wishes and motives. Similarly, reaction-formation towards selfish tendencies may be manifested in extreme generosity.

Thus, by resorting to reaction-formation as defence, an individual, in spite of suspected meanness, may behave very nobly such that no one may possibly doubt the purity of his motives. It may be added that his self reaction-formation is not, however, to be confused with hypocritical pretence. The individual casually resorts to such mechanism rather than in full awareness and there is usually little doubt of the sincerity of his desire and care for the protection of his self-esteem which compels him to resort to reaction formation instead of facing the things as they are or behaving as he tends to behave.

REPRESSION

The automatic inhibition of a threatening impulse is called *repression*. It is an unconscious forgetting or blocking from consciousness of internal impulses, feelings or thought which are unacceptable to the conscious self. In this way, repression as a defence mechanism is that mechanism in which the threatening or anxiety producing experiences, conflicts and unfulfilled wishes are pushed down into one's consciousness and, as a result, one tries to forget the things that might be painful or threatening to one's self.

Forgetting one's date of marriage or appointment with a friend may be associated with such repression. A person who has painful experiences attached to his school or teacher may not be able to recall even the name of the school or the teacher. In another situation, a girl who has repressed the painful memories of her first love affair may not be able to write a love letter to her husband.

Therefore, repression serves by providing relief, though temporarily, from the tension or anxiety by making one believe that the tension producing situation does not exist. It saves us from distressing thoughts, feelings, and from engaging in certain actions which might prove dangerous or painful. It helps us to hide our thoughts and feelings and actions from ourselves just as we sometimes more consciously attempt to conceal certain things from others. However, in certain cases, repression as a defence may prove detrimental in the long run. What has been repressed may prove more dangerous and threatening at a later stage. Commenting on this possibility, Carroll writes *"Repressed desires, fantasies, and experiences constitute a burden sometimes light, sometimes heavy, which each human being carries. For some the burden becomes too heavy and responses are made to the strain which may be neurotic or psychotic. Such persons need professional help."* (1967, p. 75)

REGRESSION

Regression means going backward or returning to the past. It is, in a way, a retreat for an individual from the complexities of the present to an earlier and simpler form of behaviour or a more fortunate and pleasant period of one's life. Thus, used a defence, *regression may be defined as a mechanism by which an individual, longing for the earlier, happier period of life, begins to behave in a manner more appropriate to his earlier age or period of life for protecting himself from the threatening situations involving frustration, conflict, anxiety or tension.*

A man failing in his love affair resorts to regression when he exhibits his love for a doll. An older boy may regress when his new brother is born and he feels neglected or deprived. Although he has been walking for several years, suddenly he may insist that he is unable to do, that he is too small and must be carried. He may even abandon the toilet habits and insist on breast feeding. An adult earning member of the family may also show signs of regression when, after a hard day, he wants to be nurtured, pampered and otherwise cared for at home. A young woman may be said to resort to the regression mechanism when she returns to her parent's home after finding it impossible to meet the demands of her marriage and the new environment.

A person who resorts to the mechanism of regression is introvert, timid and lacks self-confidence. He feels secure only in old and tried situations and strives to avoid new experiences. He avoids adventure and is fearful of the future, turns around and retreats to the world of his past.

The extreme cases of regressive behaviour tend to develop into a disorganized personality where the individual may retreat to very early patterns of behaviour so successfully that he loses touch with reality and believes as well as behaves like a child or an infant.

AGGRESSION

Expression or demonstration of one's angry behaviour through verbal dialogue or physical assault or both may be termed as *aggression*. Some of us may try to adopt such type of expression as defence mechanism. Such over assertiveness may help one deal effectively with other persons, situations and problems etc. Others may get influenced or become fearful of his aggressive behaviour and thus may fall in line with him or they may avoid unnecessary dialogues or conflicts leading to spoiled relationship or bitterness with him. Reinforced by such impact of his aggressive behaviour, one may then be tempted to adopt it as an important component of one's behaviour. However, it is not essential that his resorting to such mechanism may always prove a boon to him. It has an equal chance of going otherwise. If the situation is a trying one or the rival personality is a tough guy, his aggressiveness may cost him dear.

The question arises as to from where do we pick or learn such aggressiveness. The reason lies well in our environmental surroundings where an individual from the very beginning of his life encounters or perceives the aggressive behaviour of his elders in the real life of screen. Knowingly or unknowingly, this type of aggressiveness is then transferred in one's behaviour by way of imitation and this becomes his style of coping with the environmental situations. This picked up style of ours may often get due reinforcement when we get desired success through our aggressive behaviour and consequently we may adopt it as a way of behaving with others.

As a defence mechanism, our aggressiveness may provide us temporary defence against our repressed wishes, mounted tensions and pressures, conflicting desires and frustrations etc. Our sudden outburst of foul and aggressive language or fighting may provide us a certain type of relief from the mounted pressure built up in our psyche, but the ultimate consequences are always negative and painful both to the individual as well as others who are subjected to such aggressiveness. In this way, it is always wise to give up aggression for being better adjusted to one's self and others.

Displacement

It refers to the process of displacing or shifting of thought, feeling or action from one person or situation to another. When an individual is unable to react or express his emotion or impulse in a particular situation, he may resort to displacement mechanism for relieving himself of the anxiety or frustration by its transfer or displacement to another situation or object—neutral, vulnerable, or less dangerous than the original. For example:

- A youngster rebuked by the mother, being unable to attack or react directly, may trample her flower-bed.
- A little boy, beaten by one of his schoolmates, may kick or slap his younger brother on returning home.
- A clerk, being ill-treated by his boss, may displace his anger towards the peon or his wife or children.
- A child who fears his father or teacher may displace his fear to animals.
- An inherent fear of committing suicide may be transferred to a fear of knives and other sharp instruments.
- A boy who is unable to get attention from his father may turn his attention to a teacher or some other adult male.

In this manner, displacement is a kind or substitution of one outlet for another, and works as a safety valve for the pentup emotions and impulses which otherwise may prove harmful to the self and the society.

Fantasy and Daydreaming

Fantasy or daydreaming is a kind of withdrawal of one's self in a private and satisfying world of imagination. Thus, instead of facing the realities he may become satisfied with unreal, imaginary success or satisfaction that he gets in wandering in the make-believe world of imagination. Commenting on the use of the mechanism, Arkoff writes:

"As a defence, our fantasy life provides us with an escape from the dangers, threats, and problems of the real world. In our fantasies we can meet our unmet needs and reach our un-reached goals. We can picture ourselves as a different sort of person and the world as a different sort of world.." (1968, p. 162)

An individual may turn to daydreaming or fantasy when the present he is living in is uninteresting and frustrating. Fantasy permits him to escape to a dream world where exciting things occur and he is able to achieve whatever he desires.

In general, there are three common types of daydreaming or fantasies—roaming in the past, conquering hero, and suffering hero or martyr type.

- In the roaming type, an individual, while considering the present as bitter and painful, tries to roam in his happy past. In such fantasies, an elderly person may relieve the happy experiences of his past, sometimes making them even more pleasant than they really were.
- In the conquering hero type, the individual imagines that he is the master of some situation. He says and does all the things that he failed to say and do during the actual experiences. He is the managing director of a factory, a great player of hockey, a gold medal winner in a convocation or a great cine actor. He is applauded, acclaimed and sought after. In such daydreaming a young man who fails to get married may imagine about the love affair, marriage and the affection to be shared with a beautiful girl who was once seen by him in a marriage party. Similarly, a single woman may dream that she is married, has a good husband, beautiful children and a decent home.
- In the suffering hero or martyr type of daydreams, the individual imagines himself to be the victim of some situation. It is resorted to by the individual who pities himself. As a result, a child who feels that he gets maltreatment at home may imagine himself as seriously ill or even dead. Similarly, an adult may see himself undergoing great hardships or miseries and thus get satisfaction by imaging himself a martyr or the victim of the circumstances. The suffering hero type of daydreaming is a form of aggression turned inward and therefore may prove more dangerous than the conquering hero type.

Daydreaming or fantasy may prove detrimental when it becomes a substitute for the real world and the actual efforts for achievements. Not only does it lead to the wastage of precious time and energy but also paves the way for maladaptive behaviour and disorganization of the personality.

SUBLIMATION

You may have used the term 'sublimation' in your chemistry textbook as a process of purifying the solids and gases through desired heating and evaporation. That is why, it is also named as purification. In psychology, we use this term as a way or means of purifying or modifying our undesirable or unsocial desires and feelings. In this way, as a means of purification, *sublimation may be considered as a special type of mental or adjustment mechanism which helps in the re-channeling or redirection of our repressed and undesirable wishes, impulses, drives, emotions or actions in some socially acceptable form and thus saving us from the mental agony and other troublesome physical consequences.* As a result of the adoption of sublimation as an adjustment mechanism, one may be successful in channeling or redirecting one's so-called undesirable behaviour involving the emotion of love and lust towards love for humanity or God.

We have example of Tulsidas, the author of great epic *Ramayana* before us who successfully redirected his love or lust towards *Rama* the God after getting rebuked by his wife Ratnavali for his undesirable lust. In our day-to-day life also, we may have enough examples to demonstrate the role of sublimation. By adopting this mechanism, a woman who is experiencing trouble playing the roles of wife and mother may direct her energies to social or professional activities, a student quite brave but aggressive in behaviour may turn into a good player, boxer, wrestler, saviour of the weak, and martyrs. By re-directing and channeling his tremendous energies and strong will power, a young man may be found to write beautiful poems and sketch beautiful portraits and in this way may discharge or sublimate some part of the strong sexual desire he was unable to discharge directly to his beloved.

Conclusion about Defence Mechanism

All the defence mechanisms discussed above are used unconsciously by a person to protect himself, although for the time being, from psychological dangers. They are not the permanent cure of the trouble as *Morgan* observes, but "*they merely conceal or disguise the real problem. It is still there, ready to produce anxiety again and again.*" (1961, p. 143). In this way, defence mechanisms may be regarded as temporary defence against anxiety and inadequacies. Moreover, the use of such mechanisms may create new difficulties for the individual who frequently resorts to them like a person who tells a lie to save himself from a particular situation but falls on to the series of troubles on account of his telling lie.

MENTAL DISORDERS

Meaning and Definition

As emphasized earlier, an individual is said to be in satisfactory mental health to the extent he feels satisfied with himself and his environment. The disequilibrium of this balance leads to his maladjustment with the self and the environment paying the way for one or the other kind of mental disorder and mental illness. Defence mechanism, as we have just discussed, is nothing but temporary measures for defending or protecting oneself from the possible maladjustment or behaviour disorders. However, these measures often either do not prove successful or get damaged in the long run resulting into one or the other type of mental disorder or mental illness. Let us know in detail about these mental disorders that are notorious for turning an otherwise normal personality into an abnormal one.

As a matter of definition, *mental disorders represent certain types of abnormalities, malfunctioning of deficiency in the behaviour or personality of an individual resulted from his maladjustment with the self and the environment.*

Classification of Mental Disorders

For the sake of diagnosis, prevention and treatment of the various mental disorders various attempts have been made to put them into some definite categories. Mentionable among those are the attempts made by the American Psychiatric Association and World Health Organization (WHO). While the former has developed Diagnostic and Statistical Manual of Mental Disorders DSM-I (1952), DSM-II (1968), DSM-III (1980) and DSM-IV (1994), the latter has brought such classification in the chapter V of International Classification of Diseases ICD-8, (1965) and ICD-9 (1979). A close analysis of these attempts of classification may reveal that all types of mental disorders may be broadly classified into two major types—organic and psychogenic.

The organic disorder involves damages to the tissues of the brain as a result of infectious disease, injury, mental retardation, hormonal or toxic disturbances etc. As a result of such damage, the person demonstrates disturbed or disoriented behaviour like disturbance of memory, perception and thought, sometimes mild and sometimes severe. The organic disorders are incurable in the sense that there is no way of regeneration of brain tissue once it is damaged.

The Psychogenic disorders also referred to as functional disorders involve no such brain damage or proven physical cause and the disorder does not prove as helpless and refractory to treatment as in the case of organic disorders. These disorders may be further divided into subtypes like neurotic disorders, psychotic disorders, psychosomatic disorders and personality disorders. The first two terms are quite popular in describing abnormal personalities and mentally ill. For the purpose of distinguishing, the rest two from the popular ones, neurosis and psychosis, let us give them a common name simple mental disorders (where the etiology, i.e. the causation of disorder and its treatment, is not too difficult or impossible). We are thus in a position to classify the psychogenic disorders into three types (i) Simple disorders incorporating disorders like psycho-somatic and personality disorders, (ii) neurotic disorders, and (iii) psychotic disorders. Let us now have some discussion on the above-mentioned types and sub-types of the psychogenic disorders.

PSYCHO-SOMATIC OR PSYCHO-PHYSIOLOGICAL DISORDERS

The term 'psycho-somatic' or 'psycho-physiological' disorders refer to those disorders in which both organic and psychological factors may work side by side in terms of their origin as well as treatment. Usually in such disorders, we come across changes in the psychological functioning of the individual resulting from the emotional factors and stress. Since the physical disorders are the result of the psychological factors, medicine is also required to join forces with psychology for getting desired success in the treatment. As a matter of definition, The American Psychiatric Association DSM-III, Publication States: *"Psycho-physiological disorders are characterized by physical symptoms that are caused by emotional factors and involve a single organ system, usually under automatic nervous system innervations. The physiological changes involved are those that normally accompany certain emotional states, but in these disorders the changes are more intense and sustained."* (1968, p. 46)

This definition leads us to the following characteristics of psycho-physiological disorders:

1. Psycho-physiological disorders always exhibit one or the other typical physical symptoms like pain, vomiting, difficulty in breathing, diarrhoea, etc. It is the severity of the distress caused by these symptoms that usually compels the individual to seek medical help.
2. Though the physical symptoms developed on account of the psycho-physiological disorders appear similar to those reflected in certain emotional states (anxiety, anger etc.), the visceral effects of emotional conflict in these disorders are so pronounced that actual and irreversible damage may be done to the body's structure. In this way, a so-called psychological illness or disorder turns into "a real" illness or disorder with identifiable tissue pathology.
3. In psycho-physiological disorders, emotional conflict affects the viscera through the autonomic nervous system which has two main divisions known as sympathetic and parasympathetic systems. These two systems of the autonomic nervous system are controlled by the brain in such a way that in normal conditions, the effects of the two systems are kept in approximate balance. It results in the predominance of either sympathetic or parasympathetic activity flooding a single organ system-respiratory, circulatory, etc.
4. The psycho-physiological disorders are neither exclusively caused by psychological factors nor by the organic ones but in all cases, they are brought about by an interaction of psychological and organic factors.

Major Types of Psycho-Physiological Disorders

1. **Respiratory disorders** like bronchial asthma, hay fever, common cold, rhinitis, hyperventilation etc.
2. **Gastrointestinal disorders** like peptic ulcer, mucus colitis, chronic gastritis, anorexia nervosa etc.
3. **Cardiovascular disorders** like hypertension, heart attacks, vascular spasm, migraine etc.
4. **Genitourinary disorders** like urinary disorders, menstrual disorder in women, and disorders associated with sex (impotence in men and frigidity in women).
5. **Skin disorders** like eczema, hives, dandruff, acne, herpes simplex, etc.
6. **Musculoskeletal disorders** like backache, muscle cramps, and arthritis.

For illustrating the nature of these above mentioned different types of psycho-physiological disorders, let us mention a few popular ones.

- **Migraine:** It involves extremely painful headaches. The pain usually occurs on the side of the head. Sometimes it is associated with nausea and blurred vision. The attack rarely lasts more than twenty four hours and is often much briefer. It is generally caused by the sympathetically innervated contraction followed by dilation of blood vessels in the brain. Emotional disturbance, early psychological experiences and genetic influences may be the other causes of migraine disorders in addition to or absence of the known bodily causes.
- **Anorexia nervosa:** Loss of appetite is known as anorexia. In the absence of organic disorder when it is caused by emotional factors it is referred to as anorexia nervosa. The more severe cases of anorexia nervosa are characterized by weight loss to the point of emaciation. This disorder is much more frequent among girls and young women of the middle and upper socio-economic classes with symptoms of menstrual disturbances, slow heart beat rate and constipation. Its onset often occurs during or shortly after adolescence, at the time when a young girl becomes very conscious of her weight. She goes on "crash" starvation diet. As she starves herself for becoming thinner, she may adamantly deny that she is underweight and may seem almost phobic to weight gain. Consequently, she resorts to a kind of voluntary self-starvation many times complaining that food disgusts her, or that she is afraid of choking on it or of vomiting after eating. In some cases self-induced vomiting are frequent rituals to cleanse one's body of food after the 'sin' of eating.
- **Peptic ulcer:** Peptic ulcer is an open sore (an inflamed wound) on the lining of the stomach or more frequently in duodenum (the upper portion of the small intestine). An important symptom is pain which a person experiences after meals and which can be eased only by eating. There may be nausea or vomiting along with pain. There is bleeding in severe cases. It is caused by the corrosive action of the overactivity and excessive secretion of the digestive acids on the protective mucous membranes of the stomach and small intestine. The ulcers arise from a complex interplay of emotional and organic factors. Emotional states are closely related to the physiological factors responsible for the cause of ulcer. A strong and sustained conflict evokes a chronic emotional response usually of hostility or anxiety. The inability to reduce the emotional tension in some harmless ways (like defence mechanisms or proper channelization) causes the stomach or duodenum to be susceptible to injury by its own acid secretions. It has often been found that the persistent emotional stress and the resulting autonomic nervous system activities are responsible for the

overactivity and excessive secretion of digestive acids. They cause ulcer by weakening the mucous membranes and breaking down the digestive tissues.

- **Impotence and Frigidity:** Only a few cases of these disorders are found to have an organic cause while in most cases psychological factors play a key role. Hostility towards the partner, anxiety and fear of disease, injury or pregnancy and guilt feeling concerning sex are the major sources of such disorders. As a result, the impotent male is unable to perform the sexual act and derive pleasure out of it. Similarly, in the case of frigid females there is either a pathological lack of sexual desire or a diminished desire for sex. In chronic cases, it leads to dyspareunia (painful intercourse) in which the establishment of normal heterosexual relationships becomes difficult or impossible on account of the local neuromuscular reaction in the form of vaginal spasms.

Causes underlying psycho-physiological disorders

Psycho-physiological disorders are caused by a close interaction of organic (genetic and other biological factors) like body structure, its chemical functioning, allergies and infections and psychological factors (like conditioning and reinforcement, early deprivations, emotional problems and psychological stress).

Prevention and treatment: Genetic influences are beyond one's control. However, reasonable control may be exercised over biological and other psychological factors for the prevention.

For the treatment of these disorders, there are measures like biomedical, psycho-analytic, behaviour modification, psycho-therapies and bio feedback, etc.

PERSONALITY DISORDERS

These disorders are also often named as 'conduct' or 'character disorders'. *These are characterized by lifelong impairment of the ability to maintain normal social relationships and repeated conflict with the mores and values of the society in which one lives* (Levin, 1978, p. 526). So the individuals suffering from these disorders are those who suffer from a general failure to acquire effective habits of adjustment and adequate social relationships and as a result are found to display a lifelong pattern of disturbed or anti-social behaviour.

Adams (1972, p. 348), while describing these disorders as behaviour anomalies, brings out the following four main features of the persons suffering from these disorders:

(i) These individuals violate or do not conform to the moral or legal codes of society.
(ii) They do not complain about their disorder (not feeling discomfort) on account of their behaviour and therefore are not usually motivated to change their behaviour.
(iii) There is no failure of the cognitive apparatus as seen in the psychotic individual although their acts are often considered bizarre.
(iv) There is little evidence that they exhibit more neurotic characteristics than would be expected in the general population.

Main Type or Classes of Personality or Conduct Disorders

Usually the following types of mental disorders are included into the broad concept of personality or conduct disorders:

1. The passive-aggressive personality disorder
2. Criminal behaviour-delinquency and crime

3. Sociopathic disorders
4. Alcoholism and drug addiction
5. Sexual deviations and disorders

Let us know about these disorders in brief:

The passive-aggressive personality, according to Lazarus (1976, p. 146), shows extensive inability to deal with inter-personal relations expressing itself in one of the three patterns, passive-dependent, passive-aggressive and aggressive. All these three patterns lead to adjustive failure and maladaptive behaviour.

In the passive dependent pattern, one may be habitual to show his helplessness, indecisiveness and carelessness inviting constant emotional support and direction from others. In the passive-aggressive pattern, one is aggressive but his aggression (constant hostility) is demonstrated in passive and indirect ways like stubbornness, inefficiency, indirect obstructionism, inciting others not to follow or cooperate etc. In the last pattern, one is openly hostile and aggressive to the things, events and persons and his such behaviour is easily demonstrable through one's imitation, temper tantrums and destructive acts. The aggressive personality, whether his aggression are passive or violent, is a typical maladjusted and maladaptive personality. The causes of his such maladaptive behaviour pattern are all most psychological, the roots of which are lying in his defective socio-cultural environment.

Similarly criminal or delinquent behaviour, as we have already discussed in this text, is definitely a coefficient of friction between the psychological self and the defective socio-culture environment.

Sociopathic Disorder or Antisocial Personality

It has been defined by the American Psychiatric Association in DSM-II (Diagnostic and Statistical Manual of Mental Disorders-II) as below:

"Sociopaths (the persons suffering from sociopathic disorder) or anti-social personalities are "the individuals who are basically un-socialized and whose behaviour pattern brings them repeatedly into conflict with society." (1969, p. 43)

Explaining further D.M.S.-II mentioned the following characteristics of these individuals as below:

- They are incapable of significant loyalty to individuals, groups or social values.
- They are grossly selfish, callous, irresponsible, impulsive and unable to feel guilty or to learn from experience and punishment.
- Their frustration tolerance is low. They tend to blame others or offer plausible rationalization for their behaviour.
- A mere history of repeated legal or social offences is not sufficient to justify their diagnosis as anti-social personality, meaning hereby that they are not professional criminals. However, they (while posing as quite innocent, calm and quiet and normal) always engage themselves in anti-social activities.

Causes of the Sociopathic Disorder

There seems to be no significant positive correlation between sociopathy and defective heredity or biological make up. Sociopathy is a behavioural problem involving social and psychological maladjustment and, as a learned pattern of behaviour, is liable to be caused by environmental factors inherent in one's family, neighbourhood, school, society or community. The child may imitate the antisocial behaviour of his father, mother or other members of the family by accepting it as a model. The uncongenial and defective family environment on account of poverty, broken or emotionally disturbed homes, faulty parent child relationships, improper upbringing, and denial of the basic needs may put a child on the track of antisocial behaviour. Thereafter, environmental factors outside the family perpetuate and nourish this tendency by encouraging and luring him into learning sociopathic behaviour.

Treatment: Punitive measures show no favourable results. Therefore proper medical or socio-psychological measures need to be taken. Anti-convulsant or depressant helps in stabilizing behaviour and reducing antisocial trends. Psychotherapy, under psychological measures, does not prove much effective with sociopaths. However, for behaviour modification of the sociopaths, behaviour therapy shows favourable results. This measure should be taken in a controlled and well-supervised special institution instead of a jail or a mental hospital.

ALCOHOLISM AND DRUG ADDICTION

Alcoholism is classified as a disorder or personality where an individual becomes addict to alcohol to the extent of harming the self and the society. The World Health Organization (WHO) in ICD-8 (International Classification of Diseases-8) brought out in 1965 has defined alcoholics as *"excessive drinkers whose dependence on alcohol has attained such a degree that they show noticeable mental disturbance or an interference with their mental and bodily health, their interpersonal relations and their smooth social and economic functioning, or who show the prodromal (beginning) sings of such developments."*

Stages in the development of the habit of alcoholism

One gradually becomes the victim of alcoholic disorder by passing through the major stages or phases, popularly known as pre-alcoholic, prodromal, crucial and chronic.

The initial **pre-alcoholic** phase lasts from two months to up to two years and is characterized by a gradual shift from infrequent or light to frequent or heavy drinking. In the second **prodromal phase**, alcohol is used more as a drug and less as a beverage. In the third **crucial phase** the dependency on alcohol increases to the extent that there is a danger of losing everything that one values. In the last **chronic phase** the individual lives only to drink.

Consequences of alcoholic disorder

An alcoholic is likely to be ruined in terms of his physical or mental health, emotional and social relationships and economic and moral assets.

Causes of alcoholic disorder

No person is born alcoholic and therefore the causes of alcoholism are purely environmental. Drinking is learned and acquired like many personality traits and later maintained on account of its physiological and psychological dependence that it provides.

Treatment of alcoholic disorder

Alcoholism is a medical and psychological problem rather than a law and order problem. For treatment, beginning is made with the diagnosis of the early warning signals of alcoholism and then followed with (i) keeping away alcoholics from any adverse life situation and controlling their behaviour; (ii) providing essential clinical investigations; (iii) detoxificating; (iv) using deterrent measured in the form of aversion therapy; (v) providing group or individual psycho-therapy for gaining insight into behaviour and adequate adjustment; and (vi) providing socio-therapy involving modification of environmental situation and improvement of social adjustment.

Drug addiction

The American Psychiatric Association in its DSM-II has kept drug addiction in the category of personality disorders by naming it as Drug dependence. Drug addiction, like alcoholism, is also detrimental to the individual and the society. It concerns with the abnormal use of certain drugs like hashish, charas, marijuana, cocaine, LSD, mandrax, valium, dexedrine and methidrine. Excessive use of these intoxicating drugs leads to increased tolerance and physiological or psychological dependence. With prolonged use, the body system gets habituated to a particular drug so that larger doses are necessary to maintain similar intoxicating effects. Consequently, the individual develops an increasing physiological and psychological dependence on them to the extent that he feels miserable whenever the drug is not administered. He begins to show withdrawal symptoms like lack of appetite, loss of weight, constipation, restlessness, nervousness, nausea, vomiting, diarrhea, disinterest in sexual and social relationships and even epileptic seizures or acute brain syndromes in some cases. Besides, there is intense craving, anxiety, pleasant reverie and short-lived pleasing effects or state of euphoria created by the drug. Gradually, larger and larger doses are needed for similar results and one becomes dependent, physiologically as well as psychologically, on a particular drug. Thus, what begins as an innocuous experiment ends in disaster.

Causes of drug addiction

These are purely environmental and drug addiction is a matter of learned behaviour and an inadequate adjustment to the stresses of life and style of living.

Prevention and control

It involves measures like (i) Making the public aware about the causes and consequences of drug addiction; (ii) Re-structurization of unhealthy environmental conditions and reduction in the problems leading to frustration, tension and anxieties; (iii) Prohibition of drugs that have low medicinal value and are harmful; (iv) Different panel provisions against the smuggling of and trade in drugs.

Treatment

It involves (i) compulsory hospitalization; (ii) detoxification; (iii) adoption of medical measures; (iv) introduction of psychological treatment; and (v) arrangement for long-term therapy and rehabilitation.

Sexual deviations and disorders

The American Psychiatric Association has kept both sexual deviations and disorders (in its DSM-II and III) in the category of personality disorders as they are bound to affect the behaviour, conduct and personality of the individual to the extent of proving harmful to the self, others or both. Let us briefly describe both these maladaptive sex behaviours.

Sexual deviations as a term may be defined as the learned persistent habit patterns of sexual behaviour which compel an individual to seek sexual gratification from unconventional sources and means other than the genital coitus with an adult member of the opposite sex irrespective of the fact that such natural gratification is available.

Major Sexual Deviations

1. **Pedophilia** involves the deviant behaviour in which an adult is sexually attracted to a child.
2. **Homosexuality** refers to the deviation in which one prefers to derive sexual pleasure from the members of the same sex.
3. **Oralism** is the dependence on oral genital contacts for gratifying sex needs.
4. **Analism** refers to exclusive reliance on anus instead of vagina for penile insertion.
5. **Sadism** is sexual gratification from the infliction of pain upon the sexual partner.
6. **Masochism** is sexual gratification from being punished or experiencing pain.
7. **Fetishism** is a compulsive and irrational sexual attraction and obtaining sexual gratification from intimate objects or part of the body other than the genitals.
8. **Bestiality** means using animals for the achievement of sexual excitation and gratification.
9. **Necrophilia** is obtaining sexual gratification through viewing or actually having sexual relations with a dead body.
10. **Incest** is sexual activity between close blood relations.
11. **Exhibitionism** is sexual gratification obtained by exposing the genitals publicly usually to member of the opposite sex or children who are involuntary observer or complete strangers.
12. **Voyeurism** is sexual gratification obtained through peeping, observing genitals or sexual behaviour of others.
13. **Frotteurism** is sexual gratification obtained by rubbing or pressing against a member of the opposite sex.
14. **Transvestism** is sexual gratification obtained by wearing clothes appropriate to the opposite sex.
15. **Transsexualism** is behaving and believing firmly in the change of his or her sex.

Causes of sexual deviations

Sexual deviations are, to a great extent, produced by the interaction of several psychological factors. The dynamics of these factors involves patterns like (i) pathogenic family environment, (ii) earlier traumatic sex-experiences, (iii) generalized inhibitions and sexual ignorance, (iv) deprivations of outlet for normal sex behaviour, (v) fears and complexes associated with opposite sex and normal sex behaviour; and (vi) conditioning and fixation of suitable abnormal pattern of sex behaviour.

Treatment

Treatment measures are psychological. Psychotherapies like behaviour therapy, analytical therapy and group therapy prove effective in dealing with the sexual deviates. These psychological treatments should be followed by an adequate follow-up programme of proper rehabilitation.

Sexual Disorders

These are psycho-physiological disturbances that interfere with the complete enjoyment of the conventional sexual relations. Impotence and frigidity are the two main disorders of such nature.

Impotence causes an impairment in desire for sexual gratification in a man or an inability to achieve it. Frigidity, the counterpart of impotence, is found in females. It creates in them a lack of interest and desire for sexual gratification or difficulty in achieving it.

Causes

In some cases, impotence and frigidity may be attributed to physical damage to sex organs or nervous system. But more often they are caused on account of psychological effects resulting from the interaction of one's environment. These disorders involving the feeling of inadequacies are the learned responses involving factors like sex guilt, fear, complexes, depressions, conflicts, frustrations, sexual perversion and bedroom mistakes.

Prevention

Preventive measures should be adopted for the avoidance of physical injury to the sex organs and nervous system. In psychological measures of prevention, proper sex education of parents, and adults members (before and after the marriage) may prove fruitful.

Treatment

The treatment often involves establishing a stable, intimate, affectionate relationship involving confidence, security and love. A number of psychological therapies like behaviour, analytical, family and couple therapy may be successfully attempted for this purpose. In some cases of impotence and frigidity, medical measures may also prove effective.

NEUROTIC DISORDERS

Neurotic disorders like psychotic disorders are purely psychogenic disorders. There is no relevant organic pathology present in these disorders and thus may be clearly distinguished from psycho-physiological disorders which are known as the disorders of the psyche as well as the body. They can also be well distinguished from the personality or conduct disorders in the sense that their maladaptive pattern of behaviour does not lead to discomfort and harm to others and they do not violate legal or moral rules any more frequently than normal individuals.

Actually in the sequence of the behavioural disorders of psychogenic origin, neurosis falls midway between minor emotional maladjustment and psychotic disorders. Consequently, it is known as more serious than a minor emotional maladjustment and less serious than a psychotic disorder. Neurotic disorders in the real sense represent the typical ways of dealing with frustrations and conflicts and the anxiety which results from these frustrations and conflicts. However, in spite of its extreme anxiety content, neurotic behaviour is not disorganized nor is neurotic personality a split personality like that of a psychotic. Most of the neurotics function adequately in the majority of life situations and unlike psychotics, their perception of reality is generally accurate and that only rarely can their behaviour be considered bizarre. However, unlike psychotics, they are usually distressed by their behaviour and in most cases realize that it is deviant.

Although the symptoms of neurosis differ from individual to individual, the common factor is a maladaptive and self defeating life pattern. Generally the neurotic reactions and disorder "anxiety" as described in DSM-II is the chief characteristic of neuroses. It may be felt and expressed directly, or it may be controlled unconsciously. It is in this context that George W. Kisker has defined neurosis as *"a pattern of maladaptive behaviour in which a person responds to life stress with persistent anxiety or other behaviour representing attempts to control the anxiety."* (1964, p. 194)

Anxiety is closely linked to an individual's needs and motives. If the essential needs linked with affection, security, self-esteem, achievement and freedom are not satisfactorily gratified, it may give rise to the feeling of excessive anxiety or guilt which in turn results in a neurotic behaviour. But it is not to be concluded that every anxiety reaction leads to neurotic behaviour. We are occasionally quite anxious, irritable, down or restless, but it does not mean that we are neurotic. It is only when the anxiety behaviour patterns become more persistent and interfere with our ability to lead a normal life and thus depict "break downs" in the adjustment mechanism, that they are usually labeled as "neurosis."

Basic Characteristics of Neurotic Behaviour

Neurotic behaviour is assumed to be characterized with certain typical personality characteristics. In this sense Coleman (1970) has narrated the following characteristics of a neurotic personality:

1. Inadequacy and low stress tolerance.
2. Egocentricity and disturbed interpersonal relationships.
3. Lack of insight and rigidity.
4. Dissatisfaction and unhappiness.
5. Anxiety and fearfulness.
6. Persistent non integrative behaviour.
7. Presence of psychological and somatic symptoms.
8. Tension and irritability.

Major Types of Neurotic Disorders

In the list of the major types of neurotic reactions (neurosis), we generally include the following sub-types:

1. Anxiety neurosis
2. Hysterical neurosis—conversion and dissociative type
3. Phobic neurosis
4. Obsessive compulsive neurosis
5. Depressive neurosis

Let us discuss these sub-types in brief:

ANXIETY NEUROSIS

Anxiety neurosis represents a maladaptive behaviour pattern dominated by chronic apprehensiveness with recurring episodes of acute anxiety, helplessness and resentment so much so that it interferes seriously with the individual's personal and social adjustment and well-being. An interesting feature of the anxiety as Lazarus (1976) puts is that it is free floating in the sense of its being non-attracted to a single situation or specified object. Neurotic person may have fear and apprehension of every or anything without having an idea of the source of danger or why he feels this way. The length to which he goes to find things to worry about is remarkable. As soon as one cause for worry is removed, he finds another until his kith and kin lose patience with him.

Similarly, while suffering from the feeling of helplessness, an anxiety neurotic does not know which way to turn. He is sure that anything he attempts will result in failure. He is likely to be dependent on others, which he does not like to do. So, resentment builds up within him and ultimately results in aggression towards the self as he does not have enough courage to attack those upon whom he is dependent.

Ultimately, the free floating excessive anxiety coupled with the feelings of helplessness and resentment leads him to an intense state of tension, stress and discomfort well exhibited through physical reaction like increase in blood pressure and pulse rate, suffocation and difficulties in breathing, disturbances of sleep and appetite, heart palpitation and faintness, skeletal motor disorders including tremors of hands and limbs, facial tics, excessive eye blinks and lip biting. In the acute anxiety reaction or panic state, these symptoms may become so severe that the individual believes that he is having a heart attack or is dying.

HYSTERICAL NEUROSIS

Hysterical neurosis represents such neurotic reaction in which the individual exhibits behaviour that mimics physiological illness or disease (without an organic basis) for controlling his anxiety or solving psychological conflicts. There are two types of hysterical neurosis—conversion hysteria and dissociative hysteria.

Conversion hysteria

In such type of neurotic behaviour, the person in a threatening situation tries to convert his anxiety of psychological conflicts into physical symptoms like paralysis of legs, inability to see or hear or becoming faint and unconscious. His gains are often two-fold. First he gets to escape from the confronting problem and the second, being sick he is offered desired sympathy and comforts. An unemployed youth, for example, may become paralyzed in his legs. He now no more feels any guilt over his repeated failures in getting employment and finds desired support and comfort from his family. A newly married girl may become deaf so as to avoid listening to the bitter criticism from her in-laws and relatives for not bringing enough dowry.

Dissociative hysteria

The hysterical dissociative neurosis is maladaptive cognitive behaviour in which a person tries to control his anxiety or psychological problem by the dissociation of his self. Disturbances in consciousness and/or loss of personal identity are the main characteristics of such dissociative reactions. The four major types of such reactions are somnambulism, amnesia, fugue and multiple personality.

Somnambulism is sleepwalking. In their sleepwalk, people are known to travel long distances and do many complex activities.

Amnesia refers to the loss of memory. Here the individual forgets information causing distress and may remain in the state of not remembering for just a few minutes or for hours or days.

A fugue is combination of amnesia and physical flight. In this state, the loss of identity continues for a long period of time (may be for several years) and it is accompanied by actual flight from the customary surroundings. The person may suddenly leave home, travel to another place and sometimes begin a 'new life'.

Multiple personalities are the coexistence of two or more personalities in an individual each of whom may or may not be aware of the other.

PHOBIC NEUROSIS

The term "phobia" comes from the Greek word *phobos* which means panic, flight or fear. Phobic neurosis may be defined as a disorder of the behaviour in which a person experiences persistent, intense, irrational fear of a specific situation or object. In spite of his rational knowledge that his fear is unrealistic and overwhelming, he is forced to experience great apprehension and anxiety symptoms while in contact with the phobic object or situation.

One cannot draw any limit regarding the types or varieties of phobias as almost any object event or situation surrounding one's life may become stimulus for a phobic behaviour. As a result a neurotic may have fear of high places (Acrophobia) while others may be suffering from agoraphobia (fear of open places), claustrophobia (fear of closed spaces or confinement), hydrophobia (fear of water), nyclophobia (fear of darkness), ochlophobia (fear of crowds), pyrophobia (fear of fire), zoophobia (fear of animals or some particular animal) etc.

Obsessive compulsive neurosis

Obsessive behaviour represents maladaptive behaviour in which an individual is haunted with the persistent recurrence of unwelcome, absurd and disturbing idea or thought. For example, a wife may have an obsessive idea of stabbing or poisoning her husband, a mother of hurting her little girl, a son of wishing his mother's death, a husband of pushing his wife down a flight of stairs. Although the patient realizes the absurdity and irrelevance of such thoughts, he is still unable to get rid of them. The more desperately he tries to rid himself of them, the more they haunt.

Compulsive behaviour, on the other hand, represents maladaptive behaviour in which an individual is seen to perform repeated acts of unreasonable and irrelevant nature such as washing his hands again and again, checking the alarm clock several times to ensure it has been wound or returning to his house again and again to be certain that the door has been locked or following an elaborate ritualistic sequence before going to sleep. Such patterns of behaviour are maladaptive in the sense that they are unnecessary and irrational. Even the person realizes the absurdity of his compulsive acts, but he feels uncomfortable unless he performs them.

As a neurotic mental disorder, obsession and compulsions are classified together because they unusually tend to occur together. Thereby symptoms of both obsessive and compulsive behaviour are present in the obsessive and compulsive neurosis. For example a neurotic may not only worry constantly about germs and dirt (an obsession) but also be compelled to constantly wash his hands (compulsion). In doing so, he is fully assured that if he does not perform the act (like hand washing), something terrible will happen or by performing the act he has prevented certain disaster.

Depressive neurosis

This is a neurotic disorder characterized by disproportionate reactions to distressing stress situations like death of a loved one, an occupational failure or a financial set-back. In such distressing stress situation, it is not abnormal to have feelings of grief and despair in a reasonable amount. It is when these feelings become much exaggerated in intensity and duration and begin to interfere with the personal or social adjustment of an individual, that they turn into behavioural disorder—neurotic and psychotic.

Neurotic depression may be considered midway between normal depression and psychotic depression. Neurotic depressive reactions are neither too severe in degree or in duration as the psychotic depressive reactions nor as mild and simple as in normal depressive reactions.

Time is found to be a great healing factor in normal depressive reactions. In neurotic depression, however, the depressed mood does not return to normal even after a reasonable period of time as it ordinarily does in normal depressive reactions. Here the symptoms concerning depression of mood are also relatively severe. The patient may have intensive feelings of dejection, discouragement and sadness. There is a high level of anxiety and apprehensiveness and extreme feelings of self-condemnation. The person is unable to concentrate and his level of activity and initiative is lowered. In its more severe form, the anxiety and depressions are heightened to such an extent that the person is unable to work, and sits in despair viewing the dark side of life alone and sometimes thinks of committing suicide.

Depression may be viewed as hospitality or anger directed towards the self instead of being turned outward. Instead of blaming others, the person blames himself for the loss and the distressing situation. Thus, the formula for neurotic depression is self-condemnation plus an external loss. Here, the person may be viewed as punishing himself by feeling responsible for the loss or for the distress situations.

CAUSES OF PSYCHONEUROTIC DISORDERS

The most important causative factors of all neuroses are psychological. The early unhappy experiences, repressed wishes and unresolved conflicts initiate the process. Later, unfavourable circumstances, stresses and strain provide sufficient cause for learning reactions. In many cases psychoneurotic reactions often represent learned maladaptive behaviour patterns.

TREATMENT

The psycho-neurotic disorders vary from each other in relation to their nature and causation. No common treatment can therefore be prescribed for all these disorders. However, neurotic patients are curable. They respond more favourably to behaviour therapy and other psycho therapies than the patients suffering from conduct disorders or functional psychosis.

PSYCHOTIC DISORDERS

Meaning

Psychotic disorders (referred to as insanity in the lay man's as well as the legal language) represent the more serious disorders of the mind and in this sense are considered the most severe form of adjustive failure and a major illness in comparison to the neurotic disorders. A psychotic behaviour is characterized by serious forms of personality disturbance in which the patient shows (i) periodic or prolonged loss of contact with the world of reality, (ii) manifests symptoms of severe nature in the form of delusions (beliefs contrary to reality), hallucinations (perception contrary to reality like hearing voices in a completely silent room), stupor (state of immobility with partial or complete unconsciousness) incoherence (disconnected and unrelated thoughts) or violent reactions. Such patients require compulsory hospitalization.

Types

Functionally, there are three main types or categories of psychotic disorders: the affective disorders, paranoid disorders and the schizophrenic disorders. Let us have a brief idea of these types of disorders.

AFFECTIVE DISORDERS

The affective disorders involve disorders of the mood or the dimension of elation and depression. Accordingly, there are three sub-types of affective disorders, namely, manic disorder, depressive disorder and manic depressive disorder.

(i) **Manic disorder** or mania is associated with the elation of mood and excessive excitement. The patient is high in spirits, overactive and bursting with energy. He is very jovial, mobile, impatient when dealing with restrains or criticism, agitated and silly to the point of being a bore. In its most extreme form, a manic patient in his wild excitement may shout and laugh constantly, tear his clothes and is likely to become dangerous both to himself and to others (quite fit for being isolated and kept in a room).

(ii) Depressive disorder: Depression is the polar opposite of mania. The patient remains in low spirits, feels discouraged and sad. He loses his interest in things around him and may even neglect appearance and body care. The patient's movements become slow. He may either sit doing nothing or even remain in bed in a state of stupor ignoring his surroundings and need for food and hygiene. There is a marked retardation of thought process, he has difficulty summoning enough energy to think. He talks slowly and hesitantly or not at all. Contrarily, some patients with severe depression may also show signs of agitation. They pace up and down restlessly wringing their hands in despair. Agitation and retardation have some common elements also. The element of anger (rage) is likely to be present in both as the depressed individual may express hostility inwardly and outwardly. The other common feature exhibited through retarded or agitated behaviour is a severe lack of useful energy. Loss of appetite, loss of weight and constipation are common. Sexual desire tends to diminish and the patient is likely to become frigid or impotent. The patient suffers from insomnia. Early morning wakefulness is a characteristic found in severe forms of depressive disorder.

Depressive disorder also involves delusions and hallucinations usually associated with feelings of guilt. The patient may hear voices accusing him of sins that he has committed. The ideas related with disease, unworthiness and poverty are also found. The patient may be preoccupied with disease and retains his convictions despite medical examination. Feelings of depersonalization are coloured by the mood of depressive illness, Declarations like "my mind is dead", "my legs have been turned to lead", "my liver has been taken away", often reflect the state of affective disorder in individuals. Another common feature of depressive disorder is loss of confidence and pessimistic outlook. The world looks gloomy for the patients and nothing gives delight. The profound helplessness and ideas of unworthiness may lead to suicidal attempts or passive contemplation of suicide.

(iii) Manic depressive disorder: This category of affective disorder involves reactions which are neither manic nor depressive but a blend of the two occurring in a cyclic order. Consequently in this disorder there is a manic reaction (mood of elation) followed by a depressive episode (morbid ideas and despair), which may be followed by normal affect and behaviour for a period of days or months. However, all these episodes always remain cyclic in nature having all possibilities of their reoccurrence.

PARANOID DISORDERS

Paranoid disorders involves highly systematized and stable delusions of persecution or grandeur. In the delusion of persecution, the affected person feels that an individual or a group is attempting to harm him. As a result he becomes over cautious, inordinately suspicious and on a lookout for evidence to prove that his hypothesis is true. On the other hand, under the influence of grandeur delusion the person may feel that he has been endowed with some special ability, talent, gift or that he has been chosen by the Almighty, or a supernatural or earthly power to perform a great task, an invention, some reform or rule in one way or the other.

However, here it should be made clear that a paranoid person, unlike the paranoid schizophrenic, does not suffer from hallucination, has no emotional blunting and keeps his or her personality relatively intact.

On the basis of the degree or level of the severity or disorder, the paranoid disorder may be further sub-divided into two groups—paranoia and paranoid state.

Paranoia

Paranoia, sometimes called true paranoia, is rare. It is a quite developed state achieved after passing through the paranoid state. The delusion system here becomes highly systematized, organized and stable and the patient shows little or no signs of personality disorganization or incoherence in his thinking and behaviour. Contrarily, thus the paranoid individual is very well integrated. In fact, he is better integrated than normal individuals. He is cool, calculating and well controlled. He knows his enemies and plans aggression with great care and cunningness. It is in this sense that he is to be considered dangerous. His emotional reactions are in accordance with expressed ideas. The majority of them are self supporting and capable. They often go unidentified in general population and usually try to maintain their 'crazy' behaviour despite hospitalization and treatment. It is in this sense that paranoia is considered a continuous and incurable disorder.

Paranoid state

In comparison to paranoia, a person passing through paranoid state remains in it for a brief period and then recovers. It is thus less dangerous than true paranoia. The paranoid state lies between paranoia and the paranoid schizophrenia with respect to abnormalities in behaviour and resistance to deterioration. A paranoid state is neither very logical nor complex as true, bizarre and changeable than those observed in schizophrenia, and is less reasonable and is logically elaborate than those found in paranoia. Although thinking here is somewhat disconnected and hallucinations are common, yet the patient does not show any sign of impairment in intellectual and emotional spheres with the passing of years.

SCHIZOPHRENIA

In comparison to affective and paranoid disorders or the disorders described so far in this chapter, schizophrenia represents the most serious and severe mental disorder which requires a long or sometimes the whole life hospitalization of the patient.

The term *schizophrenia* literally means "splitting of the mind". Here splitting of the mind does not mean a split personality as an amnesia and multiple personality, but a marked separation of the self from reality. "The term schizophrenia," according to Coleman, *"is now used to include a group of psychotic reactions in which there are fundamental disturbances in reality relationships and in emotional and intellectual processes.* (1970, p. 275)

Schizophrenia as a rule manifests a number of symptoms, the significant ones of which are:

1. Lack of coherence in the thought process.
2. Disorganized patterns of thinking and feeling.
3. Apathy-absence of feeling.
4. Disorganized pattern of speech.
5. Peculiarities of movements of bizarre actions.
6. Autism-preoccupation with private fantasy.
7. Withdrawal from reality or seclusiveness.
8. Neglect of conduct and personal habits.
9. Delusions and hallucinations.

Types of schizophrenia

For diagnosis as well as treatment, the schizophrenic disorders are divided depending upon the severity of the symptoms and incurability of the disease.

Simple schizophrenia, as the name suggests, is the simplest type of schizophrenia characterized by an attitude of indifference or in advanced stages by extreme apathy and complete withdrawal from social relations. In this stage the person remains occupied with his self all the time by cutting off from the surrounding events.

There remains nothing to wish for, nothing to fight for and the person is contented to lead a simple, irresponsible, indifferent and dependent life often cared for by his or her family.

Hebephrenic schizophrenia: In this disorder, the affected person retreats from the stress of life by regressing to a silly, childish level of behaviour and by withdrawing into a fantasy world of his own, with accompanying emotional disintegration and psychological symptoms of schizophrenic behaviour.

Catatonic schizophrenia: The catatonic schizophrenia is diagnosed mainly by the patient's behaviour fluctuating between stupurous depression and wild excitement.

During his periods of stupor, the patient may remain for hours in a bizarre posture. For example, he may sit, stand, or keep his limb in a particular position for hours on end or he may manifest symptoms like muscular rigidity (rigidity of the muscles and a general resistance to movement), waxy flexibility (remaining in any position in which he is put), echopraxia (mimicry or imitation of what other do), echolatia (automatic repetition of words said by another) and negativism (resisting even the simplest request). He may repeatedly carry out complicated stereotyped movements such as hanging the parts of his chair in a certain sequence symmetrically with both hands or walking endlessly up and down the ward; some steps in one direction and an equal number of steps in the other.

In the excited phase of catatonic schizophrenia patients display typical schizophrenic thinking and affect. They may frequently experience fears, hallucinations and delusions involving ideas of grandeur and persecutions.

Paranoid schizophrenia: This type of schizophrenia resembles the already discussed paranoid reactions in so many aspects but differs in being less systematic and more bizarre delusions and/or hallucination, as well as greater disintegration of behaviour pattern.

As a result, paranoid schizophrenia is diagnosed mainly by the disorders of thought content involving frequent systematic delusions and hallucinations of persecutory nature resulting in loss of critical judgement and an unpredictable behaviour.

In the beginning, the individual who develops paranoid schizophrenia feels unworthy and suffers from the feeling of inferiority. He resorts to the defence mechanism of blaming others for his failure to achieve. He carries this defence to extremes by distrusting everyone to the extent that he feels certain that they have designs against him. Suspicion gradually grows into ideas of reference and ideas of reference, in turn, become delusions of persecution.

Hallucination and the delusion of persecution of paranoid schizophrenic may take many forms, sometimes of very peculiar nature. The patient falsely believes that an event has a particular significance for him individually. He may believe that the events described by the newsreader on the television are oblique references to his own life; the newspapers say things about him in code; there is a special meaning for him in the nods and glances exchanged by others on the train.

The persecutory beliefs and the element of mystery combine to produce a preoccupation with plots to kill or injure the patient. A businessman was sure that his partner trying to get rid of him and take over the company. Another patient used to wear a rubber suit at home to protect himself from the rays of an "influenced machine" which a spiteful neighbour was directing against him. A labourer declared that some people were going to lower him into hot acid and make hot iron out of him. The more interesting case is of a woman patient who remarked that "one of the doctors has stolen my mind out of my head and he is going to use it to make a lot of money."

The paranoid schizophrenic is inclined to be very verbal about his or her ideas and beliefs. Such patients are generally alert, agitated, talkative, aggressive but also confused and afraid. At times when they believe that someone wants to destroy them they destroy them first in order to save themselves. The hostile attitude and aggression shown by some of the paranoid patients reflects such trends. However, as the personality deteriorates with time, the paranoid schizophrenics tend to become withdrawn, apathetic rather than aggressive.

Causes Underlying Psychotic Disorders

The causes for one's maladaptation psychotic behaviour may be first looked into one's genetic makeup. However, it can be safely said that the genetic influences are a necessary, but not sufficient cause for the development of psychotic disorders. What is acquired as predisposition to the disorder in the form of defective genes and improper biological structure is further subjected to environmental influences. The early childhood experiences and family situations coupled with the stress events of later life acts as causative as well as precipitating factors in the development of psychotic disorders. In all cases therefore, the likelihood of an individual becoming a psychotic depends upon the magnitude or degree of the genetic predisposition (genetic plus biologically makeup) and socio-psychological factors including stressful events.

Treatment of Psychotic Disorders

Psychotic disorders, besides being a learned behaviour, have a hereditary and biological base. The treatment of such disorders may, therefore, involve the physical as well as psychological methods.

Physical method or Medical therapy carries out the physiological and medical treatment of the psychotic disorders. Some of the main measures belonging to this category are drug or chemotherapy, shock therapy and brain surgery.

In drug therapy, various drugs may prove effective in reducing the severity of symptoms and make the management of the patient convenient in the hospital or at home. **Shock therapy** involves an artificial induction of deep comas, convulsions or bath by shock inducing drugs (e.g. Insulin shock therapy IST) or electric current (e.g. Electro-convulsive therapy – ECT). It is recommended to patients who are difficult to be controlled or do not benefit from drug therapy.

Psycho-therapy involves surgical operation of the patient's brain for reducing the emotional torment of disturbing thoughts, apathy, delusions and hallucinations. However, it involves considerable risk and negative consequence and should therefore, be taken as a method of last resort.

Psychological methods or psycho-therapy provides psychological treatment of the mental disorders by a trained person (therapist) through a number of systematic approaches like psychoanalytic, client centered behaviour and group therapy etc. All these different psychotherapies aim to bring about changes in the patient's perception of himself and of his environment and thus resulting in positive enduring changes in his behaviour for achieving adequate adjustment and regaining better mental heath.

DIRECT AND INDIRECT METHODS OF TENSION REDUCTION

There is a saying that "if you remain tense, you will soon become past tense". It has quite a wide meaning and important lesson for all of us. It reflects the harmful consequences and impact of being overtensed to the extent that it may end our lives. Tension, in this sense, may be viewed as such harmful psychotical state of our mind or psyche that goes in a short or long way to impair the mental and physical health of the individual.

Ordinarily, we all face some or the other types of tense moments in our life. Our life, in general, is full of struggles. We have to struggle and strive for the satisfaction of our physiological and socio-psychological needs. However, there is not always a smooth way or sailing for the satisfaction of these needs, desires or wants. One may have to cross one or the other hurdles, or may suffer unwanted failures or frustrations, conflicts and contradictions giving birth to one or the other tensed moments in one's life. One's well-being in such a situation lies in the proper management and reduction of one's tension.

In case one manages to overcome and reduce his tension, he may remain adjusted with his self and the environment. Failure to do so can drift him towards maladjustment and impairment of his mental and physical health. It is therefore quite desirable that all of us right from our school days be acquainted with the ways and means of tension reduction.

In general, the methods used for reducing tension may be grouped into two categories, direct or problem-oriented methods and indirect or defence-oriented methods. Let us have an idea about these.

Direct or Problems-Oriented Methods

Direct methods are those methods that are employed by the individual intentionally at the conscious level to hit at the very source of tension producing situation. These are rational and logical and help the individual in finding a way out of the conflicting and stressful situation, ultimately resulting in the reduction and elimination of his tension. These are:

- **Adopting attacking behaviour:** Attack is said to be best form of defence against any stress or tension generating source or situation. The tension to win a game in competitive sports can be reduced better by adopting attacking behaviour and thus by taking initiative to go ahead of others. It also happens in other competitive situations in business, education and other professions. For example, in military combat, the tension regarding the fear of being attacked by the enemy may be released and reduced by firing the first shot. Similarly, in situation of facing tension regarding problem-solving, the attacking behaviour pays suitable dividend. One has to try with all his energy and resources for finding the solution. In some cases one may have to increase trials or improve efforts regarding the ways of attacking the problem or behavioural process.
- **Adopting compromising behaviour:** One may be able to reduce his tension by coming to terms or compromising with the tension generating source or situation in either of the way given below:
  - — He may altogether change his direction of efforts by changing the original goals i.e. an aspirant for IAS may direct his energies towards becoming probation officer in a nationalized bank or by seeking a partial substitution of goal like selection for the provincial civil service in place of the IAS.
  - — He may satisfy himself by an apparent substitute for the real thing e.g. in the case of a child, by toy car in place of a real car and in the case of an adult by rented house in place of an owned one.
  - — In case of rejection and ill-treatment in comparison to her brother, a girl child may learn the ways of reducing her tension by thinking that she is a girl and has to adjust in a male-dominated society.

- **Adopting withdrawal behaviour:** One may be able to reduce his tension by withdrawal from the tension generating situation by just accepting defeat and surrendering oneself to the powerful forces of environment and circumstances as cited below:
  - — One may altogether abandon the task of solving the problem, leave the idea of participating in a competitive game or facing interview.
  - — One may leave his or her spouse or flee from the home or the environment which is putting one under unbearable stress and tension-building situation.
  - — One may declare bankruptcy to free himself from the repayment of loans.
  - — In case one is not able to face a situation with his own resources, one may turn to other people for help by accepting defeat and narrating his despair and agonies.

Indirect of Defence-Oriented Methods

Indirect methods of tension reduction are those methods which instead of helping an individual face the tension-inducing problematic situation, directly provide one or the other defence for the well-being of his self, may be for the time being against a psychological danger. These are as below:

- **ADOPTING RELAXATION TECHNIQUES**

  One can reduce his tension and protect his self from the possible psychological and physiological damage on account of the build up tension by learning and practicing therapeutic relaxation methods, including bio feed-back, hypnosis or meditation and thus gain the required mental and physical energy so as to face the tension-inducing situation.

- **ADOPTING SELF TALK PROCEDURE**

  By talking to himself, one can gain sufficient control over his emotional arousal and other tension related reactions and it may help him to protect his self against the possible psychological and physiological damage.

- **ADOPTING DEFENCE MECHANISMS**

  Defence mechanisms can prove a big helping hand in providing desired defence (although temporarily) for protecting one's self from the possible psychological and physiological damage under tension and stress building situations. These defence oriented reactions are in fact the unconsciously learned responses. Although they involve self-deception and reality distortion, they may still be considered quite normal and even desirable except in cases where these are used to such an extreme degree that they begin to injure the self instead of protecting it. How these mechanisms are able to protect the self against the possible damage by taking control of the tension inducing situations may be clearly visualized through the detailed description of these mental or defence mechanisms given earlier in this chapter.

Role of Home, School and Society in Mental Health

Development of good mental health is to be cared for from the early childhood like the development of physical health. If this foundation remains weak, then one has to pay a heavy price at the later stage. Therefore, every effort should be made to help the children in acquiring desirable behaviour patterns and enjoying good mental health from the very beginning. The task is not so simple. It requires all-round efforts on the part of all – parents, teachers, school authorities and other members of the society – who are concerned with the welfare of the youngsters in one way or the other. They have to join hands for this greater cause as today's children are tomorrow's elders on whose shoulders the future of the nation and humanity rest. Now the question arises—what role can be played by these agencies in helping the youngsters to maintain a proper mental health? Their role as such may be visualized in taking care of the following measures aiming towards the development of good mental health among the youngsters.

1. **Good physical health:** A sound body is said to possess a sound mind. Therefore, children should be helped in maintaining good physical health. For this purpose, there should be provisions in their schools and communities for their regular physical and medical care and children should be made to imbibe proper health habits.
2. **Proper emotional development:** Youngsters should be helped in acquiring balanced emotional development. They should learn to exercise control over their emotions and to express them in a socially desirable way.
3. **Proper social relationship and acceptance:** Nothing is more sad to the child than being rejected from a group. He wants to be accepted and admired by the group. Therefore, proper care should be taken to help the child in the adjustment with his classmates and others.
4. **Behaviour of teachers and parents:** Teachers are said to be the second parents. Mental health of the children is quite influenced by the attitudes and behaviour of their teachers in the school and parents at home. Therefore, the teachers and parents should take care of the following things about their own behaviour:
   (i) Their behaviour must be sympathetic. They should always have feelings of warmth and affection for their students and children. Moreover, they should be as impartial as possible since favouritism and partisan attitude of the elders always disturb the children.
   (ii) They must not play authoritarian and dictatorial role. They should try to understand the children and render them desirable help and guidance. Children must get opportunity to talk about their worries and problems without the fear of being ridiculed or rebuffed.
   (iii) Nothing is more disturbing to a child than the inconsistency in the behaviour and attitude of his elders. Sometimes they praise a child for an act but punishes him for substantially the same act some other time depending upon their own mood. Such situations seriously disturb the child as he cannot understand what the elders expect from him. Therefore, the parents and other elders must ensure consistency in their behaviour.
5. **Proper level of aspiration:** Children should be helped to set a proper level of aspiration for themselves. They should know themselves properly. Their interests, aptitudes, strengths and limitations should be known to them. Accordingly, they should neither struggle to achieve the unexpected or difficult goals nor should they set a very low level of aspiration by selecting most easy and insignificant tasks or problems to solve.
6. **No emphasis on perfection:** The teachers and parents get their children constantly worried about the nature of their work and behaviour when they unduly emphasize complete perfection. They should keep in mind that complete perfection is an ideal state. The children should be accepted as imperfect as the rest of all of us are.
7. **Checking unhealthy competitions:** Unhealthy competitions make children uneasy and perturbed. In the blind race of outperforming others, children lose their patience, acquire

negative characteristics like jealousy, envy, dishonesty and telling lies etc. Therefore, children should not be made to engage themselves in the blind race of unhealthy competitions.

8. **To avoid the use of defence mechanisms:** Children are usually found to blame their own fates or teachers or parents or illness for their failure in examination. Such type of defence mechanisms are often used by them to protect themselves from the anxieties and worries created through their failures and frustrations. But such type of false protection is temporary. It leads to serious mental conflicts and disorders. Therefore, children should be helped to develop proper patience and power of tolerance to face the failures and frustrations in life.
9. **Appropriate Homework:** Children remain worried over their home assignments. Therefore, teacher should assign the homework with great care. It should always suit the abilities and capacities of the students and in no case, should be made a burden on their part. Parents should also provide suitable environment and help for completing their assignments.
10. **Freedom and Self-discipline:** An atmosphere of reasonable freedom and spontaneity should prevail in the school and home. Teachers and parents should seldom use corporal and capital punishment in maintaining discipline. They should encourage self-discipline on the democratic lines. Children should be made to feel the necessity of maintaining discipline and order. A sense of belongingness should be developed in them towards the school, home and society and they should be made to share responsibilities.
11. **Sex Education:** Sexual adjustment of the adolescents is also a great necessity in schools and the society for realization of their proper mental health. Therefore, provision should be made for imparting adequate sex education to them by the parents, schools and the society.
12. **Religious and Moral Education:** Loss of moral and spiritual values results in dishonesty, corruption, nepotism, favouritism, unhealthy rivalry and fighting which breeds mental conflicts, tensions and disorders. Therefore, there must be adequate provision for a balanced religious and moral education for inculcating moral and human values in children.
13. **Need for proper Guidance services:** In schools and community, there must be adequate provision for guiding and helping children in their day-to-day problems. They should be helped in removing their mental tensions, conflicts and disorders by the parents, teachers and special counsellors.
14. **Efficient methods of teaching:** Sometimes improper teaching techniques and methods bring dissatisfaction and tension in the minds of the children. Therefore, teachers should try to adopt psychological methods in their teaching. Maxims like learning by doing, from concrete to abstract, from known to unknown etc. should be followed and the child should be made to feel the joy of discovery and self-learning. The problem of individual differences should also be kept in mind and the instructions should always be planned according to the abilities and capacities of the students.
15. **Improvement and enrichment of the curriculum:** The present day curriculum is also responsible for the casualties in the mental field. Therefore, attempts should be made to bring desirable changes and modifications in the existing curriculum. The state and national educational agencies should take lead in this direction. The teachers and school authorities can also do something by paying attention to the extra-curricular aspect of the

school programme. Adequate provision for the proper outlet of emotional energy and creative expression in the form of cocurricular activities bring positive results in helping children in the acquisition of proper mental health.

16. **Mental health of the teachers and the parents:** Teachers, parents and other elder members of the society cannot be expected to improve the mental health of the youngsters unless their own mental health is sound. Therefore, as elders in the home, school and the society we should set an example by becoming models of good mental health and well adaptive behaviour. Maladaptive behaviour, patterns, the solid ground work for the poor mental health, are in fact the true learned behaviour. These are acquired and nourished like bad health and hygienic habits and caught easily like wild fire. Therefore, as far as possible we must set good example of proper and adaptive behaviour before the youngsters by keeping ourselves in good mental health.
17. **Overall improvement in the environmental conditions:** Uncongenial environmental conditions, whether at home, in school, neighbourhood, community or society, have direct bearing on the children's mental health. The behaviour and mental health of the parents and elder members of the family, the family atmosphere, the peer group relationships, school and its atmosphere, mental health of the teachers and classmates, the environment prevailing in neighbourhood, community and the society—all cast significant impact on the mental health of children. Under uncongenial and improper conditions, children's basic needs are not satisfied. They do not get adequate adjustment and development and consequently develop inferiority feelings, unusual conflicts, anxieties and complexes that lead them to mental illness and disorders. It is, therefore, the duty of the parents, teachers and other responsible members of the society to provide congenial and proper environmental conditions at home, school and the society for the development of good mental health among the youngsters.

As a matter of conclusion, we can again emphasize that the acquisition as well as maintenance of adequate mental health of children is a gigantic problem that needs all-round efforts. The cooperation of the state authorities, parents and other responsible members of the society is an urgent necessity to achieve success at this point. Uncongenial atmosphere at home and in social situations bring harmful impact on the tender minds of the children. Therefore, parents should be taken into confidence for achieving proper mental health of their children. State can also provide financial assistance to the parents or schools for upbringing the children. Establishment of Child Guidance Clinics by the state or some welfare organizations of psychiatric and mental experts in schools may also bring desirable results. In this way the problem of maintaining proper mental health of children should be tackled from all the possible sources and measures.

SUMMARY

Mental hygiene is that branch of hygiene which deals with the mental health of the individuals in the same way as physical hygiene is concerned with their physical health. Accordingly it takes care of the prevention as well as treatment of mental illness, disorder and maladjustment and also suggests ways and means of maintaining proper mental health and efficiency.

Mental hygiene aims (i) to suggest preventive measures for saving us from mental illness, maladjustment and disorders (ii) to find out the ways and means of preserving and promoting our mental health and (iii) to provide ways and means for the cure and treatment of our mental illness, maladjustment and disorders ultimately, helping us in the attainment of fuller, happier, more harmonious and more effective existence.

Mental health is concerned with the health of one's mind and its functioning in the same way as the physical health is concerned with the health of one's physical organs and their functioning. A mentally healthy person is supposed to possess an integrated personality and balanced behaviour identified on the basis of the level of his adjustment to his self, others and environment. However, there is nothing called perfect mental health. Therefore, it is always better to strive for the *optimum* mental health in place of *perfect* mental health.

A mentally healthy individual can be distinguished from others easily through his mode of living, behaviour and personality characteristics typically associated with a good mental health. We can also make a list of all the opposite negative features and characteristics of one's behaviour indicative of his good mental health to list the symptoms of one's poor mental health. Attainment of good mental health occupies a very important place in one's life. His overall adjustment to his self and the environment essential for leading a happy and contended life depends upon the acquisition of his good mental health. One has to observe certain basic principles for the attainment of good mental health specifically meant for seeking adjustment with one's self and environment.

Defence of mental mechanisms refers to the devices in the shape of a certain pattern of behaviour employed at the unconscious level by an individual for providing temporary relief from the psychological tension, conflicts and stresses and make him feel adjusted for the time being. Some of the important defence mechanism employed for this purpose may be named as rationalization, projection, reaction formation, repression, regression, aggression, displacement, fantasy and day dreaming and sublimation etc. It is not at all a good practice to employ those mechanism for protecting oneself from the psychological dangers. The relief providing them is quite temporary and resorting to such mechanism may create new difficulties for them.

Mental disorders refers to certain types of abnormalities, malfunctioning or deficiency in the behaviour or personality of an individual resulted from his maladjustment with the self and the environment. These disorders may be broadly classified into two major types — organic disorders (involving damage to the tissues of the brain for the abnormalities of the behaviour) and psychogenic disorders (also referred to as functional disorders involving no such brain damage or proven physical cause). Psychogenic disorders may be further divided into sub-types like psycho-physiological disorders and personality disorders; neurotic disorders and psychotic disorders.

Psycho-Physiological disorders refer to those disorders in which both organic and psychological factors may work side by side in terms of their origin as well as in their treatment. Migraine, anorexia nervosa, peptic ulcer, impotence and frigidity etc. may be cited as some glaring examples of such disorders. *Personality disorders* are often named as conduct or character disorders. Delinquent and criminal behaviour, sociopathic disorders, alcoholism and drug addiction, sexual deviation and disorders, etc. may be cited as examples of such disorders. *Neurotic disorders* fall midway between minor emotional maladjustment and psychotic disorders. As examples of such disorders we may cite the names of anxiety neurosis, hysterical neurosis, phobic neurosis, obsessive compulsive neurosis, depression neurosis etc. *Psychotic disorders* (referred to as insanity in the layman's as well as legal language) represent the more serious disorder of the mind. There are three more types of psychotic disorders—affective disorders, paranoid disorders and schizophrenic disorders.

The methods used for reducing the tension may be grouped into two categories — direct or problem-oriented methods (like adopting attacking behaviour, compromising behaviour or withdrawal behaviour etc.) and indirect or defence-oriented methods (like adopting relaxation techniques, self talk procedure or defence mechanisms).

Home, school and society need to join hands for the proper development of the mental health of the children by helping them in the attainment of good physical health, proper social and emotional development and adequate level of aspiration, mending their own behaviour and progress, laying no emphasis on perfection and accepting the children with their strength as well as limitations, providing due encouragement help and guidance at the time of their needs.

References and Suggested Readings

Adams, Herry E., *Psychology of Adjustment*, Ronald Press, New York, 1972.

American Psychiatric Association, *Diagnostic and Statistical Manual of Mental Disorders* (DSM-I), Washington D.C., 1952.

———, *DSM-II*, Washington DC, 1968.

———, *DSM-III*, Washington DC, 1980.

———, *DSM-IV*, Washington DC, 1994.

———, Quoted by Singh, Labh and Tiwari, G.P., *Essentials of Abnormal Psychology*, Vinod Pustak Mandir, Agra, 1971.

Arkoff, Abe, *Adjustment and Mental Health*, McGraw-Hill, New York, 1968.

Carrol, H.A., *Mental Hygiene—The Dynamics of Adjustment*, Prentice-Hall, New Jersey, 1967.

Coleman, James, C, *Abnormal Psychology and Modern Life*, D.B. Taraporewala & Sons, Bombay, 1970.

Crow, L.D. and Crow, Alice, *Mental Hygiene*, McGraw-Hill Inc., New York, 1951.

———, *Child Psychology*, Barnes & Noble, Inc., New York, 1969.

Cutts, N.F. and Moslay, P., *Practical School Discipline and Mental Hygiene*, Hoghton Mifflin, Boston, 1941.

Davison, Gerald, C. and Neale, John, M., *Abnormal Psychology*, 2nd ed., John Wiley, New York, 1978.

Drever, James, *A Dictionary of Psychology*, Penguin Books, Middlesex, 1952.

Good, Carter, V., *Dictionary of Education*, McGraw-Hill, New York, 1959.

Hadfield, J.A., *Mental Health and the Psychoneurosis*, George Allen & Unwin, London, 1952.

Kartz, Barney and Lehner, G.F., *Mental Hygiene in Modern Living*, Ronald Press, New York, 1997.

Kisker, George, W., *The Disorganized Personality*, McGraw-Hill, New York, 1964.

Klein, D.B., *Mental Hygiene*, Revised edition, Henry Holt, New York, 1965.

Lawkan, P.B., *Mental Hygiene in Public Health*, McGraw-Hill, New York, 1949.

Lazarus, Richard S., *Patterns of Adjustment*, McGraw-Hill, Kogakusha, *International Student Edition*, Tokyo, 1976.

Lehner, George and Ela Kubo, *The Dynamics of Personal Adjustment*, Prentice-Hall, New York, 1964.

Levin, M.J., *Psychology—A Geographical Approach*, McGraw-Hill, New York, 1978.

Mangal, S.K., *Abnormal Psychology*, Revised ed., Sterling Publications, New Delhi, 1987.

Menninger, K.A., *Human Mind* Quoted by R.N. Sharma in Shiksha Manovigyan, Rastogi Publications, Meerut, 1967.

Morgan, C.T., *Introduction to Psychology*, 2nd ed., McGraw-Hill, New York, 1961.

Munn, N.L., *The Fundamentals of Human Adjustment*, Georg G. Harrap, London, 1968.

Page, James, D., *Abnormal Psychology*, Tata McGraw-Hill, New Delhi, 1976.

Walten, N.E.W., *Personality, Maladjustment and Mental Hygiene*, 1951.

World Health Organization (WHO), *International Classification of Diseases (ICD-8)*, 1965.

World Health Organization (WHO), *International Classification of Diseases (ICD-9)*, 1979.

38

Sex Education

CHAPTER COMPOSITION

NEED AND IMPORTANCE OF SEX EDUCATION

Among the many inner urges and drives of human being, sex is the most universal and powerful drive. Leaving aside the extravagant claims of Freud, we can observe that one's interest in sex is instinctive and starts from early infancy. It can be revealed through his interest in playing with his genital organs and asking questions like—where do babies come from? Why does the baby not possess the similar passage to urinate as I? This spontaneous curiosity about sex related things is generally taken as a sign of great danger. The children get rebuked by the parents or are given wrong information in a state of great hush and embarrassment. This intensifies their curiosity in a much greater force than earlier.

Now they try go get information from other sources. In doing so, they more often knock wrong doors and thereby gather wrong and dangerous information. This does not happen with small children alone. Even adolescents and mature adults suffer a lot on account of improper or many a time incorrect information received from misleading literature, movies and sexually perverted, ill-motivated or inexperienced companions. Such inaccurate, inadequate and even distorted information about sex from unwholesome sources (even parents can misguide their children for saving their prestigious position) not only creates unhealthy attitude towards sex and sex problems but also runs a risk of serious mental disorders, complexes and behavioural maladjustment. The fear of impotency, frigidity, diseases, neurotic maladjustment, sex perversions, eve-teasing, excessive sexual interests, to a great extent, are the product of unnecessary repression, taboos, secrecy and guilt environment surrounding the topic of sex.

Therefore, there is a need to break the silence and remove the veil of unnecessary secrecy surrounding sex. We are not to allow sex to grow as a subject of excessive curiosity in the minds of youngsters. They should get correct and appropriate answers to their queries from the right sources. Moreover, we cannot leave the youngsters perplexed and bewildered at the onset of puberty. They have to be made to feel at home with their bodily changes and natural phenomenon like nocturnal emission and menstruation etc. There is a great need for proper sublimation of powerful sex instinct at this age. It is the age where the need for sex information and guidance is strongly felt by the youngsters themselves. The parents, teachers and other responsible members of the society have to remain vigilant. Instead of engaging themselves in eve-teasing; writing obscene remarks and sketching obscene scenes, the youth should be made to develop a healthy social attitude towards sex. One should not be allowed to view the sex aspects of life with distaste, horror, sly interest, excessive interest and one should not have guilt feeling or complexes in maintaining socially approved sex relations. All this need a well knitted scientific programme of sex education for youngsters so that they can grow as balanced individual in feeling, thoughts and deeds.

HOW TO IMPART SEX EDUCATION?

In the foregoing discussion we have realized the need of sex education. Now to give it a practical shape, it is needed that the problem be viewed from different angles. Normally, we are required to concentrate on the following questions:

- What is to be imparted in sex education?
- When should it be started or what is the appropriate age for imparting such education?
- By whom should it be imparted?

Let us try to seek answers to these questions.

What is to be Imparted in Sex Education?

What type of sex education should be imparted to the youngsters? What should they be told or what information should they get, is the basic problem of sex education. Let us try to think over the problem through the following systematic steps:

SATISFACTION OF CHILD'S SEX CURIOSITY

As discussed earlier, the sex interest of a child can be revealed through his utmost curiosity about sex. Therefore, answering these queries of small children should be regarded as an essential beginning in imparting sex education. It must be remembered that a child's curiosity about mother's pregnancy, birth of a new baby in the family and difference in genital organs of opposite sex, is not a sign of sexuality. It is a natural desire to discover an important scientific fact as Kenneth Walker puts it, "*It is as natural as his desire to know where the sun has gone to when it drops down below the horizon.*" (1949, pp. 148-49)

Therefore, elders should not feel embarrassed in answering such questions. They must be answered as simply and naturally as possible without involving unnecessary details. Neither the children should be given wrong information by the elders to keep their images as idealistic, ethical and valuable, nor should they be rebuked.

One of the important areas of extreme curiosity for small children is the genital organs. They are curious about the differences between the genital organs of the two sexes. Therefore, an early attempt should be made to satisfy their such curiosity. Mother can play the leading role in explaining these differences. Moreover, small boys and girls should be made to bathe together naked, so that they can know the difference in each other and do not have unnecessary curiosity about the sex organs of opposite sex. Some parents also adopt the plan of bathing naked with their small children. Some enthusiasts go further ahead and advocate that children should be allowed to watch their parents in their sex act. But it is too much. It not only leads them to premature serious sex interest but can also create emotional and mental complexes as Uday Shanker explains it, *"It may look like intimidation her, be labouring her and doing some serious harm by handling her in that unusual manner."* (1958, p. 155). Therefore parents as elders should not give any opportunity to the child to vitiate his mind by exposing serious adult sex activities.

SEX EDUCATION IN ADOLESCENCE

After traveling along the path of childhood, the child enters adolescence. It is the period of intensive sex consciousness as the sex impulses are strongly felt during this age. Moreover there are typical changes in their internal as well as external bodily organs. These sudden changes and strange sensations in their sense organs accompanied by occasional seminal emissions in boys and menstruation in girls make them perplexed and restless. Therefore, it is strongly needed that they must be given proper information about these changes before they are caught unaware. The following things should be taken into consideration for this purpose:

(a) Initially, these grown-up children should be given adequate information regarding general hygiene and growth, the function of the glands of internal secretion, working and functioning of the reproductive organs and sex processes concerning the birth of a baby, in a simple and most natural way.

(b) They should be given prior information about all the anatomical and physiological changes that take place during adolescence so that they may not be caught unaware.

(c) The seminal discharge through the process of nocturnal emissions also known as wet-dreams, and masturbation brings a lot of anxiety and creates unnecessary complexes in adolescent boys. Even some religious literature also, like the one I read which said, "Brahmcharya is life and sensuality is death", creates lot of misunderstanding by exaggerating the harms of seminal discharge. Therefore adolescents need to be told beforehand that such occasional discharges are absolutely natural and are an indication that they are not small children now but are growing into men to play their role as fathers. "They should be told," as Prof. Uday Shanker puts it, "*that as they are eating every day, the semen will be formed and it will accumulate but it cannot go on accumulating indefinitely and must have a safety valve and so this over-flow of the accumulated semen is the nocturnal emission.*" (1958, p. 157)

Similarly masturbation should not be thought as a sinful act and adolescents should be saved from unnecessary worry and anxiety about this act. Observation made by Kretschmer in the connection may prove quite beneficial to such adolescents. He writes, "*Masturbation is a harmless physiological transitional phase and byproduct of the healthy sexual impulse: it acts as safety-valve when sexual intercourse is prevented by one of the many inevitable obstacles created by civilized communal life. Masturbation can only be counted as perversion when it is practiced for its own sake, i.e. when it acquires a greater value than sexual intercourse, and is substituted for it even when coitus (intercourse with opposite sex) is legitimately possible.*" (Walker Kenneth, 1949, p. 156).

But with the above discussion, it should not be concluded that masturbation is a useful and essential act to be practiced by adolescents for their proper growth and development. They should never be persuaded to do this. In any case, this unusual practice should not be given importance and paid unusual attention. The adolescents should be asked to avoid unnecessary excitement like use of intoxicants, watching sexmovies, obscene pictures and reading cheap sex literature. They should also be made to realize that lonely and unoccupied moments motivate one to masturbate, therefore, they should try to engage themselves in work of some kind.

(d) While adolescent boys have an excessive fear of becoming impotent due to wet-dreams or masturbation, adolescent girls are noted to be afraid of 'being pregnant' at any time. Like seminal discharges in boys, the first sight of menstruation flow may also cause a shock to the unprepared adolescent girls. Therefore, girls should be made to understand that the flow of menstrual blood is not an abnormality but it is an indication that they are getting ready to play part of mothers. Also the conditions and processes of pregnancy and child birth should be explained to them clearly when they are haunted with unusual abnormal fears.

Knowledge of Venereal Diseases

Young children as well as adolescents and adults need to be told about the veneral diseases in a scientific way. They should learn the causes, measure of prevention and treatment of these diseases.

Appropriate Sex Behaviour

The adolescents as well as adults should be told the basic difference between the sexual behaviour of human beings and that of animals.

Right Attitude Towards the Members of Opposite Sex

Right attitude towards members of the opposite sex should be developed among young boys and girls. They must learn to pay due regard to the opposite sex. We have to make them realize that both males and females are equal and superior physical strength gives men no right over women. Such dangerous ideas like women are not to be trusted in sex matters, they are animals endowed with strong sex impulses and appetites; they are made to suffer and tolerate and men are always cruel in sex acts, etc., should be removed from the minds of the youths.

Healthy Attitude Towards Love and Marriage

Last, but not the least, is the inculcation of healthy attitude towards love and marriage in adolescent boys and girls and thus they should get pre-education for playing the role of marital partners. Ignorance of sex process or the feeling of guilt, sin and unusual shame creates complicated problems. Sometimes it results in fights, emotional and mental disorders and turbulence in marital relationships. Therefore, adolescent boys and girls should be educated, as Uday Shanker puts it, "*to have no ideas of impurity and no inhibition or sense of guilt or shame in functioning as sex partners and they should be made to think that they are created by nature for such cooperation in the vital enterprise and that to love and to enjoy sex life is their privilege*". (1958, p. 158)

When Should Sex Education be Imparted?

At what age should sex education be started is a controversial question. Many fears are expressed about starting it at an early age. It is believed that talking to an immature child about sex processes creates excessive curiosity and interest in the sex matters and thus brings harmful consequences. It may be true to some extent, if we try to give young children more than needed information for the immediate satisfaction of their curiosity. Their instinctive curiosity does not need to know about the processes of sex acts or its physiological satisfaction but we must not hesitate to answer the spontaneous and innocent questions of our children. Frankly answering, without involving unnecessary details, does not involve any risk. Therefore, in my opinion, sexual guidance of the youngsters should begin at a very early age.

The starting of sex education from an early childhood can also be supported on other grounds. The sexual behaviour of childhood gets a typical turn in adolescence. The child needs a pre-preparation to face the strange sensations of adolescence. Therefore, there is a strong need of sex education before one attains puberty, not only for the sublimation of one's powerful sex instinct but also to equip him or her with correct scientific sex information in order to pass through the challenging phases of adolescence.

Moreover, sex education cannot bear the desired fruit unless it is imparted in a natural and frank atmosphere without involving emotional reactions. But with the onset of puberty, the child becomes very sensitive and emotional and already develops an emotional attitude towards sex of healthy or unhealthy type. Thus adolescence is too late a period for beginning sex education. Therefore by all means and in all cases, it should be started from a much earlier period.

But this does not mean that we should not impart sex education to adolescents or adults. Sex knowledge, with its utmost importance, is essential at all stages of human life. It is as much essential to the adults as to the adolescents. Therefore, sex education should always be taken as a continuous process from infancy till the old age.

By Whom Should Sex Education be Imparted?

Who is to be assigned the responsibility of imparting sex education to the youngsters is again a controversial question. Tucker and Pout beautifully describe the attitudes of elders in this connection:

'The father often expresses the opinion that training children is mother's job.

'Mothers say they feel it is the teacher's task to instruct adolescent children;

'Teachers generally feel that it is the work of an outside specialist teacher'.

In other words, everybody realizes the necessity of moral (sex) education and everybody wants to shift the work on to some one else." (1937, p. 17)

The opinions expressed above do not only reveal the general human tendency of shirking from the responsibility but also signify the difficulty of the task.

It is really very difficult to face the embarrassing questions of the girls and boys related to sex and find suitable words to answer them. We elders always take sex as a matter of top secrecy and attach it with morality. Society has also made sex a subject of top secrecy by placing so many restrictions and taboos. Conditions in countries like India are more conservative where sex is taken as the negation of moral sense. In such atmosphere, it is difficult to talk about sex by teachers and outsiders. Even parents feel difficulty in imparting necessary sex education to their wards due to their own attitude towards sex. They fear that they will lose their prestige and respect if they talk to their children about sex matters.

But whatever the difficulties may be, they ought to be faced by the parents, responsible elders and teachers for the welfare of children.

The initiative should come from the parents. During infancy and early childhood, mothers can take the lead in satisfying the spontaneous curiosity of their children about sex. Later on, as the adolescence approaches and the child requires some special essential sex information and guidance, both mother and father can take the responsibility of educating their children. Father can take the responsibility of male children and mother can reveal the sexual realities to the daughters. In many cases, grandparents may also prove quite helpful in this task.

The help from other responsible elder members can also be taken. *Bhabhi* (the wife of the elder brother), *chachi* (wife of the father's brother) or elder sisters are more close to young adolescent girls and can frankly talk about such delicate issues of sex and help in removing unnecessary fears and doubts related to sex. Similarly, adolescent boys can be helped by their uncles and other elder male relatives. Thus parents as well as elder relatives have the primary responsibility of developing a better sexual life for their children and only they can be the best teachers for their children.

The teachers, also to some extent, should try to share the responsibility of imparting sex education to youngsters. In schools, there should be some arrangement for sex education (separately for girls and boys if they are co-educational). Classes of general hygiene and physiology and programmes related to physical education and personal guidance can be utilized for this purpose. There must be standard literature related to sex in school libraries so that students may discover the secrets of sex and acquire correct information. They should also be helped in developing healthy attitude towards sex and the opportunities should be provided for the sublimation of their sex instinct.

The desired help may also be taken from professional like sexologists, medical practitioners or other specialists for providing expert and first-hand knowledge of sex to the youngsters.

But the suggestion that sex education should be left to the outside specialists is quite impracticable and uneconomical in our country. However, school authorities should try to get the help of the above-mentioned experts by occasionally inviting them for delivering talks about sex processes, problems and diseases etc.

Therefore, parents and to some extent the teachers and school authorities should come forward for sharing the responsibility of imparting sex education to the children and I am sure, if they are determined they will have a smooth sailing. Hesitation, if any, can be removed by arranging some orientation courses for them.

SUMMARY

There is a great need of imparting sex education to the children. It can help the children in getting proper information about their sex related curiosity and problem. The children and adolescents especially can be helped in developing healthy desirable attitude towards sex with the help of the proper sex information and guidance. Moreover, by doing this they can be saved from a number of physiological and psychological dangers associated with the denial of proper access to sex information and education.

Sex related interest and sex urge is felt by the human beings from the very early age. Therefore sexual guidance and education of the youngsters should be initiated at a very early age. The sex curiosity of small children should be satisfied as simply and naturally as possible without involving unnecessary details. Adolescence is regarded as the period of intensive sex consciousness on account of the typical bodily changes and feeling of strange sensations in their sex organs. Therefore, there is urgent need of providing necessary knowledge about the anatomy and physiology of the changes related to their sex organs, health and hygiene including dangers related to unsafe and pre marital sex etc. They must be helped in developing right attitude towards members of the opposite sex along with the inculcation of very healthy attitude towards love and marriage for leading a happy married life as an adult.

The initiative for imparting sex education from an early age should essentially come from the parents. Father can take the responsibility of male children and mother for the female ones. Grand-parents and other responsible elder members may also usefully, cooperate in this task. For the adolescents, valuable help can be provided by other mature members of the family and relatives like sister-in-law, brother-in-law, uncle and aunt etc. School education should also be geared for imparting necessary age-related sex education to the youngsters. There must be standard healthy literature related to sex in school libraries. Curriculum and experiences related to general hygiene, physiology, biology and physical education should be linked to provide necessary healthy sex education to the youngsters. In addition, there must be provision of desirable cocurricular programmes, lectures and seminars from the experts in providing useful sex information and guidance to the youngsters.

References and Suggested Readings

Kretshmer, Quoted by Kenneth Walker, *The Physiology of Sex*, Penguin Books, Middlesex, 1949.

Shankar, Uday, *Problem Children*, Atma Ram, Delhi, 1958.

Tucker, T.F. and Pout, Muriel, *Sex Education in Schools*, 2nd ed., Gerald Howe, London, 1937.

Walker, Kenneth, *The Physiology of Sex*, Penguine Books, Middlesex, 1949.

39

Guidance and Counseling

CHAPTER COMPOSITION

- Meaning and Definitions of the Term Guidance
- Need of Guidance in Schools
- Counseling—Meaning and Definitions
- Relationship between Guidance and Counseling
- Spheres of Guidance
- Summary
- References and Suggested Readings

MEANING AND DEFINITIONS OF THE TERM GUIDANCE

There are problems and problems in human life. The confrontation between the needs, abilities and resources of an individual on one hand and the conditions prevailing in his environment on the other starts from quite an early age and continues till one's death. An individual makes his best efforts to overcome the difficulties or adjust to his environment. He may, for this purpose, try to develop his abilities or capacities or formulate plans. But there arc times when he realizes that the path leading towards his goal is not visible unless he learns or acquires certain abilities and capacities. In such a situation, he needs someone to illuminate his path or assist him in the process of acquiring desired knowledge or skills. In other words, he needs guidance to enable him to overcome his difficulties and develop his abilities and capacities. Thus the term 'guidance' is referred to as a process of rendering any kind of assistance, help or advice to any individual by another individual. It is a simple meaning of the term guidance. To get a little more insight into the meaning of this term, let us try to look at some of the definitions given by eminent scholars.

Crow & Crow

Guidance is assistance made available by properly qualified and adequately trained men or women to an individual of any age to help manage his own life activities, develop his points of view, make his own decisions and carry his own burdens. (1962, p. 14)

Jones

Guidance is the help given by one person to another in making choices and adjustments and in solving problems. (1951, p. 85)

Skinner

Guidance is a process of helping young persons learn to adjust to self, to others, and to circumstances. (1968, p. 67)

Secondary Education Commission

Guidance involves the difficult art of helping boys and girls to plan their own future wisely in the full light of the factors that can be mastered about themselves and about the world in which they are to live and work. (1953, p. 139)

Analysis of these definitions reveals the following facts about 'Guidance':

(i) Guidance is personal assistance. Whether given individually or in group, it aims to render personal help or assistance.

(ii) To render guidance is not everybody's job. It is the work of the most competent, mature and able persons. Moreover, in the field of psychology, guidance occupies a technical position and requires the services of trained guidance personnel, career masters, psychologists and counselors etc.

(iii) Guidance can be rendered to any person of any age who is in need of it. In this way its scope is very wide and it covers different individuals of both of the sexes with varying age and temperaments.

(iv) Guidance aims at developing the individual to his capacity for self direction. It helps him become independent and self-reliant so that he can solve his own problems and carry his own burdens. It should not, therefore, be understood as synonymous to direction. Crow & Crow has emphasized this fact in the following words:

"Guidance is not giving directions. It is not the imposition of one person's point of view upon another person. It is not making decisions for an individual which he should make for himself. It is not carrying the burden of another's life. (1962, p. 14)

In this way a person who gives guidance neither makes an individual dependent on him nor does he impose his will. The person who is guided is free to accept or reject the advice given to him.

(v) Guidance is the process of helping a person in adjusting to himself, to others and to his own peculiar environment. First of all, it renders him help in understanding himself. Then it helps him in his acquaintance with the things and world around him. Then finally it helps the person to seek harmony between his personal needs and ambitions and the peculiarities of his own environment. In this way, guidance can be described as a process of assisting an individual with his adjustment problems.

(vi) Guidance aims to prepare individuals for their future. It helps them acquire essential abilities and capacities for the tasks to be accomplished in future. It also helps the individuals in the selection of proper future profession and role in the society and enables then to play their roles successfully.

In this way, guidance has both personal and social significance. It aims to help an individual in the process of this adjustment with himself and his environment. It helps him to develop his strengths and abilities to achieve utmost personal and social efficiency. It also aims to stop wastage of human power and physical resources by helping individuals fit themselves suitably in the society.

Taking such wide meaning and implication, guidance must be regarded to possess a very wide and comprehensive scope. It takes into consideration every problem of human life and is concerned with the assistance given to any individual of any age. But as far as the field of education and psychology is concerned, we are only required to care for the welfare of the students' community. Therefore, in the present text, we would confine ourselves to the guidance given to the students as far as possible in school situations for their welfare and progress.

For this purpose let us establish a workable definition of the term 'Guidance'.

Guidance is referred to as a process of assisting or helping the students by properly trained teachers, career masters or special guidance personnel in planning their own future wisely and in developing their potentialities to the maximum for them to solve their immediate or future problems and to lead a successful personal and social life.

NEED OF GUIDANCE IN SCHOOLS

Guidance is defined as the process of helping an individual in his adjustment to self and to his environment. It helps him to solve his problems and fulfil his needs. If we try to analyze the problems faced by the students, we can conclude that they can be categorized under three heads, viz. educational problems, vocational problems and personal or psychological problems. Consequently, students need help for their educational, vocational and personal or psychological adjustments as well as development.

Therefore, in general we can summarize the need of guidance in the following three ways:

Educational Need

While getting their education, students are confronted with numerous problems like selection of subjects or courses, making choices for improving their handwriting, pronunciation and study habits. They also desire to be helped in the process of learning and acquiring specific knowledge and skills. In this way, students' needs and problems in the educational field can be both adjustive and developmental and thus guidance is needed for helping them in their proper educational adjustment as well as in the proper educational development.

Vocational Need

One of the important aims of education is to equip children so that they can earn their livelihood in future. There are a number of occupations and professions that can be adopted by them. Proper knowledge of these job options and opportunities is very essential for the maximum utilization of personal as well as national resources. Guidance services can help a lot in this direction by imparting valuable vocational information. Besides, for helping in the selection of future jobs, proper guidance is needed by the students. Every individual is not fit for every job. Round pegs should be fitted in round holes and square pegs in squares holes. Professional adjustment is essential for succeeding in life as well as for bringing prosperity to the nation. It is possible only through the right choice of the job suiting one's abilities, interests and aptitudes and for this one needs guidance by competent people at an early age.

PERSONAL OR PSYCHOLOGICAL NEEDS

Guidance is also needed for the personal as well as psychological adjustment of the children. Emotional as well as social adjustment is very essential for their proper development and success in life. Maladjustment creates serious problems. It may turn them into problem children or may breed mental illness. Therefore, children need help in relieving themselves from their mental conflicts, tensions and anxieties. They need assistance for making proper social and emotional adjustment. All such assistance or help makes guidance a necessary requirement of the youngsters.

In this way, rendering of guidance to the students should be regarded as a great necessity if we really want to help them in their proper adjustment to self and to the peculiarities of their environment by developing their abilities and capacities. This need becomes more urgent in countries like India where most of the parents are illiterates or semi-educated. Therefore, the responsibility of rendering guidance to the youngsters should be felt by the teachers and steps should be taken to provide regular guidance in our schools.

COUNSELING—MEANING AND DEFINITIONS

The word 'counseling' in its general interpretation stands for the act of giving advice, providing suggestion and consultation, expressing opinion etc. In our day-to-day life, we generally make use of this term in the above referred senses. When we are confronted with a personal or family problem, we approach an experienced and respectable aged person in our neighbourhood or village for necessary counseling (his valuable suggestions, opinions or piece of advice) for solving our problem. Whether it is a problem or a matter concerning the marriage or service, selection of a proper school, course or occupation for our children, financial matters, or setting a dispute regarding property or occupation, we always consult (take counseling) someone on whom we have the required faith. Here it is not necessary that all these persons whom we approach are sufficiently trained professionals or experts in the matter of our concern. The main thing is that we believe that their consultation will certainly help us in some way or the other. However, there are also professionals and trained personnel available as lawyers, doctors, auditors, social workers, brokers, commission agents etc. who, solely deal in providing counseling in the matters related to their respective fields. Thus in our day-to-day life, counseling is seeked by each of us at different occasions for help in the hours of the need. However, as far as the use of the term 'counseling' in the field of education or psychology is concerned, it is used as simple as referred above. A few definitions of this term put forward by eminent authors and psychologists may be cited to make it clearer:

Rogers

Counseling may be defined as a series of direct contacts with the individual which aims to offer him assistance in changing his attitudes and behaviour. (1942)

Shostrom and Brammer

Counseling is self-adjustive process which helps the client become more self-directive and self responsible. (1952)

Apart from the above definitions, a comprehensive definition cited in a textbook published by NCERT (1998) will certainly help us in understanding the meaning and concept of the term 'counseling'. This definition given by E.G. Vedanayagam runs as under:

"Counseling is an accepting, trusting and safe relationship in which clients (or the counselees) learn to discuss freely what upsets them, to define their goals, to acquire the essential social skills, and to develop the courage and self-confidence to implement desired new behaviour."

The above cited definitions can now substantially help us for arriving at the following conclusions about the meaning and nature of the term.

- Counseling is that behavioural process which involves at least two persons namely counselee and the counselor.
- The two persons, counselee and the counselor, must have a very cordial and satisfying relationship based on mutual understanding, acceptance, faith and trust.
- In counseling, the counselee must be provided with the essential facilities and opportunities for clearly putting up his problem before the counselor or the counselor should have such guts, courtesy and skills to know on his own about the problem of his counselee.
- It is very essential to have a continuous and direct contact between the counselor and the counselee for the proper give and take of the required counseling.
- Counseling should not be misunderstood as a task of providing some immediate solution or accepting the burdens of the problems of the counselee by the counselor himself. His task is only to help him by providing valuable suggestions, in the form of ideological and psychological support for equipping him to gain proper insight and strength for solving his problem.
- Counseling provides ways for self adjustment by enhancing the abilities and capacities of the counselee for facing the problems and challenges himself. Counseling thus aims for the development of self-dependence in the counselee instead of remaining dependent on the counselor.
- In counseling, all possible attempts are made to bring such desirable modifications in the interests, attitudes, abilities and the overall behaviour of the counselee so that he may be able to develop his abilities and capacities for gaining proper confidence in solving his problem and proceeding further on the path of his personal and social development.

Hence as a conclusion we may consider counseling in the form of a *such helping and developing process in which the counselor (by way of establishing cordial and satisfying relationship) tries to bring desirable modification and improvement in the interests, attitudes, abilities and other behavioural aspects of the counselee aimed to make him quite independent in solving his immediate problems and proceeding properly on the path of self and social progress.*

RELATIONSHIP BETWEEN GUIDANCE AND COUNSELING

Guidance and counseling both serve the same major purpose of helping a guidance or counseling seeking individual in developing his capacity for effectively facing and solving his problems independently with his own efforts. Both thus aim at providing valuable suggestions and guiding such that he can sort out his problems independently. None of these desires to make the individual dependent on the guidance worker or counselor.

The question arises now as if they are so similar in their purpose then what is the need of employing the two terms—guidance and counseling. If these are synonymous then why not use any one for avoiding any confusion. The answer lies in negative. Both may have same aims, but there definitely lies some difference in their methodologies and approaches. Let us try to see and note these differences.

Guidance in all its forms and shapes refers to a process of guiding such a needy person (guidance seeker) who has lost his path or got confused in making the right choice while standing on a crossway. The duty of guidance worker here lies in pointing out to him the most appropriate way suiting to his abilities and capacities so that he can go ahead to achieve his targets. He neither gives directions nor walks along with him for attaining the goal but only guides, i.e. points out the right way by providing proper information, knowledge and techniques. Such type of guidance can be given to any guidance seeker individually or in groups. We can organize proper guidance services for this purpose in our schools. The students here can receive various types of information and guidance for the solution of their personal, educational and vocational problems. However, such type of information sharing does not necessarily demand the establishment of closeness, support or mutually satisfying trustworthy cordial relationship between the guidance worker and guidance seeker as happens in the case of a counselor and counselee.

Thus counseling demands something more in comparison to guidance in the following ways:

(i) Firstly, counseling has to be done purely on individual basis. Guidance may be given in groups but counseling can't be arranged in such a way. It is an individual phenomenon. In counseling, the counselee is treated as a unique person in a unique situation. Here he has to approach the counselor in his personal capacity, open up his self for disclosing his problem, discuss it without any reservation for getting in return the appropriate unique advice, help and assistance for solving his problem. It is needless to say in case of consultation and advice that there lies a dire necessity of having mutually satisfying, cordial and trustworthy relationship between the counselor and the counselee.

(ii) There is an urgent need for a continuous face to face direct relationship between the counselor and the counselee for getting desired results from the counseling. Guidance can be sought otherwise, despite not having any such personal direct contact, many a times through postal means or telephones.

(iii) In comparison to a guidance worker, a counselor's task is more serious, technical and specialized. It can't be performed satisfactorily by the teachers who do not possess necessary educational background and professional training as counselors.

Thus in close scrutiny, we may observe some apparent differences between guidance and counseling. However, on the practical ground, we don't assume any much difference between them. Guidance services, in their comprehensive meaning and applications, automatically include counseling. Similarly, in providing counseling services a counselor has to resort to all the guidance related techniques like providing direction, guidance and advice to the counselee depending upon the needs of the situation. The only mentionable difference between guidance and counseling lies in the fact that in counseling, there is a dire need for more cordial, and mutually satisfying as well as trustworthy relationship between the counselor and the counselee for providing proper counseling than needed in the case of giving guidance.

However, as far as their mutual relationship is concerned, they may be regarded as complementary to each other. Somewhere starting is done with counseling and it graduates into guidance or guidance is made into use as its helping hand. In other situations, starting is made with guidance and it finally ends with some appropriate counseling services. As far as school situations are concerned, generally the group guidance takes the lead and then it is followed by individual guidance. It helps in providing the students some essential general information about the school, its resources and functioning, educating them in terms of prevention and treatment of physical, physiological and psychological deficits in their behaviour and health and providing desired vocational and educational guidance etc. Going in this direction if the students are confronted with such a problem that needs a lot of personal contact and mutually satisfying and somewhat confidential exchanges between them and the guidance worker, then such personal guidance may take the form of counseling. Counseling deals with the problems of children in a more systematic and professional way by going deep into their nature and possible causes. A counselor understands his counselee well and has sufficient skills, ability as well as experience for providing better advice and consultation to him for the proper adjustment. Counselee, on account of the very nature of the counseling setup, has full confidence in the counselor and is thus likely to be benefited more with the counseling services in comparison to the guidance. However, if guidance session can be arranged with the necessary inner spirit of counseling, and guidance workers are equipped with necessary skills and educational background, then there remains hardly any difference between such well-organized guidance services and counseling. Therefore we must try to make use of the available guidance as well as counseling services in schools in their proper mutual coordination for serving the interests of the students in the maximum effective way.

SPHERES OF GUIDANCE

To whom guidance is to be provided and what should be the main areas or spheres of such guidance should be dealt with at this stage. As far as imparting of guidance is concerned, it is the necessity of all the human beings. Therefore, it needs to be provided to all, irrespective of their wide individual differences related to age, caste, colour, creed, religion, sex, education and socio-economic status etc. It can be provided on an individual basis or in groups by taking into consideration the individual or group needs. These individual and group needs may be quite diversified and distinctive in nature and therefore it is quite difficult to draw a definite boundary for limiting the fields and scope of guidance. However, as far as the needs as a student is concerned, we can limit our discussion here for making provision of certain guidance services usually provided in the schools. In this connection, the Bureau of Educational and Vocational Guidance has suggested to divide the guidance services provided in schools in the following three main spheres:

(*i*) Educational Guidance, (*ii*) Vocational Guidance and (*iii*) Personal Guidance.

Let us try to now understand the nature, composition and functioning of the above three types or spheres of guidance services provided in our schools.

Educational Guidance

WHAT IS EDUCATIONAL GUIDANCE?

Let us try to understand its meaning and nature on the basis of some popular definitions given below:

Jones

Educational Guidance is concerned with assistance given to pupils in their choices and adjustment with relation to schools, curriculum course and school life. (1951, p. 85)

Myers

Educational Guidance is a process concerned with bringing about between an individual pupil with his distinctive characteristics on the one hand, and differing groups of opportunities and requirements on the other, a favourable setting for individual's development or education. (1947, p. 19)

These two definitions reveal the following facts concerning the nature of educational guidance:

(i) This kind of guidance is only rendered to the students community.

(ii) It helps the pupils in their attempts to make wise selection and right choices regarding various educational programmes and situations. There are many situations where they may feel difficulty in taking proper educational decisions. In what school or college should one take admission? What type of subjects or courses of study should be chosen? In which particular curricular activity, hobby or club should he participate? In this way, help of educational guidance is needed to enable the students to take important educational decisions at each of the many forks in the road.

(iii) Educational Guidance not only assists the pupils in making educational choices but it also guides them to achieve maximum educational growth and development according to their own capacities and abilities.

(iv) Main function of educational guidance is to help the pupils in their educational adjustment so that they may feel quite at home and achieve maximum educational success. There are many difficulties and novel situations in the environment that may demand a particular mode of adjustment on their part. A public school product may face difficulty in adapting himself to the educational environment of any ordinary school. Similarly a new entrant in a college may find difficulty in adjusting himself to the lecture method or taking notes rapidly or selecting a book in the library. In all such situations, children need active assistance through the guidance services.

With all the above knowledge regarding the nature and meaning of educational guidance, we can now give a simple definition of the term 'educational guidance'.

Educational Guidance is a process of rendering help to the students in their proper educational development and adjustment.

NEED OF EDUCATIONAL GUIDANCE

The question as to why is it essential to impart educational guidance to the students can be properly answered in the light of the above discussion. However, we can summarize the reasons justifying such guidance as follows:

In checking the wastage and stagnation in education

We find that there is huge wastage and stagnation in education. Many students fail repeatedly and remain in the same class for a number of years. They feel difficulty in learning or acquiring some or the other piece of knowledge and skill. It leads to the wastage of human as well as national resources. Such wastage and stagnation can only be checked through a suitable programme of educational guidance.

In realizing the aims and objectives of education

Now the teacher's function is not limited to merely giving instructions in some school subjects. It has quite a broader base. The all-round progressive and harmonious development of all the innate abilities and capacities of an individual is only possible through a well-organized programme of educational guidance. With its help, the teacher can realize the maximum educational development of their students within the specific time and limited resources.

In making right educational choices

Educational guidance is necessary for making right educational choices. The students, while taking education, are often confronted with the problem of making the right selection or choice. There are diversified courses from which they have to select subjects or activities. The wrong choice of a subject or activity may doom their career and future. Therefore, they should be helped by guidance in making right choice with regard to subjects or courses of study, cocurricular activities, methods of learning, style of speaking, writing and reading books and other literature for study etc.

For proper educational adjustment

Adjustment to prevailing educational environment is essential for the proper educational growth and well-being of the children. A child enters a school directly from his home environment. Here he finds a formal environment of education and gets experiences that are quite novel and strange to him. He needs to be adjusted to these educational situations and environmental conditions. He has to read, write, speak and participate in the learning process. Drill work and home assignments have to be completed. Participation in curricular activities is required. Regularity and punctuality in educational process is to be observed. Sometimes he has to derive benefit from new techniques and devices of teaching. He has to prepare himself for desired tests and evaluation. Thus the child faces many adjustment problems with regard to his educational environment and therefore needs proper educational guidance.

How to Impart Educational Guidance?

The process of educational guidance, like the general pattern of guidance process, involves three important phases:

(a) Collecting information or data.
(b) Rendering guidance on the basis of this information.
(c) Follow-up programme.

Collecting information or data

In the first phase, it is required to collect full information or data regarding the pupil. The information like the following can be collected for this purpose:

- Details concerning his health and physique.
- His intelligence and other cognitive abilities.
- Details concerning his scholastic attainments.
- His interests, aptitudes, attitudes and other personality characteristics.
- Family history and background.
- Details regarding his social and emotional development.
- Details regarding the previous school attended.
- Details regarding his company and his friends.

Various techniques like personality tests, achievement tests, intelligence tests, aptitude tests, attitudes scales, interviews, questionnaires, rating scales, inventories, observations etc. can be employed for collecting these information or data.

The knowledge of the above mentioned aspects are not sufficient for an educational guidance worker. He also has to obtain useful information regarding the following educational aspects:

- Curriculum and subjects taught in the school.
- Cocurricular experiences and other activities performed in the school.
- Information regarding future courses of study, occupation and professions.
- Information regarding the admission in specialized institutions and their environment.
- Information regarding various techniques and methods of learning.
- Collecting necessary knowledge and techniques for rendering help to the students in removing their educational weaknesses and problems.

Rendering Guidance

The next phase deals with the work of actual guidance imparted to the needy. It is a difficult task. It requires complete analysis of the information gathered about his personality make-up and adjustment. These conclusions further provide a base for making decisions about the nature of guidance to be given to the individual in question. For example, he is guided to select a course or a method of learning or mode of study that suits his individuality as well as his peculiar environment.

Follow-up programme

The work of a guidance worker does not stop with the rendering of guidance but it requires some efforts in the follow-up programme as well. Under this programme, the progress made by the child on account of the guidance given to him is evaluated. On this basis, required step, if necessary, are taken for giving him any further guidance or necessary changes are introduced in the previous guidance programme. In every situation, it is to be seen that the child becomes able to solve his educational problem—developmental or adjustive. If it happens, then and only then can we think about the success of a guidance programme.

Vocational Guidance

WHAT IS VOCATIONAL GUIDANCE?

To know the meaning of the term 'Vocational guidance', let us first try to acquaint ourselves with the definitions suggested by some eminent thinkers. These definitions are:

National vocational guidance association (U.S.A.)

According to the definition accepted by this association in 1937, *"Vocational Guidance is the process of assisting the individual to choose an occupation, prepare for it, enter upon and progress in it."* (Myers, 1947, p. 3)

Committee of the international labour organization

According to the definition accepted by this organization in 1954, *"Vocational Guidance is an assistance rendered by an individual to another in the latter's solving of problems related to his progress and vocational selection, keeping in mind the individual's peculiarities or special abilities and their relation with his occupational opportunity."*

Myers

"Vocational Guidance is fundamentally an effort to conserve the priceless native capacities of youth and the costly training provided for youth in the schools. It seeks to conserve these richest of all human resources by aiding the individual to invest and use them where they will bring greatest satisfaction and success to himself and greatest benefit to society." (1947, p. 7)

Super

"Vocational Guidance is a process of helping the person to develop and accept an integrated and adequate picture of himself and of his role in the world of work, to test this concept against reality and to convert into reality with satisfaction to himself and benefit to society." (1957, p.197)

In this way, vocational guidance is a kind of guidance that is concerned with the vocational needs and problems of the individuals. In strict psychological and educational sense, we can define it as the *process of helping a pupil to get adequate information regarding the world of work around him, make a proper choice for his future vocation, get adequate training or preparation for it, get entry into it, and achieve maximum success and satisfaction in it.*

Nature and Purposes of Vocational Guidance

The definitions and meaning of the term 'Vocational Guidance' may help us to derive the following conclusions regarding its nature and purposes:

1. Vocational Guidance is a sort of assistance that is given to an individual by a competent individual.
2. The assistance, given through vocational guidance, helps an individual in getting information about the world of work around him.
3. It helps him to know himself, his strengths and limitations etc. so that he can develop an adequate concept of himself and his role in the world of work.
4. It further helps him to make a proper decision regarding his occupation.
5. It also helps him to prepare for entering into the desired profession.
6. Hence forth, vocational guidance helps an individual get absorbed in the occupation of his choice. He is acquainted with the sources and methods of utilizing job opportunities or is helped in seeking self employment. In this way, he gets opportunity for realizing his long cherished ambitions regarding his career or occupation.
7. After entering into a vocation, the individual is further helped by vocational Guidance in his vocational adjustment. He is helped in making satisfactory progress in his vocation in such a way that it can bring greatest satisfaction and success to him and greatest benefit to the nation.
8. Vocational Guidance aims to bring economic prosperity to the individuals as well as to the nation.
9. It aims to utilize all the available natural resources of the nation. For this purpose, it helps the individuals to get acquainted with all such opportunities.
10. It aims to stop the huge wastage and mis-utilization of the time, money and labour that may occur in the preparation or training of the individuals for a particular profession, who are not suited to it. On the other hand, it aims to conserve human as well as national resources by placing the proper person at a proper place.

Need of Vocational Guidance to Pupils

What we have said above in connection with the nature and purpose of vocational guidance is sufficient for us to understand the necessity of vocational guidance to our youngsters. However, we would make fresh attempts to justify this requirement on the following grounds.

- Vocations have ceased to be *empirical*. The son of a tailor would not necessarily be a tailor. He may like to enter some other field of his interest. Also many of the occupations that happened to exist earlier have now become extinct. Moreover, with the growing technical and scientific advancement and complexity of life, the world of work has become very extensive and wide. There have been multiple growth of many new and novel occupations that need the services of our young men and women. Therefore, there is an urgent need of guidance services for rendering necessary information regarding all such job areas and opportunities.

- We are astonished to see great number of engineering graduates and postgraduates unemployed. We blame national planning or state governments for the huge problem of unemployment in our country. There may be some truth in this allegation but the major cause of such devastating situation is the lack of proper vocational guidance to the youngsters. The knowledge of the parents and these youngsters regarding the world of work is too narrow and specific. A few professions and occupations are considered to be lucrative and reputable, while others are neglected or are unknown to them. Therefore, we find unnecessary crowding in some occupations. Thus there is an urgent need to acquaint the students with the growing trend in the employment market and job opportunities so that they may be saved from unnecessary frustration and aimless wandering.
- Vocational maladjustment is another problem that is alarming and injurious to the well being of the individuals and the society. The persons who are not competent enough or do not possess interest and aptitude for the professions of medicine or engineering are working as doctors, nurses or engineers. Most often it is the result of high ambitions and desires on the part of their parents. Sometimes, young men and women opt for a profession simply because they have not been absorbed in any of the other occupations known to them. It brings round pegs into square holes and square pegs into round holes. In fact, there is a great dearth of vocational guidance that can help students choose the occupations best suited to their abilities, personality characteristics and circumstances of life. They should be helped to select the subjects and other activities in schools in the light of their future vocations. They should get adequate training or preparation for getting success in their future vocations and should be helped in entering and afterwards progressing in their chosen occupation. Such help or assistance can only be given through a well organized programme of vocational guidance. Our schools and teachers must play their due role in organizing such guidance services for the benefit of their students and the nation at large.

HOW TO IMPART VOCATIONAL GUIDANCE TO PUPILS

Vocational guidance like educational guidance can be accomplished in three phases, namely: (i) Collecting data, (ii) Rendering guidance on the basis of this information, and (iii) Follow-up programme.

(i) First of all, necessary information regarding the nature of the child like his abilities, interests, aptitudes, personality characteristics and circumstances of life are obtained carefully. Meanwhile, the guidance worker also tries to get all the adequate and relevant information regarding the world of work and job opportunities. He make himself well-informed with the help of all the current literature and publications. He has contacts with the counseling services and is well acquainted with the current trends of employment market and the demand and supply position.

(ii) Equipped with all such information and knowledge, he may engage himself in the actual guidance work. For this purpose, he may utilize both individual guidance and group guidance methods. Pupils are informed about the world of work and job opportunities through lectures, display of literature and pamphlets or library reading. They are now helped to know about different jobs or occupations and this helps them in making adequate vocational choices. Further, they are helped to select courses and activities related to their vocational choices. Many a time, they are helped to join special courses and vocational training for the necessary pre-preparation. Vocational guidance work also shares the responsibility of helping the pupils in entering the vocations of their choice by rendering adequate information about the employment opportunities and having an intimate contact with the employment agencies. In some cases vocational guidance helps in seeking self-employment. All this work comes within the area of active Vocational Guidance or follow-up programme.

(iii) The evaluation of the process of such guidance is also essential not only for evaluating the merits and demerits of administered guidance but also for the benefit of the individual concerned. One may be further helped in his proper adjustment to his vocation through such follow-up programme.

In this way we see that the task of rendering vocational guidance to the pupils is quite extensive and laborious. It cannot be left only in the hands of career masters or separate guidance workers appointed in the schools. Parents, teachers and head of the institution should also play their due roles in rendering vocational guidance to the pupils. Guidance services in schools should be properly established and the cooperation of all the essential forces should be secured to draw maximum benefit from these services.

Personal Guidance

Nature and Meaning of Personal Guidance

As the name suggests, Personal Guidance is that guidance which is rendered to a person for solving his personal problems. But, there is no end to the personal problems. In this world of struggle and competition, one has to strive hard for the satisfaction of his personal needs. For this purpose, he has to make adjustment in so many aspects in different situations. There are occasions when one feels problems in making adjustment to himself, others and his peculiar environment. In this way one needs personal assistance or help for satisfying one's personal needs as well as for solving one's adjustment problems.

Taking all such aspects into consideration, personal guidance may be found to cover all the problems and aspects concerning the development and adjustment of a person. It has a very comprehensive and wide meaning. Crow and Crow emphasize such broad meaning in their attempts of making correct interpretation of this term. In their words, *"Personal Guidance refers to help given to an individual towards a better adjustment in the development of attitudes and behaviour in all areas of life."* (1962, p. 164). Thus, in its wider sense, personal guidance may be interpreted to include all kinds of guidance that may be rendered to a person.

In our previous discussion in this text, we mentioned that personal guidance is one of the three parts or aspects of the total guidance programme. The other two aspects—educational and vocational guidance—deal with the educational and vocational needs or problems of a person. Such problems or needs can also be described as personal problems or needs. Therefore, we can interpret the term "personal guidance" in such wide sense as it has been interpreted above.

But for making it quite distinct from educational and vocational guidance and to maintain its separate identity, the term 'personal guidance' should either be used in a specific narrow sense or it may be replaced by some other suitable term like 'psychological guidance' or 'emotional and social adjustment guidance.'

In this sense it should concern itself with the satisfaction of emotional and social needs of the individual and help him in his emotional and social adjustment. It can extend valuable help in reducing tension, mental conflicts and anxieties of our students. It may also help them to grow as emotionally stable and socially desirable personalities and thus prove as an important preventive measure against problematic and abnormal behaviour. It may also help in dealing with the exceptional children and can prove useful in the treatment of abnormal or maladjusted personalities.

HOW TO RENDER PERSONAL OR PSYCHOLOGICAL GUIDANCE?

The following five steps are involved in a personal guidance programme:

Collection of all the information or data

First of all, relevant information or data concerning the individual, who needs personal or psychological guidance, should be collected. It may be concerned with his physical, intellectual, social and emotional development, academic achievement, personality characteristics, interests and aptitudes, family and school background and other environmental conditions. Thus an adequate picture of the background and personality make up of an individual should be drawn properly for the solution of the problem faced by the individual.

Diagnosis of the causes of the problems

Now the problem of the individual is analyzed with respect to the collected information. The causes lying within the individual or his environment are detected. For correct diagnosis, personal interview or other techniques may also be adopted and more information may be acquired.

Thinking about the remedial measures

In view of the detected possible causes, remedial measures are chalked out. The guidance worker now thinks about the personal guidance that may be provided to the individual so that he can get rid of his problem.

Rendering personal guidance

By establishing proper rapport, the guidance personnel makes the individual realize the main cause of his difficulty or trouble. Sometimes on this basis he is made to realize or even think about the possible changes in his behaviour or attitude. For this purpose, many valuable techniques like suggestions, imitation, sympathetic and affectionate advice, sublimation or catharsis, psychoanalysis or other psychological therapy can be adopted. The sole purpose of such guidance is to help or assist the individual in getting rid of his difficulty either by modifying his behaviour or by bringing some changes in his environment.

Follow-up service

After rendering personal guidance to an individual, it is essential to evaluate the progress or outcome of such guidance through personal interviews, contact or any other suitable technique. It is such follow-up programme that helps in knowing the strengths and weaknesses of the administered personal guidance. It may also suggest the need of further guidance to him or any alteration in the proposed guidance.

The knowledge about the above mentioned process of personal guidance is not only needed by the guidance personnel specially appointed in the school, but the headmaster and teachers should also make themselves acquainted with it. Teachers with their unique position in the school are able to develop close contacts with the students and may be able to know the real causes of a trouble. With a little training, they can learn the area of rendering personal guidance to their students. Therefore, our schools are required to play their due role in this direction. In every school, the head of the institution should try to organize a personal guidance programme with the active help of his staff and cooperation of the parents and state guidance services.

Types of Counselling

In schools, teachers as well as trained counselors try to provide various types of counseling to the students depending upon the nature of their problems, needs and situations. The four main types of such counseling may be named and described as follows:

EMERGENCY COUNSELING

It is also termed as the counseling at the time of crises. As the name suggests, it is necessarily provided by the counselor to the counselee in those hours of need when he feels quite an emergency to save himself from adverse situations, happenings or crises.

Crises, accidents and adverse situations are the informidable components of human life. Students may have some mishappening in their homes, confronted some accidental crises, fallen victims to some ailments and diseases, been threatened by some miscreants or anti-social elements, face serious maladjustment problems or may have found themselves at the crossroads on account of their failures and frustrations etc. Such crises or adverse situations are the real tests in our lives. Every one of us, while banking upon ourselves and the resources in hand, always need some outside support, suggestions, advice and consultation for meeting the adversities of crises. In the case of immature youth and children, it is predominantly essential. Hence we need proper provision for a form of counseling exclusively meant for the times of crises. Therefore in every school, there must be a trained counselor who can provide necessary moral and psychological support to the counselee for facing the adversities of the crises. He must help him in retaining his confidence and making him stand on his own for coming out of these hours of crises. Such type of counseling provided for meeting some or the other emergency is referred to as emergency counseling. It is provided on the lines of emergency services of the hospitals without wasting time and in view of the available circumstances by the person specially trained for the purpose of helping the children in coming out successfully from the emergent distresses and crises.

PROBLEM SOLVING OR CURATIVE COUNSELING

Many a time, students are confronted with some or the other problems related to their studies and other activities of the school, their educational and vocational choices and adjustment, their difficulties in making proper adjustment to the self and the environment etc. They feel that their own attempts and means of solving these problems are not adequate. In such a need of hour, they look for somebody who can advise and help them.

In such a situation, there arises the necessity of special type of counseling services known as problem solving, curative or adjustment related counseling. It can provide necessary help to the counselee for (i) facing his problem with his own efforts; (ii) bringing necessary modification in his behaviour for the rectification of his problem; (iii) inducing properly other curative measures; and (iv) thus finally helping him in his proper adjustment with his self and the environment.

PREVENTIVE COUNSELING

It is a well-known and well-tested saying that prevention is always better than cure. Therefore serious attempts should always be made for providing such counseling to the students that may help in the prevention of probable disasters, distresses and crises. It is no wisdom to search for ways and means after getting into trouble. The wise thing is to remain cautious and use preventive measures to avoid the expected difficulties or troubles. Preventive counseling aims at all such precautionary and preventive steps and measures. Under such counseling, children are told about the ways and means of remaining physically and mentally healthy and strong. They are made to learn healthy and hygienic habits through regular exercise, avoidance of illness and diseases, balanced diet and its availability from the local food stuff etc. They are told about the proper ways and means of learning, using their potentials to maximum capacity, making right educational and vocational choices according to their needs, interests, aptitudes and abilities etc. for making them adjusted to their educational, vocational and personal lives. They are also prevented and saved from the evil effects of bad company, social or emotional maladaptation and picking up of the unsocial and undesirable habits through systematically planned and preventive counseling. In this way, preventive counseling may help in avoiding various problems and crises that may otherwise affect the children in the absence of the required preventive measures.

DEVELOPMENTAL OR FORMATIVE COUNSELING

This type of counseling has a complete positive and constructive approach. It works on the assumption that if a child's abilities and capacities are planned to develop a positive direction, then he will be so capable, efficient and satisfied that he would not approach anybody for any help for the solution of his problems, or for further development or actualization of his potentialities for making adjustment to his self and the environment. Through a systematic, well-planned and organized counseling service of this type in the school, we can certainly aim for (i) the all-round harmonious growth and development of the innate powers of the child (ii) providing the children opportunities for the actualization or expression of their constructive and creative energies; and (iii) providing them a constructive, formative and developmental direction for picking up right habits and desirable behaviour in the interest of their self and the society.

In tune with this, most of the formal and informal education related to health education, personal and social hygiene, value education, education for personality development, activities and hobbies meant for serving diversified interests etc. may be included in the contents or methodology of developmental or formative counseling.

Approaches of Counseling

Counseling may take a particular form, shape or style, known as approaches of counseling, depending upon the relative roles of the counselor and counselee, the need and objectives of such counseling and the facilities, situations or environment prevalent at the time of counseling. Mainly there are three approaches of counseling named as below:

1. Directive Counseling
2. Non-directive Counseling
3. Eclectic Counseling

Let us discuss these approaches of counseling.

DIRECTIVE COUNSELING

Directive counseling as the name suggests involves clearcut directions on the part of the counselor to lead the counselee in the direction and the way decided by the counselor in order to help him in solving his problems, developing his capacities or modifying his behaviour. In this way, this type of counseling is very counselor-centered who plays the role of the sole director, controller and organizer of the total process of counseling. The main assumptions, characteristics and operational procedure of such an approach may be briefly outlined as under.

Basic Assumptions

Directive counseling mainly works on the assumption that the counselor is a more knowledgeable, intelligent and capable person in comparison to the counselee. Moreover, he has enough experience and professional training. Therefore, he is in a position to control and direct the counseling process for providing proper advice, help and consultation to the counselee according to the needs and demands of the situation.

Procedure

Working on the above assumption, the counselor takes full command and operation of the counseling process in his hand. When a less mature and problem-ridden counselee approaches the counselor to consult with regard to the solution of his problem, he proceeds in the following way:

(i) The counselor concentrates his energies on knowing and analyzing the problem of his client. What really is his problem? What is the intensity or gravity and seriousness of the problem? Through which observable behavioural or situational sysmptoms is it being reflected? What are the possible underlying causes for the eruption or development of this problem? etc.

(ii) After the careful and systematic analysis of the problem, the counselor engages himself in search for the ways and means of finding solution to the problem. With the help of his experience, education and professional skills, he arrives at a solution of his problem. Then he chalks out the details of his plan for advising the counselee to follow.

(iii) In between, the counselor remains quite alert and careful in ensuring that the counselee is following the directions and going on the right path laid down by him. The counselor also from time to time evaluates the progress and outcome of his suggested way. In case not much fruitful results are obtained from his suggested plans, he may suggest another way or plan for the solution of his client's problems. In this way, he almost feels his utmost responsibility for directing and leading the counselee in the whole journey of finding ways of getting rid of the difficulties or problems.

(iv) While doing so much effort and hard work with the counselee, the counselor never forgets that in no case the counselee may be unnecessarily forced to accept his plan of action. The counselor must try to win his confidence, faith and trust and then persuade him to follow the directions and the plan of action. Similarly he should also be careful in ensuring that the counselee works well on the suggested lines without becoming much dependent on him. However, he tries to exercise necessary control on him for the proper implementation and follow up of the chalked plan.

Merits and Limitations

The main merits and limitations of this approach can be summarized as follows:

Merits:

1. The counselee gets immediate attention as well as plan of action for the solution of his problems based on the vast experiences, competencies and profession skills of the counselor.
2. Counselor directs the whole procedure right from analyzing the problem and the plan of action to the final solution of the problem. Thus no time and energy of the counselee is unnecessarily wasted in thinking over the possible solution or plan of action for his problem.

3. It saves the counselee from the situations or consequences of getting frustrated and unnecessarily tensed on account of the gravity of his problem. The counselor is there to provide direct guidance and assistance to him within no time. Such assurance makes him psychologically strong for successfully coping with this problems and adjustment to his self and the environment.
4. Such type of counseling proves more effective where the functions of counseling are limited to the dissemination of information and knowledge or for imparting suggestions, consultation or advice.

Limitations:

1. Such approach expects too much from the counselor as the whole process from beginning till the end is totally initiated, directed and controlled by the counselor. He must have thorough knowledge, experience, necessary skills not only for the solution of various problems but of the practical human psychology. In the absence of such knowledgeable, experienced, educated, professionally trained counselor, it becomes quite difficult to have desirable outcomes from directive counseling.
2. Since the plan of action for the solution of the problem is directly drawn by the counselor without any democratic consultation with the counselee, very little or no consideration is paid to the interests, abilities and capacities of the counselee for implementing the plan. In such a situation, the counseling may fail to achieve its objective on account of lack of proper involvement and capacity of the counselee.
3. In directive counseling, counselor behaves like a planner, director or administrator dictating and directing the counselee in a particular direction and path for the solution of his problem. He feels no need of coming into direct personal contact or seeking his total involvement with him for the planning of action or its implementation on the part of the counselee. With the lack of such emotional bonds and mutually satisfying close relationship, this type of counseling may prove effective only to the extent of providing consultation, giving advice or imparting necessary knowledge and information for the solution of one's problem. The wholesome purpose of counseling in terms of the desired modification of the behaviour and development of proper independent problem solving ability and adjustment capacities can be hardly achieved through such type of counseling.

NON-DIRECTIVE COUNSELING

Quite contrary to directive approach, this non-directive approach is a counselee-centered approach. Here the controlling key of the whole operation of counseling does not lie with the counselor. He does not formulate an action plan or issues directive to counselee for his observation but adopts such techniques and builds up such environment that can help the counselee solve his problems with his own efforts. The basic assumptions underlying this approach alongwith its characteristics and procedure are briefly described as follows:

Basic Assumptions

The basic assumptions underlying the non-directive approach may be summarized as follows:

(i) Counseling can achieve its desired objectives only when it is planned and executed in tune with the needs, interests, abilities and capacities of the counselee.

(ii) There must be a close and constant interaction between the counselor and the counselee. Although both need to remain quite active during such interaction, the leading role should be played by the counselee. He must be quite ready and willing to share his problem, take decision about the plan of action and work on his own towards the solution of his problem.

(iii) It is the present and not the past of the counselee that should be more cared for the problem solving and behaviour modification of the counselee. Instead of wasting time in finding out the origin of his problem, the counselor should try to know well about the existing needs, feelings and behaviour patterns of the counselee for seeking identification and winning his active cooperation in the process of counseling.

(iv) Every individual as a counselee is unique in himself carrying with him a vast treasure of goodness, abilities and capacities. The duty of the counselor lies in awakening and acquainting the counselee with his hidden and dormant powers for going ahead in solving his problems.

(v) Counseling can better realize its objectives if efforts are made to make the counselee realize the real nature of his problem and he should be properly motivated to work actively to get rid of his problem.

(vi) The counseling outcomes may be more effective when the contribution and efforts of the counselee are given more weightage and importance than the advice or consultation related activities of the counselor.

Procedure

In the non-directive approach the counseling activities may proceed as under:

(i) At the initial stage instead of providing information, giving direction or advice or lecturing on his own, the counselor takes the initiative of providing proper opportunities to the counselee for opening the dialogue and saying something about himself and his problem.

(ii) It is followed by necessary reinforcement. The counselor again persuades and encourages the counselee for expressing and discussing his problem more freely with the counselor by establishing a rapport and providing other facilities for doing so.

(iii) The counselee after being assured of the mutually satisfying, supporting and confidential relationship with the counselor freely expresses himself and discusses his problem with the counselor. Such expression works as a catharsis for relieving him from the stress and tensions, pent up desires and emotions etc. Now he is in a position to take an objective view of his self and his problem. He can now fully cooperate with the counselor in chalking out an action plan for the solution of his problem. His eagerness and determination to get rid of the problem helps much in this direction.

(v) With such preparation on the part of the counselee now, the counselor wisely takes steps to generate adequate motivation and energy in the form of developed abilities and capacities in the counselee aiming to make him quite capable of introducing modification in his behaviour and organizing his resources for achieving the desired ends.

Merits and Limitations

Merits: Non-directive counseling has the following credit points on its side.

1. It provides proper opportunities to the counselee for playing the leading role in the process of counseling. Here he finds full opportunities to look into his self and the problem, and to take interest in solving his problem with his own efforts. This readiness and total willingness on his part makes the counseling task quite easy and as a result counselee can get the desired relief.

2. Non-directive counseling helps the counselee to follow the right path of self-dependence, self-instruction, self-consciousness and self-development for the proper development of his own powers to meet the problems and challenges.
3. In comparison to directive counseling, here the counselor feels much relieved in the matter of exercising his responsibilities for the success of counseling. He need not do everything by himself by playing the leading role and remaining always at the helm of the affairs. The counselee here remains very active, cooperative and interested in looking after his interests of solving his problem mostly with his own efforts, in close cooperation of the counselor.
4. There is more close, trustworthy and active cooperation and rapport in this type of counseling than in directive counseling. It helps much in building a more proper and conductive environment for the better organization of the desired counseling services.
5. In this type of counseling, one gets full opportunity to express himself and his problem quite openly. This brings all the psychological advantages for providing relief to the counselee from the tension, anxieties and pressures mounted by repressed feelings, desires and emotions.
6. Such type of counseling is adjudged as the most appropriate approach for solving emotional and behavioural problem of the counselee by bringing desired modification in his behaviour and building a self-dependent integrated personality.

Limitations: Non-directive counseling is said to suffer from some of the following limitations:

1. Such type of counseling takes more time. Behaviour modification and self-development are quite lengthy processes. It is not like lecturing, providing information or issuing directions or instructions as happens in directive counseling. Here, counselee has to be motivated and equipped for taking the lead. In this way, much time may be wasted in preparing and equipping the counselee for running the entire show of counseling.
2. On account of the immaturity, lack of experience, abilities and skills etc. on the part of the counselee, much time and energy is unnecessarily wasted in seeking his cooperation and allowing him his independent efforts in the solution of his problem.
3. The success of the non-directive counseling depends upon the degree of intimacy, close, trustworthy and mutually satisfying as well as confidential relationship maintained between the counselor and the counselee. In the absence of such satisfied rapport, the counselee can't open himself and put his heart and soul along with the counselor for the achievement of the desired success through counseling.

ECLECTIC COUNSELING

Both the above mentioned directive and non-directive approaches have their own advantages and limitations. Hence it is not appropriate to recommend the exclusive use of one or the other approach in all the situations. In achieving the most satisfying results, we can't afford to make our counseling process entirely counselor-centered or counselee-centered. We have to strike the mean by incorporating all the goodness of the available counseling approaches and doing away with their possible limitations and defects to the extent as possible. Such well thought properly integrated approach has been referred to as eclectic approach. Let us try to postulate the underlying assumption, procedure, merits and limitations of such an approach.

Basic assumptions

Eclectic approach is mainly based on the following assumptions:

1. There are wide individual differences among the counselees with regard to their behavioural and personality characteristics. The range of problems faced by them is also

quite wide and diversified. In such a situation, it is difficult as well as futile to prescribe a single way or approach for their counseling. They need counseling according to the nature of their problem and the self. Moreover, the organization of the counseling services also rests on the availability of the resources as well as on the need of the existing situation or environment. Hence it is not appropriate to depend entirely upon one or the other type of counseling approaches.

2. The individual has the best solution for his problems. He has enough guts and ability for doing this. Therefore it is always better to motivate the counselee to take initiatives in this direction.
3. It is an undeniable fact that counselor is more mature, experienced, capable and professionally trained in comparison to the counselee. In this situation where the counselee is not getting any way or insight for the solution of his problem, it is not proper to allow him further to unnecessarily waste his time and energy. Here the counselor should come forward to take control of the counseling process by adopting directive approach.
4. During counseling, a counselor can achieve better results if he gets due cooperation from other persons and the environmental condition associated with the counselee and his problem.
5. In the task of solving the problem, modifying the behaviour and helping in the proper adjustment of the counselee, his past and the present both carry equal weightage. Therefore, the counselor should try his level best to go deep into his problem by equally exploring his past as well as the present.
6. The environmental conditions, situations and means are always in the process of change. As a result the counseling process should also be kept quite flexible according to the needs of the situation. Therefore, it is wise for the counselor not to depend on a single approach but try to incorporate various approaches according to the demands of the situation, *e.g.* at one time the counselor should try to give a patient hearing to the counselees, give weightage to their opinion and accept their action plan while emphasizing on his view points, giving them necessary direction about his action plan or allowing them to proceed in their own way by keeping a constant vigil and proper supervision of their activities.

Procedure

The task of counseling in this approach may proceed on the following lines.

1. The problem of the counselee is deeply studied and investigated by the counselor. All types of relevant information related to the past and present of the counselee's problem are therefore collected objectively by all possible means. In addition to the outside sources, the counselee is provided full opportunities and encouragement for expressing and discussing his problem.
2. The counselee is then helped in analyzing and knowing well about the nature and dimensions of his problem in quite an objective way. He is given due encouragement through advice and environmental facilities for chalking out an action plan to solve his problem by bringing desired modification in his behaviour or developing his abilities and capabilities accordingly.
3. The counselor then tries to take the counselee with him along the path of counseling. He tactfully plans, coordinates and controls in such a way that counselee always takes the lead in making action plans and work for their implementation to achieve the desired goals.

    However, in all situations and at all occasions he remains quite alert and attentive for guiding and controlling the activities of the counselee in the right direction with the minimum wastage of time and resources. He may, for this purpose, change the approach from non-directive to directive or vice versa according to the need of the time.

4. All the relevant data incorporating past and the present of the counselee and his problem are now well coordinated and integrated to find the solution of the problem. The counselee is made an active partner in the ongoing counseling process. It is ensured that the counselee remains properly motivated, takes genuine interest in making action plan, works for its proper implementation and cooperates fully with the counselor in achieving the goals of counseling by having proper faith in him. It is also taken care of that counselee remains quite active, takes the lead and is quite independent in his efforts but where there is any need, he may be given proper direction, suggestion and active help by the counselor for remaining well on the track of reaching the goal.
5. In the task of counseling, the counselor may take the necessary help from any person, or other available sources according to the needs of the situation. The action plan may also be modified or replaced in tune with the demands of the changed circumstances. The implementation procedure can also be modified and improved in view of the needs of the time and resources.
6. At last the counseling process may be put to an end after ascertaining that the counselee is now in full control of the situation. He may go ahead independently for facing and solving his problem. His behaviour stands desirably modified or he has been able to develop his abilities and capacities to the extent of proceeding well on the path of further progress.

Merits: The eclectic approach is credited with the following points in its favour:

1. It gives emphasis on the roles of counselor and counselee. Both remain equally active and work in close cooperation. As a result here the counseling task may be carried out more effectively in comparison to other approaches.
2. The flexibility permitted in this approach is quite unmatchable. The action plan and its implementation can be modified or replaced at any time depending upon the needs of the changed situations. Such flexibility provides sufficient mobility and strength to the process of counseling for achieving its desired ends.
3. In such counseling, attempts are made to seek and integrate the cooperation from all the corners, men and material resources etc. Such integration of resources and attempts help in the desired objectives of helping the counselee according to his needs and abilities.
4. In this approach neither the counselor is overloaded with the single handed responsibilities of conducting counseling nor the counselee is left to his own for making unwise attempts resulting in the unnecessary wastage of time and energy. It calls for the mutual coordination and cooperation of both the counselor and the counselee. Here they work unitedly for achieving the common goal by harnessing all the available men and material resources.
5. Eclectic approach can be easily employed for all types of counseling activities. As a result we can utilize it in all the dimensions, educational, vocational and personal, for helping the counselee according to his varying needs at different times and situations.

Limitations: The eclectic approach may be said to suffer from a few limitations:

1. The success of this approach expects too much on the part of the counselor. He has to remain constantly on his legs for switching over from one approach to another or integrate various approaches in a suitable way for achieving the desired success with the counselee.

It is not an easy task. It needs a lot of preparation, zeal and enthusiasm, sincerity and professionalism on the part of counselor, the lack of which may adversely affect the results of the counseling.

2. Too much flexibility in the role and duties of the counselee in tune with the changes in the adoption of direct or indirect approaches may make him quite uncertain and confused about his role and functions. Sometimes he may be asked to follow the readymade solutions and instructions without any comments and at other times he may be supposed to be entirely on his own. This indecisiveness may cost him dear in taking proper decision about himself and his problem.

In this way we may see that there are certain difficulties and limitations in adopting one or the other approaches of counseling. However, a close analysis may reveal that eclectic approach may prove quite practicable as well as beneficial in all types of counseling problems. Its flexibility should be adjudged as a boon and not a hurdle in the process of counseling. If the counselor is properly educated and trained and the counselee's cooperation and confidence is properly secured then this integrated approach may surely prove effective in the complete realization of the counseling objectives.

SUMMARY

Guidance may be taken as a process of helping a guidance seeker by a person capable of providing such guidance for solving his problems, developing his potentialities to the maximum, adjusting to his self and the environment and thus making him capable of a successful personal and social life.

The need of providing guidance to the children in schools can be grouped into three types namely educational, vocational and personal aimed for seeking their needed educational, vocational and personal adjustment as well as development in the schools and life.

Counseling may be understood as such helping and developing process in which the counselor tries to bring desirable modification in the behaviour of the counselee by establishing proper rapport with him for making him capable of solving the problems independently and proceeding properly on the path of the self and social progress.

Guidance and counseling may be regarded as complementary to each other both aiming to achieve similar purposes. The only mentionable difference between them lies in the fact that (i) in counseling, there is a dire need of more cordial, and mutually satisfying as well as trustworthy relationship between the counselor and the counselee for providing proper counseling than needed usually in the case of giving guidance and (ii) counseling deals with the problems of counselee in a more systematic and professional way by going deep into their nature and possible causes. In case a guidance process is also able to meet the above two conditions then practically there remains no difference between a work of guidance personnel and counselor.

Educational guidance is a process of rendering help to the students in their proper educational development and adjustment. It may serve various purposes like checking huge wastage and stagnation in education, helping in the proper realization of the aims and objectives of education, helping the students in making right educational choices and seeking proper educational adjustment etc. The task of providing educational guidance to pupils may involve three important phases namely collecting full information or data regarding the pupil, rendering appropriate guidance and then resorting to a follow up programme in the light of the evaluation of the guidance results.

Vocational guidance refers to a process of helping the students in getting adequate vocational information, making proper vocational choices, get needed training or preparation for entering as well as achieving maximum adjustment and progress in their chosen vocations. Vocational guidance may prove quite useful in furnishing lot of information regarding the available job opportunities and areas in the world of work to the students. It may help them choose the occupation best suited to their abilities, personality characteristics and circumstances of life. They can be helped in term of doing proper preparation in getting entry to particular vocations and feel properly vocationally adjusted with the help of proper vocational guidance services. The task of rendering vocational services like educational may also involve the same phases, namely collecting necessary information regarding the nature of the students, providing individual or group guidance on the basis of the collected information and then resorting to follow up work after evaluating the results of imparting guidance.

Personal guidance refers to a process of assisting a person for meeting out his personal needs and problems specifically concerned with his emotional and social adjustment and development. The steps involved in rendering personal guidance may be listed as collection of all the information or data, diagnosis of the cause of a problem, thinking about the possible remedial measures, rendering personal guidance, and then finally resort to follow up service.

The task of counseling like guidance may be grouped into certain definite types and categories like Emergency Counseling (provided at the time of crises, accidents and adverse situation), Problem solving or curative solving (helping in solving the problem or taking curative measures), Preventive Counseling (helping in the avoidance of various problems and crises) and Developmental or formative Counseling (helping in the desired formation of behaviour and development of the personality).

Mainly three approaches namely Directive Counseling, Non-directive Counseling and Eclectic Counseling are employed for providing counseling by the counselors at different times. *Directive Counseling* is too much counselor-centered. Here a counselor is required to provide clearcut directions to lead the counselee in the direction and the way decided purely by the counselor for helping the counselee in solving his problem, developing his capacities or modifying his behaviour. *Non-Directive Counseling* is a counselee-centered approach. Accordingly counselor here is required to adopt such techniques and build up such environment that can help the counselee to solve his problems with his own efforts and pick up his developmental directions according to his own individuality. *Eclectic Counseling* is an attempt to strike proper balance between the extremities propounded by directive and non-directive counseling in the name of purely counselor and counselee centered approaches. Here neither the counselor is overloaded with the single-handed responsibilities of conducting counseling nor the counselee is left to his own for making unwise attempts resulting in the unncecessary wastage of his time and energy. It calls for the mutual coordination and cooperation of both the counselor and counselee for achieving the common goal by harnessing all the available men and material resources.

References and Suggested Readings

Crow, L.D. and Crow, Alice, *An Introduction to Guidance*, Eurasia Publishing House, New Delhi, 1962.

Dave, Indu, *Basic Essentials of Counseling*, Sterling Publishers, New Delhi, 1984.

Jones, A.J., *Principles of Guidance*, McGraw-Hill, New York, 1951.

Kulshrestha, S.P., *Vocational Interest Record*, National Psychological Corporation (Reprint), Agra, 1994.

Mehta, P.H., Wadia, K.A. and Odgers, J.D., *Handbook for Counselors*, NCERT, New Delhi, 1967.

Myers, G.G., *Principles and Techniques of Vocational Guidance*, McGraw-Hill, 1947.

National Vocational Guidance Association (USA), Quoted by Myers, G.E. in *Principles and Techniques of Vocational Guidance*, McGraw-Hill, 1947.

Rogers, Cart, R., Counseling and *Psychotherapy*, Houghton Miflin, Boston, 1942.

Shostrom, Everett, L. and Brammer, Lawrence M., *The Dynamics of the Counseling Process*, McGraw-Hill, New York, 1952.

Skinner, C.E. (Ed), *Essentials of Educational Psychology*, Prentice-Hall, New York, 1968.

Super, D.E., *The Psychology of Careers*, Harper & Brothers, New York, 1957.

Traxler, A.E., *Techniques of Guidance*, Rev. ed., Harper & Brothers, New York, 1957.

40

Group Dynamics and Group Behaviour

CHAPTER COMPOSITION

INTRODUCTION

It has been commonly observed and also established through various experimental studies that there are differences in the behaviour of individuals when they are alone and when they are together with other individuals. An individual, as a member of a group, behaves quite differently from what he would otherwise do. As a member of the group he exhibits group behaviour. Group behaviour is not a mere sum total of the behaviour of the individuals who constitute that group. Under the influence of group behaviour, even the most disciplined and obedient students have been found indulging in the most irresponsible and undesirable behaviour. On the other hand, the most coward, unsocial or irresponsible ones are found contributing significantly when observed to work in a group. Therefore, it should be clearly understood that in a group, the behaviour of the individuals rests on a different psychic level and is governed by a unique force operating in the group called as group dynamics.

In this chapter let us try to know something about the term 'group dynamics' and the mechanism of group behaviour.

WHAT IS GROUP DYNAMICS?

Group Dynamics is a relatively new concept in the socio-psychological field. It is, in fact, a new approach to the study of groups that has gained popularity since World War II. Various attempts have been made to define the term 'Group Dynamics'. The attempt made by Cartwright and Zander seems to be more appealing. In their words *"Group dynamics should be defined as a field of inquiry dedicated to advancing knowledge about the nature of groups, the laws of their development, and their inter relations with individuals, other groups and larger institutions."* (1968, p. 7)

In this sense, group dynamics is that branch of knowledge that deals with the study of groups. It tries to answer the host of questions concerning the nature and working of groups. How are groups formed? What conditions are necessary for their growth and effective functioning? How do groups affect the behaviour of individuals? In this way Group dynamics acquaints us with the human behaviour and social relationships that exist in the group.

DEFINING THE TERM GROUP DYNAMICS

Etymological Speaking

'Dynamics' is derived from a Greek word meaning *force*. Hence 'group dynamics' stands for the forces operating in a group. The meaning of the term may be made more clear in the light of the some of the following definitions:

Good, C.V.

Group dynamics implies an interactive psychological relationship in which members of a group develop a common perception based on feeling and emotions. The inter-simulative relationships may be described by the term group dynamics. (1959)

Kretch, Crutchfield and Ballachey

Group dynamics implies changes that take place within groups. (1950)

Otto Klineberg

It is not easy to define or delimit the important area of group dynamics. From one point of view it represents a field of inquiry, a series of inter-related problems : from another it includes a set of techniques; from a third, a theory of the nature of groups and of interaction within groups.

Based on the ground work laid down by these definitions, we can consider *group dynamics as the study of the forces exerted by the individual on the group or by the group on the individual.* Accordingly the aspirations, attitudes, beliefs, characters, emotions, personality and values of an individual are influenced by the group and vice versa.

The group helps a person satisfy his fundamental needs and achieve the sense of accomplishment. It helps to transform the original nature of the person to human nature. Expression of instincts and emotions, formulation of ambitions, attitudes, character, habits and sentiments, values and the development of personality of the individual is influenced by his interaction with a group.

BASIC ASSUMPTIONS OF GROUP DYNAMICS

The basic assumptions related to group dynamics may be outlined as below:

1. **Groups are inevitable and ubiquitous (omnipresent).** Individuals form certain groups.
2. **Groups mobilize powerful forces producing effects of utmost importance to individuals.** The very sense of identity of a person is shaped by the groups significant to him — his family, school, occupation and profession, and religious groups. The position of a person in a group may influence the way others behave towards him, his self-esteem and level of aspiration.
3. **Groups may produce good as well as bad consequences.** There is convincing evidence to show that groups can be completely good and completely bad.

Correct understanding of group dynamics allows the possibility that desirable consequences from groups can be knowingly increased. Through a knowledge of group dynamics, groups can be made to serve better ends because knowledge gives power to modify human behaviour and social institutions.

EDUCATIONAL SIGNIFICANCE OF GROUP DYNAMICS

According to A.I. Gates (1947), *Group Dynamics* offers the best means available for the development of social skills essential for democratic living, better social understanding, and preparing individual members of the group for democratic citizenship.

Group dynamics is an educational method that is being specially attempted at these days. Its aim is neither to produce leaders nor to find ways in which a person can get work done by a group. Its purpose is to promote democratic activities. It is based on the assumption that only those persons can help in social progress who have learnt to make the most precious sacrifice for the welfare of the people and are prepared to do the same. It is also supposed that qualitative as well as quantitative individual differences in the abilities of persons are present. Every member of the group takes active part in the activities of the group. It is for this reason that the total work done by a group is more than the sum of work done by them individually. Besides this, actually the process by which one must consider other individuals in a group, and a problem at the same time not only tends to increase understanding to the problem, but also creates a solution which the individual has practiced in bringing about the emotional balance.

The techniques used in group dynamics are such in which there is little mutual conflict. Conflict hinders proper working of a group because it does not allow defining and having independent thinking for solving the problem. When we think alone we tend to accept our own thoughts. On the other hand when we express our own thoughts before a group, we have to give reasons for our thinking. With the help of such experience, we come to know those thoughts and feelings about which even we did not know earlier. We learn to think by paying more attention to facts and aims. It may not appear good in the beginning but exchange (give and take) is good for us.

When the members of a group develop familiarity and come closer, the feeling of enmity decreases and may even come to an end. Not only this, it is replaced by new feelings of respect for others and others also start thinking about us in good terms. In this way group dynamics teaches us to solve the problems of the group with the help of others. More work is accomplished in a group than is done individually. This is the aim of group dynamics.

By the study of group dynamics, teachers and counselors can take proper advantage of specific abilities of the students. The organizer should remember that he should not ignore individual effects in the possibilities of group dynamics. The organizers and the supervisor should understand that each is important in his or her own place.

Besides focusing on the groups as the object of study, group dynamics pays attention to the questions concerned with the dynamics of group life. It tells us about the different centripetal and centrifugal forces that try to change the structure of the group. How does an influential member or a leader bring change in the composition or working of the group? What are the pressures that a group may exert in bringing uniformity of thinking, feeling and acting among its members? If a change of membership or leadership occurs in a group, which other features of the group will change and which will remain stable? What changes in a group encourage creativity or heighten productivity? In what conditions does democratic structure of the group change into an autocratic one or vice versa? In what respect is the group structure and behaviour influenced if there is a change in the size or objective of the groups? There are a number of such questions that relate to the enquiries made about the possible changes in the group life on account of some variations, interactions, inner communication and pressures that are experienced within the group or exercised by other groups or factors outside the group.

In general it tries to answer the following types of questions related with the change that take place within the group:

(i) What kind of groups tend to change?
(ii) Under what conditions do they change?
(iii) What is the likely direction of change?

By answering such questions and presenting a body of information and knowledge, group dynamics aims to make the groups serve better and to bring dynamic changes in them in order to attain their legitimate goals.

To delve into the mechanism of group dynamics and related group behaviour, let us know about the meaning of the term *group* and the terms associated with group behaviour. Let us first begin by defining the term 'group'.

What is a 'Group'?

In an ordinary sense, a *group* is said to be a collection or aggregate of two or more objects or persons. But from the socio-psychological angle, mere collection or aggregate of people does not form a group. A psychological group in the opinion of Kretch, Crutchfield and Ballachey may be defined *as two or more persons who meet the following conditions*:

- *The relations among the members are interdependent—each member's behaviour influences the behaviour of each of the others.*

- *The members 'share an ideology'—a set of beliefs, values and norms which regulate their mutual conduct.* (1950, p. 283)

In this sense, members of a psychological group are said to be interdependent to some significant degree. They share common interests and aims and observe agreed rules of conduct and behaviour. In more clear terms, the members of a psychological group must have a common psychology *i.e.* they must feel, think and act together. *A group, therefore, may be defined as the collection or aggregate of two or more interdependent individuals who usually feel, think and act together.*

Defined in this manner, a number of children independently playing their respective games in a public park cannot be regarded as the members of one group. Similarly, a number of people passing through a street, each pursuing his or her own way or passengers unrelated and unfamiliar to one another in a railway carriage cannot be said to form a group. They are merely in the togetherness situation at a particular place at a particular moment. Unless they feel and act together and thus share experience of each other, they cannot be said to form a psychological group.

In a situation when the fellow passengers of a railway carriage take note of and accommodate one another, resist a newcomer trying to enter their compartment and thus begin to think, feel and act together, their simple togetherness turns into a psychological group. Similarly, those passing a street at a particular moment may be found to form a psychological group when they are faced with a common danger. The children playing in the park are said to form such a group when they engage themselves in a common game.

Moreover, a sort of belongingness or we-feeling is essential for the formation of a psychological group. When people say, *we* teachers, *we* Rajasthanies, *we* labourers etc, it means that they are the members of a psychological group. Under such feelings they can feel, act and think together and, therefore, can be called as the members of a psychological group. Hence the essential characteristics of a psychological group may be summarized in the following way:

- It is the collection or aggregate of two or more individuals.
- The members of the group have relations with one another that make them interdependent to some significant degree.
- There is a feeling of belongingness or we-feeling in the members of a group.
- It possesses a set of values or norms of its own that regulates the behaviour of individual members to seek the common goal or purpose.
- On account of group psychology, the members of psychological group merge their individualities and begin to feel, think and act together at least in a particular moment at a particular place.

KINDS OF GROUPS

Every one of us is a member of group that exists in the society. Various attempts have been made to classify these groups on one ground or the other. Some of these classifications are discussed below:

Sumner's Classification

W.G. Sumner classifies the groups into two main categories. (Brown, F.J., 1960, p. 92)

(i) In-group or we-group
(ii) Out-group or others-groups

In-group or we-group is the group with which we identify ourselves. The out-group or other-group is the group, the members of which are considered outsiders by us. Therefore, there are only two categories 'we' and 'they' and individual might belong to either in-group or out-group. Those not members of the 'we-group' are of the 'they-group'. Antagonistic feelings are often common between these groups. We do not try to understand the members belonging to out-group and show an attitude of indifference or scorn or even hate. For example, to the white American child a Negro child belongs to the out-group and therefore he hates him. In schools where segregation is observed, the girls or boys form two opposite groups. For the girls they belong to in-group and boys are considered to be the members of out-group. Similarly, boys consider the girls to be belonging to out-group.

Cooley's Classification

The classification suggested by Cooley is based on the degree of intimacy which the individual feels with other persons or groups or a we-feeling. (Brown, F.J., 1960, p. 94). On this basis groups may be classified as primary, secondary or tertiary.

In *Primary groups* there is an intimate face-to-face relationship and cooperation. We-feelings are found to a maximum degree among the members of such groups. Also they are bound with a mutual bond of interest. The family, play-group of children and village community are some of the examples of primary groups.

In *Secondary groups* the relationships are more or less casual. Here the relationships are usually marked by a single bond of interest. Examples of this type of groups are trade unions, professional associations, social organizations and associations, lodges and clubs.

In *Tertiary groups*, the degree of intimacy or relationship is quite marginal and transient in character. The group of audience in a cinema hall or passengers in a railway carriage, etc. are the examples of such groups.

Organized v/s Spontaneous Groups

Groups may be classified as organized group and spontaneous group. In a spontaneous group, the individual belonging to it come together naturally without any previous planning or specific purpose. But organized groups exist for some specific purposes and are formed as a result of careful pre-planning. The family, the army, the school etc. are the examples of such organized groups.

Formal v/s Informal Groups

Psychological groups, according to another mode of classification, can be classified as formal and informal groups.

In *formal groups*, the members of the group observe formalities and are bound by some specific rigid rules, values and norms. On the other hand in *informal groups* members are not bound by specific rigid rules. They may enjoy liberty of thought and freedom of action and are very informal in their relationships and behaviour.

Semi-formal groups fall in between these two categories. The group of the students in a classroom is an example of a formal group. Various kinds of work organizations also belong to this category. In informal groups we can include family, play or peer group, hobby and recreational groups etc. Semi-formal groups can include lodges, temples, social clubs, and so on.

By this sort of classification, it should not be concluded that an individual is a member of only one group and he cannot belong to more than one group. An individual may belong to many groups and can be a member of many groups at a particular time. He may be the member of his family group, class or school group, play group, club and association and other so many primary, secondary or tertiary groups; formal or informal groups, spontaneous or organized groups, in-groups or out-groups etc. Similarly, it should not also be considered that the classification of groups suggested above is rigid or static. The groups, whatever their structure or composition may be, are always dynamic in nature. For example, a formal group like participants in a seminar may turn into an informal group while taking tea or lunch. Similarly, a spontaneous group that has been formed incidently may take the shape of an organized group and a secondary group like a lodge or a hostel may perform the functions of a primary group.

SCHOOL AS A GROUP

School is a social group. All the students and teachers are its members. A school has a purpose, *i.e.* imparting education. It binds its members with its traditions and forces them to behave properly. The atmosphere of school persuades new members to join the group and continues making efforts to modify the behaviour of elder members. The success of a school depends upon the fact that its members accept and follow its traditions.

Utility of School Group Behaviour in Education

Besides being an educational institution, school is also a social group. Therefore, group behaviour of the school is of utmost importance in education. This behaviour helps the children in acquiring suitable education.

The social aim of education depends on proper group behaviour. Education aims at making such members of the society who are highly skilled, expert and useful. Training, this end in view, can be given through group behaviour in school.

Conditions Essential for Building an Organized School Community

Several types of conditions are essential for building an organized school community. Four important conditions have been discussed below:

Continuous Existence of the Community

The school community is not like a crowd. It has stability. Teachers remain in the school for a long time. A large number of students study in the school and in this way it is stable. For its stability it is essential that the teachers are not changed often and students do not leave it in short span of time. Their stay at school for considerable time is necessary so that they can understand the value of school society and acquire its good virtues.

Ideals of School

The school should have some aims and ideals. It is necessary that the children understand them. They should form a sentiment for the school. In order to achieve this purpose, functions such as celebration of national days, morning assembly, drama, prize distribution day, etc. should be organized in the schools. Such activities acquaint the students with the ideals of the school.

Social Feelings and Pride in Traditions

Even the youngest student of the school feels proud of his school. The students of different schools compare the activities etc. of their respective schools and each student tries to prove that his school is the better one. Individual competitions in debates, sports, games, one act plays etc. develop love in the students for the school.

Traditions of the school, results, sports, cultural activities of higher order etc. generate healthy rivalry and competition among the students.

All the students wish to see their schools as winners. They are ready to do many things to bring respect and glory to their alma mater. All these things help in the development of social feeling in them.

Co-operative and Creative Atmosphere

The school is an organized group. It is essential that the students work in co-operation with each other. In order to achieve this, teachers will have to lead them. As far as possible, individual competition should not be encouraged but group games like inter-class game competition should be organized.

It is essential for the school environment to be creative and progressive. It should change with time so that it remains the mirror of the school. Its aim should be decided. It should lead the society. Such a thing is possible only if there exists creative atmosphere in the school.

CLASSROOM AS A GROUP

There are many kinds of groups in a school e.g. clubs, teams, literary societies, subject societies, classroom groups etc. Classroom group is the most important of all these groups.

Importance

According to **Kuppuswami** (1971), classroom as an instructional group helps its members to satisfy their needs and achieve the goals. In school programme, the classroom group has a special place of importance.

Causes of Importance

The classroom is specially considered important due to its contribution in the following eight ways:

To improve the behaviour of students

In a classroom group, the students come in contact with each other and acquire appropriate type of education.

To develop mental processes

Some exchange of thoughts goes on in the classroom group through which intellectual activities like reasoning, memory, judgement, decision, thinking and imagination develop.

To develop the feeling of self sacrifice

The students in a classroom group remain in close contact with each other. Therefore, so much love, goodwill and sympathy develop in them that in the time of need, they do not hesitate to sacrifice something for the sake of others.

To prepare for future social life

Children in a classroom group live together for a long period of time and try to adjust their thoughts, habits and viewpoints to others. Such a type of experience prepares them for future social life.

To induce empathy of members

A student starts feeling and doing as other students do. This tendency is called empathy of the members.

To develop qualities of leadership

Students in classroom groups plan or organize a number of co-curricular activities. Thus qualities of leadership are developed in them.

To acquire more knowledge

In a classroom group, the students learn the habits of competition and imitation and get an inspiration to acquire more knowledge.

To develop the feeling of co-operation

The teacher encourages all the members of a classroom group to work together and thus a feeling of co-operation is developed in them.

SOCIAL DISTANCE IN GROUPS

What is social distance? Groups possess strong likes and dislikes for other groups. Members of a group like to keep the members of some other group and the group itself at a distance. This distance is called social distance in the world of sociology and social psychology. In this way *social distance* as a term can be defined as *the distance to which members of a particular group try to hold another group and its members.* In the true sense this distance represents the degree of social intimacy or understanding between the members of the different groups.

Measurement of Social Distance

Social distance scales are helpful in measuring social distance of one group from the other. These scales differ from the scales of attitude measurement (like Thurstone or the Likert type) in the sense that they do not represent the exceptional attitude of a single member or any group towards other groups or its members but they represent the attitude or feeling of a group as a whole towards other groups or their members.

Bogardus Social Distance Scale may be regarded as an earliest attempt in the measurement of social distance. He asked the people belonging to different social groups of United States to indicate to which of the following classifications would they admit members of the various racial groups.

1. To close kinship by marriage,
2. To my club as personal chums,
3. To my street as neighbours,
4. To employment in my occupation,
5. To citizenship in my country,
6. As visitors only in my country,
7. Would exclude from my country.

A close analysis of the above seven categories reveals that in social distance scales statements are constructed to measure the varying degrees of social intimacy or distance. The respondents have a wide choice ranging from a fairly close degree of relationship with the other group or their members to an extremely remote relationship or none at all.

In India too, attempts have been made to devise social distance scales for measuring social distance between different groups. B. Kuppuswamy in 1951 devised a scale in which he asked his respondents, (students in Madras) to indicate as to what extent would they admit Brahmins, Christians, Harijans, higher caste non-Brahmins, Muslims, Parsis and Sikhs to the following social relationships:

1. To kinship by marriage,
2. To take food in your own dining room,
3. As an intimate personal friend,
4. As a guest in your house,
5. As your neighbour,
6. As an acquaintance.

In this way in the social distance scales we find two different types of individuals.

(i) Those who are relatively willing or unwilling to be exposed to other group or their members.

(ii) Those who are relatively willing or unwilling to be identified with other groups or their members.

Factors Responsible for Social Distance

Social distance among various groups is the creation of the social condition and environment. Traditions, old beliefs, biased attitudes, discriminations or atrocities suffered by one group at the hands of others and stereotypes, all contribute towards widening the gulf between different groups and thus increasing the social distance. In brief, prejudices of any kind lead to social distance. It is the prejudice that manifests itself in an attitude unfavourable to the other group. A prejudiced individual keeps other groups at varying distances depending upon the intensity of the unfavourable attitude towards each group. In this way prejudices are responsible for creating a huge social distance that is very persistent in nature. The examples of such social distance can be found in the social distance manifested between Harijans and lower caste Hindus and between Muslims and Hindus.

GROUP INTERACTION

Groups are formed out of individuals. The mutual interdependence and action between and among the members of a group is responsible, to a great extent, in determining the nature, purpose and organization of the group. Every member of a group tries to influence the behaviour of the other group members and in turn is influenced by their behaviour. Thus, there is a sort of give and take between the members of a group on one hand and between different groups on the other. Such sort of give and take give rise to the phenomenon of group-interaction. Borrowing the words of Brown (1960) it can be safely said that *group interaction is a two-way process whereby each individual or group stimulates the other, and, in varying degree modifies the behaviour of the participants.*

Thus the process of interrelations and associations within the group and between and among different groups, is taken as group interaction and consequently it is supposed to include:

(i) The influence or impact of the group on their individual members;

(ii) The influence or impact of individual members on other members or on groups as a whole;
(iii) The mutual influence or impact of one group over the other.

In every society the groups, formal or informal, exert great influence on the behaviour and conduct of their members. They persuade their members to conform to the norms established by them. Groups influence personal goals, interests, attitudes and thus mould the personality and character of their members. Moreover, socialization of the individual takes place in groups as interpersonal relationships are learnt in group membership. The family, childhood, gang, peer group and other socio-psychological groups thus play a big role in shaping the personality and behaviour of its members.

The behaviour and personality characteristics of individual members of a group affect the behaviour of others and cast a significant impact over the functioning of the groups as a whole. The individual's influence on the group or its members depends on his status, strengths and weaknesses. Leader of the group exerts a great impact on the group members and behaviour of the group is moulded by him accordingly. Powerful members other than their leader also influence the decision of the group and can bring serious changes in the entire structure or functioning of the group. Sometimes, a single member, by his exceptionally bad or good personality characteristics and relationship within and outside the group may leave a mark on the life of the group. Students, teachers or head of the institution as an individual member may bring a lot of change in the group life of a school and similarly, in other walks of life, groups are formed, they make progress or fail and die as a result of the effect of their individual members on them.

There is also constant interaction among different groups. The structure, norms and values of one group exert influence on other groups. For example, family exercises great influence on the school life of the children. Peer-group relationships have impact upon the adjustment of children in other formal or informal groups. Community and its religious and social groups decide the working of the school as a group. On the other hand, school as a group also casts desirable impact on the community and society at large. In this way there is a constant give and take between the different formal or informal groups that exist in the society.

GROUP MIND

Group Mind is a term in social psychology that has been used to express group psychology by sociologists and psychologists. Let us see how this term has been used.

1. Firstly, we have sociologists like Lebon who used this term for explaining the various characteristics of crowd behaviour. This French sociologist asserted that individuals behave in a peculiar way when they are members of a crowd. Explaining the reason for such behaviour he said that individuals as members of a crowd are in the grip of "collective" or "group mind" and thus behave differently. At this time, as members of a crowd, their conscious personality disappears and it is their unconscious, moved by the group mind, that is responsible for their peculiar behaviour.
2. In the second category, we have sociologists and psychologists like McDougall who use this term as a concept to explain the behaviour of individuals as members of highly stable enduring groups like the army of some political and religious organizations. He asserted that members of these highly organized, well-integrated groups behave differently in these groups as they would otherwise behave as an individual outside these groups. "*The reason*" he said, "*is that as a member of these highly organized groups his behaviour is directed by the Psychology of Group Mind, viz. he behaves as others behave.*"

So, the concept of group mind has been made into use for explaining our peculiar behaviour as members of a crowd or a highly organized and integrated group. But there have been some difficulties in explaining the behaviour of individuals in the group by this concept named as *group mind*. It has been now clearly admitted that the concept of group mind, a mind over and above the minds of the individuals in that group, is not necessary to explain the behaviour of the individuals forming the group. The concept of group mind is now under attack. Kuppuswamy refutes this concept in the following way.

"*If we accept the concept of group mind we will have to speak of a Bengali mind or a Panjabi mind or Kerala mind and probably also of a Brahmin mind or a Harijan mind. Again, we will have to speak of the mind of each area in the town or the city or even of each road or part of a road in a city. Thus the whole problem reduces itself into absurdity.*" (1971, p. 361)

Therefore, it is difficult to coin a new type of group mind for explaining the behaviour of the individuals in that group. Moreover, an individual is a member of different groups at the same time and behaves differently as the situations or conditions undergo changes. In this way, even for explaining the behaviour of an individual as a member of different groups or the member of the same group in different situations, we will have to invent a number of group minds.

Due to some of these practical difficulties, the concept of group mind has been abandoned by the sociologists and psychologists. It has now been replaced by a more comprehensive and general term 'group behaviour'. Now it is understood that people behave differently as members of a special group under the influence of "group behaviour." In the pages to follow, we will study the factors affecting 'group behaviour' but let us first gain more insight into the importance and development of group mind as a prevalent term.

Importance of Group Mind

For the Country

A strong group mind elevates a country. The progress of Germany and Japan, after the second World War, took place as a result of strong group mind.

A group mind may pull a country down. It is for this reason that India is lagging behind other countries in terms of progress. In India we have many castes, sub-classes, religions and groups and so, there cannot be one 'group mind' in the country. In other words, there is diversity in the thoughts, feelings and actions of the countrymen which is a great obstacle in the way of group mind.

For the society

A strong group mind elevates a society and a weak mind brings the downfall of a society.

For the school

A strong group mind makes it easier for a school to attain high position. On the contrary, a school can reach the position of pride only by directing weak group mind and strengthening it.

Development of Group Mind in School

Group mind can be developed in schools in the following ten ways:

Acquainting the students and teachers with the high traditions of the school

Every school should have some high traditions and the students and teachers should be fully acquainted with them.

Writing model sentences

Mottos pertaining to group mind such as 'Union is strength' etc. should be written at important places in the schools.

Organizing functions

Some functions should be organized in the school, e.g. birthday celebrations of great leaders, annual functions, prize distribution function, parents' day, meeting of Alumni (Old Students) association.

Entrusting jobs of responsibility to students

Students should be entrusted with jobs of responsibility in the school so that leadership traits and group mind can be developed in them.

Appointing teachers on permanent basis

Teachers should be appointed on permanent basis in schools. Only then will they take greater interest in the affairs of the school.

Discouraging change of schools among students

It is essential for the development of group mind among the students that they continue their education in one school for a number of years. Development of group mind is impossible in children who change their school every year.

Giving opportunities of expression of feelings of rivalry and co-operation

At times the school should provide the students with opportunities of expression of feelings of healthy rivalry and co-operation in play, cultural and other activities in class groups.

Developing the feeling of group consciousness

The feeling of group consciousness should be developed in schools in order to have a group mind.

Enrolling the students as members of various groups

Students should be enrolled as members of many such groups as having own aims, traditions and methods.

To arrange for hostel accommodation

Hostel accommodation should be arranged in schools so that students may develop group mind by community living.

GROUP BEHAVIOUR

Meaning

The behaviour of a person in a group is different from his individual behaviour. In the individual behaviour, a person is free to think, feel and act but his freedom to do so is lost in a group. This individual is compelled to give up his individuality and his behaviour is governed by social rules. Therefore, when a person is the member of a club, he behaves in quite a different way because he obeys the rules of the club. Similarly, when a person becomes the member of a crowd he is ready to do the meanest of actions. He indulges in actions which he would feel very shy of doing in an individual capacity. Individuality is lost in a crowd and the group dynamics becomes uniform. Here, sympathy and suggestion play an extremely important part. The level of intelligence goes down in the case of a crowd, and so, susceptibility to suggestions increases. This type of behaviour seen in a group is called group behaviour.

Characteristics of Group Behaviour

Common goals, interest and ideals

The goals, interests and ideals of a group are common. They do their best to achieve them.

Similar behaviour

The members of a group show similarity of behaviour because they have common aims, interests and ideals.

Control of the group

The actions of members are controlled by the group. All the members of the group follow the ideals and traditions of the group.

Mutual obligation

It is such a power that not only keeps the members of a group united but provides them with energy, e.g. the relationship between the parents and children in a family or the love of husband and wife. In spite of differences on many issues they have certain common aims, ideals and values.

Sense of oneness

There is sense of oneness in a group because of the similarity in interests. A member looks upon others as related to him. In this way good feelings, devotion, faithfulness, adjustment, suggestions and imitation develop.

Psychological relationship

The behaviour of one member of a group influences that of the other and in this way his own behaviour is also influenced. This type of relationship is known as psychological relationship.

Influence of group characteristics

The characteristics or features of a group affect all its members.

Factors Affecting Group Behaviour

Man is a social animal. He has an instinct of gregariousness that compels him to live in a group. He needs society and socio-psychological groups for the satisfaction of his biological, social and psychological needs. In fact, the desire to satisfy various needs and motives brings people on the common platform and they join hands to form different formal as well as informal groups. Later on, psychological factors work as a motivating force for sustaining these groups. People derive satisfaction from belonging to a group. In group life, their tensions and anxieties are greatly reduced or eliminated and they get enormous opportunities for proper growth and development under proper care and suitable direction. For some people, group life provides opportunity to satisfy their need of dominating over or leading others. In this way for the satisfaction of their instinctive and other basic needs, people prefer to form different groups. Interdependence of the members of the group, their common interests and purposes, and shared common experiences give birth to group behaviour. Now they begin to feel, think and act together.

How a group will behave depends upon so many social and psychological factors. The individual members of the group and leader, ideals and norms of the group and the environment or situation in which it functions, are some of the factors that influence the structure of the group and its behaviour at a particular time. But most often, group behaviour is motivated by different psychological functions as those of sympathy, suggestions and imitation besides others. Below we shall try to describe their influence in detail.

SYMPATHY

Sympathy influences group behaviour by arousing collective feelings. It enables an individual to perceive the psychological state of another person. He begins to feel as others feel without caring to know why others are feeling in such a way. In this way sympathy leads the individuals to feel together. In the playing group of children, when someone screams "snake" and exhibits the emotion of fear, others perceiving the psychological state of their fellow member begin to exhibit the emotion of fear as well. They are persuaded to feel collectively and share the common experience on account of the phenomenon of sympathy. And in this way, sympathy is said to influence the behaviour of the group.

SUGGESTION

The phenomenon of suggestions influences the behaviour of the group by making the individual members think collectively. Suggestion makes the individual think like others. The thinking of an individual member in the group is merged with collective thinking. In a group, members share the thought with each other. When someone puts an idea or solution of the problem then others in the group begin to think that way. Particularly, the suggestions put forward by the leaders of the group are readily accepted and thus suggestions play a leading role in influencing the group decisions and behaviour. Moreover, the group norms and rules of conduct and behaviour are enforced through the phenomenon of suggestions. Through suggestion a person behaves in a group in accordance with the pre-practices and ideals and in this way also the phenomenon of suggestion plays a major role in influencing the group behaviour.

IMITATION

Phenomenon of imitation influences the behaviour of the group by making the individual members act collectively. Imitation involves copying others. By imitating the behaviour of others, a member in the group does as others do and thus members of the group indulge in common action by imitating each other. Like suggestion and sympathy, imitation also proceeds unwittingly. The acts of a superior person in the group or of a leader are imitated blindly and thus individuals in the group exhibit uniformity in their behaviour. They share the same conative experience with the help of the psychological phenomenon of imitation and in this way group behaviour is said to be influenced by imitation.

INDIVIDUAL AND GROUP GOALS

All individuals and all groups have their goals. The personal goals of individuals can be satisfied in a group. So, they willingly join groups. The goals in the classroom have been laid down in the form of goals of the curriculum. At present the students who do not come up to their mark of these goals form the majority of drop-outs, problem children etc. and are punished. A teacher well-versed in group psychology would think of modifying these goals so as to make them acceptable to all and such that the pupils as group members develop strong bonds of interpersonal relationships.

COHESIVENESS

The degree to which the members of a group wish to remain in the group is called cohesiveness. A cohesive group is one in which

(1) There are common goals.
(2) Members have similar background.
(3) In spite of changing conditions, it remains intact.
(4) The members are concerned with their membership and have strong motivation for contributing to the group's welfare, to take part in its activities and to further its objectives.

Group cohesiveness is useful because

(i) it contributes to the potency and vitality of a group.
(ii) it increases the importance of membership for group members.

FACTORS OF COHESIVENESS

Cohesiveness is influenced by the following seven factors:

Goals

Commonly accepted goals contribute to cohesiveness. Self-determined goals establish group unity more than imposed goals.

Size of the group

A group should be large enough to present diverse views but small enough to make provision for all the members of the group to participate in its deliberations. The size of the group should be determined by the purpose, individual needs, leadership and the sensitiveness of the teacher in diagnosing group action.

Discussion

Zander (1950) discovered that there was less aggression and interpersonal resentment in groups which are discussion oriented.

Effectiveness of sub-unit communication

Socio-metric groupings increase the solidarity and productivity of the group. As a result, the members of the group like to live with one another in comfort.

Participation and loyalty

The cohesiveness of a group is directly proportional to the participation and loyalty of its members.

Spirit of interpersonal competition

The modern era is the age of competition. In order to enable the pupils to meet the exigencies of life, it is desirable to inculcate in them the spirit of interpersonal competition. But excess of everything is bad and much emphasis on competition inhibits effective group action.

Democratic procedures

These imply maximum participation and involvement of group members in group activities, determining objectives, encouraging and reinforcing interpersonal contacts and relations, showing due regard for the individual specialists, employing the techniques of affection, warmth of feelings and persuasion etc.

Satisfaction of common needs

Group members have certain common needs on the existence of which depends group action.

LEADERSHIP

Every group, whether formal or informal, spontaneous or organized, has a leader. He is the person who manages the group activities and is responsible for intensifying the feeling of belongingness and interdependence among the group members. He persuades the members to feel, think and act together. In fact, the leader is one of the members of the group who, by virtue of his exceptional qualities or unique position in the group, rises to occasion, influences the behaviour of the group and directs the energy of the group to any channel—desirable or undesirable.

The group gets integrated and flourishes or gets disintegrated or perishes as a result of the efficient or inefficient leadership. A school in the able leadership of a headmaster can make tremendous progress while the unwise leadership may doom its future. Similarly, the family, class, playing group, hobby club and so many other groups can make progress or fail in their objectives as a result of the leadership they avail. Therefore, it is essential to know more about leadership and the characteristics of a good leader so that we can train children for effective leadership.

Types of Leadership

Different authors have adopted different modes for the classification of leaders in various types. Some have classified them as political leaders, social leaders, religious leaders and intellectual leaders depending on the field of their activities. Writers like Prem Pasricha and Kuppuswamy assert that leaders should be classified into the following four types:

Institutional leaders like head of the school, district collector, president of a country, manager of a factory etc. Their orders are obeyed through the hierarchies of ranks and the decisions are based on the established precedents.

Dominant leaders like Napoleon, Stalin, Nasser etc. They lead the group due to an urge to dominate. They are autocrats and dictators.

Persuasive leaders like Gandhi, Lincoln and Nehru. They do not aim to dominate and dictate the group but to persuade the members to help and follow them.

Experts. They lead the group on account of their acquired proficiency and skill in science, art or any other sphere. They are recognized as the authorities in their respective fields and have a line of followers among the people who are interested in that type of work.

The categories suggested above are not mutually exclusive and Kuppuswamy himself admits that "*such a classification cannot be said to be a sound classification*." (1971, pp. 461-62). Therefore, a more appropriate ground is needed to classify the leaders. In my opinion, the behaviour and the personality characteristics of the leaders or the way they lead their groups should be made a criterion for their classification. On this ground, I agree with the simplest classification suggested by Kretch and Crutchfield in their text "Theory and problems of Social Psychology". According to them, leaders can be classified as Authoritarian and Democratic.

Authoritarian leaders are very dominant and aggressive. They determine policies without counting their followers and dictate every step and assign duties. They do not tolerate any debate and believe in action rather than planning and thinking. They typically forbid direct communication or interaction among their followers. All communication and directions must flow through them. In this way they become indispensable to the followers and the group they lead. In their absence, the group cannot function. All the autocrats and dictators belong to this category. It has been found that such type of leadership does not care for the wishes and ambitions of the members of the group or followers. It makes the members either submissive or secretly aggressive towards it. Either they depend on him entirely and lose all initiative; or they feel frustrated and aggressive towards the leader. When practiced in the classroom by the teacher or headmaster, such type of leadership makes the children quite dependent and submissive. In some cases it leads to the problematic behaviour and maladjustment of children.

Democratic leaders, on the other hand, are very cooperative and accommodating. They do not dominate or dictate but persuade the members to follow them and share the power with other individuals in the groups. They win the hearts of their followers and identify themselves completely with the group they lead. They encourage group discussion and collective decision on matters of policy, allow members to choose their own work and also themselves actively participate in the work. They encourage freedom of thought and action and thus cultivate democratic values in the groups. Unlike the authoritarian leaders, the democratic leaders are flexible. They bring desirable changes in their ideas in the light of the needed group changes. They encourage interpersonal relationships and communications among the members and make them strive hard to achieve the desired objectives. Such type of leadership, if practiced in schools, may be very conductive and helpful in the proper growth and development of children.

Traits or Qualities of Leadership

Attempts have been made to discover the essential qualities or traits that different type of leaders possess. For this, it has been tried to list the traits of leadership. Various mental, physical, emotional, social and moral qualities are thus generalized. But such generalization, however general it may be, does not fit for all types of leaders. There is no single kind of skills and personality traits that will make a man always a leader. Leadership, besides the important trait of one's personality, is a function of the situation. Specific situations require specific qualities in a leader. However, the following four characteristics or traits are essential for becoming a successful leader:

Identification with the Group

The leader must belong to the group he leads. He should have membership character of the group and should be able to make the members feel that he is one of them. He must share the values, attitudes and interests of the group and thus try to completely identify with the group.

Superiority over the Members of the Group

The leader, while completely identifying with the group and being perceived by group members as one of them, must be able to show his superiority to the group members in the qualities esteemed by them. On account of his superior qualities and virtues, he can be able to exercise effective control and coordination of the work of the group. Moreover, he can win confidence and cooperation of the members. But he apparently must not be very superior or talented. In such cases, group members do not consider him as one of them and thus do not accept his leadership.

Knowing the Psychology of the Group

The leader must have an adequate knowledge of group psychology. He should have a functional knowledge of the group mind or group behaviour. Moreover, he should be able to utilize his knowledge of group psychology for proper organization and working of his group.

Dynamic and Flexible

The leader should be dynamic and flexible in his attitude, interests and other behaviour patterns. In every case, he must meet his followers' expectations. He must be able to play democratic or authoritarian role depending upon the need of the situation. He should be able to bring changes in line of action according to the demands of situation and common wishes of his followers.

Training For Leadership

The notion that traits of leadership are inherited and therefore, leaders are born and not made is wrong. Similarly, the belief that by mere training or education under suitable environment any person can be made to become a successful leader is also erroneous. The truth lies between these two extremes. Both heredity and environment coupled with adequate training or education is essential for helping children become successful leaders. In this way the initial step, in any programme of imparting training for leadership to children, consists in the location of the would-be-leaders. Children, who exhibit the basic traits of leadership in the classroom as well as in other extra-curricular group situations should be well attended by the teachers and school authorities. The following few suggestions may work well in helping these potential leaders:

1. These children should be given opportunities for playing the role of leaders in curricular or extra-curricular group situations. They can be made monitor of the class or assigned leadership role in the hobbies groups, games or other extra curricular group situations.
2. The biographies and auto-biographies of national heroes, political, social and religious leaders and other great men educate and inspire the youngsters. Thus they should be encouraged and provided opportunities of reading, stimulating and inspiring literature.
3. Example is better than precept. Therefore, the teachers and headmaster should produce a living example of successful leadership before children. Student leaders belonging to higher grades of the school may also stimulate and educate the would-be-leaders belonging to the lower grades.
4. Religion and moral education and the organization of social services may also help in the cultivation of proper social and moral traits as well as group tendencies among these children.
5. Cooperation of the parents and other social agencies should also be secured in the proper cultivation of desirable leadership traits among these children.

In this way, school can play a big role in training the potential leaders by formal as well as informal techniques. In an advanced training programme the potential leaders may be given an adequate knowledge of group psychology and the various experiences for role playing can also be arranged. Teacher as well as other responsible elders can take a lead by putting self-examples and regulating the behaviour of these trainees for acquiring the necessary skill, knowledge and other personality traits.

SUMMARY

Group dynamics refers to a mechanism that tries to explain dynamics within a group on account of nature of the group, group interaction and factors responsible for influencing the functioning of the group. Knowledge of the group dynamics may prove quite helpful to the teachers for organizing classrooms, other learning situations and school as a whole as an effective as well as efficient group for bringing desired behaviour changes in terms of students' proper growth and development, particularly in inculcating social skills, democratic values and leadership qualities.

In layman's language, *a group* is said to be a collection or aggregate of two or more people. However, from the socio-psychological angle, a *group* refers to a collection or aggregate of two or more interdependent individuals who usually feel, think and act together. Groups may be classified as (i) In group (the group with which we identify ourselves) and out group (the group the members of which are considered as outsiders by us) (ii) Primary (intimate face to face relationship among members), secondary (relationship are more or less casual) and tertiary (relationship is quite marginal and transient in character) (iii) Organized and spontaneous groups and (iv) Formal and Informal groups.

School as a miniature society can act as a very influencing social group for exercising desirable impact on the growth and development of the children. Many of its sub-groups like classroom group, literary society, dramatic club, subject societies etc. can also work effectively on this front. The school and its sub-groups with all their dynamism help the children as members of the group to satisfy their socio-psychological and educational needs as well as for attaining the goals of schooling.

Social distance refers to the distance at which members of a particular group try to hold another group and its members. For the measurement of such social distance between the members of the two groups, we can make use of the social distance scales especially constructed for this purpose. In these scales, statements are so constructed so as to measure the varying degrees of social intimacy or distance. Prejudices of any kind in the relationship between the members of two groups give birth to an attitude unfavourable to each other and it then becomes a potent source of increasing social distance between these groups.

Group interaction may be understood as a two-way process whereby each individual or group tries to stimulate and modify the behaviour and structure of another on the basis of a mutual give and take relationship. As a result of such interaction, groups may be seen to exert great influence on the behaviour of their members. The behaviour of individual members of a group may exercise great impact on influencing the behaviour of others and also over the functioning of the group as a whole. Similarly interaction between and among different groups may also exert great influence on the structure and working of the other groups.

Group Mind as a term is used to express group psychology in the field of social psychology. It indicates that as members of a group, we have a different set of mind called 'group mind' as a result of which members behave in a particular way. However, the term group mind has now been replaced by a more comprehensive and general term 'group behaviour'.

The term **group behaviour** refers to a distinct and particular type of behaviour demonstrated by the individuals as members of a group. As an influence of such behaviour, the individuals try to behave in the manner as the group as a whole behaves by giving up their individualities altogether. The group behaviour is influenced by so many psychological and environmental factors like sympathy, suggestion, imitation, dominance of group goals over individual goals, group cohesiveness, etc.

The group may get integrated and flourish, or get disintegrated or perish as a result of the efficient and inefficient leadership. Leadership by its nature and objectives may be classified as authoritarian and democratic leadership. The latter type of leadership may prove more conducive and helpful in the proper growth and development of our children. Teachers should, therefore, try to imbibe the traits essential for the development of such leadership. It may include their identification with the group, ability to show their superiority to the group members, knowledge about the psychology of the groups, and their capacity to remain dynamic and flexible according to the demands of the situation. They should also work for developing leadership qualities among these students by placing their own example of effective leadership, providing opportunities for developing and nurturing leadership traits through curricular and co-curricular means, etc. with the active cooperation of the parents and other social agencies.

References and Suggested Readings

Cartwright, D. and Zander, A., *Group Dynamics*, International ed., Harper & Row, New York, 1968.

Cooley, C.H., Quoted by Brown, F.J., *Educational Sociology*, Prentice-Hall, New York, 1960.

Gates, A.I., *Elementary Psychology*, Macmillon, New York, 1947.

Good, Carter V., *Dictionary of Education*, McGraw-Hill, New York, 1959.

Kretch, D., Cruchfield and Ballachey, E., *Individual in Society*, International (Students ed.), McGraw-Hill, Tokyo, 1951.

Kuppuswamy, B., *An Introduction to Social Psychology*, Asia Publishing House, Bombay, 1971 (Reprint).

McDougall, William, *Introduction to Social Psychology*, Methuen, London, 1946.

Summer, W.G., Quoted by Brown, F.J., *Educational Sociology*, (5th printing), Prentice-Hall, New York, 1960.

41

Statistical Data—Meaning, Organisation and Presentation

CHAPTER COMPOSITION

MEANING OF THE TERM STATISTICS

Usually the word *statistics* carries the following three meanings:

1. In the first place, it refers to numerical facts. State as well as Central statistical departments and various other agencies can be seen engaged in collecting valuable statistics (numerical facts) concerning the birth and death, school attendance, employment market, output of industrial plants, agriculture fields, etc.
2. The word *statistics* also refers to the method or methods of dealing with numerical facts. In this sense, statistics is considered a science of collecting, classifying, summarizing, analyzing and interpreting numerical facts.
3. Thirdly, *statistics* also refers to the summarized figures of numerical facts such as percentages, averages, means, medians, modes, standard deviations etc. Each of these figures is separately (average or mean etc.) referred to as 'statistics'.

In this way, the word 'statistics' can be referred to as numerical facts or science or methodology of dealing with numerical facts or summarized figures of numerical facts. Tate has beautifully summarized these different meanings of 'statistics' in the following witty way: *"It's all perfectly clear; you compute statistics (mean, median, mode etc.) from statistics (numerical facts) by statistics (as a science or methodology).*" (1955, p. 5)

MEANING OF TERM DATA

The dictionary meaning of the word 'data' is facts (plural of datum, meaning fact). Thus in wider sense, the term data designate the evidence or facts for describing a group or a situation, but in a particular sense, it is generally used for numerical facts such as heights, weights, scores on achievement tests, intelligence test, etc.

METHODS OF ORGANIZING AND PRESENTING DATA

The data from tests and experiments in the form of scores need to be classified and organized in a systematic way for understanding the meanings and deriving some useful conclusions. In general, the following four methods are used for organizing and presenting statistical data:

1. Presentation in the form of Statistical Tables.
2. Presentation in the form of Frequency distribution.
3. Graphical presentation of ungrouped data.
4. Graphical presentation of Frequency distribution (Grouped data).

Statistical Tables

In this form of presentation, the data are tabulated or arranged in some properly selected classes, and the arrangement is described by a title and sub-titles. Such tables can list the original raw scores as well as the percentages, means, standard deviations, etc. Below we have explained this with the help of Table 41.1.

Table 41.1 Pass Percentage of High Schools of Rohtak City in the High School Public Examination

High school of Rohtak	*Name of the school*	*Pass percentage*	*Girls pass percentage*	*Boys pass percentage*
	A			
	B			
	C			
	D			
	E			

Frequency Distribution

In this form of presentation, we group the quantitative data in some arbitrarily chosen classes. For this purpose usually the scores are distributed into groups of scores (classes) and each score is allotted a place in the respective group or class. It is also seen as to how many times does a particular score or group of scores occur in the given data. This is known as the frequency of score or group of scores. In this way, *Frequency distribution may be considered as a method of presenting a collection of groups of scores in such a way that it shows frequency in each group of scores or class.* Various steps for presenting quantitive data by a frequency distribution can be understood properly with the help of the following problem:

Problem. The marks obtained by 50 students in an Achievement test are given below:

62, 21, 26, 32, 56, 36, 37, 39, 53, 40, 54, 42
44, 61, 68, 28, 33, 56, 57, 37, 52, 39, 40, 54
43, 43, 63, 30, 34, 58, 35, 38, 50, 38, 52, 41
51, 44, 41, 42, 43, 45, 46, 45, 47, 48, 49, 45
46, 48.

Tabulate these scores in Frequency distribution by clearly explaining the various steps involved.

Steps for grouping data into Frequency distribution:

1. **Finding the range.** First of all, the range of the series to be grouped is found out. It is done by subtracting the lowest score from the highest. In this present problem, the range of the distribution is 68 – 21, i.e. 47.

2. **To determinate the class interval or grouping interval.** After deriving the range, the number and size of the classes of groups to be used in grouping the data are determined.

There exists two rules for this purpose.

First rule: For gaining an idea of the size of the classes, i.e. class interval, the range is divided by the number of classes. Class interval is usually denoted by the symbol '*i*' and is always a whole number. Thus the formula for deciding the class interval is

$$i = \frac{\text{Range}}{\text{Number of Classes Desired}}$$

Now the question arises as to how much classes or groups should one distribute a given data. As a general rule, Tate writes *"If the series contains fewer than about 50 items, more than about 10 classes are not justified. If the series contains from about 50 to 100 items, 10 to 15 classes tend to be appropriate. If more than 100 items, 15 or more classes tend to be appropriate. Ordinarily not fewer than 10 classes or more than 20 are used."* (1955, p. 44)

If by dividing Range by the number of classes we do not get a whole number, the nearest appropriate number is taken as class interval.

Second Rule: According to the second rule, class interval i is first decided and then the number of the classes is determined. For this purpose usually the class intervals of 2, 3, 5 or 10 units in length are used.

Both of the above mentioned rules are practiced. In my opinion, it is better to use a combined procedure made out of both the rules. Actually the range, the number of classes and the class interval – all should be taken into consideration while planning for the frequency distribution and we must aim to select a proper class interval i that can yield appropriate categories (number of classes) as mentioned above by Tate.

Considering in this way, the proper class interval i in the present example is 5.

[Here, Range = 47. Scores are 50 in number and thus about 10 classes are sufficient. Therefore $i = 47/10 = 4.7$, i.e. Nearest whole number = 5].

Writing the Contents of Frequency Distribution

After deciding on the size and number of the class interval and locating the highest and lowest scores of the given data, we proceed to write down the contents of the Frequency distribution. For this purpose, three columns are drawn and work is carried out as under:

(a) *Writing the classes of distribution.* In the first column, we write down all the classes of distribution. For this purpose, first of all the lowest class is settled down and afterwards other subsequent classes are written down. In the present problem, 20–24 can be taken as the lowest class and then we can have classes as 25–29, 30–34, etc, up to 65–69.

(b) *Tallying the Scores into proper classes.* In this step, the scores given in the data are taken one by one and tallied in their proper classes as shown in the second column of the table given below. These tally marks against each class are then counted. These counted numbers are called the frequencies of that class. They are written in the third column as shown in Table 41.2.

Table 41.2

Class or Scores	*Tallies*	*Frequencies*
65–69	|	1
60–64	|||	3
55–59	||||	4
50–54	~~||||~~ ||	7
45–49	~~||||~~ ||||	9
40–44	~~||||~~ ~~||||~~ |	11
35–39	~~||||~~ |||	8
30–34	||||	4
25–29	||	2
20–24	|	1
		Total Frequencies (N) = 50

(c) *Checking the tallies:* The total or third column should be equal to the number of individuals whose scores have been tabulated. Under the above tabulation, total frequencies, i.e. 50, agrees with the total number of students given in the problem.

SOME MORE THINGS REGARDING FREQUENCY DISTRIBUTION

1. *Class limits of the frequency distribution:* The designation of classes, i.e. 20–24, 25–29, 30–34 etc., are called the indicated or written class limits. The actual class limits are always taken as 0.5 units below and 0.5 units above the written class limits. For example, the actual limit of class 20–24 is 19.5–24.5 (19.5 as lower and 24.5 as higher class limits).
2. *Mid-point of a class in a frequency distribution.* In a frequency distribution, classes are sometimes indicated by their mid-values or mid-points. The formula of determining the mid-point of a class—

   Mid-point of a class = Indicated or written lower limits + [Upper limit – Lower limit/2]

[Note: We don't consider actual class limits in calculating mid-point. Thus, for the class 20–24, the mid-point is 20 + [(24 – 20)/2] = 20 + 2 = 22.

Graphical Presentation of Ungrouped Data

For the data which is not grouped into a frequency distribution, we use the following common graphs or diagrams.

(i) Pictographs or Pictograms.
(ii) Bar graph or Bar Diagrams.
(iii) Circle or pie graphs/diagrams.
(iv) Line graphs.

Let us discuss these four types of graphical representation.

PICTOGRAPHS OR PICTOGRAMS

Pictographs or pictograms are the graphs or diagrams used for presenting an ungrouped statistical data in pictorial (picture like) form. A picture is said to be worth more than 1000 spoken or written words. Thereby the pictorial representation of the data is always considered better than its description in words or figures. Let us illustrate this fact through an example.

Example 41.1

In a data collection process, it was found that there are 100 students in class VI, 85 students in Class VII, 80 in VIII, 90 in IX and 70 in X. Present this data through a pictograph.

Solution

Table 41.3 Presentation of data in a Tabular Form

Class	*VI*	*VII*	*VIII*	*IX*	*X*
No. of students	100	85	80	90	70

Presentation of Data in the pictorial form

Step 1: Let us represent a student with a picture (indicative of a student figure)

Step 2: For the sake of brevity and simplicity, let us have a scale, a picture (of student) equal to 20 students in number:

Following these steps the pictorial presentation (pictograph) of the given data will be as under:

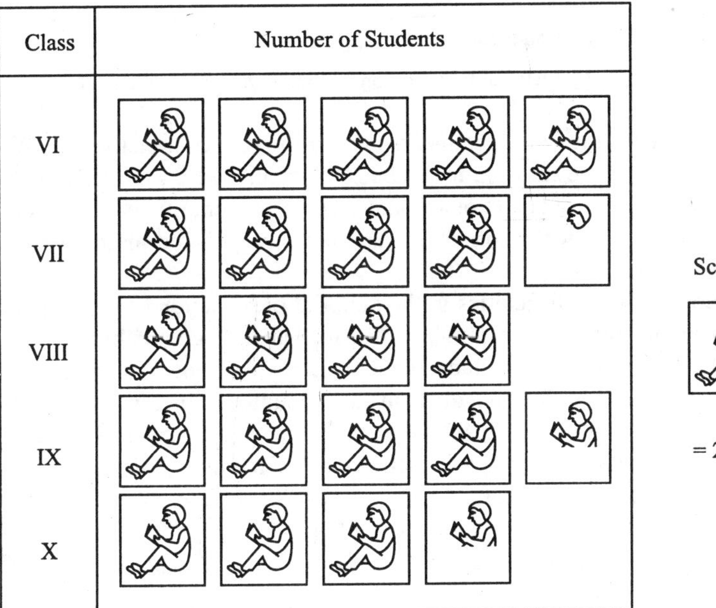

Fig. 41.1 Pictorial presentation of the data given in Example 41.1

Example 41.2

At a parking place at New Delhi Railway Station, the following statistical data (about the number of cars from different states) was collected and arranged in tabular form. Make a pictogram of this tabular data.

Table 41.4 Presentation of Data in Tabular Form

State	*Number of Cars*
Delhi	140
Uttar Pradesh	60
Punjab	30
Haryana	100
Others	70

The pictograph showing the number of cars belonging to different states is presented below:

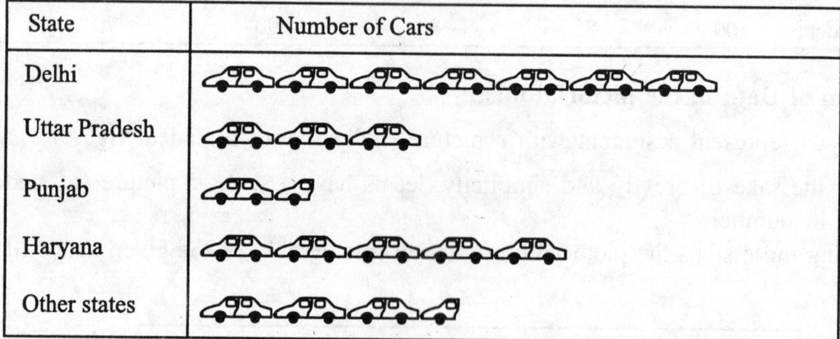

Fig. 41.2 Pictorial presentation of data given in Example 41.2.

You can now very well imagine the merits and advantages of a pictograph. A mere glimpse of the pictograph reveals that the maximum number of cars parked on the railway station were from Delhi. It was followed by Haryana and other states. The minimum number of cars parked were from Punjab. Hence valuable statistical information can be easily gathered in an interesting and pleasing way from the pictograph.

However, there lies some difficulties in the pictorial presentation of data especially in choosing a suitable scale (picture for a given number of units) and its comprehension. In the above two examples, we have chosen figures of students and cars representing a strength of 20. In both these pictographs, we can easily notice the difficulties encountered in representing the numbers not wholly divisible by 20 i.e. 30, 50, 70, 85, 90 etc. We have represented the strength of 85 (in the first example) students with four complete pictures and a fraction (only head). Similar is the case with the incomplete pictures of cars. Here we just have approximation and not the exact measurement of the pictorial figures for representing the scaled fractions numerical data. This difficulty can be somewhat removed in other forms of graphical representation of data as will be discussed soon.

BAR GRAPHS OR BAR DIAGRAMS

Instead of using pictures, we can use bars (rectangles of similar breadth) for the representation of numerical data. This mode of presentation, statistical data through bars is known as bar graphs or bar diagrams. For illustration, let us try to have a bar graph of the tabulated data given in example 41.1. It may take the following shape as given in Fig. 41.3.

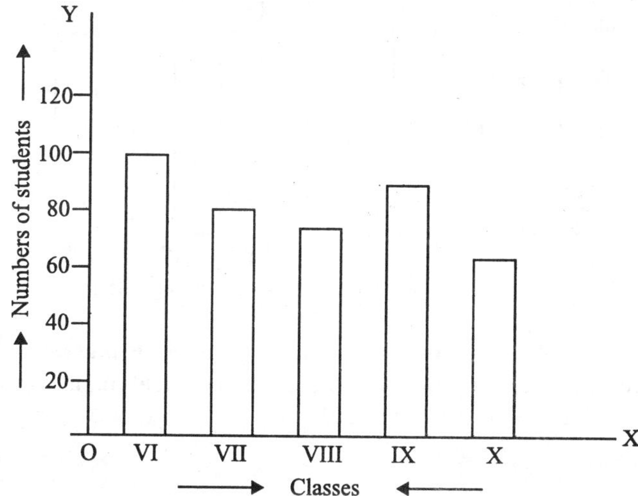

Fig. 41.3 Bar graph or bar diagram showing the strength of students in various classes.

How to draw bar graph?

(i) Try to use a graph paper for drawing the bar graph.

(ii) On one of the axes X or Y, try to plot numerical data by choosing a proper scale and have the other variable like classes in this example on the other axis. Here in this example, the numerical strength of students has been potted on the Y axis. The number of students in different classes are then represented by bars (rectangles of similar breadth) constructed on the X axis.

What can be inferred from the bar graph?

A bar graph shown in the figure above may provide the following information in quite a simple and quick way.

- It shows the strength of students in a particular class of the school, i.e. there are 70 students in class X.
- The class having highest strength, i.e. class VI.
- The class with lowest strength, i.e. Class X.
- It also reveals that the strength of students gets decreased as we pass from class VI to VIII. It once again increases in class IX but lowers down once again in class X.
- The relative strength of the students studying in different classes of the school may also be adjudged easily for one or the other type of comparison.

Example 41.3

Let us have another bar graph for further illustration. Can you think abut various types of information revealed to you just through its glimpse and useful interpretation?

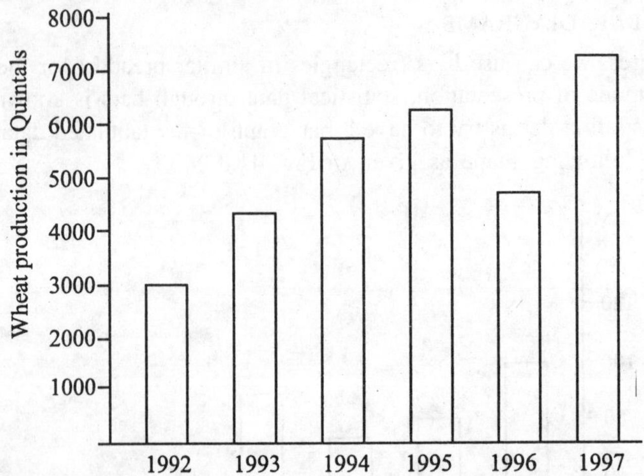

Fig. 41.4 Bar graph showing wheat production during different years.

One can easily infer from the above bar graph that the years of the highest and the lowest yields are 1997 and 1992 respectively and in comparison to the yield in the year 1992, there is approximately double production in the year 1995.

CIRCLE GRAPH OR PIE DIAGRAM

Circle or pie graphs/diagrams provide us an opportunity to represent statistical data through the figure of a circle and its constituents, i.e. proportionate sub-divisions. These are specifically helpful in the cases in which the question of proportion is of much interest. Constructing them requires a working knowledge of angle measurement and percentages.

The process of the construction of a pie graph may be understood with the help of an example given below.

Example 41.4

200 B.Ed students of a college of Education were asked to give their options for the participation in one or the other types of cocurricular activities. The preferences data was tabulated as under:

Activities	Debate	Dance	Music	Painting	Models	Excursion
No. of students	42	36	36	12	6	68

Present this data through pie diagram.

Solution

The steps for the construction of the required pie diagram may be outlined as below:

(i) A circle has the value of 2π (2 pie) i.e. 360°. In the present example, the total sample is 200 which has to be represented through a complete circle having 360°.

(ii) The various constituents of the collected data, i.e. preference for one or the other cocurricular activities, may then be assigned varying values of pie in terms of the degrees as computed below:

Debate: No. of students = 42 out of 200

Proportion out of 100 = 42\200 × 100 = 21%

Proportion out of 360° = 42\200 × 360° = 75.6°

Dance & Music : No. of students = 36 out of 200
Proportion out of 100 = 36/200 × 100 = 18%
Proportion out of 360° = 36/200 × 360° = 64.8°

Painting : No. of students = 12 out of 200
Proportion out of 100 = 12\200 × 100 = 6%
Proportion out of 360° = 12/200 × 360° = 21.6°

Modeling : No. of students = 6 out of 200
Proportion out of 100 = 6/200 × 100 = 3%
Proportion out of 360° = 6/200 × 360° = 10.8°

Excursion : No. of students = 68 out of 200
Proportion out of 100 = 68/200 × 100 = 34%
Proportion out of 360° = 68/200 × 360° = 122.4°

(iii) Now all these above proportions 75.6°, 64.8°, 64.8°, 21.6°, 10.8° and 122.4° may be represented as the different sectors of a whole circle with the help of the knowledge of the measurement of angles.

(iv) These may be taken as the final figures for drawing the required pie diagram.

Fig. 41.5 Pie graph showing preferences of B.Ed students for the curricular activities.

Example 41.5

A researcher collected the data from 1000 people fond of pets and tabulated the findings as under:

No. of people	Cats	Dogs	Snakes	Turtles	Fishes	Parrots	Other birds
	180	320	50	50	90	180	130

Represent the above data through pie graph.

Solution: Following the procedure suggested in the previous example, the pie diagram may take the following shape:

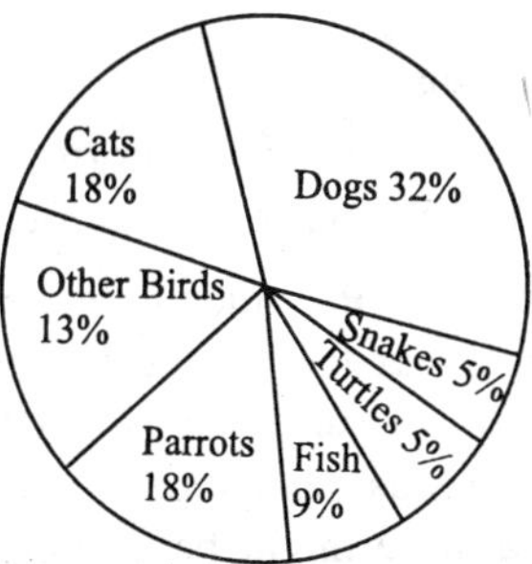

Fig. 41.6 Pie graph showing people fond of different pets.

LINE GRAPHS

Line graphs can be better used in describing the concommitted relationships between two variables by plotting their respective values on the X and Y axes of a graph paper (After choosing appropriate scales). Let us illustrate this fact through examples.

Examples 41.6

Science students of the IX class of a school collected data about weather on a cold day of the month December by recording the room temperature at various hours of the day and obtained the following line graph as the results of their survey.

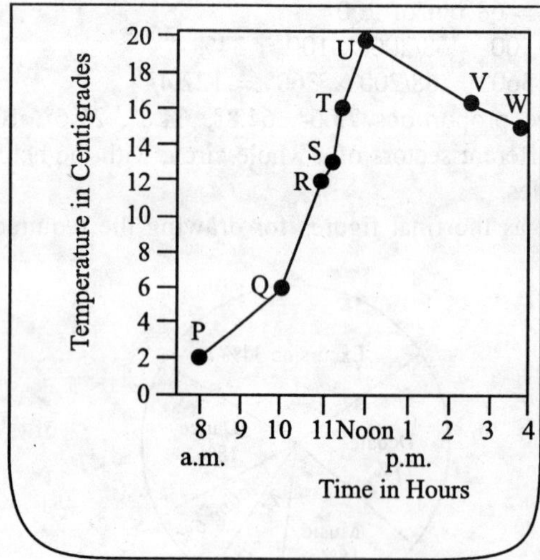

Fig. 41.7 A line graph showing the temperatures on a day in December.

Process of construction

(i) Here, time in hours has been plotted on X-axis while the corresponding temperatures in centigrade have been plotted on Y-axis.

(ii) The five small squares of the graph paper have been taken equivalent to 1 hour on X-axis and 2 centigrade on Y-axis.

(iii) The facts like 2°C recorded at 8.00 a.m., 6°C recorded at 10.00 a.m. etc. have been plotted at the varying points and then these points have been joined by continuous straight lines (see the placing of the points P, Q, R, S, T, U, V, W as the intersection points of paired data and their joining).

What can be inferred from the linegraphs?

Line graphs like above can reveal many facts and information about the collected data and consequently we can be able to provide answers to the queries like below:

1. For which hours during the day did the students collect data?
2. What was the highest temperature of the day according to the graph?
3. Between what hours was the temperature increasing/decreasing?
4. About what time in the morning was the temperature about 10°C?
5. What do you predict the temperature might be at 5.00 p.m, lower or higher than 16°C?

Example 41.7

The line graph given below in Fig. 41.8 depicts mastery of multiplication facts by a particular student in the course of learning. Here the time spent in weeks for having mastery over the multiplication facts is shown on X-axis and the achievement in terms of mastery (known through the percentage of facts mastered) is shown on Y-axis by choosing appropriate scales.

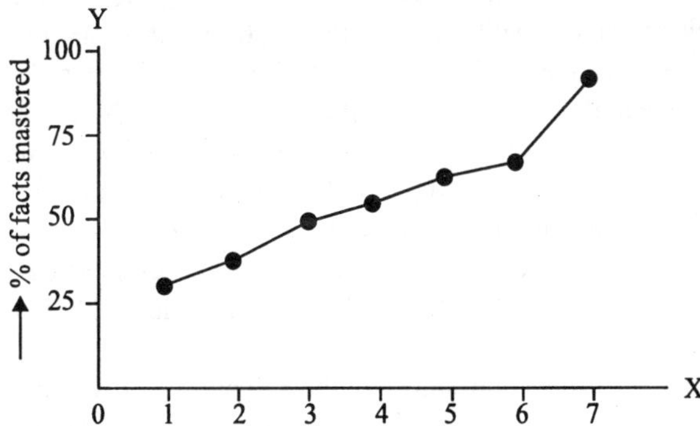

Fig. 41.8 Line graph showing progress about mastery over the multiplication facts.

Choosing a mode for ungrouped data

Each of the graphical mode, pictograph, bar graph, pie graph and line graph described above have their own merits and limitations for being utilized in the representation of a given ungrouped data at a particular occasion to furnish useful information. Therefore, a wise decision should always be made before the employment of a particular graphic mode in a particular situation. Take the last example of representing the data concerning mastery over the multiplication by a line graph. Here it would make no sense if one turns these weekly mastery figures into a pie or a bar chart. There is also no possibility of representing these through pictograph. Similarly in the case of representing facts regarding the percentage of fondness of pets, there will be no sense in displaying them through a line graph. Here the decision for representing them through a pie graph seems quite appropriate as there stands a whole of which the different figures concerning pet's choices are collectively a part. Contrarily, in the cases showing concommitment changes occurred in one variable in relation to the changes introduced in the other, it is always advisable to use line graph as the mode of representation. In this way, while trying to determine how to best display a particular data, one must decide whether or not to graph the data, and if yes, what kind of graph to use.

The Graphical Presentation of Frequency Distribution (Grouped Data)

There are four methods of representing a frequency distribution graphically:

1. Histogram or column diagram
2. Frequency Polygon
3. Cumulative Frequency Graph
4. Cumulative Frequency Percentage Curve or Ogive

Out of these methods, we would take up the most common ones, namely Histogram and Frequency Polygon, for discussion in the present text.

HISTOGRAM

A histogram or column diagram is essentially a bar graph of a frequency distribution. The following points are to be kept in mind while constructing the histogram for a frequency distribution:

(i) The scores in the form of actual class limits as 19.5-24.5, 24.5-29.5, etc. are taken in the construction of a histogram.

(ii) It is customary to take two extra intervals (classes) one below and the other above the given grouped intervals of classes (with zero frequency). In the case of frequency distribution given in table 41.2, we can take 14.5-19.5 and 69.5-74.5 as the two required extra-intervals.

(iii) Now we take the actual lower limits of all the class intervals (including the extra-intervals) and try to plot them on X-axis. The lower limit of the lowest intervals (one of the extra intervals) is taken at the intersecting point of X-axis and Y-axis.

(iv) Frequencies of the distribution are plotted on the Y-axis.

(v) Each class or interval with its specific frequency is represented by a separate rectangle. The base of each rectangle is the width of the interval '*i*' and the height is the respective frequency of that class or interval.

(vi) It is not essential to project the sides of the rectangles down to the base line.

(vii) Care should be taken in selecting the appropriate units of representation along the X-axis and Y-axis. Both X-axis as well as Y-axis should be neither too short nor too long. "A good general rule for this purpose" as suggested by Garrett "is to select X and Y units which will make the height of figures approximately 75% of its width." (1971, p. 11).

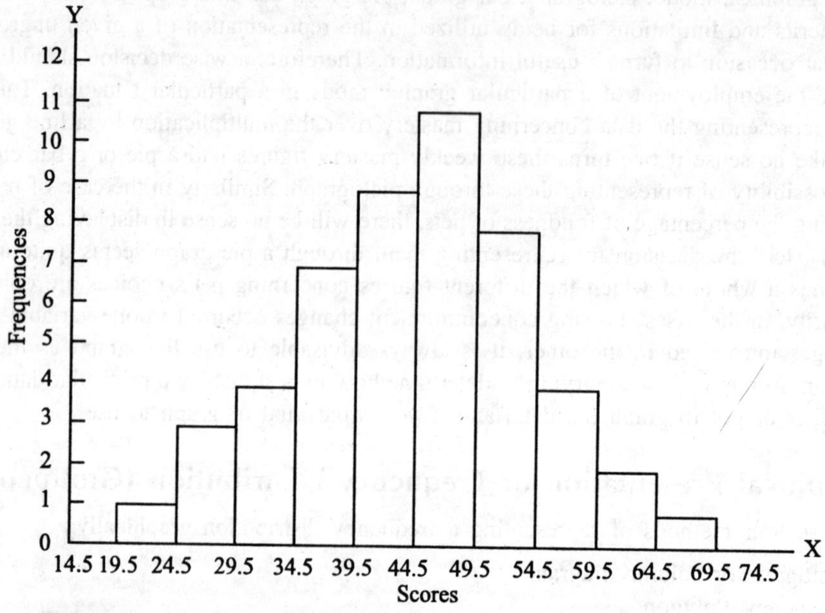

Fig. 41.9 The Histogram of Frequency distribution given in the Table 41.2.

FREQUENCY POLYGON

A *frequency polygon* is essentially a line graph for the graphical representation of the frequency distribution. We can obtain a frequency polygon from a histogram if the mid points of the upper bases of the rectangles are connected. But it is not essential to plot histogram first to draw a frequency polygon. We can construct it directly from a given frequency distribution. The following points are helpful in constructing a frequency polygon:

(i) Like histogram, two extra intervals or classes one above and the other below the given intervals are taken.
(ii) The mid-points of all the classes or intervals (including two extra intervals) are calculated.
(iii) The mid-points are marked along the X-axis and the corresponding frequencies are plotted along the Y-axis choosing suitable scales on both the axes.
(iv) The various points obtained by plotting the mid-points and frequencies are joined by straight lines to get the frequency polygon.
(v) For the appropriate height of the figure and selection of X and Y units, the rule emphasized earlier in the case of histogram should be followed.

SCALE: ON X-AXIS → 3 SCORES=5 SMALL SQUARES = 0.5″
ON Y-AXIS → FREQUENCY=3 SMALL SQUARES = 0.3″.

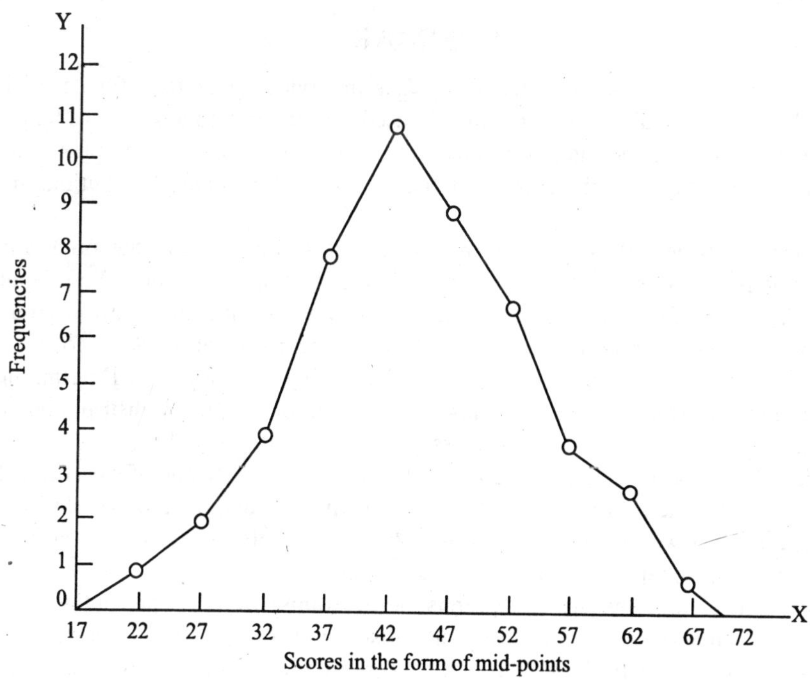

Fig. 41.10 The Frequency polygon of the frequency distribution given in Table 41.2.

COMPARISON BETWEEN HISTOGRAM AND FREQUENCY POLYGON

Although both histogram and frequency polygon are used for the graphic representation of the frequency distribution and are alike in many aspects yet they possess points of difference. Some of these differences can be cited as below:

1. While histogram is essentially the bar graph of the given frequency distribution, the frequency polygon is a line graph of this distribution.

2. In frequency polygon, we assume frequencies to be concentrated at the mid-points of the class interval. It merely points out the graphical relationship between mid-points and frequencies and thus is unable to show the distribution of frequencies within each class interval. However, the histogram gives a very clear as well as accurate picture of the relative proportions of frequency from interval to interval. A mere glimpse of the figure of the Histogram answers such questions as:
   (i) Which group of class-interval has the largest or smallest frequency?
   (ii) Which pair of groups or class intervals has the same frequency?
   (iii) Which group has its frequency double than another?
3. In comparing two or more distributions by plotting two or more graphs on the same axes, frequency polygon is more useful and practicable than the Histogram as in such cases vertical and horizontal lines in the histogram tend to coincide.
4. In comparison to histogram, frequency polygon gives a much better conception of the contour of the distribution. With a part of the polygon curve, it is easy to know the trend of the distribution but a Histogram is unable to tell such a thing.

SUMMARY

The term *statistical data* in a wider sense designates the evidence or facts for describing a group or a situation but in a particular sense, it is mostly used for numerical facts such as heights, weights, scores on achievement tests and intelligence tests etc. For the organization and presentation of these statistical data, we usually take the help of statistical tables, frequency distribution, and graphical presentation.

In presenting statistical data through *statistical tables,* we can tabulate or arrange the data collected in some properly selected classes and then describe this arrangement by title and subtitles. In presenting data in the form of *Frequency distribution,* we present a collection of groups of scores in such a way as to show the frequency in each group of scores or class. Steps for presenting data through frequency distribution may be named as (i) Finding the range (ii) Determining the class interval or grouping interval and (iii) Writing the contents of frequency distribution (in the form of classes, tallying the scores into proper classes and checking the tallies).

Both types of data, whether organized in tabular form or in the shape of frequency distribution, may be very well presented through some or the other picture diagrams or graphs. Generally, for the former type of data we make use of the four types of graphs or diagram namely pictographs, bar graph, circle or pie graphs/diagrams and line graphs.

Pictographs or pictograms are the graphs or diagrams used for presenting an ungrouped statistical data (data not grouped into a frequency distribution) in pictorial (picture like) form. The mode of presentation of statistical data through bars (rectangles of similar breadth) is known as Bar graphs or bar diagrams. In circle graphs or pie diagram, statistical data is presented through the figures of a circle and its constituents, i.e. proportionate sub-divisions. Line graphs are mostly used in describing the concommitted relationship between two variables of the collected data. These are drawn by plotting the respective values of these variables on the X and Y axes of a graph paper (after choosing appropriate scales).

For the graphical presentation of grouped data (data organized in the form of frequency distribution), four different methods, namely the histogram, the frequency polygon, the cumulative frequency graph and the cumulative frequency percentage curve or ogive, may be used. Out of these four, the first two are the most common. A histogram or column diagram in practical sense is nothing but a bar graph of a frequency distribution. Here scores in the form of classes are plotted on X-axis and respective frequencies of the distribution (different classes) are plotted on the Y-axis. The frequency polygon, on the other hand, may be understood essentially as a line graph of a frequency distribution. For constructing a line graph of a given frequency distribution, the mid points of all the classes are marked on the X-axis and their respective frequencies are plotted on the Y-axis.

In comparison to histogram, frequency polygon is more useful and practicable in comparing two or more distributions by plotting two or more graphs on the same axes. It also gives a much better conception of the contour of the distribution than the histogram. However, histogram proves much better to frequency polygon in providing a very clear as well as accurate picture of the relative proportions of frequencies from interval to interval (class to class). Frequency polygon on the other hand is unable to show the distribution of frequencies within each class interval.

References and Suggested Readings

Garrett, H.E., *Statistics in Psychology and Education*, Indian ed., Vakils Feffer & Simons, Mumbai, 1971.

Guliford, J.P., *Fundamental Statistics in Psychology and Education*, 5th International Student ed., McGraw-Hill, New York, 1973.

Mangal, S.K., *Statistics in Psychology and Education*, 2nd ed., Prentice-Hall of India, New Delhi, 2002.

McNemar, Q., *Psychological Statistics,* 3rd ed., John Wiley, New York, 1962.

Tate, M.W., *Statistics in Education*, Macmillan, New York, 1955.

Assignment Problems

1. Discuss in brief the different methods of organizing and presenting statistical data.
2. What is Frequency distribution? How can you present a data in the form of a frequency distribution? Illustrate your answers with an example.
3. Tabulate the following 25 scores into a frequency distribution using an appropriate interval:

   72, 75, 77, 67, 81, 68, 65, 86, 73, 67, 76, 76, 70, 83, 71, 63, 72, 72, 61, 67, 84, 69, 64.
4. Name the different graphs or diagrams used for the graphical presentation of ungrouped data. Discuss any one of them by taking a hypothetical data.
5. What are pictographs or pictograms? Illustrate the procedure of drawing a pictograph with the help of an example.
6. Make a pictograph of the following tabular data:

Name of the Work Experience	*Gardening*	*Book Binding*	*Cooking*	*Clay Modeling*	*Art and Painting*
No. of Students opted	60	30	40	45	25

7. What is a bar graph or bar diagram? Illustrate the procedure of representing ungrouped data through a bar diagram with the help of some hypothetical data.
8. What is a circle or pie diagram? Illustrate the procedure of representing ungrouped data through a pie diagram with the help of some hypothetical data.
9. What is a Histogram? How does it differ from a Frequency polygon?
10. Plot Histograms and frequency polygons separately on the different axes for the following distributions.

(a)

Scores	*f*
75–79	1
70–74	3
65–69	5
60–64	8
55–59	11
50–54	18
45–49	10
40–44	8
35–39	6
30–34	3
25–29	1
20–24	1
	N = 75

(b)

Scores	*f*
60–69	1
70–79	2
80–89	3
90–99	4
100–109	7
110–119	12
120–129	8
130–139	5
140–149	3
150–159	3
	N = 50

(c)

Scores	*f*
37–39	2
34–36	4
31–33	6
28–30	10
25–27	12
22–24	7
19–21	7
16–18	3
13–15	2
10–12	1
	N = 54

11. The data shown in the given table presents the figure of the merit positions earned in the X and XII classes by a school in different years. Draw a bar graph for representing this data:

Year	*1997-98*	*1998-99*	*1999-2000*	*2000-2001*	*2001-2002*
No. of Merit positions	4	11	24	13	16

12. Draw a line graph for the data presented in the problem 11.
13. Draw a pie diagram for representing the data presented in the problem 16.
14. What is a line graph? How can it be used for representing an ungrouped data? Illustrate the process by taking some hypothetical data.
15. Name the various methods used for presenting a frequency distribution (grouped data) in a graphical form. Discuss any one of them in detail.
16. What is a histogram? Illustrate the procedure of drawing histogram for the presentation of a given frequency distribution with the help of an example.
17. What is a frequency polygon? Discuss the procedure of its construction with the help of an example.

42

Measures of Central Tendency and Percentiles

CHAPTER COMPOSITION

INTRODUCTION

If we take the achievement scores of the students of a class and arrange them in a frequency distribution, we can easily find that there are a few students who either score very high or very low. The marks of most of the students lie somewhere between the highest and the lowest scores of the whole class. This tendency of a group of distribution is named as 'central tendency' and the typical score lying between the extremes and shared by most of the students is referred to as a measure of central tendency. In this way, a measure of central tendency, as Tate defines "*is a sort of average or typical value of the items in the series and its function is to summarize the series in terms of his average value*" (1955, p. 78).

The most common measures of central tendency are:

(i) Arithmetic mean or mean (ii) median and (iii) mode. Each of them in their own way can be called a representative of the characteristics of the whole group and thus the performance of the group as a whole can be described by the single value which each of these measures gives. The values of mean, median or mode also help us in comparing two or more groups or frequency distributions in terms of typical or characteristics performance. In the present chapter, we will study these measures of central tendency.

ARITHMETIC MEAN (M)

It is the simplest but the most useful measure of central tendency. It is nothing but the 'average' which we compute in our high school arithmetic and therefore can be easily defined as the "sum of all the values of the items in a series divided by the number of items". It is designated by the symbol M.

Computation of Mean in the Case of Ungrouped Data

Let X_1, X_2, X_3, X_4, X_5, X_6, X_7, X_8, X_9, X_{10}, be the scores obtained by 10 students in Achievement Test. Then the Arithmetic mean or Mean scores of the group of these students can be calculated as

$$M = \frac{X_1 + X_2 + X_3 + X_4 + X_5 + X_6 + \cdots + X_{10}}{10}$$

In this way, the formula for calculating mean of an ungrouped data is— $M = \Sigma X/N$, where ΣX stands for the sum of the scores of values of the items and N for the total numbers of items in a series of group.

Computation of Mean in the Case of Grouped Data (Data in the Form of Frequency Distribution)

(i) In frequency distribution where frequencies are greater than 1, the mean is calculated by

$M = \frac{\Sigma fX}{N}$, where X represents the mid-point of class interval, f is its respective frequency and N, the total of all the frequencies.

We can illustrate this formula by taking the frequency distribution previously given in Table 41.1.

Table 42.1 Computation of Mean in Grouped Data

Scores	*f*	*Mid-(Point) (X)*	*(f.X)*	
65–69	1	67	67	
60–64	3	62	186	
55–59	4	57	228	
50–54	7	52	364	M = ΣfX/N
45–49	9	47	423	= 2230/50 = 44.6
40–44	11	42	462	
35–39	8	37	296	Arithmetic mean
30–34	4	32	128	= 44.6
25–29	2	27	54	
20–24	1	22	22	
	N = 50		Σ fX = 2230	

Short Cut Method of Computing the Mean of Grouped Data.

Mean for the grouped data can be computed easily with the help of the following formula:

$$M = A + \frac{\Sigma fx'}{N} \times i$$

where *A* stands for assumed mean, i for class interval, f for the respective frequency of the mid-value, N for the total frequency and x′ for X – A/i (the quotient obtained after division of the difference between the mid-value of the class and assumed mean by i).

The use of this formula can be easily understood through the following illustrations: Let's assume that Mean (A) = 42

Scores	*f*	*X*	*x' = X – A/i*	*fx′*
65–69	1	67	5	5
60–64	3	62	4	12
55–59	4	57	3	12
50–54	7	52	2	14
45–49	9	47	1	9
40–44	11	42	0	0
35–39	8	37	–1	–8
30–34	4	32	–2	–8
25–29	2	27	–3	–6
20–24	1	22	–4	–4
			Σ*fx′* = 26	

$$M = A + \frac{\Sigma fx'}{N} \times I$$

$$= 42 + \frac{26}{50} \times 5$$

$$= 42 + 2.6 = 44.6$$

MEDIAN (M_d)

If the items of a series are arranged in ascending or descending order of magnitude, the measure or value of the central item in the series is termed as the median. In this way, as Bloomers and Lindquist define:

"The Median of a distribution is the point on the score scales below which one-half or 50 percent of the scores fall."

Thus, median is the score or value of the central item which divides the series into two equal parts. In this connection, it should be clearly understood that central item itself is not the median. It is only the measure or value of the central item that is known as median. For example, if we arrange in ascending or descending order the marks of 5 students, then the marks obtained by the third student from either side will be termed as the median of the scores of the group of students under consideration.

Computation in the Case of Ungrouped Data

(i) When N (the number of items in series) is odd

In the case where N, *i.e.* number of students, as in the above example, is odd (not divisible by 2) then the median can be computed by the formula:

M_d = The measure of value of the $(N + 1)/2^{th}$ item.

Example Let the scores obtained by 7 students in an Achievement test be 17, 47, 15, 35, 25, 39, 44. Then first of all, for calculating median we have to arrange the scores in the ascending or descending order like 15, 17, 25, 35, 39, 44, 47. Here N (=7) is odd and therefore the score of the $(N+1)/2^{th}$ or 4th student, i.e. 35 is the median of given scores.

(ii) Where N (the number of items in a series) is even

In the case where N is even (divisible by 2), the median is determined by the following formula:

$$M_d = \frac{\text{The value of (N/2)th and (N/2 + 1)th item}}{2}$$

Example Let there be a group of 8 students, whose scores are 17, 47, 15, 35, 39, 50, 44, 25. For, calculating the median of these scores, we will proceed as under:

Arrangement of scores in proper order 15, 17, 25, 35, 39, 44, 47, 50

The score of the (N/2)th = 35

i.e. 4th students

The score of the (N/2+1)th = 39

i.e. 5th student

Then, Median = (35 + 39)/2=37.

Computation of the Median for Grouped Data (Data in the form of a Frequency Distribution)

If the data is available in the form of a frequency distribution like the following, then calculation of median first requires the location of median class.

Scores	*f*
65–69	1
60–64	3
55–59	4
50–54	7
45–49	9
40–44	11
35–39	8
30–34	4
25–29	2
20–24	1
	N = 50

Actually as defined earlier, median is the measure or score of the central item.

Therefore, central item whose measure we aim to determine is needed. It is located through the formula given above in the case of ungrouped data depending upon the odd and even nature of total frequencies (N). Here in the present distribution, N (=50) is even, therefore median will fall somewhere between the scores of 25th and 26th items in the given distribution. In the present example, if we take all the frequencies from the above or below we can know that the class interval designated as 40–44 can be labeled as the class where the score representing median lies.

After estimating the median class, the median of the distribution can be determined from the following formula:

$$M_d = L + \frac{N/2 - F}{f} \times i$$

where

L = Exact lower limit of the median class
F = Total of all the frequencies before the median class
f = Frequency of the median class
i = Class interval
N = Total of all the frequencies

By applying the above formula, we can compute the median of the given distribution in the following way:

$$M_d = 39.5 + \left[\frac{50/2}{11}\right] \times 5$$

$$= 39.5 + \frac{10}{11} \times 5$$

$$= 39.5 + \frac{50}{11} = 39.5 + 4.55$$

$$= 44.05.$$

Some Special Situations in the Computation of Median

(a) Scores	f	(b) Scores	f	(c) Scores	f
55–59	5	45–49	2	20–21	2
50–54	3	40–49	5	18–19	1
45–49	8	35–49	6	16–17	0
40–44	18	30–49	0	14–15	0
35–39	15	25–49	8	12–13	2
30–34	10	20–49	3	10–11	0
25–29	7	15–49	2	8–9	0
20–24	2		N = 26	6–7	1
	N = 68			4–5	1
				2–3	1
				0–1	1
					N = 10

Let us consider the medians of the above distributions.

(a) We know by definition that median is the point on the score scale below and above which 50% cases lie. Observing through this definition we can determine the score above which 50% cases lie. So, the score representing median should be a common score falling between the classes 35–39 and 40–44. This score is nothing but the upper limit of the class 35–39 which is also the lower limit of the class 40–44. Therefore, in this case median is 39–5.

(b) In the second distribution, if we try to add the frequencies from below we see that up to class interval 25–29, 13 cases lie and by adding frequencies from above we also find that up to the class interval 35–39, there are 13 cases. In this way, the class interval 30–34 divides the distribution into two equal parts below and above which 50% cases lie. It leads us to conclude that median should be the mid-point of the class interval 30–34 and therefore 32 is median of this distribution.

(c) In the third case, if we add the frequencies from below we find that up to the class interval 6–7, 5 cases lie and by adding the frequencies from above, we also find that up to the class 12–13, 5 cases lie. The median should fall mid-way between the two classes 8–9 and 10–11. It should be the common score represented by both these classes. This score is nothing but the upper limit of the class 8-9 and lower limit of the class 10–11 and therefore, it should be 9.5.

MODE (M_O)

Mode is defined as the size of the variable (say a score) which occurs most frequently. It is the point on the score scale that correspond to the maximum frequency of the distribution. In any series it is the value of the item, which is the most characteristic or common and is usually repeated for the maximum number of items.

Computation of Mode

IN CASE OF UNGROUPED DATA

In the case of ungrouped data, mode can be easily computed by merely looking at it. All that one has to do is to find out the score which is repeated the maximum number of times.

Example Suppose we have to find out the value of the mode from the following scores of the students:

15, 29, 24, 25, 27, 25, 28, 25, 29.

Here the score 25 is repeated maximum number of times and thus the value of mode in this case is 25.

IN CASE OF GROUPED DATA

In the cases where data is available in the form of a frequency distribution, the mode is computed from the following formula:

Mode (M_0) = $3M_d - 2M$ where M_d is the median and M, the mean of the given distribution.

In this way, for the computation of mode in the case of frequency distribution, first of all mean as well as median of the distribution are computed and then with the help of the above formula, mode is calculated. For illustration, we can take distribution previously given in the Table 41.2. We know the mean and median of this distribution. Now we can use these results for the computation of the mode.

$$M_d = 44.05 \quad M = 44.6$$

Therefore,

$$M_o = 3 \times 44.05 - 2 \times 44.6$$

$$= 132.15 - 89.2$$

$$= 42.95$$

WHEN TO USE THE MEAN, MEDIAN AND MODE

Computation of any of the three—mean, median and mode provides a measure of central tendency. Now which of them should be computed for a particular distribution is a question that can be raised quite often. Below we discuss this aspect in the light of the characteristics and nature of these measures.

When to Use the Mean

(i) Mean is the most reliable accurate measure of the central tendency of a distribution in comparison to median and mode. It has the greatest stability as there are less fluctuations in the means of the samples drawn from the same population. Therefore, in cases where reliable and accurate measure of central tendency is needed, we compute mean for the given data.

(ii) Mean can be given an algebraic treatment and is better suited for further arithmetical computation. Therefore, it can be easily employed for the computation of various statistics like standard deviation, coefficient of correlation etc. Hence, when we need to know such statistics, mean is computed for the given data.

(iii) In computation of mean, we give equal weightage to every item in the series. Therefore, it is affected by the value of each item in that series. Sometimes, there are extreme items which seriously affect position of the mean. Therefore, it is not proper to compute mean for the series that have extreme items. It should be calculated only when the series has no extreme items and each score carries equal weight in determining the central tendency.

When to Use Median

(i) Median is the exact mid-point of a series as 50% cases lie below and above it. Therefore, when the exact mid-point of the distribution is desired, median is to be computed.

(ii) Median is not affected by the extreme scores in the series. Therefore, when a series contains extreme scores, the median is perhaps the most representative central measure.

(iii) In case of an open-end distribution (incomplete distribution "80 and above" or "20 and below" etc.), mean is impossible to be calculated.

(iv) Mean cannot be calculated graphically. But in case of median we can compute it graphically. Therefore, when we have suitable graphs like frequency curve, polygon etc. we should try to compute median.

(v) The median is specifically useful for the data, the items of which cannot be precisely measured quantitatively e.g. qualities like health, culture, honesty, intelligence, etc.

When to Use Mode

(i) In many cases, crude mode can be computed by just having a look at the data. It gives the quickest, although approximate, measure of central tendency. Therefore, in cases where a quick and approximate measure of central tendency is all that is desired, we compute mode.

(ii) Mode is that value of the item which occurs most frequently or is repeated maximum number of times in a given series. Therefore when we need to know the most often recurring score or value of the items in a series, we compute mode. On account of this characteristic, mode has unique importance in the large scale manufacturing of consumption goods. In finding the sizes of the shoes and ready-made clothes which will fit most men, the manufacturer makes use of his average indicated by mode.

(iii) Mode can be computed from the histogram and other frequency curves. Therefore, when we already have a graphical representation of the distribution in the form of such figures, it is appropriate to compute mode instead of mean.

COMPUTATION OF QUARTILES, DECILES AND PERCENTILES

As we have discussed earlier, median is the point on the score scale which divides the series into two equal parts such that 50 per cent of the cases lie below and the rest above it. Proceeding on the same principle, the series may be divided into four, ten or hundred parts and the values of these items (scores) are respectively known as Quartiles, Deciles and Percentiles. These values are computed by the same procedure as adopted for computing median. Even the formulae for calculating these values are similar to that for computing median. Below we give all these formulae along with the formula for computing median.

$$M_d = L + \left(\frac{N/2 - F}{f}\right) \times i$$

$$1^{st} \text{ Quartile or } Q_1 = L + \left(\frac{N/4 - F}{f}\right) \times i$$

$$\text{2nd Quartile or } Q_2 = L + \left(\frac{N/2 - F}{f}\right) \times i$$

$$\text{3rd Quartile or } Q_3 = L + \left(\frac{3N/4 - F}{f}\right) \times i$$

$$\text{1st Decile or } D_1 = L + \left(\frac{N/10 - F}{f}\right) \times i$$

$$\text{5th Decile or } D_5 = L + \left(\frac{5N/10 - F}{f}\right) \times i$$

$$= L + \left(\frac{N/2 - F}{f}\right) \times i$$

$$\text{1st Percentile or } P_1 = L + \left(\frac{N/100 - F}{f}\right) \times i$$

$$\text{50th Percentile or } P_{50} = L + \left(\frac{50N/100 - F}{f}\right) \times i = L + \left(\frac{N/2 - F}{f}\right) \times i$$

$$\text{75th Percentile or } P_{75} = L + \left(\frac{75N/100 - F}{f}\right) \times i = L + \left(\frac{3N/4 - F}{f}\right) \times i$$

In all these formulae, L represents the lower limit of the class where approximately the value or score of our required median, Quartile, Deciles or Percentiles; N stands for the total of all the frequencies; F for the total of all the frequencies before this class; *f* for the frequency of this particular class and *i* for the class interval. Now we illustrate the computation of different Quartiles. Deciles and Percentiles by taking the following distribution:

Scores	*f*
70–79	3
60–69	2
50–59	2
40–49	3
30–39	5
20–29	4
10–19	3
0–9	2
	N = 24

(i) **Ist Quartile (Q_1)**

$$Q_1 = L + \left(\frac{N/4 - F}{f}\right) \times i$$

Here, $$N/4 = \frac{24}{4} = 6$$

Adding frequencies from below, we see that up to the upper limit of the class 10–19, 5 cases lie. Therefore, 20–29 is the class where Ist Quartile falls.

$$\text{Hence } Q_1 = 19.5 + \left(\frac{6-5}{4}\right) \times 10 = 19.5 + 2.5 = 22$$

(ii) **3rd Quartile (Q_3)**

$$Q_3 = \left(\frac{3N/4 - f}{f}\right) \times i$$

Here, $$3N/4 = \frac{24 \times 3}{4} = 18$$

Adding frequencies from below we see that up to the upper limit of the class 40–49 we have 17 frequencies. Therefore, the third Quartile of the series is the interval 50–59.

$$Q_3 = 49.5 + \frac{18-7}{4} \times 10 = 49.5 + 5 = 54.5$$

(iii) **Ist Decile (D_1)**

$$\text{Formula } D_1 = L + \left(\frac{N/10 - F}{f}\right) \times i$$

Here $$N/10 = \frac{24}{10} = 2.4$$

It is easy to locate that D_1 lies in the interval 10–19.

$$\text{Hence } D_1 = 9.5 + \left(\frac{2.4-2}{3}\right) \times 10 = 9.5 + 4/3 = 9.5 + 1.33 = 10.63$$

(iv) **25th percentile (P_{25})**

$$P_{25} = L + \left(\frac{25N/100 - F}{f}\right) \times i = 19.5 \left(\frac{25 \times 24/100 - 5}{4}\right) \times 10$$

$$= 19.5 + \frac{5}{2} = 22.$$

(v) **60th percentile (P_{60})**

$$P_{60} = L + \left(\frac{60N/100 - F}{f}\right) \times i$$

Here $\quad 60^{th}$ per cent of 24 $= \dfrac{60 \times 24}{100} = \dfrac{72}{5} = 14.4$

Adding the frequencies from below we see that up to the upper limit of the class 30–39, 14 cases lie. Therefore 60th percentile of the distribution should fall in the interval 40–49.

Hence
$$P_{60} = 39.5 + \left(\frac{14.4 - 14}{3}\right) \times 10$$

$$= 39.5 + \frac{4}{3} = 39.5 + 1.33 = 40.63.$$

Percentile Rank

Computation of a particular percentile say p gives us a point on the scale of measurement, i.e. a score below which p per cent of the cases lie. For example, 75th percentile (P_{75}) provides us a specific score below which 75% of the cases lie. Now in case we are provided with a specific score on the scale of measurement and we are required to find out the percentage of the cases lying below that score, we are supposed to compute percentile rank of that specific score.

In this way, the procedure followed in computing percentile rank is just opposite to that of percentiles. Percentile rank, as the name suggests, is essentially a rank or the position of an individual on a scale of 100 decided on the basis of individual's own score.

For illustration, we will take the distribution that has been taken for the computation of Quartiles, Deciles and Percentiles etc.

Let us calculate the Percentile Rank of the score 22.

Solution. By adding frequencies from below we see that up to the score 19.5 i.e. upper limit of the class 10–19, 5 cases lie. Our problem is to find out the number of cases that lie below the score 22.

The difference between the scores 19.5 and 22 is 22–19.5 = 2.5.

Now by observing the frequency distribution, we see that in the class interval 20–29, 10 scores are shared by 4 individuals. This knowledge helps in our problem and we can proceed as under:

Since an interval of 10 is shared by 4 individuals

$\therefore$ Interval of 2.5 is shared by $\dfrac{4}{10} \times 2.5 = 1$ individual.

Therefore, up to the score 22, 5+1=6 cases lie.

For expressing these cases on the scale of 100, we have to multiply them by 100 / N. In the present problem, our N is 24.

Therefore, the required Percentile Rank $= \dfrac{6 \times 100}{24} = 25$

By comparing the results of 1st Quartile (Q_1) or 25th Percentile (P_{25}) of this distribution, we can easily conclude that Percentile Rank and Percentiles are opposite to each other.

SUMMARY

Measures of the central tendency refer to those average or typical values of the items included in a given series which may be employed for summarizing or representing all the items of this series. We may name Mean, Median and Mode as examples of such measures of central tendency.

Mean is the most simple but useful measure of central tendency. It can be computed from the data of scores in the same way as we compute average in our school classes. In the case of ungrouped data all the values of the items in a series divided by the number of items can provide us the simple average, i.e. mean. In the case of grouped data (given in the form of frequency distribution), mean can be best computed with the help of a short cut method by using the formula $M = A + \Sigma fx'/N \times i$ (where A is the assumed mean, $x' = (X - A)/I$, X is the mid point of the class interval, i the class interval and N is the total frequencies of the distribution).

Median is the score or value of the central item which divides the series into two equal parts. In computing median in the case of ungrouped data, we first consider the odd and even nature of N (total number of item in a series). If N is odd, then (N+1)/2th measure and if N is even, then (N/2+1)th measure provides us the value of our median. In case data is given in the form of frequency distribution, then median can be computed by using the formula: $M_d = L + \frac{N/2 - F}{f} \times i$ (where L is the lower limit of the median class, F, the total of all frequencies before the median class, f, the median class, i the interval and N, the total frequencies of the distribution).

Mode refers to the size of the variable which occurs most frequently. As a result we can compute crude mode by just having a look at the data. In the case of grouped data, it can be computed with the help of the formula $M_o = 3M_d - 2M$ signifying that if we know the mean and median, then mode can be easily be computed. Mode can also be computed easily with the help of histogram and other frequency curves.

Mean, median and mode all represent the measures of central tendency. Each of them have unique characteristics and importance as a measure of central tendency and are computed according to the nature of the data available and the purpose served in a particular situation. For example, in case we need a very quick and approximate measure of central tendency in the form of the most often recurring score in a series or we have an appropriate graphical representation of data, then the computation of mode should always be preferred to mean or median. But in case we need a reliable and accurate measure of central tendency, and also need to compete further statistics like standard deviation, coefficient of correlation etc., then computation of mean should be preferred to that of median or mode. However, in case a series contains extreme scores, a distribution with open end, then for getting an exact mid point of the distribution we should aim for the computation of median.

Statistical measures like Quartiles, Deciles and Percentiles represent some fixed points on the score scale (like median) below which a definite proportion of cases lie. While in the case of median, (50% of the cases lie below and above it) the series is divided into two equal halves by the median score, it is divided into 4, 10 and 100 equal parts, in the case of quartiles, deciles and percentiles respectively. The formulae for computing these can be developed on the pattern of the formula used for computing

$$\text{Median, i.e. } M_d = L + \frac{N/2 - F}{f} \times i,$$

For example in the case of computation of percentiles, we will be making use of the formula

$$P = L + \left(\frac{PN/100 - F}{f}\right) \times i$$

Computation of a particular percentile, say p, may then give us a point on the scale of measurement i.e. a score below which p per cent of the cases lie. Contrary to this, if we are provided with a specific score on the scale of measurement and are required to find out the percentages of cases lying below that score; then we are supposed to compute percentile rank of that specific score. In this way the concept of percentile rank presents an altogether reverse picture of the various percentile points and it is why the procedure followed in computing percentile rank in just opposite to that of percentiles.

References and Suggested Readings

Garrett, H.E., *Statistics in Psychology and Education*, Mumbai, Vakils, Feffer and Simons (Indian ed.), 1971.

Guliford, J.P., *Fundamental Statistics in Psychology and Education*, McGraw-Hill, New York, (5th International students ed.), 1973.

Mangal, S.K., *Statistics in Psychology and Education*, 2nd ed., Prentice-Hall of India, New Delhi, 2002.

Tate, M.W., *Statistics in Education*, Macmillan, New York, 1955.

Assignment Problems

1. Compute Median for the following ungrouped data:
   (i) 16, 2, 10, 9, 4, 7, 12, 14, 15
   (ii) 8, 3, 10, 5, 2, 11, 14, 12
   Ans. (i) 10 (ii) 9
2. Find the crude Mode for the following data:
   15, 14, 8, 14, 14, 11, 9, 9, 11.
   Ans. 14
3. Compute the Mean, Median and Mode for the following distribution:

(a) Scores	f	*(b)* Scores	f	*(c)* Scores	f	*(d)* Scores	f
70–71	2	120–122	2	45–49	2	135–144	1
68–69	2	117–119	2	40–44	3	125–134	2
66–67	3	114–116	2	35–39	2	115–124	8
64–65	4	111–113	4	30–34	17	105–114	22
62–63	6	108–110	5	25–29	30	95–104	33
60–61	7	105–107	9	20–24	25	85–94	22
58–59	5	102–104	6	15–19	15	75–84	9
56–57	1	99–101	3	10–14	3	65–74	2
54–55	2	96–98	4	5–9	2	55–64	1
52–53	3	93–95	2	0–4	1		
50–51	1	90–92	1				
	N = 36		N = 40		N = 100		N = 100

Ans.:	(a)	(b)	(c)	(d)
	M = 61.11	**M = 106.00**	**M = 25.05**	**M = 99.3**
	M_d = 61.21	**M_d = 105.83**	**M_d = 25.17**	**M_d = 99.3**
	Mo = 61.41	**Mo = 105.49**	**Mo = 25.41**	**Mo = 99.3**

4. What do you understand by mean and median? Explain by computing these for the scores in a test given below. (Taking 2 as class interval).

72	75	77	67	72
91	78	65	86	83
67	82	76	76	70
83	71	63	72	72
61	67	84	69	64

Ans.: M = 72.94;
M_d = 71.9

5. What do you mean by measures of central tendency? Name different measures of central tendency and discuss them in brief.
6. What is Arithmetic mean (M)? How is it computed in the cases of ungrouped and grouped data? Discuss with hypothetical examples.
7. What is median (M_d)? How is it computed in the cases of ungrouped and grouped data? Discuss with the help of a hypothetical example.
8. What is Mode (Mo)? How is it computed in the cases of ungrouped and grouped data? Discuss with the help of a hypothetical example.
9. Explain which of the three mean, median and mode should be computed for a particular distribution in a specified situation.
10. Calculate the mean, Median and mode of the following frequency distribution.

Class Interval	*Frequency*
195–199	1
190–194	2
185–189	4
180–184	5
175–179	8
170–174	10
165–169	6
160–164	4
155–159	4
150–154	2
145–149	3
140–144	1

Ans.: M = 170.8
M_d = 172
Mo = 174.4

11. Calculate the mean, median and mode of the following distribution

Class Interval	*Frequency*
35–39	4
30–34	8
25–29	15
20–24	10
15–19	8
10–14	5

Ans.: **M = 24.5**
M_d = 28.83
Mo = 37.49

43

Measures of Variability or Dispersion

CHAPTER COMPOSITION

NEED OF THE MEASURES OF VARIABILITY OR DISPERSION

Measures of central tendency—mean, median and mode—provide central value or typical representative of a set of scores as a whole. Through these measures, we can represent a characteristic or quality of the whole group by a single number. By comparing such typical representatives of the different sets of scores, we can compare the achievement of two groups. But these representative numbers merely give us an idea of the general achievement of the group as a whole, and does not show how the individual scores are spread over. Therefore, through measures of central tendency we are unable to know much about the distribution of scores in a series or characteristics of items in a group. Hence measures of central tendency provide insufficient base for the comparison of two or more frequency distributions or sets of scores. It can be made more clear from the following examples:

Let there be two small groups of boys and girls whose scores in an achievement test are as follows:

Test scores of Group A (boys) — 40, 38, 36, 17, 20, 19, 18, 3, 5, 4.

Test scores of Group B (girls) — 19, 20, 22, 18, 21, 23, 17, 20, 22, 18.

Now the value of the Mean in both the cases is 20 and thus, as far as the mean goes, there is no difference in the performance of the two groups. Now the question arises: can we take both sets of scores as identical? Definitely there is a lot of difference between the performance of the two groups. While the test scores of group A are found to range from 30 to 40, the scores in group B range from 18 to 23. First group is composed of individuals who have wide individual differences. It comprises either very capable or very ordinary individuals. The second group, on the other hand, is composed of average individuals. Individuals in the latter group are less variable than those of the former. Looking in this way, there is a great need to pay consideration to the variability or dispersion of the scores in the sets of scores or series if we want to describe and compare them.

DIFFERENT MEASURES OF VARIABILITY OR DISPERSION

There are chiefly four measures of indicating variability or dispersion within the set of scores. These are:

(a) Range (R)

(b) Quartile Deviation (Q)

(c) Average Deviation (AD)

(d) Standard Deviation (SD)

Each of the above measures of variability gives us the degree of variability or dispersion by the use of a single number and tells us how the individual scores are scattered or spread over throughout the distribution or given data.

In the following pages, we will briefly discuss these measures.

Range (R)

Range is the simplest measure of variability or dispersion. It is calculated by subtracting the lowest scores in the series from the highest. But it is a very rough measure of the variability of a series. It takes only extreme scores into consideration and tells nothing about the variation of individual items.

Quartile Deviation (Q)

It is computed by the formula $Q = (Q_3 - Q_1)/2$ where Q_1 and Q_3 represent the 1st and 3rd Quartiles of the distribution under consideration. The amount Q_3 and Q_1 is the difference of range between 3rd and 1st Quartile. It is designated as the inter quartile range. For computing Quartile Deviation, this inter quartile range is divided by 2 and therefore, Quartile Deviation is also named as semi-inter quartile range. In this way, for computing Q, the values of Q_1 and Q_3 are first determined and then by applying the above formula, we obtain the value of Quartile Deviation.

Average Deviation (A.D.)

Average Deviation or A.D. as Gerrett defines it, *is the mean of the deviation of all the separate scores in the series taken from their mean (occasionally from the median or mode).* (1971, p. 481)

It is the simplest measure of variability that takes into account the fluctuation or variation of all the items in a series.

COMPUTATION OF AVERAGE DEVIATION (AD) FROM UNGROUPED DATA

In the case of ungrouped data, AD is calculated by the formula:

$$AD = \frac{\Sigma |x|}{N}$$

where x = X – M = Deviation of the score from the mean of the series and |x| signifies that in the deviation values, we ignore the algebraic signs +ve or –ve. The use of this formula can be explained through the following examples.

Problem. Find out the Average Deviation of the scores 15, 10, 6, 8, 11 of a series.

Solution. The mean of the given series = $\frac{15 + 10 + 6 + 8 + 11}{5} = 10$

Scores (X)	*Deviation from the mean (X – M) = x*	|*x*|
15	5	5
10	0	0
6	– 4	4
8	– 2	2
11	1	1
N = 5		Σ|x| = 12

$$\text{Hence, } AD = \frac{\Sigma |x|}{N} = \frac{12}{5} = 2.4$$

COMPUTATION OF AVERAGE DEVIATION FROM GROUPED DATA

From grouped data, AD can be computed by the formula

$$AD = \frac{\Sigma |fx|}{N}$$

Use of this formula can be understood through the following illustration:

Score	*f*	*Mid-Point (X)*	*fX*	*x (X – 100.06)*	*fx*	|*fx*|
110–114	4	112	448	11.94	44.76	47.76
105–109	4	107	428	6.94	27.76	27.76
100–104	3	102	306	1.94	5.82	5.82
95–99	0	97	0	–3.06	0	0
90–94	3	92	276	–8.08	–24.18	24.18
85–89	3	87	261	–13.36	–39.18	39.18
80–84	1	82	82	–18.06	–18.06	18.06
	N = 18		ΣfX = 1801			Σ|fX| = 162.67

First of all, mean is computed.

Here, $$\text{Mean} = \frac{\Sigma Fx}{N} = \frac{1801}{18} = 100.06$$

Then we calculate the values of x by subtracting Mean from the respective values of X and entering them into column V. By multiplying these values by the respective class frequencies and ignoring the algebraic sign, we get the value of $\Sigma|fx|$. Afterward, we apply the formula as below:

$$AD = \frac{\Sigma fx}{N} = \frac{162.76}{18} = 9.04$$

Standard Deviation (SD)

Standard Deviation of a set scores is defined as the square root of the average of the squares of the deviations of each score from the mean.

Symbolically we can say that $SD = \sqrt{\Sigma}\,(X - M)^2/N = \sqrt{\Sigma x^2/N}$ where X stands for individual scores, N for total number of scores and x for the deviation of each score from the mean.

Standard Deviation is regarded as the most stable and reliable measure of variability as it employs mean for its computation. It is often called as Root—mean square deviation and is denoted by the Greek letter sigma (σ).

COMPUTATION OF STANDARD DEVIATION (SD) FROM UNGROUPED DATA

SD can be computed from the ungrouped scores by the following formula

$$\sigma = \sqrt{\frac{\Sigma x^2}{N}}$$

Below we illustrate the use of this formula with the help of a problem.

Problem. Calculate SD for the following set of test scores:

52, 50, 56, 68, 65, 57, 70.

Here, Mean of the given scores = 480/8 = 60

Scores X	*Deviation from mean (X–M) or x*	*Squares of the Deviations x^2*	
52	–8	64	
50	–10	100	Now $\sigma = \sqrt{\Sigma x^2/N}$
56	–4	16	
68	8	64	$= \sqrt{382/8}$
65	8	64	
62	2	4	$= \sqrt{47.75}$
57	–3	9	
70	10	100	= 6.91
		$\Sigma x^2 = 382$	

(b) Computation of S.D. from the grouped data S.D. in case of grouped data can be computed by the formula $\sigma = \sqrt{\Sigma fx^2/N}$.

The use of the formula can be understood through the solution of the following problem.

Problem. Compute SD for the frequency distribution given below on the extreme left. The mean of this distribution is 115.

I.Q. Scores	*f*	*X*	*M*	*x*	x^2	fx^2
127–129	1	128	115	13	169	169
124–126	2	125	115	10	100	200
121–123	3	122	115	7	49	147
118–120	1	119	115	4	16	16
115–117	6	116	115	1	1	6
112–114	4	113	115	–2	4	16
109–111	3	110	115	–5	25	75
106–108	2	107	115	–8	64	128
103–105	1	114	115	–11	121	121
100–102	1	101	115	–14	196	196
	N = 24					$\Sigma fx^2 = 1074$

Now $\sigma = \sqrt{\Sigma fx^2/N} = \sqrt{1074/24} = \sqrt{44.75} = 6.69.$

In the above computation work we have made use of M, the mean of the distribution. If not given in the problem, it can be computed in the following way:

Calculation of mean. Let us assume that Mean is 116.

Scores	*f*	*X (Mid value)*	*x′ = (X–A)/i*	*fx′*
127–129	1	128	4	4
124–126	2	125	3	6
121–123	3	122	2	6
118–120	1	119	1	1
115–117	6	116	0	0
112–114	4	113	–1	–4
109–111	3	110	–2	–6
106–108	2	107	–3	–6
103–105	1	104	–4	–4
100–102	1	101	–5	–5
	N = 24			fx′ = –8

So, $$\text{Mean} = A + \frac{\Sigma fx'}{N} \times i = 116 - \frac{8}{24} \times 3 = 116 - 1 = 115.$$

Mean = 115.

Computation of SD from Grouped Data by Shortcut Method

SD from grouped data can also be computed by the following formula:

$$\sigma = i\sqrt{\frac{\Sigma fx'^2}{N} - \left(\frac{\Sigma fx'}{N}\right)^2}$$

Here the notation have the same meaning as desired earlier. The use of this formula can be explained by solving the problem given under the case (b).

Scores	*f*	*X*	*x′ = (X—A)/i*	*fx′*	*Fx′²*
127–129	1	128	4	4	16
124–126	2	125	3	6	18
121–123	3	122	2	6	12
118–120	1	119	1	1	1
115–117	6	116	0	0	0
112–114	4	113	–1	–4	4
109–111	3	110	–2	–6	12
106–108	2	107	–3	–6	18
103–105	1	104	–4	–4	16
100–102	1	101	–5	–5	25
	N = 24			Σfx′ = –8	Σfx′² = 122

$$\text{Formula } \sigma = i\sqrt{\frac{\Sigma fx'^2}{N} - \left(\frac{\Sigma fx'}{N}\right)^2}$$

$$= 2\sqrt{\frac{122}{24} - \left(-\frac{8}{24}\right)^2}$$

$$= 3\sqrt{\frac{122}{24} - \left(\frac{64}{24 \times 24}\right)}$$

$$= \frac{1}{8}\sqrt{2864} = \frac{53.51}{8}$$

∴ Standard deviation = 6.69.

SUMMARY

Measures of central tendency like mean, median and mode provide insufficient base for the comparison of two or more frequency distributions or sets of scores. It is because there may lie considerable variability or dispersion in the sets of scores or series around the average or the central value represented by means, median or mode. Such tendency of the sets of scores is known by the term dispersion or variability. It needs to be measured appropriately for describing and comparing two or more frequency distributions of sets of scores.

Different measures adopted for indicating variability or disperson may be named as Range, Quartile Deviation, Average Deviation and Standard Deviation. **Range** is the simplest but a very rough measure of variability. It can be computed by subtracting the lowest scores in the series from the highest. It can't be termed as a good measure of variability on account of its dependency on the two extreme scores at the cost of the variation of the individual items of the series.

Quartile Deviation is designated as the semi-inter quartile range. It can be computed by the use of the formula $Q = (Q_3 - Q_1)/2$ (where Q_1 and Q_3 represent the 1st and 3rd quartiles of the distribution). It is known as more stable than the range, but it also takes no care for the fluctuations or variations of all the items in a series.

Average Deviation is the mean of the deviation of all the individual scores in the series taken from the mean or some other measures of central tendency. It takes into account the dispersion or variation of all the items in a series and is computed by the use of formula $SD = \Sigma x/N$ (in case of ungrouped data) and $AD = \Sigma| fx |/N$ (in case of grouped data or Frequency distribution), where $|x|$ stands for the deviation of the raw scores, irrespective of positive or negative sign, from the mean of the series. This type of measure of variability is usually criticized for ignoring of algebraic signs.

Standard Derivation of a set of scores is defined as the square root of the average of the squares of the deviations of each score from the mean of the distribution. It is designated by the Greek letter σ pronounced as sigma. It is considered the most stable and reliable measure of variability on account of its employing mean and also not ignoring algebraic signs for its computation. It can be computed by use of the formulae, SD or $\sigma = \sqrt{\Sigma x^2/N}$ (In the case of ungrouped data) and $\sigma = \sqrt{\Sigma fx^2/N}$ (In the case of grouped data or Frequency distribution). There is also a short cut formula for the computation which runs as

$$\sigma = i\sqrt{\frac{\Sigma fx'^2}{N} - \left(\frac{\Sigma fx'}{N}\right)^2}$$

(where $x = X - M$ = Derivation of the raw score from the mean of the distribution) and $x' = (X - M)/i$.

References and Suggested Readings

Garrett, H.E., *Statistics in Psychology and Education*, Indian ed., Vakils, Feffer & Simons, Mumbai, 1971.

Guliford, J.P., *Fundamental Statistics in Psychology and Education*, 5th international students ed., McGraw-Hill, New York, 1973.

Mangal, S.K., *Statistics in Psychology and Education*, 2nd ed., Prentice-Hall of India, New Delhi, 2002.

McNemar, Q., *Psychological Statistics*, 3rd ed., John Wiley, New York, 1962.

Assignment Problems

1. What do you understand by dispersion or variability of the scores in a given series? Discuss in brief the different measures of variability.
2. Calculate average Deviation from the following Data:

   (a) Scores 30, 35, 36, 39, 42, 44, 46, 38, 34, 35

(b)

Scores	f
80–84	4
85–89	4
90–94	3
95–99	0
100–104	3
105–109	3
110–114	1
	N = 18

Ans. (a) 3.9 (b) 2.04

3. Compute standard deviation from the ungrouped data under the above problems (a).

   Ans. 4.68

4. Calculate standard deviation for each of the four frequency distributions a, b, c, d given in the problem 3 of chapter 42.

   Ans.: (a) 4.99 (b) 7.33 (c) 7.7 (d) 13.4

5. What are the measures of variability or dispersion? Discuss the need for their computation.
6. What is average deviation? Discuss the procedure of its computing from the ungrouped as well as the grouped data with the help of hypothetical examples.
7. What is Standard Deviation? Discuss the procedure of its computation from the ungrouped as well as grouped data with the help of some hypothetical data.
8. Calculate Mean and Standard Deviation for the following data.

(a) Scores	*Frequencies*	*(b) Scores*	*Frequencies*
60–69	4	40–44	1
50–59	4	35–39	2
40–49	4	30–34	3
30–39	10	25–29	4
20–29	8	15–19	15
10–19	5	10–14	5
0–9	5	5–9	8

Ans. (a) M = 36.75, SD = 17.815 (b) M = 18.98, SD = 8.52

9. Calculate Mean and Standard Deviation for the following data:

(a) Scores	*f*	*(b) Scores*	*f*
45–49	2	55–59	1
40–44	3	50–54	1
35–39	5	45–49	3
30–34	9	40–44	4
25–29	6	35–39	6
20–24	4	30–34	7
15–19	1	25–29	12
		20–24	6
		15–19	8'
		10–14	2

Ans. (a) M = 32 (b) M = 29.6
SD = 7.415 SD = 10.45

10. Compute Mean and Standard Deviation for the following data.

(a) Scores	*Ff*	*(b) Scores*	*f*	*(c) Scores*	*f*
45–49	2	90–93	1	85–87	1
40–44	3	86–89	3	82–84	3
35–39	2	82–85	8	79–81	2
30–34	6	78–81	5	76–78	3
25–29	8	74–77	7	73–75	3
20–24	8	70–73	6	70–72	2
15–19	7	66–69	4	67–69	2
10–14	5	62–65	2	64–66	3
5–9	9			61–63	1

Ans. (a) M = 22.4 (b) M = 77.06 (c) M = 74.15
SD = 11.3 SD = 7.13 SD = 6.936

11. Compute Quartile deviation from the following data.

(a) Scores	*f*	*(b) Scores*	*f*
45–49	2	135–144	1
40–44	3	125–134	2
35–39	2	115–124	8
30–34	17	105–114	22
25–29	30	95–104	33
20–24	25	85–94	22
15–19	15	75–84	9
10–14	3	65–74	2
5–9	2	55–64	1
0–4	1		

Ans. (a) 4.5 (b) 8.85

12. Compute Standard deviation for the data presented in the problems 10 and 11 of the chapter 42.

Ans. Problem 10, SD = 12.62
Problem 11, SD = 7.017

44

Correlation

CHAPTER COMPOSITION

INTRODUCTION

In education as well as psychology, there are times when it is needed to know whether there exists any relationship between the different abilities of the individual or they are independent of each other. Consequently, there are numerous questions like the following which have to be answered:

(i) Does scholastic achievement depend upon the general intelligence of a child?
(ii) Is it true that the height of the children increases with the increase in their age?
(iii) Is there any relationship between the size of the skull and general intelligence of the individuals?
(iv) It is true that dull children tend to be more neurotic than bright children?

The questions and problems like the above in which there is a need to find out the relationship between two variables (age and height, intelligence and achievement etc.) can be tackled properly by the method of correlation.

There are many types of correlation like Linear, Curvilinear, Biserial, Partial or Multiple correlation that are computed in statistics. As we aim to only have an elementary knowledge of the statistical methods in this text, we will discuss only the Linear correlation in the following pages.

LINEAR CORRELATION

This is the simplest kind of correlation to be found between two sets of scores or variables. Actually, when the relationship between two sets of scores or variables can be represented graphically by a straight line, it is known as Linear Correlation. Such type of correlation clearly reveals how the change in one variable is accompanied by a change in the other or to what extent is the increase or decrease in one accompanied by the increase or decrease in other.

The correlation between two sets of measures of variables can be positive or negative. It is said to be positive when an increase (or decrease) in one corresponds to an increase (or decrease) in the other. It is negative when increase corresponds to decrease and decrease corresponds to increase. There is also possibility of a third type of correlation, i.e. zero correlation between two sets of measures of variables if there exists no relationship between them.

COEFFICIENT OF CORRELATION

For expressing the degree of relationship quantitatively between two sets of measures of variables, we usually take the help of an index that is known as *coefficient of correlation*. It is a kind of ratio which expresses the extent to which changes in one variable are accompanied with changes in the other variable. It involves no units and varies from –1 (indicating perfect negative correlation) to +1 (indicating perfect positive correlation). In case the coefficient of correlation is zero, it is indicated by zero correlation between the two sets of measures.

Computation of Coefficient of Correlation

There are two different methods of computing co-efficient of (linear). These are:

(A) Rank Difference Method.
(B) Product Moment Method.

RANK DIFFERENCE METHOD OF COMPUTING COEFFICIENT OF CORRELATION

In computing coefficient of correlation between two sets of scores achieved by individuals with the help of this method, we require ranks, i.e. positions of merits of these individuals in the possession of certain characteristics. The coefficient of correlation computed by this method, as it considers only the ranks of the individuals in the characteristics A and B, is known as Rank correlation coefficient and is designated by Greek letter σ pronounced as Rho. Sometimes it is also known as Spearman's coefficient of correlation after the name of its inventor.

In case we do not have scores and have to work with data in which differences between the individuals in the possession of certain characteristics can be expressed only by ranks, rank correlation coefficient is the only correlation coefficient than can be computed. But this does not mean that it cannot be computed from the usual data given in scores. In case the data contain scores of individuals, we can compute by converting them into ranks. For example, if the marks of a group of 5 students are given as 17, 25, 9, 35, 18, we will rank them as 4, 2, 5, 1 and 3. We determine the rank or position of the individuals in both the given sets of scores. These ranks are then subjected to further calculation for the determination of the coefficient of correlation.

The method can be understood properly through the following illustration:

Example 1

Individual	*Marks in the subject of History X*	*Marks in the subject of Civics Y*	*Rank in History R_1*	*Rank in Civics R_2*	*Difference in Rank irrespective of sign+ve or −ve $\|d\|$ $\|R_1 - R_2\|$*	*Difference squared d^2*
A	80	82	2	3	1	1
B	45	86	11	2	9	81
C	55	50	10	10	0	0
D	56	48	9	11	2	4
E	58	60	8	9	1	12
F	60	62	7	8	1	1
G	65	64	6	7	1	1
H	68	65	5	6	1	1
I	70	70	4	5	1	1
J	75	74	3	4	1	1
K	85	90	1	1	0	0
N = 11						$\Sigma d^2 = 92$

$$\text{Formula } \rho = 1 - \frac{6\Sigma d^2}{N(N^2 - 1)}$$

$$= 1 - \frac{6 \times 92}{11(11^2 - 1)} = 1 - \frac{6 \times 92}{11 \times 120}$$

$$= 1 - \frac{23}{55} = 1 - 0.42 = 0.58$$

Example 2

Individuals	*Scores in Test X*	*Scores in Test Y*	*Rank in X_1 (R_1)*	*Rank in X_2(R_2)*	*$R_1 - R_2 = d$*	*d^2*
A	12	21	8	6	2	4
B	15	25	6.5	3.5	3	9
C	24	35	2	2	0	0
D	20	24	4	5	1	1
E	8	16	10	9	1	1
F	15	18	6.5	7	0.5	0.25
G	20	25	4	3.5	0.5	0.25
H	20	16	4	9	5	25
I	11	16	9	9	0	0
J	26	38	1	1	0	0
N = 10						$\Sigma d^2 = 40.5$

Since, $$\rho = 1 - \frac{6\Sigma d^2}{N(N^2 - 1)}$$

$$1 - \frac{6 \times 40.5}{10(10^2 - 1)} = 1 - \frac{6 \times 40.5}{10 \times 99}$$

$$= 1 - \frac{8.1}{33} = 1 - 0.245$$

$$\rho = 0.755.$$

Steps for the calculation of ρ

1. First of all it is required to assign position of merit or rank to each individual on either test. These ranks are put under column 3 (designated as R_1) and 4 (designated as R_2) respectively. The task of assigning ranks in the cases like example 1 is not difficult. But in cases like example 2, where two or more individuals are found to achieve the same score, some difficulty arises. In the above example, in the first test X, B and F are two individuals who have the same score i.e. 15. Therefore, score 15 occupies sixth position in order of merit. But now the question arises as to which of the two individuals B and F should be ranked as 6th or 7th. In order to overcome this difficulty we equally share the rank 5th and 7th between them and thus rank each one of them as 6.5.

   Similarly, if there are three persons who have the same score and share the same rank, we take the average of the ranks claimed by these persons. For example, we can take the score 20 in the second example which is shared by three individuals D, G and H. It is ranked third in the whole series and therefore the ranks 3, 4 and 5 are shared equally by D, G and H and hence we attribute rank 4 to each of them.
2. After writing down the allotted rank to all the individuals on either of the two tests, the differences in these ranks are calculated. In doing so we do not consider the algebraic signs + ive or –ive of the differences. The differences is written under column 5 (designated as $|d|$).
3. In the next column (designated as d^2) we square up the Rank difference of the values of d written in the column five.
4. Now we calculate the total of all the values of d^2 and this sum is designated as Σd^2.
5. Now the value of ρ is calculated by the formula $\rho = 1 - \dfrac{6\Sigma d^2}{N(N^2 - 1)}$

Where Σd^2 stands for the sum of the squares of differences between the ranks of the scores on two different tests and N for the number of individuals whose scores are under consideration for computing.

Product Moment method of computing coefficient of correlation. This method is also known as Pearson Product Moment method in the honour of the English statesman Karl Pearson who is said to be the inventor of this method. The coefficient of correlation computed by this method is known as Product Moment coefficient of correlation symbolically represented by r.

(a) **The calculation of r from ungrouped data.** The basic formula for the computation of r for the ungrouped data by this method is

$$r = \frac{\Sigma xy}{\sqrt{\Sigma x^2 \times \Sigma y^2}}$$

where x and y represent the deviation of scores in the tests X and Y from the means of each distribution.

The procedure of calculating r by this formula can be understood by the following illustration:

Individuals	*Scorers in Text X*	*Scores in Text Y*	*x*	*y*	*x.y*	*x^2*	*y^2*
A	15	60	–10	10	–100	100	100
B	25	70	0	20	0	0	400
C	20	40	–5	–10	50	25	100
D	30	50	5	0	0	25	0
E	35	30	–10	–20	–200	100	400
					Σxy =–250	Σx^2 =250	Σy^2 =1000

Mean of series X, $(M)_x = 25$

Mean of series Y, $(M)_y = 50$

$$\text{Formula } r = \frac{\Sigma xy}{\sqrt{\Sigma x^2 \times \Sigma y^2}}$$

$$= \frac{-250}{\sqrt{250 \times 1000}} = \frac{-250}{\sqrt{250000}}$$

$$= \frac{-250}{500} = \frac{1}{2} = -0.5$$

Computation of r directly from raw scores when deviations are taken from zero (without calculating deviations from the means). Here we apply the formula.

$$r = \frac{N\Sigma XY - \Sigma X.\Sigma Y}{\sqrt{[N\Sigma X^2 - (\Sigma X)^2][N\Sigma Y^2 - (\Sigma Y)^2]}}$$

Subject	*Scores in 1st Test X*	*Scores in 2nd Test Y*	*XY*	*X^2*	*Y^2*
A	5	12	60	25	144
B	3	15	45	2	225
C	2	11	22	4	121
D	8	10	80	64	100
E	6	8	108	36	324
N = 5	$\Sigma X = 24$	$\Sigma Y = 66$	$\Sigma XY = 315$	$\Sigma X^2 = 138$	$\Sigma Y^2 = 914$

$$r = \frac{5 \times 315 - 24 \times 66}{\sqrt{[5 \times 138 - 576] \times [5 \times 914 - 66 \times 66]}}$$

$$= \frac{1575 - 1650}{\sqrt{[690 - 576] \times [4570 - 4356]}}$$

$$= \frac{-75}{\sqrt{24396}} \frac{-75}{\sqrt{156.2}} = -0.48$$

Ans. r = – 0.48

SUMMARY

In social sciences including education, there arise many situations where we have to find out the relationship between two set of scores or variables e.g. intelligence and achievement etc. It can be done by using various methods of correlation like linear correlation.

Linear correlation represents the simplest type of correlation found between two sets of scores or variables. Such correlation is designated as linear on account of its capacity for being represented by a straight line. It reveals how the change in one variable is accompanied by changes in the other in terms of direction as well as magnitude. The relationship is generally expressed by a ratio known as coefficient of correlation. It involves no units and varies from –1 to +1 (perfect negative to perfect positive correlation). A zero value signifies absolutely no relationship between two sets of scores or variables.

There are two methods of computing coefficient of correlation (linear) namely the Rank difference method and Product Moment method. Use of Rank difference method requires rank, i.e. position of merit earned by the individuals with respect to the possession of certain characteristics say A and B. For only considering the ranks of individuals to compute coefficient correlation between the set of scores A and B, it is called as Rank Correlation Coefficient and often symbolically designated by the Greek letter ρ (pronounced as Rho). For its computation, it employs the formula

$$\rho = 1 - \frac{6\Sigma d^2}{N(N^2 - 1)}$$

(where d is the difference between the rank of individuals whose scores are under consideration for computing).

The coefficient computed by Product Moment Method, (also known as Pearson's product moment method) is known as Product Moment, Coefficient of correlation. It is symbolically represented by r and computed in the case of ungrouped data by using the formula:

$$r = \frac{\Sigma xy}{\sqrt{\Sigma x^2 \times \Sigma y^2}}$$

where x and y represent the deviation of scores in the tests X and Y from the means of each distribution. It can also be computed directly from the raw scores (without calculating deviations from the means) by using the formula $r = \frac{N\Sigma XY - \Sigma X \cdot \Sigma Y}{\sqrt{[N\Sigma X^2 - (\Sigma X)^2][N\Sigma Y^2 - (\Sigma Y)^2]}}$

References and Suggested Readings

Garrett, H.E., *Statistics in Psychology and Education*, Indian ed., Vakils, Feffer and Simons, Mumbai, 1971.

Guliford, J.P., *Fundamental Statistics in Psychology and Education*, 5th International Students ed., McGraw Hill, New York, 1973.

Mangal, S.K., *Statistics in Psychology and Education*, 2nd ed., Prentice-Hall of India, New Delhi, 2002.

McNemar, Q., *Psychological Statistics,* 3rd ed., John Wiley, New York, 1962.

Assignment Problems

1. What is correlation in Statistics? Discuss its types? How is it useful in the field of education?
2. Find the correlation between the following two sets of scores using product moment methods.

Subject	*A*	*B*	*C*	*D*	*E*	*F*	*G*	*H*
Test X	15	18	22	17	19	20	16	21
Test Y	40	42	50	45	43	46	41	41

Ans. r = 0.65

3. Find the correlation between the following two sets of raw scores without computing deviation from the mean.

A	*B*	*C*	*D*	*E*	*F*	*G*	*H*	*I*	*J*
13	12	10	8	7	6	6	4	3	1
7	11	3	7	2	12	6	2	9	6

Ans. r = 0.14

4. Compute the coefficient of correlation between the following two series of test scores by Rank difference method.

(a) Pupils	*Test X*	*Test Y*	*(b) Pupils*	*Test X*	*Test Y*
A	40	42	A	12	16
B	36	35	B	26	25
C	27	28	C	21	15
D	18	27	D	23	21
E	13	15	E	25	22
F	48	48	F	15	21
G	43	50	G	18	27
H	25	27	H	22	30
I	29	32	I	18	28
J	17	21	J	19	23

Ans. 0.985 **Ans. 0.188**

5. Find the correlation coefficient between the following set of scores using product moment method.

Subject	A	B	C	D	E	F	G	H	I	J
Test x	13	12	10	10	8	6	6	5	3	2
Test y	11	14	11	7	9	11	3	7	6	1

Ans. 0.76

6. Find the Rank correlation coefficient from the following data

Individuals	*A*	*B*	*C*	*D*	*E*	*F*	*G*	*H*
Marks in Hindi	30	40	50	20	10	45	22	18
Marks in English	55	75	60	12	11	38	25	15

Ans. 0.86

7. What is coefficient of correlation? Calculate the coefficient of correlation by Rank order Method in the following groups:

Group (x)	*Group (y)*
50	24
62	20
68	22
69	18
73	18
73	18
78	19
81	10

Ans. – 0.756

8. Calculate the coefficient of correlation by Rank difference method from the following data:

Students	*X – Scores*	*Y – Scores*
A	32	27
B	28	25
C	35	26
D	26	22
E	22	15
F	20	18
G	30	24

Ans. 0.893

9. Compute the coefficient or correlation by Rank difference method from the following data:

Students	*X – Scores*	*Y – Scores*
A	20	35
B	22	40
C	24	32
D	18	30
E	27	38
F	30	39
G	28	34
H	23	33

Ans. 0.357

45

Administration and Interpretation of Psychological Tests (Practical Work)

CHAPTER COMPOSITION

INTRODUCTION

There is no exaggeration in Kant's saying that "experiment without theory is blind and theory without experiment is lame." Theory and practice, related to any field of knowledge, present idea and action. One is necessary for the other, not only for their own survival but also for rendering some service to the humanity. Therefore, in any scheme of study there should be a close integration of theory with practice. Psychology is not an exception. Here too we must pay due emphasis on the practical work besides theoretical insight into the subject. Being a student of educational psychology you must be well-versed in using and employing the theory and contents of psychology in a practical way. You may yourself be curious to know your intellectual level, your interests and aptitudes, your personality make up, your adjustment to your self and the environment etc. You can know such things through measurements, possible with the relevant psychological tests. Many of these tests have been constructed and standardized by psychologists and researchers in India as well as abroad. In their test manuals, they have described all about their tests, their usability, methods of administration, scoring and interpretation etc. for the benefit of their users. In your interest we have selected a few psychological tests related to your B.Ed. syllabus here. In the following pages, we are going to discuss the methodology of conducting and reporting these tests.

MEASUREMENT OF INTELLIGENCE

Introduction

What is intelligence? It has been discussed and interpreted by the psychologists and scholars in their own ways. While some have described it as an ability to learn, or ability to adopt or adjust, others have accepted it as the ability to think, reason, imagine or problem solving. While agreeing with all such views about one's intelligence, we can globally consider it as a complex blend of all the mental abilities and capabilities of an individual which help him perform all the tasks needing the use of such mental abilities and capacities of an individual. Hence, one's intelligence is nothing but his intellect put to use.

Nothing definite can be said about the number of different mental or cognitive abilities and capacities comprising one's intellect. Various theories of intelligence have tried to throw light on this aspect from their own angles. Factor theories have tried to point out a definite number of elements or factors present in human intelligence. The nature, degree and amount of such factors present in one's intelligence may thus become the measuring yardstick of one's intelligence in relation to other individuals belonging to his group.

Intelligence tests in this way are designed so as to find out the extent and level of these various elements or factors in one's intellectual performance. The performance related behaviour may be either verbal or non-verbal. Consequently, intelligence tests are mainly grouped into two main categories, verbal and non-verbal. These can be used for testing the intelligence of an individual one at a time or in group according to their nature.

While verbal tests are language dominated, the use of language is strictly prohibited or is very much limited in the non-verbal tests. Instead of language, we make use of pictures, signs and symbols to judge one's intelligence through his performance in activities requiring some use of his intellect.

Let us now discuss the process of using the intelligence tests with the help of two different tests, verbal as well as non-verbal in the present chapter.

Verbal Intelligence Test

The reporting work of the use of such a verbal intelligence test can be illustrated as below:

OBJECTIVE

To test the intelligence of a subject by making use of a verbal intelligence test.

NEEDED TEST MATERIAL AND ENVIRONMENTAL SITUATIONS

(i) A copy of the Group Test of General Mental Ability constructed and standardized by Dr. Shyam Sunder Jalota comprising test booklet, answer-sheet, scoring key and test manual.

(ii) A subject whose intelligence is to be tested.

(iii) The arrangement of proper environmental conditions and material facilities for conducting the test.

(iv) A table clock or stop watch.

Identifying Data of the Subject

Name of the Subject:	Ramesh	Name of the School
Date of Birth:	5.7.1994	Model School, Rohtak
Date of the testing:	5.1.2006	Class: VIII

Description of the Test Material

This verbal intelligence test has been constructed and standardized by Dr. S.S. Jalota. It can be used to test the intelligence of the Hindi speaking students of VIII, IX and X classes. It is a group test meaning thereby that we can test the intelligence of a group of students at a time by using this test. It can also be used for testing the intelligence of a single student like in the present case where we are testing the intelligence of our subject Ramesh studying in class VIII. Its test material can be divided into four parts for its proper description.

Test Booklet

It is a reusable booklet. The testees are instructed not to write anything in it or damage it in any way.

The starting page contains all the necessary instructions regarding the administration of the test. The examinees are asked to read them carefully. On the second page, there are 20 questions given for illustration purpose to let the examinees know how to answer the test items. On the third page, there is an instruction which reads as "Unless asked, do not turn this page." From fourth page onwards, there are test items in the form of verbal questions. Every page contains 20 questions and there are 100 questions in all in this test. Most of these questions are multiple choice type. Out of the given four alternatives, only one is correct. The examinees are required to search for this correct response. A few questions are not the multiple choice type and the examinees are required to provide their answer by writing a number or digit. The examples of both these types of questions included in this test are as follows:

1. तट का अर्थ है - (i) गंगा (ii) किनारा (iii) बाँध (iv) पर
2. 19, 17, 15, 13, 11 इन संख्याओं के क्रमानुसार आगे की एक संख्या उत्तर पत्र (Answer Sheet) पर लिखें।

Answer Sheet

This sheet is given to the subject for writing the answers of the 100 test items. The top of the sheet contains columns to write name, class, school, date of birth, date of the testing etc. for ascertaining the identity of the subject. This information is to be furnished by the examinee. Then, there is blank space for answering the 100 test items. In each column, there is a serial order of 20 items page wise and in front of it in the next column there is a blank space. The subject has to write his response either by writing the serial number of the chosen alternative or by writing the number or digit in the blank space provided adjacent to the test item.

Scoring Key

Scoring key lies with the examiner or administrator of the test. He provides numerical scores to the student's responses by checking their correctness through this key. Every question or test item is scored as 1 if correct and 0 if incorrect. In this way, the maximum and minimum score in the test ranges from 100 to zero.

Test Manual

It also lies with the examiner. It contains all the essential details about the test like how the test items have been selected? How the test has been standardized? What type of subjects can be tested through this intelligence test? How can this test be administered? How is the scoring done? How can we interpret the intelligence of the subjects with the help of the computed scores? This manual also contains a conversion table which helps the examiner convert the test scores of the students into their mental age scores. This manual contains another table meant for converting original test scores of the subjects into the respective stanine scores. It also contains the norms for the VIII, IX and X class of students which may help in grading a subject on the basis of their stanine scores as poor, very dull, superior, very superior and excellent etc.

ADMINISTRATION OF THE TEST

For the administration of the test, the following procedure was followed:

(i) The environmental situations and seating arrangement etc. were so arranged that the examinee feels quite at home. The necessary rapport was established and he was told that the objective of this test is to measure his intelligence.

(ii) He was given a test booklet and an answer sheet. He was told that nothing should be written on the test booklet. He is to use it as a question paper and return it safely along with his answer-sheet.

(iii) He was then asked to carefully read all the instructions given on the first page of the test booklet. All these instructions were also explained to him verbally and he was clearly told that there is a time limit of 20 minutes for answering all the 100 items of the test.

(iv) He was then given full opportunity to go through all the 20 examples for letting him know the way of answering the test items. These illustrations were also properly explained verbally to the subject.

(v) Now the subject was asked to start responding to the test items. It was properly taken care of that the subject provides answers correctly on the answer-sheet, items and page wise as per the instructions. After 20 minutes, he was asked to submit his answer sheet along with the reusable booklet.

SCORING OF THE TEST ITEMS

For scoring the responses of the subject of all the 100 items, proper help was taken from the scoring key. Every correct answer was scored as 1 and incorrect as zero. Since our subject Ramesh provided correct responses for 53 test items, he was awarded 53 marks.

Interpretation of the result

For the necessary interpretation and drawing conclusion about the intelligence of the subject from his earned scores, following procedure was adopted.

(i) First of all this score was used to determine his mental age. The help of the conversion table provided in the test manual was taken for this purpose. It was read as 15 years for his scores of 53. Next his chronological age was computed with the help of his date of birth furnished by him in his identifying data. It was 12 years and 6 months. Now his I.Q. was computed as below:

Mental Age = 15 years = 180 months.
Chronological age = 12 years 6 months = 150 months.

$$\text{IQ} = \frac{\text{Mental age}}{\text{Chronological age}} \times 100 = \frac{180}{150} \times 100 = 120$$

(ii) Now to know about the nature and degree of the intellectual potential of our subject on the basis of his so computed I.Q., necessary help was taken from the classification table given by Terman (given earlier in this text). It can be inferred from this table that Ramesh with his I.Q. of 120 can be adjudged as superior.

(iii) For interpreting in another way, Ramesh's original score of 53 was converted into stanine score. Ramesh is the student of VIII class, hence for his scores of 53, his stanine score was computed as 6. Now this stanine score of 6 was converted into grade and it was bright according to the interpretation given in the test manual (It has been also mentioned right on the page of answer sheet). Judging on this line of interpretation also, Ramesh can be adjudged as superior or bright.

CONCLUSION

Ramesh may be adjudged as a bright superior child in terms of his intellectual capacities on the basis of the present test. This fact may be further ascertained with the help of some other measure of intelligence.

Non-Verbal Intelligence Test

The non-verbal intelligence test can be used for testing the intelligence of a subject in the following way.

OBJECTIVE

To test the intelligence of a subject with the help of a non-verbal intelligence test.

NEEDED TEST MATERIAL AND ENVIRONMENTAL SITUATIONS

(i) A copy of the (CIE) Non-verbal Group Test of Intelligence containing practice booklet, test booklet and test manual.
(ii) A subject under testing.
(iii) Appropriate and conducive environment and facilities for the administration of the test.
(iv) A stop watch.

IDENTIFYING DATA OF THE SUBJECT

Name of the Subject :	Satish	Name of the School
Date of Birth :	15.8.2002	Govt. High School,
Class : VII : Age :	11 years	Rohtak

DESCRIPTION OF THE TEST

This test was originally designed and constructed by J.W. Jenkins. Here we are using its Hindi adaptation prepared and standardized by Central Institute of Education (CIE), New Delhi. It can be used only with the Hindi speaking, school-going Indian children. This test contains the pictorial items as given below:

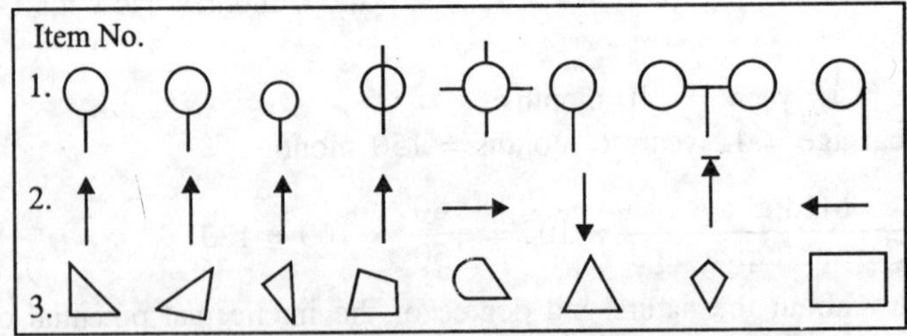

Fig. 45.1 Test items of the CIE non-verbal intelligence test.

For responding to these items, instruction like below is issued to the examinees.

"The three figures in each lines (rows) given on the left hand side are somewhat similar. On the right hand side, there lie five figures. One of these five belongs to the family of the three given on the left hand side. You have to locate and mark its serial no. (i), (ii), (iii), (iv) or (v) on the answer-sheet against the S. No. of the item."

The test material used in this test can be divided into three main components: (i) Practice Booklet, (ii) Test Booklet, and (iii) Test manual.

ADMINISTRATION OF THE TEST

The subject was made to feel comfortable and a good rapport was established with him and he was made acquainted with the objective of the testing. The administration of this test was done in the following two phases:

(a) Preliminary practice test.
(b) The main proper test.

Administration of the Preliminary Practice Test

It was done in the following steps:

(i) The subject was given the preliminary practice test booklet and instructed not to open it unless asked to do so.
(ii) He was then asked to carefully read the instructions given in this booklet. The same was again well-explained to him and he was instructed to follow them carefully. He was also told that he should strictly follow the time schedule. He must begin and end the moment he is asked to do so.
(iii) The subject was then asked to begin with responding to the questions related to Group 1. After two minutes he was asked to stop responding. For moving further he was asked to respond to the questions related to group II, III, IV and V one by one by following the time schedule to the questions related to single group.
(iv) Thus, after 10 minutes, the practice test booklet was taken back from him. It was not scored but the subject was not told that practice test is not scored.

Administration of the Proper Test

The proper test was administered by keeping the following points in consideration:

(i) After 10 minutes the subject was given proper test booklet. He was instructed not to open it unless asked to do so.
(ii) He was then asked to carefully read the instructions given on the first page of the booklet. The same was explained to him again verbally.
(iii) He was then asked to begin with responding to the questions belonging to different groups starting from group I to V by strictly sticking to the following time schedule for responding to the questions of a particular group.

Sub-tests of Group	*Page*	*Time*
I	2 pages	5 minutes
II	2 pages	5 minutes
III	2 pages	5 minutes
IV	2 pages	5 minutes
V	3 pages	10 minutes
		Total Time = 30 minutes

(iv) After 30 minutes, he was asked to hand over the proper test booklet to the examiner.

Scoring of the Response

The responses of the subject were scored with the help of the scoring key by assigning one mark to correct responses and zero for the incorrect, incomplete and ambiguous answers, i.e. providing no or more than one answer. The total scores were thus computed as under:

Sub-test or group	I	II	III	IV	V	Total score
Scores	10	11	13	13	8	57

These test scores were then converted into standard scores with the help of the conversion table provided in the manual. (This table provides the standard scores for the scores earned in the test separately for boys and girls in view of their different ages and grades with a mean of 100 and S.D. as 15).

Summary of Results

The total scores Obtained in the test	Agewise Standard Scores	Gradewise Standard Scores
57	125	130

Interpretation of the Results

By comparing the standard scores of 125 and 130 with the mean and S.D. of the standardized group, we can come to the conclusion that our subject Satish is quite an intelligent boy. By taking into consideration the percentile values of 125 and 130, we can have some more ground for the verification of his good intelligence.

APTITUDE MEASUREMENT

Introduction

We usually come across individuals who are found to excel in one or the other sphere of everyday life. It may be attributed on account of many factors or reasons. One such important reason may lie in their possession of certain specific abilities or aptitudes more than others due to which they acquire more success in certain fields.

Therefore, simply put, aptitude may be considered as the special ability or specific capacity of an individual, other than his general intellectual capacities, interests, life opportunities, hard work, etc., which help him acquire a required degree of proficiency or achievement in a specific field.

So, if we can know about the range of aptitudes of our children, in different fields, it may help us a lot in planning and organizing proper educational and vocational guidance and counseling services to them. We can surely predict that a particular child has abilities or aptitude for doing a particular job or judging a particular subject. Hence, it will be quite beneficial for him if he chooses that particular subject or vocation.

Judging in this way, the measurement of the aptitudes of the children becomes a necessity in the field of education, psychology and guidance. As a student of psychology you must also be well-versed in the measurement of aptitudes.

Measurement of Aptitude

The students may possess different types of aptitudes like mechanical aptitude, musical aptitude, artistic aptitude, aptitude for learning a particular subject and getting success in a particular profession or vocation etc. These aptitudes can be measured through various types of specific aptitude tests. For example, if we intend to know for a student of XII class about his level of teaching, we have to take the help of suitable standardized teaching aptitude test for this purpose. Such measurement of his teaching aptitude may then help us to take a judgement about whether or not he should take admission in a teacher-training course. Similar guidance can also be provided to other students choosing engineering, medical, computer or management courses on the basis of the measurement of their aptitudes with the help of relevant aptitude tests.

Measurement of Aptitude with the Help of an Aptitude Test

To illustrate the process of measurement of aptitude, we would like to use a teaching aptitude test for measuring teaching aptitude of a subject here. The use of the test along with its reporting can be done in the way given ahead.

Objective

To find about the teaching aptitude of a subject with the application of a teaching aptitude test.

Test material and environmental situations:

(i) A copy of the teaching aptitude test constructed and standardized by Dr. R.P. Singh and Dr. S.N. Sharma containing test booklet, answer-sheet and test manual.
(ii) A subject whose teaching aptitude is to be measured.
(iii) Proper environmental situations and facilities for conducting the test.

Identifying data of the subject

Name :	Arti Sharma	Age : 17 years
Name of the School :		Date of Testing : 8.9.2005
Govt. Girls Hr. Sec. School, Rohtak		Class : XII

Description of the test

The present test named as Teaching Aptitude Test Battery has been constructed and standardized by Dr. R.P. Singh and Dr. S.N. Sharma of Patna University, Patna (Bihar). It has been published by National Psychological Corporation, Agra. This test can only be employed with the Hindi speaking testees. Its objective is to test the teaching aptitude of teachers working in elementary schools or those who wish to intend to become elementary school teachers in the near future. In this sense, it can be used as a measure of selecting trainees for the J.B.T. or Diploma in Education Teacher's training course. Test material of this test can be divided into three sections for the necessary description.

Test Booklet

It is meant to provide necessary instructions to the examinee regarding answering the questions (test items) given in this test booklet on a separate answer sheet. The title page of this booklet contains the names of the test, author and the publisher along with the necessary instructions regarding the test. The next 16 pages of this booklet contain test item. This test has its five sub-tests each having a special type of test item. In the first sub-test, there are 32 items, in the second 20, 28 each in third and fourth and 12 in the fifth. In this way, there are 120 total test items (questions) in this aptitude test. In the beginning of the each section (sub-test), the necessary instructions for responding to the items in the sub-test are given for the benefit of the examinees. The nature of the items and instruction related to each sub-test or section is hereby illustrated by reproducing some sample items from this aptitude test.

खंड 1: प्रश्न 1 सूची 'क' में रिक्त स्थान की पूर्ति हेतु सूची 'ख' में अंकित शब्दों में से किसी एक उपयुक्त शब्द को उत्तर पर लिखें –

सूची क	सूची ख
पान : हरा दूध : ?	गाय, बकरी, उजला, मीठा

प्रश्न 25 एक बिजली की गाड़ी पूना से मुम्बई जा रही है। हवा पश्चिम की ओर बह रही है तो गाड़ी का धुआँ किस ओर उड़ेगा?

खंड 2: प्रश्न 2 यदि आप प्रश्न से बिल्कुल सहमत हैं तो उत्तर में 5 को यदि सहमत हैं तो 4 को यदि उदासीन हैं तो 3 को, यदि असहमत हैं तो 2 को तथा बिल्कुल असहमत हों तो 1 को गोले से घेरें।

शिक्षकों के स्नेह के कारण बच्चे बिगड़ सकते हैं।

खंड 3: प्रश्न 4 मान लीजिए कोई शिक्षक प्रतिदिन देर से आता है। क्या आप,

(क) उन्हें समय पर आने की राय देंगे?
(ख) विद्यालय प्राचार्य को सूचित करेंगे?
(ग) अन्य शिक्षकों के सामने उन्हें लज्जित करेंगे?
(घ) छात्रों तथा अभिभावकों में इसका प्रचार करेंगे?

खंड 4: प्रश्न 2 शिक्षक में विषय का अच्छा ज्ञान आवश्यक है, इसलिए कि-

(क) वे छात्रों को अपने बस में रख सकें।
(ख) वे छात्रों की शंकाओं का समाधान कर सकें।

खंड 5: प्रश्न 2 आपने अध्यापन पेशा अपनाया है, क्योंकि

(क) आपके पिता शिक्षक थे।
(ख) आपके कॉलेज (प्रशिक्षण संस्थानों) में पढ़ने का साधन था।
(ग) आप शिक्षक बनना चाहते थे।
(घ) आपको कोई अन्य नौकरी नहीं मिली।

Answer-Sheet

There are two pages in the answer-sheet. On the top of the Ist page, there are various columns meant for collecting identifying data of the subject. It is to be filled by the subject before responding to the test items. The remaining space of the Ist page contains the serial number of the test items or questions related to sections or sub-items I and II, alongwith the spaces for writing responses to these items. (Questions in one column and the space for answers in the other). On the second page of this answer sheet, there is appropriate provision for the serial no. of the questions related to section III, IV and V and the needed space for writing responses of these questions by choosing one alternative out of the given four.

Test Manual

It is meant for the examiner or test administrator. It mentions all about the need of constructing this test, procedure for construction, its standardization, reliability and ability and validity of the test, its main objectives, purposes and all about the application and administration of this test. It clearly explains the process of administration, scoring, interpretation and drawing conclusions on the basis of one's scores in this test. There is a scoring key for marking the responses of the examinees in this manual. Besides this, it also contains the necessary norms for converting original scores into standard scores and percentiles.

Administration of the Test

The test was administered in the following ways:

(i) Environmental situations were so arranged as to provide quite congenial environment for the administration of the test. The subject was made to feel quite at home and comfortable. The essential rapport was established and he was made aware of the objective of testing.

(ii) He was then given test booklet and answer-sheet. It was clearly told to him that he was not to write anything on the booklet or damage it in any way.

(iii) Then, he was asked to carefully read the instructions given in the test booklet. These were also clearly explained to him by the examiner.

(iv) The subject was clearly told that the five sub-tests of this aptitude test are not all alike. They contain items of different nature. They have to be responded in different ways. For understanding the nature of these items and the method of providing responses, illustrations were given in the beginning of the each sub-test or section. The subject was instructed to read all the instructions carefully and then respond accordingly. Although there is no time limit for the completion of this test, subject should finish his work as early as possible. On an average, this test takes about 90 minutes.

(v) During the administration of the test, it was ensured that the subject provided all information related to identifying data and gave responses to all the 120 items of the test on the given answer-sheet. It was also seen that he gave only one response to each test item. The incompleteness in any way was removed by asking him to do so. After such thorough inspection, the answer-sheet and test booklet were taken from the subject.

Scoring of the Responses

Help was taken from the scoring key given in the test manual for scoring the responses of the subject. The scoring work so done can be presented as below:

Sub-tests	I	II	III	IV	V	Whole test
Raw Scores	19	13	16	15	8	71

Interpretation of the test scores

For the interpretation of the test scores, help was taken from the norms given in the form of standard scores and percentiles in the manual. Our subject scored 71 marks in the present aptitude test. These original scores were subjected to conversion as below:

Raw Scores	Standard Scores	Percentile
71	116.42	P_{80}

The level of the teaching aptitude of our subject can now be properly interpreted with the help of his standard scores and percentile.

Our subject has 116.42 as his standard scores. The similar standard scores can be computed for other candidates. It may then help to prepare a merit list for selecting the candidates for a teacher training course or their recruitment as a teacher.

Our subject's percentile is P_{80}. This knowledge can help us to locate where does this boy stand in the group in relation to other candidates. The percentile P_{80} clearly indicates that only 20 per cent of the boys from the whole group possess more teaching aptitude potential in comparison to him. In this respect, he is superior to 80 per cent candidates of the group.

ASSESSMENT OF PERSONALITY

Introduction

In general, we have quite a lot of misconception about the term 'personality'. We often say 'poor' or 'magnetic' personality on the basis of one's outward appearance of behaviour. It is a very superficial approach. We must have a total picture of a person for the assessment of his personality. This picture should include all the aspects of his personality in physical, mental, social, emotional, moral and aesthetic dimensions, and the nature of his total behaviour, inner and outer, conscious and unconscious, in all the three cognitive and affective domains. Consequently, it is proper to say that personality is all that a person is in his total self.

To throw light on its meaning and nature, various scholars and psychologists have tried to define the term 'personality' in their own ways. The definitions given by Allport, Cattle and Eysenck are quite mentionable and popular among these definitions. Through the study of these popular definitions, we can reach the conclusion that personality is such a complex blend or organization of one's psychophysical systems—body, mind and soul, which provides him an identity of his own through his unique style of living and making adjustment with his self and the environment.

Here question may arise as to how can we know about one's personality for labeling or describing it as good or poor. It can be done through various methods and techniques available for the assessment of one's personality like observation, questionnaire and inventories, interview and various other projective techniques and tests. How these tests and techniques may be employed for the assessment of one's personality can be understood through an example given in the following text. Here we are making use of a personality inventory for the assessment of a subject.

Assessment of the personality of an individual through personality test

The administration and reporting work of the assessment of the personality of an individual can be done by the following steps discussed below:

Objectives

To assess the personality of a subject with the help of a written verbal test of personality

Required Test Material and Environmental Situations

(i) A copy of the Personality Dimensional Test constructed and standardized by Dr. S.P. Kulshrestha and R.P. Kothiyal containing test booklet, answer-sheet, scoring key and test manual.

(ii) The subject whose personality is to be assessed.

(iii) The appropriate and congenial environmental situations for the proper administration of the test.

Identifying data of the subject

Name of the Subject	: Arun	Name of the School
Age	: 15 years	DAV School, Rohtak
Date of the testing	: 10.8.2005	Class : X

Description of the test material

This test named as Personality Dimensional Test has been devised and standardized by Dr. S.P. Kulshrestha and R.P. Kothiyal for the assessment of the personality of Hindi speaking, school-going students of not more than 16 years old. It has been published by ISPT, Dehradun and can be employed both in individual or group tests for testing one's personality in 12 dimensions. The main components of the test material can be divided and explained as under:

Test Booklet

The title page contains the name of the test, the authors of the test, the name and address of the publisher, and so on. On the second page, there are 10 instructions meant for the examinees regarding the test. In the third page, there is an illustration to explain the way of responding to the items of the test. In the pages four to seven, there are 122 test items or questions. Every question is in the form of a compound sentence containing contradictory statements joined by 'or'. The subject is to select any one of these statements (lying left or right) which appears true for describing his self and marking in the left or right boxes. Such test items (originally in Hindi) are of the following nature:

1. I easily get angry or I take the steps after careful consideration.
2. I usually remain happy or I become happy and sad quite soon.
3. I begin to weep soon or I live my life laughing.
4. The numbers 22, 25, 28 should be followed by 38 or 31.

Answer-Sheet

The top portion of this sheet is meant for collecting identifying data from the subject. In the remaining portion, there is a provision for writing responses for the all 122 items or questions. In the first column, there are serial numbers (from 1 to122) of the test items and in the second, there is a provision of two blank rectangles. The subject has to tick in the left or right box to specify telling whether he considers the left or right statement of the item as true description of his self.

Answer Key

Every response is marked as one or zero in the way as shown in the given answer key or sheet. It is of the following nature:

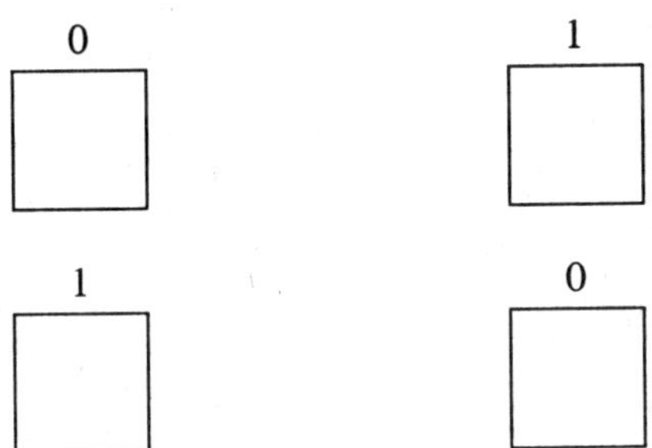

In case the subject marks the left box, he will earn zero score but if he puts it in the right box he will be awarded a score of 1. In Q. No. 2, the scoring will be just reverse. The test has a total of 122 items or questions to assess 12 personality dimensions. To facilitate the process or computation, scoring is not made for two questions (S. No. 31 and 32). Remaining 120 questions are scored and divided into 10 groups. Each group consists of 10 items. The total scores of these 10 items called factor score provide assessment for one of the factors or dimensions associated with one's personality.

Test Manual

In the test manual, the authors of the test have mentioned the objectives and purposes of the construction of the test, the procedure of construction and standardization, the ways of the test administration, scoring and interpretation etc. This test manual is meant for the examiner.

ADMINISTRATION OF THE TEST

The following steps were taken for the proper administration of the test.

(i) The subject was made to feel quite at home by providing congenial environment and establishing a proper rapport. He was made to realize that it was not a testing or examination for ascertaining something good or bad about his personality but to know about his liking or disliking about certain behaviour acts. He was to show his liking by marking the statements written on the left and right sides of the word 'or'.

(ii) The subject was asked to carefully read all the instructions about the test and he was also helped to understand the way of responding to all the 122 test items through the help of an illustration.

(iii) He was allowed to respond freely to all the 122 items. It was well assured that he had responded to all these items by putting mark on the assigned places. It was also examined that he had not written anything on the test booklet or damaged it in any way. Once completed, both the test booklet and the answer-sheets were taken back from the subject.

SCORING OF THE RESPONSES

Scoring was done with the help of the scoring key. Score of 1 or 0 was awarded to the mark put up by the subject in the left or the right rectangular box strictly on the basis of what was written on the top of the mark. The scores of 10 questions was then totaled for computing the total scores of the Dimension or Factors. In this way 10 Factor Scores were computed and tabulated as under:

S. No. questions and the total of their responses		*Name of the Factor*
Total for the responses of the questions 1 to 10 =	5	A
Total for the responses of the questions 11 to 20 =	6	B
Total for the responses of the questions 21 to 30 =	5	C
Total for the responses of the questions 33 to 42 =	8	D
Total for the responses of the questions 43 to 52 =	7	E
Total for the responses of the questions 53 to 62 =	8	F
Total for the responses of the questions 63 to 72 =	5	G
Total for the responses of the questions 73 to 82 =	5	H
Total for the responses of the questions 83 to 92 =	6	I
Total for the responses of the questions 93 to 102 =	7	J
Total for the responses of the questions 103 to 112 =	8	K
Total for the responses of the questions 113 to 122 =	5	L

Interpretation of the Test Scores : It was done as under:

(*i*) The factor scores were converted into stanine scores. In this task due help was taken from the conversion table provided in the manual.

Table for converting factorwise Raw Score into Stanine

Stanine Scores	*Factor*	*I*	*II*	*III*	*IV*	*V*	*VI*	*VII*	*VIII*	*IX*
5	A	0	1	2	3	4	5	6	7	8–10
6	B	0–1	2	3	4	5–6	7	8	10	10
5	C	0	1	2-3	4	5	6	7	8–9	10
8	D	0	1	2	3	4	5	6	7–8	9–10
7	E	—	0	1	2	3	4–5	6	7	8–10
8	F	0–2	3	4	5–6	7	8	9	—	10
5	G	0–1	2	3	4	5	6	7	8–9	10
5	H	0–1	2	3	4	5	6	7	8	9–10
6	I	0–2	3	—	4	5	6–7	8	9	10
7	J	0	1	2	3–4	5	6	7–8	9	10
8	K	0	1	2	3–4	5–6	7	8	9	10
5	L	0–1	2	3	4	5	6	7	8–9	10

In this way, was the stanine scores of our subjects alongwith their original factor scores can be tabulated as under:

Factor	*A*	*B*	*C*	*D*	*E*	*F*	*G*	*H*	*I*	*J*	*K*	*L*
Total Scores	5	6	5	8	7	8	5	5	6	7	8	5
Stanine Score	VI	V	V	VIII	VIII	VI	V	V	VI	VII	VII	V

(II) These stanine scores were then used to describe the personality traits of the subject on the following pattern as suggested in the manual. This pattern is being produced below:

Low Score Description	I	II	III	IV	V	**Stanine Scores Average**	VI	VII	VIII	IX	**High Score Description**
Emotionally Less stable	...	...	...	...	...	A	...	..	..	..	Emotionally More stable
Submissive	...	...	...	...	...	B	...	..	..	..	Dominant
Inactive	...	...	...	...	...	C	...	..	..	..	Over active
Less Intelligence	...	...	...	...	...	D	...	..	..	..	More Intelligence
Introvert	...	...	...	...	...	E	...	..	..	..	Extrovert
Tensed	...	...	...	...	...	F	...	..	..	..	Relaxed
Poor Mental Health	...	...	...	...	...	G	...	..	..	..	Good Mental Health
Poor Adjustment	...	...	...	...	...	H	...	..	..	..	Good Adjustment
Insecured	...	...	...	...	...	I	...	..	..	..	Secured
Superstitious	...	...	...	...	...	J	...	..	..	..	Non-Superstitious
Less Creative	...	...	...	...	...	K	...	..	..	..	More Creative
Low Moral ability	...	...	...	...	...	L	...	..	..	..	High Moral ability

Now with the help of the above pattern, we can use the stanine scores (for the original factor scores) of our subject for describing her personality traits factorwise, as below:

Factor	*Stanine Score*	*Personality Traits*
A	VI	Emotionally more Stable
B	V	Dominant and Assertive
C	V	Over active
D	VIII	More Intelligent
E	VIII	Extrovert
F	VI	Relaxed
G	V	Good Mental Health
H	V	Good Adjustment
I	VI	Secured
J	VII	Non-Superstitious
K	VII	More creative
L	V	High Moral ability

MEASUREMENT OF LEARNING

Introduction

Learning is defined as a process that brings relatively permanent changes in one's behaviour through experience or training. How we learn may be explained on the basis of the theories propagated by various psychogists. One of these theories propagated by Thorndike is trial and error. According to this theory one learns through stamping out of the incorrect responses and stamping in of the correct responses while making efforts and trials in learning a thing or task. This type of learning can be demonstrated through the experiments categorized as maze learning.

A maze consists of several paths and turnings. A few of these paths are blind, i.e. having no opening. In order to get out of the maze, one has to follow the right path or turning. In case he chooses a wrong path he is led to a blind alley, i.e. blind path. There are different kinds of human mazes available for the experiments in maze learning, e.g. punch, board maze, pursuit rotor, jungle mazes, metallic mazes and electric mazes. In the present experiment, we are going to make use of an electric maze.

Objective

To demonstrate the process of learning through an experiment on maze learning.

Name of the experimenter: Date :
Name of the subject: Sex :
Educational qualifications: Age:

Apparatus and Materials

An electric maze, dry battery of 1.5 volts, battery bulb, bulb holder, connecting wires, screwdriver, blade, stylus, stop watch and writing material.

Preliminary Set-up

The electric maze is connected with our terminal of the battery cell. The other wire is connected with one wire of the bulb holder. The other wire of the bulb holder is joined with one wire of the stylus and the other wire of the stylus is connected with the remaining terminal of the battery cell. Now a bulb suitable for a battery of 1.5 volts is fitted in the bulb holder. Before making its use, the electric circuit of the apparatus is properly tested.

Procedure

1. The following instructions were given to the subject after he was made to sit comfortably near the starting point of the maze.

   "It is an electric maze. The letter 'S' written on it stands for the starting point of the maze and the letter 'G' indicates the goal where you are to reach. Here it is a 'Stylus'. You have to make its use for searching the path to reach the goal. However, you have to touch with it only the points comprising the right path. In case you happen to touch the wrong knob, you will at once see red light in the bulb showing thereby that you have gone wrong. As soon as you see the red light in the bulb, come back on the right knob touched by you just before the wrong knob. In any case you are not to skip the knobs for finding out your path to the goal. In this way, go on fresh knob to knob but do not return unless you have commited an error. Try to reach the goal 'G' as quickly and accurately as possible. Once you reach the goal 'G' take rest for 30 seconds and then start again from the starting point 'S'. Repeat the process till you are told to stop after having made these successive errorless trials. I have a stop watch with me and you have to start only when the 'ready' signal is given to you. You are neither to touch the knobs nor count them. At the end of the experiment, I will also ask you to give an introspection report about the method by which you learn the maze and your own feelings and experiences etc. If you have any doubts, kindly clarify before I say 'ready' to you."
2. After setting the apparatus, making the subject sit comfortably and giving him proper instructions, the experiment was conducted in a cool and calm environment. The subject was made to search the right path and reach the goal with the help of the stylus. The time taken in each trial and the number of mistakes committed (appearnce of red light) were properly recorded by the experimenter. In all twelve trials were made. The trials were stopped when the subject reached the learning stage of three errorless trials.

Precautions Observed

1. It was kept in mind that the subject selected for the experiment might not have any previous experience of working as subject in the similar experiments.
2. The subject was provided with a comfortable seat not the starting point of the maze.
3. It was checked before performing the experiment that the apparatus was in working order alongwith completion of its electric circuit.
4. The subject was not allowed to count the number of knobs or touch the maze.
5. It was tried to control all the possible sources of distraction.
6. Stopwatch was regulated properly and the time and errors were recorded as accurately as possible.

Introspection Report

The introspection report obtained immediately after the completion of the experiment was of the following nature.

"I found the experiment quite interesting. When I was touching the knob with the stylus, I was surprised to see the red light when I went wrong. It made me uncomfortable. However, I tried to be very cautious in reaching the goal but every time in the beginning I committed a number of mistakes. In the latter trials, I somehow knew the nature of my path and tried to eliminate as much errors as possible."

Recording of the Experimental Data

The observation data of the experiment was recorded and tabulated as follows:

Table 45.1 Performance in Maze Learning

S. No. of Trials	*Time taken in seconds*	*No. of errors made*
1.	25	7
2.	25	5
3.	23	6
4.	21	4
5.	20	4
6.	20	3
7.	18	2
8.	18	2
9.	15	1
10.	14	0
11.	14	0
12.	13	0
Total 12 Trials	226 Seconds	34 Errors

Interpretation of the Results and Discussion

It can be seen from the recorded observations that in 12 trials, the subject committed 34 mistakes. The last three trials were errorless and, therefore, it can be concluded that the subject learned the maze after committing 34 mistakes in 226 seconds. It can also be seen that almost every subsequent trial required less time and the subject committed fewer errors. The relationship of trials with the passage of the time and mistakes committed can be properly interpreted through the learning curves as shown in the next figures.

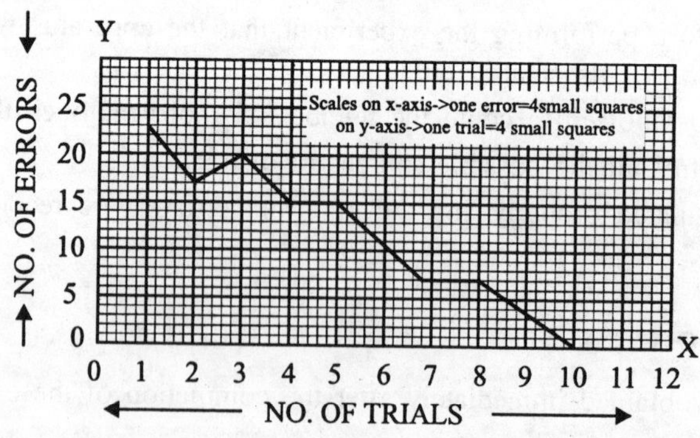

Fig. 45.2 Graph showing relationship between trials and time during maze learning.

A close observation of these graphs may at once reveal that the subject requires lesser time and commits fewer mistakes with the increase in the number of trials thus leading us to conclude that the practice is helpful in maze learning.

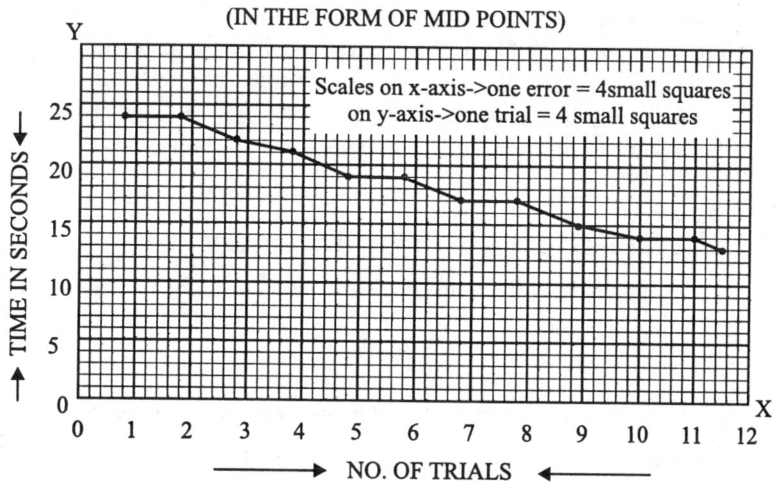

Fig. 45.3 Graph showing relationship between trials and error committed during maze learning.

MEASUREMENT OF ADJUSTMENT

Introduction

What is known as 'adaptation' in biological sciences is termed as 'adjustment' in the subject psychology. According to Darwin's theory of evolution, our life represents a continuous chain of struggle for our existence and survival. In this struggle only the species, which tried to adapt to the changing demands of the environment, were able to survive while others who did not adapt completely suffered their extinction. In this way, if we want to live or live in a better way in this physical world, we have to adapt ourselves all the demands of our physical environment. However, man is somewhat different from other species. He needs to live well physically as well as socially and psychologically. For him the psychological survival is as much essential as his physical survival. Therefore, the term adaptation used for biological or physical survival is somewhat small and narrow for the description of the physical, social and psychological survival of the human being. Therefore, it has been now replaced by a more comprehensive term 'adjustment'.

Adjustment, in this way, refers to the state of one's body and mind in which he remains adapted to the physical and socio-psychological demands of his self and the environment. In this way, for one's adjustment, the satisfaction of his self and his environmental needs are quite essential. One remains adjusted as long his basic needs are gratified or he has a hope for their gratification. Once this balance is disturbed or seems to be in danger, the individual gets maladjusted resulting into the deterioration of his mental health.

In this way, while a good adjustment to one's self and the environment is the key to one's good mental and physical health and the overall well-being of the individual, the maladjustment may drift him towards abnormal behaviour and poor mental health. The welfare of our children thus lies in seeking proper adjustment with their self and the environment. Since prevention is said to be better than cure, our efforts should be directed towards knowing well about the adjustment level of our children well in time. It is equally true for the children. They must also know their adjustment level with their self and the environment.

Hence, we must be acquainted with the measures of adjustment. The use of adjustment inventories in this direction has been found quite practicable. There are various inventories available for measuring the adjustment of the individuals belonging to different ages, grades, professions, and categories. For examples, we have inventories for measuring the adjustment of school-going children, college-going students, adults, teachers, and so on. We are illustrating here the task of the measurement of adjustment with the help of an inventory meant for measuring the adjustment of college students.

Measurement of Adjustment by Using Inventory

The measurement of adjustment with the help of a suitable adjustment inventory can be done and reported through the following steps:

Objective

To measure the adjustment of a college student with the help of an adjustment inventory.

Needed Test Material and Environmental Situations

(i) A subject (studying in a college) whose adjustment we want to measure.

(ii) A copy of the adjustment inventory (meant for college students) divised by Dr. A.K.P. Sinha and Dr. R.P. Singh which includes a test booklet, answer-sheet and test manual.

(iii) The proper congenial environment and facilities for the administration of the test.

Identifying Data of the Subject

Name : Somesh — Institution : Vaish College, Rohtak
Age : 17 years — Class : XII
Sex : Male — Date of Testing : 10th September, 2005
Occupation of Father : Service
Income : Rs. 4,000 per month

Description of the Test Material

This inventory has been devised by Dr. A.K.P. Sinha and Dr. R.P. Singh. It has been published by National Psychological Corporation, Agra. It can be used for measuring the adjustment of Hindi as well as English speaking college students. It measures their adjustment in five areas related to home, health, social, emotional and educational adjustments. The test material of this inventory can be divided and described as under:

Test Booklet

It contains 8 pages. The title or front page contains the name of the test, name of the authors and name and address of the publisher. Besides, there are instructions related to the administration of the test on the page. Nothing is written on the back of the front page. Similarly, the back cover page also does not have any thing written on it. In this way, the test items are given only on the pages 3 to 7. These are 102 in number. All the 102 items have been identified and marked with either of the five bracketed letters as (a), (b), (c), (d) or (e) written in front of them. Such identification is done for indicating that a particular item aims to measure one's adjustment in a particular area symbolized by that bracketed letter like home, health, social, emotional or educational. This booklet is a reusable one and hence examinees are instructed not to write anything on it. For response, they are provided an answer sheet. The test items are available in Hindi as well as in English.

Answer Sheet

It is given to the subject along with the test booklet. The top of this sheet is meant for collecting the identifying data from the subject. The rest of this sheet is meant for the responses of the subject. For this purpose, there are S. Nos. of the 102 test items in the left column and in the second column, there are two rectangular boxes printed in front of each item. On the top of these boxes, yes or no is already written and one has to simply put mark in either of the boxes depending upon his response. The bottom of this answer sheet contains scoring table meant for the use of the examiner.

Test Manual

In this test manual, the authors of this inventory have described the need and objective of this inventory, the way of its preparation and standardization, the methods of administration, scoring and interpretation etc. Every examiner should carefully read this manual for the required success in his task.

ADMINISTRATION OF THE TEST

This inventory was administered to the subject in the following way:

(i) First of all care was taken for proper and congenial environment needed for the administration of the test. Then the subject was made to feel relaxed. A good rapport was established with him and he was made aware of the objective of the testing.

(ii) Then he was given a copy of the test booklet and an answer sheet.

(iii) Then he was asked to fill the columns meant for his identifying data. It was observed and assured that he had completed this work in a desired way.

(iv) Then he was asked to read the instructions given in the test booklet carefully. These were again well explained to him so that he might not feel any difficulty in responding to the test items.

(v) He was allowed to work at his own speed. It was fully taken care of that he provides his answer in yes or no by marking in the appropriate column. After the completion of the work, the test booklet and answer sheet were taken back from him. It was again ensured that he had not written anything on the test booklet and provided responses to all the test items.

SCORING OF THE RESPONSES

The responses of the subject were scored with the help of five transparent scoring keys provided in the test material of this inventory. Each of these scoring keys is used for scoring the responses of the items meant for measuring one's adjustment in a particular area. Hence the respective keys were employed for scoring the responses of the items identified and marked as (a), (b), (c), (d), or (e). For this purpose, we first made use of a key meant for scoring the items related to home adjustment. This transparency was placed on the answer sheet of the subject. We counted all the marks with the help of the circles of the key. The counting of these marks then provided us the home adjustment scores of our subject. Similar practice was adopted for the computation of the scores related to the other four adjustment areas.

The scores so computed were tabulated as under:

Areas of Adjustment	*Scores*
(a) Home Adjustment	7
(b) Health Adjustment	6
(c) Social Adjustment	10
(d) Emotional Adjustment	15
(e) Educational Adjustment	11
General Adjustment	49

INTERPRETATION OF THE TEST SCORES

It was done in the following two ways:

Interpretation through percentile norms

In the manual percentile norms tables were given separately for males and females. With their help, we converted the original scores of our subject (both Area wise and General Adjustment Scores) into percentiles. Percentiles thus computed and conclusions then derived for our subject can be summarized as under. It is also to be remembered that this inventory provides one's maladjustment scores meaning thereby that more the scores one gets, more maladjusted he is.

- Our subject Somesh scored 7 in the area of home adjustment. By consulting table 3 of the manual, we converted his raw scores of 7 into the percentile value P_{80}. The percentile value P_{80} clearly reveals that in this area of adjustment, there are only 20% students who are more maladjusted than him.
- The same is true for his adjustment in the area of health adjustment, social adjustment and educational adjustment where our subject has earned the same percentile value i.e. P_{80} (on the basis of his original scores in these area as 6, 10 and 11 respectively).
- In the area of emotional adjustment, the original scores of our subject is 15. The percentile value of this score is P_{80}. It means that he has somewhat less maladjustment in this area is comparison to all the other areas of adjustment. However, in this area also, only 30% students are more maladjusted than him.
- In terms of total general adjustment, our subject's score is 49. The percentile value of this score, known from the conversion table, is more than P_{80}. In this way, he may be adjudged as quite maladjusted even in terms of his total general adjustment.

Interpretation through Adjustment Categories

Tables of the manual help in converting the raw scores (Total General Adjustment Scores and Areawise Adjustment Scores) of the male and female subjects into some specific adjustment categories for describing them as Excellent, Good, Average, Unsatisfactory or Very Unsatisfactory in terms of their level of adjustment. We took the necessary help from both these tables for the interpretation of the respective original scores of our subject. The results may be summarized as below:

Adjustment Area	*Raw Scores*	*Adjustment Categories*	*Adjustment Description*
(a) Home Adjustment	7	C	Average
(b) Health Adjustment	6	D	Unsatisfactory
(c) Social Adjustment	10	D	Unsatisfactory
(d) Emotional Adjustment	15	C	Average
(e) Educational Adjustment	11	D	Unsatisfactory
General Adjustment	49	D	Unsatisfactory

Discussion

Somesh is average and normal in terms of his adjustment in the areas of home and emotional adjustment. However, in all the other three areas of adjustment—health, social and educational—his level of adjustment is unsatisfactory. In terms of total general adjustment also, his level of adjustment is unsatisfactory. In this way, it may be concluded that he is not properly adjusted with his self and the environment.

Conclusion

With the result of the administration of the present adjustment inventory, it can be concluded that our subject Somesh is not properly adjusted with his self and the environment. He is the victim of maladjustment. Therefore, attempts should be made to help him in his proper adjustment by finding out the root causes of his maladjustment.

MEASUREMENT OF ATTITUDES

Introduction

Our attitudes play quite a significant role in shaping our behaviour and personality make-up. The nature of our reactions and responses towards things, ideas or persons depends much on the formation of our attitudes towards them. As a matter of definition, we may understand by the term attitude a determining acquired tendency which prepares us to behave in a certain way towards a specific object or class of objects, subject to the conditions prevailing in the environment. Consequently if we keep positive and favourable attitude towards an object, we will be attracted towards it, admire it and try to achieve it. On the other hand, if we have a negative or unfavourable attitude towards it, we will try to avoid it and even feel hostile towards it. Summing in this way, we can conclude that attitudes are, to a great extent, responsible for the particular behaviour of a person towards an object, idea or person.

Measurement of Attitudes

Attitudes are learned behaviour. What type of attitude, favourable or unfavourable, positive or negative does one possesses towards an object, idea or person is a thing of investigation. Its objective assessment needs a type of measurement that can help us to determine to some extent in a reliable and accurate way the nature of one's attitude towards a given object, idea or person. It needs the administration of a properly constructed and standardized attitude scale. Research workers and investigators have devised a number of attitude scales for the measurement of one's attitude towards a number of objects, ideas or persons. Let us learn the way of measuring one's attitude towards a thing with the help of a practical illustration given ahead.

Measurement of Attitude with the Help of an Attitude Scale

To illustrate the process of measurement of attitude, we would like to use an attitude scale here for measuring one's attitude towards science. The use of this test alongwith its reporting can be done in the way given ahead.

OBJECTIVE

To find out the attitude of a subject towards science with the help of an attitude scale.

TEST MATERIAL AND ENVIRONMENTAL SITUATION

(i) A copy of the Science Attitude scale constructed and standardized by Mrs. Avinash Grewal, containing test manual and test booklet cum answer sheet.

(ii) A subject whose attitude towards science we want to measure.

(iii) Proper environmental situations and facilities for conducting the test.

IDENTIFYING DATA OF THE SUBJECT

Name	:	Aruna Verma
Age	:	16 years
Name of the School	:	Girls Hr. Secondary School, Rohtak
Date of Testing	:	8-2-2006
Class	:	X

DESCRIPTION OF THE TEST

The present test named as Science Attitude Scale has been constructed and standardized by Mrs. Avinash Grewal, Lecturer Regional College of Education, Bhopal. It has been published by National Psychological Corporation, Agra. It has both English and Hindi version and thus can be used with the English as well as Hindi speaking testees. Its objective is to measure the attitude of the individual students towards science so that we can guide them in their selection of the subjects for their future study or professions.

The test material of this attitude scale may be divided into two sections for the necessary description.

Test Booklet cum Answer Sheet

It consists of two pages (one for English speaking and the other for Hindi speaking testees). The top contains space for the identifying data of the subject like his name, class, age, sex, school or college etc. It is followed by necessary directions regarding getting response of the test or scale items from the testees. Below, there are 20 statements for measuring one's attitude towards science. One has to provide one's degree of agreement or disagreement through the five alternatives ranging from strongly agree to strongly disagree by encircling his chosen option. These direction along with 12 statements (out of 20) are reproduced below to give an idea about the nature of the material of the test booklet cum answer-sheet of the Science Attitude Scale.

Directions

Given below are some statements about science. Some of these statements describe how you might feel about science. We are interested in knowing your valuable opinion about science as a subject of study. You may agree with some of the statement, carefully decide whether or not you agree with the statement.

If you agree strongly with a statement, put a circle (O) around the category SA (Strongly Agree); if you agree, put a circle around A (Agree); if you undecided, put a circle around U (Undecided); if you disagree, put a circle around D (Disagree); and if you strongly disagree, put a circle around SD (Strongly Disagree).

You are requested to give your free and frank opinion.

1.	Scientists are persons without human considerations.	SA	A	U	D	SD
2.	Scientific careers are more useful to the society than other careers.	SA	A	U	D	SD
3.	Study of science subjects is rather a dull affairs.	SA	A	U	D	SD
4.	Other subjects cannot be properly understood without the knowledge of science.	SA	A	U	D	SD
5.	Science subjects are very difficult to study.	SA	A	U	D	SD
6.	Science subjects are more exact than others.	SA	A	U	D	SD
7.	Science is bound to lead our society to Godlessness.	SA	A	U	D	SD
8.	Science subjects provide more recreation than other subjects.	SA	A	U	D	SD
9.	Scientific knowledge alone cannot improve a man's life.	SA	A	U	D	SD
10.	Science sharpens our reasoning power and logical thinking.	SA	A	U	D	SD
11.	Science fails to solve all our problems.	SA	A	U	D	SD
12.	Science subjects are useful for getting success in competitive examinations.	SA	A	U	D	SD

Test Manual

It is meant for the examiner or test administrator. It mentions all about the need of constructing the attitude scale, procedure for its construction, and standardization, reliability and validity of the measurement through this scale, its main objectives, purposes and all about the application of this scale etc. It clearly explains the process of administration scoring interpretation and drawing conclusion on the basis of one's score on this scale. It provides guidance for scoring each item of the scale on the basis of one's degree of agreement or disagreement to the given 20 items. Besides this, it also contains the necessary norms for converting original raw scores into standard scores and percentiles.

Administration of the Test

The Test was administered in the following way:

(i) Environmental situations were so arranged that provided quite congenial environment for the administration of the test. The subject was made to feel quite at home and comfortable. The essential rapport was established and she was made aware of the objective of testing.
(ii) She was then given test booklet cum answer-sheet. She was asked to first fill up the identifying data and then carefully read the given instruction carefully before responding to the 20 statements of the scale. The same was also verbally explained to her. The procedure of encircling her choice out of the five alternative was clearly emphasized and demonstrated to her.
(iii) She was told that she had to respond to each and every statement given in this scale. Although there is no time limit for the completion of the test, subject was asked to finish her work as early as possible. On an average it takes about 5 minutes to explain the test and the subject required about 15 minutes for giving responses to the 20 times of the scale.
(iv) During the administration of the test, it was ensured that the subject provided all information related to the identifying data and gave responses to all the 20 items of the scale by properly encircling her choice. It was also seen that she gave only one response to a scale item. The incompleteness in anyway was removed by asking her to do so. After such through inspection, the test booklet cum answer sheet was taken from the subject.

Scoring of the Responses

Scoring work of the responses of the subject was carried out by observing the following procedure given in the manual.

Each of the even numbered positive items (No. 2, 4, 6, 8, 10, 12, 14, 16, 18, 20) of the scale were assigned a weight ranging from 4 (strongly agree) to zero (thoroughly disagree). In the case of the remaining ten odd numbers negative items (S. No. 1, 3, 5, 7, 9, 11, 13, 15, 17, 19) the scale scoring was reversed ranging from zero (thoroughly agree) to 4 (strongly disagree). In this way, for our subject her total score on this science attitude scale was obtained by summating her scores for the individual items. Computing in this way, our subject Aruna got her individual and total scores on the attitude scale as below:

Item No.	*1*	*2*	*3*	*4*	*5*	*6*	*7*	*8*	*9*	*10*
Scores	(4)	(1)	(3)	(3)	(1)	(3)	(3)	(1)	(1)	(4)
Item No.	*11*	*12*	*13*	*14*	*15*	*16*	*17*	*18*	*19*	*20*
Scores	(3)	(1)	(4)	(4)	(3)	(1)	(4)	(4)	(3)	(4)

Total of all individual items Scores = 55.

Interpretation of the Test Scores

For the interpretation of the test scores, help was taken from the tables 1 and 2 given in the test manual. Table 1 helped in converting the raw score (original total score earned by our subject on the scale) into percentile rank (PRS). The table 2 provided norms for interpreting the attitude of our subject towards science in terms of her position in the standardized population along with a verbal description of her behaviour (related to her attitude towards science).

Both the tables are presented here for the purpose of required information and illustration.

Table 45.2 Percentile Rank (PRS) Equivalent to the Raw Scores

Percentile Rank	*Raw Score*	*Percentile*	*Raw Score*
Above 99	*Above 65*	*Rank 33*	*46*
99	64	30	45
98	63	25	44
97	62	22	43
96	60–61	18	42
89	59	14	41
87	58	10	40
86	57	6	39
85	56	5	38
84	55	4	36–37
72	54	3	35
70	53	2	31–34
65	52	1	27–30
63	51	Less than 1	25–26
43	49		
40	48		
36	47		

Table 45.3 gives the complete norms of the scale in Percentile Ranks, Standard Scores and Stannic. Verbal description and interpretation of the rank obtained by a subject is also given in this table.

Table 45.3 The Various Norms of the SAS and Their Interpretation

Attitude Scores	*Range of PRS and standard scores (in brackets)*	*% of cases includeed*	*Stanine*	*Verbal Description*	*Interpretation*
65–64 and above	99 and above (+2.29 to +2.85)	1%	9	Superior	Extremely Favourable
60–64	96.28 – 99 (1.59 to +2.15)	5%	8	Above Average	Decidedly Favourable
55–59	84.08 – 89.20 (+0.89 to +1.45)	12%	7	Above Average	Fairly Favourable
50–54	60.12 – 72.72 (+0.18 to + 0.75)	24%	6	Average	Somewhat Favourable
45–49	30.24 – 42.40 (–0.52 to + 0.5)	30%	5	Average	Just Favourable
40–44	10.28 – 5.50 (–1.22 to – 0.66)	18%	4	Average	Somewhat Favourable
35–39	3.18 – 5.50 (–1.92 to – 1.36)	7%	3	Below Average	Unfavourable
30–34	1.16 – 1.96 (–2.63 to – 2.06)	2%	2	Below Average	Decidedly Unfavourable
25–29	0.0 – 1.0 (–3.33 to – 2.77)	1%	1	Low	Extremely Unfavourable

The attitude of our subject can now be interpreted in the light of her total scores earned on the Science Attitude Scale as below:

- Our subject earned 55 as the raw scores. Similar scores can be computed for other students desiring to seek admission to science section or any science subject related professional course. It may then help to prepare a merit list for their selection or providing vocational and educational guidance.
- The percentile rank (PRS) of our subject equivalent to her raw scores 55 is 84. The knowledge can help us to locate where our subject stands in the group in relation to other students. The percentile P_{84} clearly indicates that only 16 per cent students from the whole group possess more favourable attitude towards the science subject in comparison to her. She is superior in this respect to 84 per cent students of the group.
- The range of her standard scores (for the raw scores of 55) as read from the table is 0.89 to 1.45. The further interpretation of these standard scores reveals the following things about our subject.

She is above average in terms of her total scores earned on this science attitude scale and her attitude towards the subject science is fairly favourable.

MEASUREMENT OF CREATIVITY

Introduction

All of us possess creative abilities whether in lesser or greater amount. The creative process and its output is very much linked with creative thinking. One who can think creatively and constructively is sure to lead and progress well on the path of creativity. However, we may find wide individual differences regarding the abilities and capacity to think creatively and constructively and that is why only a few of us are recognized as creative, the one who can create, discover or produce a new idea or object (including the re-arrangement or reshaping of what is already known to us). The question then arises is that how can we identify the students or persons who can be labelled as creative? How can we say that a particular child possesses so much creativity? This is done through some tests or measures available for assessing the degree of the creativity level among the testees. Through these tests, we try to make an assessment of creativity like originality, fluency, inventiveness, flexibility, elaboration, divergent thinking, etc. Both verbal as well as non-verbal tests are available for the measurement of creativity. In the following pages, we would be illustrating the use of a creativity test for measuring the creativity level of a subject.

Illustrating the Use of Creativity Test

OBJECTIVE

To determine the level of a subject by using a creativity test.

Identifying Data

Name of the subject :__________ Age :___________

Class : ___________ School : ______________________

Name of the Experimenter : ________________ Dated : ___________

Required Test Material and Environmental Situations

(i) The subject whose creativity level is to be identified.

(ii) A copy of creativity test standardized by Dr. Baquer Mehdi including a test booklet, scoring sheet, scoring guide and test manual.

(iii) The desirable situation and environment conductive to the administration of the test.

Description of the Test Material

The present test has been prepared by Dr. Baquer Mehdi. It is a verbal test that attempts to measure the level of creativity held by an individual. It has been published by National Psychological Corporation, Agra. Its test material can be well understood by making a three-fold division like below:

TEST BOOKLET

The introductory page of the test booklet contains the essential directions regarding the administration of the test. The pages to follow contain problematic questions (alongwith the space for the responses) based on four different types of activities as below:

Activity I. If it happens, then

The following three problems are mentioned under this title.

1. What will happen if men begin to fly like birds?
2. What will happen if your school gets wheels?
3. What will happen if the need to take food is vanished among the human beings?

Enough space is provided for responses to each of these three unprobable events. If needed, the responses can be extended on extra sheets.

Activity II. Innovative use of the objects

The following three objectives have been mentioned and subjects are required to think and write the types of noble, strange and innovative unusual uses they can make of these three objects.

(i) A piece of the stone

(ii) Wooden Stick

(iii) Water

Activity III. Discovering new relationships

The following three pairs are mentioned and subjects are required to discover new, noble and unusual relationships existing between them.

(i) Tree and house

(ii) Chair and the stair

(iii) Air and water

Activity IV. To make a given product or object more interesting, strange and playful

Here in this problematic task, the subject is given a horse play toy and asked to suggest how can it be made more interesting, strange and playful. The responses are to be written in the space provided in the test booklet.

In this way this test booklet serves the function of a question paper as well as the answer sheet and thus can be used only once.

Scoring Sheet

This one page scoring sheet remains with the experimenter. Here he writes the scores of the subject's responses computed with the help of scoring guide (provided in the manual) in three different categories namely fluency, flexibility and originality separately and then compute their total for getting category wise and composite scores.

Scoring Guide

It is that part of the test manual which helps an experimenter to score the responses of the subject. With its help, the responses can be scored in terms of three categories namely, fluency, flexibility and originality.

Administration of the Test

It was conducted as under:

(i) The subject was allowed to sit comfortably and was told about the objective of the test.

(ii) He was given a test booklet and asked to go through the given instructions carefully.

(iii) The four types of tasks mentioned in the test were explained to him with regard to their problematic nature and type of responses required from the subject with the help of the illustrations given in the booklet.

(iv) He was specifically told about the time limit required for giving responses to the problems related to the four types of activities, *i.e.* 15 minutes for activity I, 12 minutes for activity II, 15 minutes for activity III and 6 minutes for activity IV.

(v) He was asked to hand over the test booklet after the expiry of the total time, *i.e.* 1 hour 18 minutes.

(vi) He was also given two or three extra sheets in case he required more space for responding to the test problems.

Scoring of the Test

It was done as per provision of the scoring guide by computing three types of scores: (i) Originality scores (ii) Fluency scores and (iii) Flexibility scores. The task was carried out as under:

Computation of Originality Weight for Each Response

In the scoring guide, all the probable responses of the given problems related to the four activities have been provided separate alphabetical categories as A, B, C, D, E, F ...and also given the name as (i) Effect on Transport and Travel (ii) Thrill of new experience (iii) Effect on Economy (iv) Effect on Sanitation (v) Saving of Life (vi) Destructive use etc. Therefore, at the time of scoring, the task of the scorer is to first find out the category (alphabet and title of the category) in which a particular response is falling and then read out the originality weight given to that category from the last column of the scoring guide table. A portion of the specimen of such scoring guide for the calculation of originality weight is reproduced as follows:

Table 45.4 Scoring Guide (List of Categories and the Responses on Verbal Test of Creativity)

Activity No.	*Item No.*	*Category Alphabet Serial*	*Category*	*Responses*	*Originality Weight*
I Conse- quences	1	A	Effect on Transport and Travel	1. Disuse of vehicles 2. Disuse of aeroplanes 3. Disuse of parachute 4. Ease in travel	 4
If it happens then....	If men is able to fly like birds	B	Effect on Communi- cation	1. Disuse of telephone 2. Disuse of postal communication	5
		C	Effect on Living Habits	1. No walking 2. Less privacy 3. No use of stairs 4. Living on trees possible 5. Need for tight clothes	 1 2
		D	Thrill of New Experience	1. Moon travel made easy 2. Travel to fairly land 3. Meeting with angels	4 3
		E	Man-Bird Relationship	1. Competition between species 2. New friendships 3. Hostility with birds	 2

The originality weight thus read from the scoring guide for each response of our subject were in this way entered on the score sheet. For the responses which were not present in the scoring guide for the computation of originality weight, the following procedure was adopted.

(i) Since originality is defined as uncommonness of a given response hence responses given by less than 5% of the group were to be treated as original (as per instructions given in the manual).

(ii) Then original weights were assigned as below:

Nature of Response	**Originality weight**
Responses given below 1%	5
Responses given below 2%	4
Responses given below 3%	3
Responses given below 4%	2
Responses given below 5%	1
Responses given by 5% or more	0

Scoring for Fluency

Fluency in this test refers to the number of relevant and unrepeated ideas reflected through the responses of the subject. Consequently from the responses, an item found irrelevant and repeated was struck off and the remaining ones was counted and entered on the scoring sheet as the fluency score.

Scoring for Flexibility

From the scoring guide, alphabetical serial of the category awarded to each response just as A, B, C, D, E etc. was noted down (for a response belonging to an entirely new category a new alphabet serial was given). Then flexibility score was computed by using the following formula

Flexibility score = Total number of different alphabet serials used

Now proceeding as above, the originality, fluency and flexibility scores for different items belonging to each of the four activities or task I, II, III and IV were noted down on the scoring sheet. The specimen of the scoring sheet is given below:

Table 45.5 Scoring Sheet used in Creativity Test

		Task or Activity I	
	Fluency	Flexibility	Originality
Item 1.	....	....	....
Item 2.	....	....	....
Item 3.	....	....	....
Total			
		Task or Activity II	
	Fluency	Flexibility	Originality
Item 1.	....	....	....
Item 2.	....	....	....
Item 3.	....	....	....
Total			
		Task or Activity III	
	Fluency	Flexibility	Originality
Item 1.	....	....	....
Item 2.	....	....	....
Item 3.	....	....	....
Total			
		Task or Activity IV	
	Fluency	Flexibility	Originality
Item 1.	....	....	....
Item 2.	....	....	....
Item 3,	....	....	....
Total			
		Score Summary	
	Fluency	Flexibility	Originality
Task of Activity I.	....	....	....
Task of Activity II.	....	....	....
Task of Activity III.	....	....	....
Task of Activity IV.	....	....	....
Grand Total			

Interpretation of the Test Scores

Thus, we obtained three types of factor scores namely originality scores. Fluency scores and Flexibility scores of the subject along with the total creativity scores by summing up these three factor scores. These scores can now help us to derive the desired conclusions regarding the creativity level of the subject in the manner detailed below:

1. The test manual contains the norms for interpreting the scores earned by a subject in the creativity test. We can safely interpret the earned scores of the subject in terms of these given norms and conclude about the creativity level of our subject.
2. In case we are administrating this creativity test to a subject or group of subjects not covered in the norms given in the test, e.g. a group of B.Ed. students, then you as an experimenter should yourself build up the required norms for the interpretation of the derived creativity scores. The adopted procedure for this purpose may be laid down as under:
   (i) Suppose you have administered this creativity test on a group of 100 B.Ed. students, then the first task is to compute three factors scores namely Originality scores, Fluency scores and Flexibility scores for the responses of all the students separately and enter them into respective score sheets.
   (ii) These raw scores on originality, fluency and flexibility are then converted into T scores (standard scores) by using the formula

$$T = \frac{10(X - M)}{\sigma} + 50$$

   Here X means raw scores, M and σ stand for the mean and standard deviation of the scores earned by 100 students. (For computing σ you may use the formula

   $\sigma = \sqrt{(X - M)^2/N}$.

   (iii) Now these three T scores belonging to originality, fluency and flexibility factors are added for providing composite creativity scores on the creativity test.
   (iv) The composite creativity scores of the students can be used for making comparison of the creativity level of the students within the examined group. For this purpose we can also compute percentile rank.

We can also employ an alternative method for the required interpretation in which we can make use of raw scores directly without converting these into T scores. It is based on high and low scores earned in the test. For this purpose we have to compute mean and standard deviation (SD) of the scores of the group and then use the following rule.

"Scores which are 1 σ or SD above the mean are taken as high creativity group and those which are 1 σ or SD below the mean are designated as low creativity group."

Therefore in case your group is a B.Ed. students group, and norms are not available in the manual you can employ this alternative method for the interpretation of the creativity scores and then may be able to determine the creativity levels of the students of your class.

Index